The Beat of a Different Drum

Playing the bongo drums. (Courtesy: California Institute of Technology, Pasadena, California.)

The Beat of a Different Drum

The Life and Science of Richard Feynman

JAGDISH MEHRA

CLARENDON PRESS · OXFORD

Oxford University Press, Walton Street, Oxford OX2 6DP

Oxford New York Toronto
Delhi Bombay Calcutta Madras Karachi
Kuala Lumpur Singapore Hong Kong Tokyo
Nairobi Dar es Salaam Cape Town
Melbourne Auckland Madrid

and associated companies in
Berlin Ibadan

Oxford is a trade mark of Oxford University Press

Published in the United States
by Oxford University Press Inc., New York

A catalogue record for this book is available from the British Library

Library of Congress Cataloging in Publication Data
Mehra, Jagdish.
The beat of a different drum: the life and science of Richard
Feynman/Jagdish Mehra.
1. Feynman, Richard Phillips. 2. Physicists—United States—
Biography. I. Title.
QC16.F49M45 1994 530'.092—dc20 [B] 93-282
ISBN 0 19 853948 7

Printed in the United States of America

To Marlis,
in love and friendship

ACKNOWLEDGEMENTS

I N WRITING this book I have received assistance from many people who knew about this or that aspect of Richard Feynman's multifaceted life and scientific work or had collaborated with him in some venture. It is impossible for me to thank them all adequately for sharing with me their knowledge of Feynman's life, work, and personality, and what I can do here is no more than record my gratitude to them. Although I had the opportunity of talking to a lot of people on whose memories and impressions I have drawn, I alone am responsible for the context in which I have made use of conversations and interviews with them and the conclusions I have drawn.

More than anybody else, I owe my greatest debt of gratitude to Richard Feynman himself for sowing the seed of this book in my mind and for many extensive conversations and interviews I had with him in preparation for writing this work. Among these conversations and interviews, the last ones I had with him in January 1988, shortly before his death, were the most important. Feynman cooperated with me in answering all the questions I posed to him, and encouraged me in writing about his life and scientific work, in particular about his unique and special way of contemplating and thinking about nature and the problems of physics. I had the good fortune of learning directly from Feynman himself about the origin and execution of his various scientific projects and the varied adventures of his life and thrills of the mind.

While I had the opportunity of talking to many people about various aspects of Feynman's life and work, it was with Feynman alone that I was able to talk about *all* of them. With this general acknowledgement of my indebtedness and gratitude to Feynman for opening up to me, I shall mention in the following the names of people who have contributed to my knowledge and understanding of his life and work treated in the different chapters of this book.

For Chapters 1 and 2, dealing with Feynman's childhood, upbringing, and family life in Far Rockaway, New York, I learned most of the details from Feynman himself, but numerous essential ingredients were filled in by Mrs Adele Curott (née Rosenbaum), a distant cousin of Feynman's, with whose family Feynman had close interactions in his early boyhood. Elmer Heller, Harold Gast, David Leff, and Jessica Fleischmann (née Soffer), all of whom attended Far Rockaway High School with Feynman, shared with me their recollections of him, as did Abram Bader, Feynman's physics teacher in the last year of high school. I also learned a good deal about Feynman's relationship with Arline Greenbaum, whom he later married, during their high school years from Elmer Heller and Harold Gast; Heller also shared with me the letters and other details which Feynman had communicated to him during his studies at MIT.

Theodore Welton attended MIT with Feynman and became his closest friend there. Later on he worked in the Technical Computations Group in the Theory Division, of which Feynman was the group leader, at the Manhattan Project in Los Alamos during the war years. He kindly shared with me an unpublished manuscript dealing with his memories of Richard Feynman, and answered a number of my questions dealing with that period of Feynman's life. Feynman's stay and studies at MIT are treated in Chapter 3, where the details of Feynman's senior thesis on 'Forces and stresses in molecules' are also given; G. Ray Allcock of the University of Liverpool gave me a tutorial on Feynman's thesis and the so-called Hellman–Feynman theorem which emerged from it.

John Archibald Wheeler and Eugene Wigner shared with me their recollections of Richard Feynman as a graduate student at Princeton, a topic which I have treated in Chapter 4. Feynman himself retained very vivid memories of his graduate studies and the writing of his dissertation at Princeton, during the course of which he encountered Herbert Jehle, a physicist recently arrived from Europe.

In Chapters 5 and 6 have been treated the Wheeler–Feynman action-at-a-distance theory of electrodynamics (on which I received a tutorial from Fritz Rohrlich), and the principle of least action in quantum mechanics, respectively. The principle of least action had become a focal point of much of Feynman's scientific work, and its roots went back to the last year of his high school when he learned about it from his physics teacher Abram Bader. For much of the background information on these topics I have greatly benefited, apart from conversations with Feynman himself, from John Wheeler.

Almost all of my information about Arline Greenbaum and Feynman's marriage to her, her stay at the Deborah Hospital near Princeton, New Jersey, and the clinic in Albuquerque, New Mexico, where she died, comes from Richard Feynman himself. Certain details were furnished by Elmer Heller, Feynman's class and fraternity friend in high school. The touching memories of Feynman about his relationship with Arline are treated in Chapter 7.

In Chapter 8, dealing with Feynman's stay and work at Los Alamos during the building of the atomic bomb, Feynman himself has been the best source of information, especially his talk 'Los Alamos from below', which was subsequently published. I also learned a great deal about Feynman's work, relationships, and adventures at Los Alamos from Hans Bethe, Frederick Reines, Theodore Welton, and Robert R. Wilson. I also wish to acknowledge a conversation about Los Alamos, and his memories of Feynman there, with the atomic spy Klaus Fuchs in December 1975 at the Academy of Sciences in East Berlin.

Feynman himself was the best source of information about his stay at Cornell as a physics professor (Chapter 9), but I obtained many valuable details also from Hans Bethe, Philip Morrison, Freeman Dyson, Theodore Schultz, and Herbert Corben. Corben also provided me with information concerning the writing of Feynman's paper on the space–time approach to nonrelativistic quantum mechanics in Chapter 10. Douglas Fitchen, chairman of the Department of Physics at Cornell University, kindly made available to me a copy of Feynman's dossier dealing with his relations with Cornell.

Almost all the background information concerning Feynman's role in the development of quantum electrodynamics, treated in Chapters 10–15, comes from conversations with and lectures by Feynman himself. However, numerous valuable details were provided by Paul Dirac, Hans Bethe, Freeman Dyson, Viktor Weisskopf, Julian Schwinger, and Willis E. Lamb, Jr. Plamen Petkov Fiziev of the University of Bulgaria, Sofia, Bulgaria, greatly assisted me with the technical details of the formalism of quantum electrodynamics and path integrals, and Feynman's work in this field, by giving me tutorials on them: I am very grateful for my association with him and for his invaluable assistance.

I learned about Feynman's adventures in Brazil and Japan (treated in Chapter 16) from Feynman himself. J. Leite Lopes, of Centro Brasiliero de Pesquisas Fisicas in Rio de Janeiro, answered my queries concerning Feynman's visits to and stay in Brazil.

Feynman's work on the superfluidity of liquid helium is treated in Chapter 17. I interviewed Michael Cohen, who had worked on liquid helium with Feynman, and requested Russell J. Donnelly to provide me information about his recollections of Lars Onsager's and Richard Feynman's work in this field, which he very kindly did. R. M. Mazo and W. F. Vinen contributed additional notes to Donnelly's account. I requested Raj K. Pathria to help me put together all the material concerning the technical details and my interviews with Feynman and Cohen on this subject. It turned out that Pathria's contribution to my understanding of Feynman's work on superfluidity of liquid helium and its rich background became vitally important, and he very kindly agreed to be coauthor of this chapter, for which I am very grateful to him.

For Feynman's contributions to the polaron problem, in which his interest had been aroused by certain remarks of Herbert Fröhlich in a review paper, I interviewed Theodore Schultz, Robert Hellwarth, Carl Iddings, and Phil Platzman. I also had occasion to discuss this subject with Herbert Fröhlich and Ray Allcock in Liverpool, England. I requested Gerard J. Hyland, of the University of Warwick, Coventry, England, who had worked extensively with Fröhlich on numerous problems, to give me tutorials on all aspects of the polaron problem, culminating in a joint major historical study of the polaron problem from Lev D. Landau to Richard Feynman. I also discussed the polaron problem in detail with Josef T. Devreese of the University of Antwerp, Antwerp, Belgium, and he gave me an extensive tutorial on Feynman path integrals and the polaron, a field to which Devreese and his collaborators have made important contributions. My indebtedness to all concerned, but above all to Gerard Hyland, is sincere.

For Chapter 20, I discussed Feynman's work on the geometrical representation of the Schrödinger equation and the theory of a general quantum system interacting with a linear dissipative system with Robert Hellwarth, and I received clarifications of Feynman's adventure into biology from Robert S. Edgar, Francis Crick, and Matthew Meselson. Feynman told me about these problems himself, as well as about his interest in nanotechnology—'There's plenty of room at the bottom'—and his service on the the State of California Curriculum Commission.

I discussed the history of the V–A theory of weak interactions with Richard Feynman, Murray Gell-Mann, Robert E. Marshak, C. S. Wu, and C. N. Yang. Robert Marshak responded in detail to all the questions I posed to him about this field, as did Gell-Mann and Madame Wu. Feynman had already given me the details of his own direct involvement with the V–A theory in conversations with me. I am also grateful to Martin Block for telling me about his discussions with Feynman at the 1956 Rochester Conference about the violation of parity, and sharing with me the notes of a talk entitled 'Why be even-handed?', which he gave on the occasion of his sixtieth birthday. I have greatly benefited from all this information in writing Chapter 21.

Feynman's celebrated lectures on physics had been a great event at the California Institute of Technology. Conversations with Matthew Sands, Robert Leighton, and Richard Feynman elicited the details of how these lectures came to be conceived, organized, delivered, and published. In Chapter 22, I have also discussed Feynman's Messenger Lectures on 'The character of physical law' at Cornell University, and the Alix G. Mautner Memorial Lectures on 'QED: The strange theory of light and matter' at the University of California, Los Angeles, about which I had occasion to talk to Feynman.

In Chapter 23, I have treated three large themes: Feynman's work on the quantum theory of gravitation (on which I received tutorials from Bryce DeWitt, Ludwig Faddeev, Gerard 'tHooft, Christopher Isham, and Jamal Islam); partons and the parton–quark model (which I discussed with J. D. Bjorken, Emmanuel Paschos, and Trivan Pal, all of whom answered my questions in detail); and the quark jets (which I discussed with Geoffrey Fox, E. Reya, and Trivan Pal). Feynman himself gave me an overview of his contributions to these fields in January 1988.

In Chapter 24 is treated the subject of the fundamental limits of computation and Feynman's work on the quantum computer. After discussing this field with Feynman, I pursued it in detail with Charles Bennett, Ed Fredkin, Rolf Landauer, Paul Benioff, John Hopfield, and Steven Wolfram, and received a tutorial on this subject from Krzysztof Heller.

Chapter 25 summarizes Feynman's reflections and viewpoints on science, religion, culture, and modern society. Here the source is Feynman himself and his addresses on diverse themes contained under the rubric of 'culture and modern society'. One of the important addresses given by Feynman in this connection was on the occasion of the celebration of the 400th anniversary of Galileo's birth, which was held in Pisa in 1964. There, Feynman's remarks aroused the displeasure of the representatives of the Soviet Union; I got an account of the details of this controversy from H. B. G. Casimir and V. F. Weisskopf.

Chapter 26, 'The beat of a different drum', celebrates Feynman as a unique and distinctive personality. In writing about the various themes discussed in this chapter, I have drawn on conversations with Feynman himself, and those with Albert Hibbs, Jirayr Zorthian, and Tom Van Sant. In order to determine Feynman's relations with his colleagues at Caltech and his work as a faculty member, I talked to Murray Gell-Mann, William Fowler, Robert Christy, Robert Walker, Matthew Sands, Robert Leighton, and Feynman's long-time secretary, Helen Tuck. I learned about Feynman's relations with and his handling of students from conversations with numerous former Feynman students, including Albert Hibbs, Michael Cohen, Phil Platzman, Carl Iddings, Gerald Speisman, Elisha Huggins, Sam Berman, Daniele Amati, and Alberto Sirlin. For the section 'The last journey of a genius', I have found the PBS Broadcast of that title and Ralph Leighton's book *Tuva or bust!* very useful; Christopher Sykes kindly provided me with a complete tape of this broadcast.

To all the people mentioned in the foregoing I extend my heartfelt thanks. In addition, I am grateful to the Librarian, Sealy G. Mudd Library, Princeton University, for providing me copies of the lectures delivered in the session on nuclear science on the occasion of the Bicentennial Celebration of Princeton University in 1946. I also wish to thank the staff of the Archivist, Millikan Library, California Institute of Technology, especially Paula Hurwitz, for help in consulting the Feynman archives held at Caltech, and for making copies of the requested documents available to me; my grateful thanks are also due to Caltech for permission to quote from the Feynman archives in their possession. I would also like to thank the American Institute of Physics for allowing me, at Richard Feynman's request, to consult Charles Weiner's interview with him, which took place in 1966.

Finally, I wish to thank the staff of Oxford University Press for their cooperation in all phases of the publication of this book.

1993 J.M.

CONTENTS

Plates fall between pages 320 and 321

Introduction

This book is about the life and scientific work of Richard Phillips Feynman. It is divided into twenty-six chapters dealing with his life, science, personality, and achievements.

Just as Josiah Willard Gibbs was assuredly the greatest American physicist of the nineteenth century, Richard Feynman was arguably the greatest American-born theoretical physicist of the twentieth century. Feynman was among the truly great physicists of the world.

Mark Kac, the eminent Polish-American mathematician wrote: 'In science, as well as in other fields of human endeavor, there are two kinds of geniuses: the "ordinary" and the "magicians". An ordinary genius is a fellow that you and I would be just as good as, if we were only many times better. There is no mystery as to how his mind works. Once we understand what he has done, we feel certain that we, too, could have done it. It is different with magicians. They are, to use mathematical jargon, in the orthogonal complement of where we are and the working of their minds is for all intents and purposes incomprehensible. They seldom, if ever, have students because they cannot be emulated and it must be terribly frustrating for a brilliant young mind to cope with the mysterious ways in which the magician's mind works. Richard Feynman [was] a magician of the highest caliber.'[1]

Richard Feynman was born in Far Rockaway, Queens, New York, on 11 May 1918, and died on 15 February 1988, in Pasadena, California, a few months before his seventieth birthday. He was a very charismatic person, widely loved and admired, not only by the members of the physics community—in which he was famous for his scientific achievement, brilliance, humor, and showmanship—but also by members of the public who had either heard about him or had the opportunity of listening to one of his inimitable public lectures (Chapters 22 and 25).

I had the good fortune to see Feynman in action, as it were, since I first went to southern California in the fall of 1958, and began to attend the theoretical physics seminars and physics colloquia (called the Physics Research

Conferences) every week at the California Institute of Technology. During the next few years I developed a nodding acquaintance with Feynman, but on 10 May 1962—on the eve of my departure for Switzerland for a couple of years— we spent an entire day together at Caltech talking about his life and scientific work. From that time on, I visited him at Caltech every few years, and saw him occasionally at conferences and symposia at other places such as Rochester (New York), Austin (Texas), and Geneva (Switzerland), where I talked to him about his role in the development of quantum field theory (Chapters 10–16), as well as the other things he had been working on such as liquid helium (Chapter 17) and the theory of weak interactions (Chapter 21).

On 10 April 1980 I gave a physics colloquium at Caltech on the birth of quantum mechanics, which Feynman attended and seemed to enjoy. After my talk, as we walked together to his office, he half seriously asked me if I wouldn't do for him what I had done for Heisenberg, Dirac, and Pauli—that is, write about him. I told him that I would find it a great pleasure to do so, and our discussions about his life and science were resumed.

On 19 December 1987, I telephoned Feynman from Houston and asked if I could visit him to talk to him about a number of questions about his scientific biography which I hoped to write. He said that he felt tired and depressed, and would rather not talk about the past. Knowing that he had recently undergone his fourth operation for abdominal cancer, I did not wish to insist. But a few days later, on 23 December, he called me and said that he had been reading my book on Erwin Schrödinger,[2] and if I still wanted to visit him I was welcome. Regarding Schrödinger, Feynman commented that he had been like Harry Truman, who, though not an extraordinary man himself, rose to the occasion as president of the United States of America after the death of Franklin D. Roosevelt; similarly Schrödinger rose to the occasion in meeting the challenge of developing his version of quantum mechanics.

A colloquium to be given by me on Erwin Schrödinger and the creation of wave mechanics was arranged at Caltech for 21 January 1988 but, having arranged with Feynman the plan for a long series of conversations, I had already arrived in Pasadena about ten days earlier. When I saw Feynman, I was shocked by his haggard looks, weak voice, and limping gait. I soon learned what suffering he had been through since his last operation for cancer, which had returned.

We determined a schedule according to which we would have tape-recorded discussions during the following days. We were to meet each day at 10 a.m., except the mornings of Tuesdays and Thursdays, when he taught a class on quantum chromodynamics, and we would then go on through the day, with a break for lunch, as long as his strength and interest would permit. Thus our discussions began right away. Before we started to record the conversations, Feynman proposed a deal. He said, 'You may ask me anything you want, and I shall answer you. But at lunch I will relax, and you will have to tell me stories to entertain me.' The bargain was struck.

This last and, unfortunately, final set of conversations and interviews began by my telling Feynman that, like Mozart, a good part of him was a showman, prankster, joker, and clown, but about seventy percent of him—that is, his science—was divine music. (Freeman Dyson revised his estimate of Richard Feynman from being a 'half genius and half buffoon' to 'all genius and all buffoon').[3] Most of Feynman, the prankster and buffoon, he had covered himself in his anecdotal book, '*Surely you're joking, Mr. Feynman!*', but his biography had also to cover other aspects of his life, science, and personality. And this, I told him, had to be captured and written about. He said, 'You are welcome to any false gold there is.'

So we began in the mid-morning of 11 January. From that moment, over the following days, until 4.30 p.m. on the afternoon of 27 January, several hours every day, except Tuesdays and Thursdays, when we talked only after lunch, the discussions covered many topics.

We discussed Feynman's family and growing up in Far Rockway, New York (Chapters 1 and 2), including his hobbies, friends, family and influences upon him, especially the influence of his father, who instilled in him the love of rational inquiry about natural phenomena and a hatred of all fuzziness in thinking. Feynman adored his father, who taught him a deep dislike of ceremony and distrust of all authority.

I talked to him about his teachers at the Far Rockaway High School, especially the physics teacher, Abram Bader, who, in a private conversation after class with the boy Feynman, had told him about the beauty of the principle of least action—a principle which would become a continuously running thread in Feynman's later scientific work (Chapter 2).

We covered his studies in high school (Chapter 2), at MIT (Chapter 3), and Princeton (Chapter 4). After Mr Bader in high school, the great influence at MIT was that of Phillip Morse, who gave special lectures on quantum mechanics to Richard Feynman and his friend Theodore Welton in their sophomore year. Morse gave them actual problems to solve: to determine the spectra of low-atomic-number elements, up to 10 or 12. They had to determine the energy levels by a variational principle, using hydrogen-like wave functions and parameters. Feynman said that he 'was so excited to get numbers reasonably close to the real world, which was to me very exciting, because to me the real world was always so complicated. To be able to figure out what's actually happening, that was impressive.' For quantum mechanics, he studied Pauling and Wilson's *Introduction to quantum mechanics*. Feynman also studied Ruark and Urey's *Atoms, molecules and quanta* and P. A. M. Dirac's *The principles of quantum mechanics*. He learned statistical mechanics from Richard Tolman's book on that subject, and relativity from A. S. Eddington's *The mathematical theory of relativity*. For nuclear physics, he studied Hans Bethe's articles in the *Reviews of Modern Physics* on that subject. He learned quantum electrodynamics from Heitler's book and from Enrico Fermi's article in the *Reviews of Modern Physics*. During his years at MIT, from 1935 to 1939, Feynman learned about the whole of theoretical physics on his own. He even published a couple of articles. He coauthored an article on 'The scattering of cosmic rays by the stars of the galaxy' with the cosmic ray physicist Manuel Sandoval Vallarta, and published his senior thesis on 'Forces in molecules'; both of these articles were published in the *Physical Review*. From his senior thesis, a theorem—called the Hellman–Feynman theorem—became well known (Chapter 3).

At Princeton, Feynman was supposed to become a research assistant to Eugene Wigner, but was instead assigned to John Archibald Wheeler, who had just recently joined the Princeton physics faculty. Wheeler profoundly influenced Feynman, and the latter gave as much as he got (Chapter 4). At Princeton, Feynman perfected his path-integral approach to nonrelativistic quantum mechanics and wrote a doctoral dissertation on 'The principle of least action in quantum mechanics'; he took his Ph.D. degree from Princeton in 1942 (Chapter 6). Feynman and I discussed all aspects of his personal and scientific life at Princeton, including the seminar he gave on his work with Wheeler on the action-at-a-distance theory of electrodynamics that was attended by 'monster minds' such as Einstein, Pauli, Henry Norris Russell, John von Neumann, and Eugene Wigner (Chapters 5–7).

Already during his last year at Princeton, even before he had completed his doctorate, Feynman was persuaded to join the atomic bomb project by R. R. Wilson. In the Manhattan Project at Los Alamos, Feynman became the leader of the Technical Computations Group in the Theory Division headed by Hans Bethe (Chapter 8). Feynman developed a special rapport with Bethe and was deeply influenced by him. He came to have a great affection and respect for Bethe and, after Los Alamos, followed Bethe to Cornell, where Bethe had arranged an appointment for him as an 'acting' assistant professor—the prefix 'acting' to be dropped after a year's satisfactory performance. Actually, the prefix 'acting' was dropped long before Feynman joined the Cornell University faculty, and he received several raises in salary (before actually joining); Bethe was keeping an eye on what was happening in the academic market to bright young physicists, and he was looking out for Feynman's interests. Although at the beginning of his stay at Cornell (where he arrived in November 1945), he did not know in which direction to go scientifically, he later spent a beautiful, satisfying, and productive period of five years there, having been promoted to an associate professorship in February 1947 (Chapter 9).

In a major experiment, performed by Willis E. Lamb, Jr., and his graduate student Robert Retherford at Columbia University in the last week of April 1947, the Lamb shift had been discovered and measured. It became one of the principal themes of discussion at the Shelter Island Conference on the fundamental problems of quantum mechanics, which was organized by J. Robert Oppenheimer with the sponsorship of the National Academy of Sciences, in the first week of June 1947. On the return trip from Shelter Island,

Bethe took the train from New York to Schenectady, and during the three or four hours' ride on the train he made the initial nonrelativistic quantum electrodynamical calculation of the Lamb shift. Bethe had gone for consulting work at the General Electric Company's Research Laboratory in Schenectady, from where he sent a copy of a manuscript to Willis Lamb and a few others, in which he gave an amazingly short calculation of the $2S_{1/2}-2P_{1/2}$ shift amounting to 1040 MHz. From Schenectady Bethe called Feynman on the telephone and told him about his calculation, and upon his return to Cornell he gave a lecture and explained his calculation in detail. Bethe pointed out that if a means could be found to make electrodynamics finite with the help of a relativistic cut-off procedure then a relativistic quantum field-theoretic calculation of the Lamb shift could be carried out quite simply. Bethe's lecture really got Feynman started on his research again, for he knew how to introduce a relativistically invariant cut-off into the Lagrangian of classical electrodynamics by his path-integral method (Chapters 11 and 12).

Feynman immediately began to perfect his space–time approach to quantum electrodynamics, in which his path-integral formulation of non-relativistic quantum mechanics played a fundamental role (Chapters 6 and 10). During the academic year 1947–48, Feynman often discussed his methods with anyone who would listen. One attentive listener was Freeman Dyson, who had arrived from Cambridge, England, with a Commonwealth Fund Fellowship to work as a graduate student with Hans Bethe at Cornell. Bethe gave him the problem of calculating the Lamb shift for a spin-0 electron by using the correct relativistic wave equations. All that Dyson had to do was to take Bethe's nonrelativistic calculation and repeat it by using relativistic electrodynamics and doing the mass renormalization a little bit more carefully. Of course, there was no experiment to compare it with since there were no spin-0 electrons. Dyson recalls that he interacted with Feynman 'mostly by listening. At that time he [Feynman] was working extremely hard to develop his version of quantum electrodynamics; at that time it was still not finished. He had the relativistic cut-off and he knew how to deal with positrons, pair creation, and closed loops by means of his diagrams. But he hadn't yet got it all together into a workable scheme. It was still something that only he knew how to do, and he had problems communicating with other people. He had ideas that were so different from the conventional ones. I listened a great deal to him and I was convinced that he had something valuable, but that it needed to be understood. That was one of the things I set out to do. During that year I spent a fair amount of time just listening to Feynman talk about all kinds of things. I was in Cornell just nine months, from September to June; during that time I picked up everything from Feynman.'[4]

In the spring of 1948, from 30 March to 2 April, the second conference on the fundamental problems of theoretical physics, which was organized by Oppenheimer, took place at Pocono Manor, Pennsylvania, a site located between Scranton and the Delaware Water Gap; Pocono Manor offered the same kind of setting as had Ram's Head Inn on Shelter Island, where the first conference had been held. By the time of the Pocono Conference, both Julian Schwinger and Richard Feynman had developed their relativistically invariant calculational schemes. At the conference, Schwinger presented his scheme in a marathon lecture; this scheme was rooted in the earlier work of Dirac, Fock, and Podolsky, and Schwinger proceeded to present a systematic approach based on a series of canonical transformations. He gave an exact calculation of the anomalous magnetic moment of the electron on the basis of his methods. All those present at the conference—including the new participants who had not attended the Shelter Island Conference in 1947, such as Paul Dirac, Niels Bohr, Walter Heitler, Gregor Wentzel, and Eugene Wigner—were deeply impressed by Schwinger's ideas and talk. Feynman made a hurried presentation of his ideas at Pocono, including his way of looking at the positron as an electron moving backward in time; it followed Schwinger's brilliant marathon talk, and was received with skepticism and hostility, especially by Bohr. Niels Bohr got the impression that Feynman was using concepts in his theory—such as paths and trajectories—which had been abandoned already in the formulation of quantum mechanics in the mid-1920s. Feynman compared his results with those of Schwinger and they agreed, but on account of the skepticism and hostility that he encountered at the conference he returned to Cornell rather depressed and resolved to publish a detailed presentation of his theory (Chapter 12).

By the beginning of 1948, the early papers of Sin-Itiro Tomonaga, published in the first two issues of the Japanese journal *Progress of Theoretical Physics*, had become available in the United States.

In the early summer of 1948, Freeman Dyson traveled west from Cleveland to Albuquerque by car with Richard Feynman on a completely unplanned trip, which took three or four days, and 'that was the time when I really got to talk with Feynman—twenty-four hours at a stretch. We talked about everything: his theory and his whole approach to life and physics. Then I came back on the bus from Albuquerque to Ann Arbor, Michigan, and spent four weeks at the summer school listening to Schwinger, and there I had very close contact with Schwinger.'[4] At Ann Arbor, Schwinger gave 'his very polished lectures describing his way of doing the Lamb shift and his version of quantum electrodynamics. The lectures were in the mornings, and I sat in the afternoons working through them, calculating myself and reproducing what he had done. So I understood it, so to say, from the inside. The methods of Schwinger and Feynman led to the same results, but it was not at all clear why, because they looked so different. Also Tomonaga was doing essentially the same thing that Schwinger was doing, only Tomonaga explained things in a much less elaborate fashion so that it was easier to understand, but he did not go much into detail. But Tomonaga's way and Schwinger's way were essentially the same. They were based on the standard field theory formalism translated into covariant language and that basic formalism was the same, but Feynman was totally different. He didn't even write down a Hamiltonian or anything; he just wrote down the answer, just gave you a set of rules for writing down the answer.'[4]

From Ann Arbor, Dyson went to Berkeley. On the bus ride back from Berkeley to Chicago, where he was going to stay with friends for a week, 'it became clear in my head what the situation was with Feynman, what Feynman's theory really was ... It all came together more or less simultaneously. It became obvious to me [Dyson] that the theories [of Schwinger, Tomonaga, and Feynman] must in some way be identical. It was an obvious thing for me to try to clean up the whole thing and to show what was the same and what was different. Since I was more in contact with Feynman than anybody else, I realized quite soon that it was a very great opportunity to translate Feynman into the language that other people could use. That was essentially my job ... Then in Chicago I really worked out the essential outline of the published paper which I put together.'[4]

Feynman's work on quantum electrodynamics (Chapters 13 and 14) was still unpublished when Dyson wrote his paper. 'That was a little bit delicate because I was publishing his work before he did. But he always behaved extremely generously; that was one thing that impressed me deeply, that I never had the slightest problem with Feynman about publishing his ideas first though I was certainly a little bit apprehensive about that. But he was as generous as could be.'[4] Dyson went to Princeton, where he got installed to work at the Institute for Advanced Study. Then he went to Ithaca to talk to Feynman and tell him what had happened. 'He was absolutely delighted. He just had no qualms about giving me a free hand to publish whatever I liked. He just said: "Well, that's great! Finally I am respectable!"'[4] Dyson wrote up the paper on 'The radiation theories of Tomonaga, Schwinger, and Feynman' in Princeton in September 1948; it was received by the *Physical Review* on 6 October and published early in 1949.

Early in 1949, Richard Feynman completed his papers on 'The theory of positrons' (Chapter 13) and the 'Space–time approach to quantum electrodynamics' (Chapter 14), which were received by the *Physical Review* on 8 April and 9 May 1949, respectively. By means of his methods, quantum electrodynamic effects could be calculated to any order. Feynman had introduced the diagrammatic technique to visualize mathematical terms. He told me: 'In private I had great amusement in thinking that my silly-looking diagrams, when published in the *Physical Review*, would poke fun at that august journal. I liked to think that my diagrams were the equivalent of sheep's livers and entrails into which the ancient Greek and Egyptian priests used to look for predicting the future!' (Chapters 13–15). It was through the use of the so-called 'Feynman diagrams' that, as Julian Schwinger once remarked, 'Feynman brought calculation to the masses.'

Another remark concerning his work on quantum electrodynamics that Feynman made was the following: 'I knew that Pauli and Heisenberg had formulated the theory of quantum electrodynamics correctly in the late 1920s, and had recognized the difficulties that arose with the infinities. However, like a Watusi tribal warrior I psyched myself up by saying that Pauli, Heisenberg, and Dirac were all wrong and knew nothing; I could do better. I fought them like a warrior in my mind. This was my way of psyching myself to triumph over the difficulties of quantum electrodynamics.'

Feynman and I discussed the details of his work on the theory of liquid helium (Chapter 17), his work (with Murray Gell-Mann) on the vector–axial vector (V–A) theory of weak interactions (Chapter 21), work on bacterio-phages (Chapter 20), quantum gravity, partons, and quarks (Chapter 23), polarons (Chapter 19), and quantum computers (Chapter 24). On the basis of his work on partons and quark jets (Chapter 23), he declared, 'I am now a confirmed quarkanian!'

We talked about the various series of lectures—scientific and popular—he had given (Chapters 22 and 25), and his work on the presidential commission to investigate the space shuttle *Challenger* disaster (Chapter 26). With evident pleasure, he showed me the private notebooks he kept about his ideas and work in progress. 'Physics is my only hobby; it is my work and entertainment. I think about it all the time, as you can see from my notebooks. Most of the ideas lead nowhere; some do, and I publish them', said Feynman. One problem which he had wrestled with for many years, which he would have liked to solve, and which still rankled with him, was the problem of superconductivity. 'When the Bardeen, Cooper, Schrieffer paper came out, I could not read it for several weeks; I had an emotional feeling about that problem', he said. But the V–A theory of weak interactions had given him a great deal of pleasure. 'It was nothing like the work of Maxwell or Dirac, but it was the only time in my life that I discovered a law of nature. In the case of quantum electrodynamics, I had shoved the problem [of infinities] under the rug', Feynman said with excitement.

Feynman held forth a lot concerning his notions about science, the physical interpretation of quantum mechanics (which, he said, he often discussed with Murray Gell-Mann), and what the pursuit of the understanding of nature meant to him.

He talked about his travels to Europe, Brazil, and Japan (Chapter 16), his great adventure with the desire to travel to Tannu Tuva in Central Asia (Chapter 26), and what he thought about the different cultures. He discussed his interest in the civilization of the Mayans, and talked about his abiding enthusiasm in deciphering Mayan hieroglyphics (Chapter 26). Cultures of antiquity and a comparative study of them fascinated Feynman.

Feynman said that prizes, honors, and election to academies did not mean anything to him; the real honor was the pleasure and excitement he derived from his work in science. He had quite early resigned his membership in the US National Academy of Sciences (Chapter 18), and had felt like refusing the Nobel Prize in 1965, until it was pointed out that he would make more of a fuss by refusing it than by accepting it (Chapter 26). He asked me if there were other examples where someone had wanted to refuse the Nobel Prize. I told him about the two I knew. The first was about George Bernard Shaw. When Shaw was awarded the Nobel Prize for literature in 1925, he said: 'As for the money of it, I have enough; as for the reputation it entails, it is like throwing a rope to the sailor who has already reached the shore.' And, further, Shaw had remarked: 'I can forgive Alfred Nobel for inventing dynamite, but only the Devil in human form could have invented the Nobel Prize!' The second example, I told Feynman, was that of Paul Dirac. Dirac had been genuinely afraid of the publicity that the Nobel Prize would bring him, and he went to Rutherford for advice. Dirac told Rutherford that he wanted to refuse the award. Rutherford advised him against doing any such thing by saying, 'You will get more publicity by refusing the prize than by accepting it.' Feynman thought that his views corresponded exactly with those of George Bernard Shaw and Paul Dirac. He especially liked it when I told him what Dirac had told me about his Nobel Prize: 'It has been a nuisance,' Dirac had said on several occasions. Feynman told me that the only pleasure he found in the Nobel Prize was to discover how many people loved him; he had found a genuine thrill in the messages of congratulations, expressing love and affection and admiration, many of them from school children, students, and boyhood friends and acquaintances. The students at Caltech had hung a banner from the top of Throope Hall, proclaiming: 'WIN BIG, R.P.F.' Feynman had loved that (Chapter 26).

I asked Feynman about his scientific heroes. He said there were essentially three: Sadi Carnot, James Clerk Maxwell, and Paul Adrien Maurice Dirac. Carnot obtained a general principle of nature from the nuts and bolts of the thermal efficiency of steam engines; Maxwell, in one stroke, unified electric, magnetic, and optical phenomena. Dirac had discovered the relativistic equation for the electron, which made possible the prediction of the existence of antimatter. During the Symposium on the Past Decade in Particle Theory at the University of Texas at Austin in April 1970, I had occasion to bring Dirac and Feynman together for a discussion at dinner. Dirac told Feynman that the relativistic quantum electrodynamics in its present form was an ugly theory, and before tackling the more difficult problems of elementary particle physics 'one must try to solve the problems of quantum electrodynamics. Electrodynamics is something we know most about, and we must find a consistent theory of it rather than get rid of the infinities in an arbitrary manner.' Feynman agreed with Dirac. Dirac then asked him: 'What would *you* have liked to do most if you had the choice?' Feynman: 'I would have liked to have discovered the Dirac equation for the electron!' Dirac: 'Things were simpler then.'† Paul Dirac had always been Richard Feynman's hero since he

---

† Almost exactly the same exchange of remarks took place between P. A. M. Dirac and W. E. Lamb, Jr., at the 1959 Lindau meeting of Nobel Prize winners in physics. Lamb related this story in his talk on the fine structure of hydrogen at the Fermilab Conference on the Birth of Particle Physics.[5]

first came across Dirac's book *The principles of quantum mechanics* in his first year at MIT.

Feynman and I talked a lot about education and teaching methods in schools, and he described in detail his experiences as a member of the State Curriculum Commission in California (Chapter 20). He was particularly against what the psychologists and sociologists were doing to schools with half-baked antiscientific theories in the name of science. He was one of those who hold the view that anybody who wishes to see a psychiatrist should have his head examined! Relating to intelligence tests, Feynman told me the story of an occasion when he was visiting Santa Barbara for a scientific meeting. As they were about to leave for Santa Barbara, the wife of a friend took Feynman aside and said that her husband would probably not ask it of him, but wouldn't he like to have his name proposed for the membership of MENSA, an organization whose members all have IQs of 150 or more. Feynman told her, 'But you know, when I was tested in high school, my IQ was found to be 125, so I cannot be elected a member of your organization.' Feynman had a good laugh as to what these high IQ people talked about with each other and thought about people with lower IQs than their own. He was glad that he was not one of them.

Feynman and I discussed his showmanship, pranks, and hustling. I told Feynman the story concerning the Indian mathematician Srinivasa Ramanujan when he lay sick in a clinic in Putney in London and G. H. Hardy went to see him there. Hardy thought that anything having to do with numbers would amuse Ramanujan and said, 'Ramanujan, the number of the cab I came by was peculiarly uninteresting. It was 1729.' To which Ramanujan immediately responded, 'No, Hardy, that's a most interesting number. It is the smallest number which can be expressed as the sum of two cubes in two ways!'

Feynman at once took up the theme. He recalled that at Princeton he and John Wheeler once went to a seminar on number theory in the mathematics department. An acquaintance, a pure mathematician, came up to Feynman and exclaimed, 'You, Feynman, are you *also* interested in number theory?' Feynman: 'Yes, a little bit.' The conversation then turned to Ramanujan and the mathematician mentioned the number 1729. Then Feynman said, 'I told him not to tell me any further. Then I acted as if I was thinking very hard. I creased my forehead, raised my eyebrows, tapped my head, and whistled, all in a gesture of instantaneous creativity. Then, with some effort, I said, "I believe it is the smallest number which can be expressed as the sum of two cubes in two ways!" The poor mathematician was floored; he thought I was a number theory genius.'

I kept my bargain about telling Feynman stories at lunch. One story was about Feynman's own first visit to Zurich, Switzerland, in 1949, which I had learned from Valentine Telegdi. In Zurich, at the joint ETH–University colloquium on theoretical physics, Feynman gave a talk on his space–time approach to nonrelativistic quantum mechanics. After the lecture, Walter Heitler very diffidently and respectfully turned to Feynman (then about age thirty) and said: 'What you said, Professor Feynman, didn't sound like orthodox quantum mechanics to me.' Feynman, a tall man, stooped down to the height of the short, seated Heitler and, rolling a chalk between the palms of his hands, said ironically, 'Listen, Heitler, what you just heard was not orthodox quantum mechanics; it's something *I* figured out by myself.' When I told this story, Feynman laughed at his behavior at the expense of Heitler and told me, 'It seems you have been talking to Telegdi', which I had been.

I related to Feynman other anecdotes about physicists. Some of these were Pauli stories. I told him what I had learned from Pauli when I asked him about his opinion of various physicists. Feynman especially enjoyed the following remarks of Pauli. About Oppenheimer, Pauli had said: 'He always acts like the caricature of God in action!' About Hermann Weyl: 'One must first penetrate his façade [literally 'makeup', *Schminke* in German] in order to understand his thoughts.' About Léon Rosenfeld: 'He is the choirboy of the Pope [Niels Bohr]!' About Freeman Dyson, which I had heard from Telegdi: 'Everyone wants to learn something from me; no one wants to teach me anything. I had hoped Dyson would do it, but he's only a mathematician!' By now, Feynman was becoming quite eager: 'Did you ask Pauli about me?' I said, 'Yes.' 'Well, what did he say?' I replied, 'When I asked Pauli what he thought of you, he was amused, and replied, "Oh, Feynman, that Feynman, he talks like a gangster!"' This story made Feynman's day; nothing could have pleased him more.

During these two and a half weeks, Feynman had told me hundreds of details about the conception and execution of various ideas connected with each of his scientific works; he had allowed me to ask him intimate questions about his thoughts, motivations, and feelings of suffering and elation in the pursuit of scientific discovery—and many of these details are recaptured throughout this book.

On 26 January, he lay down on the chaise longue on the patio of his house, while I sat nearby in a chair, with the tape-recorder on the table between us. The scene was uncannily Freudian. Feynman closed his eyes and said, 'Now, Professor, psychoanalyze me!' I took up the theme of scientific creativity and discovery as applied to his own experience. 'Do you feel a sense of power when you attack a new scientific problem?' I asked him at one point. 'No,' he said, 'I feel utterly dopey most of the time, but if it comes out all right I feel happy. Each time it is a fresh experience of feeling stupid and finding joy or despair.' But the despair wouldn't last long; Feynman would move on to something else that excited him.

Feynman described his interactions with other physicists. He expressed candid opinions, mostly charitable, about the various scientists he had known. It would be impossible to say here much more about the myriad topics we covered in our discussions; many of them are treated in this book.

On the last day of our discussions, 27 January 1988, Feynman and I left for lunch at the Athenaeum, the Caltech faculty club, at about 12.30, as had become our custom. As we walked down the stairwell of the Lauritsen High Energy Physics Laboratory, Feynman asked me what I thought about

Whittaker's account of the early history of special relativity theory in his book
A history of the theories of aether and electricity. I told him that I thought that
Whittaker had given a fair account of the work of Lorentz and Poincaré, but
had failed to point out clearly that Einstein had been the first to abandon the
use of the concept of aether in deriving the equations of special relativity
theory; in doing this, Einstein had been much bolder than either Lorentz or
Poincaré. Whittaker had been completely fair in discussing the background of
Einstein's general relativity theory. Feynman said that he entirely agreed. He
asked me: 'Why are the historians of science so much up in arms against
Whittaker?' I replied: 'For a number of historians of science, as for some
physicists also, Einstein represents their own private territory, a kind of a
hallowed personality who belongs *to them alone*; they believe that it is their
burden to protect Einstein's reputation from all criticism, however just or
mild?' Feynman thought that no one, not even Einstein, should be put on a
pedestal to be worshipped.

As we walked towards the Athenaeum, we saw a young couple coming
towards us, with their arms wrapped around each other's waists. From a
distance Feynman shouted in mock disapproval: 'Gee, what have morals
come to on our campus!' The young couple burst into laughter and hugged
each other more closely. Feynman smiled and said: 'Isn't life wonderful?' At
lunch he ordered a bowl of bortsch, which he said his father used to like. 'But
this bortsch does not look like the one I used to know,' he said, and swallowed
only a couple of spoons of that concoction. Then he ordered for himself a
chocolate éclair. A Korean student, a devout Christian, came over from an
adjacent table and respectfully asked Feynman: 'Are you Richard Feynman?'
Feynman said, 'Many people think I am.' The student said that he was at one
of the California state universities, where the teacher made the students learn
from the *Feynman lectures on physics*. Feynman said that the teacher should
not '*make* you do it; you should read them only if you find pleasure in doing
so.' The student then said that he was a fervent Christian and he believed that
Christ was ever present. Feynman said that if that was so, could the student
give him Christ's address and phone number? The student remarked that it
was a matter of faith. Feynman wished him well in his faith.

After lunch we returned to Feynman's office in the Lauritsen Laboratory.
Before entering the building, Feynman stood outside while I took a couple of
pictures of him. Then, in his office, we resumed the discussion of the last items
on my list. I asked him, 'Which people have exercised the greatest influence on
you, and where have you enjoyed your life the most?' Feynman: 'First of all,
my father. Then my physics teacher, Mr Bader. At MIT, Phillip Morse and
John Slater. At Princeton, it was John Wheeler. I greatly appreciated the brief
contact I had with Einstein and Pauli; they were very nice gentlemen. At Los
Alamos and Cornell, it was Hans Bethe; I came to have great affection and
admiration for him. But science is a collective enterprise, and I have learned
from many people. I have been very happy at Caltech. It is a one-dimensional

school, which is ideally suited for a one-dimensional guy like me. No clutter with philosophy, history, psychology, and sociology—just the emphasis on science and engineering. I have made many friends here.'

I asked him about his scientific work and the things that had given him the greatest pleasure. Feynman: 'The most exciting thing was the space–time (path-integral) formulation of nonrelativistic quantum mechanics; the work on quantum electrodynamics followed from that. The work on liquid helium was very exciting, too. In the V–A theory I discovered the only law of nature I could lay a claim to, but other people discovered that law at the same time.[6] I would really have liked to have solved the problem of superconductivity, and develop a quantum theory of gravity. I enjoyed the work on biology; when I began to pursue it, I became a full-time graduate student of that field. What do *you* think of my contribution to physics?' I said, 'My answer would be what Einstein wrote to Langevin about Louis de Broglie's thesis when the former asked Einstein's opinion of it. Einstein wrote: "He has lifted a corner of the veil of Nature." I believe that's what you have done also.' Feynman replied: 'I have been trying to dance with and woo her [Nature] all my life, but she doesn't let you lift her veil.'

Finally, after our last discussion on 27 January in his office at Caltech, I drove Richard Feynman to his house at about 4:30 p.m. On the ride to his house, he told me how awful he felt. During our conversations he would seem to revive and become animated. Then he returned to his brief exchange with the young Korean student. He said that a faith like that was admirable if it could sustain one. As for himself, he said, 'I'm a little curious as to what is on the other side, but I think that the end of life is like the falling of a leaf into eternity.' We reached Feynman's house. We went through the garage into the kitchen, where I wished him well and said goodbye. He said: 'Mehra, I am very grateful that you find me *in-ter-es-ting* and wish to write my scientific biography. All the best.' I left him standing in the kitchen, hunched over with his hands resting on the table. As I closed the door behind me, I stifled a sob; the thought crossed my mind that I had seen the last of a great physicist and a most extraordinary man.

I flew back from Los Angeles to Houston the next morning. On 16 February I was in Boston, ready to fly to New York, from where I had to go to give lectures at the State University of New York in Stony Brook and at Cornell. I turned on the television for news: the world learned of Feynman's passing on the previous day. That evening, from Stony Brook, I telephoned Valentine Telegdi, who was in Pasadena. He informed me that the students at Caltech had hung up a banner from the top of the Millikan Library, which proclaimed: 'We love you, Dick.' Indeed, we all do.

Jagdish Mehra
Houston, Texas
9 October 1993

Notes and References

1. Mark Kac, *Enigmas of chance: An autobiography*. Harper and Row, New York, 1985, p. xxv.

2. Jagdish Mehra and Helmut Rechenberg, *The historical development of quantum theory*, Vol. 5, *Erwin Schrödinger and the rise of wave mechanics*, Parts 1 and 2. Springer, New York, 1987.

3. Freeman Dyson, *From Eros to Gaia*. Pantheon Press, New York, 1992, p. 314.

4. Freeman Dyson, Conversations with Jagdish Mehra, in Princeton, New Jersey, 25 February 1987.

5. W.E. Lamb, Jr., The fine structure of hydrogen. In: *The birth of particle physics* (ed. L.M. Brown and L. Hoddeson). Cambridge University Press, 1983, p. 326.

6. E.C.G. Sudarshan and R.E. Marshak developed the V–A theory of weak interactions at the same time as Richard Feynman and Murray Gell-Mann. See Chapter 21.

1

'If it's a boy, he'll be a scientist'

Richard Phillips Feynman's father, Melville Arthur Feynman, came to the United States of America as a child of five from Minsk, in Byelorussia, with his parents in 1895. His father, Jakob (Louis) Feynman, a Lithuanian Jew, had settled in Minsk with his family. Many of the Russian and Polish Jews at that time had a great faith in the new science that was developing, and Jakob Feynman had fallen in with a group of rationalists. Times were hard in Minsk, especially for the Jews, and Jakob —with his wife Anne and son Melville emigrated to America, where, on arrival, he settled in Patchogue, Long Island, New York. It was in Patchogue that Melville grew up. He was taught at home by his father and then by special tutors. He attended a regular high school in Patchogue. Melville never successfully went to college. His ambition was to go to medical school, but not having much money, he enrolled in a homeopathic institute. He lived in a house where people were very poor, and he became involved in helping them. For lack of funds he discontinued his medical education at the homeopathic institute. However, he was eager to learn and absorbed a great deal of knowledge, especially in the sciences; he learned from his father and other people, or taught himself. Like his father Jakob, Melville had a rational mind, and liked those things which could be understood by clear thinking.

Melville Feynman had different jobs and occupations; apparently he never became a very successful man. He lived through the Depression, and he was forced to make a living in different ways, such as shirt manufacturing or running drycleaning stores. Richard Feynman recalled: 'My earliest memory is that he sold Whiz, which was some kind of agent for cleaning and polishing automobiles. We had a garage full of Whiz of different kinds; it was something like Simonize polish.'[1] In partnership with a friend, called Brockman, Melville opened a real estate business, which did not work out. Then, again with Brockman, he started a chain of cleaning stores called 'Sanis Cleaners, New York'. This was a chain of drycleaning stores, the first 'dollar cleaners'. This was in the 1920s. The cleaning business flourished, until a third man, Paul, was brought in, who was clever enough to put out first Melville and then his partner Brockman. 'So my father got put out of his tree. Ultimately, he got his most permanent job as a sales manager for a large uniform company, called Wender and Goldstein. From then on he was in the uniform business most of his life.'[1]

Melville Feynman married Lucille Phillips. Her parents had come from Germany at a young age. Her father, Henry Phillips, became a very successful businessman; he manufactured shirts as a partner in the Phillips-Jones-Van Heusen Company, and was called 'the father of the trimmed-hat business'.[1] Lucille was born in New York and, being the daughter of a relatively successful man, she received a fine education. She went to the Ethical Culture School in New York City, which had a considerable influence upon her.[2] However, she did not go to college.

Lucille had an elder sister named Pearl. She was a woman of superior intellect, and liked plays and reading. She married a man called Harold Levine, whom she thought was compatible intellectually, 'but he was rather dull, uninteresting, and not a very able man'.[1] Henry Phillips and his wife lived with their two daughters and their families in their large house with a big garden. The house, situated in rural surroundings in Far Rockaway, Queens County, New York, was a couple of miles from the beach.

Richard Phillips Feynman, the first child of Melville Arthur Feynman and his wife Lucille, was born on 11 May 1918 in Far Rockaway. Before Richard was born, Melville had told Lucille, 'If it's a boy, he'll be a scientist,' and he guided Richard in that direction during his childhood.[1] When Richard was three or four, another son was born to his parents, but he died very young, only a month or so after his birth. Richard would remember that that child cried all the time and had a finger bleeding constantly; it was some kind of disease that did not heal. Richard's sister Joan was born when he was nine years old. When Joan was born, 'I remember asking the nurse how they knew whether it was a boy or girl, and being told that one knew it by the shape of the ear; even then I thought that was strange. It didn't sound like a sensible thing.'[1] As Richard grew up, he had no brothers or sisters to play with. 'But we lived in this house where there were cousins, the children of my mother's sister, and we lived together, so it was very much as if there were brothers and sisters. Their father worked in the shirt business for a while. There was a cousin three years younger than I, a girl called Frances, and a boy, Robert, three years older than I. We all played together.'[1]

At first all of them lived together in this big house in Far Rockaway for a few years when Richard was very young, and had started elementary school. Then, when he was about ten, his father moved his wife and children to the nearby town of Cedarhurst, where they lived separately from the rest of the family for a couple of years. Then they returned to Far Rockaway again. Richard recalled: 'The husband of my mother's sister was not able to provide a fine home for his family, with adequate finances; they had troubles, and he held rather mundane jobs in the shirt factories, maybe as head of shipping in the shirt business. Both sisters had married men who did not have financial luck. The husbands were not as successful businessmen as their father had been. This explains why they lived together. The house had been left by the father to the two daughters—my mother and my aunt—as part of his estate.'[1]

Melville played a lot with little Richard, whom he and his wife always called Richy or Ritty, never Dick. They fooled around a lot and had a very good relationship with each other. When Richard was very small, Melville went to a company that made bathroom tiles and got a lot of extra old tiles. He would stand them up on a tray of the high chair on end, in a long row as one does with dominoes. Then they would all get ready. Richard was allowed to push it at the end, and the whole pile would go over. Melville would play this game over and over again. He would play other games with the tiles as well. 'He would say, "Now we put a white one, now a blue one." Sometimes I'd want to put two blue ones together and he would say, "No, No. There must be a white one now." My mother would say to him, "Now let the boy put a blue one." He would say, "No, we have to get him to understand patterns." This was the only thing I could do at that age, to think about patterns and to recognize them as being interesting. After a short time with this game, I could do extremely elaborate patterns. Once I got to pay attention, I would put two blues, two whites, and so on, and repeat the pattern. So my father started as early as he could to interest me in a kind of mathematics, sort of shadow mathematics.'[3]

When Richard went to kindergarten at about six years of age, they had something that in those days was called weaving. They used a kind of colored square paper, with about quarter inch slots made parallel, and then quarter inch strips of paper. One was the woof and the other was the warp. One was supposed to weave it and make designs that were regular and interesting. Apparently this kind of weaving was extremely difficult for a child, but Richard seems to have done it very well; the teacher was surprised and excited by his designs and commented favorably on them. He found it easy, whereas for most of the other children of the kindergarten it was a difficult exercise.[1]

Ritty was not good at drawing at this time. His father was good at it though, and he would try to show him some tricks with drawing. He showed him how to make the sort of letter signs one found in a butcher shop.

Melville had books in the house, though they were not scientific books in the conventional sense. He had books like *Devils, drugs and doctors*, or *Men and medicine*. Ritty became interested in mathematics and science quite early on. 'My father had interested me in patterns from the beginning. Then, later, we would turn over the stones and watch the ants carry the little white baby ants down deeper in the holes. We would look at the worms. It was all part of playing. When we would go for walks, we would look at things all the time, and then my father would tell me about things of every kind: the stars, bugs, geometry. He was always telling me interesting things: the way the birds fly, the way the oceans work. I don't know why, but there was always talking about the world, from every angle. My father talked not only about mathematics, but the whole range of things he was interested in. He was always telling me things.'[1]

In the summer the Feynmans would take their vacations in the Catskill mountains. There would be a large group of people there, but the fathers would all go back to New York to work during the week and only come back again over the weekend. 'On weekends, when my father came,' recalled Richard, 'he would take me for walks in the woods. When the other mothers saw this, they thought it was wonderful and that the other fathers should take their sons for walks. They tried to work on them but they did not get anywhere at first. They wanted my father to take all the kids, but he didn't want to because he had a special relationship with me. So it ended up that the other fathers had to take their children for walks the next weekend.

'The next Monday, when the fathers were back at work, we kids were playing in a field. One kid said to me, "See that bird? What kind of bird is that?" I said, "I haven't the slightest idea what kind of bird it is." He says, "It's a brown-throated thrush. Your father does not teach you anything!"

'But it was the opposite. He had already taught me: "See that bird? It's a Spencer's warbler." (I knew he didn't know the real name.) "Well, in Italian it's *Chutto Lapittida*. In Portuguese, it is *Bom da Peida*. In Chinese, it's *Chung-long-tah*, and in Japanese it is *Katano Tekeda*. You can know the name of that bird in all the languages of the world, but when you are finished, you'll know absolutely nothing whatever about the world. You'll know about the humans in different places, and what they call the bird. So let's look at the bird and see what it's doing—that's what counts." I learned very early from my father the difference between knowing the name of something and knowing something.'[1,3]

Feynman explained: 'My father understood that knowledge was different from the names of things. The names of things are only a convention that human beings use to discuss things, and of course that is important. But when he would tell me about looking at the birds, it was not just to look at them but to see what they were *doing*. As an example, he said, "Look, see the birds walking around there. They seem to be pecking their feathers all the time. Why do you think they do that?" And I said, "Well, I don't know." I was a kid of ten or eleven. I said, "Maybe their feathers get ruffled when they are flying." I made an attempt at an explanation. He then said, "If that were the case, they would peck more when they just landed after they flew. And after they got straightened out, walking around, they wouldn't peck so much. So let's see, watch those that land and then see how long they go on pecking and whether or not they peck in their feathers at the same rate." After a while we discovered that indeed they did. So it was not due to a need to straighten out their feathers just after flying. You see, he had made a little experiment, learning how to observe and discuss. But he finally had to tell me that the reason why they pecked their feathers was that they had little lice, that in their feathers they had protein scales that would fall off, and the lice eat that stuff. And, as a matter of fact, in between the joints of the louse leg, there is a kind of grease and, in there, there is a tiny red spider-like mite, very tiny, that eats that, and now that mite is so successful, it doesn't digest all its food very well, so it emits a lot of sugar at the rear end. And in that there is a bacterium or something, which eats that. And then he said that "wherever there is any source of food, where there is any way to live, something will find a way to live there."

'I *knew* that the names of birds he was giving me were not right. And that exactly whether it was a louse or beetle that it was going after was not important. The leg of the louse might not exactly have a mite, but the principle was always right, the spirit was always right, and so that was a lesson about life. And I thought that was very exciting.'[1,3]

On another occasion, 'we were walking somewhere and he picked up a leaf off a tree. This leaf had a flaw—a thing we never look at much—a little brown line that started in the middle of the leaf and like a C-shape. They are sort of deteriorated, a leaf has become brown from something. This little brown line was like the shape of a C, starting somewhere in the middle of the leaf in a curl and came to the edge. And my father said, "You look at this, and you see it is narrow at the beginning and it's wider as it goes to the edge. Now what this is," he said, "is that a fly, a blue fly with yellow eyes and green wings, comes and lays an egg on this leaf. Then the egg hatches into a small maggot-like thing, whose whole life is spent eating this leaf—that's where it gets its food. That's why the egg is left there, and, as it eats along, it leaves behind this trail of eaten leaf which is brown. And, as the maggot grows, the trail grows wider and wider, until it has grown to full length at the end of the leaf, where it turns into a fly—a blue fly with yellow eyes and green wings; it flies away and lays an egg on another leaf." Now I know that he didn't know that it was a blue fly with green wings and yellow eyes, but the idea that he was trying to tell me was the amusing part of life, that the whole thing was just reproduction. No matter how complicated this business is, the main point is to do it again, to have it come out again.'[3]

What Feynman's father taught him as a child was to notice things. 'One day when I was playing with what we call an "express wagon", which is a little wagon with a railing for children to play with. It had a ball in it, and I pulled the wagon and noticed something about the way the ball moved. So I went to my father and I said, "Say, Pop, I noticed something. When I pull the wagon, the ball rolls to the back of the wagon; it rushes to the back of the wagon. And when I'm pulling it along and I suddenly stop, the ball rolls to the front of the wagon, why is that?" And he said that nobody knows. He said, "The general principle is that things that are moving try to keep on moving and things that are standing still tend to stand still unless you push them hard." And he said, "this tendency is called *inertia*, but nobody knows why it's true." Now that's a deep understanding. He didn't give me a name. He knew the difference between knowing the name of something and knowing the thing itself, which I learned very early. He went on to say, "If you look close, you'll find that the ball does not rush to the wagon, but it's the back of the wagon that you are pulling toward the ball—that the ball stands still or, as a matter of fact, from the friction, starts to move forward really and doesn't move back." So I ran back to the little wagon and set the ball up again and pulled the wagon from under it and looking sideways and seeing indeed that he was right. The ball never moved backwards in the wagon when I pulled the wagon forward. It moved backward relative to the wagon, but relative to the sidewalk, it moved forward a little bit, it's just that the wagon caught up with it.'[3]

The Feynmans had the *Encyclopaedia Britannica* at home, and even when Richard was a small boy his father used to seat him on his lap and read to him from the encyclopedia. They would read, say, about dinosaurs, maybe about the *Brontosaurus* or *Tyrannosaurus rex*, and the encyclopedia would say something like this: 'This thing is twenty-five feet high and the head is six feet across.' So Melville would stop the reading and say, 'Let's see what that means. That would mean that if he stood in our front yard he would be high enough to put his head through the window, but not quite, because the head is a little bit too wide and it would break the window as it came by.' Everything that they read, Melville would translate as best he could into some reality, and little Ritty learned to do that; everything he read he would try to figure out what it really meant, what it was really saying by translating it. So he got used to reading the encyclopedia when he was a little boy, but with proper translation, so it was very interesting and exciting to think that there were animals of such magnitude. Ritty wasn't frightened that there would be one coming in through his window as a consequence of this exercise, but he thought it very interesting that they all had died out by that time and nobody knows why.[1,3] 'And I learned from my father really that if you look at anything closely enough and keep working and turning over and over, there's gold down there. You get something very interesting out at the other end, if you look deeply enough. And that was, of course, a motivation: trying to answer questions as far as possible.'[1]

Melville would often take Ritty to the Museum of Natural History in Manhattan. For Ritty, the Museum was a great place. They would look at the dinosaur bones. 'That was great. I remember my father talking, talking, talking. When you go into the Museum, for example, there are great rocks, which have long cuts and grooves in them, from the glaciers. When I was there the first time, my father stopped and explained to me about the ice moving and grinding. He would explain all the stuff to me, that this ice moves, it might look solid but it moves; with its tremendous height and weight it moves gradually, year by year, an inch every year, grinding and pushing. He described vividly what was going on. That's the way he did it, not just "These are glacier cracks!" His approach was quite different. The ice had to be felt as you saw the top of it. Then he would ask me: "How do you think that we know that there were glaciers all over the world at a certain time?" I don't remember what I answered, but he would point out, "Look at that. These rocks are found in New York. And so there must have been ice in New York." He understood. Something that was very important about him was not the facts but the process, the meaning of everything, how one finds out things, what is the consequence of finding such a rock. He would give us a vivid description of the ice, which was probably exactly right. Perhaps the speed was not an inch a year but ten feet per year. I never knew. But my father would describe anyway, in a vivid way, and with always a lesson about it like, "How do you think we ever find these things out?" And there, of course, would stand in front of me the method. That's the kind of guy he was. It is therefore not hard to understand that I have been interested in science. It was very good.'[1,4]

Melville had started taking Ritty out to the Museum of Natural History quite early and, in fact, a visit to the City meant a visit to the Museum. Feynman recalled that once, when he was twelve, a cousin, who lived in New York, invited him to visit her there. She was six years older. She thought that she'd show him New York and the buildings and everything else. As soon as he got there, she asked him, 'What would you like to see?' His answer was: 'I want to go to the Museum.' He thought that the Museum was the only good thing in New York: 'to me New York was the Museum of Natural History.' But his cousin 'probably spent a dull day'. Richard usually went to the Museum with his father alone. Actually the science did not spread to the other members of the family, to the cousins the Feynmans were living with. Richard's sister Joan ultimately did catch the scientific interest, but Melville's influence was not direct in her case; she would overhear their father and Richard talking, and then she would ask Richard various things, and he would explain them to her.[1]

Feynman always remained very proud to admit that he had been trained by his father. 'I find him now, when I look back, a very remarkable man, because I have since met many scientists and trained people and there are only a few, *but they are very few*, who understand deeply what science is about, so to speak. And he had a complete understanding of what not to pay attention to, the difference between naming things and the facts, the fact that if you looked into things you always found exciting things. He had a complete understanding of the deeper flavor of science, which he communicated to me, and he liked it so much that he couldn't stop telling me things to illustrate all those things. Although formally not a scientist himself, he had the spirit of a scientist. I don't believe that he did any particular research; he just thought about everything. And he understood its flavor, and knew what it was all about. In a way, he never knew the *facts* very well. But he knew *truths*. A truth like that wherever there is any source of food, some form of life finds its way to live on it. That's a truth, but which form finds which food? That he did not particularly know, but he could make it up, and I always knew where he was making up the details. And I knew that he was telling me a fundamental fact at the same time. We had a good relationship. There was always certain humor in it, there was a certain pathos in it, interesting twists in nature always. There was always fun that when you start with something dumb like why birds peck in their feathers you end up with a fundamental principle of life. It was great.'[1]

There was no doubt that the first major, perhaps the greatest, influence on Richard was his father. 'He influenced all the other influences. First of all, he was motivating me. He was telling me, not by forcing me, not by saying "You should be a scientist" or this or that, but by telling me these terrific things, making me learn that if I looked into this stuff it would be exciting and so I acted on that from then on. So he motivated me that way. He also got me to the point of reading with him the *Encyclopaedia Britannica*, which is a kind of heavy book, at bedtime. As he would read, he would explain. He would stop and explain what the words meant. He would translate words, ideas, concepts, etc., in terms that I could comprehend. Everything we read had to be translated into understandable things, and this also became a characteristic of my own and my work all the time. I find great difficulty in understanding most things that other people are doing or how they do them. I always try to translate it back, back, back, into some way that I can understand.'[1]

One of the things that Melville taught his young son, besides science and nature, was a disrespect for the seemingly respectable—irreverence for certain kinds of authority. For example, Richard recalled that when he was little his father once showed him a picture from a newspaper of the Pope with everybody bowing in front of him, and asked him why the Pope was different from other people. 'It was only because of the name and his position, because of his uniform, not because of something special he did, or his honor, or something else like that.' It was the same for all figures of authority: 'The difference is epaulets', he would say in the case of a general, for example. It was always the uniform that gave the person authority; otherwise he was like anyone else. 'He, by the way, was in the uniform business. So he knew what the difference was with the man with the uniform off and the uniform on: it was the same man for him.'[3]

There was no stopping Feynman once he got started talking about his father. 'The old man had a kind of strictness about how to look for reality, look for what is real and permanent and experimentally verifiable, the logic behind all that, and disrespect for authority. It didn't make any difference who had said something; you had to watch the reasoning, the reasoning alone, never mind the name of the man who said it. Just because so and so said this and thought this doesn't mean that the logic is any good; you have got to look at the logic. There were positive efforts not to pay attention to who said it. It was not just disregard, it was an understanding that it was irrelevant. It's just the same as a name. As a result, I have always had a great deal of difficulty: I don't know the names of things. It's rather silly, because when you get in the outside world and you have to talk to other people, it's very easy to have a shorthand and not to have to wave your arms or describe things in utter detail. But I don't remember the name of a certain theorem; I don't know what that theorem is called. Oh! You mean the total number of particles coming in is equal to the total number of particles going out! So I can't remember the names; I was taught not to pay attention to them.'[1]

Although his father had been paramount in Feynman's growing up, his mother also exerted some important influence. 'My mother had a great sense of humor, much better than my father's. I am sure that she influenced me in appreciating the importance of humor, but my father had an aspect of humor that she didn't use much because he didn't have the full flavor of humor. He looked at things in a screwy way, a strange way. You look at it funny and it looks quite different, and that's always a little humorous because of the surprise. So that, combined with my mother's sense of humor, makes me have a lot of fun looking at things the wrong way around and having it come out right. But my mother was a compassionate person whom everybody liked and whom everybody could talk to because she was a good listener. I didn't learn that. My mother was one of those wonderful people that many others seek out to discuss their inner problems with, but I did not learn from her how that works. I can't do it.'[1]

When Richard was ten or eleven, Melville took the family to live in the nearby town of Cedarhurst. When Richard first came to Cedarhurst, he had to meet new boys and learn to get along with them. He had accidentally learned a trick, which they had never seen. A clothesline, lighted at one end, burned like a cigarette, and would go on and on. For Richard, it acted like a clock. He would mark it off, and know when to return home—he used to carry this thing around! The other kids saw it at Cedarhurst, and said, 'Oh, that's a neat idea!' Then they all got the clothesline, which they began to use to burn each other with; it shocked and disturbed Richard. He also discovered at the same time that when he put the lighted clothesline on his bicycle and drove around, it burned too fast; he thus discovered a fault in the design of his clock.

Richard, now called Ritty by all the children at school, had a chemistry set in Far Rockaway before he went to Cedarhurst. His father had given it to him as a birthday present. The earliest chemistry set was too early. 'I played around with it a little bit, and a lot of kids from the neighborhood came and I showed them the chemistry set. They were big boys, and they took the thing outside, while I stood helplessly by; they mixed up everything with everything else, poured it on the sidewalk, and tried to put a match to it. I stood back, because I was afraid it would explode. But it was full of water and it did not explode. I still remember that it was brownish and made bubbles when you mixed everything together.'[1,4]

This was not Richard's way of doing things; this, for him, was sheer destruction. This was not what the chemistry set was meant for. He never played that way; he never played chaotically with scientific things. 'I realized that their real value was in doing things carefully and systematically and watching what happened, and that was a real pleasure. It was worth it. And this other way, what the older kids did, was just terrible, a silly way to behave.'[1]

In any case, at that time he was too young to want another chemistry set or to do anything with it. 'In Cedarhurst, science developed really consciously, and I began to do a lot of things.'[1] In the basement of the house at Cedarhurst, Richard had a laboratory, where he would test chemicals. 'We put ferrocyanide in the towels, and another substance, an iron salt, probably alum, in the soap. When they come together, they make blue ink. So we were supposed to fool my mother. She would wash her hands and when she dried them, her hands would turn blue. She was horrified, and screamed, "My good linen towels!"'[1,4]

But Richard's mother was generally very cooperative. She was never afraid of these experiments. She used to play bridge, and her bridge partners would ask her: 'How can you let the child have a laboratory? He might blow up the house!' She would just say, 'It's worth the risk.'[1,4] She understood that Ritty's curiosity was worthwhile. Of course, she didn't like it when he ruined her good towels, not at all. They tried to get the stains out, they boiled the towels, they did everything, but nothing helped; the towels just turned yellow from the oxide.

The science teacher at the Cedarhurst Elementary School was Major Connolly, a heavy-set, loud kind of fellow. The students had to call him 'Major' Connolly, because he had been a major in the World War I, and still liked his title; it was important to him. Once Major Connolly tried to explain on the blackboard how the projection system works, how the projector makes pictures on the wall. So he drew a light bulb and a lens, and the other things to explain. Then he drew parallel lines coming out of the bulb. Ritty or one of his friends said, 'But that can't be right. The rays come out of the filament radially, in all directions.' Major Connolly turned around and said, 'I say they go parallel!' But that was the level of the class. The students were ahead of it, and they knew the errors in everything that was taught. Ritty did not learn anything in this class, except that a meter has 39.37 inches. Major Connolly was very good at teaching memory. He had a little side course in which he taught memory training. He said, 'Now, we're going to remember how many inches there are to the meter. This is public school No.39, so that helps with the first two digits.' And then there was some other rule for the last two digits. But the number was definitely 39.37.[1,4] Science came only in the eighth grade in the school. By that time Richard was considerably beyond what was being taught by Major Connolly.

Major Connolly was a liar. He would tell stories about the time he was in the war. He was in an airplane, and he helped to invent the machine gun that shot bullets between the propeller blades as the blades went round, because at first they used to shoot the propellers off. And he was in the plane when they were making the tests, and something went wrong, and they shot the propeller off, and all kinds of things. 'I don't remember whether I believed all this stuff or not. He was difficult. One had to be careful with him. He wouldn't tell you anything right. I knew that.'[1,4] The scientific things that Major Connolly talked about were cockeyed, and his stories were often incredible. Amusing but incredible stories about his exploits in the war: he made himself out to be such an important character, he was always in the forefront of everything. One had to be careful with him.

When Richard was at Cedarhurst, he used to read science fiction, which, because of his love for science, he found interesting. As time went on, he became very upset with it, because often it got more and more ridiculous and anything could happen. Every once in a while there would be an idea that was scientifically interesting in the science fiction stories, but he gradually stopped reading them. After he reached high school, he did not read science fiction anymore.

Richard had confidence in himself to know what was right and what was not. Not just that he was smart; he also had confidence that scientific things are rationally correct. It was not like learning the facts of history which, right or wrong, one learned from the book. The fact that light had to come out of the filament radially never seemed to him as something he had to learn; from his other knowledge, it seemed to him to be obvious. How could it come out parallel? This thing was not a matter of confidence in knowledge; it seemed to be obvious. It was simply an understanding of the material world, a world view by which this was evidently false. It was obviously cockeyed and wrong. Richard had already learned from his father that what one looks at is what one sees. 'To look at things carefully is the way to know what's right; many people have said things without looking that they were wrong, simply because they didn't look. That aspect is vital to science. And that I knew. I knew that people, authorities, often stated things that weren't true, because they didn't know, and they would just say them. So what Major Connolly said was just one of those things to me, his claiming to know something which he didn't, but he had to say it. I know what he was worried about. He was just upset because my friend and I had caught him in front of the whole class. We both understood that he was defending himself against criticism. He could have just said it's true, but he didn't.'[1,4]

So, in grade school, it was this one big general science course. It was one day a week and was meant for boys, who had science and shop, while the girls had cooking, dressmaking, or sewing.

When Richard was in the arithmetic class, the kids had to learn decimal fractions for the first time. One of the problems was to express $3\frac{1}{8}$ as a decimal fraction. Richard wrote 3.125. Then it hit some chord in his memory, and, to show off, he wrote 'equals pi, the ratio of the circumference to the diameter of the circle'. The teacher came by, looked at this, crossed it out, and said, 'No, pi is 3.1416.' Melville had told Richard about pi before he learned decimals for fractions at school; he had also explained decimals to him. Richard was really ahead in arithmetic. He remembered Melville telling him about pi as a great and marvellous property. Everything was always dramatic, that all circles have the same ratio of the distance around to the distance across, and this strange number is a marvellous number and has great significance; pi was something that was written in gold letters. So, when the number 3.125 occurred in school, Richard thought he had hit upon pi again.

At some period the bullies at school began to have some fun at the expense of other kids. When Richard would come into the yard to play, they would hit him and knock him over. One of them would stand behind him, and say, 'What are you going to do today?' and boom! Richard did not know how to handle it; he couldn't. It was really quite a miserable and unhappy experience for him. Approximately at that time, one day he overheard some older kids from a higher grade, as they were going to school, and one of them was saying to the other, 'Rust? Rust is iron chloride.' They were talking about their classroom things. So Richard told them, 'No, excuse me, rust is iron oxide. Oxygen comes from the air and mixes with the iron and it makes iron oxide.'[1,4] The eyes of these kids popped out and they asked him a lot of other questions. They were seniors, in a higher grade. The next time Richard came into the courtyard, and the bullies started to fool around, these other fellows came over and stopped them, and said, 'No, we want to talk to him.' They talked to Richard quite a bit, and would always do so because he was competent in their science subjects. Actually, Richard was making it easy for them to pass the questions in the examinations. But they got interested in him, which stopped the bullies from molesting him, and everything became all right after that. This was still in the elementary school, in fifth grade, while the older kids were in seventh grade.

Richard was good at school. He was always very upset if something went badly, or if he had done something wrong. He always tried to be good. This was because of family and personal discipline. He was above average in most subjects at school, but in arithmetic he was especially good. For instance, when he was ten or eleven, he was called from his class to a previous class which he had attended, in order to explain how to do subtraction. The teacher apparently liked the way Richard did subtraction and wanted him to show it to his class. He had learned subtraction in the Far Rockaway School, but in Cedarhurst they were using a different method at school. 'At any rate, I was already known as some kind of whiz-kid at arithmetic in elementary school.'[1] And his grades reflected this.

Although the school in Cedarhurst was an intellectual desert, Richard became very interested in science there, and did a lot of experiments. He would take bottles of water with oil mixed in them; he would shake them, and the oil would separate. He had a chemistry set, and he would do experiments. At Cedarhurst he acquired a friend by the name of Leonard Mautner. It was Mautner who first really taught him about atoms. As Richard remembered, 'Leonard Mautner explained to me about water. If you keep on breaking it, and breaking it, at the end, "Well, it turns out that there are particles." I remember him telling me about the atoms, so I learned.'[1] And then, he knew about chemicals quite a lot. There used to be a box of calcium oxide. Mautner discovered that calcium oxide was the same stuff they used in mortar for buildings. So he and Richard would go out at night and steal a mayonnaise jug full of that stuff, which was worth at least a few dollars. In his chemistry set, Richard had many boxes full of chemicals, and big bottles of calcium oxide, borax, and other things, which Leonard had found out from his brother were commonplace objects.

Once, Richard got one of the chemicals from his chemistry set in his mouth. He was horrified, thinking it might be poisonous. But Leonard Mautner was not worried. He asked, 'Does it taste a little sour and salty?' That's exactly how it tasted. It was sodium hyposulphate, partly acid, partly salt. Leonard was very good in chemistry; he knew enough about it to allay Richard's fear of poisoning. He was not much older than Richard, there being one year's difference between them at school.

Richard also became interested at that time in electrical things. He bought a pair of earphones from a man to do experiments. The earphones did not work, so he took them apart. He was a child really, fooling around, sometimes breaking and at other times making things.

He was not interested in sports. He was not good at drawing or working with clay. He didn't have any hobbies or interests other than in science, but this didn't take up all his time. He used to run around the streets with his friends and talk about various things. He would discuss the world—the world of school children—or hang around the drug store and drink sodas otherwise he would work in his laboratory.

Richard had a laboratory at home when he was in elementary school in Cedarhurst. He would repair radios in the neighborhood to make a little money to buy things for his laboratory. He had a photoelectric cell. He made amplifiers, though not good ones. Nothing really worked well for him, but he struggled with it. He had a laboratory bench, and batteries and old radios and motors, and so on. Electrical stuff. His laboratory had developed from a chemical laboratory into an electrical one, which he would continue to use, even through high school.

A cousin of his, Adele Curott (née Rosenbaum), who lived in Far Rockaway and was a year older, recalled that when Ritty was ten or eleven he would come by their house to see if they had any radio to give him; he explained that he wanted to take it apart and put it back together. Adele remembered that he was the recipient of their first radio, a De Forest, with a green strung aerial and earphones, which he liked to fiddle with on her family's library table.[5]

Richard did have an interest in repairing radios, but it was connected with his laboratory and equipment. Everything he did at that time was connected with his laboratory. He had become interested in repairing radios in Far Rockaway, and carried this interest to Cedarhurst. It was the Depression, and people could not have their radios repaired by the regular repairman. They discovered that Richard, even though a youngster, could repair them, and they would hire him to repair their sets. 'The first person who hired me was my aunt, who ran a resort hotel. She called me up one day and said that her radio was out of commission. Actually she had somebody else call. 'This is such and such hotel, do you know anything about radios?' 'Well, a little', I said. 'Would you come and repair our radio, please. It doesn't work.' I said, 'But I am only a little boy.' They said, 'That's all right, we understand from good authority that you know something. Would you like to fix our radio?' I said, 'Very well, I'll try.' And I went. I, a little boy, went with a large screwdriver sticking out of my pocket; I took my tools in my pocket! I went to see the radio. They had a handyman in the hotel, who was a nice fellow. I found out rather quickly that the switch wouldn't work, only because the knob slipped on the shaft. I could see that it couldn't work because the screw was broken. After I pointed out what the trouble was, the handyman fixed it up. He figured out a way to fix it that I might not have been able to do. He helped me. And so I was successful in my first repair job.'[1,4]

Following this, Richard had good luck with things like this. For the next person who called him up, it was only the plug in the wall that had to be fixed up. The jobs became more and more complicated in the right order; it was almost as if a course had been prepared. 'Otherwise I might have been horribly discouraged at the beginning, but by sheer luck the jobs grew only gradually in difficulty.'[1,4] Richard put up a new antenna. That just meant climbing up the roof. One day he was fixing up the antenna on the roof and, as his mother was coming home, she saw him climbing up somebody's roof and fixing things; she was horrified. Gradually, he got more and more difficult jobs, because people, such as his mother's friends, had heard of his talent for repairing radios. Finally, he got jobs that were outside the family circle. Richard and his friend Bernard Walker were working for a painter, and another painter, to whom they had something to deliver, wanted to help Richard out. He found out that Richard could fix radios, so he got him some jobs, and they were people whom Richard did not know at all.

There was an amusing incident in one of his jobs. The man, who wished to have his radio repaired, called for Richard to take him to his place in a car that was a wreck. They got into the car, and the man said, 'You are only a child, How can you expect to fix radios?' All the way to his house he was muttering about 'only a child fixing radios'. Finally they reached his place. Richard asked him, 'What's the matter with the set?' 'Oh', the man said, 'It makes noises when you first turn it on, but the noise then stops and everything becomes all right.' Richard thought, 'How can this fellow worry about a mere noise when he's got no money.' He turned the radio on; it gave out a blood-curdling noise, a terrifying racket, and one could see why the guy wanted to have it fixed. After a while, the noise quieted down, and the radio would play all right. So Richard turned it on, listened to it, turned it off, and started to walk back and forth, thinking. 'What are you doing? Can you fix it?' the man asked. 'I'm thinking,' Richard answered. He tried to figure out how there could be noise that disappears? Something is changing with time, something is heating up before something else. He guessed that the amplifiers were heating up before the information came in from the grids, from the earlier circuits, thus it was picking up some kind of noise. So, it was probably due to the heating up of the tubes; if he could reverse the earlier tubes, maybe it would be all right. It would then heat up the other way round. He changed the tubes around and put them back, and switched the radio on. It was just as quiet as you please! 'When a man is angry at you and thinks you can't do something and when you *do* do something, he just loves you; there are people of that kind. Afterward you are a god. They are the kind of people that if you succeed, they are absolutely the opposite than they were before. He went crazy. He recommended me to everybody. He said, 'This fellow is a genius! I never saw a man who repaired a radio first by thinking.'[1,6]

For Richard, it was a success of the mind. He loved that. It was a big success, especially after all the things the man had said earlier. 'I love challenges. I always have. In fact, later hobbies at the beginning were not scientific but were always challenges—picking locks, cracking codes, analyzing hieroglyphs that nobody knows how to translate, they were there all the time.'[1,4,6]

In kindergarten and elementary school, Richard used to attend the Sunday School at the synagogue. There he would learn about the stories of the Old Testament, and apply his imagination to try to understand rationally the various accounts of the miracles. Even before he finished elementary school he had decided that he did not want to have anything to do with religion; for him science was much more important, as it reflected his own temperament and questioning attitude to every phenomenon.

The Cedarhurst period had been very fruitful. From Cedarhurst, the family again returned to Far Rockaway. This had to do with the precarious financial situation of the families who lived in the big house there.

The Feynman family did not travel much at this time. In the summer they would go off to the beach. 'We weren't too well off. At that time, my father was making about $5000 a year; I knew it because he sometimes let me take the check to the bank, and it was about $100 per week. This was in the 1930s. I was twelve or thirteen, 1931–32. It was the period of the Depression. My father was in trouble. That was why we moved back to Far Rockaway. There was probably trouble between the two families, I guess. And they moved back because of still higher financial difficulties; that was the logical solution. But I never felt poor. In fact, I remember distinctly, when I used to go to the bank that it was very good. My father knew how to teach me. He would say, "You take the check to the bank." In this way I knew how much money was what. And I remember thinking that that was a very nice amount, that everything was all right, we lived fine, and my ambition was to earn that much money. So I knew I wanted about $5000 a year, that's all I needed. I recall all these dopey things.'[1,4]

At Far Rockaway, Richard got a real laboratory, a better one, in his room. Melville got an old radio packing case, a big box about five feet long and three feet high, and Richard started out by making things of erector set motors and playing.[1] His father had told him that electrochemistry was a very important new field, that it combined the action of electricity on chemicals. Richard remembered that. He loved his father. Everything he told Richard, the latter found great. Richard remembered having a little pile of some chemical, from a chemistry set. He took two wires from the electric plug, and put them into the dry chemicals. Nothing whatever happened. But that was his first attempt to discover what electrochemistry was, especially since his father had told him that it was a big thing.[1]

When Richard got his new laboratory, he put everything into it. He had this laboratory for years, even when he was in high school, but he was developing electrical interests. He had a crystal set in the house, on which he used to listen all night to the program 'The Shadow', and Eno's effervescent salts were being advertised on the radio. Then, by buying in rummage sales, he gradually obtained a tube set, and things like that, which he would fix, and connect to the storage battery he had.

He learned to fix all these things. They were probably not broken in an obvious way. When one looked inside, there would be a wire hanging off, where there should have been a connection. It began that way and went deeper. Richard became more and more involved and learned more about it. At the beginning he would fix simple things in a simple way, and would be very excited if it worked. Then he would try distant radio stations and sit up all night with his speakers and electrical gadgets. Thus he found that if he put the 110-volt line through the electric light bulb into water, it would boil the water; that was his (faulty) understanding of electrochemistry at that time. He also used to develop pictures in those days in their basement; his cousins Robert and Frances took part in this.

Richard enjoyed working with his hands. He liked his laboratory immensely. He worked all the time. He connected the whole house with wires to his lab, so that he could plug in with his earphones to his radio upstairs, anywhere in the house. Then he would use that system in many ways. He would put a loudspeaker somewhere in the house, and go to his laboratory upstairs and broadcast from there.

Richard always remembered something from approximately his last year in the elementary school. 'My dentist, Dr Marx, was the scientist [to me] in town; he was the professional man, who had something to do with science. He was a very nice man but a very poor dentist. I looked at him as though he were a scientist, but I knew no better. When I got a rash on my face, he would tell me that it was impetigo or something and I thought the word was good, and I would try to find out about it, and we would discuss how the teeth worked and what he was doing. He was a sort of "the scientist" for me; that was the level. One has to appreciate that in my town there weren't many scientific books. There were some books in the public library about quantum theory and other things that were coming out, by people like James Jeans, that were almost readable and I struggled with these.'[1,4]

Since Richard asked Dr Marx so many questions, the latter realized that he was interested in science. The dentist had a patient, a chemistry teacher in the Far Rockaway High School, by the name of William LeSeur. LeSeur told Dr Marx, 'Let Richard come around after school one day a week to the chemistry laboratory where I teach, and he can play in the laboratory; sort of help out as a laboratory assistant while we clean up.'[1,4]

So Richard used to go one day a week to the Far Rockaway High School, where LeSeur taught. He was actually an English teacher, but was also assigned to teach general science in the chemistry laboratory. He was really neither very scientific nor very profound. Another man there, Joseph Johnson, who taught real chemistry, took a great interest in Richard, and let him play with the apparatus and do experiments. Richard also met Dr Edwin Barnes, the head of the science department. He found that both Johnson and Barnes were serious people, good teachers of science; they had studied their science and knew it pretty well. So he learned a lot from them and loved to listen to them about scientific and other matters. Richard would clean up the apparatus and they would talk about how the different things worked.

In his science class at the elementary school at Cedarhurst, Richard gave a demonstration of electrolysis for the kids, for which he borrowed the apparatus from the Far Rockaway High School and carried it through the streets on his bicycle. He thought it was the most expensive and remarkable piece of apparatus. It was like the standard equipment, like a big H, with graduated tubes and two stopcocks. It had platinum electrodes at the bottom. 'That was to me valuable and marvellous. I carried it as best as I could through the streets on my bicycle, and took it to the school to make the demonstration. But I pushed the cork up, that held the electrodes, too high and broke the glass. I was terrified and upset by this. I remember very distinctly—it was very serious. I tried to wax it closed. It was leaking while the demonstration was going on. When I took it back to the High School, I was rather upset and unhappy. But they comforted me by saying that it was no so bad. It was all right; "these things happen", they said.'[1,4]

With Johnson and LeSeur, Richard talked about all kinds of things that would come up. They would talk to each other, and Richard would listen in. He remembered a question to which they did not give a satisfactory answer, this being the only one he remembered. 'If everything is made up of atoms, and they are always moving about, how is it that something you find that is very old—like a screw that has been left around for a long time—still retains the sharp corners of the screw. Or you make sharp things. How do these things stay sharp for all that period of time, if the atoms are always moving about?' In answer, they told Richard about the fusion of metals, that if you put gold and silver together there is gradual mixing. But Richard did not feel that was an answer to his question. That's the kind of level at which the whole thing was. 'I was asking a lot of questions, and in spite of everything I learned a great deal.'[1]

In the seventh grade, the last but one of the elementary school, Richard made a scientific discovery. One day he was playing with various pieces of equipment. In the rummage sale he had obtained a loudspeaker, which had no tube, and a microphone. He also had earphones. He connected this system over the entire house. He would try changing the earphones and the speakers around; he had them both connected to a two-way double plug. He was going to plug into the line, to listen, while he had them both connected. Now, while he had the earphones on, he had his fingers accidentally probing the hole of the loudspeaker and touching it, making a noise, and he heard the noise in the speaker. The loudspeaker had a permanent magnet; when he shook it, he generated a current, so he had a telephone. He discovered he could hear that; he could talk into the thing and hear it. He had discovered a kind of microphone, and he used it to talk from upstairs to downstairs.

Richard remembered this discovery in particular, because in the history class they were learning about the discovery of the telephone. He told them that he would give them a demonstration of the telephone. So he got a long vacuum cleaner cord and two plugs at each end, and plugged his loudspeaker to one end (to talk into) and the earphones on the other end (to listen). He went out of the room, and had the wire running under the door, and listened; somebody said something, and he came back and told them what had been said. 'This device was mine, I had invented it.' But he learned later that this was the design of the first telephone. 'If I had known that, which I didn't, I would have been even better in my history class, because I explained to them that my telephone was not really the right kind. I knew that it wasn't. But I didn't know that, in fact, historically it was the right kind.'[1] Richard gave a demonstration of his telephone in a couple of classes at the invitation of the teachers.

Richard's cousin Robert could never get hold of algebra. 'I always pitied the poor fellow. He was terrible in algebra and flunked it most of the time.' Because of Robert's difficulties, a tutor, Mr Albert Maskett, used to come to teach him. Since Richard was fascinated with mathematics, he was allowed to sit in and listen; just listen, not say anything. Richard asked his cousin, 'What are you trying to do?' He said, 'What do you know? $2x + 7$ is equal to 15, and you are trying to find what x is.' Richard told him, 'You mean 4.' The cousin said, 'Yeah, but you did it with arithmetic. You have to do it by algebra.' Robert was forced in school to have to try to find a mystical way of doing it, which was supposed to be 'algebraic'. That's why he was never able to do algebra, for he never understood how he was supposed to do it. 'There was no way', said Feynman. 'I learned algebra fortunately by not learning it at school, and knowing that the whole idea was to find out what x was, and it didn't make any difference how you did it. There is no such thing as doing it by arithmetic or doing it by algebra. That was a false thing that they had invented in school so that the children who have to study algebra could all pass it. They had invented a set of rules which, if you followed them without thinking, could produce the answer. Subtract 7 from both sides; if you have a multiplier, divide both sides by the multiplier, and so on—a series of steps by which you could get the answer if you didn't understand what you were trying to do.'[1,4]

After the tutoring session was over, Richard would talk to Mr Maskett, who became very interested in him and helped him a great deal. What Richard talked to him about was the following. He had discovered a formula for doing the following problem. Suppose you want to add 1 plus 2 plus 3 plus 4, and so on, up to some number. He had discovered that with an odd number of terms, like $1 + 2 + 3$ is 6, $1 + 2 + 3 + 4 + 5$ is 15, a certain rule worked: the rule was that you multiply the odd number by half of one more than the odd number. Eventually, Richard also found a rule for an even number of terms: multiply half the even number by one more than the even number. He made up the following problem. Suppose a theater has a new idea. Instead of charging a definite amount for the movie, it charged 1 cent from the first person who comes, 2 cents from the next one, 3 cents from the third one, and so on, until 100 people come. How much money will he collect from this scheme in the movie?

Richard showed this problem to Mr Maskett, and he showed him how the two rules Richard had could be made into one: you multiply the number by one more than the number and then divide by 2. Richard had two rules, and was now excited to have just one rule. But Mr Maskett was also very pleased by the fact that the little boy had cooked this thing up. So he would always tell him little things and help him along; he kept on encouraging Richard in various ways to discover things.

Richard felt disconnected from the beginning from the conventional way of doing things. 'I was trying to find a formula for adding integers together because I wanted to find the formula. I didn't care whether it had been worked out by the Greeks or even by the Babylonians; that didn't interest me at all. It was *my* problem, and I had fun out of it. It was always the same; I was playing my own independent game.'[1,4]

When Richard was about twelve and was going to bed one night, he asked his father what algebra was. Melville said, 'It has to do with solving problems that you can't do with arithmetic.' 'Like what?' asked Richard. He said, 'Like a house and garage rent for $15 000. How much does the garage rent for?' Richard said, 'But you can't do it that way at all!' Melville left Richard with that vague answer. 'So I knew that algebra was something interesting, and therefore I was somewhat frustrated in discovering what it was. So it was perfectly natural that when I found a book marked "Algebra", that I would become interested in that book.'[1]

When the family returned to Far Rockaway, Richard was doing arithmetic at school, but he had taught himself enough algebra as well. Towards the end of the last grades of the elementary school, he had learned how to solve simultaneous equations, linear equations, like two equations and two unknowns. Then he made up a problem with four equations and four unknowns; he took these equations and went through a formal procedure for solving them. He made up the problem so that the answers would be all integers, and not just arbitrary, and he showed it to the arithmetic teacher in the elementary school. She thought that it was very impressive, but she did not really know much about it. She took it to the principal, who apparently still remembered a little algebra; she went over it and said it was correct, signed her name to it, and complimented Richard for being able to do that. 'I had done that just to show off', recalled Richard.[1]

Near the end of the last grade of the elementary school, Richard became curious about learning how to take square roots. He asked a man teacher about it, who was quite good and also taught science. He knew how to do it numerically, and told Richard the rules. But Richard did not quite trust him; he thought that what the teacher had told him about square roots was false. However, when he tried the method at home it worked.

By the time he was twelve, in the second period of stay in Far Rockaway, Richard had a friend, Bernard Walker, who was interested in science. He and Richard did a lot of things together, including chemistry experiments. Bernard later on went into a semi-engineering business. He did not follow through on his scientific and technical education. This was probably due to family influences, the importance of money and business, so that he became more of a salesman than an honest scientific man, in fact a mixture. At first he developed a process for metal-plating plastics and did some research to develop it. Several years later, shortly before graduating from the Massachusetts Institute of Technology, Richard worked during the summer at Bernard Walker's company, called the Metaplast Corporation. This was Bernard's intermediate stage, when he was still connected with science and engineering. After that he went entirely into business.

Bernard Walker had an encyclopedia, too; he had a thing called *The book of knowledge*, which was designed for children. It was arranged to make things a little bit easier; but you never felt right with it. The thing that bothered Richard the most about it was the index. His father had taught him how to use the index. In this book, under W, for example, you would find What's a horse? or What's the history of a horse? 'People say that I don't respect authority. I also realized that there are stupidities in the world, that people make dumb books. Before reaching high school I had already learned how to have disrespect for authorities, for certain authors, for the opinions of people. I knew that the world was a dopey place, and that there were only a limited number of people who had rational views, like the *New York Times* was a good newspaper, that the *Encyclopaedia Britannica* was *the* encyclopedia. My father read the *New York Times*, so I knew that was a good newspaper; the same with the encyclopedia.'[1,4]

Richard went through the elementary school, enjoying learning all he could and looking forward to high school. Loved dearly by his parents, having the security of a good home life, he had a very cheerful and pleasant childhood. He had already formed a number of attitudes that would follow him throughout life, foremost among them being a rationalistic outlook, disrespect for authority, disdain for ceremony, love of intellectual achievement, and a happy and cheerful disposition. Both of his parents, and his growing success at school and the cultivation of a creative outlook, had begun to contribute greatly to an enlarging world view.

Notes and References

1. R.P. Feynman, Interviews and conversations with Jagdish Mehra, in Pasadena, California, January 1988.

2. J. Robert Oppenheimer also attended the Ethical Culture School, in New York City, as a young boy.

3. R.P. Feynman, in the Public Broadcasting System broadcast, WGBH Boston, 'The pleasure of finding things out', 25 January 1983.

4. R.P. Feynman, Interviews with Charles Weiner (American Institute of Physics), in Pasadena, California, 1966.

5. Personal communication to Jagdish Mehra from Mrs. Adele Rosenbaum Curott, Lynbrook, New York, 3 October 1988.

6. R.P. Feynman, 'Surely you're joking, Mr. Feynman!' (abbreviated as SYJMF). Norton, New York, 1985, p. 20.

2

'What one fool can do, another can do better'

In the fall of 1931, Richard began high school. He was thirteen and a half years old. 'When I was in grade school I looked upon high school as an important stage. I was interested in learning, and the high school offered the opportunity. After all, in high school kids were learning algebra, the same business of which my cousin Robert had the opportunity. So I went to the high school and liked it. I already knew some of the teachers. It was just great to be in high school.'[1]

Richard attended the Far Rockaway High School. It was a mile away from his home, and he walked to it every day. The principal of the school was Mr Ellsworth. He was called 'Pussyfoot' by the students, 'because of his habit of sneaking around and peeking through the windows of the classes to see what was going on. He was a martinet of a pedant, rather than a real disciplinarian, the latter being somebody who has a code of ethics and enforces it.'[2]

Joseph Johnson was the chemistry teacher at Far Rockaway High School; William LeSeur was the general science teacher, and Edwin Barnes taught physics. Richard had already met Messrs Johnson, LeSeur, and Barnes when he was in the elementary school. In 1934, Richard's senior year in high school, Edwin Barnes was joined by Abram Bader as another physics teacher; Barnes was also the head of the science department. Geometry and trigonometry were taught by Dr Earl Augsberry, head of the mathematics department. Lillian Moore was the algebra teacher; she was called 'Battleship Moore' because 'she was built like a battleship—short, stout, and hostile, but she was an excellent teacher; she minded her own business and expected you to mind yours.'[2] Myrtle Simendinger was the teacher of advanced algebra and calculus.

Richard found that the algebra class was boring, because he had already learned algebra. He could see the answers before the teacher wrote down the equations on the blackboard: 'It was just terrible!'[1] Richard suffered this for an entire semester, then he went to the teacher and told her that he knew all that stuff. The teacher sent him to Dr Augsberry, head of the mathematics department and dean of the school, who was called the 'Iron Duke', because he was a strict disciplinarian. 'He had the habit of taking a yardstick and bending it back and forth. You would think that he was going to break it right under your nose. While bending the stick he would say, "You little kids, what do you know!" We had lots of jokes about him.'[2] Dr Augsberry gave Richard an algebra problem, which he had made up; it made Richard sweat. It went to a quadratic equation, but Richard did not know how to solve quadratic equations at that time. He couldn't figure out how to solve the darned thing, and he went around in circles.

Dr Augsberry looked at Richard's papers. He noticed that he had taken a few right steps to solve the problem. He decided that Richard did not have to go to Grade I, but to a class called 2X. This class had Lillian Moore as a teacher, who was especially effective with students who were not very good. She was prim, proper, and purposeful, and could not be made to change her course: she was not called 'Battleship Moore' for nothing. Richard was put in her class. The students in her class had taken everything before, but they had been at the lower end of the class and were repeating it. Richard learned some things from her, because there were things that came up in that class that he did not know, like the quadratic equations; other things he learned on his own.

Something happened in Miss Moore's class. She wrote down a problem: $2^x = 32$, what's x? Nobody could make head or tail of it; it was a new problem, and the students did not have the slightest idea of how to solve it. Richard, however, immediately said, '$x = 5$', and explained that he found it by taking the product of the 2's. He understood what the problem meant. The fact that Richard was able to solve the problem made all the other students angry and a little jealous, but perhaps a few of them admired him. He immediately became somebody special in the class. They thought that Richard had learned how to solve such problems somewhere else, but to him the solution was obvious. When he explained it to them, they still couldn't see. It was the same type of problem as to how he knew that the rays from the light bulb came out radially. It was one of the facts of the world; it was almost self-evident. He never understood what the trouble was.

The thing that bothered the other students was that this was an entirely new matter, and how could this fellow know it? Only by having studied it before could he have known it. But to Richard it was not something new at all, it was the same principle: you use x for a number that you don't know, and the answer to '2 to what the power is 32?' was not something he had to have studied before. He remembered this occasion distinctly, because it gave him a feeling of difference between himself and the other students.

Richard had learned that calculus was a big thing. Now that he was in high school, he wanted to learn it right away. 'I knew by this time by reading the encyclopedia that calculus was an important subject and it was an interesting one, and I ought to learn it. Sometime early in high school my father took me to New York. It was only twenty miles away, but it was a big event to go to Macy's! I wasn't old enough just to go by myself to buy a book. We bought a book called *Calculus made easy*.[3] I had by that time learned how important calculus was, and it wasn't easy to learn it from the encyclopedia. There it was explained why it was interesting and important. So I got this little book and came home very excited. For me, it was a source of information. Nowadays there are books on everything all over the place readily available, but it wasn't like that then. It was much harder. Each thing was a gift; you could take this one book and work on it. I worked on it and made notes. So I learned elementary calculus. My father started to read the beginning of this book and found it rather confusing, and that bothered me a little bit. That's the first time I discovered my father's limitations. He had told me many interesting mathematical things; they were funny little curiosities—about triangular numbers, tetrahedral numbers, etc. We would go to visit the park where they had cannon balls piled into pyramids. He said, "How can we figure out ahead of time that we want to have n balls across at the bottom, how many balls are there altogether in this pile?" I would go home and figure it out after a while. And I discovered a large number of interesting things. Numbers are great! There were all kinds of wonderful things in that book, and I learned elementary calculus from it. It was a very good book. On the first page, the fly-leaf, it said in quotes "*What one fool can do, another can*" (Ancient Simian proverb). I had a certain fear. In those days, Latin and calculus were the impossible things; calculus was the impossible thing in college that nobody could get through. It was a tremendous problem, and everybody was talking about it: "You're going to learn calculus? Calculus is impossible." And this book said, "What one fool can do, another can!" It meant that calculus was done by fools, of course, and you can do it too. I changed this quotation a little bit for my students. I said to them just the other day: "When you read all this stuff, don't just try to learn it. Think of it this way: *What one fool can do, another can do better!*"

'Everything broke down and I learned it easily. I have since realized that that particular calculus book had its especially screwy methods of rates for finding derivatives, not by the usual method of taking limits, and it invented proofs which really weren't proofs; there were errors in proofs. But the author knew the answers all the time, so it always would come out right. But, of course, the proofs were not important. Calculus is really a mechanical process for differentiating and integrating and learning how to do it, and the fact that this book, from the mathematical point of view was a shambles, really made no difference in screwing up my education.'[1,4]

The public library then got a series of books, called *Mathematics for self-study*, which started with *Arithmetic for the practical man*, then *Algebra for the practical man*, and then *Trigonometry for the practical man*. Richard studied the book on trigonometry and promptly forgot it; this was long before he had trigonometry in high school. Then came *Calculus for the practical man*.[5] Richard went to borrow the calculus book from the library, and the librarian said, 'Oh, you are just a child! What are you taking this book out for?' Richard felt uncomfortable. He lied and told her that the book was for his father. He learned from this book also. When he actually came to have calculus from Miss Myrtle Simendinger in high school, she gave him her copy of *Differential and integral calculus* by Clyde E. Love.[6]

Richard's friend Leonard Mautner was with him at Far Rockaway High School; he had come from Cedarhurst. Then he was with him at MIT. Later on in life, Mautner went to live in Pasadena, California, where Feynman was. It was all a pure coincidence. Richard and Leonard learned geometry together. Melville had told Richard that it was impossible to trisect a triangle, that it was impossible to find three pieces which are the same area together as the original triangle. Richard and Leonard managed to do it for an equilateral triangle. They thought that it had never been done before, and dreamed that it would make news in all the papers. Leonard Mautner was about the same age as Richard Feynman, and they did things together.

It was in solid geometry that Richard first encountered mathematical difficulties. In the beginning, solid geometry was for him complete and absolute chaos. 'It was my only experience of how it must feel to the ordinary human being', he recalled.[1] Then he discovered what was wrong. The diagrams that were being drawn on the blackboard were three-dimensional, and he had been thinking of them as diagrams in a plane. Suddenly he realized what was going on; it was child's play again. He had made a mistake in orientation; once he understood it, things became very easy. Richard caught on after about two or three weeks, but during that period it seemed to him to be terrifying. He had made the same kind of mistake as his cousin had made in algebra, but corrected himself fast. Once he realized what was going on, he had no problem in visualizing; he had the perception of depth in solid geometry. Later on he exercised for the purpose of conceptually visualizing things in four dimensions; he discovered that he could do so, although the visualization remained poor and coarse.

In trigonometry, Richard knew the definitions of sine, cosine, and tangent, and applied them to illustrate the practical problems of triangles that he would formulate himself. By knowing the sine of $5°$, he worked out a table for the sines, cosines, and tangents of all the angles. These were the kinds of games he played. By the time he actually got to the trigonometry class, it was a waste of time. In most of the classes he attended, he would do other things on the side; he didn't care, it was too easy!

Dr Earl Augsberry was his teacher in the trigonometry class. There was another student, by the name of Herbert Harris, with whom Richard had become friends now; Leonard Mautner was away somewhere. Herbert was a year older, but because Richard was good in arithmetic, he was in the higher class with him. Dr Augsberry gave them both a challenge. He said that he had two problems which he had given to students from time to time, but they had never been able to solve them. He thought he would like to give them again to Richard and Herbert. He would first give one problem, and if they solved it, he'd give the other. It was a dramatic business.

The first problem was this: given a parallelopiped, and the angles of the three faces and the lengths of the three sides, what is the volume of the parallelopiped? Richard Feynman and Herbert Harris worked for three weeks on this problem. They developed theorems and methods, and gradually worked out a formula for the volume, which was very beautiful. It was the square root of a complicated expression, but it was beautifully symmetric in the angles α, β, γ and the sides A, B, C. However, the method which Feynman and Harris employed was very unsymmetrical, and they attacked the problem in a clumsy manner. In any case, they worked out the problem, and showed it to Dr Augsberry, who was very impressed.

Then he gave them the other problem, which was to find the formula relating the dihedral angles in regular solids and the number of sides in the polyhedron. Feynman and Harris worked that one out too, using many of the same theorems which they had formulated earlier. Dr Augsberry was very impressed; none of his students had ever solved these problems before, but these two youngsters had solved them. For students in high school they were good and substantial problems and really excellent challenges. It was not self-evident how to solve them, but Feynman and Harris pursued them doggedly and got closer and closer to solving them until they got the final answer.

Feynman tried to solve these problems in his head in later years; he thought of the old problems while taking a shower and worked them out in fifteen minutes. The first problem, especially, was beautiful in the sense of symmetry. Richard appreciated the problem of calculating the volume of the parallelopiped, and loved the symmetrical solution, but he did not like the second problem. By this time Richard had already developed a sense of taste about what he liked. He felt that he had a special ability in this area, and was beginning to feel that he would become a scientist somehow. He felt that, of all things, he wanted to do this kind of thing all his life.

Richard did not have any particular area for future work in mind. When, for instance, his father told him that electrochemistry was the up-and-coming field, he would daydream that he would one day become a great electrochemist. He would play around with electric wires and salt, probably to find out what would happen, and think about preparing for this field. Whatever his father told him became a part of his dreams, the other part being what he was doing at school. Although Melville himself was not a scientist, he inspired Richard to become one. The specific field, whether physics or chemistry, was not clear, nor was it clear how he would earn his $5000 per annum. He had decided, however, that it was important for him to do science, though he was not career-minded in high school; he did not know and did not care where the best opportunities lay. When the teachers gave him challenges, he loved them for their own sake, for the fun and excitement of working them out. There was also some conceit involved, some one-upmanship, some showing off, in making other people aware of what he had done. Still, from the beginning he appreciated mathematics and science and wanted to pursue them wherever they might lead him.

Just before the high school period, Richard read *The book of knowledge*, which belonged to his friend Bernie Walker. He also read another book called *The boy scientist* by A. Frederick Commons, which interested him very much. It had a big circle on the front page, in which was inscribed 'Knowledge is power'; then it had arches going out, which said 'chemistry', 'electricity', etc. *The boy scientist* was his own book. Then he got hold of *The boy electrician*. Bernie Walker had another book, in which there were formulas for electric power and resistance, as well as the resistance–voltage relation: the ohms are volts divided by amperes; the watts are amperes squared times ohms, and so on. There were about eight of these formulas. Richard realized at once that these formulas were not all independent, they were restatements of each other. 'I had to learn that these relations were only mathematically interchangeable formulas. You could derive one from the other. So I became interested in the relation of mathematics to physics.'[1]

Later on, in high school, he found the formula for the frequency of the oscillating circuit in a book. At that time he was making oscillators and radio receivers and things like that. For the frequency it said, '[the reciprocal of] 2π times the square root of L (inductance) $\times C$ (capacitance)'. Where did the π come from? He had been told by his father that π was a 'golden circle', and here was π. The watts—volts times amperes—that was a childish formula. But the frequency—2π times the square root of LC—that bothered him, especially the inclusion of π. Then, one day he realized that the coils, the inductances, were circles, that's probably where the π came from! But, in his book, there were listed the inductances of square coils, round coils; whatever the inductance, π came in. He realized that the inductance had nothing to do with the shape of coils, be they round or square. This π, the relationship of mathematics to physics, fascinated him. Richard became more and more interested in mathematics, but always with some relation to physics. However, he still did not understand why π was there in the inductance. Although Richard was always interested in the practical aspects of things, of how to make things go, 'mathematics and science were of one piece'.[1]

Richard's cousin, Adele Rosenbaum Curott, recalled that when he was twelve or thirteen and thereafter 'Richard used to come regularly for the *Scripta Mathematica*, a scholarly magazine which my father subscribed to on account of his longtime friendship with Ed Kasner, a mathematics professor at Columbia University. Richard would always ask if we were done with it, and I'd reply, 'Let me ask Edith and Jerome (my siblings).'' Though none of us ever looked at the magazine, for it was totally beyond us. Richard would finally go off happily with it, having been told to keep it. When I last spoke to Richard in the fall of 1984, he said, "Where else, in those days, could I have gotten what I did from *Scripta mathematica*?".'[7]

Richard's first science course, taught by William LeSeur, was on general science. First he took biology, which he did not find particularly interesting. Later on he would not remember much of this course, except some experiment in which egg white was dissolved in stomach enzymes. It had seemed to him that egg white could not dissolve in anything, and to see it dissolve was of some interest. Osmosis, with its explanation in terms of atoms, seemed to be a fascinating process, but on the whole he did not find biology interesting—certainly not at that time. This was not because he was not interested in living things; in fact, his father had greatly interested him in plants and animals and in the living processes of life, but somehow the biology course did not *do* anything. Later on, as a famous professor of theoretical physics at the California Institute of Technology, Feynman would devote many months to experiments in biology and enjoy working as a 'graduate student' in this field.

Then he took chemistry and physics. In these courses he learned a little bit. He knew a considerable amount already, which he had learned on his own, especially by studying the articles in the *Encyclopaedia Britannica*, so he didn't learn much directly from these courses. The Feynmans possessed the 1914 edition of the *Britannica*; it was the thirteenth edition, which was really based on the famous eleventh edition. It did not contain any modern physics, such as the quantum and relativity theories. There was an article on electrostatics by James Clerk Maxwell, which was much easier than the whole section on electricity and magnetism. Richard found the article on electrostatics rather difficult; he tried to read it several times and made a notebook on it. After going over it a few times, he understood it all, things like tubes of force and all the rest. Everything was sharp and concise, not just a jumble of words. there were many ingenious demonstrations of things that would be demonstrated with vector analysis later. There was an ingenious explanation of why the force is zero inside the surface of a charged sphere. Richard thus learned to look at electrostatic phenomena in an unconventional way. The *Britannica*'s influence on Richard's education 'was second only to that of my father.'[1]

In the physics course at Far Rockaway High School, Richard did enjoy the working of coupled pendula. You pull one out and the other starts to oscillate. This was shown to him by one of his teachers in physics, and he found it wonderful. He had a lot of fun making it go, playing with it and trying to understand it.

Richard would work out the theory of everything he learned about. 'I remember when I was first learning calculus. We had a toaster, which had a place to put the bread in. One had to push the lever and it turned around, lifted out, and turned back in. It was done by four levers, two movable levers at an angle, and it pulled the thing out and turned it around, then it would go back in. I tried to figure out the curve it made. This was the hardest thing I attempted to do at that time. It was so very complicated. It was a quartic curve or something, just terrible. Most of the things I tried to figure came out nice, but not that. I remember working on it because it was so hard. I would work out things like the shape of water coming out of a faucet. Every time I would see something that was pretty, I would try to find if I could understand it. I was always playing around to see what I could do, and I did an awful lot of playing at things. That was my hobby: looking at things and seeing if there might be a simpler way to understand them.

'But I didn't learn any physics in high school. By the time I got there, I knew everything they were talking about. Mathematics was somewhat similar, but I did learn there because they pushed me into it. The rigor of the high school was pretty good, so I learned a few formulas by memorization and so forth. I would say, I did learn some mathematics.'[1,4]

In the public library there was a book by James Jeans, which discussed quantum theory and talked about the Heisenberg matrices, and mentioned that unlike classical mechanics the dynamical quantities in quantum theory were to be described by pairs of quantities called matrices. But the discussion was not very clear, and Richard did not understand it very well. There was also some treatment of the Bohr orbits. Richard had bought a book called Smith's *College chemistry*. From it he learned more about Bohr's orbits, quantum mechanics, and energy levels. There was also a discussion of the periodic table of elements, and how the levels from element to element were filled up.

One day, the students were allowed to bring any book that they pleased to the class. Richard brought a college level book on physical chemistry, and opened the chapter on ionic equilibrium, which he did not understand at all, but he liked the sound of the words 'ionic equilibrium'; he was, of course, just showing off to others. He probably learned something about the subject of ionic equilibrium from that book.[1]

There were several clubs in Far Rockaway High School: chemistry club, physics club, mathematics club, and chess club, where those students who were interested would stay after school to participate in activities. They would work up demonstrations and give lectures to other students. It gave them good practice. In one demonstration, Richard made phosphene gas, which explodes and burns when it comes into contact with air, and makes a flame and a smoke ring. Elmer Heller, a friend of Richard's, who was a year older and whom Richard addressed as 'Helmholtz', was elected president of the physics club and Richard was vice-president in the fall of 1934. Heller recalled: 'We worked together in planning the program for meetings which consisted of groups of experiments and demonstrations. For the first meeting, we prepared experiments on light, one of which was to show the polarizing effect of reflection from a stack of glass plates. I tried to produce interference by introducing a strain in the plates and the plates broke and cut my finger rather seriously, and I had to leave to see the doctor immediately. Richard continued the meeting, which he assured me went well and without further disasters, but I still have the scar on my finger, 54 years later.'[8]

The second meeting of the physics club was much safer and consisted of several demonstrations on the properties of sand. Heller recalled: 'The first two were to illustrate loose and close packing. We filled a rubber balloon with sand till it was about four inches in diameter and then sealed the neck to a long-stemmed glass funnel. The sand was closely packed by slapping with a ruler. Water, colored with copper sulfate, was poured into the balloon until it reached about halfway up the stem of the funnel. The question then was put to the audience: What would happen if the balloon were squeezed? The obvious answer was that the water would be squirted out through the funnel. Of course, the obvious did not happen. Rather, the level of the water dropped to the amazement of the audience and I explained that when the close packing was deformed and became loose packing the volume of the void increased and was filled by the water, thus dropping the level in the funnel stem.'[8] The other demonstrations on the properties of sand were equally ingenious. Feynman recalled: 'It was a beautiful lecture. This is the kind of thing we did in these clubs, and that's the way we'd learn something, either from the other fellow— about sand in this case—or by yourself in preparing the lecture. Some of these lectures were pretty good.'[1]

Richard was still known as Ritty or Richy in high school. As Elmer Heller recalled, 'It was about this time that Richy discovered Bertrand Russell's *ABC of relativity* and *Introduction to mathematical philosophy* in the public library and we both read them with relish. The latter was a deep book and Richy read it with avid pleasure. We admired the brilliance of Russell in going in the opposite direction from most other scientists who worked towards more and more complex problems. Here was Russell asking simpler and simpler questions: Why one and one make two? One times two, two, but two times two, four? What is a number? We had a marvelous time working through these ideas. Richard developed the habit of always asking the same kind of fundamental questions, and always going back to fundamentals in his analysis of a problem.'[8]

Elmer Heller had met Ritty Feynman in the Far Rockaway High School chess club during the fall semester of 1932. A few weeks later, he mentioned to his mother: 'I have a new friend. He's a skinny little kid, but so smart in science that some day he'll win a Nobel Prize. When Richard did win the Nobel Prize, I reminded my mother of what I had said about him many years ago.'[8] Again Elmer Heller: 'He was pretty good in chess; he wasn't a great player, but he was very ingenious and daring. He did have a good background in chess. There was a fellow by the name of Morris Jacobs, who was a good chess player but, strangely enough, he became a superb chess player. He was called Jake, and his father owned a luggage store. We used to hang around Jake's store and play chess with him, while he was minding his father's business. We would go in the back and play chess and that was nice. Ritty used to be there and all the other chess players, and we would have a lot of fun playing chess.

'We used to go out with various girls together, double date and triple date and have parties together.

'Ritty's father was a wonderful man, very kind, patient, friendly. He was very friendly with us boys. We'd come over and we'd sit around and talk for a while and then we'd go off on our own interests after that. I liked him very much and I liked his mother very much, too.

'In their Crossways apartment, Ritty had his clock that ran backwards, which everyone complained about, that his clock was out of order, didn't keep time. He would say, "Oh, no, it's quite correct. It's a quarter after three." You would look at it and it wasn't. It was running backwards, so he would compute in his mind because he had changed the gears around so it would run backwards. It was an electric clock. He had it on the wall of his room, and it ran counterclockwise. He had reversed the numerals, but when he read them it was accurate. It was always the right time, but whenever you'd come into the room, you'd look at the clock and, let's say it was 3:15, but on his clock it would be a quarter of nine. You would say, "My God, your clock is all wrong, it's a quarter of nine there." He'd say, "No, it's not a quarter of nine, it's 3:15." He liked to get a new guy to see his clock and that would always be an attention-getter. There would always be a big argument about the time. Then, finally, Ritty would say, "Well, it goes counterclockwise, that's all!" Of course, he wouldn't tell them this in the beginning, and anybody who knew about it always kept quiet and let this argument go on until the newest victims had been taken through the process. No one ever dreamed that he did that until he told us and then he made us keep quiet so he could fool the next guy.

'Politically, Ritty was not as radical as most of the kids were in those days. It was the Depression and many of our friends were members of either the Young Socialist League or the Young Communist League. We were not members of any of those organizations, but we had friends who were and so we talked about politics. Politics was really important. But Ritty Feynman had no interest in it. He liked mathematics and girls, and with girls it soon narrowed down to Arline.

'We were always involved in long scientific discussions on all kinds of weighty questions. We decided that thinking was such a mechanical process, rules of logic were so well worked out, that we could build a machine to do that. So we decided to build a thinking machine, a machine that would work out syllogisms. It had a bank of three switches across and two rows of three horizontal switches. It was made on a panel and below that there were three lights. There were double-throw switches: either yes or no. Maybe there was perhaps a zero, a neutral one in between. "All men are mortal; Socrates is a man; therefore Socrates is mortal." We had three switches; there had to be three pieces of information. The first premise, the second premise, and the lights lit up the conclusion. How that was going to work I cannot remember. We didn't finish the machine in high school, but we worked on it little by little until we forgot all about it.'[2]

In the fall of 1934, the last year of Richard's high school, Abram Bader joined the Far Rockaway High School as a physics teacher. It was the Depression. He had wanted to become a trained physicist and was trying to get his Ph.D. degree under Isidor Isaac Rabi at Columbia University. Bader had majored in physics at the City College. 'Upon graduation I was granted a fellowship for one semester. The money enabled me to attend Columbia and undertake graduate work. Among the courses I took were statistical mechanics and quantum mechanics, both from Professor Rabi. I also attended a summer symposium at the University of Michigan, where I attended a course on advanced quantum theory taught by Professor Enrico Fermi (who had no trouble beating me at tennis) and atomic theory taught by Professor Samuel Goudsmit. Lack of money kept me from going on with the doctorate. My father had died a few years before this and I had to take a job teaching in high school. Prejudice [against the Jews] was prevalent in those days and so I couldn't obtain a position at City College, since I was Jewish. I told Professor Rabi that I had been forced to take a job and would come for research only late in the day. I had been helping another student finish his project on the use of a molecular beam method of measuring molecular size, and anticipated being given some work in this field. However, Professor Rabi informed me that he could not see giving a room and apparatus for only half a day. I turned around and walked out on him and the field of physics.'[9]

Feynman recalled: 'It was rather sad. He went into teaching in high school. Those days were different. Given the Depression, it was difficult to achieve one's goals. He was teaching this physics class, which I attended; he understood it well all the way. He wasn't like William LeSeur who didn't know much, or Joseph Johnson who knew the stuff from many years ago. He knew more than he was teaching.'[1]

Abram Bader remembered Richard, too: 'Feynman became my student in the fourth and final year of his high school. I had heard a bit about the unusually bright boy from his chemistry teacher, Joe Johnson. Johnson and Feynman had worked together on a project to measure the size of the molecules, using the thickness of a thin layer of oil. I was about to start teaching a class in honor's physics and looked forward to having a group in which all the students would be bright. After my first day I realized that Feynman was *sui generis*. In only one day he stood out as the top student in a class of top students.'[9]

One day, when they were discussing the index of refraction, Abram Bader called Richard down from the class and told him that he was making too much noise and was being a disruptive influence on the other students. Bader realized, however, that this was because he found the lesson too easy, so he gave him a book to read by himself and sent him to the back of the class. Feynman recalled: 'So he gave me a book; he knew that I had learned calculus from other books. I was a senior then. He gave me a book entitled Woods's *Advanced calculus*,[10] which had Fourier series, Bessel functions, gamma functions, wondrous things that came out of calculus and all the juice, wonderful stuff. What a good time I had back there with that book! What wondrous things I learned and played with! So that was a wonderful thing he did to me!'[1] Richard found Woods's *Advanced calculus* most interesting. 'I worked very hard on that, and learned a great deal of mathematics in high school, mathematics of an advanced kind.'[1] As Abram Bader still recalled late in life: 'I had used that book to study the subject since I did not take much mathematics in college. I had often written a brief note or question in the margin of the book. I spent a year trying to master the subject while working. Feynman returned the book to me in less than a month and expressed surprise at some of my questions. He went through the book with me, clearing up the problems I had!'[9]

On another occasion, 'when we were hanging around in the laboratory, Mr Bader said he wanted to show me something very interesting. He explained to me the principle of least action—that there is a number, the kinetic energy minus the potential energy, the action, which when averaged over the path, is least for the true path. This is philosophically a delightful thing. It is a different kind of way of expressing the [dynamical] laws. Instead of differential equations, it tells the property of the whole path. And this fascinated me. That was one of the greatest things ever. The rest of my life I have played with action, one way or another, in all my work. I have loved it always. Afterwards, I found in the *Encyclopaedia Britannica* a statement that the laws of electricity are such that the potential is distributed to make the integral of the energy a minimum. And I proved from the formula—it wasn't in the book—that, in fact, you would get a differential equation of electricity from that. It was stated, but it wasn't there; I derived that.

'Anyway, I learned advanced calculus from Woods's book—the determinants, Fourier series, and so on. I already knew something about the Fourier series from the *Encyclopaedia Britannica*. I struggled with every article in the encyclopedia that was scientific. I could understand everything except the article on gyroscopes and the article on group theory. The article on electrostatics gave me great difficulty, but by making a notebook on that, and going through it several times, I learned the method until I understood it.'[1]

Feynman recalled further that 'Mr. Bader did not *assign* anything to me. He just gave me Woods's book to study. In all my time there, in these schools, the terrible thing was the lack of supplies. Perhaps it was good, so that I had plenty of time to worry about elementary things before I was swamped by advanced things. I couldn't get books. The library had no books on calculus. When they got one it was within a week or two that I took it out; *Calculus for the practical man* was the first calculus book that was in the public library in town, and I was the first guy to borrow it. I had the thirst; I could not satisfy it.

'I had heard about vector analysis, for example, but I did not know what it was. But I knew somehow that it was important and useful, and Albert Maskett—my cousin's tutor—who, by this time, was getting his degree at Columbia University in mathematics, wrote a thesis on vector analysis; and I learned vector analysis from his thesis. There was one part of that thesis that was some complicated business about transforming coordinate systems, which I did not think was very important and left out. When Maskett got his thesis back and asked me what I thought of it, I said: "It was very good and thank you very much, but the stuff about transforming coordinates I didn't pay much attention to." He said, "That's what the thesis was about, the rest was introduction!"'[1]

Somehow Richard had always the sense about what was central and what was peripheral, what were the complicated details that were not useful and what were the great ideas of each subject. He paid no attention to Maskett's reciprocal coordinate system when he read his thesis; what Maskett had contributed was interesting, but more advanced, whereas the description of vector analysis which was in there, Richard knew was really worthwhile for him.

Feynman recalled: 'Mr Bader explained the principle of least action to me only once. Whenever a thing is exciting to the mind, such as the principle of least action, you remember all the subsidiary things that have nothing to do with it. Like, I remember exactly where the blackboard was (it was in the laboratory), where he was standing, where I was standing, and everything else, while he was telling me this. It was after class, in the room where the laboratory was. I don't remember how it came up, but Mr Bader told me about this principle, and explained it by drawing curves of the motion of a particle on the blackboard, and two different curves, and the one that gives the least number is the right one. He just explained; he didn't prove anything. There was nothing complicated; he just explained that such a principle exists. I reacted to it then and there, that this was a miraculous and marvelous thing to be able to express the laws in such an unusual fashion.'[1]

Abram Bader had done immeasurable good to Feynman by doing these two things: first by asking him to study Woods's book on calculus, and second by telling him about the principle of least action. By being exposed so early to the methods of advanced calculus, Feynman became a great expert on doing any integral if it could be done at all. The principle of least action became a kind of 'mantra' for him; in all the great problems of theoretical physics that he treated, he invoked this principle wherever he could. This principle became his very own in every way.[11]

Abram Bader remembered Feynman fondly. 'I gave Feynman problems involving advanced calculus. They were child's play to him. One I remember in particular involved the envelope of curves formed when a beam of light is reflected from the inner surface of a cup containing a liquid such as milk. The envelope is a cardioid. Feynman found this problem as well as other difficult problems child's play, and shared my love for mathematical ideas. He was my student for one year. His intellectual promise was clear enough.'[9]

Richard did not make demonstrations for science fairs, but he visited them from time to time. 'There were a few visiting science fairs in those days, with students doing scientific things. I remember in particular visiting a science fair, going around and seeing a boy who had made crystals, beautiful octahedra, and had a big demonstration of them. Then I looked carefully at the octahedra, and there was something funny about the lines, the crystal axes. I looked very closely, and I realized that it was painted wood. So I said to the boy, "Is this yours?" He said, "Yeah." I said, "But this is just painted wood!" "Yeah, I know", he said, "but it looks good, makes a nice demonstration." I was horrified. I was very much an idealist and a purist. I thought this was so unscientific, antiscientific—it was an evil thing. It bothered the heck out of me. That's why I wouldn't enter those things. I had a great feeling of respect for science, a love for it, and when someone would fiddle with it like that it hurt me. I was hurt by this, because he was trying to fool people. If he had grown small crystals, then it would have been nice. That was the only way for me. You don't have to build it up; you don't have to fake it. It's great the way it is; there's a sort of feeling that comes with it. This was some kind of terrible falseness. It just bothered me. I didn't enter into that kind of thing.

'What I did do, in high school as well as earlier, was to cut out of the newspaper things that had to do with science. One of these things was called "Explore Your Mind", which was a sort of silly thing. They would ask questions, make up something, and then try to explain. I still remember an article, "Scientists Meet, Find Atom Is A Wave", and there was a picture of a diffraction pattern. I didn't understand, but I was interested enough in science that I kept a newspaper scrapbook of science articles.'[1,12]

The great handicap was finding books to read. 'There was no consistent pouring out from libraries. There was nowhere to find such a library that I knew of. I think it's just as well. I try to imagine what would have happened to me if I had lived in today's era. I am rather horrified. I think there are too many books, that the mind gets boggled. If I got interested, I would have so many things to look at, I would go crazy. Maybe, maybe not. Maybe this is just an old-fashioned point of view. There are always these things. But it does bother me a little bit that there are so many things, and it's so easy, and they are watered down.'[1]

The thing that pleased Richard was that everything he read was serious, it was not written for a child. He never read anything that was written for a child except *The boy scientist* book, which was actually pretty good. 'I very rarely found things written for children interesting. There were books on the cavemen, *Cave man living* and *People who live on trees*, and there was a book with a series of families in different circumstances that I found interesting. That was obviously for children. In general, I didn't like children's things, because I was—and still am—very sensitive and worried that the thing be dead honest, that it's not fixed up to look easy, that it's not fixed up and partly faked so that the explanation can be made more simply for a child. Details purposely left out, or slightly erroneous explanations, in order to get away with it. So, ultimately, I had only to trust the completely mature and odd old things, even though I was only in high school. I think most kids in high school are very mature. I know my friends who were in literature—who wrote plays—they would read great plays. Anybody who's any good in high school already knows that he has to look at the real stuff.'[1]

Richard was not very intrigued by courses in physics and chemistry in high school. It was only a little bit of work, like exercises, to do the things. They were not difficult and he got very good grades. The physics and chemistry courses were a year each. 'I was just recently reading about Einstein, who was an individual who did not like the educational system and came through without it. But I went through the educational system all right. In my particular case, it is true that it was stifling, but because of the accidents, starting with my father and so on, I had always been ahead enough that the labor of doing the ritual for schools, working out, doing whatever I had to do, was relatively easy; I could do it so easily that it didn't disturb me. I didn't work at it really. I just did it. It was easy enough. And then I had time to play at a much higher level. I was always like that through the rest of my education, for example learning advanced calculus in high school. Later on when I got to college it was exactly the same. I was always ahead, so that I didn't learn much in courses, and I found it relatively easy to satisfy all the necessary requirements as I went along, without it being a labor, without it being hard work that would take up a lot of my time. Then I had plenty of time to do other things. The classes and courses were just nothing; they were so simple, and it was always so slow. It was a pitiful business altogether.'[1]

In the beginning Richard was only familiar with the neighborhood kids, but in high school he gradually became a member of a group of four or five guys, all good friends. They would walk around together in the streets and talk about things, or go for walks and do other things together. There was Harold Gast, who was interested in writing plays. Later on he would write for television, Playhouse 90, Kraft Theater. Then there was a literary fellow, David N. Leff, who was the editor of the school newspaper; he was very interested in writing, but not plays. Leff would continue his writing career; later on in life he became the editor of a biochemical newsletter for McGraw-Hill. There was Elmer Heller; he was a year older than Richard, and was one semester ahead. Then there was a scientific type, Robert Stappler, who was a very good student, but because of his mother's interest and influence he was driven out of the group and wasn't able to go on to college. Feynman, Heller, and Stappler were the scientific guys; the others belonged to the humanities. On the periphery of the group, there were also Gerald Robbins and Marty Stecher. As in any school, there were cliques, other guys coming in and out of the group. They didn't have any enemies; their group activities were simple and friendly.

A group of older boys, whom Richard got to know, took an interest in him and tried to develop his interest in girls. There were parties among them. A dancing school teacher, a friend of Richard's mother, tried to make some money by having dances on some Friday evenings in her studio, and Richard's mother encouraged kids to go there to dances. Richard had a great sense of rhythm and became a very good dancer; he would always enjoy dancing as a pastime.

The boys used to meet at the beach, and would hang around with each other. For his first date, Richard got the idea that he liked a certain girl. Richard happened to say, 'Gee, I would like to take her out, make a date.' So the kids grabbed him by the hair, and grabbed her too, and brought them together and said, 'Ritty wants to ask you for a date.' It was a difficult situation, but in any case they made a date, and Richard took her to the movies. His mother had taught him how to conduct himself politely with the girl, help her out, and so on. It was his first experience of dating. She asked him if he played the piano. He told her that he had tried to learn and had taken lessons for a while. When he was older, after many months of learning to play, he could only play something called the 'Dance of the Daisies', which did not seem to him to be a very good thing, so he no longer continued to play the piano. Later on, as they were saying goodbye, his date said, 'Thank you for a lovely evening.' Richard was very impressed and happy. Then on his second date with another girl, the girl said, 'Thank you for a lovely evening.' On the third date, when Richard and the young lady were saying goodnight at the door, he said to her, 'Thank you for a lovely evening', and she got paralyzed, unable to say anything, because that was what she was going to say. 'So I quickly learned the formal from the truth.'[1]

At that time Richard and his family were no longer living in the big house with the cousins and the other family. In about the second year of high school, they had moved to an apartment house that was only a block or so away; it was the Crossways Apartment House, situated on 1502 Mott Avenue with Conaga Avenue as the nearest cross street. Richard brought his laboratory with him. It was a tight squeeze in the apartment; he had a small room, but he was satisfied and happy. He still used to see his cousins, for they were close by.

In high school Richard worked part-time for a printer. He did odd jobs. He swept the floor, put the furniture—such as it was—away, and delivered the circulars that had been printed. He did this in the afternoons. He tried to collect the bills that were owed, and he would take things that were too hard for this jobbing printer to the Linotype typesetter, and return after about four miles on his bicycle. That's the kind of thing he did.

The job with the printer came about because he and his friend Bernard Walker decided that they had to get some work. They went around from store to store asking if they had any circulars to deliver, because in those days they used to advertise by hand the things that had to be sold. They met with some success, but not too good. Bernie Walker, who later went into business, said, 'Hey, I've got an idea. Why do we go from store to store asking if they have any circulars to deliver? We'll go to the printer, who prints the circulars and we'll ask him whom he wants us to deliver his order of circulars to. We'll do it for nothing. Then, when we come in we'll say, 'We're delivering your circulars from the printer, do you need a boy to deliver them?' The printer said, 'That's a

great idea!' Bernie Walker had a businessman's mind; Richard would not have
thought up the scheme. So that's the way they did it, and the printer was so
impressed with their ingenuity that he said he needed a boy to take care of the
place, and so he hired both of them, alternately, to do this.[1,4]

The money that Richard earned was spending money. There was the
attitude that you should do something, some work; to hang around and do
nothing was somehow not acceptable; there was a feeling of some sort of
responsibility to earn money. This was also the Depression; it was good to do
some work like that, and the feeling was that one should do it. Richard would
have received the spending money from his parents, because what he earned
was not a lot really, but the idea that one should get a job somehow felt the
right thing to do.

Apart from hanging out with some of his friends from high school, Richard
had had no social life before going to college. He thought he had been rather a
sissy and was a bit worried about his relationship with girls. The opportunity
to round out his angularities was provided by the Jewish Center in town. They
got the idea of making a Junior League, which was formed to make the young
high school kids happy. This organization, the Junior League, was supposed
to be run by them, with their own president and so on, but they could use the
buildings that belonged to the Jewish Temple. It was a wonderful effort. They
had their teachers to come in to help, and the young people were divided into
units, like a drama unit, an art unit, a writers' unit, where the young people
who liked to write (such as Harold Gast and David Leff) would get together;
they would tell the story they would write, and the next week some other guy
would write a story and tell it. They'd discuss it. In the art unit, which Richard
joined, they started to make plaster casts of heads, of faces. You'd lie on the
floor and put plaster on, and have straws out of the nose to breathe and all that
kind of thing. And then they'd try to make artistic things, for which Richard
had no talent whatsoever.

The reason why Richard joined the art unit was that he had met a beautiful
girl, who was very interested in art and was going to join the art unit. He did
not know her too well; she was the girlfriend of some other guy. She and her
boyfriend were really close to each other, and it was really hopeless for
Richard. But he joined the art unit anyway so that he could be close to her. 'I
think that the first time I met her was at a party at which somebody was
teaching her how to neck, and showing us how to kiss a girl—the lips should be
at right angles, and that kind of stuff. Then we sat and practiced with some
girls. The older fellow who was demonstrating it did it before the group. Then
we would sit and we'd try to neck. I had a girl I was practicing with. Then, just
at that moment, there was a little excitement—'Arline is coming, Arline is
coming!'—and everybody jumped to greet her. I decided that nobody was so
important, that this was not the way to behave, and I just kept on sitting and
practicing necking. She remembered later on that, as she came in, there was
one person in the party who did not get up, because he was necking in a corner;

nobody else was doing such a thing. She did not know that a few moments before everybody was doing that!'[1,4]

The young lady, who thus made her appearance, was Arline Greenbaum, and Richard started on the wrong foot with her. However, at another party, he understood why everybody had jumped when she came in: she was very beautiful! By that time he had seen this Arline several times, and was really impressed with her. At this other party, where she was, for some reason which Richard did not know, she sat on the arm of his chair. 'So there was hope. I was excited as the devil. She was with this older group. She belonged to the Jewish Center, and it was because of her that I had joined the art group. There was no science group. There were dances, because it was a social center. It was a good thing to join, even though Arline was going out with Jerome.'[1]

In this way Richard got to know Arline and also made the acquaintance of her boyfriend Jerome. It turned out that she broke up with Jerome, and Richard got to know her better. He took her to a dance at the studio of his mother's friend, and introduced her to his friends, including the playwright Harold Gast, who later approached Richard very carefully and told him that he realized she was his girl and he was not interested in her. Anyway, 'he turned out to be my competitor after his assertion that she was my girl and he would not interfere, something which I had not asked for. But he was a competitor, and Arline would go out either with me or with Harold.'[1]

It was only on the day of graduation that Richard realized that he was getting ahead of Harold Gast in Arline's affections. They were both graduating together. 'Being a sensible girl, Arline sat between the two sets of parents. It so happened that I won a lot of medals, for best in physics, best in chemistry, and best in mathematics. Harold had written a play, but I was being called to the platform every few minutes: "Now the prize for physics", "Now the prize for chemistry", "Now the prize for mathematics", and so on. I was constantly getting up and down to receive the prizes. Then came the announcement for English. The examiners had decided the award on the basis of the Regents' examination and nothing else. I had been relatively poor in English. But neither of my two friends—Harold Gast, the playwright, and David Leff, the writer for the newspaper—received honors in English because they did badly on the Regents' examinations, but I did. This was a freakish accident.

'I knew why I got the honors, because for one time in my life I broke down in English; I thought I could not perform as well as I was expected to. I listen to everybody talk, and they talk a kind of baloney. In the English class, they don't talk straight, while I always tried to talk straight. In the Regents' examination, they had two things: take a book and write a review, and I took the simplest freshman book, *Treasure island*, while my friends took something like Sinclair Lewis's book about the stockyard or something. Mine, though dull, was all right, so the dull teachers said OK, but the bright teachers had objections to my friends' interpretations of social relations, in which they were much more interested. However, the real place where I faked was the following. They gave us a list of compositions that we could write [essays] on different subjects, and for a change they had a few scientific subjects, one of them being "The importance of aviation". To me, this seemed incredible, that the man who made up the title was an ass, because it was so obvious. It was a dumb kind of subject. But I figured for once I'm going to see what my friends do. So I wrote an article in which I talked about the importance of science in the analysis of vortices, eddies, turbulence, and the swirling motions of the air—all the same thing! So I made up those big words and repeated myself and I did all that baloney, and the teacher who examined my essay gave me a mark of 91—while my literary friends, Harold Gast, and David Leff, who chose topics the English teachers could more easily take issue with, both got 88. That year, a new rule had come out: if you got 90 or better on a Regents' examination, you automatically got honors in that subject on graduation! I was called up once again and received honors in English.'[1,12]

These awards seem to have impressed Arline, but the thing that impressed her the most was the following. "She was with my parents and Harold's parents, when the head of the mathematics department, Dr Augsberry, came over. Mrs Gast said to him, 'Hello, Dr Augsberry, I am Harold Gast's mother and this is Mrs Feynman . . .'". He completely ignored her and turned to my mother: "Mrs Feynman, I want to impress upon you that a young man like your son comes along very rarely. The state should support a man of such talent. You must be *sure* that he goes on to college, the best college you can afford!" He made a great speech. He was very impressed with me. And Mrs Gast kept saying, "What about my Harold?" "Oh, Harold is all right, never mind Harold. Now Mrs Feynman, listen . . .". He was concerned that my parents might not be planning to send me to college, for in those days lots of kids had to get a job immediately after graduation to help support the family. (That, in fact did happen to my friend Robert Stappler. He had a lab too, and taught me all about lenses and optics. One day he had an accident in his lab. He was opening a bottle of carbolic acid and the bottled jerked, spilling some acid on his face. He went to the doctor and had bandages put on for a few weeks. The funny thing was, when they took the bandages off his skin was smoother underneath, nicer than it had been before—there were many fewer blemishes. I've since found out that there was, for a while, some kind of beauty treatment using carbolic acid in a more dilute form. Robert's mother was poor; his father was dead. He had to go to work right away to support her, so he couldn't continue his interest in the sciences.) Anyway, my mother assured Dr Augsberry: "We are saving money as best we can, and we are trying to send him to Columbia or MIT." '[1,12]

Arline was listening to all this. After that Richard had a little easier job against Harold Gast. In an interview with Harold Gast on 14 June 1990, I sought to verify Richard Feynman's story about his competition with Gast for the affections of Arline. 'We were not competitors in any way. I myself have never been that competitive, and Feynman's talents were not in the area which interested me. Feynman was a very happy and civilized young man. The thing that I remember fondly about Feynman was that he sort of loved nonsensical things, typified later by his taking up the bongo drums. Before that, he used to say little nonsense rhymes. Arline had much more in common with Richard than she had with me. She used to enjoy his silly things. She was a very lovely and pleasant girl, rather sweet. She had deep dimples, and everybody liked her. But she was not very bright, that's the plain truth. I couldn't converse with her at great length without wondering what to talk about next. But she and Feynman were together a lot, and one could tell after a while that they were really very fond of each other and nobody was going to interfere, least of all I. Nobody was going to take her away from Feynman. His story is plain silly.'

Feynman: 'Anyway, I fell in love with this girl, and it took me six years before we got engaged. I met her when I was thirteen, she was thirteen and a half, and we got engaged six years later, and we married another five years later. I knew her for eleven years before we got married. It was quite an unusually long duration. We were very much in love by this time. She was a most marvelous woman. She was the editor of the newspaper at Nassau County Lawrence High School; she played piano beautifully, and was very artistic. She made decorations for our house, like the parrot on the inside of our closet. As time went on, our family got to know her better, she would go out to the woods to paint with my father, who had taken up painting later on in life.'[1,12]

The medals that were given at the high school graduation were sponsored by various companies or organizations. Thus, for example, the Exchange Club of Far Rockaway would give the chemistry medal by donating money for the medal. The Bausch and Lomb Optical Company gave the medal for science. Richard always remembered that Bausch and Lomb Company gave the medal for science because his father continued to ask him to write them a letter of thanks, which he never did.

At the time of graduation, the class book, *DOLPHIN*, for June 1935 noted the achievements of Richard Feynman. They recorded: 'Einstein [Richard] is good, too! Mathematics Club President, Captain of Mathematics Team, First Place in City for Mathematics Team Competition; President, Chemistry Club; German Club; Chess Team; Arista (this was the honor society of top students, to which the election was made by fellow members); Chairman, Mathematics Tutoring; Program Committee, Laboratory Squad.' The magazine further noted: 'In May, a team consisting of Richard Feynman, Jessica Lee Soffer, Walter Targoff, and Frederick Gelberg was sent to the annual Pi Mu Epsilon contest which was held at New York University. In this contest, to which every public and private high school in New York City sent representatives, Feynman finished first. The other members also finished in high standing but not quite high as Ritty. Many of the members are being graduated this term, and we depend upon the lower terms to maintain the standard set so high by the present members of the Math Club.' *DOLPHIN* closed with the remark: 'We bequeath . . . Ritty Feynman's math wizardry, not only to grace the schools annals, but for Mr Augsberry when he needs help.'[13]

Thus laden with honors in high school, Richard Feynman got ready for college. After graduation, Feynman worked during the summer in the hotel run by his aunt, where several years before he had been called to repair a radio. At the hotel, he alternated eleven hours one day and thirteen the next as a desk clerk or as a busboy in the restaurant. He earned about twenty-two dollars per month. 'That's the way the world was: You worked long hours every day and got nothing for it.'[14] This was a resort hotel, by the beach, on the outskirts of New York City. 'The husbands would go out to work in the city and leave the wives behind to play cards, so you would always have to get the bridge tables out. Then at night the guys would play poker, so you'd get the tables ready for them—clean out the ashtrays and so on. I was always up until late at night, like two o'clock, so it really was thirteen and eleven hours a day.'[14] Richard did not like the tipping; he would have preferred to have been paid more. Richard liked desserts, and if any desserts were left over at any evening, the pantry lady would leave them for him in the refrigerator, and he would eat them after work. One evening she left six desserts: 'There was chocolate pudding, a piece of cake, some peach slices, some rice pudding, some jello, there was everything! So I sat there and ate the six desserts—it was sensational.'[14] The pantry lady had left all six desserts because she did not know which one Richard really liked, but he was glad to have all of them! From that time on she continued to leave six desserts for him, and he greatly enjoyed that. One time when he was desk clerk a girl left a book by the telephone at the desk while she went to dinner, so he looked at it. It was *The life of Leonardo*, which he could not resist reading. The girl let him borrow it and Richard read the whole thing.[14]

Notes and References

1. R.P. Feynman, Interviews and conversations with Jagdish Mehra, in Pasadena, California, January 1988.

2. Elmer W. Heller, a former schoolmate of Richard Feynman's, Interview with Jagdish Mehra, in Los Angeles, California, 23 November 1988.

3. Silvanus P. Thompson, *Calculus made easy*. St. Martin's Press, New York, 1st edn., 1910; many editions since then, including one in 1931.

4. R.P. Feynman, Interviews with Charles Weiner (American Institute of Physics), in Pasadena, California, 1966.

5. J.E. Thompson, *Calculus for the practical man*. Van Nostrand, New York, 1931.

6. Clyde E. Love, *Differential and integral calculus*. Macmillan, New York, 1924.

7. Personal communication from Mrs. Adele Rosenbaum Curott, Lynbrook, New York, to Jagdish Mehra, 3 October 1988.

8. Letter from Elmer W. Heller to Jagdish Mehra, 8 January 1989.

9. Letter from Abram Bader to Jagdish Mehra, 8 December 1988.

10. Frederick S. Woods, *Advanced calculus*. Ginn & Company, Boston, 1932, 1934.

11. In the *Feynman lectures on physics* (Addison-Wesley, 1963), which Feynman gave to freshmen and sophomore students at Caltech in the early 1960s, he devoted a special lecture to the principle of least action and recalled what he had learned from Mr. Bader (Volume II, Chapter 19). Mr Bader also discussed the principle of least time with Feynman, and both of these principles became special to him.

12. R.P. Feynman, *What do you care what other people think?* (abbreviated as *WDYCWOPT*). Norton, 1988, pp. 31–32.

13. *DOLPHIN*, Senior Will, June 1935, pp. 25, 35. I am grateful to Mrs. Jessica Fleischmann (née Soffer) for telling me the details of Richard Feynman's exploits on the mathematics team and sending me a copy of *DOLPHIN*, June 1935.

14. R.P. Feynman, *SYJMF*, pp. 25–27.

3

Undergraduate at MIT

3.1 Applying to college

During his last semester at Far Rockaway High School, Richard applied for admission to various colleges. Among the colleges he considered were the Massachusetts Institute of Technology, Columbia University, and the City College of New York. He applied to CCNY because of financial limitations and in case he wouldn't be accepted elsewhere. At that time, there used to be the State Regents' examinations for graduation from high school. In mathematics and science Richard did the absolute tops, 99 percent, even 100 percent sometimes. In the other subjects, he scored in the 80's. He did better in the Regents' examinations than in the courses themselves. If there was pressure enough, Richard was perfectly able to work very hard and temporarily absorb enough information, say in German, to make a strong passing grade—by cramming—and then promptly forget the whole thing. With decent Regents' scores, fair in most courses, but really outstanding in science and mathematics, he applied for admission to these various institutions.

At Columbia, he had to take an admission's examination, for which there was a fee of fifteen dollars. He paid the required fee and took the entrance examination, but admission was denied to him; it had something to do with the Jewish quota for the freshman class at Columbia.[1] At MIT, there were a few scholarships, which he applied for but did not get. However, he was admitted as a regular student at MIT with a small scholarship (about a hundred dollars per annum); he did not get the big scholarship he had hoped for. For admission to MIT, they required a recommendation from a former MIT graduate. Richard's father found such a man: he was the vice-president of Barrett Roofing Company, whom he knew and who had gone to MIT. Richard visited him at his office and talked to him for about ten minutes, and got his recommendation: 'This guy is a good man.'[1] Richard thought that such a practice was evil, wrong, and dishonest. He was bothered that MIT would request such a thing and that he had to go through such falseness; that was the one thing he didn't like in applying to MIT.

Richard applied to MIT because it was supposed to be one of the best schools of science and technology in the country. 'My father probably knew that. My parents discussed it. MIT was more expensive than local schools. I remember how the two of them sat down and tried to figure out how, with their budget, they could send me to the best school. Although they did not know anyone at MIT, they just knew it was a good school.'[1]

Richard graduated from high school in June 1935. He thought he would major in mathematics, his strongest subject, if he were accepted at MIT, and in the summers he would work to supplement his allowance. During the summers in high school, he had usually tried to work. In his last summer at Far Rockaway after completing high school he had worked in his aunt's resort hotel as a waiter.[2]

At MIT there were fraternities, and two of them were Jewish. These fraternities were looking for good students, good pledges, and would hold 'smokers' or gatherings to meet them. Only the Jewish fraternities were interested in Richard. Both of them held their smokers, and Richard went to them. One of these smokers was for the Phi Beta Delta fraternity, which he later joined. The upper classmen from these fraternities would look for the New York boys going to MIT, and they were very kind to freshmen. At the smoker for Phi Beta Delta, two boys—Art Cohen, a science major, and Bill Crossman, a mathematics major—who were going to be seniors, started to talk to Richard. This was in the summer of 1935. Crossman asked Richard questions about mathematics; he told Richard that since he knew calculus it would be silly to take a regular course in mathematics in the first year. Crossman advised him to take examinations at MIT in first year mathematics courses, so that he could start in the second year right away.

When Richard was about to leave for MIT, the boys from the other fraternity, Sigma Alpha Mu (SAM), also came around. They were going to drive up to Boston, and they invited Richard to drive up with them. So he got into the car with these fellows. 'My mother always remembered the day her little boy left home —the cars and strangers that were going to drive him all the way to Boston. It was the big day! But to me, it was only a great, happy excitement. We had quite an adventure in the car, because it snowed and the car skidded; it was a long trip and we talked about various things. I was treated more like a man. It was a big deal; you are grown up!'[1,3]

3.2 Bright college days

When they got to Cambridge, Massachusetts, Richard stayed at the Sigma Alpha Mu house. The young men from that fraternity had driven him up, and they asked him to stay at their fraternity house temporarily. When he woke up in the morning they were very upset. They said, 'Two men are here looking for you.' They were Cohen and Crossman from the Phi Beta Delta house, who took Richard to their house with them. 'I guess I was a little dumb. I didn't realize the trouble these fellows were having rushing me. But I was wanted by both houses, which was a pleasant feeling. Formerly I had a sissyish feeling, but at MIT it disappeared because of all this attention.'[1,3] Finally, Richard became a pledge at the Phi Beta Delta fraternity, where Art Cohen and Bill Crossman were.

The day Richard pledged to become a member of his fraternity, everything changed. Then he had to do errands for the other boys, and the friendliness disappeared. There were various forms of hazing at the fraternity, which all the new pledges had to suffer. One of the things that they did to the new pledges was to take them, blindfolded, far out into the countryside in the dead of winter and leave them by a frozen lake about a hundred feet apart. They would be in the middle of nowhere and were supposed to find their way back to the fraternity; they ultimately found their way back into town. On the following day, there took place a schoolwide freshman versus sophomore 'mudeo' (various forms of wrestling and tug of wars that take place in the mud). Late in the evening, a whole bunch of sophomores came into the fraternity house, some of them from Richard's own fraternity and some from outside; their idea was to kidnap the freshmen. The sophomores tied up all the freshmen relatively easily—except Richard. He didn't want the guys in the fraternity to find out that he was a 'sissy'. He had never been good at sports, and he had always avoided encounters that might lead to physical conflict of any kind. He decided that this was a new situation, a new world, and he could make a new reputation by saying goodbye to the old one from Far Rockaway of being a sissy. So, in order that he wouldn't look like he didn't know how to fight, he fought like hell as best he could not quite knowing what he was doing, and it took three or four men many attempts before they were able to tie him up. The sophomores took them all to a house, far away in the woods, and tied them all down to a wooden floor with big tacks. By the time the night was over, there were only three sophomores guarding about twenty tied-up freshmen. It was a terrible night, but Richard made a new reputation for being a 'tough' guy with whom it would not be good to mess around; 'I never had to worry about that sissy business again—a tremendous relief.'[4]

In social matters the fraternity was good for Richard. Phi Beta Delta had had difficulties and had almost disintegrated, but they had forged a compromise. They had two groups of fellows in the house, the academic, studious type, who knew something, and the wild, social guys with cars, who would zip around and knew all about girls and so on. The fraternity had almost broken apart because of the differences in the interests of these two groups. The compromise they made was that the wild social fellows had to maintain certain grades, and if they didn't they would get lessons from the other guys, and they would have to work a certain number of hours and not go out unless they got such grades. Whereas, the other fellows, the studious types—and this was the most important thing—would have to take a date to every dance, and do socially desirable things; the other fellows would get them dates if they could not find them themselves. But they had to. This was an interesting environment for Richard. The pledges had to earn certain grades, which was easy for him, but they also had to find dates for the dances. They had formal dances, and they would have to get dressed up in tuxedos.

The dates came from the schools in the neighborhood and girlfriends of fellow students' girlfriends—those who already had girls—and their sisters. Richard was frightened of girls when he went to MIT. 'I remember, when I had to deliver mail at the dormitory. I had to take the mail from upstairs. It happened to be a time when some of the juniors had their girlfriends. They were just sitting on the steps and talking, and I just didn't know how the heck I was going to be able to carry those letters past them. Girls scared me. This whole business of getting past them scared me. I did get the letters through, and the way they said 'Oh, look, isn't he cute!' scared and worried me.'[1,5]

The fraternity had the rule that the pledges had to learn to dance. So they would get the girls, their girlfriends and friends of their girlfriends, to come on certain days of each week, and they would turn on the records and teach the pledges how to dance. This was really impressive, and it was a very important thing for Richard; from it he gained social confidence. The fraternity became a very important thing in his life. It was hard to do all the social things, but he was forced to do them. He had learned how to dance in his mother's friend's studio, but at the fraternity he became an accomplished dancer. The confidence came rapidly. He *had* to spend time with the girls, and everything became all right after a while.

Richard recalled: 'My first date was a blind date. But they were careful not to make me embarrassed by having some harlot. They were really serious about it, so that they got for me a pretty good girl for the first date. Since I couldn't get my own dates in the beginning, they found the first date for me, a girl called Pearl. Since I came from New York, I said, "Oh, Poil, Poil." They said, "No, no, you must say *Pearl*, because she will be horrified if you say *Poil*." So I made them believe that I couldn't do it, and I said, "All right, stop in the middle, I'll go through and say her name, Pearl, Pearl, Pearl, Poil, Poil, Poil," and they would hit me when I wouldn't get it right. Then, when I met the girl, I told her, "Listen, I understand your name is *Pearl*." She said, "Yes." I said, "You see, I say it very nicely—Pearl!" She said, "Yes." Then I told her that the guys at the fraternity were worrying about how I was going to pronounce it, "so you don't mind, when I introduce you, I'll do it peculiarly, you'll see." So, to every guy I would say, "This is my goil, Poil. This is Poil so and so." Of course, she knew I was kidding, but they were horrified. Anyhow, all these experiences relaxed me a lot, and did a lot of good for me socially.'[1,3]

While Richard was at MIT in Cambridge, Massachusetts, his girlfriend Arline was back home in Lawrence, New York, and they were writing letters to each other every week. 'She was probably out of high school, or maybe she was one more year in high school after me. But we wrote letters to each other during the whole MIT period. Later on at MIT I had her up to visit me at school for dances. I went out with other girls when she was not around. We became engaged somewhere along the way, but in spite of that I kept on going out with other girls. It was understood between us that that was all right, because it was impossible that any other girl could mean anything to me. It was just clear. Maybe naive, but it was true, and it worked out that way. She wasn't upset by it.'[1,3]

By December 1935, in his first semester, Richard was well established at MIT. On 8 December, from Far Rockaway, New York, he wrote to his friend Elmer Heller, who, after graduation from high school, had joined Purdue University in Lafayette, Indiana: 'Herr Helmholtz, . . . You sound like a fish out of water with respect to the sex situation where you are. The gentiles don't give a damn, they go out with us, but we don't go out much with them. We have plenty of Jewish dames. In short, religion is unimportant. There is a college called Wellesley, which is a concentration of beautiful girls just made for Tech [MIT] fellows. There is also a girls' college called Simmons around here. There are millions of wimmin [*sic*] in Boston and Brookline. In short, the supply is greater than demand, therefore we can get them easily. . ..

'I take physics, math, chemistry, ROTC, English; in decreasing order of pleasure I get out of them. The math is not as interesting as it might be. I take integral calculus too. There is too much dog work calculating goddamn integrals. It's like trig[onometry]. The theory is very interesting but the work of figuring out the numerical triangles is not. The physics is O.K. They don't try to get us all balled (or bowled) up by giving a problem in which some of the values are like grams and centimeters, and others (in the same problem) like foot-pounds and slugs, so that you have to convert before you do the problem, as you have described. The chemistry is just sloppy (academically too) a subject as it always has been to me, but we learn it much faster than in high school. Smith's *College chemistry* is one of our textbooks. So far I've gotten along without it, but I would appreciate your sending it to me.

'. . . We were sent on a scavenger hunt yesterday, a hell of a lot of fun until we got back to the damn fraternity. I had to get a wiffle tree, a ball-bearing mousetrap (i.e. a cat, male), an egg plant, a projectile which when uniformly accelerated from a 30-foot cannon will acquire a velocity of 500,000 foot-pounds, the number of windows in the Suffolk County jail divided by the square root of two to ten places. That will be all, Ritty.'[6]

When school started, Richard had declared mathematics to be his major. At first he was in the mathematics courses. It didn't matter very much what course you were in, really. For the first year or so, you had to take more or less the same thing. One had to take physics, chemistry, electrical engineering, mathematics, English, and so on. Somewhere during the first year, Richard began to get upset. He looked at what he was going to do next in the mathematics program. He found that he would be learning about manifolds and integrals and he could not decide what it would be good for. It occurred to him that this stuff wasn't good by itself; it was only good to teach to somebody else. He would retain this feeling about mathematics throughout his life.

The mathematical things Richard looked at were all too abstract; they weren't connected to anything. He went to the head of the mathematics department and asked him: 'Sir, what is the use of mathematics if not to teach more mathematics?' This was 1936, so it was still the Depression. The department head replied: 'Well, you can become an actuary, calculating insurance rates for an insurance company.' This did not sit well with Richard. The head of the department also said that a man who asked that kind of question was perhaps not right for mathematics. Richard liked to make his hands dirty; he had had a laboratory. The physical world was 'real'; he had become enthralled with mathematics, but not for its own sake. Mathematics was fascinating, but his heart was elsewhere. He couldn't stand abstract things. So he changed his major to electrical engineering, because that was something 'real'. A few months later, however, he realized that he had gone too far in the opposite direction, and that something in between—like physics—was really the right thing. So he ended up with the physics course. Electrical engineering and physics being so close, he was allowed to make the change without penalty.

The physics course that Richard took at MIT wasn't very new to him. It was mechanics about inclined planes, statics, and dynamics—and it was rather boring. He had learned this stuff before. The laboratory, however, was interesting. In the past he had used the laboratory to play around and build and repair radios; he had never used the laboratory for experimental, numerical research. His first experiment, which was to measure the acceleration due to gravity, by dropping weights, was mildly interesting. The most beautiful experiment for him in the laboratory, which Richard always remembered, was about a ring. There was a hook in the wall—which was just a nail driven into the wall—and a ring of metal, an annulus, like a big washer. The experiment was to 'hang the ring on the wall, measure the period [of oscillation], calculate the period from the shape, and see if they agree.' Richard loved that. 'I thought that was the best doggone thing. I liked the other experiments, but they involved sparks and other hocus pocus, which was too easy. With all that equipment you could measure the acceleration due to gravity. The remarkable thing is that physics is so good, in that not only can you figure out something carefully prepared but something so natural as a lousy old ring hanging off a hook—that impressed me! Now I had the power not only to figure out what would happen if I had a lot of oscillators and other apparatus to measure something precisely but that, in a dirty world, where nothing special existed other than a crummy ring hanging from a hook, I could do experiments with it. That impressed me a lot. So I liked that experiment, and I did like some other experiments in physics, because I had not done quite that kind of thing before.'[1,3]

Sometime later, in an experiment in electricity, Richard had to work with Faraday's rotating disk. He had to measure the ratio of electrostatic and electromagnetic units, which he knew was related to the speed of light in a vacuum. For this, one produced an electric current by means of a changing magnetic field; one had to measure the current by charging a condenser to a certain voltage a number of times. 'I remember that I was working on it with my friend Ted Welton, when the instructor, John Wolfe, came, and asked, "Do you know what you are doing?" I said, "Yeah, we're measuring the speed of light." We knew that. He was happy to learn that somebody knew what the heck it was, because the whole arrangement was rather poor. There were a lot of wires that had to be connected to terminals. There was a paper full of instructions that told you what to measure next, and unless you knew a certain amount, you couldn't get any pleasure out of it.

'In order to get some pleasure out of the hanging ring, I had to know what physics could do and what it couldn't do. I had to be very advanced to appreciate that ring. Also, I had to be advanced enough to appreciate that it was marvelous that we were measuring the speed of light by rotating a wheel at hand speed; that's some miracle, where those high numbers like the speed of light come from. It was quite exciting to do that experiment in an ordinary-sized room. That's why I feel that somehow education is not right—there is not sufficient motivation and appreciation. Motivations are not carefully handled. And motivation is the whole thing. It makes one love physics, or whatever else; it makes the good that comes out of something. I was motivated because I had had other experiences.'[1,3] The other guys in the laboratory just did all these things without appreciating what was involved. The sophomore year included a lot of other people, not only physics majors, people such as the students of electrical engineering.

At the beginning of his studies at MIT, Richard was taking sophomore mathematics courses because of advanced placement, and he had spare time. 'In my freshman year, my friends Art Cohen and Bill Crossman, with whom I roomed at the fraternity, were in the senior year. They were taking an advanced course in theoretical physics, taught by John Slater. They were studying for this course, and I, a dumb freshman, used to sit near them. One day, a month or two into the semester, I heard them talking. They were worrying about a problem they couldn't do. I had heard what the problem was, and I knew something about it, so I said, 'Hey, why don't you try Bernoulli's equation?' I had read everything in the encyclopedia, but in talking to them I mispronounced everything, and my notations were cockeyed. Finally, we communicated. "He means Bernoulli's equation", one of them said. So they tried that equation, and it solved their problem very nicely.'[1,3]

After that, Cohen and Crossman would always discuss their problems with Feynman. He couldn't do them fully—he wasn't that good—but he did do little bits and pieces, and because they discussed their physics problems with him he learned a tremendous amount. 'So I decided to take that course in my sophomore year; after all I had discussed the problems with my room-mates. I knew what the level was; I wasn't making a mistake, I was getting confidence. I had decided to take the senior course in my sophomore year. MIT was free enough that, if you had the guts, you could do it. One probably had to obtain the permission of the instructor to do so.'[1,3]

On the first day, going to that class, Richard wore his ROTC uniform; only the first or second year people had to take ROTC, and the uniform was compulsory for them. Richard had his uniform on, and it was a perfect giveaway. Besides, he looked very young. All the other students were seniors, and Richard was a sophomore. Although it was rather worrisome, in his own heart and mind he was quite proud. All the seniors and graduate students had green and brown cards to fill out. There were many graduate students in the class, and graduate students from other schools would take this course to get practice. It was a good course, being at the top of the heap of advanced undergraduate physics. Richard had a pink card. It was all very obvious, and Richard felt very good about it. Seated next to him was another guy in a ROTC uniform with a pink card. His name was Theodore (Ted) Welton. So there was someone else in the school who thought himself good enough to take the course based on Slater's book.

'So we started to talk to each other, happy to discover the existence of another peculiar nut. The conversation started by my noticing that he had a book on tensor analysis, which I was trying to learn. I said to him: 'Oh, you have got Levi-Civita's book on *The absolute differential calculus* (i.e. tensor analysis). I was trying to learn it. I wanted to get it at the library but could not find it.' He said, "Yeah, I'm bringing it back. I am trying to get another book that somebody has checked out called such-and-such something." And, sure enough, it was the book that I had borrowed. So, really, we were made for each other. That was terribly exciting, because then we would walk and talk together; he had a different background, but he was very good. He had learned quantum mechanics, while I had learned [special] relativity theory. I had learned relativity theory at MIT in the freshman year by reading books in the library, especially A. S. Eddington's *The mathematical theory of relativity*.'[1,3,7] Richard had A. P. Wills's *Vector and tensor analysis* in his stack, and that was the reason Ted Welton had been unable to find it in the library.

They began to teach each other, and within a few weeks both of them had achieved the same level of understanding in relativity and quantum mechanics. 'Since we were the only two sophomores in that class, it apparently simultaneously occurred to both of us that cooperation in the struggle against a crew of aggressive-looking seniors and graduate students might be mutually beneficial. Our friendship dated from that almost instantaneous recognition.'[1,3] Welton and Feynman had lots of conversations. 'It was a terrific educational experience to have somebody of your own type to argue back and forth with, to learn. I learned tremendous amounts from Ted Welton, and vice versa.'[1,3]

Julius Stratton, later on to become the president of MIT, was the lecturer in that introductory course on theoretical physics, which was taught from the book by J. S. Slater and Nathaniel Frank. 'In fact, Stratton, who was certainly an admirable lecturer, would occasionally skimp on his preparation with the usual consequence that he would come to an embarrassed halt, with a little red creeping into his complexion. With only a moment's hesitation he would ask, "Mr Feynman, how did you handle this problem?", and Dick [Feynman] would diffidently proceed to the blackboard and give his solution, always correct[ly] and frequently ingeniously. I note that Stratton never entrusted his lecture to me or to any other student.'[8]

Welton recalled that Feynman and he quickly found that their interests, aspirations, and general state of physical knowledge were remarkably similar, or overlapped to such an extent that their conversations on such matters were enormously profitable to both of them. Later on, Feynman 'would occasionally claim that I taught him quantum mechanics. The truth is that we learned it together, and this process was so pleasant that we never thought [of it as] work.

'In our first conversation [on the afternoon of that remarkable first class with Stratton], Dick announced that he wanted to learn general relativity. I already knew a bit and with proper superiority, announced that I wanted to learn quantum mechanics. Dick promptly announced that he had read a good book on the subject by somebody named Dirac and intimated that I should try my hand at it. Somewhat miffed at never having heard of Dirac or his book, I secretly resolved to get it and remedy this defect in my preparation. We talked for several hours about Einstein's work on gravitation of which, of course, neither of us had any deep appreciation. The mathematical manifestations of the general theory were, however, clear and interesting so that we considered ourselves real professionals. Dick, had, by the way, ended his vacillation between the too practical (engineering) and the too abstract (mathematics), and decided that theoretical physics was just right. I had previously come to the same conclusion, so we had no argument there.

'The next day I got Dirac's book from the library and rather quickly found myself in over my head. Shortly thereafter, one of us located Pauling and Wilson's *Introduction to quantum mechanics*, and this was the level we chose for our entry into the mysterious realm of quantum mechanics. We wandered, without external guidance (except for the ideas of orthogonal functions and such we were encountering in Stratton's course), through much of quantum mechanics, with naturally some enormous gaps in our understanding. Around Christmastime, one of our fellow students in Stratton's course announced that he had found a new book that seemed to have answers for most of the fundamental problems of physics. Its title was *The relativity theory of protons and electrons*, and its author was Arthur Stanley Eddington, whom we had already identified as a true prophet of the new physics from his book *The mathematical theory of relativity*. We got this book of promised revelation and took turns trying to make sense of it. We were both enormously impressed and so far too immature to recognize it as garbage. It perhaps reflects faintly to our credit that we never fooled ourselves into believing we understood the book, but we did suffer through several agonizing months, tantalized by Eddington's claimed results, but convinced that we were somehow too dumb to understand his methods.

'One amazing (in retrospect) quirk displayed by Dick in Stratton's course was his maddening refusal to concede that Lagrange might have something useful to say about physics. The rest of us were appropriately impressed with the compactness, elegance, and utility of Lagrange's formulation of mechanics, but Dick stubbornly insisted that real physics lay in identifying all the forces and properly resolving them into components. Fortunately, this madness appears to have lasted only a few years. [It must have been a brief "madness", because Richard Feynman had already become deeply enamored of the principle of least action in high school.]

'For the second semester, the introduction to theoretical physics was taken over by Phil[lip] Morse, who had been trained as a quantum mechanician and had worked extensively in several aspects of that field. Morse took proper advantage of his opportunity and included a section on elementary wave mechanics to complete the year. Dick and I already had acquired a fair grasp of the subject at that level, but Morse's systematic presentation did us no harm and further allowed Morse to see (from our problem sets and questions) that we were ready for greater things. Consequently, Dick and I were invited, with Al Clogston (a year ahead of us) to come to Morse's office for one afternoon a week the next year (our junior year) to be *properly* exposed to quantum mechanics. We accepted with alacrity and Phil Morse thereby can claim an important role in Feynman's training.

'After a run through Dirac's book, Phil [Morse] suggested we might be ready for a little research and suggested some calculations of atomic properties using a rather convenient formulation of the variational method, which Morse had worked out in a previous paper. Dick and I set to work with a will, first learning how to use the "chug-chug-ding-chug-chug-ding" calculators of those prewar days. Morse's scheme involved use of kinetic and potential energy integrals calculated with hydrogenic functions, and tabulated for various values of the coefficients occurring in these functions. For Dick, these were "hygienic" functions, and my efforts to convert him to "hydrogenic" were totally unavailing.

'The result of this work was, of course, a gradual realization that quantum mechanics was more than a romantic dream and might have something to do with life outside the college years. By this time, I had naturally learned one lesson well, namely that I was not going to be able to compete with Dick in his chosen field. . . . We, of course, learned much together in addition to quantum mechanics, and I have always recognized elements in his later work which clearly came directly from some of the well-organized and well-taught MIT courses, particularly the physics courses but also the elementary electrical engineering courses we were required to take. Many of the chapters in the *Feynman lectures [on physics]* stem directly from the material we were subjected to (rather pleasurably, I should add) during these years.'[8]

Richard remembered this period of his life quite well also. 'We learned this course [the introduction to theoretical physics] together, too, and the course began with Lagrange's equations. Being always a practical fellow, all I was interested in was the problems. A ball rolls down an incline, and I would work it out directly. I didn't have to learn the Lagrangian. My friend [Welton] would always do it the other way. As the problems went on, they got harder and harder. About a ball, spinning around in a paraboloid. Then it would take me an hour, him half an hour. But I really learned the Lagrangian very well, because I wanted to make sure that it was necessary to solve something that was really worthwhile. I always had the feeling of judging the thing against its actual applicational use. That's a very amusing thing. I had the same relation with Welton. I was challenging the Lagrangian for him to show me that it was necessary. Welton would do it his way, and I mine, and we would compare the times we took to do something. But, of course, my way would take ingenuity, whereas the trick of the Lagrangian was that you could do it blindfold. It's like analytical geometry compared to ordinary geometry: it's slower, but it's surefire. Well, this was the same situation. I still think that you can do it better than the Lagrangian. Anyway, there were one or two problems where I was behind, near the end. But it was worth it; it was a good experience.'[1,3]

The course on theoretical physics, given by Stratton and Morse, was for seniors and graduate students. Richard found that 'that was about the level at which I could learn something when I was a sophomore.'[1,3] Richard did not have any contact with John Slater at the time the course was given from his book; it was later that Slater was to supervise Feynman's senior thesis.

No good course on quantum mechanics existed at that time. This was the period around 1936–37, and still there did not exist a proper course on this subject. There was no place for Feynman and Welton to learn it right. They asked Morse where they could learn it, other than teaching it to each other. It was then that Morse said, 'I will teach you.'[1] Morse would sit in his black chair in his office, and his audience of three—Feynman, Welton, and Clogston—would also sit in chairs; he would teach quantum mechanics for at least one hour each week and give them problems. 'Welton had a little problem: narcolepsy. He would fall asleep incontrollably. Sitting in his chair, he would fall asleep. So one of the worst embarrassments to him was that we would take these lectures of Morse, and there were a few chairs set in the middle of the room and there was a blackboard on Morse's office wall. He would stand there and explain this stuff, and that poor friend of mine could not help but fall asleep. It was biological. He asked me to poke him when he fell asleep, but it wouldn't do. I did the best I could. He has since discovered that all he has to do is to get up and walk around. If he had known it at that time, he would have been able to pace back and forth while Morse was talking, but Morse would have been somewhat chagrined that he made this special effort for these guys and one of them falls asleep. But it was not boredom; it was this disease.'[1,3]

Phillip Morse gave Feynman and Welton a research project in quantum mechanics: to calculate the energy levels of light atoms by a variational method which he had invented and which was new and different. Morse knew how to teach. He was just great for them. When they found results that were useful for the astronomers at Harvard, he would send them there to discuss the atomic energy levels with them. They would give the astronomers the information, and find out what else they could calculate for them, such as the intensities of lines and so on. It was a very good arrangement.

At Harvard Feynman reported the results to the astronomers. 'I remember that as soon as I started to talk, everybody laughed at me. I was talking about "hydrogenic atoms". I wanted to say, "the kind of wave functions we are using are like those of hydrogen," but I said, "well, we start with *hygienic* wave functions", and so on. I was always careless with words and pronunciations, and they teased me a little bit about that. It wasn't very serious. This was at the Harvard Observatory. I said, "The way we are doing this, we start with hygienic wave functions, with parameters which we varied to get a minimum energy." We had done these calculations. We had also worked on an old-fashioned computing machine. Welton and I learned a lot. It was an extracurricular course, but Morse brought us to calculate really interesting things. He made a lot of effort for us. He came across somehow; he knew quantum mechanics.

'We had a regular course in atomic physics, which consisted in telling us that the square of the angular quantum number was $l(l+1)$, but we didn't learn much in that course. But in the quantum mechanics course from Morse, we learned a great deal. This was about the time of my junior year.

'Now, a thing happened between Welton and me, in which Welton taught me something of first-rate importance. By fooling around with relativity and quantum mechanics, I had cooked up an equation which I claimed must be the relativistic quantum mechanics. The Schrödinger equation was not relativistic. And by making relativistically varying forms, I obtained a great equation. It was the equation, which, in fact, Schrödinger had originally written, but I found it, I didn't look it up; it's called the Klein–Gordon equation. I cooked it up; it was easy. You generalize Schrödinger's equation to relativity; I worked it out and showed it to Welton. I said, "this is it, this is relativistic quantum mechanics." So he said, "All right. Let's calculate the energy levels of hydrogen, and see if they agree with the right energy levels."

'This was a terrible shock to me, that in fact we could actually do a real problem. At first, in spite of my practical attitude—learning relativity, quantum mechanics, gauge invariance, and all these wonderful things—the wonder of the formal things was impressive for me, but not the question what would actually come out. That we could actually figure out something had not occurred to me. So, Welton said, "Well, let's see. For hydrogen, we have to use the potential $V = Ze^2/r$ in the equation." We sat down, the two of us, and Welton showed me how to do a real problem with an esoteric equation. It gave the wrong fine structure, and that was the end of it.[9]

'It was a very important lesson, which was not just to rely on the beauty of the equation and marvel at its formality, but to bring it down to test against the real thing. We were not doing too badly for young fellows.'[1,3]

As for the other courses, Feynman studied analytical chemistry. He did pretty well in it, and since it was science he liked it. He had to learn all kinds of things in chemistry; it was not something he could do by logic alone. As Feynman got into more and more advanced courses at MIT, he was really learning new things. He took a course in optics, with an experimental laboratory, and this course was so detailed that he learned the technique of the Wallenstein prisms, as well as the methods for measuring the index of refraction, things which he had not learned before by himself. For the course on electricity and magnetism, they were using Smythe's book which for some reason he did not like.[10]

MIT had a course in theoretical nuclear physics, given for the first time in 1938 or 1939. It was the first course in nuclear theory ever given there, and they took the material for it from H. A. Bethe and R. Bacher's famous articles in the journal *Reviews of Modern Physics*. 'As a matter of fact, I remember that one because I wanted to take that class. It was a graduate course, but I was only an undergraduate and I had to have special permission. I thought, maybe I wouldn't be allowed in this. So I walked into the class and the room was full of students. Professor Morse was sitting on the window sill; the course was going to be given by him and someone else. All the students were there. I came in just a little late. As I came in, Morse looked at me and said, 'Are you going to take this course?', as if he was saying, 'What the hell!' So I said, 'Yes, I expected to.' He asked, 'What about your friend Welton?' I said, 'I think he intends to take it, too.' 'Good, we've got three; now we can proceed!' He needed three people to register, and all these goddamn graduate students were frightened that if they registered they might flunk this terrible course. So the course that was given in the graduate school was supported two out of three by little undergraduate seniors who were taking it. But the lectures were not very advanced.'[1,3]

Near the senior year, Feynman did not have much to do; he had already taken all the necessary senior courses as well as several graduate courses, so he pursued other things that interested him. He wanted to study metallurgy. He studied metallography, just because it was a field he did not know anything about. He was always interested in learning things about which he did not know anything. In these courses he discovered for the first time the great use of the knowledge of physics, its universality. He had thought that metallurgy would be a different subject, dealing entirely with metals. The metallurgy boys were now studying for their senior course in metallography. There they learned how to grind samples and look at them under the microscope. These guys had worked in the foundry, where they would take a sample of steel, pound it, and see what happened. Feynman had had no such experience, so he thought he was at a disadvantage. But he didn't fully realize what a great advantage he had because he knew about atoms. He knew that these metallic substances were nothing but piles of atoms. He would intuitively understand many things that were possible or impossible without having actually studied metallurgy. However, while he was taking the course he didn't have the confidence that he really understood it. When the final examination came, he tried to answer every question that he could on the basis of what seemed to him to be the most logical and reasonable grounds.

After the examination, the metallurgy students, who were the experts, were talking amongst themselves. They would say, 'How'd you answer the question why nickel does not corrode?', and Feynman answered, 'I think because of the face it allows, and there's different packing on the surface, so that the oxygen has no effect on it.'[1,3] The experts did not agree and would express other opinions. Feynman thought he was really demolished, because these 'experts', whom he thought knew everything, told him that what he thought was cockeyed. In the end it turned out that he had been right about these things and received an excellent grade. So he learned that physics provided a very useful background for what appeared to be, at first sight, different fields: the world is the same, the physical laws are universal, and they work. One can use these ideas in different fields, and one who knows physics is ahead of those who don't know it; they have to learn a large number of things in an unconnected manner. But, of course, you have to have experience too. Both together are far better than anything else.

In physics, there was especially one course in which Feynman learned something very important. This was a course on experimental physics, given by George Harrison. It was a lecture-cum-laboratory course, but the lectures were fascinating. There were lots of interesting ideas about experiments. And there were challenges. The storage battery: How much energy would it be possible to store per cubic centimeter of material? How much energy can one store in a storage battery? Harrison knew how to teach the subject. He discussed the challenges of experimental physics. Feynman learned about many problems that needed to be solved from Harrison, as well as about the beauty of the experiments. The laboratory itself was quite good. On the wall, there was a list of fifty problems; you had to pick one out and work on it. Feynman selected two of them. One was the diffraction of light from sound waves generated in a liquid, say benzene, by a high-energy oscillator. When sound waves are generated, the refractive index of the liquid varies; light passing through the liquid produces a diffraction pattern. Feynman and Welton did this experiment together. The second challenge that Feynman took was to build a machine to measure the ratio of the velocities of two rotating shafts. It had to be built from scratch; Feynman had to design and build the apparatus. However, the bearings he used were all too loose, and his machine-shop work was poor; as a result, the apparatus did not work properly. It required precision and Feynman was not good enough at it. Harrison complimented him on the design: it was a very cleverly conceived device. That was some solace to Feynman. This course offered other problems to work on, which other students took, such as constructing a photometer that could detect a candle at six miles. 'It was good, just great, and the guys would figure it out. It was within range. These things were all real, they were all possible—at the limits of the possible, and a fellow would get a lot of excitement from working on them. It was an excellent course.'[1,3] Feynman and Welton also took courses on X-rays and other topics; these were senior or graduate courses. MIT offered a good opportunity to learn the sciences.

There were also courses in the humanities, but Feynman had little patience with them. The excuse given for the courses in English was that they would be useful if one had to write applications for obtaining patents. Some of Feynman's fraternity brothers liked the courses in English and French literature, but he didn't. For him, the humanities were a pain in the neck, which he preferred not to be subjected to.

At the beginning of the English class, there was a ten-minute quiz everyday, to ascertain whether the students had read the assigned material. So Feynman would peek and have a look at what the neighboring student had written about the assigned book; for a while, in the English course, he felt that he had lost his moral sense. It was all forced, and he felt that it was all a bit illegitimate. He didn't like it. He felt that he had really to fight the humanities in order to pursue the things he really wanted to work on.

Feynman was not good at English spelling, and it always bothered him that it would arrest his progress. He felt that English spelling was irrational and should be modified. He did not have the same feeling of progress or self-development in the humanities as he had in the sciences. English spelling was ridiculous and unnecessary to learn, and did not represent intellectual development, or so he thought.

And philosophy. He had looked at books on philosophy before going to MIT. In high school he thought that he had become a sort of philosopher. He had the notion that he had grown from biology to chemistry to physics to mathematics, and finally to philosophy—having pursued a hierarchy of intellectual climbing. So he did a little philosophy. For example, he tried to prove by logic that God does not exist. He used to look a little bit at the writings of Reade. But when he read, he thought he realized how stupid things really were. His girlfriend, Arline, was trying to read Descartes, and Feynman started to look at the first few paragraphs of his philosophy, in which, starting from only the fact that he is, he proves that God is perfect. He felt that he knew enough logic to realize that some things don't come out of some other things.

You can usually guess from the axioms what kind of thing is going to come out, and it was not possible to get out what Descartes did. Therefore, he felt there was something wrong with Descartes's reasoning. He came to the conclusion that even some respected philosophers were really quite poor and rather stupid people, as far as he was concerned. They had obvious, trivial errors in logic.

At MIT, they had Randall's *The making of the modern mind* as a textbook in the English course to learn about the development of philosophical ideas. Feynman thought there was so much nonsense there while the modern mind was being made, and he thought of his own modern mind. He was required to remember what dumb things various dumb guys had said.

Feynman learned how Francis Bacon understood that experiments should be done. So he took up Gilbert, the author of *De magnete*, who actually did experiments in those days, and looked up what he had said about Bacon. Gilbert said that Bacon was a good philosopher and a good scientist for a politician. 'He writes science like a lord chancellor', Gilbert had said of Bacon, and Feynman agreed. 'Gilbert was actually doing something real, while Bacon was telling people what they ought to do. And we get the idea in history that science was developing because they followed Bacon's principles of how to do it!'[1]

The more Feynman learned, the less he believed anything. He did not wish to go on reading, because he did not like what he read; in fact, he objected to what he read. In the humanities, there were options. Not only were there things like French literature, but there were subjects like philosophy and descriptive astronomy. Feynman chose astronomy, because that provided a minimum escape from the humanities requirements for graduation. He also took philosophy. A man by the name of Stewart taught astronomy, which was based on a book by Baker. Feynman was glad to learn new things in this course, for after all it was science.

The philosophy professor, Robinson, was an old man with a beard; he spoke in a mumbled fashion, which was incomprehensible to Feynman. Only once in a great while a few words ever hung together. There used to be a lecture every day. One day, Feynman heard him go: 'bmbmobmobo; the stream of consciousness, *rmbmoomb* . . . .' That's all. The other students had gradually begun to understand him; they had learned how to hear him. But Feynman, who had a block against philosophy in the first place, never got to understand him. He thought it was a waste of time. The students would sit for an hour in Robinson's class, then get out. That day, when Robinson said something, which sounded mumbo-jumbo to Feynman, there was great excitement among the students. Feynman asked around what was said, and learned that they had to write a theme for the final grade.

Feynman had heard the words 'stream of consciousness', and that was a problem which had always interested him. What happens when one goes to sleep? His father had taught him to think about the world from the point of view of a Martian coming down and asking one questions. Suppose the Martians did not sleep. The Martian would be very interested in the question of sleeping. He would ask, 'How does it feel?' You go along, your mind is working, and all of a sudden what do you do? Turn off suddenly? And turn on suddenly? What happens to your ideas when you go to sleep? Do they suddenly turn off?' So, Feynman found the idea of 'stream of consciousness' interesting! And he decided to write something on this theme.

He would work on his philosophy paper by going to his rooms in the afternoon, pulling down the shades, getting into bed, and watching, introspecting, what would happen when he went to sleep. Thus he would fall asleep in the afternoon for a nap, and again at night, and he would work for this theme—the students had quite a long time to work on it—and he kept on introspecting. He noticed a lot of things—'because, if you practice, you can think deeper and deeper about the depths of consciousness.'[1,3] For his theme, he pondered about the difficulties of introspection. He wrote up his essay and made up a poem which summed it all up by saying:

> *I wonder why, I wonder why.*
> *I wonder why I wonder.*
> *I wonder* why *I wonder why*
> *I wonder why I wonder!*

Feynman turned in his paper. After a few days, Professor Robinson brought back some of the themes, and read one of them to the class. Then he read another. Finally he read:

> *Uh wugga wuh. Uh wugga wuh.*
> *Uh wugga wugga wugga.*
> *I wugga* wuh *uh wugga wuh*
> *Uh wugga wugga wugga.*[11]

From his rhythm, Feynman judged that his theme was being read. At first, he had not recognized it, until Robinson came to the poem. Feynman got an A on the theme, and wondered how little one needed to pass philosophy.

In one of the humanities courses on the history of thought, the students were supposed to read Goethe's *Faust* and write a theme about it. Feynman read *Faust*, but could not make head or tail of it. He told his fraternity brothers that there was no way he was going to write a theme about it. His fraternity brothers suggested that he should write a long theme—the number of words required—on an entirely different subject, and then somehow connect it with *Faust*. So he sat down and wrote a theme on 'The limitations of reason'. He thought that there were certain problems that could not be solved by thinking about them alone—such as aesthetic meaning, value judgments, and other such things. He developed the ideas about the limitations of the methods of science, and wrote up this theme.[12]

3.3 'The limitations of reason'

On the theme 'The limitations of reason', Feynman wrote:

'Reason, it has been said, is what distinguishes man from other animals. It is usual to consider reason to mean logical thinking. This will enable us to conclude that the outward signs that lead us to recognize ourselves from beasts have their source in logical thought. What are these things that we possess that animals lack? They seem to consist mainly in store of material capital, a social, political, and moral system of mutual relations (which animals do not entirely lack), artistic creations, and partial knowledge of the laws of material nature. Is the basis of all this logical thought? Have all these things been produced solely by rational deductions, as the idea of reason being characteristic of man implies?

'It is certain that our partial knowledge of natural laws does certainly claim to have sprung from rationalization. Scientists have been classified as logical thinkers and analysts. The basis of most sciences that are able to predict has been mathematics. And mathematics is logic. It must be clear that science is apparently of purely logical origin.

'How does this apply to our supply of material capital? Does it have its source in man's ability to reason? To a great extent it does. Most of the modern physical objects that man has made for himself are of logical design. They have been devised by thinking men and, therefore, owe their existence to man's ability to think in a logical manner.

'It is not very different in political and social ideas. They are usually thought out ahead of time (at least in modern times), and a great deal of mental effort goes into them. Hence the relation of man to man is in some ways logical. In other ways, it is moral and religious; then it is not rational. Most moral principles do not seem to come from logical thought. We *feel* very strongly about certain (or, more accurately, uncertain) moral principles. We are, to an extremely great extent, morally intolerant. The animals have no moral sense (at least to the extent human beings have), yet we do not use reason to obtain our moral ideas. Where do they come from?

'Art also does not spring from rationality. The sense of beauty has almost completely escaped the gamut of logic. Beauty is undefinable; it is impervious to logic. We certainly have logical ideas about what is beautiful, and argue about them, but not logically. Our ideas on these subjects do not come from reason. Animals show no aesthetic sense. Man has another faculty besides reason that animals don't: appreciation of art.

'We have found, then, at least two instances of ideas in man that are not bestial, and do not come from reason: moral and aesthetic principles. Reason is impotent to tackle certain problems. It is not the sole source of knowledge and civilization. It does not deal in aesthetics, in feeling. But the thing that distinguishes man from animals is reason. Reason must then be the sole prime mover of all of man's non-animal endeavors. Reason must be the sole fundamental and indispensable characteristic behind what we proudly call our "civilization".

'By civilization we usually mean our technological and physical constructs, our social and political scheme of things, our artistic principles, our store of knowledge of Nature, etc. Is reason, then, the important, the most important, constituent of these things? It is true that our knowledge of Nature has been obtained by rational means. However, I question the idea that reason is the primary influence in politics and society.

'It is also quite impossible to analyze spirit and religion. Moral ideas also do not yield to its attack. If morals were 'reasonable', I'm sure that they would be very different.

'What, then, is the other human faculty? It is the understanding of things that are not known by the senses, but are felt intuitively. It is the understanding of spirit and feeling. An age of reason alone would therefore have no place for feeling and religion (other than a rational religion). But men have feelings and emotions, which lead them with a much more powerful attraction than does reason. They must rebel.

'So it was at the end of the eighteenth century. The first part of the century was convinced that reason, and reason alone, was the way to happiness, to pleasure, and to a full life. The thinker was the happy man. The non-thinker was no better than an animal. All could be done by thought. But all was not done with thought. Thought could only take away religion; it could substitute very little in place of it. Thought could not lead to a happy life. It could not lead to rich emotional feeling and active participation in the life one was to enjoy. It could only contemplate life objectively, almost physiologically. This was not living, it was watching life [go by].'

With this paen to the glory of reason, Feynman turned to the immediate theme, which was *Faust*. He continued:

'The principle, that life was [to be] lived to the full was recognized by the Romanticists of the latter eighteenth century. They felt, not thought. They felt that man was more than just a thinking machine. Man could appreciate art. Science had so far been unable to do so. Scientific morals were unacceptable. Scientific religion was practically no religion [at all]. Religion is simply feeling and intuitive emotionalism. It is not to be a logical doctrine of axioms and conclusions.

'Goethe lived at a time that just bridged the gap from the rationalistic age to the romantic period that followed. He was a part of the Romantic revolution. He realized the limitations of thought and materialism of his time. He was a poet, an emotionalist, and a philosopher of sorts. One may therefore gain an insight into the characteristics of the change by studying the life of Goethe and what he wrote.

'One of the most interesting of his works, from the point of view of allegorical significance, and of the insight it gives into the spirit of the age, is *Faust*. Faust is just the story of the importance of reason and of the importance of feeling in the striving for happiness. Faust himself at first represents a man who has had his fill of knowledge, and yet is unhappy. The infinity of the universe confuses him. The goal of happiness is not to be approached only through reason. Faust is therefore unhappy. In attempting to end his life he is interrupted by the Easter bells. They give him an indication that there is something more in life than [mere] thought; there is feeling, religious feeling.

'Mephistopheles, the portrayer of cruel, cynical, and sardonic reason, tells Faust that he can show him the path to happiness. He tries to show Faust happiness in frivolity and drink, but this only disgusts Faust. Faust finds almost no pleasure in woman; he almost appreciates the high worth of woman's nature, woman's beauty, and woman's companionship in the adventure of life, as college humor says it. Mephistopheles, however, cannot see this, and urges Faust on to the more material pleasures with women. Mephistopheles bungles it entirely; he cannot show Faust true happiness and only brings tragedy and unhappiness. Mephistopheles fails again and again to bring happiness to Faust. Faust, however, does not find it even in spite of the devil's arrangements. He finds true contentment in the happiness of others. It is the spirit of doing things, not the reason for doing them, that is life. Feeling and emotion are true life. As Goethe says,

> My dear young friend, gray is all theory
> The golden tree of life alone is green.'

Feynman sent a copy of the above theme to his friend Elmer Heller at Purdue University, with a covering letter dated 9 March 1937. He wrote: 'I am sure you will not believe me but I've been working my proverbial balls to the bone. For this reason I have not written to you.

'When I first got your letter on the unimportance and limitations of logical reasoning, I thought that you were full of beer (for variation). However, after considering it further I was very much convinced that you're all OK. There must be something funny there, however, because reasoning logically does provide a check on work. A very fruitful check at that. It does seem damn strange that we can get ideas (so easily and illogically) that can be logically checked. I'm sure the mind does not think the problem out logically first, then suddenly presents the answer to the consciousness as if it were impulsive. The mind is inherently illogical and intuitive. Why does it only accept logical doctrines as being reasonable ones?

'Logic has been analyzed very completely, yet, as you point out, nothing has been done with the other "sight". How can we approach the problem? I haven't much of an aesthetic sense, so that I can only appreciate the action of this "sight" when it is applied to my solution of mathematical and physical problems. It is very rapid and defies analysis so far. I'll give it a good "think" sometime when I have time.

'I'm taking a course (a crappy course) on [the] history of thought. We had an assignment to read Goethe's *Faust* and then write a theme on it. I wrote one of my usual shit themes. The ideas of the first part are your ideas. Thanks very much for them. I've looked at the question in a little different way, but I owe the inspiration to you. You only need to read up to where I have it marked. It is enclosed. It does not stress the idea that scientific ideas are, in their source, illogical, but otherwise it is OK.

'I'm going along with the dames as per usual. Arline (? doubt exists) is coming for the Inter-fraternity Dance here. It's the biggest dance of the year. It looks like a very pleasant weekend and therefore (since pleasure is derived from woman) very expensive.

'There is a dance around here every weekend or so. I'm having my usual good time. . ... Fraternally, R. Feynman.'

In his theme, Feynman concluded that 'This problem of the limitation of reason is well illustrated in *Faust*. Faust represents reason. . ..' But the original theme on 'The limitations of reason' had been written completely independently of this, and he put this connection at the end. The professor read Feynman's essay, and wrote on the top: 'The introductory material is excellent, but the connection with *Faust* is not too satisfactory. I would advise a better proportion between the *Faust* material and the introduction . . . .'[1] Feynman received a good grade, something like B$^+$, on his theme. The professor did not notice how the theme was artificially put together. Feynman always had to struggle like this in the courses on humanities.

On another occasion, he had to make a commentary on any one of a series of themes. One of these was Thomas Huxley's 'On a piece of chalk'. He had to write an analytical analysis of this work. He found that he couldn't do that. Instead of that, he wrote a kind of parody of the work, an imitation, on dust, in which he told all the things that dust did. Huxley had talked about how an ordinary piece of chalk he is holding is the remains from animal bones, and how the forces inside the earth lifted it up so that it became part of the White Cliffs, and then it was quarried and is now used to convey ideas through writing on the blackboard. In his parody, 'On a piece of dust', Feynman discussed how dust makes the colors of sunset and precipitates rain. 'I was always a faker, always trying to escape' from such chores in the humanities.[13]

At MIT, Feynman did not take part in any extracurricular activities, such as clubs and student activities, execpt the ROTC. He did try to play some squash for a while, with a couple of friends from the fraternity, but never got on to the squash team. His principal extracurricular activities there were girlfriends and going for walks in the city, and learning how to drive a car. In his spare time he carried on rather intensive discussions on physics with friends like Ted Welton.

Feynman had only a small scholarship at MIT, worth about one hundred dollars per annum. His parents had worked very hard to collect the money to send him to MIT. He thought of augmenting his finances by working with a professor on research projects. In those days, there was a body called the National Youth Administration, which financed projects in universities like MIT. Students would obtain jobs for assisting professors in some way in their research projects. Feynman and Welton got a job to help Professor Warren in the X-ray department. Their task was to make tables of universal lattices of some crystals by working on computing machines. They developed faster and faster methods of computation for this purpose. They worked on the problem which Professor Warren had given them, calculating as fast as possible, and estimated that the work they were doing would take seven years to complete. So they talked themselves out of a job, but Warren gave them other things to do, which they did in off hours after school.

Later on Feynman got the same NYA job in the laboratory of Professor Stockbarger, a man who grew large single crystals of lithium fluoride and other alkali halides. In his laboratory, Feynman did odd jobs like putting in shelves, fixing lights, etc. Stockbarger gave Feynman some experimental scientific work to do as well, like making a certain substance out of lithium oxide by using a furnace. He built the furnace and tried to make the substance, but it did not work out. Feynman was not able to do the scientific things which Stockbarger asked him to do. Stockbarger also asked Feynman to design a device to measure the position of a shaft that oscillated in a lathe. One could buy such things, but Stockbarger thought it should be made; there was always money trouble. Feynman designed it, but because of his imprecise machine work it didn't function properly. Because of his failure in machine work, in spite of trying hard, he developed a great respect for it and for the machinists who could do it.

Feynman always wanted to be a machinist. On one occasion, he gave crucial help to a machinist who was working on a great brass ring in a lathe, in which Feynman's sense of rhythm and timing came in handy. On another occasion, in another machine shop, they had a circular disk, a copper ring with a screening over it, and they wanted to drill a hole in the center of the screening; they were building some kind of a gas generator. But the machinist did not know how to find the center of the screening. Feynman showed him how to find the center of the circle without using a compass, visually, by using a lathe wheel with a pulley. He gave the impression that he was a great machinist himself and enjoyed the game. What Feynman loved was the practical man. He believed that the man who could really do things, like machine-shop work, possessed some deep knowledge of a special kind.

In his own machine work, Feynman was helped by his sense of rhythm. It is not clear when his actual drum-playing started. He used to play bang–bang against the wall, and he had played a toy drum. He used to make rhythms by hitting something against something else, but he did not play real drums with music at that time; he was not that kind of drummer. He never listened to music for recreation or relaxation, nor did he do so even later in life. Music was not played in his parents' house, but he did like rhythms and did listen to drums from time to time. He could listen to good drum music from Africa, but not the usual classical or modern music.

3.4 Chief chemist at the Metaplast Corporation

Every summer, Feynman would try to obtain some employment during the long vacation. While he was wondering what to do during the long summer vacation early in June 1938, he met his old friend from high school days, Bernard Walker, on the beach in Far Rockaway. Walker had just returned from a trip to France, and he told Feynman that he knew how to 'metal-plate anything'. He picked up the pit of a peach from the sand at the beach and said that he could even metal-plate that pit. Feynman wondered how he would get metallic contact with such a surface, but Walker assured him 'that's the secret' and told him a lot of other things. He offered Feynman a job in his newly established business, the Metaplast Corporation, which he had started for metal-plating various plastics. Bernie Walker's company was situated on the top floor of a building in New York City. There were just four or five persons in the company: Bernie's father got the money together for the enterprise and was the president; Bernie himself was vice-president; there was another fellow who was the salesman; Feynman became chief research chemist; and Bernie's brother, who was not very bright, was bottle-washer and cleaner. The company had six metal-plating baths altogether.

Feynman recalled that the process for metal-plating was as follows: 'First, deposit silver on the object by precipitating silver from a silver nitrate bath with a reducing agent (as one does to make mirrors); then stick the object with silver on it as a conductor into the electroplating bath, and the silver gets plated. The problem was: Does the silver stick to the object? It doesn't. It peels off easily. So there was a step in between to make silver stick better to the object. For things like Bakelite, which was a well-known and important plastic in those days, my friend had found that if he sandblasted it first, and then soaked it for many hours in stannous hydroxide, which got into the pores of the Bakelite, the silver would hold onto the surface very nicely.

'But it worked only on a few plastics, and new kinds of plastics were coming out all the time, such as methyl methacrylate (which we call plexiglass, now), that couldn't plate directly, at first. And cellulose acetate, which was very cheap, was another one we couldn't plate at first, though we finally discovered that putting it in sodium hydroxide for a little while before using the stannous chloride made it plate very well.'[14]

Feynman was quite successful as a 'chemist' at the Metaplast Corporation. His great advantage was that Bernie Walker did not know any chemistry nor had he tried to do any experiments. Feynman, on the other hand, by keeping track of everything he did to plate a wider range of plastics than Walker had done, tried to do things in the only scientific way he had learned at MIT. Feynman also tried to simplify the various processes he had used by reading chemical literature: for instance, he changed the reducing agent from glucose to formaldehyde, and was able to recover 100 percent of the silver immediately, instead of having to recover the silver left in the solution at a later time. He also found that he could dissolve stannous hydroxide in water by adding a little bit of hydrochloric acid, something which he remembered from his chemistry course at MIT; with the help of this step he was able to do in minutes that which had taken several hours before. Feynman's chemical experiments were continually interrupted by the salesman, who would bring different kinds of plastics for plating from prospective customers. Feynman had neatly arranged his bottles of chemicals and planned his experiments, when the salesman would come and ask him to do some other 'super job' which the 'sales department' wanted done as soon as possible. Such new assignments would lead to trouble from time to time, since the salesman would go around boasting all over the place that their company 'could metal-plate *anything*'! For instance, once an artist, who had in mind to make a picture for the cover of an automobile magazine, had very carefully built a plastic wheel and wanted to have the hub of the wheel metal-plated so as to make it look like a shiny silver hub. The artist had made the wheel of a certain plastic with which Feynman was not familiar. The salesman did not know what could be plated, but would go around promising all kinds of wild things which could be done at the first try. On this occasion, Feynman tried to remove the old silver by using concentrated nitric acid, which took off all the silver all right but made pits and holes in the plastic, thus causing troubles for the company. 'In fact we had lots of "hot water" experiments.'[15]

It was decided that the company would run advertisements in *Modern Plastics* magazine. Some of the things which Feynman had metal-plated were indeed 'very pretty', and they looked good in the advertisements. Some of these good-looking items were also placed in the showcase in front of the company offices for customers to look at, but neither from these items nor from the advertisements could one decide how long the plating would stay on, although some of these jobs had been done very carefully and were not the regular products of the company. Soon after Feynman left the company at the end of the summer to go back to MIT, the company received a good order from a client who wanted to have plastic fountain pens metal-plated, so that people could buy light and cheap 'silver' pens. These pens immediately sold very well everywhere, but since the company did not have prior experience with silver-plating this special plastic, which was not pure and had a special filler, it would develop blisters that would peel off the pens. This gave rise to an emergency problem at the company, and Bernie Walker decided that he needed a large microscope to examine the problem with the silver-plated pens, although he had no idea what he was going to examine or how, and the company spent a lot of money on this 'fake research'. With Feynman no longer there, they were never able to solve the problem. This had been a big order for the company, and failure to solve the problem led to the failure of the company.

Several years later, when Feynman went from Princeton to Los Alamos to work on the Manhattan Project, he met Frederic de Hoffman, an emigré scientist from Austria. Although de Hoffman was scientifically not very accomplished, he liked mathematics and compensated for his lack of training by hard work. Later on he became an important administrator, first as director of the General Atomics Laboratory in San Diego and, finally, president of the Salk Institute for Biological Sciences at La Jolla, California. But at that time in Los Alamos, 'he was just a very energetic, open-eyed, enthusiastic young man, helping along at the project as best as he could.

'One day we were eating at the Fuller Lodge, and he told me [Feynman] that he had been working in England before coming to Los Alamos.' Feynman asked him what kind of work had he been doing in England? De Hoffman told him that he was working on a process for metal-plating plastics, and was one of the guys in the laboratory. 'How did it go?', asked Feynman. De Hoffman: 'It was going pretty well, but we had our problems. Just as we were beginning to develop our process, there was a company in New York . . .' Feynman: 'What company in New York?' De Hoffman: 'It was called Metaplast Corporation. They were developing further than we were.' Feynman: 'How could you tell?' De Hoffman: 'They were advertising in *Modern Plastics* with full page advertisements showing all the things that they could plate, and we realized that they were further along than we were.'

Feynman: 'Did you have any stuff from them?' De Hoffman: 'No, but you could tell from the advertisements that they were ahead of what we could do. Our process was pretty good, but it was no use trying to compete with an American process like that.'

Feynman: 'How many chemists did you have working in your laboratory?' De Hoffman; 'We had six chemists working.' Feynman: How many chemists do you think the Metaplast Corporation had?' De Hoffman: 'Oh! They must have had a real chemistry department!'

Feynman: 'Would you describe for me what you think the chief research chemist of the Metaplast Corporation might look like?' De Hoffman: 'I would guess that they must have twenty or fifty chemists, and the chief research chemist has his own office—special, with glass. You know, like they have in the movies—guys coming in all the time with research projects that they're doing, getting his advice, and rushing off to do research, people coming in and out all the time. With twenty-five or fifty chemists, how the hell could we compete with them?' Feynman: 'You'll be amused to know that you are now talking to the chief research chemist of Metaplast Corporation, whose staff consisted of one bottle-washer!'[16]

3.5 Research on cosmic rays as an undergraduate

While Feynman was still an undergraduate at MIT, he published two papers in the *Physical Review*. One of these was with Manuel Sandoval Vallarta. Vallarta was interested in cosmic rays. Feynman had attended one of Vallarta's classes, and the two had become sort of friends. Vallarta told Feynman about a cosmic ray problem that he had, but he had not fully analyzed it. It appeared that cosmic rays, after the correction for their bending in a magnetic field was taken into account, were still energetic enough and were isotropic in all directions. That bothered Vallarta. He said to Feynman, 'Look, there are lots of stars in the Milky Way. If the cosmic rays are isotropic outside the galaxy, then they would be scattered by the stars and they would be less (or more) so in the Milky Way.' So he said, 'I want you to figure out that if cosmic rays were isotropic at infinity outside the galaxy, how the stars in the galaxy would just change the distribution so that we would be able to know how much more of them we would detect.'[1] Feynman worked on it a bit and proved the theorem that if cosmic rays are isotropic outside the galaxy then they would be isotropic inside as well. In their published note, entitled 'The scattering of cosmic rays by the stars of a galaxy', Vallarta and Feynman formulated the problem as follows.[17]

Imagine a galaxy of N stars, each carrying a magnetic dipole of moment $\mu_n (n = 1, 2, \ldots, N)$ and assume that the density, defined as the number of stars per unit volume, varies according to any given law, while the dipoles are oriented at random because of their very weak coupling. Under this condition the resultant field of the whole galaxy almost vanishes. Let there be an isotropic distribution of charged cosmic particles entering the galaxy from the outside. The problem is to find the intensity distribution in all directions around a point within the galaxy. Its importance arises from the fact that if the distribution should prove to be anisotropic a means would be available for determining whether cosmic rays come from beyond the galaxy, independent of the galactic rotation effect, which had been considered earlier by Compton and Getting.[18]

Consider a particle sent into a volume element dV of scattering matter in a direction given by the vector R. Let the probability of emerging in the direction R' be given by a scattering function $f(R, R')$ per unit solid angle. Conversely, a particle entering in the direction R' will have a probability $f(R', R)$ of emerging in the direction R. Let us assume that the scatterer (magnetic field of the star) has the reciprocal property so that $f(R, R') = f(R', R)$. In the present case this property is satisfied provided the particle sign is reversed at the same time as its direction of motion. That is, the probability of an electron going by any route is equal to the probability of a positron's going by the opposite route. If it has the reciprocal property for each element of volume it will also have it for any extended distribution of matter, that is, $F(R, P; R', P') = F(R', P'; R, P)$, where $F(R, P; R', P')$ is the probability that a particle going in the direction R at the point P will emerge in the direction R' at the point P'. This is because the probability of following any route is equal to the probability of following the reverse route, through the same element of volume. Thus the probability of a certain end result from a number of possible routes will equal the probability of the reversal of the result occurring through the reverse routes.

If the scatterer (the star) is to a large extent nonabsorbing and non-capturing, as in the case considered, all particles starting in a direction R at point P, sufficiently far from all neighboring stars, have only a small chance of being either absorbed or captured in a periodic orbit (of finite or infinite period), so that the great majority of them will emerge at infinity. For almost all particles, therefore, the probability of emerging at infinity must be unity, or

$$\int_{R'} F(R, P; R', \infty) \, dR' = 1 \tag{3.1}$$

almost always.

Now consider a beam of particles at infinity whose intensity in a direction R' is $I_\infty(R')$. The intensity at P observed in the direction R will be

$$I_P(R) = \int_{R'} F(R', \infty; R, P) I_\infty(R') \, dR'. \tag{3.2}$$

Using equation (3.1) and assuming an isotropic distribution at infinity such that $I(R')$ is a constant (independent of R'), we find that equation (3.2) becomes

$$I_P(R) = I_\infty \int_{R'} F(R, P; R', \infty) \, dR' = I_\infty \tag{3.3}$$

by equation (3.1). Therefore the intensity in any direction at P is the same and the distribution is isotropic at P if it is isotropic at infinity.

It is clear that if the distribution of positive and negative particles at infinity is isotropic, it will also be isotropic at any point P, except for small irregularities due to absorption by collision and by capture into periodic orbits. The conclusion is that particle scattering by magnetic fields of the stars is unable to contribute anything to the solution of the problem whether or not cosmic ray particles come from beyond the galaxy. These considerations hold so long as the scattering centers (stars) satisfy the conditions of being nonabsorbing and noncapturing, irrespective of the law of force which is responsible for the scattering.

Feynman felt very good about the proof he had found, although all he was proving was Liouville's theorem. Vallarta thought that this was very interesting, and it was the solution of the problem he had in mind. There was no effect due to the scattering by the stars of the galaxy; the net effect was zero, the only assumption being that the stars do not absorb cosmic rays. Vallarta wrote up the note, and they published it jointly. No referee commented upon the fact that the result was based on Liouville's famous theorem. It was published as a letter in the *Physical Review*, and appeared on 1 March 1939.

When the note was being written, Vallarta said to Feynman, 'Listen, since I am the senior scientist, I'll put my name first, that's the convention.'[1] Feynman found it a bit funny, but it presented no problem to him: 'So he put his name first, and the letter was published in the names of "Vallarta and Feynman". Then, many years later, Heisenberg edited a book on cosmic rays. He commented on every [worthwhile] paper, and our paper had no place anywhere. He did not know where to put it. So, at the end of the book, he mentioned that "another possibility for such fluctuations would be given by magnetic fields in the galactic system; in case the magnetic moments of individual stars are randomly oriented such an effect is not expected according to Vallarta and Feynman".[19] Thus I was the last word in the cosmic ray book of Heisenberg. When I saw Vallarta some time afterwards, I said, "Did you see the book by Heisenberg?" He said, "Yes. You're the last word in cosmic rays." He had noticed it too; "that's what I get for being the senior scientist," he said. He even remembered the joke he had pulled.'[1]

3.6 Feynman's senior thesis: 'Forces and stresses in molecules'

When the time came that Feynman had to write a senior thesis, as a requirement for his graduation, he went to John Clarke Slater to get a problem. Slater explained to him that he had an idea for a problem. Quartz, he told Feynman, was a remarkable substance, because when you heat it up it doesn't expand too much; it's very stable. And he thought that the reason quartz had an abnormal expansion rate was that there was a free vibration of the silicon atom, like a gyro, that would turn. If you turn a gyro around it tightens; similarly, as the atom vibrates, it tightens the bond, thus opposing the normal expansion which arises from the force law, and makes the expansion increase rapidly but not as rapidly as one would expect. Slater wanted Feynman to determine quantitatively the estimates whether this idea would work or not. It seemed like an interesting problem, and Feynman accepted to work on it for his senior thesis. 'Then I began to think, how am I going to calculate the expansion? The way to do that would be to imagine that the crystal is fixed in space, fixed in size, and ask what forces and stresses are generated to hold it. But for the compressibility, it's just the same thing as expansion. Then I began to wonder about the compressibility of crystals and their elastic constants.

'My mind was wild about the problem. I realized that if I assumed forces between the bonds like springs that wouldn't be so bad, since there were enormous thrusts like the ones I had learned about in bridge design, and I worked out elastic constants of certain substances by assuming springs between them. I knew that my formulation of the problem was getting away from the quartz, but I was able to work out the theory of the elastic constants. Of course, it had been done before, but I did not know that. I worked out the theory by myself, and it felt good to compute the properties of substances from fundamentals.'[1] Feynman proceeded to work out the problem as follows.

In his thesis,[20] Feynman started out with an apology for studying the forces and stresses within molecules. The concept of force is said to be 'more qualitatively illuminating than the energy concept'. This motivation is evidently a reflection of Feynman's wish at the time to feel what is going on; fortunately, as soon as as he got down to business, he turned to the energy $W(\lambda)$ from which the generalized force is derived,

$$f_\lambda = -\partial W(\lambda)/\partial\lambda. \tag{3.4}$$

Here the parameters λ are geometrical variables describing the spatial disposition of the various nuclei within the molecule.

Feynman remarked that a usual method to compute the right-hand side of equation (3.4) would be to obtain the numerical values $W(\lambda)$ for at least two different but neighboring configurations λ, from which the required derivative (3.4) might then be obtained by differencing. The numerical values $W(\lambda)$ would themselves be obtained by the variational method or by some perturbation scheme.

In contrast to this, Feynman set out to calculate the right-hand side of equation (3.4) directly in terms of a single configuration λ. This, as he pointed out, will avoid the necessity of obtaining wave functions for two separate configurations, so that the labor involved will be approximately halved.

In point of fact, Feynman's approach achieved far more than this, for the basic theory which he obtained for equation (3.4) was very powerful, enabling rapid and straightforward derivations to be given for various approximate force formulas. That this is indeed so may best be understood from the vantage point afforded by the variational principle of quantum mechanics. The thesis itself, however, contained no reference to this principle, so that we may safely deduce that, at the time he wrote this thesis (1939), Feynman had yet to make full acquaintance with the use of variational concepts, to which he was later to make his own very special and unique contributions.

The primary motivation of the thesis appears to stem from the following intuitively appealing theorem, which Feynman enunciated and proved:

'The force on any nucleus (considered fixed) in any system of nuclei and electrons is just the classical electrostatic attraction exerted on the nucleus in question by other nuclei and by the electron charge density distribution.' (i)

Clearly, this theorem embodied Feynman's claim that he needed only one configuration λ; nevertheless, as we shall see, the principal import of Feynman's approach went far beyond the particular statement of the theorem.

In view of the profound connection with the variational principle it will be useful for us here to invoke the latter. Let the ground state of the molecule in the nuclear configuration be described by means of the Schrödinger equation

$$H(\lambda)\psi(\lambda) = W(\lambda)\psi(\lambda), \tag{ii}$$

with the normalization condition

$$\int_V \psi^*(\lambda)\psi(\lambda)\,dV = 1. \tag{iii}$$

Then, multiplying both sides of equation (ii) by $\psi^*(\lambda)$ and integrating over the electron coordinates, we get

$$W(\lambda) = \int_V \psi^*(\lambda)H(\lambda)\psi(\lambda)\,dV, \tag{iv}$$

from which it follows that the required generalized force (3.4) is given by

$$f_\lambda = -\int_V \frac{\partial \psi^*(\lambda)}{\partial \lambda} H(\lambda)\psi(\lambda)\,dV - \int_V \psi^*(\lambda)\frac{\partial H(\lambda)}{\partial \lambda}\psi(\lambda)\,dV$$

$$- \int_V \psi^*(\lambda)H(\lambda)\frac{\partial \psi(\lambda)}{\partial \lambda}\,dV. \tag{v}$$

Now, the immediate interpretation of the first and third terms on the right-hand side of equation (v) is that they relate the infinitesimal change in the expectation value of the energy operator H consequent upon an infinitesimal change $[\partial\psi(\lambda)/\partial\lambda]\,\delta\lambda$ in the electronic wave function $\psi(\lambda)$. It is precisely this type of change which the variational principle of quantum mechanics asserts to be equal to zero. Indeed, the variational principle states that the energy expectation is stationary in the infinitesimal neighborhood of any of the eigenstates and, therefore, in particular in the infinitesimal neighborhood of the molecular ground state. The first and third term thus mutually cancel, leaving us with the simple formula

$$f_\lambda = -\int_V \psi^*(\lambda)\frac{\partial H(\lambda)}{\partial \lambda}\psi(\lambda)\,dV, \tag{vi}$$

in which the λ derivative of ψ is no longer required.

Suppose now that the molecular problem be coordinatized within a single Cartesian frame, and suppose further that the λ are Cartesian coordinates of the nuclei with respect to this frame. In such a coordinatization, the kinetic terms in $H(\lambda)$ make no reference to λ, and the only terms containing the λ are the energies of the Coulombic repulsion between the nuclei and the electrons.

If we denote the sum of these energies in the coordinatization by $V(\lambda)$, we then get

$$f_\lambda = -\int_V \psi^*(\lambda)\, \frac{\partial V(\lambda)}{\partial \lambda}\, \psi(\lambda)\, dV, \tag{3.5}$$

which is precisely the Feynman theorem quoted verbatim earlier under (i), since the right-hand side in equation (3.5) is manifestly the expectation value of the sum of the Coulomb forces mentioned.

Nowhere in the thesis did Feynman invoke or even suggest the role of the variational principle mentioned above. Instead he carried through explicitly the partial integrations pertaining thereto, which have to do with the hermiticity of the operator H, and which, in conjunction with equations (ii) and (iii), provided him with his proof that the first and third terms of the right-hand side of equation (v) do indeed cancel as stated.

The next section of the thesis dealt with the case in which that part of $H(\lambda)$, which contains λ, can be counted as a small perturbation $P(\lambda)$ on an otherwise solvable problem, whose unperturbed energy eigenvalues are denoted by E_k, and whose unperturbed groundstate energy E_0 is assumed to be non-degenerate. The Feynman force formula (vi) here leads, correctly to the second order, and with delightful directness, to the compact result

$$-f_\lambda = \langle 0|\partial P/\partial \lambda|0\rangle + 2\mathrm{Re} \sum_{k=0} \frac{\langle 0|P|k\rangle\langle k|\partial P/\partial \lambda|0\rangle}{E_0 - E_k}. \tag{3.6}$$

The perturbative force formula (3.6) is then applied to the evaluation of the van der Waals force between two neutral atoms. In order that we might grasp the significance of what follows, it is important to make note of an intriguing subtlety, the full significance of which (had Feynman noticed it at the time) could have led to considerable simplifications and economy of effort in the later parts of Feynman's thesis, especially the appendix.

The subtle point at issue is that the internuclear separation R, which is here the relevant configurational parameter λ, is confined within an identifiable small perturbation $P(\lambda)$ only by virtue of special choice of coordinates for the problem. A double system of Cartesian coordinates is suitable, wherein the electrons of the first atom are referred to the first nucleus as the origin, while those of the second nucleus are referred to the second nucleus as origin. This coordinatization is the natural and obvious one to use for the van der Waals force, and was of course the standard choice in the literature at the time (1939) when Feynman wrote his senior thesis. With it the only part of the energy operator to contain R comprises the sum of the various Coulombic interactions between the constituents of the one atom and the constituents of the other. This acts then as a perturbation $P(R)$, in which the leading term is the dipole–dipole interaction energy containing a small overall factor R^{-3}, to which there are corrections of higher order of smallness, starting with a term

R^{-4}. In contrast to this, the undoubled Cartesian frame relevant to the proof of Feynman's force theorem (i) gives the R-dependence also in the Coulomb interactions between the nuclei and their *own* electrons, i.e. within terms which cannot at all be counted as small perturbations. Thus, in spite of the obvious similarity of concept, the term $\partial V/\partial R$ of the Feynman force theorem (3.5) must not be identified with the term $\partial P/\partial R$ of the Feynman perturbative calculation (3.6), at least not where the van der Waals force is at issue.

In view of this subtlety, it is pertinent to ask whether Feynman's proof of his basic formula (3.5) through partial integrations, etc., was formulated in such a way as to demonstrate its equal validity in the two differing types of coordinate systems. To such an inquiry, one has to reply that the proof which Feynman gave left much to the reader, being based only on a one-electron system.

It is also pertinent to ask whether Feynman enumerated the Coulombic forces which his term $\partial P/\partial R$ contained. Strangely, he did not do so anywhere in the thesis. What he did do was to embark straight away upon the evaluation of his formula (3.6). The calculation was swift and direct. The first nonzero contribution came in the second-order perturbation theory, giving therefore an overall factor R^{-6}, to which the derivative $\partial/\partial R$ adjoined an extra factor R^{-1}. The force so obtained thus contained the familiar factor R^{-7}; in full, it is

$$f = -\frac{6}{R^7} \sum_{k,l} \frac{|\langle 00|Q|kl\rangle|^2}{E_0 \quad F_0 - E_k - F_l}, \tag{vii}$$

where the quantum numbers k and l, and the unperturbed energies E_k and F_l refer to the two atoms respectively, and where Q is the dipole–dipole operator, which in more obvious notation reads as

$$Q = e^2 \sum_{i,j} (x_i x_j + y_i y_j - 2x_i z_j). \tag{viii}$$

Equally effective was Feynman's application of his formula (3.6) to a system of several atoms, wherein it was quickly verified that the van der Waals forces are central and additive.

Following these applications, Feynman also used the perturbative formula (3.6) to provide a derivation of the 'usual expression'

$$\alpha = \sum_R 2\frac{|\langle 0|eZ|k\rangle|^2}{E_0 - E_k} \tag{ix}$$

for the electric polarizability of an atom. Here we find already an example of the extraordinary dexterity or crafty manipulative power which characterized so many of Feynman's later contributions. The problem at issue was the polarizability, but instead of first defining a dipole moment and then working out its expectation value in a uniform electric field, Feynman very efficiently achieved the same end by evaluating the force f exerted on the nucleus when the atom was placed in a nonuniform field. As in case of the van der Waals force, two parallel Cartesian frames were in fact used, and again this was done without any comment.

Following these expeditious applications of the universal concept (vi), we find an evaluation of the van der Waals force as it is given by a direct application of the specialized formula (3.5) of the theorem (i). In contrast with what has gone on before, this evaluation is extraordinarily complicated, and was incorporated into the thesis by way of a substantial mathematical appendix. In order to assess the situation, let us recall that the theorem (i) pictured the force on one nucleus as being due to its Coulomb interaction V with the other nucleus and with all the electrons (including its own). On the other hand, Feynman's treatment in terms of the perturbation P and the formula (3.6), if analyzed in a similar spirit, would evidently picture the same force as being due to the sum of all the Coulomb interactions linking mutually the constituents of one atom with the constitutents of the other; this difference in the physical picture arises solely by virtue of the different system of coordinatization of the electrons (one Cartesian frame versus two, and hence a different action of $\partial/\partial R$).

It thus follows that, whereas equation (3.5) includes the force exerted by the nucleus by its own electrons, the formula (3.6) includes instead the force exerted on these same electrons by the other atom. While the first of these forces can be described, according to the Feynman theorem, as the Coulomb force exerted by a static charge cloud, the second may only be pictured as due to the correlation between the motions of the respective electrons of the two atoms, diminishing the probabilities for finding energetically unfavorable configurations wherein both sets of electrons are simultaneously present in the space region between the nuclei. This concept cannot be formulated in any static picture, since the quantum laws forbid us to say which of the two sets of electrons is to be excluded.

Since the electron cloud is in equilibrium under the difference of the two forces it follows nevertheless that they must anyhow be equal, and of this a formal proof may easily be constructed, merely by considering the vanishing of the expectation value of the commutator $[p, H]$, where p is a momentum component for the said electron cloud. There is, therefore, from this point of view, no further problem to be examined.

However, as we have indicated, these illuminating connections did not feature in the thesis, wherein the original conception seems rather to have been to set forth and illustrate the theorem (i). The above-mentioned complications arise at just this juncture because equation (3.5) requires a perturbative evaluation of the force exerted on the nucleus by its own distorted electron cloud, in which context the R derivative $\partial/\partial R$ moves only the nucleus, and therefore does not produce the extra factor R^{-1}. It follows that not only the R^{-3} terms, but also R^{-4} terms of the perturbation, must be taken into account in calculating the distortion of this electron cloud. It would be pointless to go into the details of the requisite calculations; it is, however, a salutory testimony to Feynman's mastery of algebraic manipulation that he was able to get through this calculation, and to get it right, and all moreover in a bachelor's thesis! Some of the mathematical identities used in the end to prove equivalence with equation (3.6) were in essence of the same nature as suggested above, but with the relevant commutator (or, rather, something equivalent thereto!) evaluated between various of the unperturbed constituents of the overall perturbed state. Others, which were equally necessary, were certain identities expressive of the fact that the R^{-4} perturbation and the R^{-3} perturbtion have a common origin in certain Coulomb interactions, thus leading to a relationship between them. The successful exploitation of these and other identities discussed in the thesis demands adroit manipulations. How Feynman was led to these identities is not really apparent; they seem to have been concocted *ad hoc* in order to establish the necessary equivalence.

It is only fair to comment that the complexity and difficulty thus encountered with equation (3.5) did not at all bear out Feynman's expressed hope that his theorem (i) might provide an effective calculational tool. The latter is found, as we have seen, in the more adaptable general force formula (vi) or its perturbative extension (3.6). On the other hand, we must also in fairness allow that the theorem (i) does open up a new and physically appealing picture or explanation of the van der Waals force. Feynman developed his new physical picture in some detail in the main body of the thesis, where he showed that the electron clouds acquire both p-wave and d-wave admixtures, so that s–p and p–d interferences give rise to dipolar distortions in order R^{-7}, and correspondingly to an R^{-7} pull on the nucleus at the center.

A second part of the thesis dealt with the concept of stress, which, Feynman suggested, might help to understand such things as bonding angles or elastic constants. A stress tensor was sought such that its inward surface flux gives rise to the forces of the formula (3.5) plus (in case of time-dependent systems) the rate of increase of electronic momentum within the surface. Feynman found a symmetric stress tensor: it comprised a wave-mechanical part plus some Maxwell stresses. The wave-mechanical part, in the case of a one-electron system was that given by Pauli in his *Handbuch* article.[21] In the case of n electrons, Feynman showed that a straightforward integration over $n-1$ sets of electron coordinates gives a satisfactory analog of the Pauli stress from the nth electron. The n contributions of this type are then added to the Maxwell stresses to give a satisfactory total stress.

Feynman tried out his stress tensor within a hydrogen atom and found, as one might anticipate, a state of radial compression and transverse tension. He noted that a similar attempt in the case of the hydrogen molecular ion led to very difficult integrals in connection with the electronic cloud. Apparently, the use of elliptical coordinates did not substantially ameliorate this situation.

There was also the question of nonuniqueness of the stress, since a divergence-free and symmetric term could be added without introducing higher derivatives of ψ. Feynman gave an example of one such addition.

Feynman's theorem (i) opened up a new and more revealing picture of the physical mechanism of the van der Waals force. The same may be said of the physical mechanism of the covalent or homopolar chemical bond, in which connection Feynman's theorem is held in considerable esteem among the physical chemists. In order to understand why this should be so, it is only necessary to observe that the older textbooks treating the bond tended to display the bonding effect as a somewhat mysterious quantum mechanical concomitant of the exchange antisymmetry of the overall wave function and the pairing of electron spins, whereas Feynman focused attention solely on the charge distribution engendered by the spatial factor of the wave function and the chemically desirable Coulomb forces exerted by this charge distribution.

Feynman's theorem (i) is referred to in the literature as the 'Hellman–Feynman theorem'.[22] This terminology may be inexact, in so far as Hellman did not envisage the Feynman force theorem (i).[23]

John Slater thought that 'the thesis was good and ought to be published. So I wanted to publish it. Now, I had put in a hell of a long section in which I proved some quantum mechanical theorems concerning the Hamiltonian. Slater asked me to show it to Conyers Herring, who was a good student in those days, and let him comment on my paper. He said, "You don't have to prove all this. You just write down what you have said, and say that it is so because H is self-adjoint." I said, "What does it mean that H is self-adjoint?" He said, "What you have said means that." I asked, "Does everybody know that?" He said, "Yes." It just shows the level at which everything was being figured. So it was elementary and I didn't know anything, but I could prove it. Afterwards, I felt very ashamed, because it's really an obvious result of the Schrödinger first-order perturbation theory, and so I thought that the paper was dead. Anyway, it was published in the *Physical Review* under the title "Forces in molecules",[24] but I never heard it referred to by anybody.'[1]

Many years later, in summer 1949, Feynman went to give lectures on quantum electrodynamics at the University of Michigan summer school at Ann Arbor. There, 'Ted Berlin, who was in physical chemistry, said, "Have you heard all the debates about your Feynman–Hellman theorem?" I said, "What theorem?" He said, "It's called the Feynman–Hellman theorem, the force law between molecules." Everyone was arguing it across the ocean. The Americans were saying I was right and the Germans were saying that I had made two mistakes: I left out the kinetic energy and something else. But anyway, they thought that things cancelled out and I was just lucky. But my proof was really sound, and it wasn't just a matter of luck. There was no mistake. Hellman had discovered it independently. However, it was nothing but perturbation theory.'[1,3]

3.7 Pastures new

John Slater was impressed by Feynman's work. When the time came to choose a graduate school, 'I wanted to go to MIT, because one learns at MIT that it's the best place in the world. I told Slater that I wanted to go to MIT, and he said, "Why do you want to do that? You are not going to be accepted here." I asked him why. He said, "Because you should go to a different school for graduate work than for undergraduate work." He wouldn't let me in. And he asked, "Why do you want to go to MIT?" I said, "Because MIT is the best school in the country for science and engineering." He said, "Do you think so?" I said, "Yes." He said, "That's why you have to go to another school for your graduate work." Then I went to Princeton, and Slater was right. I learned that the world is bigger and there are many good places. MIT has its wonderful spirit and it's OK to keep you motivated and feeling wonderful, but it's slightly false. It's like the New Yorker's idea of the United States of America, that there is really nothing interesting west of the Hudson River, and one has to learn that it's not true. So Slater was a good influence in keeping me from going to graduate school there. Otherwise, Slater did not have any influence on me directly; he did not have the kind of influence that Morse had. Morse had the greatest influence upon me at MIT.'[1,3]

Upon graduation from MIT, Feynman spent the summer in Boston. He had obtained a summer job with the Chrysler Company to measure friction. The Chrysler Company had developed a new method of polishing to get a super finish, and Feynman's task was to determine how much better it was. 'It turned out that the "super finish" was not significantly better.'[25]

Feynman decided to go to Princeton. At Princeton he had been offered a research assistantship, 'which was wonderful. You got paid to help some poor bastard with his research. It was suggested that I should work with Eugene Wigner. When I got there, it turned out that they had shifted it around and I worked with John Archibald Wheeler, which was just fine.'[1]

Notes and References

1. R.P. Feynman, Interviews and conversations with Jagdish Mehra, in Pasadena, California, January 1988.

2. See Chapter 2, Ref. 14.

3. R.P. Feynman, Interviews of Charles Weiner (American Institute of Physics), in Pasadena, California, 1966.

4. R.P. Feynman, *SYJMF*, pp. 32–34.

5. R.P. Feynman, *SYJMF*, p. 31.

6. R.P. Feynman to Elmer W. Heller, 8 December 1935. Courtesy of Mr Heller.

7. A.S. Eddington, *The mathematical theory of relativity*. Cambridge University Press, London, 1923.

8. T.A. Welton, 'Memories of R.P. Feynman', unpublished manuscript, 1983.

9. Erwin Schrödinger had reached the same conclusion when he tried to calculate the spectrum of the hydrogen atom with his relativistic equation, and had to abandon it before he discovered the nonrelativistic equation. See Jagdish Mehra and Helmut Rechenberg, *The historical development of quantum theory*, Volume 5, Part 2, *The rise of wave mechanics, 1925–1926*. Springer, New York, 1987.

10. R.P. Feynman, Ref. 1. Feynman thought that Smythe's book was rather dry and unimaginative, that it emphasized routine exercises more than the fundamental principles of the subject.

11. R.P. Feynman, *SYJMF*, pp. 48–49.

12. Feynman sent a copy of it to his friend Elmer Heller at Purdue University. Mr Heller kindly shared it with me.

13. R.P. Feynman, *SYJMF*, pp. 45–46.

14. R.P. Feynman, *SYJMF*, p. 55.

15. R.P. Feynman, *SYJMF*, p. 56.

16. R.P. Feynman, *SYJMF*, pp. 57–58.

17. M.S. Vallarta and R.P. Feynman, The scattering of cosmic rays by the stars of a galaxy. *Phys. Rev.* **55**, 506 (1939).

18. A.H. Compton and I.A. Getting, *Phys. Rev.* **47**, 817(1935); M.S. Vallarta and S. Kusaka, *Phys. Rev.* **55**, 1(1939).

19. W. Heisenberg (ed.) *Cosmic radiation, Fifteen lectures* (trans. T.H. Johnson). Dover, New York, 1946, p. 180.

20. R.P. Feynman, Forces and stresses in molecules. Thesis submitted in partial fulfillment of the requirements for the degree of Bachelor of Science, Course VIII, at MIT, 1939.

21. W. Pauli, Jr., *Quantentheorie, Handbuch der Physik*. Springer, Berlin, 1933. In the 1958 revised edition the equations are cited as 11.3, 11.3′, and 11.3″.

22. J.O. Hirschfelder, C.F. Curtiss, and R.B. Bird, *Molecular theory of gases and liquids*. Wiley, New York, 1954, p. 932.

23. H. Hellman, *Einführung in die Quantenchemie*. Deuticke, Leipzig, 1937.

24. R.P. Feynman, Forces in molecules. *Phys. Rev.* **56**, 340 (1939).

25. R.P. Feynman, *WDYCWOPT*, p. 34.

4

Arrival in Princeton as a graduate student

4.1 Settling in

In the fall of 1939, with his summer job at the Chrysler Company, working on the so-called 'super finish', behind him, Feynman went to Princeton. His father, Melville, drove him there by car on a Sunday and saw him installed in the Graduate College of Princeton University, where all the graduate students lived. It was like an imitation Oxford or Cambridge college, complete with accents: the Master of the Graduate College was a professor of 'French littrachaw'! There was a porter downstairs, everybody had nice rooms, and all the residents had their meals together, wearing their academic gowns, in a great hall which had stained-glass windows. Princeton itself had a great aspect of elegance. Partly with its imitation Gothic architecture, it looked like an old English university town. Before his going to Princeton from MIT, Feynman's fellow fraternity members, who knew about his rough and informal manners, had started to make remarks like: 'Wait till they find out whom they've got coming to Princeton! Wait till they see the mistake they have made!'[1] So Feynman decided to be specially nice and well behaved when he got there.

One of the things in the first few days had to do with his social life. Feynman had been barely an hour in his room in the Graduate College after arrival, trying to get settled, when the Master dropped by to see him and said: 'The Dean is having Tea and would like you and your room-mate Mr Serrette to come.'[2] Feynman had not yet met his room-mate up to that time; he was a chemist of some renown. Feynman was scared by the announcement: 'The Dean's Tea'. To him it sounded rather silly and high class, but his room-mate took it in his stride. Together they went down to the Dean's tea on the very afternoon that Feynman arrived in Princeton. The Dean, Professor Eisenhart, was in the line going in to receive people and greet the new students. Feynman told him his name, and he said, 'Oh, yes, you're Mr Feynman from MIT. We're glad to have you.' The fact that the Dean recognized him pleased Feynman and helped in breaking the ice. As he went in, Feynman was thinking about where he should sit, because he wanted to do things right. Inside, there were some matrons and girls around, and Feynman felt rather stiff. It was all very formal, and Feynman was still wondering where to sit down, whether he should sit next to this girl or that, or not, when he heard a voice behind him say, 'Would you like cream or lemon in your tea, Mr Feynman?' This was Mrs Eisenhart pouring tea. Feynman absentmindedly answered, 'Both please, thank you!' Still deciding on where to sit, he heard the sound of giggling and laughter, 'Heh, heh, heh, heh, heh, heh. Surely, you're joking, Mr Feynman!'

'Joking? Joking? What the hell did I say?' Feynman wondered; then he realized what he had done, and that was his first experience of this 'tea business'.[3]

After Feynman had been at Princeton a little while longer, he got to understand what this 'heh, heh, heh' meant; it meant, 'you're making a social error', because the next time he heard the same 'heh, heh, heh' from Mrs. Eisenhart was when someone was kissing her hand before leaving.

Another time, Feynman went out to buy supplies, and after shopping he was carrying a wastepaper basket and some other things, when Eisenberg, a theoretical physicist, passed him in the street, and said: 'Ah, you look like you're going to be a good theoretical physicist. You have bought the right tools—there is an eraser and a wastebasket!'[1] Before going to Princeton, Feynman had indeed decided that he was going to become a theoretical physicist, because his interests and talents as a theoretical physicist had by then outstripped his capabilities as an experimental physicist.

At the Graduate College they wore academic gowns to dinner. The first evening 'it scared the hell out of me, because I did not like formality.'[1] But Feynman soon realized that wearing the gowns had advantages. Young men who had been out doing sports could rush into their rooms, grab the gown, and put it on, without having to take a shower or change their clothes, and underneath the gowns they wore their T-shirts or other sportswear. As a rule, the gowns were never cleaned or repaired, 'so you could tell a first-year man from a second-year man, from a third year man, from a pig!'[4] The first-year men had very nice gowns, but by the time one got to the third or fourth year the gown was nothing but cardboard on the shoulders with tatters hanging down from it. 'So when I got to Princeton, I went to that tea on Sunday afternoon and had dinner that evening in an academic gown at the "College". But on Monday, the first thing I wanted to do was to see the cyclotron.'[4]

The reason why Feynman had chosen to go to Princeton University was that among the papers published in the *Physical Review*, he had seen many very good articles from Princeton, which appeared quite regularly. At MIT, in addition to many wonderful books on all aspects of physics, he had become used to studying journals, and from these he learned the kind of things that were going on at various places; and he knew that a lot of good work was reported from the research done at the Princeton cyclotron. They seemed to be very proud of what they were doing there. At MIT, everyone, including

Feynman, was proud and self-confident that great work was being done there. 'The cyclotron at MIT was "gold-plated" essentially, though not literally.'[1] The control board was in the other room, with special glass panels and shiny knobs. Feynman had seen the cyclotron at MIT and thought that it was very nice, but he knew from the journals that—relatively speaking—not many new results were being reported from there. Therefore, he thought that 'the Princeton cyclotron must be something extraordinary',[1] although the MIT one was large and occupied much space.

So, upon arrival in Princeton, the first thing that Feynman did was to go to the physics building, and there he asked someone: 'Where is the cyclotron? I want to see it.'[1] He was very excited. They told him to go down to the room at the end of the basement to see it. It seemed to be incredible to him that such an important thing was stuffed away at the far end of the basement. He walked into the basement where the cyclotron was, and he understood immediately 'why so many new results were being reported from the Princeton cyclotron' and why John Slater had told him to go to another school for graduate work. For Feynman, 'the whole idealism that MIT was the greatest school collapsed, because I recognized in that room the same kind of atmosphere as I had had in my laboratory at home.'[1]

The cyclotron was in the middle of the room and wires were hanging in the air all over the place, just strung up together. There were automatic water coolers and switches, so that if water stopped it would automatically shut off, and there were some pipes from which one could see the water was dripping. Wax was hanging all over the place, where they were fixing things. 'The whole place was completely different from MIT; it was a place where somebody was working! The person working there was close to the machine and he could fix it with his own hands; it was not an insulated box with knobs.'[1] Feynman understood immediately that this was a place for research; it had the atmosphere of a laboratory, with all the necessary tools lying around. 'At MIT I had been fooled: they had very good engineering design in an abstract sort of way, but the real work was not being done with that machine. Researchers at MIT were remote from their experiments. Experiment is fiddling around and therein lies the answer; it's not a totally organized program or elegance. That's what I noticed right away at Princeton. I loved it and felt that I had come to the right place, and I realized right away that Slater had been right. I had believed that MIT was the best school in the world; at the same time I had imagined that Princeton must have a cyclotron five or ten times as large as the one at MIT and must have more elegant facilities in order to produce that much more research. But, as I saw it, it was much smaller and completely inelegant, and that was the secret! So I loved it right away.

'It was like Frederic de Hoffman's description of the Metaplast Corporation, the image from the advertisements. The fact of the matter was that later on the Princeton cyclotron had a fire, because of all the wires that were hanging around in space, and they had a great deal of trouble on account of that fire, so in a certain way I was wrong. But, of course, I became friends right away with the people running the cyclotron at Princeton and the graduate students working there.'[1]

Later on, when Feynman went to teach at Cornell, he noticed that the cyclotron there hardly required a room. 'It was about three feet in diameter, perhaps the smallest cyclotron in the world, but they also got fantastic results from their small machine. At Princeton it was a lot harder to work with the cyclotron than at Cornell, but at MIT one had to have a crane that came rolling across the ceiling, lower the hooks, and it was just a "hell of a job". MIT was good, but Slater was right to warn me to go to another school for my graduate work. And I advise my students in the same way: learn what the rest of the world is like; the variety is worthwhile.'[1]

Feynman had started reading the *Physical Review* regularly from cover to cover already at MIT—'it could be done in those days!'[1] From it he learned about the work that was being done at different places. 'There were papers from all over the country, from important laboratories including Princeton, but there were not many papers from MIT. MIT had the spirit that it was a big deal to be there. I myself had thought that MIT was the biggest thing, certainly in engineering, perhaps in its relation to industry. But when it came to deeper scientific things, they were a little behind. I had not realized it, *but they were.* When I got to Princeton, I found that Princeton was more advanced somehow. They were doing more fundamental problems and, in general, the physicists there had a deeper thinking about physical matters. There were good people at MIT also, but there weren't enough of them. I got the feeling that physics at Princeton was more profound. Of course, there was also the Institute for Advanced Study at Princeton, with [H. P.] Robertson, [Hermann] Weyl, and [Albert] Einstein, but they were not part of the University. But they had [Rudolph] Ladenburg and [Eugene P.] Wigner, and [John Archibald] Wheeler had recently joined the physics department.'[1]

Before coming to Princeton Feynman had been informed that he would work as a research assistant to Eugene Wigner, but upon arrival there he found that he had been assigned to work with the 27-year-old John Archibald Wheeler, who had joined the physics department at Princeton in 1938 as an assistant professor of theoretical physics. It would turn out that Wheeler and Feynman were ideally matched to work with each other. 'I learned all kinds of things at Princeton that I had not learned at MIT. Wheeler was a wonderful man. Morse was nice, too, he gave me special attention at MIT, and brought me to his house from time to time to eat. Wheeler was similar. I went to his home very often. We discussed physics a lot and worked out things together. He was trying to write a book on scattering theory, and we worked out all kinds of things and discussed them together. I'm sure I got educated quite well.'[1]

4.2 Graduate studies

All the graduate students lived together in the Graduate College. They belonged to all the diverse fields, except theology, and ate their supper together in the great dining room in their academic gowns, the wearing of which used to bother Feynman a great deal. He always had a feeling that in such artificially contrived, socially elegant situations there were always some people, like himself, who were uncomfortable and who, in their hearts and minds, laughed at such customs. After all, Feynman's father, Melville, had been the sales manager of a uniform making company, and he had brought up young Feynman to disdain authority, stultifying and 'elegant' customs and rituals, and 'always be himself'.[1] In Princeton, he met quite a few so-called 'elegant' and 'superior' people who realized that a custom like wearing academic gowns for dinner was just a meaningless show. In any case, Feynman found it quite pleasant to live together with other graduate students in the same house. There were always many people to talk to in all kinds of fields, including the sciences, archaeology, mathematics, and the humanities. For instance, Feynman and a number of other graduate students had great fun in carrying on arguments with a Catholic priest, who would often drop by the Graduate College.

When Feynman first met Wheeler he was very surprised to see how young he was and looked. Feynman went to see Wheeler in his office by appointment, and Wheeler told him that they would get together on certain days of the week for discussions at a fixed time for a given duration. Feynman went to Wheeler's office at the appointed time, and Wheeler took out his pocket watch and placed it on the table so that he could see how much time had elapsed; then he explained what they should think about and discuss. Feynman found Wheeler to be a very nice fellow, from whom he thought he would learn a great deal. For their next meeting, Feynman also bought for himself a 'dollar watch'. When Wheeler came in, he took out his watch and placed it on the table; Feynman also took out his watch and put it in front of himself on the table. 'I was imitating him a little bit, and when I put my watch on the table he laughed very hard.'[1] Both of them laughed at each other and, like two teenage kids, they could not stop laughing. They realized that it was a ridiculous thing, and both of them collapsed with laughter at initially being so formal and a bit pompous, and they could not start discussing their work for a while. The ice was broken and they got down to business; but, by starting out in this manner, they became very good friends and remained so throughout life.[1]

Princeton had no requirement about how many or what courses one had to take for working towards a Ph.D. degree. Courses on various subjects were offered, but there was no pressure whatsoever to take anything. One had, of course, to pass the preliminary or qualifying examination—which was partly written and partly oral—to become a candidate for the doctorate. These examinations were far-ranging and rigorous, and one had to prepare well for them in order to pass them, that being the only prerequisite for work towards obtaining the Ph.D. When Feynman had to take the written and oral qualifying examinations, he prepared by taking several weeks off from Princeton and going back to MIT, where he was now unknown and nobody bothered him; he could organize his knowledge of physics away from the bustle of activities in Princeton.

Since there was no compulsion to take this or that course, Feynman took only a few courses. Being Wheeler's assistant, he had to attend his course on nuclear physics and write up the notes of his lectures. At Princeton, many people were closer to the forefront of nuclear physics, unlike MIT where Bethe and Bacher's articles in the *Reviews of Modern Physics* had served as the basis of the course on nuclear physics.[1] In Princeton at that time Eugene Wigner was developing the abstract theory of nuclei and the notion of 'Wigner forces', etc., and the subject was being created in front of one's eyes; one did not have to borrow the course material from anywhere. Feynman also took Wigner's course on solid state physics, from which he 'learned many things, including such deep questions as to why a solid is a solid.'[1] However, he was not able to master a number of things in group theory, Wigner's special tool, and he had always to find his own way to understand things, something which he would often do later on in his own creative work in theoretical physics.

Most of all, Feynman's graduate education was completed by discussing intensely and incessantly with fellow research students and working on research problems. For instance, he heard from someone that Heisenberg was working on the problem of the deuteron, and that he had encountered a terrible difficulty. Wigner had made a suggestion as to why the deuteron had a quadrupole moment, and after working with Wigner's idea for over a year a research student was not able to get the quadrupole moment. The students would commiserate with each other about their difficulties; if the professor made a suggestion, which did not turn out to be correct, it was the student's tough luck!

There were many cases in which Feynman himself was able to provide helpful hints to some of his fellow research students. One of the experimental physicists encountered the following problem: in the experiment he was doing there occurred something called K conversion, a phenomenon in which the nucleus captures an electron. But he had an atom (i.e. atomic nucleus) which captured the electron from the L shell and not from the K shell; he had L conversion but not K conversion. So, Feynman calculated the rate of L conversion when the energy level is close to the K conversion, or just a little higher, so that the conversion to the K level would not occur, and gave the experimentalist the answer he was looking for. Feynman felt very good, because that was the first time really that he had computed what was needed for an experiment; it was a very interesting puzzle, because until then he did not know how to calculate something that was going on in current research and which would agree with experiment. 'I felt that I really had the power to calculate things in a real situation. It was a nice feeling. Maybe the guy published it, or finally discovered the same thing in a book, but that didn't make any difference. The important thing was that I did it, that was the beginning of the real stuff, and it felt good.'[1, 5]

By the time Feynman arrived in Princeton in the fall of 1939, he knew quantum mechanics quite well. He enjoyed learning solid state physics, but there also the prevailing concepts were quantum mechanical. In his senior thesis at MIT, he had already worked on the problem of the forces between molecules, in which he had discovered the quantum-mechanical Feynman–Hellmann theorem. Once he was set on the path to quantum mechanics, he never left it.

Sometimes Feynman interacted with people at the Institute for Advanced Study. He talked to H. P. Robertson from time to time, and also went to see Einstein once or twice when he had a question. 'With Einstein, it was like this. He had invented general relativity, and thereafter it had degenerated because it was being done by mathematicians. And they were making all kinds of theorems putting everything in doubt, questioning whether there were gravitational waves or not, and not much of anything was coming out. After all, there were no new experiments. It was one of those things: a field can get elitist, esoteric, full of big smart guys who are going nowhere. But Einstein would give a talk from time to time and explain some things, and I got the feeling that, of all the people who were talking about relativity at that time, he made more sense than anybody else. They were all off on some mathematical tangent, but I could understand him and what he was trying to say.

'I had the problem that I had no respect for reputation or authority, something my father had taught me. For example, once Einstein gave a lecture on something in gravity theory at the Institute for Advanced Study, and the place was packed with people hanging off the rafters, and I was in the middle of the audience. Einstein proved a theorem that, if the potential falls as $1/r$ at large distances, the total amount of mass inside is the coefficient of $1/r$ blah, blah, blah! Very interesting! It didn't make any difference how the mass was distributed. And I got up and said, "Haven't you disregarded or have you assumed something about radiation, because we could get gravitational radiation with amplitudes and potentials of the order of $1/r$, which represent the internal effects. So where is the statement of assumption? Have you disregarded that?" "Oh, yes," he said, "I guess I have disregarded the radiation. I suppose, we'll have to assume dc [i.e. a constant over r]. On the other hand, it can't be dc, because nothing is stable; masses always move. That's not easy." It cannot be a constant over r because the masses move, so it's a question of whether they move fast or slow. To what extent had the energy been radiating during the time he was computing the mass? How much was left in there and when? Because it radiates. So there was a real question because it was supposed to be a mathematical theorem, and I noticed that there was radiation.

'OK? I was just so dumb, I simply asked a question, an honest question, a real difficulty. And, as a matter of fact, he answered it as best he could and tried to explain that "yes, there was this point" that he had to straighten out, and so on. But afterwards other people came up to me and said, "How could you ask Einstein such a question, blah, blah, blah?" That never struck me when I was asking it; I thought that I was just talking to another guy about a problem and it didn't matter who he was; it did not matter whether it was Einstein or someone else. It had nothing to do with [my trying to show off]; it was a question about what the theory was, and if it was true or not, that's all. It did not enter into my mind at that time really that I was challenging the great Einstein or anything like that. It was like a friend who was talking and I was asking him a question. But everybody else, they made all kinds of remarks about it. It was a reasonable question too, not a dumb question!'[1,5]

Feynman himself was not entirely a novice concerning the problems that existed in the field of general relativity theory. At MIT he had learned the details of the theory from Eddington's book *The mathematical theory of relativity* and had taken more than a passing interest in Eddington's other ideas on the theory of the fine structure constant. At MIT and soon after arriving in Princeton Feynman had flirted with the idea of pursuing Eddington's notions further, but was saved from this pitfall by Herbert C. Corben, who had studied under both Dirac and Eddington at Cambridge for his doctorate, and had learned the details of Eddington's theory directly from him. Corben was at the Institute for Advanced Study in Princeton, working with Wolfgang Pauli, and Feynman learned all about Eddington's ideas from him; Corben dissuaded Feynman from falling into the trap of these ideas. 'Many years later Feynman thanked me for having saved him a lot of time by advising him not to waste his time on Eddington.'[6]

As John Wheeler's assistant, Richard Feynman was supposed to, and did, work only on problems of theoretical physics, but he continued to learn from every source he encountered.[1] After a while, Feynman got the reputation that he was good at calculating integrals, that if an integral could be done he would be able to solve it; this went back to Abram Bader's physics class at Far Rockaway High School, where Feynman had mastered Woods' book on advanced calculus. One day he saw an integral written on a blackboard in the physics department, but he did not pay much attention to it. Later on he saw the same integral on various blackboards and concluded that some mathematician was trying to solve it. When he saw John Wheeler next, Wheeler told him, 'Oh, by the way, I've got an integral. I haven't showed it to you, but I have been showing it to everybody else. Can you do it?' Feynman looked at this integral, which all the other people were trying to solve, and said: 'It's a double integral; would it be all right if it comes out as a Bessel function?' He took it with him and returned in less than an hour and declared: 'It's an integral of a Bessel function, and is quite easy to express!' He knew such integrals from having studied Woods's *Advanced algebra* in high school. He recalled that 'it was just a technical thing, nothing very brilliant. It's just that I was facile at doing mathematical manipulations, having learned to do such things for six years or more. It was like the guy who is good at doing mental arithmetic. It was very useful to be able to do such things.'[1,5]

Wheeler and Feynman had immediately developed a good rapport with each other. Wheeler would give him a variety of problems, which arose in the course of his research work, and Feynman would work on them and solve them. 'Once Wheeler gave me a problem, and I got stuck and found that I couldn't do it. So, for a change, I began to think about certain ideas which had occurred to me already at MIT. At MIT, I had learned that the quantum electrodynamics of the day gave infinities, and this was the problem I wanted to work on.'[1]

4.3 Feynman's MIT program

As an undergraduate at MIT, Feynman had gradually learned about the fundamental problems of quantum electrodynamics that were being actively pursued and discussed at that time. This he gathered from the books of Heitler and Dirac.[7] 'At that young age what I could understand were the remarks about the fact that this [state of affairs in quantum electrodynamics] does not make any sense, and the last sentence of the book of Dirac I can still remember, "It seems that some essential new physical ideas are here needed." So I had this as a challenge and an inspiration. I also had a personal feeling that, since they did not get a satisfactory answer to [this very] problem I wanted to solve, I don't have to pay attention to what they did do.'[8] Feynman recalled: 'I psyched myself up like a Watusi tribal warrior, and said to myself: "these men, like Heisenberg and Pauli, who had worked on quantum electrodynamics and had been stuck with the difficulties of solving the problem of infinities, did not know anything; I'm going to show them how to do it!"'[1]

From his reading, however, Feynman gathered that two things were the source of the difficulties of quantum electrodynamics. The first was an infinite energy of the interaction of the electron with itself (the self-energy), which had appeared even in classical theory, and the second one arose from reasons which had to do with the infinite number of degrees of freedom of the field. The latter was simply the difficulty that the electromagnetic field could be regarded as a set of harmonic oscillators. If you quantized the oscillators of the field (say, in a box), each oscillator would have a ground-state energy of $\frac{1}{2}\hbar\omega$, and, since there is an infinite number of modes in the box of ever-increasing frequency ω, there would be an infinite energy in the box, which is unacceptable from the physical point of view.

This, of course, wasn't a completely correct statement of the problem; it could be removed simply by changing the zero from which the energy is measured. At any rate, Feynman believed that the difficulty arose somehow from a combination of the electron acting on itself and the infinite number of the degrees of freedom of the field. As he recalled: 'It seemed to me quite evident that the idea that a particle acts on itself, that the electrical force acts on the same particle that generates it, is not a necessary one—it is a sort of silly one, as a matter of fact. And so I suggested to myself that electrons cannot act on themselves, they can act only on other electrons. That means there is no field at all. You see, if all charges contribute to making a single common field, and if that common field acts back on all the charges, then each charge must act back on itself. Well, that was where the mistake was, there was no field. It was just when you shook one charge, another would shake later. There was a direct action between charges, albeit with a delay. The law of force connecting the motion of one charge with another would just involve a delay. Shake this one, that one shakes another. The sun atom shakes; my eye electron shakes eight minutes later, because of a direct action across.

'Now, this has the attractive feature that it solves both problems at once. First, I can say immediately, I don't let the electron act on itself, I just let this act on that, hence no self-energy! Secondly, there is not an infinite number of degrees of freedom in the field. There is not a field at all; or if you insist on thinking in terms of ideas like that of a field, this field is always completely determined by the action of the particles which produce it. You shake this particle, it shakes that one, but if you want to think of a field way, the field, if it's there, would be entirely determined by the matter which generates it, and therefore, the field does not have any *independent* degrees of freedom and the infinities from the degrees of freedom would then be removed.'[9]

Thus, Feynman's general plan was first to solve the classical problems in electrodynamics, 'to get rid of the infinite self-energies in the classical theory, and to hope that when I made a quantum theory of it, everything would just be fine . . .. The idea seemed so obvious to me and so elegant that I fell deeply in love with it. And, like falling in love with a woman, it is only possible if you do not know too much about her, so you cannot see her faults. The faults will become apparent later on, but after the love is strong enough to hold you to her. So, I was held on to this theory, in spite of all difficulties, by my youthful enthusiasm.'[10]

This way of thinking had started Feynman off. When he got stuck with the last problem that John Wheeler had given him, he went back to these earlier ideas which he had conceived at MIT. Upon arrival at Princeton, and during his early collaboration with Wheeler, he realized what was wrong with the idea that an electron does not act on itself; it does interact with itself in order to account for radiation resistance. What he soon learned in graduate school was against his principle, the principle that an electron acts only on other electrons. And then he thought maybe the action of radiation resistance was to shake one electron, which would shake another electron, and the latter would affect the former back. When Feynman calculated the effect of this, he obtained the wrong formula. It was then that he told these ideas of his to Wheeler and they began to have intense discussions about these things.

During all this time Wheeler would invite Feynman to his home to have dinner with his wife and children and work together afterwards in his study. Together they embarked upon the development of the action-at-a-distance theory of time-symmetric electrodynamics.

Notes and References

1. R.P. Feynman, Interviews and conversations with Jagdish Mehra, in Austin, Texas, April 1970, and Pasadena, California, January 1988.

2. R.P. Feynman, *SYJMF*, p. 59.

3. R.P. Feynman, '*Surely you're joking, Mr. Feynman!*', p. 60. This remark became the title of *SYJMF*, Feynman's anecdotal, autobiographical book.

4. R.P. Feynman, *SYJMF*, p. 61.

5. R.P. Feynman, Interviews of Charles Weiner (American Institute of Physics), in Pasadena, California, 1966.

6. Personal communication from Herbert C. Corben to Jagdish Mehra, 20 March 1988.

7. P.A.M. Dirac, *The principles of quantum mechanics*. Oxford University Press, 2nd edn., 1935; W. Heitler, *The quantum theory of radiation*, Oxford University Press, 1935.

8. R.P. Feynman, The development of the space–time view of quantum electrodynamics, Nobel Lecture, 11 December 1965. *Science* **153**, 699 (1966), p. 1.

9. R.P. Feynman, Ref. 8, pp. 1–2.

10. R.P. Feynman, Ref. 8, p. 2.

5

Action-at-a-distance in electrodynamics: the Wheeler–Feynman theory

5.1 Wheeler's modification of Feynman's ideas

Soon after arriving in Princeton for graduate studies from MIT, Feynman learned what was wrong with his idea that the electron does not act upon itself. The matter was that he had missed the radiation damping force. 'When you accelerate an electron it radiates energy and you have to do extra work to account for that energy. The extra force against which this work is done is called the force of radiation resistance. The origin of this force (following the work of the Dutch physicist, Hendrik Antoon Lorentz) was identified in those days as the action of the electron upon itself. The first term of this action, of the electron on itself, gave a kind of inertia (which was relativistically not quite satisfactory). But the inertia-like term was infinite for the point charge. Yet the next term in the sequence gave an energy loss rate which for a point charge agrees exactly with the rate that you get by calculating how much energy is radiated. So, the force of radiation resistance, which is absolutely necessary for the conservation of energy, would disappear if I said that a charge could act on itself.'[1]

Meanwhile Feynman had learned the glaringly obvious fault of his own theory. But he was still in love with the original theory, and was still thinking that with it lay the solution to the difficulties of quantum electrodynamics. 'So, I continued to try on and off to save it somehow. I must have some action develop on a given electron when I accelerate it to account for radiation resistance. But, if I let electrons only act on other electrons the only possible source for this action is another electron in this world. So, one day, when I was working for Professor Wheeler and could no longer solve the problem he had given me, I thought about this again and calculated the following. Suppose I have two charges—I shake the first charge, which I think of as a source, and this makes the second one shake, but the second one shaking produces an effect back on the source. And so I calculated how much that effect back on the first charge was, hoping that it might add up to the force of radiation resistance. It didn't come out right, of course.'[1]

Feynman went to John Wheeler and told him about the ideas he had conceived at MIT and the new difficulty he had encountered in proceeding with his program. Wheeler told him that the answer Feynman got for the problem with the two charges depended upon the charge and the mass of the second charge and would vary inversely as the square of the distance R between the charges, while the force of radiation resistance depended on none of these things. He also pointed out something else that bothered Feynman: 'If we had a situation with many charges all around the original source at roughly uniform density and if we added the effect of all the surrounding charges, the inverse R^2 would be compensated by the R^2 in the volume element and we would get a result proportional to the thickness of the layer, which would go to infinity. That is, one would have an infinite total effect back at the source.'[1] And, finally, he told Feynman that 'when you accelerate the first charge, the second acts later, and the reaction back here at the source would be still later. In other words, the action occurs at the wrong time.'[1] Wheeler told Feynman that what he had described and calculated was just ordinary reflected light, not radiation reaction.

After this critique of Feynman's idea, Wheeler went on to give a lecture in which he worked out the right modification of it. 'First,' he said, 'let us suppose that the return action by the charges in the absorber reaches the source by advanced waves as well as by the ordinary retarded waves of reflected light, so that the law of interaction acts backward in time, as well as forward in time.' But, as Feynman recalled, 'I was enough of a physicist at that time not to say, "Oh, no, how could that be?" For today all physicists know by studying Einstein and Bohr that sometimes an idea which looks completely paradoxical at first, if analyzed to completion in all detail and in experimental situations, may, in fact, not be paradoxical. So, it did not bother me any more than it bothered Professor Wheeler to use advanced waves for the back reaction—a solution of Maxwell's equations which previously had not been physically used.'[1]

Wheeler used advanced waves to get the reaction back at the right time and then he suggested: 'If there were lots of electrons in the absorber, there would be an index of refraction n, so that the retarded waves coming from the source would have their wavelengths slightly modified in going through the absorber. Now, if we shall assume that the advanced waves come back from the absorber without an index . . . , then there will be a gradual shifting in phase between the return and the original signal so that we would only have to figure that the contributions act as if they come from only a finite thickness, that of the first wave [Fresnel] zone. (More specifically, up to that depth where the phase in the medium is shifted appreciably from it would be in vacuum, a thickness proportional to $\lambda/(n-1)$.) Now, the less the number of electrons in here, the less each contributes, but the thicker will be the layer that effectively contributes because with less electrons, the index differs less from 1. The higher the charges of these electrons, the more each contributes, but the thinner the effective layer, because the index would be higher. And when we estimated it (calculated without being careful to keep the correct numerical factor) sure enough, it came out that the action back at the source was completely independent of the properties of the charges that were surrounding the absorber. Further, it was just the right character to represent radiation resistance, but we were unable to see if it was exactly the right size.[2]

Feynman found this to be 'quite exciting, absolutely terrific!' So, Wheeler said, 'OK, you go home and find out how much advanced and how much retarded waves we need to get the right answer.'[3] Wheeler asked Feynman to figure out what would happen to the advanced effects that you would expect if you put a test charge close to the source. For if all charges generate advanced as well as retarded effects, why would that test charge not be affected by the advanced waves from the source?

'That started it. I found that you get the right answer if you use half-advanced and half-retarded [potentials] as the field generated by each charge. That is, one has to use the solution of Maxwell's equations which is symmetrical in time and the reason why we got no advanced effects at a point close to the source in spite of the fact that the source was producing an advanced field is this: Suppose the source is surrounded by a spherical absorbing wall ten light-seconds away, and that the test charge is one second to the right of the source. Then the source is as much as eleven seconds away from some parts of the wall and only nine seconds away from other parts. The source acting at time $t = 0$ induces motions in the wall at time $+10$. Advanced effects from this can act on the test charge as early as eleven seconds earlier, or at $t = -1$. This is just at the time that the direct advanced waves from the source should reach the test charge, and it turns out that the two effects are exactly equal and opposite and cancel out! At the later time $+1$ effects on the test charge from the source and from the walls are again equal, but this time are of the same sign and add to convert the half-retarded wave of the source to full retarded strength.

'Thus, it became clear that there was the possibility that if we assume all actions via half-advanced and half-retarded solutions of Maxwell's equations and assume that the sources are surrounded by material absorbing all the light which is emitted, then we could account for radiation resistance as direct action of the charges of the absorber acting back by advanced waves on the source.'[2]

Feynman devoted several months to check the new theory. He worked hard to make sure that everything was independent of the shape of the container, and that the advanced effects really canceled in every case. Feynman and Wheeler tried to improve the efficiency of their demonstrations, and tried to see more and more clearly how and why their method worked. 'Because of our using advanced waves, we also had many paradoxes, which we gradually reduced one by one, and saw that there was in fact no logical difficulty with the theory. It was perfectly satisfactory.'[2]

In this way, Feynman and Wheeler constructed a classical theory of electrodynamics, which had half-advanced and half-retarded waves in it (classically), and which had no self-energy problem, there being no electron acting on itself. The electrons only acted on each other, and yet they were able to obtain radiation resistance from the fact that there was matter out there which did the absorbing. The next problem was to make a quantum theory of that, and Feynman started to work on it. 'Wheeler kept on giving me little assignments to try to straighten out problems of the classical theory, for he said that the quantum theory was very easy and he knew how to do it, and he kept on putting out announcements that he was going to give a lecture on it, but it always turned out that he didn't quite have it. But I started to work on it anyway, and the problem I had was that the classical theory I was starting out with was not in Hamiltonian form, not the usual form of mechanics, because the action being delayed could be represented beautifully by a minimum principle, with no action, but not by a Hamiltonian because it involved only a Lagrangian (involving only position and velocity). There was no field; it was a direct particle–particle interaction. The only coordinates in the system were [of] the particles, and there was not going to be an infinite number of degrees of freedom.'[3]

It occurred to John Wheeler that Richard Feynman should give a colloquium on their joint work on the classical time-symmetric electrodynamics in the physics department at Princeton. He told Feynman: 'You're a young man, and you should learn how to give talks. You should give the talk and I shall answer the questions. Meanwhile, I'll work on the quantum theory part and give a seminar on that later.' Feynman was frightened. 'It was going to be my first technical seminar, and I was concerned. Wheeler made arrangements with Professor Eugene Wigner, who was the colloquium chairman, to put my talk on the regular seminar schedule. A day or two before the talk I saw Wigner in the hall. 'Feynman,' he said, 'I think your work with Wheeler is very interesting, so I've invited Russell to the seminar.' Henry Norris Russell, the great, famous astronomer of the day was coming to the lecture! Wigner went on, 'I think Professor von Neumann would be interested.' John von Neumann was the greatest mathematician around. 'And Professor Pauli is visiting from Switzerland, it so happens, so I've invited Professor Pauli to come'—and by this time I was turning yellow. Finally, Wigner said, 'Professor Einstein only rarely comes to our weekly seminars, but your work is so interesting that I've invited him specially, so he's coming too.'

'By this time I must have turned green, because Wigner said, "No, no! Don't worry! I'll just warn you though: if Professor Russell falls asleep—and he'll undoubtedly fall asleep—it doesn't mean that the seminar is bad; he falls asleep in all seminars. On the other hand, if Professor Pauli is nodding all the time, and seems to be in agreement as the seminar goes along, pay no attention. Professor Pauli has palsy." '[3,4]

Feynman went to Wheeler and told him about all the big, famous people who were coming to the talk which Wheeler had committed him into giving, and told him how uneasy he felt. Wheeler calmed him by saying that there was no reason to worry, and that he (Wheeler) would answer all the questions. So Feynman prepared his talk, and on the appointed day he did something that young men who have no experience in giving talks often do—'I put too many equations on the blackboard.' For he thought that people in the audience would not be able to follow all the steps on which the theory was based. As he was writing down the equations all over the blackboard ahead of time, Einstein came in and said pleasantly, 'Hello, I'm coming to your seminar, but first, where's tea?' Feynman told him and continued writing on the blackboard. This was not Feynman's first encounter with Einstein; he had gone with John Wheeler to see him about the action-at-a-distance theory that they were developing, and Einstein gave him some hints about the relevant scientific literature on the subject.[3,4]

When everybody came in, Feynman got up and gave the lecture. 'I can still remember very clearly seeing my hands shaking as I was pulling out my notes from a brown envelope, because it was quite a thing to talk in front of all these 'monster minds'. And then, something happened, which has always happened ever since and is just great: as soon as my mind got on to the physics and trying to explain it, to organize the ideas and how to present them, there was no more worrying about the audience and the personalities! It was all in terms of physics. I was calm, everything was good, I developed the ideas and explained everything to the best of my ability. It was not very good because I was not used to giving lectures, but at any rate there was no more nervousness until I sat down. Then came the questions.'[3,4]

First of all, 'Wolfgang Pauli who was sitting next to Einstein, said: "I do not think this theory can be right because of this, that, and the other thing." It's too bad that I cannot remember what Pauli's reason was for the theory not being right; he may well have hit the nail on the head, but I don't remember what he said, because I was too nervous to listen and I didn't understand the objections. At the end of this criticism, Pauli said to Einstein, "Don't you agree, Professor Einstein? I don't believe this is right, don't you agree, Professor Einstein?" Einstein said, "No," in a soft German voice that sounded very pleasant to me, very polite. "I find only that it would be very difficult to make a corresponding theory [i.e. an action-at-a-distance theory] for gravitational interaction." He meant for the general theory of relativity, which was his baby. After all, he said, general relativity is not so well established as electrodynamics. He continued, "since at this time we do not have a great deal of experimental evidence, I am not absolutely sure of the correct gravitational theory, and with this perspective I would not use that as an argument against you." Einstein appreciated that things might be different from what his theory stated; he was very tolerant of ideas. Very nice, very interesting! I remember that. Then there were some other questions. Wheeler answered Pauli's objections and others, but it was so much like fireworks! Wheeler did answer everything, just as he had promised.'[3,5]

'I wish I had remembered what Pauli said, because I discovered years later that the theory was not satisfactory when it came to making the quantum theory [of it]. It's possible that Pauli noticed the difficulty immediately and explained to me in his question, but I was so relieved that I did not have to answer the questions that I didn't listen to them carefully. I do remember walking up the steps to the Palmer Library with Pauli, who asked me, "What is Wheeler going to say about the quantum theory when he gives his talk?" I said, "I don't know. He hasn't told me. He's working it out himself." "Oh," he said. "The man works and doesn't tell his assistant what's he doing on the quantum theory!" He came closer [to me] and said in a low, secretive voice, "Wheeler will never give that seminar!" And it's true. Wheeler didn't give the seminar. He thought it would be easy to work out the quantum part; he thought he had it, almost. But he didn't. And by the time [his turn] came around, he realized he didn't know how to do it, and therefore, didn't have anything to say. I didn't solve it either— a quantum theory of half-advanced half-retarded potentials—and I worked on it for years.'[3,5]

In a talk given on 21 February 1941, at the meeting of the American Physical Society in Cambridge, Massachusetts, Feynman made a presentation with John Wheeler on their joint work on 'Reaction of the absorber as the mechanism of radiation damping'. In the abstract of their talk, which basically reflected partially the content of Feynman's presentation in the seminar in the fall of 1940, Wheeler and Feynman noted: 'Radiation damping arises from retarded interactions between various parts of an electron of finite size, according to Lorentz. At high frequencies, this damping depends on the electron's structure. Nonelectric stresses are required to hold the electron together. Dirac abandoned this picture and postulated a point electron. Guided by considerations of relativistic invariance he proposed essentially the first term in Lorentz's expression as a possible law for radiation damping. We postulate: 1. that an accelerated point charge in otherwise charge-free space does *not* radiate energy; 2. that in general, the fields which act on a given particle arise only from *other* particles; 3. that these fields are represented by one-half the retarded plus one-half the advanced Liénard–Wiechert solutions of Maxwell's equations. In a universe in which all light is eventually absorbed, the absorbing material scatters back to an accelerated charge a field, part of which is found to be independent of the properties of the material. This part is equal to one-half the retarded *minus* one-half the advanced field generated by the charge. It produces radiative damping (Dirac's expression) and combines with the field of the source to give retarded effects alone.'[6]

Feynman discussed many of these and other ideas with fellow graduate students, like Bill Woodward and John Tookey, all of whom lived together in the Graduate College. At the same time, Feynman continued to develop the general theory of the time-symmetrical action-at-a-distance theory of classical electrodynamics. He tried to write up the work in a variety of different ways. Finally, Wheeler and Feynman appealed to a principle of least action; they represented the theory along the lines of least action instead of Maxwell's equations, because in Maxwell's equations there is one field, and one field would have to act back on its own generator, which is action on itself. But there were so many fields, one for each particle. Unlike Feynman, Wheeler was well familiar with the literature. He knew that an idea like that had been suggested by Frenkel.[7] He also found a paper by Fokker,[8] who had a least action principle, which he showed to Feynman shortly after they began to work on the problem. Fokker had noticed that if you try to write the interaction with the least action you get the advanced and retarded waves, and that's just what Wheeler and Feynman got, half and half, so that they could have an action. Feynman found a way to write Fokker's rather complicated-looking action very simply by using the Dirac delta-function.

Gradually, Wheeler and Feynman got to understand this problem in a variety of ways, until they knew it inside out; they understood all the theorems, all the paradoxes, in fact everything related to these questions, including how to prove everything involved in the clearest possible manner. 'Then Wheeler told me to write it up, and that it should not be more than twenty pages, a simple and beautiful thing. So I wrote it up, and it took me twenty-one pages to discuss and explain everything in a draft manuscript entitled "The interaction theory of radiation".'[3]

Wheeler did not like Feynman's draft of the proposed article. By the time Feynman gave it to him, Wheeler had changed his mind about what he wanted. 'He had decided that the work we had done together was such a grand and wonderful thing that it should be turned into an extensive program of five major papers, something which I did not understand; what I had written was going to be only a part of his [Wheeler's] grand design. In other words, he began by wanting a short concise paper, but ended by conceiving something really elaborate and grand.'[3,9] In the first instance, however, Wheeler reworked and expanded Feynman's draft of the paper and returned him a new, expanded, and unified manuscript in the spring of 1942. By that time, John Wheeler had become engaged upon war-related work at the Metallurgical Laboratory at the University of Chicago, and would not be able to devote any more time to this project until almost the end of World War II. The new manuscript was entitled 'Action at a distance in classical theory: Reaction of the absorber as the mechanism of radiation damping'.[10] Most of it was included in the paper submitted by Wheeler and Feynman to the *Festschrift* published in honor of Niels Bohr's sixtieth birthday.[11]

Soon after his short presentation at the American Physical Society's meeting in Cambridge, Massachusetts,[6] Feynman began to think more seriously about the Ph.D. thesis he to write. His work on the time-symmetrical action-at-a-distance theory of electrodynamics was not accept-able as a doctoral thesis to John Wheeler, since both he and Wheeler had worked upon this problem together. Feynman and Wheeler continued to discuss problems of mutual interest as they had done before. While all this was going on, Wheeler sent the abstract of a talk he intended to give at the Washington Meeting of the American Physical Society (1–3 May 1941), which was to take place at the National Bureau of Standards and the National Academy of Sciences in Washington, D.C., 'about which he never told me [Feynman]', nor did he say that he was going 'to give a talk at the meeting on the quantum theory of action-at-a-distance' or, for that matter, 'what, if at all, he was going to talk about at Washington.'[3] From the beginning, Feynman's feeling had been that 'we had to straighten out the intrinsic difficulties of classical electrodynamics, before trying to solve the difficulties with quantum electrodynamics, although both of them sounded similar as far as the problem of the self-energy was concerned. Since this difficulty was not cured by quantum mechanics, I thought that we must first cure the difficulties of the classical theory, and then see if the same ideas would apply to quantum physics. Moreover, I never thought that it would be possible to go easily and directly from the classical theory to the quantum theory, but it was essential that we should pursue it in this order if only to see what was required to solve the problem in the two cases. From the beginning Wheeler felt that the transition from the classical case to the quantum case was simple and obvious, but I just did not see how to do it, because he never explained his thoughts about this to me. From time to time he did make some remarks about the transition from the classical to the quantum case, but these were never clear to me. It may be that he had certain ideas which he thought would work but didn't, and I don't know exactly why his announced lecture in the colloquium was canceled.'[3,9]

Feynman did not see the *Bulletin of the American Physical Society*, dated 17 April 1941, in which the program of the Washington meeting was announced a couple of weeks before the actual meeting, and which contained the abstract of Wheeler's talk. This abstract must have been sent several weeks before the meeting, 'so maybe a month and a half after my talk at the Cambridge meeting of the Society, Wheeler must have announced his talk on the quantum theory of action-at-a-distance. I also went to attend the meeting. There he told me that he was going to give a talk, but he still did not tell me what it was going to be: I had to go to listen! Then, in the beginning of his lecture, Wheeler talked a little bit about our ideas about the classical and the quantum theory of action-at-a-distance. Then he changed course, and said: "Concerning this problem," and then he began to talk about the question of van der Waals forces between atoms when they are far apart, farther apart than the wavelength of virtual interactions between them changes from the usual r^{-6} law. He had talked to me about this before, but it was standard electrodynamics; it had no relation to what we had been working upon, though in his initial remarks he brought my name in. But his talk had nothing to do with our work. They were perfectly legitimate things, but I was rather upset that he had done this. He had implied that it had something to do with our theory of action-at-a-distance, but it did not. Perhaps it was not nice of me to do this, but I got up after his talk and remarked that "Professor Wheeler's introduction had nothing to do with the second part of his talk." I wanted to protect myself against the implication that our joint work on the classical theory of action-at-a-distance, when carried into quantum theory, had anything to do with what he presented, for I did not see the connection. Wheeler admitted right away that indeed there was no connection between the two things.'[3,9]

As they walked out together from the lecture room, Wheeler remarked to Feynman, 'I should not have given that talk at all. You are right. I thought that I would have the quantum theory of action-at-a-distance by this time, but I don't. I thought I could talk about this van der Waals thing under that title.'[3,9] The abstract of Wheeler's talk at the Washington meeting did indeed mix up the two things, for it read: '*Action at a distance between simple atoms.* The mutual energy of two atoms in S states varies in a complicated way for small internuclear separations but for larger distances approaches van der Waals $1/r^6$ law. In quantum mechanics this result receives a simple interpretation. . . .'[12]

All this misunderstanding occurred for two reasons: (1) Wheeler did not tell Feynman in advance what the exact topic of his talk at the Washington meeting was going to be, and Feynman had not seen the *Bulletin* listing the detailed program of the meeting. (2) Wheeler had left upon Feynman the impression that he was quite close to unveiling the quantum theory of action-at-a-distance, and would take the first opportunity of announcing it as soon as it was ready. He had already canceled his announced talk at the departmental colloquium at Princeton, and Feynman did not know what to make of his vagueness in this matter. As Feynman recalled: 'I was a little bit unhappy that he could not explain the quantum case, but I think the reason was not that he wouldn't have if he had found a way of doing it. But he didn't quite have it at any point—and the few little attempts he had made to explain it to me, I had shot full of holes right away and had seen his troubles. I think the poor man believed that it was going to be easy, to the point that he would perhaps have it the next morning; so he never told me what it was because he didn't have it until the day of his talk at the meeting, and then he was stuck with the situation. I never felt that he had been trying to do something wrong or dirty to me; I just felt that he mistakenly believed that the answer was just around the corner.'[3,9]

At the Cambridge meeting of the American Physical Society in February 1941, Feynman had already given a summary of their joint work on the classical action-at-a-distance theory. That was the first talk outside Princeton that Feynman was going to give, and the thought of having to give it had scared him. He had written the whole speech out and practiced doing it for the ten prescribed minutes in his room with a friend. 'It took me longer than ten minutes at the meeting, and I heard the bell ring, indicating that my time was up, and I became nervous, then I read the whole speech. So it felt dull, impossible for people to understand, and uninteresting. I must have sounded like a crackpot, and people were bored by listening to me read my speech on and on. At Princeton, I had literally been driven through the wringer at the colloquium; at Cambridge, there were just a few questions, and Wheeler answered one of them.'[3,9]

After the Washington meeting 'Wheeler became engrossed in writing up our work in a grand and wonderful fashion. I began to work on the quantum theory, for I had nothing else to do. Wheeler kept on giving me little problems to explain this or that, and I kept on solving them so fast that it must have driven him mad. Although I started to work on the passage of the classical action-at-a-distance electrodynamics to the quantum case, but the quantum theory was not easy to arrive at, and Wheeler's worry about how we could get the answer quickly was unnecessary.'[3,9]

When the Wheeler–Feynman paper was actually written, Wheeler wrote it.[11] 'It's a long thing, and I didn't write it. I worked with him, but it was not in the spirit in which I thought it should be written. I didn't like it; I didn't think it was a good way to present it; it made things too complicated; there was a much more beautiful way to do it.

'Later on, when I started to talk about quantum theory, I published my own paper. That was in 1948. In my paper on "A relativistic cut-off for classical electrodynamics"[13] I reviewed the classical theory of action-at-a-distance. In my paper on the "Space–time approach to non-relativistic quantum mechanics", I reviewed the 1945 paper with Wheeler again; there I said that this paper was an attempt to quantize the 1945 theory, but that the idea presented then will not work in quantum mechanics, and when I did quantum electrodynamics I was convinced of that.'[3,9]

5.2 The historical context of time-symmetric electrodynamics

Wheeler and Feynman recalled: 'It was the 19th of March 1845 when Carl Friedrich Gauss described the conception of an action-at-a-distance propagated with a finite velocity, the natural generalization to electrodynamics of the view of force so fruitfully applied by Newton and his followers. In the century between then and now what obstacle has discouraged the general use of this conception in the study of Nature?'[14]

The most important physical theory of the nineteenth century was classical electrodynamics, which had its roots in the scientific work of many scientists. From the conceptual point of view, the most important work was the earlier development of electrodynamics by Michael Faraday, who formulated the laws of electrodynamics in terms of electric and magnetic fields and, later, by James Clerk Maxwell's theory of electromagnetic interactions, which gave the complete and unified theory of these phenomena.

Faraday's basic idea was that charged particles interact through an intermediate carrier, namely some new kind of object, called the electric field E, responsible for electrical interactions, and another, called the magnetic field H, which is responsible for magnetic interactions. The sources of these fields are the charged particles and their currents.

Maxwell's main achievement was the unification of these two vector fields into a general electromagnetic field which, according to the modern relativistic point of view, is a four-tensor field in Minkowski space–time:

$$F^{\mu\nu}(x) = \begin{bmatrix} 0 & -E_1 & -E_2 & -E_3 \\ E_1 & 0 & -H_3 & H_2 \\ E_2 & H_3 & 0 & -H_1 \\ E_3 & -H_2 & H_1 & 0 \end{bmatrix} \quad (\mu, \nu = 0, 1, 2, 3). \tag{5.1}$$

Here $E_{1,2,3}(x)$ are the components of the electric field, and $H_{1,2,3}(x)$ are the corresponding components of the magnetic field. The coordinates of x in Minkowski space–time are: $x_0 = ict$, where c is the speed of light and t is the time, and $x_{1, 2, 3}$, are the usual space coordinates. Then, in the modern relativistic notation, the first group of Maxwell's equations reads:

$$\frac{\partial F_{\nu\mu}(x)}{\partial x_\mu} = 4\pi j_\nu(x) \quad (\nu = 0, 1, 2, 3), \tag{5.2}$$

where Einstein's summation rule is assumed (i.e. the summation on repeated indices is to be performed), and the second group of Maxwell's equations is:

$$\frac{\partial F_{\nu\mu}(x)}{\partial x_\rho} + \frac{\partial F_{\rho\nu}(x)}{\partial x_\mu} + \frac{\partial F_{\mu\rho}(x)}{\partial x_\nu} = 0 \quad (\nu \neq \mu \neq \rho), \tag{5.3}$$

In equation (5.2) $j_\nu(x)$ is the four-vector of the electric current, the zeroth component of which actually represents the electric charge density. Equation (5.3) may be solved quite simply by introducing the four-vector potential $A_\mu(x)$ such that

$$F_{\nu\mu}(x) = \frac{\partial A_\nu(x)}{\partial x^\mu} - \frac{\partial A_\mu(x)}{\partial x^\nu}. \tag{5.4}$$

Then, as a consequence, instead of equation (5.2), one has to consider the new equation for the four-vector potential:

$$\Box A_\nu(x) = -4\pi j_\nu(x), \tag{5.5}$$

where $\Box = \partial^2/\partial x_\mu \, \partial x^\mu$ is the so-called d'Alembert differential operator or

Dalembertian. In addition, the four-vector potential must satisfy the Lorentz condition:

$$\frac{\partial A_\mu(x)}{\partial x_\mu} = 0. \tag{5.6}$$

The above relations have to hold with certain boundary conditions, which describe the physical conditions at the boundary of the space–time domain in which one has to solve Maxwell's equations. These equations, together with the boundary conditions, give us the complete theory of all electromagnetic phenomena in the macroworld if the equations of motion of the charged particles in the electromagnetic field are also included. Suppose there is a particle with mass m and charge e, and its position four-tensor is a_v. Then the relativistic four-tensor equation of motion of this particle takes the form

$$mc^2 \ddot{a}_v = e F_{v\mu}(a)\dot{a}^\mu, \tag{5.7}$$

which is identical with the Lorentz equation, in which the three-dimensional force reads $F = e[E + (v/c) \times H]$. In equation (5.7) the dots denote differentiation with respect to the 'proper time' of the particle under consideration. Now we have got a self-consistent theory of electromagnetic interactions of the charged particles, which turns out to be extremely successful for explaining all electromagnetic phenomena in the macroworld, and has a large number of applications in engineering and other practical domains.

It should be mentioned that the whole theory given above may be derived from a single principle of least action $\delta A = 0$ (see Section 6.3), with the action functional

$$A = -\sum_i m_i \int (\dot{a}^\mu_{(i)} \dot{a}_{(i)\mu})^{1/2} \, d\lambda_i - \frac{1}{16\pi} \int F^{\mu v} F_{\mu v} \, d^4 x - \sum_i e_i \int j^\mu A_\mu \, d\lambda_i. \tag{5.8}$$

Here the first term describes the action of the classical particles, and there are supposed to be several of them. This kinetic term only describes the free relativistic particles and it is not connected with their interactions. The index i in all the quantities denotes the particle's number. The second term describes the action of the electromagnetic field $F_{\mu v}$ only. It describes the free field without the particles, while the last term in the expression (5.8) describes the interaction of the particles with the field.

But when one tries to extend this theory to the domain of the microworld of elementary particles, one encounters several fundamental difficulties, even at the classical level, before any attempt at the quantization of the theory is made. These difficulties have been thoroughly studied since the times of Alfred Liénard, Emil Wiechert, Max Abraham, and Hendrik Antoon Lorentz. The simplest and most fundamental difficulty is the one connected with the self-energy of the charged point particle, like the electron. One can easily obtain the energy of a spherically symmetric charged particle with radius a and charge e as being of the order of e^2/a. However, if we have a point particle, we have to let the radius a go to zero, and then we obtain an infinite result for the self-energy for the charged point particle. For a moving particle this self-energy appears as a coefficient in some force term, which describes the interaction of the particle with its own field, i.e. the self-interaction of the particle. This term is proportional to the acceleration of the particle and, therefore, may be combined with the left-hand side of equation (5.7). This leads to the 'renormalization' of the mass of the particle, which we represent as $m + \delta m_{\text{selfint}}$, where $\delta m_{\text{selfint}}$ is the mass term which is created by the self-interaction. But $\delta m_{\text{selfint}}$ is proportional to e^2/a and, therefore, goes to infinity for the point particle. Hence, in the classical electrodynamics of a point particle, because of the self-interaction, we are forced to make an infinite renormalization of this particle.

The next difficulty is much more sophisticated. It is connected with the radiation resistance of the moving charged point particle. Suppose we have such a particle, and it describes some trajectory $a_\mu(\mu)$ in Minkowski space–time. Because of the motion of the particle, its electromagnetic field will change, and this disturbance will be propagated in the usual three-dimensional space with the speed of light c, as follows from equation (5.5). The source of the field disturbance is the four-dimensional charged current j_μ in equation (5.5). Liénard and Wiechert[15] obtained the potential of the electromagnetic field of such a particle in a three-dimensional form:

$$A_0(x) = \left[\frac{e}{qR}\right]_{\text{ret}}, \quad A(x) = \left[\frac{e\mathbf{v}}{qR}\right]_{\text{ret}}, \tag{5.9}$$

where $q = 1 - \mathbf{v} \cdot \mathbf{R}/R$, $\mathbf{v}$ is the three-dimensional vector of the particle's velocity at some instant of time τ, $\mathbf{R} = \mathbf{r} - \mathbf{a}$ is the vector from the position $\mathbf{a}$ of the particle at the same instant of time τ to the position $\mathbf{r}$ of the point in the three-dimensional space, where the potential has to be calculated with the help of equations (5.9), and R is the distance between these two points. Here $\mathbf{v}.\mathbf{R}$ denotes the scalar product of the three-vectors, hence $\mathbf{v}.\mathbf{R}/R$ is actually the component of the particle velocity $\mathbf{v}$ in the direction of the three-space vector $\mathbf{R}$. It seems to be obvious that because of the finite velocity of light, c, the electromagnetic disturbance will spread with some delay in space. Hence, in the formulas (5.9) one ought to calculate the velocity and the position of the particle at the past instant $\tau = \tau_- = t - |\mathbf{r} - \mathbf{a}|/c$. This retardation means that the disturbance at position $\mathbf{r}$ at time t is caused by the charged particle at another point $\mathbf{a}$, but not at a simultaneous time t, rather at an earlier time τ. The difference between t and τ appears because the disturbance propagates across the intervening distance $R = |\mathbf{r} - \mathbf{a}|$ with a finite velocity c. The subscript 'ret' in equation (5.9) denotes the evaluation of all the quantitites within the brackets at the instant of time τ_-. The corresponding four-tensor $F_{\mu\nu}$ of the electromagnetic field, which one obtains for the Liénard–Wiechert retarded potential (5.9) will be denoted as $F_{\mu\nu}^{\text{ret}}$. This field also includes the field of the particle itself. Using the retarded Liénard–Wiechert potentials, one can see that the charged particle, which moves with some acceleration $\dot{v}$, will radiate electromagnetic waves. But if such a particle radiates energy in the form of electromagnetic waves, it must suffer a damping in its mechanical energy. The magnitude f_{damp} of this damping force is found to be

$$f_{\text{damp}} = \tfrac{2}{3}(e^2/c^2)\ddot{v}. \tag{5.10}$$

The coefficient $\tfrac{2}{3}e^2/c^3$ is related to the so-called relaxation time of the particle, which is usually very small; for an electron this relaxation time is about 10^{-23} seconds. This time is typical of the radiation process. The origin of this force lies in the self-interaction of the charged particles with their own fields. This self-interaction allows a charged particle to radiate energy in the absence of other charges or fields in the entire space. This radiation is a well-verified experimental phenomenon. The force given by equation (5.10) also gives a correct account of the conservation of energy, momentum, and angular momentum of the particle.

Unlike the usual forces in classical physics, the damping force depends on the second derivative $\ddot{v}$ of the velocity of the particle, i.e. of the third derivative $\dddot{a}$ of its position. This fact leads to very strange physical consequences: equation (5.7) has more solutions than are needed. For example, if there are no external forces, this equation leads to two completely different solutions. The first solution is of the usual type and shows that the free particle will preserve its velocity unchanged for an infinitely long time; for instance, it may stay at rest all the time. But the other solution shows that, because of the self-interaction, the particle, which is in a state of rest at the initial instant of time, will run away with an exponentially increasing acceleration. The solution yielding such self-acceleration is clearly unphysical and has to be excluded with the help of certain additional physical conditions.

P. A. M. Dirac proposed to eliminate such runaway solutions by fixing a special value of the initial acceleration.[16] But this approach leads to a new difficulty, called *preacceleration*. It turned out that under Dirac's condition the particle must accelerate *before* the force is applied. This notion violates the usual conception of causality. However, such acausal behavior takes too small a time to be observable. It is of the order of the time required by light to cross the distance of about the 'classical radius' of an elementary particle; hence, a quantum description becomes necessary.

This was the situation in classical electrodynamics following Lorentz's work on his old theory of the electron. The first attempts at a quantization of this theory led to new difficulties besides the old ones.†

† In this section, we have explained the Liénard–Wiechert retarded potential in equation (5.9), which gives the retarded solutions of equation (5.5) and describes the retarded solution $F_{\mu\nu}^{\text{ret}}$ of Maxwell's equations (5.2) and (5.3). But these equations also have another type of solutions, the advanced ones, which one can obtain by using formulas (5.9) but at another instant of time, $\tau = \tau_+ = t + |\mathbf{r} - \mathbf{a}|/c$:

$$A_0(x) = \left[\frac{e}{qR}\right]_{\text{adv}}, \qquad A(x) = \left[\frac{e\mathbf{v}}{qR}\right]_{\text{adv}}. \qquad (5.11)$$

At first, these solutions look quite strange. Nevertheless, given the finite velocity of light, the electromagnetic disturbance will spread with some advance in space. In the formulas (5.11) one ought to calculate the velocity and the position of the particle at the advanced instant τ_+. This means that the disturbance at position $\mathbf{r}$ at time t is caused by the charged particle at another point $\mathbf{a}$, not at a simultaneous time t, but rather at a *later* time τ_+. The disturbance propagates across the intervening distance $R = |\mathbf{r} - \mathbf{a}|$ in *advance*. The subscript 'adv' in equation (5.11) denotes the evaluation of all quantities in the brackets at the later instant τ_+. The corresponding four-tensor $F_{\mu\nu}$ of the electromagnetic field, which one obtains for the advanced potential (5.11) will be denoted by $F_{\mu\nu}^{\text{adv}}$. The advanced solutions appear to violate the usual notions of causality, because the cause of the disturbance lies in the future.

However, one cannot ignore the advanced solutions of Maxwell's equations in an *ad hoc* fashion. Actually, the general solution of these equations is a linear combination of the advanced and the retarded solutions: $F_{\mu\nu} = kF_{\mu\nu}^{\text{adv}} + (1-k)F_{\mu\nu}^{\text{ret}}$, where k is an arbitrary constant. The choice of this constant depends on the so-called boundary conditions.

Suppose we consider a collection of charged particles in some volume V bounded by the surface S. Then there will exist electromagnetic waves of two kinds in the volume V. One kind are waves that are caused by charges within the volume V, and they spread through the surface S outside the volume.

The other kind of electromagnetic waves are coming in from the space around this volume. These waves are caused by outside charges and they spread through the volume V within the surface S. If we wish to obtain only the retarded waves within the volume V, then it is necessary to choose the boundary condition on the solutions of Maxwell's equations, which eliminates the incoming waves. This boundary condition is known as Sommerfeld's radiation condition. It eliminates the advanced solutions of Maxwell's equation in the volume V in accordance with our experience in the real world. Sommerfeld's radiation condition seems to be very natural if the volume V includes the entire universe. Wheeler's modification of Feynman's idea to connect the radiation resistance of the electron with the reaction of the absorbers at a long distance from the radiating particle, in this sense, means a change of boundary conditions for the solutions of Maxwell's equations. Instead of Sommerfeld's radiation condition, Wheeler proposed to put an absorber on the boundary of the universe, and then to explain radiation resistance as a back reaction of the absorber on the radiating particle. It turned out that one can satisfy this new boundary condition with a proper choice of the constant k in a linear combination, which gives the general solution of Maxwell's equations. Feynman established that the new boundary condition will be fulfilled if one put $k = \frac{1}{2}$, that is, if a one-half retarded and one-half advanced mixture is taken as a solution of Maxwell's equations. Feynman considered the simplest model of the universe: namely, flat Minkowski space-time. It turns out that in modern relativistic models of the universe the new Wheeler–Feynman boundary condition gives some new and interesting results in cosmology.[17]

5.3 Electrodynamics without the electromagnetic field: the Wheeler–Feynman theory

In Section 5.1, we mentioned that in the spring of 1941 Richard Feynman wrote the draft of a paper entitled 'The interaction theory of radiation', in which he gave a summary of the work on an action-at-distance theory of classical electrodynamics, which he and John Wheeler had carried out during the previous few months. He stated the fundamental assumptions of this theory as follows:[18]

'(1) The acceleration of the point charge is due only to the sum of its interactions with other charged particles (and to "mechanical forces"†). A charge does not act on itself.

'(2) The force of interaction which one charge exerts on the second is calculated by means of the Lorentz force formula,‡ in which the fields are the fields generated by the first charge according to Maxwell's equations.

'(3) The fundamental (microscopic) phenomena in nature are symmetrical with respect to interchanges of past and future.§

'(4) The limit of the velocity of each charge for increasingly remote (past or future) times is less than the velocity of light.

'According to the second assumption alone, the force exerted by one charge on a second might be obtained from the field derived from the retarded potentials of Liénard and Wiechert. Thus the second charge would be affected by an amount determined by the *previous* motion of the first charge. This is not the only possibility, however; one could, for example, use the advanced potentials. In this case, the second charge would be affected by an amount depending on the *later* motion of the first charge. The requirement that the effects be unchanged if one interchanges past and future removes the ambiguity and demands that one utilize one-half the retarded plus one-half the advanced potentials to calculate the force on the second point charge due to the first. This is exactly the law of interaction that one derives from the

---

† The present theory is one to describe those phenomena which are usually considered to be due to electromagnetic effects. Forces on charged particles such as nuclear forces on protons, or "quantum effects" on electrons, will be classified as "mechanical" forces and will not be discussed further in this paper.

‡ Force $= e[E + (v/c) \times H]$.

§ The original statement was 'The fundamental equations are to be invariant with respect to interchange of sign of the time in them (symmetrical with respect to interchange of past and future),' which Feynman changed.

principle of least action of Fokker, and that principle may well have formed the starting point of this theory.'[18]

Feynman then proceeded to discuss the applications of this principle to certain idealized situations in order to get an idea of its physical meaning. In the first place, he noted that a single accelerating charge in otherwise charge-free space will radiate no energy. There can be no radiation damping, since there are no electrodynamic fields acting on the charge, no other charges being present to generate such fields. Feynman then presented the explanation which he and Wheeler had devised for the mechanism of radiation damping in their theory.

Wheeler reworked Feynman's manuscript and returned to him the new expanded version in the spring of 1942. The title of the new expanded version was: 'Action at a distance in classical theory: reaction of the absorber as the mechanism of radiation damping'.[10] War work interrupted the further development of the Wheeler–Feynman theory until 1945, when a second version of the paper was submitted to the *Festschrift* published in honor of Niels Bohr's sixtieth birthday.[11] In Wheeler's long-range plan to overhaul electrodynamics completely, this paper was intended to be Part III of a series of five papers. Part II, which should have preceded the 1945 paper, was published in 1949.[19] At about the same time, the arrival of the new quantum electrodynamics, formulated by Feynman, Schwinger, and Tomonaga, made Wheeler's program redundant.

In the 1945 paper in the *Reviews of Modern Physics*, Wheeler and Feynman gave a simple and elegant explanation of radiation damping. Suppose, there are N charged particles and each of them is the source of some advanced field $F_{adv}^{(k)}$ and some retarded field $F_{ret}^{(k)}$, with k being the number of the particle. So long as there is no self-interaction, the field acting on the ath particle is given, according to the theory of action-at-a-distance, by the sum

$$\sum_{k \neq a} \left(\tfrac{1}{2} F_{ret}^{(k)} + \tfrac{1}{2} F_{adv}^{(k)} \right). \tag{5.12}$$

This field can be broken down into three parts:

$$\sum_{k \neq a} F_{ret}^{(k)} + \left(\tfrac{1}{2} F_{ret}^{(a)} + \tfrac{1}{2} F_{adv}^{(a)} \right) - \sum_{all\ k} \left(\tfrac{1}{2} F_{ret}^{(k)} - \tfrac{1}{2} F_{adv}^{(k)} \right). \tag{5.13}$$

Of these terms the third vanishes for the complete absorber. In the case of nonrelativistic velocities, the third term had been shown by Dirac[16] to give just the Lorentz damping force, given by equation (5.10). The second term gives rise to the phenomenon of radiation damping. Thus, the charged particle interacts effectively only with the retarded field of the other charged particles, which is expressed by the first term in the expression (5.13). In addition, this particle experiences a Lorentz damping force due to its own acceleration.

At first, the last conclusion seemed to be slightly confusing. Wheeler and Feynman had started from a completely time-symmetric theory, which was time-reversible. But they arrived at a result which is obviously time-irreversible, since the interaction turns out to be effectively retarded. The explanation of this difficulty lies in thermodynamical and statistical considerations. The particles in the absorber, in accordance with thermodynamical laws, will have random motion and the absorber would tend to go from ordered to disordered states of higher entropy. For this reason, the prevalence of the retarded over the advanced potentials will be observed. In his initial draft of the article, Feynman had written:

'It may be worthwhile to make a few remarks at this point about the irreversibility of radiative phenomena. We must distinguish between two types of irreversibility. A sequence of natural phenomena will be said to be microscopically irreversible if the sequence of phenomena reversed in temporal order in every detail could not possibly occur in nature. If the original sequence and the one reversed in time have a vastly different order of probability of occurrence in the macroscopic sense, the phenomena are said to be macroscopically irreversible.

'The Lorentz theory predicts the existence of microscopically irreversible phenomena in systems which are not closed (for example, energy is always lost by the system to empty space as radiation). In our theory the phenomena are microscopically reversible in any system. It seems at first sight paradoxical that the two theories can ever lead to the same result, as they do in closed systems. The reason is that the phenomena predicted for closed systems are actually reversible even within the framework of the Lorentz theory which uses only retarded waves.† The apparent irreversibility in a closed system, then, either from our point of view or the point of view of Lorentz, is a purely macroscopic irreversibility. We believe that all physical phenomena are microscopically reversible, and that, therefore, all apparently irreversible phenomena are solely macroscopically irreversible.'[18]

The main obstacle toward the realization of Feynman's MIT program (see Chapter 4) was thus overcome in the Wheeler–Feynman absorption theory of radiation of the charged particles. They had succeeded in completely explaining the force of radiation resistance in the theory without self-interaction. However, one further step was needed for overcoming the difficulty with the infinitely many degrees of freedom in the field, which still remained in the theory of one-half retarded plus one-half advanced waves, In accordance with the expression (5.12), one has to write down the equation of motion of the charged particle, with particle number a, in the form

$$mc^2 \ddot{a}_v = e \sum_{k \neq a} (\tfrac{1}{2} F^{(k)}_{\text{ret}} + \tfrac{1}{2} F^{(k)}_{\text{adv}}) \dot{a}^\mu. \tag{5.14}$$

Now the question was: Is it possible to write down some new equations of

† 'That this and the following statement are true in the Lorentz theory was emphasized by Einstein in a discussion with Ritz.[20] Our viewpoint on the matter is essentially that of Einstein. (We should like to thank Prof. W. Pauli for calling our attention to this discussion.)'

motion of the particles, which do not include the electromagnetic field, but nevertheless have the same solutions as equations (5.14)? This question was quite old, and had its roots in Newton's theory of direct interaction between particles. The most well-known example of a direct interaction between particles at some distance is Newton's law of gravitational interaction, which says that the gravitational force between two particles with masses m_1 and m_2 equals $m_1 m_2 / |r_1 - r_2|^2$ up to some coefficient, called Newton's gravitational constant. One can see that the particles interact, being at the distance $|r_1 - r_2|$. This interaction spreads infinitely fast, because if one particle changes its position, given by the corresponding vector r, then the force, which acts on the other particles changes immediately together with the distance $|r_1 - r_2|$. No field is required to describe such an interaction. But the infinitely large velocity of the propagation of interaction is in contradiction with experiments and with Einstein's theory of relativity; therefore, one has to take into account the finite velocity of the spreading of the interaction to avoid this difficulty.

Since the work of Maxwell, it was known that the velocity of propagation of the electromagnetic interaction is the velocity of light. Hence one needs some modification of the action-at-a-distance theory to explain the finite velocity of the propagation of electrodynamic interaction without the notion of the field. Wheeler and Feynman took note of this problem by saying:

'It is easy to see why no unified presentation of classical electrodynamics has yet been given, though the elements for such a description are all present in isolated form in the literature. The development of the electromagnetic theory came before the era of relativity. Most minds were not prepared for the requirement that interactions should be propagated with a certain character-istic speed, still less for the possibility of both advanced and retarded interactions. Newtonian instantaneous action-at-a-distance with its century and a half of successes seemed the natural framework about which to construct a description of electromagnetism. Attempt after attempt failed.[21] And unfortunately uncompleted was the work of Gauss, who wrote to [Wilhelm] Weber on 19 March 1845: 'I would doubtless have published my researches long since were not at times I gave them up; I had failed to find what I regarded as the keystone, *Nil actum reputans si quid superesset agendu*: namely, the derivation of the additional forces—to be added to the interaction of electrical charges at rest, when they are both in motion—form an action which is propagated not instantaneously but in time as is the case with light.'[22] These failures and the final success via the apparently quite different concept of field were taken by physicists generally as convincing arguments against electro-magnetic action-at-a-distance.

'Field theory taught gradually for over seven decades difficult lessons about constancy of light velocity, about relativity of space and time, about advanced and retarded forces, and in the end made possible by this circuitous route the theory of interparticle interaction which Gauss had hoped to achieve in one leap. On this route and historically important was Liénard[23] and Wiechert's[24] derivation from the equations of Maxwell of an expression for the elementary field generated by a point charge in arbitrary state of motion. With this expression as the starting point Schwarzschild arrived at a law of force between two point charges which made no reference to field quantities. Developed without benefit of the concept of relativity, and expressed in the inconvenient notation of the prerelativistic period, his equations made no appeal to the physicists of the time. After the advent of relativity Schwarzschild's results were rederived independently by Tetrode and Fokker. These results are most conveniently summarized in Fokker's principle of stationary action.'[25] According to this principle, $\delta A_F = 0$, where Fokker's action functional A_F is

$$A_F = -\sum_i m_i \int (\dot{a}_i^\mu \dot{a}_{(i)\mu})^{1/2} \, d\lambda_i$$

$$-\tfrac{1}{2} \sum_{i \neq j} e_i e_j \iint \delta((a_{(i)} - a_{(j)})^2) \dot{a}_{(i)}^\mu \dot{a}_{(j)\mu} \, d\lambda_i \, d\lambda_j. \quad (5.15)$$

Here δ denotes Dirac's delta-function, and its argument is the square of the relativistic four-dimensional distance between the space–time points of the particles with numbers i and j: $[(a_{(i)}^\mu - a_{(j)}^\mu)]^2 = (a_{(i)\mu} - a_{(j)\mu})$. This means that in terms of four-dimensional space–time the particles interact only at zero four-dimensional distance. In more physical terms, this fact means that two particles interact when, and only when, their locations in space–time can be connected by a light ray.

Fokker's action, equation (5.15), looks quite different compared to the usual electrodynamical action given by the expression (5.8). Fokker's action obviously depends only on the particle's variables, not on the field's variables. Thus the electromagnetic field is eliminated from the theory with the action given by equation (5.15). Feynman recalled: 'We also found that we could reformulate [the new theory] in another way, and that is by [means of] the principle of least action. Since my original plan was to describe everything directly in terms of particle motions, it was my desire to represent this new theory without saying anything about fields. It turned out that we found a form for an action directly involving the motions of charges only, which upon variation would give the equations of motion of these charges.'[3,9]

Wheeler and Feynman noted: 'However unfamiliar this direct interparticle treatment compared to the electrodynamics of Maxwell and Lorentz, it deals with the same problem, talks about the same charges, considers the interaction of the same current elements, obtains the same capacities, predicts the same inductances, and yields the same physical conclusions. Consequently action-at-a-distance must have a close connection with field theory. But never does it consider the action of a charge on itself. The theory of direct interparticle action is equivalent, not to the usual field theory, but to a modified or *adjunct field theory*. . . .'[25]

Wheeler and Feynman actually showed that if one were to write down the second term in the action equation (5.15) in the form

$$\frac{1}{2} \sum_{i \neq j} e_i \int \dot{a}_{(i)}^{\mu} A_{(j)\mu} \, d\lambda_i, \tag{5.16}$$

where

$$A_{(j)\mu} = e_j \int \delta\big((a_{(i)} - a_{(j)})^2\big) \, da_{(j)\mu} \tag{5.17}$$

is the electromagnetic potential created by the charged particle with number *j*, then Maxwell's equations will be satisfied together with all other conditions and equations in the Feynman–Wheeler modification of electrodynamics. 'So, all of classical electrodynamics was contained in this very simple form. It looked good and, therefore, it was undoubtedly true, at least to the beginner. It automatically gave half-advanced and half-retarded effects and it was without fields. By omitting the term in the sum when $i = j$, I omit self-interaction and no longer have any infinite self-energy. This then was the hoped-for solution to the problem of ridding classical electrodynamics of infinities. . . .

'I would like to make the following remark. The fact that electrodynamics can be written in so many ways—the differential equations of Maxwell, various minimum principles with fields, minimum principles without fields, all different kinds of ways—was something I knew but have never understood. It always seems odd to me that the fundamental laws of physics, when discovered, can appear in so many different forms that are not apparently identical at first, but with a little mathematical fiddling you can show the relationship. An example of that is the Schrödinger equation and the Heisenberg formulation of quantum mechanics. I don't know why this is—it remains a mystery, but it was something I learned from experience. There is always another way to say the same thing that doesn't look at all like the way you said it before. I don't know what the reason for this is. I think it is somehow a representation of the simplicity of nature. A thing like the inverse square law is just right to be represented by the solution of Poisson's equation, which, therefore, is a very different way to say the same thing that doesn't look at all like the way you said it before. I don't know what it means, that nature chooses these curious forms, but maybe that is a way of defining simplicity. Perhaps a thing is simple if you can describe it fully in several different ways without immediately knowing that you are describing the same thing.

'I was now convinced that since we had solved the problem of classical electrodynamics (and completely in accordance with my program from MIT, with only the direct interaction between particles, in a way that made fields unnecessary) everything was definitely going to be all right. I was convinced that all I had to do was make a quantum theory analogous to the classical one and everything would be solved.'[26]

Thus Feynman's MIT program of modifying classical electrodynamics was successfully fulfilled. Besides this fundamental development, Feynman arrived at some new physical points of view, different from the customary ones. The first was the new approach to physical systems. 'In the customary view, things are discussed as a function of time in very great detail. For example, you have the field at this moment, differential equation gives you the field at the next moment, and so on—a method which I shall call the Hamiltonian method, the time differential method. We have, instead (in [(5.15)], say) a thing that describes the character of the path throughout all space and time. The behavior of nature is determined by saying her whole space–time path has a certain character. For an action like [(5.15)] the equations obtained by variation of [A_r] are no longer at all easy to get back into Hamiltonian form. If you wish to use as variables only the coordinates of the particles, then you can talk about the property of the paths—but the path of one particle at a given time is affected by the path of another at a different time. If you try to describe, therefore, things differentially, telling what the present conditions of the particles are, and how these present conditions will affect the future—you see, it is impossible with particles alone, because something the particle did in the past is going to affect the future.

'Therefore, you need a lot of bookkeeping variables to keep track of what the particle did in the past. These are called field variables. You will also have to tell what the field is at this present moment, if you are to be able to see later what is going to happen. From the overall space–time view of the least action principle, the field disappears as nothing but bookkeeping variables insisted on by the Hamiltonian method.'[27] This new point of view will play an essential role in Feynman's invention of the path integral method for the quantization of classical systems (see Chapters 6 and 10).

As a by-product of this point of view at about the same time, in the fall of 1940, Feynman received a telephone call from John Wheeler at the Graduate College in Princeton, in which he said that he knew why all electrons have the same charge and the same mass. 'Why?' asked Feynman, and Wheeler replied, 'Because they are all one and the same electron.'[3,26]

One usually describes the motion of the particles as world-lines in space-time. These world-lines depend on the change of the coordinates and proper times of the particles. One usually supposes that a particle's world-line goes only from the past to the future. Then, every such world-line describes one particle at a given instant of time. If there are several such world-lines at a given instant of time, this would mean that there are several such particles, just as many as the number of world-lines at that instant (see Fig. 5.1).

Wheeler said to Feynman: 'Suppose that the world-lines which we were ordinarily considering before in time and space, if only going up in time, were a

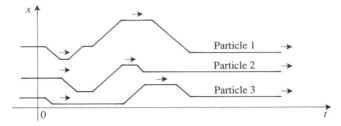

Fig. 5.1. The world-lines of three particles, which move ahead in time.

tremendous knot, and then, when we cut through the knot by a plane corresponding to a fixed time, we would see many, many world-lines and that would represent many electrons [see Fig. 5.2]—except for one thing. If in one section of this is an ordinary electron world-line, in the section in which it reversed itself and is coming back from the future we have the wrong sign to the proper time—to the proper four-velocities—and that's equivalent to change of sign of the charge,† and therefore that part of the path would act like a positron.'[26]

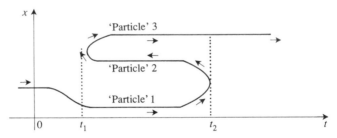

Fig. 5.2. The world-line of a particle, which turns back in the time instant t_2 and then at time instant t_1 turns in the forward direction in time. The observer will see three particles between the instances t_1 and t_2.

Feynman did not take 'the idea that all electrons were the same one from (Wheeler) as seriously as the observation that positrons could simply be represented as electrons going back from the future to the past in a back section of their world lines.'[26] Later on, in his theory of positrons, Feynman

---

† Indeed, if the increasing of the proper time has the wrong sign, then, as a consequence, we shall have a wrong sign of the four-velocity $v = \dot{a}$ and of the four-acceleration $\ddot{a}$ of the particle. But according to equation (5.7) we can include this wrong sign in the charge e of the particle, to which the right-hand side of this equation is proportional. Hence, in this part of the world-line, which goes back in time, one can think that there is one particle with the right sign for the increase of the particle's proper time, but the opposite sign of the electric charge. The mass of this imaginary particle and all its other characteristics will be the same, and we can conclude that the electron, going back in time, will behave just like a positron.

would make use of this idea in order to avoid Dirac's hole theory of positrons (see Chapter 13). However, in the conversation that fall in 1940, he said to Wheeler, 'But, Professor, there aren't as many positrons as electrons,' and Wheeler replied, 'Well, maybe they are hidden in the protons or something.'[26] Feynman's objection was based on the obvious fact (see Fig. 5.2) that each time an electron reverses its world-line in time, it will go back for some time, and then it must return to the forward direction of time. According to Wheeler's idea, the positron is part of the electron's world-line, which goes back in time. Hence, every 'positron' will correspond to another part of the world-line in the right direction, which represents another electron. Hence, if we have only one electron in the whole universe, and those positrons are parts of its world-line, which travel in the reversed time direction, we must have at each instant as many positrons as electrons minus one. So, if one were to take Wheeler's idea seriously, one needs some speculation to explain where all the positrons are.

Notes and References

1. R.P. Feynman, The development of the space–time view of quantum electrodynamics, Nobel Lecture, 11 December 1965, *Science* **153**, 699 (1966), p. 2

2. R.P. Feynman, Ref. 1, p. 2.

3. R.P. Feynman, Interviews and conversations with Jagdish Mehra, in Pasadena, California, January 1988.

4. R.P. Feynman, *SYJMF*, pp. 78–79.

5. R.P. Feynman, *SYJMF*, p. 80.

6. R.P Feynman and J.A. Wheeler, *Bull. Am. Phys. Soc.* **16**, 683 (1941).

7. J. Frenkel, *Z. Phys.* **32**, 518 (1925).

8. A.D. Fokker, *Z. Phys.* **58**, 386 (1929); *Physica* **9**, 33 (1929) and **12**, 145 (1932).

9. R.P. Feynman, Interviews with Charles Weiner (American Institute of Physics), in Pasadena, California, 1966.

10. J.A. Wheeler and R.P. Feynman, Action at a distance in classical theory, Richard Feynman Papers, Niels Bohr Library, American Institute of Physics, New York.

11. J.A. Wheeler and R.P. Feynman, *Rev. Mod. Phys.* **17**, 157 (1945).

12. J.A. Wheeler, *Bull. Am. Phys. Soc.* **16**, 21 (1941).

13. R.P. Feynman, A relativistic cut-off for classical electrodynamics, *Phys. Rev.* **74**, 939 (1948).

14. J.A. Wheeler and R.P. Feynman, Ref. 11, p. 157.

15. A. Liénard, *L'Eclairage Eléctrique* **16** (1898), pp. 5, 33, 106; E. Wiechert, *Archive Néerld.* **5** (2), 549 (1900), *Ann. Phys. Leipzig* **4**, 676 (1901).

16. P.A.M. Dirac, *Proc. R. Soc. Lond.* A **167**, 148 (1938).

17. F. Hoyle and J. Narlikar, *Action at a distance in physics and cosmology*, Freeman, New York, 1974.

18. R.P. Feynman, Draft of a paper entitled 'The interaction theory of radiation', Feynman Archives, Caltech.

19. J.A. Wheeler and R.P. Feynman, *Rev. Mod. Phys.* **21**, 425 (1949).

20. A. Einstein and W. Ritz, *Phys. Z.* **10**, 323 (1909).

21. For an instructive account of early researches on field theory and action-at-a-distance, see A. O'Rahilly, *Electromagnetics* (Longmans, New York, 1938). See also J.J. Thomson, Report of the British Association for the Advancement of Science for 1885, p. 97; J.C. Maxwell, *Electricity and magnetism* (Oxford University Press, London, 1892), 3rd ed., Chap. 23; R. Reif and A. Sommerfeld, *Encycl. Math. Wiss.* **5** Part 2, Sect. 12 (1902).

22. C.F. Gauss, *Werke*, Vol. 5, p. 629 (1867).

23. A. Liénard, Ref. 15.

24. E. Wiechert, Ref. 15.

25. J.A. Wheeler and R.P. Feynman, Ref. 19, p. 426.

26. R.P. Feynman, Ref. 1, pp. 4–5.

6

The principle of least action in quantum mechanics

6.1 Introduction

Richard Feynman had to take the qualifying examination to become a candidate for the Ph.D. degree. At Princeton, the graduate students were not restricted to pursuing any special courses, but they had to take a very stiff qualifying examination; it was a long written examination for a day or two, followed by an oral examination. Three groups of professors would examine the candidate. The graduate students used to worry about this examination, and most of them dreaded it. They had a maximum of three chances in which to pass it, and some of them had failed it once or twice. To prepare for it was a serious matter.

In order to get ready for the qualifying examination, Feynman went to Cambridge, Massachusetts, where he studied for about six to eight weeks in the library of MIT during the summer of 1940. Nobody among the young people there knew him any longer, and he had the peace of mind to work in the library. He stayed at his old fraternity, where they gave him a room to stay. He was able to study without interruption or distraction. There he fully organized his knowledge of physics, things he knew and others which he did not know. He prepared a notebook, entitled 'Things I don't know about'. In it, he summarized all the subjects as best as he could, and he was rather proud of that notebook.

Feynman tried to reduce every part of physics to its fundamentals: to learn what were the essentials and the body of knowledge that was derived from them. In this way, he was able to see the pattern of each field: electrodynamics, relativity theory, quantum mechanics, statistical mechanics—everything was in his notebook. He would use this notebook many years later to prepare the lecture courses he would give at Cornell University and, later on, at the California Institute of Technology.[1] In this way, everything became organized in his mind, never to be forgotten. He made good use of this basic knowledge when, over two decades later, he gave his famous *Feynman lectures on physics* for freshmen and sophomore students at Caltech.[2] He was able to organize everything in a logical manner, so that the effort of memorization would be minimal. That required an arrangement by means of which all the logical interconnections were clear and self-contained. He completed a summary of all of fundamental physics in a concentrated and devoted study of about two months at MIT in preparation for his qualifying examination. Then he returned to Princeton, where he took the qualifying examination in the fall of 1940.

In the oral examination, one of the professors asked him about the order of colors in the rainbow: which color was at the top and which at the bottom? Feynman answered he did not know, and proceeded to work it out by drawing the curve for the index of refraction versus the wavelength.[1,3] In the curve, Feynman mixed up the indices of refraction for the blue and the red colors, but corrected himself just in time.[1,3] H. P. Robertson asked Feynman a question about stellar aberration and relativity, which he answered incorrectly.[1,3] When you look at a star through a telescope, it appears to move in a little circle due to aberration. How would the earth look in a telescope from a star? Feynman answered that the earth would also look as if it moved in a little circle. Feynman and Robertson had much argument about it, but Feynman succeeded in persuading him that he was right. When he thought more about it afterwards, he concluded that he had been wrong. The circles in the two cases would be of different sizes, and the two observations were not related. Special relativity would fail because acceleration is involved, and the motion would appear to be in a circle in which the velocity would change.[1,3]

After Feynman graduated from MIT, he wanted to get a summer job at the Bell Telephone Laboratories, and went out a couple of times to visit there. William Shockley, who knew him from the lab at MIT, would show Feynman around each time; he enjoyed these visits very much, but he did not get a job there. In the spring of 1941, Feynman went once again to the Bell Labs in New York to apply for a summer job. Shockley again showed him around and, afterwards, some of the young research scientists took him to a seafood restaurant for lunch. They were all pleased that they were going to have oysters but Feynman, who had grown up in a town near the ocean, could not even look at oysters; he forced himself to eat a couple of oysters, but felt awful and gave up. However, 'this time, which must have been my fourth or fifth time touring the Bell Labs, they accepted me. I was very happy. In those days it was hard to find a job where you could be with other scientists.'[4] But, instead of joining the Bell Labs for summer work, Feynman joined the army for wartime work.

Even before the United States of America declared war after Pearl Harbor in December 1941, there was a lot of propaganda about joining the war effort, and a lot of patriotic feelings about helping the country's business. Many businessmen were going to Plattsburg in upstate New York to join whatever service jobs were available. Feynman also thought that his technical ability to do physics might be of some use in the war effort. As a former member of the ROTC at MIT, he did not wish to join the Signal Corps, which he could have done. He talked to an army officer, who advised him to get basic training by signing up in Plattsburg, New York, and become a second lieutenant. The officer told him that that was the way the army was organized, and if he wanted to make a contribution that was the way to do it. Instead of joining Bell Labs, where he could also have done war-related research work, Feynman chose to work as a kind of engineer at the Frankfort Arsenal near Philadelphia. His job was to check everything for making a mechanical director for directing military artillery and shooting planes down. The fuses for the director were timed and powered by airburning some powder at high altitudes from airplanes, but there was not enough oxygen in the air to burn the powder.

Towards the end of summer Feynman's boss, an army colonel, realized that he was very useful and wanted to keep him in preference to the other engineers of the same rank. He offered Feynman his support and complete freedom to design the mechanical director, and tried to tempt him into staying on by promising him that he would become a big shot and could do whatever he wanted to do. In spite of all these promises, Feynman decided not to stay there and returned to Princeton. He felt sorry that he had given up the opportunity to work at the Bell Labs, where, through his scientific work, he could have made an effective contribution.

In Princeton, Feynman continued to work on his thesis from September to the end of November 1941. One morning, early in December, Robert R. Wilson, who was a young faculty member at Princeton, came into Feynman's office. He said: 'I have something to tell you. I am not supposed to say it, because it is an absolute secret. Since, however, after I tell you, you'll work on the project anyway, there's nothing to worry about.'[1,3] Wilson told Feynman that they were getting ready to build the atomic bomb in the United States, and they needed to separate uranium-235 from the ore in which it is found with the more abundant isotope uranium-238. Wilson had a process—different from the one that was eventually used—for separating the isotopes of uranium, which he wanted to develop. He told Feynman about his ideas and he wanted him to do the theoretical work to help them along. He asked Feynman to attend a meeting at 3:00 p.m., where these things would be discussed.

Feynman told Wilson that his secret was safe with him, but that he was seriously engaged on completing his thesis and did not wish to participate in the project. After Wilson left, Feynman went back to work on his thesis, but soon he began to pace the floor and think about Wilson's words. In Germany, under Hitler, there was a real possibility of developing an atomic bomb, and it gave him a fright to think that scientists under Hitler might develop the bomb first. So, Feynman decided to attend the meeting called by Wilson at 3:00 p.m., and by 4:00 p.m. the same afternoon he had a desk in an office, and was soon at work as a junior scientist at the OSRD (Office of Scientific Research and

Development) project on whether Wilson's method for the separation of isotopes 'was limited by the amount of current that you get in the ion beam'.[5] The experimentalists at Princeton were building the apparatus right there to verify the theoretical ideas.

What had happened was that all the young physicists to whom Wilson talked decided to stop their normal research and accepted to work on problems concerning the development of the atomic bomb. Feynman did the same. It was only after a while that he took a few weeks off to complete his thesis and take the final examination.

After Feynman had been working on the atomic bomb project for a few months, he got a little tired, and thought he would take six weeks off and finish his thesis. He quit the project to take his degree. John Wheeler, who had in the meantime joined the Metallurgical Laboratory at the University of Chicago, also urged Feynman to take a little time off to complete the thesis. When Feynman returned to his thesis, he found himself entirely unable to work on it. First, he was tired from the work on the atomic bomb project; second, he could not turn from one thing he had been working on intensively to something else. 'So I lazed around and I felt very guilty. Then all of a sudden ideas began to come and I wrote it all down. I solved the [thesis] problem, whatever it was, and wrote it all up. Wheeler also kept on insisting that I had enough stuff even if I did not solve any of these problems, if I never applied my theory to electrodynamics, which was the purpose of it.'[1]

6.2 Formulation of the problem

We have noted that already as an undergraduate student at MIT in the 1930s (1935–39) Richard Feynman had realized from his reading of the books of Walter Heitler (1935) and Paul Dirac (1935) that 'the fundamental problem of the day was that the quantum theory of electricity and magnetism was not completely satisfactory' and he looked at it 'as a challenge and an inspiration'.[6] His personal feeling was, that since they didn't get a satisfactory answer to the problem he had to do it himself. In a long series of conversations a couple of weeks before he died, Feynman remarked: 'All I could remember in Heitler and Dirac, and I remember distinctly well, was that they could not solve the problems. They were getting infinities, and the last sentence in Dirac's book was that some new ideas were needed. That's the main thing I got from Dirac: that new ideas were needed. This, to me, meant that I did not have to study the old ones; I didn't have to read exactly what Dirac was doing. I didn't have to find out what Heitler was telling me, what Pauli or Weisskopf, or whoever it was, was doing with the field theory, because they were all getting infinities. So I didn't have to understand what they were doing. All that was wrong; that was going to give me trouble. So what I would learn from them, if I studied them, was *what not to learn*, and I didn't learn quantum electrodynamics from those books. I learned it from an article by Fermi in the *Reviews of Modern Physics*[7] later, that there are nothing but a bunch of oscillators, the world is made up of harmonic oscillators, and each one of them is a quantum oscillator. What could be simpler? Nothing to it! Why all this hokey-pokey?'[1]

At that time Feynman understood that there existed two kinds of difficulties in the quantum electrodynamical theories. The first one, which was the classical one, still existed, namely, an infinite energy of the electron with itself. The other difficulty, as we have also noted earlier, arose from the infinite number of degrees of freedom in the electromagnetic field. Each such degree of freedom or 'mode' has a ground state energy of $\frac{1}{2}\hbar\omega$, where $\omega = 2\pi v$ is the circular frequency, v being the frequency of the mode and $\hbar$ being Planck's constant. Because of the infinite number of modes associated with the electromagnetic field in a given finite volume, an infinite energy will be confined in this volume. Actually, the latter difficulty may be removed simply by changing the zero point, from which the energy is measured, but Feynman took this point very seriously.

The solution to these difficulties, which Feynman himself suggested, was as follows: (1) to eliminate the self-interaction of the particles—'hence, no self-energy!'; (2) to eliminate the field completely—there will be 'no infinite degrees of freedom of the field'.[6] These two steps are actually connected, because if one wishes to avoid the self-interaction of the particles, one has to avoid the field itself, otherwise each charged particle will interact with the common field, to the creation of which this particle has made its own contribution; hence, the self-interaction of the particles will still exist.

This general idea seemed to be so appealing that Feynman 'fell deeply in love with it'.[6] It seemed to be a possible solution, since the electromagnetic field of the particles is completely determined by the position and the motion of the charged particles. Then one could expect that the electromagnetic field might be expressed in terms of the particle variables and, therefore, it will not have any independent degrees of freedom, and the infinities due to the latter will be removed. Feynman's general plan was 'first to solve the classical problem, to get rid of the infinite self-energy in the classical theory, and to hope that when I made a quantum theory of it, everything would be just fine.'[8]

The resulting classical action-at-a-distance theory had its own problems, which we have discussed in the previous chapter. This theory was based on the principle of least action, with a new action but without the electromagnetic field. The main unsolved problem of this theory, that is, how to quantize it, still remained. When quantization was attempted, the electromagnetic field brought its own problems. Therefore, the idea of excluding the electromagnetic field entirely from the theory of charged material particles seemed to be quite appealing.

At the level of the classical theory, the new principle of least action that had been employed in the action-at-a-distance theory leads to an essential agreement with the usual form of electrodynamics. Besides being consistent with the description of point charges, it gives a unique law of radiation damping which could be checked experimentally. But if the electromagnetic field is a derived concept, there arise some physical questions which are in conflict with experiments at the quantum level, and which Feynman discussed in the introduction to his dissertation.[9]

After the concept of the electromagnetic field has been completely excluded, one has still to explain well-known processes such as the photoelectric effect and the Compton effect without light-quanta. Feynman's opinion was that 'since these phenomena deal with the interaction of light with matter their explanation may lie in the quantum aspects of matter, rather than requiring photons of light. This supposition is aided by the fact that if one solves the problem of an atom being perturbed by a potential varying sinusoidally with the time, which would be the situation if matter were quantum mechanical and light classical, one finds indeed that it will in all probability eject an electron whose energy shows an increase of hv, where v is the frequency of variation of the potential. In a similar way an electron perturbed by the potential of two beams of light of different frequencies and different directions will make transitions to a state in which its momentum and energy is changed by an amount just equal to that given by the formulas for the Compton effect, with one beam corresponding in direction and wavelength to the incoming photon and the other to the outgoing one. In fact, one may correctly calculate in this way the probabilities of absorption and induced emission of light by an atom.'[10]

When, however, we come to spontaneous emission and the mechanism of the production of light, we come much closer to the real reason for the apparent necessity of photons. The fact that an atom emits spontaneously at all is impossible to explain by the simple picture given above. In empty space an atom emits light and yet there is no potential to perturb the system and thus force it to make a transition. The explanation of modern quantum mechanical electrodynamics is that the atom is perturbed by the zero-point fluctuations of the quantized radiation field. 'It is here that that the theory of action-at-a-distance gives us a different viewpoint. It says that an atom in empty space would, in fact, *not* radiate. Radiation is a consequence of the interaction with other atoms (namely, those in the matter which absorb the radiation). We are then led to the possibility that the spontaneous radiation of an atom in quantum mechanics also may not be spontaneous at all, but may be induced by the interaction with other atoms, so that all of the apparent quantum properties of the light and the existence of photons may be nothing more than the result of matter interacting with matter directly, and according to quantum mechanical laws.'[10]

'Thus we see that Feynman was looking for the new physical concept of describing electromagnetic interactions between charged particles to resolve not only technical problems, but the fundamental difficulties in our understanding of the physical world. He pointed out two difficulties concerning the quantum analog of the action-at-a-distance theory of electromagnetic interactions. The first was that it might not be correct to represent fields as a set of harmonic oscillators with their own degrees of freedom, since in the action-at-a-distance theory the field is entirely determined by the particles.' On the other hand, an attempt to deal quantum mechanically directly with the particles, which would seem to be the most satisfactory way to proceed, is faced with the circumstance that the equations of motion of the particles are expressed classically as a consequence of a principle of least action, and cannot, it appears, be expressed in Hamiltonian form.

'For this reason a method of formulating a quantum analog of systems for which no Hamiltonian, but rather a principle of least action, exists has been worked out. It is a description of this method which constitutes this thesis. Although the method was worked out with the express purpose of applying it to the theory of action-at-a-distance, it is in fact independent of that theory, and complete in itself.'[11]

The second difficulty mentioned by Feynman, to avoid which the Lagrangian method should be used is, strictly speaking, not quite correct. Actually, the action-at-a-distance theories do allow the Hamiltonian prescription if one uses the generalization of the canonical formulation of classical mechanics as given by M. Ostrogradski.[12] As far as we know, no attempt in this direction has been made up to now, but one can show from Ostrogradski's formulation of the principle of least action that this argument concerning Feynman's motivation to invent the path integral method is groundless.†

6.3 Least action in classical mechanics

Feynman started his dissertation by describing the concept of the mathematical notion of a functional, which would play a predominant role in his investigations. 'To say F is a functional of the function $q(\tau)$ means that F is a number whose value depends on the *form* of the function $q(\tau)$ (where τ is just a parameter used to specify the form of $q(\tau)$). Thus, $F = \int_{-\infty}^{\infty} q(\tau) \exp(-\tau^2)\, d\tau$ is a functional of $q(\tau)$ since it associates with every choice of the function $q(\tau)$ a

---

† Action-at-a-distance theories do allow Hamiltonian formulation in the framework of a proper infinite-dimensional generalization of the canonical formalism, given by Ostrogradski.[12] The formal difference between the usual theories and the action-at-a-distance theory is that in the action-at-a-distance theory the time variable in some coordinates is shifted by a time interval which describes the retarded or the advanced interactions. By using a Taylor series expansion with respect to the time of the shifted variables in the interaction terms of the action-at-a-distance theory, one arrives at a Lagrangian with infinitely higher-order derivatives. Then, by employing all derivatives of the coordinates under consideration as new generalized coordinates, one can build canonical momenta and the corresponding classical Hamiltonian as standard formulas. In this way, Feynman could have obtained a Hamiltonian formulation of the action-at-a-distance theories, and such an approach could have been useful in overcoming some of the difficulties in formulating these theories.

number, namely the integral. Also, the area under a curve is a functional of the function representing the curve, since to each such function a number, the area, is associated. The expected value of the energy in quantum mechanics is a functional of the wave function. Again, $F = q(0)$ is a functional, which is especially simple because its value depends on the (value) of the function $q(\tau)$ at the point $\tau = 0$.' [13]

For a long time the important role of the functionals in mechanics, optics, geometry, and other mathematical and physical domains, had been realized. The concept of a functional first occurred in the papers of Johann Bernoulli, and was further developed by Leonhard Euler, Joseph Louis Lagrange, and several other mathematicians, up to Vito Volterra and David Hilbert, all of whom built the foundations of variational calculus and functional analysis. It is important to emphasize that the notion of the functional appeared in connection with the so-called variational principles in different domains, the most important of which is the principle of least action.

The first principle of such a kind in science was Pierre de Fermat's principle of least time, which explained the laws of geometrical optics. Fermat (1601–65) discovered that in every medium light rays travel from one point to another in such a way as to make the time taken a minimum. A similar law had been discovered by Hero of Alexandria (c. 125 BC) many centuries before Fermat for the special case in which a light ray is reflected by a mirror. [14] Fermat's principle of least time permits one to explain all the laws of propagation, diffraction, reflection, and refraction of rays in geometrical optics and was the first successful variational principle in science. As we know today, it is remarkable that this principle actually reflects the properties of the wave phenomenon, namely the propagation of light waves. But Fermat did not introduce the notion of a functional or give a modern formulation of his principle.

The next step toward the principle of least action was taken by Johann Bernoulli in 1696 when he had to formulate the problem of the brachisto-chrone: Given two points at different heights, not lying in the same vertical line, to find the curve, called brachistochrone, which connects these points and has the property that the body which goes down on this curve will take the least amount of time to reach the lower point starting from the upper point and moving under the force due to its weight alone. In other words, one is looking for the fastest curve of descent. The solution of this 'wonderful and unheard of' problem, as Leibniz called it, was the cycloid and was given by Leibniz himself, by Isaac Newton, Johann Bernoulli, and the Marquis de L'Hôpital.

The most important consequences for the later development of science were that, owing to Bernoulli's problem, mechanical problems were considered in the context of variational principles and the extremely useful idea of the internal connection between mechanics and optics was established.

The successful solution of Johann Bernoulli's problem led to a new question: Is it possible to derive all mechanical laws from some variational principle? The principal question was what kind of functional could one use for this purpose? This question first appeared in the seventeenth century and, after a large number of investigations, was solved at the end of the eighteenth and the beginning of the nineteenth centuries. The new mechanical quantity needed for the new variational principle was called a 'mechanical action' and the corresponding functional an 'action functional'.

The notion of mechanical action was first formulated in an incomplete form by Leibniz, which was published only in 1890 by C. J. Gerchard: Leibniz's *Dynamica de potentia et leqibus nature corporeae*, was written in 1669 during his journey to Italy. Leibniz called this quantity '*actio formalis*'. For a body with a mass m and velocity v, which travels a distance s in time t, Leibniz defined the action as mvs, or mv^2t if one employs modern conventional notation. Although he was not able to formulate the corresponding variational principle, Leibniz nevertheless tried to make some progress in this direction.

The principle of least action was first formulated by Maupertuis on 15 April 1744 in his scientific essay 'Accord de différentes lois de la Nature qui avaient jusqu'ici paru incompatibles', where he considered mainly the spreading of light. Earlier in 1740 Maupertuis had insisted that there exists some function which has an extremum in the equilibrium states of mechanical bodies. And, finally, in 1746 Maupertuis proclaimed the principle of least action as the most general principle of Nature. He declared: 'Lorsqu'il arrive quelque changement dans la Nature, la quantité d'action, nécessaire pour ce changement, est la plus petite qu'il soit possible.' In his investigations Maupertuis was looking not only for the simplest rational principles but also for the *theological* foundation of mechanics. In his opinion, 'perfection of the Supreme Being in His divine wisdom would be incompatible with anything other than utter simplicity and minimum expenditure of action'. After he had examined several simple concrete problems, namely the direct impact of two perfectly elastic bodies and the direct impact of two perfectly inelastic bodies, as well as the refraction of light, Maupertuis almost empirically derived the expression mvs for the action. His conclusion was completely independent of the work of Leibniz, which Maupertuis did not know.

The principle of least action was not strictly formulated by Maupertuis in a truly mathematical sense. His main accomplishment was that he had formulated this principle as a *general principle of nature*, but his theolological interpretation of the principle of least action has been the subject of more controversy than any other physical principle and has met great resistance from many scientists and philosophers. Among those who, in heated discussions, had different opinions and took an active part were the following: Euler, D'Arcy, König, Courtivron, Kraft, Clemm, D'Alembert, Voltaire, and even the Prussian king Frederick II, who issued the command to burn the pamphlet entitled *Histoire du docteur Akakia et du natif de Saint-Malo*, written by Voltaire against Maupertuis's theological interpretation of the principle of least action. As D'Alembert commented, the heated discussions were similar to religious discussions with respect to their fervor, and the number of people who took part in these discussions without any actual understanding of the problem was larger than any!

The first mathematician who considered the principle of least action as an exact dynamical statement in a strictly mathematical sense was Leonhard Euler. He had invented this principle independently of, and several months before, Maupertuis, but Euler's first paper on that principle was published on 12 June 1744, or two months after the paper of Maupertuis. Much earlier, in dealing with the problem of the motion of a particle with mass m between two fixed points in a gravitational field, Euler had proved that the real trajectories are those for which the integral $\int mv \, ds$ has an extremum, i.e. a minimum or a maximum. Euler was able to give strict meaning to these ideas not only because he was a great mathematician but also because he had great experience in dealing with isoperimetric problems, which he had obtained in working with his teacher Johann Bernoulli. Euler proved the general case of this problem in 1728. The problem was to find the shortest curve between two points on a certain surface, the so-called geodesic lines. Euler proved that one has to consider the path length integral, $S = \int_A^B ds$, where ds is the elementary length on the curve. The curve with a minimal or maximal length, which connects the points A and B on a given surface, is that curve for which this integral has a stationary value, i.e. an extremum.

For the mathematical formulation of the extremum conditions, one has to consider—in addition to the trajectory from the point A to the point B—another trajectory between the same points or, in other words, one has to consider the variation of the trajectory. The two trajectories pass through the fixed points A and B. Now one may examine the values of the path length integral of S for these trajectories. The difference δS between the lengths of the two trajectories, if calculated to the first-order terms with respect to the deviation between these trajectories, is called the variation of the functional S. Then the path with extremal length from point A to point B is that for which the variation of the functional S equals zero, i.e. $\delta S = 0$.

Thus we have got a variational principle which defines in general the extremal path from a point A to a point B. Euler derived a differential equation whose solution gave the extremal path; this was an ordinary differential equation of the second order which solved the isoperimetric problem completely.

Returning to the problem of the principle of least action, one can reduce Euler's discovery to the mathematical theorem

$$\delta A = 0, \qquad (6.1)$$

where δA is the variation of the action functional $A = \int mv \, ds$ in the problem of the motion of a mechanical particle between two fixed point centers in the plane in a gravitational field. Euler investigated this principle in several mechanical problems: the particle in a uniform gravitational field, in a central field, and under the action of constant horizontal and vertical forces; he was able to verify the validity of his principle in all these problems. But Euler's philosophy was basically different from that of Maupertuis. In the introduction of his paper, Euler wrote: 'Since all processes in Nature obey certain maximum or minimum laws, there is no doubt that the curves which bodies describe under the influence of arbitrary forces also possess some maximum or minimum property. It does not seem so easy, however, to define this property *a priori* from metaphysical principles. But, as it is possible to determine the curves themselves with the aid of a direct method, one should be able, upon thorough examination of these curves, to conclude what quantity in them must be a maximum or minimum.'[15]

Euler's result was that the quantity with extremal property is an action integral A, i.e. an integral of the momentum mv of the body on the path length ds. It is necessary to stress a very important justification which Euler had used implicitly in his principle. He had assumed that one can obtain the velocity v of a body as a function of its position in space from the law of conservation of energy, i.e.

$$\tfrac{1}{2}mv^2 + U(x, y, z) = E = \text{constant},\tag{6.2}$$

where E is the energy constant and $U(x, y, z)$ is the potential energy of the body with the position given by the coordinates x, y, z. Euler assumed that both the real path of the body in space and the virtual path, which is needed to calculate the variation of the action functional, obey the law of conservation of energy. The corresponding variations of the paths are called *isoenergetic* and one has to regard the variation of action, denoted as $\delta_E A$, to be strictly valid only in a mathematical sense.

Euler's interpretation of the principle of least action was expressed at the end of his paper: '... Since the bodies resist every change of their state by reason of their inertia, they yield to the accelerating forces as little as possible, at least if they are free. It therefore follows that in the actual motion the effect arising from the forces should be less than if the body or bodies were caused to move in any other manner. Although the force of this conclusion does not convince one as satisfactory, I do not doubt that it will be possible to justify it with the aid of metaphysics. I leave this task, however, to others who are proficient in metaphysical studies.'[15] Although Euler had formulated the principle of least action as a rigorous mathematical theorem in the cases he had considered, the physical meaning of this fundamental statement was not clear to him; he had not derived dynamical equations with the help of this principle.

The next step toward the justification of the principle of least action was made by Lagrange. In his famous *La mécanique analytique*, he had considered the general case of the motion of several particles interacting by means of conservative forces, derived from certain potentials. Lagrange stated that the system moves in such a way that the total action, which is equal to the sum of the actions of all the particles, is stationary on a fixed value of the total energy: $\delta_E A = \delta_E A_1 + \delta_E A_2 + \delta_E A_3 + \cdots = 0$. This first correct formulation of the principle of least action in the general case made it possible for Lagrange to derive Newton's equations of motion for each particle.

Thus Lagrange had proved that the principle of least action in his formulation is completely equivalent to Newton's dynamical laws and may be considered as a new foundation of dynamics in general. In spite of this important observation, the principle of least action was treated only as an interesting statement for the next half century, and even in 1837 Poisson spoke about it as 'a useless rule'.[16]

Lagrange had another very important success in analytical mechanics, which was also of great importance for the subsequent development of the principle of least action. He had introduced the so-called generalized *coordinates* q_1, q_2, q_3, and so on (as many as one needs to describe unambiguously the configuration of the system at any moment t). These parameters may have different physical or geometrical meaning, like distances, angles, etc., and they possess the property of being able to express all Cartesian coordinates as functions of the q's: $x = x(q)$, $y = y(q)$, $z = z(q)$. For a given mechanical system, the number f of generalized coordinates is called the number of degrees of freedom, and one may say that any generalized coordinate q_α ($\alpha = 1, \ldots, f$) describes the corresponding degrees of freedom of the system. Using D'Alembert's principle of virtual work, Lagrange had derived new equations for such systems. The new Lagrange equations read:

$$\frac{\partial A}{\partial q_\alpha} = \frac{\partial L}{\partial q_\alpha} - \frac{d}{dt}\left(\frac{\partial L}{\partial \dot{q}_\alpha}\right) = 0 \qquad (\alpha = 1, \ldots, f). \tag{6.3}$$

Here $\dot{q}_\alpha$ are the generalized velocities, i.e. the derivatives of the generalized coordinates with respect to the time t ($\dot{q}_\alpha = dq_\alpha/dt$), and L is the so-called Lagrangian of the system. It is a function of the generalized velocities, generalized coordinates, and possibly of the time; and is given by $L = L(\dot{q}, q, t) = T - U$, the difference between the kinetic and potential energy of the system. The expression $\partial A/\partial q_\alpha$ in equation (6.3) is called the variational derivative of the action functional.

Lagrange's equations have the same form as Euler's and, therefore, they are often referred to as the Euler–Lagrange equations. But their meaning is completely different. These are dynamical equations, completely equivalent to those of Newton in the case of a system without constraints, and they allow one to solve any mechanical problem, if the forces acting upon the system are conservative, in the most economical way. The other significant property of these equations is their invariance under arbitrary coordinate transformations. Therefore they have got an extremely large number of applications in different mechanical problems and also, after corresponding generalization, in field theory.

Lagrange himself did not derive his equations from a variational principle. This was done by William Rowan Hamilton, who gave us the modern form of the principle of least action, the so-called Hamilton's principle of least action. Hamilton's main achievement in this field was that he was able to avoid the *isoenergetic* restriction on the paths in the variational principle. He proved that Euler–Lagrange equations may be derived from the principle of least action (equation (6.1)) without any constraints on the virtual paths in the configuration space of the system, where the action functional may be written as

$$A[q(t)] = \int_{t_1}^{t_2} L(\dot{q}, q, t)\, dt. \tag{6.4}$$

Here t_1 and t_2 are the initial and the final instants of time and L is the Lagrangian of the given system.

Hamilton's variational principle gives us a new viewpoint on dynamics. One may consider the initial point in configuration space of the system, given by the coordinates $q_\alpha(t_1)$ $(\alpha = 1, \ldots, f)$, and the final point, given by

$$q_\alpha(t_2) \ (\alpha = 1, \ldots, f).$$

One may connect these two points with all possible paths in this space. These are just the so-called virtual paths. Then there arises the question: Which one of these paths will be the real path of actual motion of the given system? The answer is: The path which makes Hamilton's action stationary or, in other words, the path which obeys the Hamiltonian variational principle. This path is the solution of the Euler–Lagrange equations.

The final form of the principle of least action is extremely general and finds a fundamental place in a large number of physical theories. Moreover, Hamilton's principle changed the style of doing calculations in theoretical physics. All modern field theories, like classical and quantum electrodynamics, theory of gravitation, quantum chromodynamics, theory of electroweak interactions, and theories of supergravity and superstrings, were derived from the corresponding straightforward generalization of Hamilton's principle for systems with infinitely many degrees of freedom. Today the principal problem of every new fundamental theory is how to find the corresponding Lagrangian. This principle is very useful also for calculations in many practical problems.

Thus we see that Hamilton's principle of least action looks like a fundamental law of nature and there exists the great fundamental question as to what lies behind this principle, what its meaning is, and what makes its large number of applications possible. The physicists before P.A.M. Dirac and Richard Feynman were not able to answer this question, because the principle of least action is perhaps the most basic principle of classical physics, *but its full significance lies in quantum physics; one can find it only in Feynman's path-integral formulation of quantum mechanics.*

6.4 Feynman's simple 'toy' models

After the first step of Feynman's program for the resolution of the difficulties of quantum electrodynamics at MIT had been realized in collaboration with John Archibald Wheeler, the main problem was the quantization of the Wheeler–Feynman action-at-a-distance theory. In the fall of 1941, John Wheeler was still trying to solve this problem by making use of a trick of Dirac's. His idea was to replace the 'difficult' term, $(-da_\mu da^\mu)^{1/2}$, in the action functional of the action-at-a-distance theory with the linear term $\gamma_\mu da^\mu$, where γ_μ are the Dirac matrices. Therefore Wheeler advised Feynman not to bother to work on the problem of the quantization of the action-at-a-distance theory, since Wheeler thought that he already knew the solution. But since Feynman did not know what Wheeler had in mind, he still had to find it out for himself.[1] So, although Feynman had discovered the new extremely productive general method for quantization of classical systems, because of the complexities of the Wheeler–Feynman classical theory of electromagnetic interactions he first considered simple 'toy' models and sought to work out the quantum mechanics of these toy models. Feynman's idea was to 'put the essential in, but keep everything else simple'.[1]

Since the fall of 1939, when Richard Feynman went to Princeton as a graduate student, he had been assigned to work as John Wheeler's assistant. However, with the beginning of the new fall semester in 1941, Feynman received the award of a Charlotte Elizabeth Procter Fellowship open 'only to unmarried men who are in their terminal year' of graduate studies at Princeton University. 'Then I started to work on my thesis very seriously. The problem was, of course, to make a quantum theory of the classical action-at-a-distance electrodynamics, and the form I preferred to express it in was the principle of least action, involving particles only, no field, and in which the interaction occurred at two different times. It wasn't just the velocities that were involved, but coordinates at a certain time and velocity. There was no Hamiltonian for the system, and none of the standard things that you have to convert by the standard method to quantum mechanics—the Hamiltonian, the momentum operators, etc., were not there. There was no momentum operator, because the action was of a new form. It was a direct attempt to get quantum electrodynamics. I had a classical theory with an action, but not with the Hamiltonian, and the problem was how to go to a reasonable quantum analog? The standard method of going to quantum mechanics from classical mechanics assumed that there was a Hamiltonian, but in this form there wasn't. If I had expressed it in terms of fields there might have been, but I was most reluctant to do that, and I insisted upon representing only the particles. In fact, it was because I wished to get rid of the infinite degrees of freedom of the field. I had a principle of least action involving only the particles, with delayed interaction, just the way I wanted it. This was my MIT program all over again, and it was completely satisfying: to make a classical theory with action at a distance, with delays in the interaction. The only thing that had changed since MIT was that now I had delayed as well as advanced interactions, but only the coordinates of the particles were mentioned in the fundamental law, which was the principle of least action. My first step from MIT, to fix the classical theory, had been done; now I had to go on to the quantum theory.

'Since Wheeler was fiddling around to write the paper and had told me that I should not worry about the quantum part because he "already had solved it", I had a free hand. All through that year he had been having troubles with it, and I decided that I would try to find out how the quantum theory of action-at-a-distance works by myself, since he (Wheeler) had never shown me how it worked.'[1,3]

The first thing Feynman did was to consider a toy model with a particle of mass m and one degree of freedom, described by the coordinate x, which moves in a potential $V(x)$, and interacts with itself in a distant mirror by means of retarded and advanced waves. The time it takes for light to reach the mirror from the particle is assumed to be constant, and equal to $\frac{1}{2}T_0$. The action functional of this system can be written as

$$A[x(t)] = \int_{-\infty}^{\infty} \{\tfrac{1}{2}m[\dot{x}(t)]^2 - V[x(t)] + k^2\dot{x}(t)\dot{x}(t+T_0)\}\, dt, \qquad (6.5)$$

where k depends on the charge of the particle and its distance from the mirror. One can easily check in this problem that the quantity

$$E(t) = \tfrac{1}{2}m[\dot{x}(t)]^2 + V[x(t)] + k^2\dot{x}(t)\dot{x}(t+T_0) - \int_{t}^{t+T_0} \dddot{x}(t-T_0)\ddot{x}(t+T_0)\, dt \quad (6.6)$$

is conserved. The first two terms on the right-hand side represent the kinetic plus potential energy, $V(x)$, of the particle, and depend only on the state of the particle at a given moment t. But the additional terms, representing the energy of the self-interaction of the particle via the mirror, require one to know the motion of the particle for each moment from time $t-T_0$ to $t+T_0$.

'Can we really talk about conservation, when the quantity conserved depends on the path of the particles over considerable ranges of time?' asked Feynman.[17] Many quantities, which are constants may be devised, but we should not be inclined to say that they actually represent quantities of interest, in spite of their constancy. 'The conservation of a physical quantity is of considerable interest because in solving problems it permits us to forget a great number of details. The conservation of energy can be derived from the laws of motion, but its value lies in the fact that the use of it in certain broad aspects of a problem may be discussed, without going into the great detail that is often required by direct use of laws of motion.'[17]

This remark shows how Feynman had to master the mathematical treatment of physical problems. The problem why the same conserved quantity occurs in different domains has not been resolved completely up to now. In his doctoral thesis Feynman sketched the original solution of this problem, which seems to have been ignored later. He proposed that one should 'require two things if a quantity $I(t)$ is to attract our attention as being dynamically important. The first is that it be conserved, $I(t_1) = I(t_2)$. The second is that $I(t)$ should depend only locally on the path. This is to say, if one changes the path at some time t' in a certain (arbitrary) way, the change which is made in $I(t)$ should decrease to zero as t' gets further and further from t.'[18] The expression for the energy $E(t)$, written above, satisfies this condition.

Feynman considered a completely general procedure for deriving first integrals from the action functional of a given system. This procedure was based on a deep relationship between symmetries and conservation laws, which had been first realized by Emmy Noether.[19] This fundamental result showed that a conservation law corresponds to any continuous group of symmetries of the action functional of the system under consideration. For example, the law of the conservation of energy corresponds to the invariance of the action functional under time translations, conservation of the full linear momentum of the system is a consequence of the invariance of the action functional under space translations, and the conservation of the angular momentum is a consequence of the invariance under space rotations. Thus, the so-called Noether's theorem relates the fundamental conservation laws with the properties of space and time, and gives us a method of calculating the corresponding conserved quantities from the action functional.

Feynman used a similar approach to conservation laws, but he derived his own formulas for the conserved quantities, which differed from Emmy Noether's. His approach to this problem was a more general one, because he did not use the special property of the classical Lagrangian to be a function of the generalized coordinates and generalized velocities only. Feynman's approach could be used in the theories with advanced and retarded interactions, where Noether's theorem does not work without proper modifications. Feynman 'proved a thing called Noether's theorem, not knowing that it was known.'[1]

The second toy model in Feynman's dissertation described two one-dimensional particles interacting with a one-dimensional harmonic oscillator. This example is quite instructive for action-at-a-distance electrodynamics. First, Feynman supposed that he had 'two particles A and B which do not interact directly with each other, but there is the harmonic oscillator, with which both particles A and B interact. The harmonic oscillator, therefore serves as an intermediary by means of which particle A is influenced by the motion of particle B and vice versa. In what way is this interaction through the intermediate oscillator equivalent to a direct interaction between the particles A and B, and can the motion of these particles be expressed by means of a principle of least action, not involving the oscillator? (In the theory of electrodynamics this is the problem as to whether the interaction of particles through the intermediary of the field oscillators can also be expressed as a direct action at a distance.)'[20] The corresponding action functional is

$$A[x(t), y(t), z(t)] = \int [L_y + L_z + \tfrac{1}{2}(m\dot{x}^2 - m\omega^2 x^2) + (I_y + I_z)x]\, dt, \quad (6.7)$$

where $\tfrac{1}{2}(m\dot{x}^2 - m\omega^2 x^2)$ is the Lagrangian of the harmonic oscillator with a coordinate x, mass m, and frequency ω; L_y and L_z are the Lagrangians of the particles (their concrete form is not essential for the following consideration); and the last term $(I_y + I_z)x$ is the Lagrangian of the interaction between the oscillator and the particles. The coordinates y and z refer to the particles A and B, respectively. The function I_y depends on the coordinates y of atom A alone, and the function I_z on the coordinate z of atom B. Then the Lagrangian equation of motion reads

$$m\ddot{x} + m\omega^2 x = I_y(t) \mid I_z(t) = Y(t). \qquad (6.8)$$

In what way is this interaction through the intermediate oscillator equivalent to direct action between the particles A and B, and how can the motion of these particles be expressed by means of a principle of least action, not involving the oscillator? Because of its linearity, one can solve the equation of the oscillator, equation (6.8), with the arbitrary right-hand side $Y(t)$. After the oscillator equation has been solved, one can substitute the solution $x(t)$ in the equation of motion of the atoms A and B and thus eliminate the intermediate oscillator. But there exist infinitely many solutions of this type of inhomogeneous equation. Feynman showed that the proper choice of the initial conditions of the oscillator is needed to ensure energy conservation for the rest of the system after the elimination of the oscillator. For this purpose, Feynman's generalization of Noether's theorem was needed.

The next step was extremely important for all subsequent investigations of action-at-a-distance theories. We wish to derive the new equations of motion of atoms A and B from a principle of least action with a new functional which does not include the oscillator degree of freedom. The new action functional must depend only on the coordinates y and z of each of the atoms A and B. Feynman showed that it is possible to find such a new action functional only if one chooses a definitely determined solution of the oscillator equation, a symmetric one which included one-half advanced and one-half retarded interaction between the atoms A and B. This new functional reads

$$A[y(t), z(t)] = \int_{-\infty}^{\infty} (L_y + L_z)\, dt$$

$$+ \frac{1}{2m\omega} \int_{-\infty}^{\infty} \int_{-\infty}^{t} \sin \omega(t - s) Y(t) Y(s)\, ds\, dt. \qquad (6.9)$$

Feynman's main result was that one could actually completely eliminate the oscillator degree of freedom of the initial system, and thus reduce all effects of the presence of the oscillator in an action-at-a-distance between the atoms A and B of quite specific nature, namely including in equal proportion advanced and retarded interactions. Exactly the same result had been shown to take place in the Wheeler–Feynman classical time-symmetric electrodynamics.

6.5 Feynman's invention of the new method for the quantization of classical systems

Bearing in mind that in the action-at-a-distance theories 'we are faced with the circumstance that the equations of motion of the particles are expressed classically as a consequence of a principle of least action and cannot, it appears, be expressed in Hamiltonian form',[11] Feynman concluded that we need 'a formulation of quantum mechanics . . . which does not require the idea of a Hamiltonian or momentum operator for its expression. It has, as a central mathematical idea, the analog of the action integral of classical mechanics.'[21]

In the spring of 1941, Feynman was already actively looking for a new approach to quantum mechanics directly from the classical Lagrangian. One day, when he was struggling with this problem, he went to a beer party in the Nassau tavern in Princeton. There he met Professor Herbert Jehle, who had recently arrived from Europe. He sat down near Feynman and together they began to talk about various scientific problems. Feynman asked him if he knew any way of doing quantum mechanics starting with the action, or where the action integral came into quantum mechanics. Jehle said that he did not, but told him of a paper by Dirac in which the Lagrangian, at least, came into quantum mechanics.[22]

Next day Jehle and Feynman went to the Princeton Library, and Jehle showed him Dirac's paper,[23] and they studied it together. The paper began with the words: 'Quantum mechanics was built upon a foundation of analogy with the Hamiltonian theory of classical mechanics. This is because the classical notion of canonical coordinates and momenta was found to be one with a very simple quantum analogue, . . .

'Now there is an alternative formulation for classical dynamics, provided by the Lagrangian. This requires one to work in terms of coordinates and velocities instead of coordinates and momenta. The two formulations are, of course, closely related, but there are reasons for believing that the Lagrangian one is the more fundamental.

'In the first place the Lagrangian method allows one to collect together all the equations of motion and express them as the stationary property of a certain action function. (This action function is just the time integral of the Lagrangian.) There is no corresponding action principle in terms of the coordinates and momenta of the Hamiltonian theory. [This last statement is not true, but this mistake has no bearing upon what follows.] Secondly, the

Lagrangian method can easily be expressed relativistically, on account of the action function being a relativistic invariant; while the Hamiltonian method is essentially nonrelativistic in form, since it marks out a particular time variable as the canonical conjugate of the Hamiltonian function.

'For these reasons it would seem desirable to take up the question of what corresponds in the quantum theory to the Lagrangian method in classical theory.'[23]

This was exactly what Feynman was looking for. Dirac then said that in quantum mechanics there exists a quantity which describes the time evolution of the wave function $\psi(x)$. This quantity carries the wave function $\psi(x_1)$ at a time t_1 to the wave function $\psi(x_2)$ at time t_2. Dirac called this quantity $(x_{t_2}|x_{t_1})$, but later Feynman preferred to denote it as $K(x_2, t_2; x_1, t_1)$ and we will follow Feynman's notation. Dirac pointed out that this function K is '*analogous*' to $\exp[(i/\hbar)S]$, where $S = S(x_2, t_2; x_1, t_1)$ is the classical action, as a function of the intial coordinate x_1, at the initial instant of time t_1, and the corresponding final coordinate x_2 and instant t_2. This function S was first introduced by Hamilton and carries the coordinate x_1 of the classical particle at the instant t_1 to the coordinate x_2 at the instant t_2, describing the classical evolution as a canonical transformation developing in time. The function S is called Hamilton's principal function and may be obtained by calculating the classical action functional on the real classical path from the point with the coordinate x_1 at instant t_1 to the point with the coordinate x_2 at instant t_2. Hence,

$$S = S(x_2, t_2; x_1, t_1) = \int_{t_1}^{t_2} L[x(t), x(t), t] \, dt, \qquad (6.10)$$

where $x(t)$ describes the classical path of the mechanical system. Dirac also said that for an infinitesimally small time difference ε, when the initial time instant is t and the final time instant is $t + \varepsilon$, the quantum quantity $K(X, t+\varepsilon; x, t)$, x being the initial coordinate and X being the final one, is *analogous* to $\exp[(i/\hbar)\varepsilon L(X, t+\varepsilon; x, t)]$. Here one must consider the classical Lagrangian not as a function of the coordinate x and velocity v at time t but as a function of the initial coordinate x at initial time t and final corresponding coordinate X and time $t + \varepsilon$.

As Feynman read this in Dirac's paper, he asked Herbert Jehle what Dirac meant by 'analogous': did he mean that they were equal? Jehle thought not, but Feynman decided to see what happened if they were made equal.

So Feynman tried to put them equal to each other in the simplest example with the Lagrangian $L = \frac{1}{2}m\dot{x}^2 - V(x)$, and he very soon found out that they were not equal but proportional, if one chose a suitable constant of proportionality, $A = (2\pi i\hbar\varepsilon/m)^{1/2}$. By doing this, Feynman obtained the result

$$\psi(X, t+\varepsilon) = \int \exp[(i/\hbar)\varepsilon L(X, t+\varepsilon; x, t)]\psi(x, t) \frac{dx}{A}, \qquad (6.11)$$

and just calculated the integral by means of the Taylor series expansion, thus working out the Schrödinger equation

$$\left(-\frac{\hbar^2}{2m}\frac{\partial^2}{dx^2} + V(x)\right)\psi(x, t) = i\hbar\frac{\partial}{\partial t}\psi(x, t). \tag{6.12}$$

Feynman turned to Jehle, who did not quite follow, and told him that Dirac meant that they were proportional. Herbert Jehle had taken out a little notebook and was rapidly copying it down from the blackboard, and said, 'No, no, this is an important discovery. You Americans are always trying to find out how something can be used. That's a good way to discover things!'[22]

In the fall of 1946, Princeton University was celebrating its bicentennial, on the occasion of which numerous festivities, including various series of lectures were organized. In one of these sessions, devoted to science and organized by Eugene Wigner, Feynman was invited to introduce Dirac and, after his lecture, comment upon it. 'It was like the ward-heeler of the 54th district (in New York City) introducing the president of the United States. Dirac sent me his paper, in his own handwriting, to read and I had to comment on it. After Dirac's lecture, I made my comments; I tried to simplify Dirac's very technical talk for the benefit of high school teachers and others who were not familiar with the things that Dirac had talked about. But the other physicists, like Bohr and Weisskopf, who were there did not give a damn about these other people, and they criticized my attempt to 'explain Dirac' in my simplified way. After I had made my criticism, people were standing around and discussing Dirac's paper, and I looked through the window and saw that Dirac was lying on the lawn outside looking up in the sky. I had never really sat and talked to him before then. But there was this question which I very much wanted to ask him, so I walked up to him and said: 'Professor Dirac, you wrote in a paper[23] in which you talk about the analogy between exp $(i\varepsilon L)$ and the difference between two points. He said, "yes." I said, "Did you know that they are not just analogous, they are equal or rather proportional." He said, "Are they?" I said, "Yes." "Oh, that's interesting," was his comment. I wanted to know whether I had discovered something or not, but he had never sat down to find out whether they were equal or proportional. He just said, "No, I didn't know, are they? That's interesting!" That was the first time I talked to him personally.'[1]

In his paper Dirac was not able to complete this line of his investigations on quantum mechanics because his point of view was based on the opinion that the correspondence between the function K and the exponent of the classical action function is only an approximate semiclassical relation. From the very beginning of relativistic quantum mechanics it had been recognized that the expression $\exp[(i/\hbar)S]$ gave the semiclassical approximation to the exact quantum wave function. Therefore Dirac was looking for a proper and exact quantum analog of Hamilton's principal function S, and he found relations between the corresponding exact quantum Hamiltonian wave function and other quantum operators. Another step in this direction was taken by Edmund Whittaker.[24] Up to then this approach seems to have been quite formal and did not lead to any essentially new results. Hence, the crucial formal step to Feynman's new method was to look at the limit when ε goes to zero. In this limit one reaches an exact result for infinitesimal times.

Thus Feynman found the relation between the Lagrangian and quantum mechanics, which was an important result of his dissertation, but still for infinitesimal times. Several days later, when he was lying in bed, he worked out the next fundamental step. Feynman described it as follows: '. . . I'm lying in bed—I can still see the bed. And I can't sleep too well. And the bed was next to the wall. I got my feet up against the wall, leaning my head off on one side of the bed. You know that kind of stuff. And I'm picturing this thing and I'm putting more and more lengthy times, I have to do this again and again, and so I've got this exponential iL times again, times again, integrate it, integrate it. But the product of all the exponentials is the exponential of the sum of the L's, which is the action. So I go, AAAAAHHHHH, and I jumped, "That's the action!" That was a moment of discovery!'[1]

Now Feynman was able, by using N times the formula (6.11), to obtain exactly the right result for the function $K(X, T; x, t)$. He had to construct the expression

$$\int \cdots \int \exp\left((i/h) \sum_{i=0}^{N-1} L[(x_{i+1}-x_i)/(t_{i+1}-t_i), x_{i+1}](t_{i+1}-t_i)\right) \frac{dx_N}{A_N} \cdots \frac{dx_1}{A_1},$$

(6.13)

where $t=0, t_1, t_2, \ldots, t_{N-1}, t_N = T$ are certain instants of time, which divide the time interval from the initial instant t to the final instant T into a large number of small intervals from t_1 to t_{i+1} of duration ε ($i = 1, 2, \ldots, N$), such that $t_i = t + i\varepsilon$. Then, in the limit when ε goes to zero, we reach the exact quantum function K. In this limit, the expression in the exponent in equation (6.13) resembles Riemann's integral for the classical action functional:

$$A = \lim_{\varepsilon \to 0} \left(\sum_{i=0}^{N-1} L[(x_{i+1}-x_i)/(t_{i+1}-t_i), x_{i+1}](t_{i+1}-t_i) \right). \quad (6.14)$$

Feynman's conclusion was that equation (6.11) 'is equivalent to Schrödinger's differential equation for the wave function ψ. Thus, given a classical system described by a Lagrangian, which is a function of velocities and coordinates only, a quantum mechanical description of an analogous system may be written down directly, without working out a Hamiltonian.'[25]

This approach thus promised to solve the main problem, which Feynman was trying to attack in his thesis: that is, the quantization of a classical system without knowing its Hamiltonian. In addition, it turned out that he obtained a new general procedure of quantization for classical systems.† The physical meaning of expression (6.13) and the meaning of the underlying limiting procedure was treated six years later in Feynman's paper on the 'Space–time approach to non-relativistic quantum mechanics' in the *Reviews of Modern Physics.*[28]

6.6 Further development of Feynman's results in his thesis

In his Ph.D. thesis Feynman did not develop further the physical interpretation of his new method; rather he greatly developed its mathematical formalism.

First of all, he derived a new method of calculation of quantum averages. From this, Feynman derived the generalization of Ehrenfest's theorem, which says that in quantum mechanics the classical equations of motion are fulfilled by the average values of the quantum quantities. In particular, Feynman arrived at the classical Euler–Lagrange equations (6.13) and the classical Newtonian equations in the form of quantum averages. But the most unexpected result was the fact that Feynman's relation for quantum averages is fundamental, in that 'when compared to corresponding expressions in the usual form of quantum mechanics, it contains, . . ., in one equation, both the equations of motion and commutation rules for **p** and **q**.'[29] Thus Feynman actually invented a completely new formulation of quantum mechanics in terms of classical notions.

Then, keeping in mind his main point, i.e. the quantization of action-at-a-distance theories, Feynman investigated a proper generalization of the new formalism for the case when classical action is a functional of a more general type than equation (6.4). He assumed the action to be, for example, like the action of the particle in an external potential U which interacts with itself through a distant mirror, as in equation (6.5), or like the action functional in

---

† The quantization procedure is the rule which gives the quantum Hamiltonian for a given classical system. In the so-called canonical quantization procedure, one takes the classical Hamiltonian $H(p, q, t)$ and substitutes the classical coordinates and momenta in this function by means of the corresponding quantum operators. This leads to the quantum Hamiltonian $\mathbf{H} = H(\mathbf{p}, \mathbf{q}, t)$, which one can use in the Schrödinger equation. But this procedure is quite ambiguous, as Schrödinger himself mentioned in his early work on wave mechanics, because the result depends on the ordering of the noncommuting quantum operators **p** and **q** in the classical Hamiltonian, and there exist, in addition, certain ambiguities of other kind.[26] Feynman's new quantization procedure looks very attractive, because 'the form of Schrödinger equation which will be arrived at will be definite and will not suffer from the type of ambiguity one finds if one tries to substitute $(\hbar/i)\partial/\partial q$ for p in the classical Hamiltonian.'[25] Unfortunately, this belief of Feynman's was not justified, and the same ambiguity presents itself in his method, as Feynman himself showed later.[27]

equation (6.9) for two particles interacting through an intermediate oscillator after the latter's degree of freedom has been eliminated.

However, there also appeared some additional difficulties of principle, a few of which Feynman overcame in his thesis, but some others remain unsolved even to this day. One such problem was the nonexistence of the wave function for action-at-a-distance theories, which Feynman succeeded in establishing. He proposed to take the viewpoint that 'the wave function is just a mathematical construction, useful under certain particular conditions to analyze the problem presented by the more generalized quantum mechanical equations . . . but not more generally applicable. It is not unreasonable that it should be impossible to find a quantity like a wave function, which has the property of describing the state of the system at one moment, and from which the state at other moments may be derived. In more complicated mechanical systems . . . the state of motion of a system at a particular time is not enough to determine in a simple manner the way that the system will change in time. It is also necessary to know the behavior of the system at other times; information which a wave function is not designed to furnish. An interesting, and at present unsolved, question whether there exists a quantity analogous to a wave function for these more general systems. . . .

'Quantum mechanics can be worked out entirely without a wave function, by speaking of matrices and expectation values only. In practice, however, the wave function is a great convenience, and dominates most of our thought in quantum mechanics.'[30]

Feynman developed the new procedure to calculate expectation values of the physical quantities, which gives the known results in the usual cases. But he was not able to prove that in theories of the action-at-a-distance type his formulas give real values for physical quantities. Later on, in a letter to C. Kelber, Feynman wrote: 'In the thesis I was trying to generalize the ideas to apply to any action function at all—not just the integral of a function of velocities and position . . . [Feynman means the Lagrangian] I met with a difficulty. An arbitrary action functional S produces results which do not conserve probability; for example, the energy values come out complex. I do not know what this means nor was I able to find that class of functionals which would be guaranteed to give real values for the energies.'[31] This was the reason why Feynman never published this part of his thesis.

In the last section of his Ph.D. thesis Feynman discussed the quantum problem of two atoms A and B, each of which interacts with an oscillator, which we have discussed earlier (see Section 6.4). '. . . To what extent can the motion of the oscillator be disregarded and atoms be considered as interacting directly?' Feynman noted that 'this problem has been solved in a special case by Fermi,[32] who has shown that the oscillators of the electromagnetic field which represent longitudinal waves could be eliminated from the Hamiltonian, provided an additional term be added representing instantaneous Coulomb interactions between particles. . . .

'. . . Drawing on the classical analogue we shall expect that the system with the oscillator is not equivalent to the system without the oscillator for all possible motions of the oscillator, but only for those for which some property (i.e. the initial and final position) of the oscillator is fixed. These properties, in the cases discussed, are not properties of the system at just one time, so we will not expect to find the equivalence simply by specifying the state of the oscillator at a certain time, by means of a particular wave function. *It is just for this reason that the ordinary methods of quantum mechanics do not suffice to solve this problem.*' [33]

By direct calculation of the expectation values of the system of particles Feynman derived the same effective active functional (equation (6.9)) as the action functional when one eliminates the oscillator at the classical level. The final result of this investigation of Feynman's, i.e. the particles interacting through an intermediate oscillator, was that at the quantum level, just as for the classical level, one can eliminate the oscillator and describe the particles as interacting at a distance, by using an action of the type given in equation (6.9).

In his concluding remarks Feynman mentioned that 'the problem of the form that relativistic quantum mechanics, and the Dirac equation, take from this point of view, remains unsolved. Attempts to substitute, for the action, the classical relativistic form (integral of proper time) have met with difficulties associated with the fact that the square root involved becomes imaginary for certain values of the coordinates over which the action is integrated.'

Feynman reiterated the fact that 'the final test of any theory lies, of course, in experiment. No comparison to experiment has been made in [this] paper. The author hopes to apply these methods in quantum electrodynamics. It is only out of some such direct application that an experimental comparison can be made.' [34]

As Feynman found later, 'it turned out there still remained difficulties, and the thing was not satisfactory, but I didn't realize it at the time in my excitement though, of course, I had solved the difficulties I had previously seen. But it was only a temporary error, for I thought that everything was all right and I wrote up the thesis. The parts that are right, of course, are still a representation of quantum mechanics without delay and so on. But the generalizations that are contained in the thesis are probably erroneous as written.' [1]

This was the situation in the spring of 1942 when Feynman wrote up his dissertation at the strong urging of John Wheeler. At that time Wheeler was working on the first atomic pile with Fermi in Chicago, and he wrote a letter to Feynman in which he told him that he (Feynman) 'had done enough for a thesis', and Wheeler urged him 'very strongly to write up what you have in the remaining weeks before you get into the situation in which I now find myself.' [35]

Feynman had worked on the OSRD atomic bomb project at Princeton from December 1941 to March 1942. Then, in April 1942 the Manhattan

Project was established, and Feynman continued working for it, and upon graduation after completing his thesis he went back to doing war-related research. The commencement took place around the middle of June and Feynman received his Ph.D. degree. It was a regular commencement, with academic gowns and all the hoopla of graduation from Princeton. His parents came to attend the commencement from Far Rockaway, New York, and were very proud of him.

Also, soon after commencement, on 29 June 1942, Richard Feynman and Arline Greenbaum were married.

Notes and References

1. R.P. Feynman, Interviews and conversations with Jagdish Mehra, in Austin, Texas, April 1970, and Pasadena, California, January 1988.

2. R.P. Feynman, M. Sands, and R.B. Leighton, *The Feynman lectures on physics.* Addison-Wesley, Reading, Massachusetts, 1963.

3. R.P. Feynman, Interviews with Charles Weiner (American Institute of Physics), in Pasadena, California, 1966.

4. R.P. Feynman, *SYJMF*, p. 100.

5. R.P. Feynman, Los Alamos from below, *Engineering and Science*, January/February 1976, p. 12.

6. R.P. Feynman, The development of the space-time view of quantum electrodynamics, Nobel Lecture, 11 December 1965. *Science* **153**, 699 (1966), p.1.

7. E. Fermi, *Rev. Mod. Phys.* **4**, 87 (1932).

8. R.P. Feynman, Ref. 6, p. 2.

9. R.P. Feynman, The principle of least action in quantum mechanics. A dissertation presented to the faculty of Princeton University in candidacy for the degree of Doctor of Philosophy, May 1942, p. 1.

10. R.P. Feynman, Ref. 9, pp. 4–5.

11. R.P. Feynman, Ref. 9, p. 5.

12. E. Whittaker, *A treatise on analytical dynamics of particles and rigid bodies.* Cambridge University Press, 1927, 1944, p. 245.

13. R.P. Feynman, Ref. 9, p. 8.

14. W. Yourgrau and S. Mandelstam, *Variational principles in dynamics and quantum theory.* Dover, New York, 1968, p. 5.

15. L. Euler, *Methodus inveniendi lineas curves maximi minimive proprietate*

quadentes, additamentum II, Opera Omnia, Series I, Vol. 24 (ed. C. Carathéodory) 1952, LII–LV, 298–308.

16. S.D. Poisson, *Traité de mécanique*, Vol. 1, Paris, 1811.

17. R.P. Feynman, Ref. 9, pp. 13–14.

18. R.P. Feynman, Ref. 9, p. 14.

19. E. Noether, Invariante Variationsproblem, *Nach. König. Gesellsch. Göttingen, math.-phys. K1.* **2**, 235 (1918).

20. R.P. Feynman, Ref. 9, pp. 18–19.

21. Ref. 9, p. 28.

22. R.P. Feynman, Ref. 6, p. 5.

23. P.A.M. Dirac, The Lagrangian in quantum mechanics. *Phys. Z. Sowjetunion* **3**(1), 64 (1933).

24. E. Whittaker, On Hamilton's principal function in quantum mechanics, *Proc. R. Soc. Edinb. A* **LXI**, 1940/41.

25. R.P. Feynman, Ref. 9, p. 34.

26. E. Schrödinger, *Ann. Phys. (Leipzig)* **79**, 734 (1926).

27. R.P. Feynman, Ref. 26, p. 377.

28. R.P. Feynman, Space–time approach to non-relativistic quantum mechanics, *Rev. Mod. Phys.* **20**, 376 (1948).

29. R.P. Feynman, Ref. 9, p. 38.

30. R.P. Feynman, Ref. 9, p. 49.

31. R.P. Feynman, Letter to C. Kelber, 21 February 1949, Feynman Archive, Caltech.

32. E. Fermi, *Rev. Mod. Phys.* **4**, 131 (1932).

33. R.P. Feynman, Ref. 9, p. 66.

34. R.P. Feynman, Ref. 9, p. 74.

35. J.A. Wheeler, Letter to R.P. Feynman, 26 March 1942, Feynman Archive, Caltech.

7

Arline: 'A love like no other I know of'

Richard Feynman had met Arline Greenbaum when he was thirteen or fourteen years old. After that, they sort of grew up together and exchanged ideas constantly. Richard's scientific attitude influenced Arline, and the fact that she was gentle, soft, and feminine, apart from being artistic, deeply influenced Richard. Ordinarily, Richard was not interested in these softer and gentler things, but 'with the love that was developing between us', he paid great attention to these matters.[1] 'As a result of this relationship and listening to her, I became a better person.'[1,2] Arline used to play the piano and paint in watercolors. Richard and Arline developed their views of looking at the world together.

In contrast with the view often expressed that science was dull, hard, and cold, Feynman believed from the beginning that if science were used correctly it would give one a way of looking at the world and at the meaning of things that happen to one, and give one control and calmness in situations that would be difficult otherwise. This was the kind of attitude that both Richard and Arline tried to cultivate.

By the time they were in high school, Richard and Arline had fallen deeply in love. Their respective families had gotten to know each other well, and Richard and Arline began to affect each other's development. Arline had grown up in a family which was polite and sensitive to the feelings of others, and she tried to teach Richard to be sensitive towards others also. On the other hand, in her family little white lies in delicate matters were considered OK, while Richard thought that one had to be completely truthful with oneself and with others. His attitude was more like, 'What do *you* care what other people think?'[3] Arline would remind him of it time and again during the few years of their life together. Richard believed that 'one should listen to other people's opinions and take them into account. Then, if they don't make sense and we think they're wrong, then that's that,' and from there the next step was: 'What do *you* care what other people think?' Arline at once caught on to the idea of absolute candor and honesty in their relationship. 'It worked very well, and we became very much in love—a love like no other love I know of.'[4]

After the summer of 1935 Richard went to MIT. There he would receive letters from friends back home, telling him things like who Arline was dating, and what she was doing. Since Richard was also dating girls at MIT, it didn't bother him to learn that Arline went out, too. He and Arline had a deep understanding about how they were bound to each other, and no one else could take the place of one or the other.

During summers Feynman would return to Far Rockaway and live at home. The exceptions were the summers of 1938 and 1939. In the summer of 1938, Feynman worked as the chief chemist at the Metaplast Corporation, the metal-coating-of-plastics business of his friend Bernie Walker. Upon graduation in June 1939, he found a job at MIT itself, making measurements of friction for the Chrysler Corporation. During that summer Arline found a job in Scituate, about twenty miles away from Cambridge, taking care of children, so as to be close to Richard. Melville, Richard's father, became concerned that Richard would get too involved with Arline, and talked her out of taking that job. Richard was therefore able to see Arline only a few times that summer, but before he left to go to Princeton they became engaged and promised to marry each other upon the completion of his graduate studies.

As he had done at MIT, Richard would go home in vacations to see Arline. On one such occasion, he learned that she had developed a growth on one side of her neck. She was a beautiful girl and, although the growth was not painful, it bothered her. She had an uncle, who was a doctor, and she consulted him; he told her to massage the growth with 'Omega Oil', a catch-all popular remedy of the day for bites and rashes.

After some time the bump began to change and Arline developed a fever. The fever got worse and the family doctor put her in the hospital, suspecting it to be typhoid, and she was put in quarantine. Richard read up on the typhoid fever in the medical library at Princeton, and learned that the decisive test for typhoid, the Widal test, had just come out. He asked the doctor whether this test had been done, and was assured that the test was negative; she did not have typhoid fever. The doctor complained to Arline's parents that Richard was interfering in the treatment. They became very angry with him; they said that he was only her fiancé, but as parents she was their responsibility and he should not interfere with the doctor. Within a few weeks the swelling went down and the fever went away.

After a while the swelling reappeared, and another doctor was consulted. Now she had a swelling of the lymphatic glands. It could either be tuberculosis of the lymphatic glands or one of the more malignant tumors, such as Hodgkin's disease. The doctors did not know what it was. Richard read up on all the lymphatic diseases in medical texts, and concluded that she probably had a fatal disease. But the doctor and the family insisted that she should not be told that; she should be told only that she had 'glandular fever', and made Richard promise not to tell her that she had something more serious or fatal.

In view of the fact that Richard and Arline had promised to be absolutely honest with each other, it put a great strain upon him to withhold from her the information that she might be suffering from a fatal disease. Everybody told her that she only had glandular fever and she was going to be all right. Once, quite accidentally, Arline heard her mother sobbing downstairs in the living room, and, when she asked Richard what the matter was, he told her a lie that, yes, she had glandular fever. She was immediately relieved. Thereafter, Richard wrote her a letter giving the exact details of how he had been prevailed upon to lie to her. However, Arline did find out that her condition was more serious, and she asked Richard directly: 'Do I have glandular fever or Hodgkin's disease?' This time he told her that she had Hodgkin's disease and it was fatal. She realized that her family and the doctors must have exerted tremendous pressure on him to lie to her, and she asked him not to do such a thing again.

Arline was in and out of hospitals all the time. Sometimes she would feel better for a few months. She would then visit Richard at Princeton for dances and holidays; on these occasions she would stay with the Wheelers at their house and do watercolor paintings. Then the whole rigmarole of her illness would start again.

Richard's idea was to take a leave from his Princeton work and studies, take a job at the Bell Labs, rent an apartment and get married. He would then take care of Arline for the time that was left to her. But they didn't marry right away for two reasons. First, his father thought that marriage would interfere with the growth of his scientific career, and it was also not clear whether he could get married as a scholarship holder (Procter fellow), which he was in his last year at Princeton.

Feynman went to see the Dean and told him that his fiancée had this incurable disease and she had only a few years to live—two or three years at the most—and that he wanted to marry her. Could he marry and stay at the university? No, he couldn't marry and keep his scholarship. It was quite serious and Feynman was 'surprised at the cold answer'.[1,2,3] That's when he and Arline cooked up the scheme that they would rent an apartment on Long Island and he would take up a job with the Bell Telephone Laboratory. However, after a biopsy they found out that it was not Hodgkin's disease but tuberculosis of the lymphatic system, and she might live on for at least five to seven years.

Arline stayed on in the state hospital on Long Island, and Richard would visit her every week or two, just as often as he could both from Princeton and from the Frankfort Arsenal in Philadelphia. Then he arranged for her to stay at the Deborah Hospital, a charitable hospital of the Women Garment Workers' Union just south of Fort Dix in New Jersey, quite close to Princeton. His parents and friends tried to dissuade him from marrying, but he told them that, in spirit and emotions they were already married, and if he didn't actually marry her it will be like divorcing her.

After the commencement and receiving his Ph.D. degree while she was sick in the hospital, Richard picked up Arline at home in Cedarhurst. They went to Staten Island and got married there by a justice of the peace on 29 June 1942; their witness was the bookkeeper and accountant at the registry office, and they were married according to the laws of the state of New York. Their honeymoon was the trip back on the ferry from Staten Island to New York. Richard had already transferred her bed, mattress and belongings to the Deborah Hospital in a stationwagon which belonged to his friend Bill Woodward.

Although the director of the hospital did not want Richard to do so, he contributed eighteen dollars per month in savings bonds to the hospital. He did not have much money, but he tried to save and contribute what he could to the hospital. Arline stayed at the Deborah Hospital all the time. Richard would visit her every week and she used to spend her time writing letters to him. They would write letters to each other. From the start of their marriage until her death a few years later, Arline stayed on in a hospital. She tried very hard to get strength and become better, but nothing worked.

Arline would do her best to remain cheerful herself and keep Richard cheered up as well. Once she sent Richard a box of dark green pencils in which, on each pencil, in bold gold letters, were printed the words: 'RICHARD DARLING, I LOVE YOU! PUTSY'. Richard worried that he might leave one of these pencils somewhere while discussing things with one of the professors, like Wheeler or Wigner, and it would be embarrassing for him. So he tried to scrape off the gold letters from some of the pencils. As soon as Arline became aware of that, he met with her rebuff: 'What do *you* care what other people think?'

The Manhattan Project had been established in Princeton in April 1942, and Feynman continued to be associated with it, working very hard on war-related problems. In the spring of 1943, arrangements began to be made for the scientists to be moved to Los Alamos, the site chosen for the atomic weapons laboratory. The first to be moved were the theoreticians. Richard had to take Arline to New Mexico with him. When he was recruited to be sent to Los Alamos, Feynman told Robert Oppenheimer about his personal problem with Arline's sickness, and Oppenheimer helped him in making arrangements at a hospital in Albuquerque where she could stay. All her belongings were packed in boxes and she was put on a train; Richard traveled with her. They had reserved a suite on the train and went cross-country on it; it was a pleasant ride. In Albuquerque, they had to move from one hospital to another, to choose the more comfortable one, but it didn't make much difference. Richard would go down every weekend to see Arline, and sometimes one or the other of his close friends would drop by and keep Arline amused and cheerful.

The hospital rules at Albuquerque were less severe than they had been in

New Jersey; consequently, life was more pleasant for Arline. She had her many possessions, like books and a record player, in the hospital room. When Richard would visit, they would write letters, play games, and she would invent all kinds of things for them to do. She became interested in Chinese calligraphy and enjoyed doing it very much. She had a book entitled *Sounds and symbols in Chinese*, with about fifty symbols done in beautiful calligraphy; she also had a dictionary and a phrase book. With the right kind of paper, brushes, and ink, she took to practicing calligraphy, in which Richard also became very interested. He attempted to compose a message for his sister Joan (who was studying at Oberlin College) with the help of the phrase book and the dictionary.

Arline would write crazy letters to Richard trying to beat or annoy the censors at the Manhattan Project. She would send away for department store catalogues and suggest ordering out of the way items like huge kitchen equipment for restaurants or boats, yachts, and liners, which, of course, she had no intention of ordering because they were of no use to anyone, nor had anyone money enough to buy them! Ultimately, she did order a barbeque grill from a Sears & Roebuck catalogue, and Richard would broil steaks for both of them on weekends on the lawn by the roadside on Route 66 which passed by the hospital. She also had him wear an apron, emblazoned with the letters BAR-B-Q KING, chef's hat, and gloves. Whenever Richard objected to doing something, or refused to fulfil one of her whims or wishes, she would pout with, 'What do *you* care what other people think?'

On the occasion of one of Richard's birthdays, Arline had one of those mock newspapers—dozens of them—printed with a big headline screaming, 'Entire Nation Celebrates Birthday of R.P. Feynman', and sent them around to all the scientists on the Project. She had Christmas cards printed one year, saying 'Merry Christmas, from Rich and Putsy'. When he remonstrated with her on how he could send cards like that to Hans Bethe and Enrico Fermi, she gave her stock answer: 'What do *you* care what other people think?'

Feynman summed it up by saying, 'Arline had a lot of time to think. She was in her room, but she was in the world, writing me crazy letters and sending away for all kinds of stuff. . ... She was playing her game with the world.'[5]

Arline gradually became more and more ill, and grew much weaker. Her father came out from New York to visit her, although traveling during the war was difficult and expensive. One day he telephoned Richard at Los Alamos and asked him to come down to the hospital in Albuquerque. She was near her end. Her father could not take it anymore and, after a few days, he just left. Richard had foreseen such an eventuality. Normally he used to hitchhike, but now that Arline was becoming weaker and getting close to her end he borrowed his good friend Klaus Fuchs' car, an old rattletrap thing, and drove down to Albuquerque.

On the way to Santa Fe, the car got a flat tire. Richard had picked up some soldiers who were hitchhiking, and they helped him fix it. Then they got another flat tire. They went to a gas station, where one of the soldiers explained the situation to the owner. The flat was fixed again, until there were more flat tires. Richard left the car about twenty or thirty miles from Albuquerque and himself hitchhiked; someone gave him a ride into Albuquerque and he went to see his wife. He got a company to take care of the car and put new tires on it.

Arline was on oxygen, but she was weak and fogged out. She would stare ahead most of the time; otherwise she would follow movements with her eyes. She was trying to breathe. Breathing was intermittent; it would start and stop, and it went on like that for some time. Things were in a kind of slow motion. Finally, breathing stopped. Richard walked around and saw Arline die. 'This is terrible to say, but . . . it was interesting to watch the phenomenon [of death], which I had never seen before.'[1]

Richard was in Arline's room when she died. The hospital staff left him alone with her for some time. He bent down and gently kissed her and was surprised that everything smelled the same as if she were alive. He noticed another curious thing. He had given Arline a digital clock when she became sick, on which the numbers would change and one could read the time quickly. The clock had become old, but Arline still kept it. Sometimes Richard repaired it, and although it was a bit wobbly it still functioned. When Arline died, the nurse noted the time of her death; it was 9:22 (p.m.) and the clock had also stopped at 9:22. 'Since it was rather dark in the room, the nurse picked up the clock and noticed that it had stopped just at the moment when Arline died. This was something mysterious, which made an impression on me, but I thought it was explainable.'[1]

Richard was surprised to find that Arline's death did not upset him. He had anticipated it. He felt rather philosophical. He reflected what a Martian (who, let us imagine, dies only by an accident) would think if he visited the earth and saw a race of creatures who were born, lived for seventy or eighty years, then died; in the meantime they laughed, joked, and lived with the knowledge that they would die. In the case of Richard and Arline, they had been together for only a few years rather than fifty years. The difference was quantitative not qualitative. He did not think, 'What have we done to deserve this?', and dismissed such questions as basically 'irrelevant and unsolvable'. Rather, he thought that 'we had a hell of a good time together'.[6]

Richard had witnessed the whole process of Arline's dying and he tried to understand it in physiological terms—until she drew her last breath and was alive no more. Her hair smelled the same as before. Then he thought, why should her hair smell any different? Hardly any time had elapsed since she breathed her last.

Richard visited the mortuary the next day, where the attendant gave him the rings that had been removed from Arline's fingers. The attendant asked him, 'Would you like to see your wife one last time?' He said, 'But I saw her just yesterday.' 'Yes, but she's been all fixed up now', said the attendant. 'I did not want to look at Arline again; that would have made me more upset.'[7]

Feynman called up the garage, got the car back, picked up a hitchhiker, and drove back to Los Alamos. Just five miles out, there was a flat tire. Feynman cursed, and the hitchhiker said that it was only a flat tire, nothing serious. But Feynman recalled his trip down to Albuquerque, and said, 'Yeah, it's just a tire, and again another tire, and another tire!'[1] They changed the tire, drove slowly, and returned to Los Alamos.

At the laboratory, people asked Richard about Arline. He told them, 'She's dead. And, how's the [computer] program going?'[1] In the room where the calculations were being done, Feynman was head of the computations group. He asked his colleagues, 'How's it going?' They said, 'Get out, we're busy!' They did not know what had happened, and they were confused by the complicated calculation. When people learned about Arline's death, they would pull a long face and say, 'Oh, I'm sorry to hear that!' But Feynman kept on going. Upon his return to Los Alamos, he gave Fuchs's car back to him. Fuchs understood immediately how Feynman felt. His friends Nick Metropolis and Julius Ashkin asked him what had happened and he told them. They began by saying, 'Very sorry, etc.', but Feynman made a joke about the many flat tires, and they understood that he did not wish to talk about Arline's death.

Klaus Fuchs understood what Feynman wanted; he wanted to keep on going as normally as possible. He told Feynman, 'Let's visit Peierls, he's sick.' So they went to see him and wished him a speedy recovery. At Peierls's place, Feynman was sitting eating grapes and thinking, 'My wife just died, the one I love so much', and so on. But he wondered that if he were to appear so calm as if nothing was the matter then an observing psychologist would not know what happened. Later on, when the Fuchs espionage affair was revealed, Feynman reflected back on that occasion—the evening at Peierls's home in Los Alamos. He had not let out what had happened to him, nor had he realized that Fuchs was leading a double life, with his own secret locked away in his mind at that time. It really struck him that no matter how astute the observer might be—like in a Guy de Maupassant story—he would not be able to gather what people are thinking.

Given his scientific temperament, Feynman was quite philosophical. 'It has an important effect on the personality of the character. I had great faith in the scientific way of looking at the world, to make sure what the reality is. Everybody cries when someone else dies. There's no reason to cry. Why should we cry?'[1] However, a few weeks after Arline's death, Richard was in Oak Ridge and walked past the shop window of a department store, where some pretty dresses were displayed. The thought occurred to him, 'Arline would surely like one of those!', and then the pent up emotion of his loss hit him and he broke down.

Right after Arline's death, Richard returned to Far Rockaway. From his

Crossways Apartments home he called his friend Elmer Heller and asked him to get together, which they did in the late afternoon. 'Arline had died three days ago. . .. I was quite shocked at the news [but] did not ask for details. I knew about Arline's condition and so was not surprised. More importantly, I did not know how to respond. I wondered about the simple matter-of-fact way that Richard spoke. There was no emotion expressed beyond ordinary conversation and that gave me some feeling of relief because no friend of mine had died before. I admired Richard's "objectivity" about death. It was so much better than the emotional outbursts I had witnessed at the few funerals I had attended. The thought went through my mind that this is how a real scientist reacts to death. Death is inevitable. It happens to everyone. It is the end; there is nothing else. You just accept it and carry on. And that's what we did, kept on walking [towards the beach] and talking—until we came to the site of the old Tacaposha Hotel facing the beach, where Richard said, "Let's go to the boardwalk and try to pick up some girls." . . . We didn't pick up any girls, but this episode went through my mind many, many times since then. Nevertheless, even in the depths of my youthful illusions, we [Sigma, Epsilon, Xi group: Richard, David Leff, Harold Gast, Gerry Robbins, Bob Stappler, and Elmer Heller] sensed that Richard's great talents that served him so well in science were somewhat less effective in the sphere of human emotions, earning him our endearing title: T.B. (Tactless Bastard) Feynman'.[8]

Notes and References

1. R.P. Feynman, Interviews and conversations with Jagdish Mehra, in Pasadena, California, January 1988.

2. R.P. Feynman, Interviews with Charles Weiner (American Institute of Physics), in Pasadena, California, 1966.

3. This was a remark that Feynman would often make to Arline, until later on, when he would say or do anything that bothered her or made her unhappy she would remonstrate by making this remark back to him. This remark would become the title of the book *'What do you care what other people think?'*, based on Feynman's memoirs and other miscellaneous items, edited by Ralph Leighton. Norton, New York, 1988.

4. R.P. Feynman, Ref. 3, p. 33.

5. R.P. Feynman, Ref. 3, p. 45.

6. R.P. Feynman, Ref. 3, p. 51.

7. R.P. Feynman, Ref. 3, p. 52.

8. Personal communication from Elmer Heller to Jagdish Mehra, 31 August 1990.

8

Diversions and contributions at Los Alamos

Richard Feynman had not yet completed his doctorate when, in April 1942, he became member of the group working with Robert R. Wilson on the electromagnetic separation of uranium-235 and uranium-238 using the 'isotron', a device which the experimentalists at Princeton had developed for accelerating beams of ionized uranium and trying to separate the isotopes by bunching them, by applying a high-frequency voltage to a set of grids part way down a linear tube.[1] He had been engaged upon this task already since the previous December, when Wilson had invited him and other young physicists to join him in the OSRD (Office of Scientific Research and Development) project on the initial studies for building the atomic bomb. Feynman was well prepared for this task; he had taken Wheeler's course on nuclear physics, for which he prepared a detailed set of notes, as well as Wigner's course on solid state physics in which he had learned a great deal about the properties of materials. Towards the end of April, Feynman took several weeks off from the project to complete his dissertation, receive the Ph.D., and get married, after which he again returned to full-time work on war-related research.

Feynman recalled that 'one of the first interesting experiences I had in this project at Princeton was meeting great men. I had not met very many great men before.'[2] There was an evaluation committee which had to help the research work along, and help in deciding the way in which uranium isotopes were finally going to be separated. Among the members of this evaluation committee were: A. H. Compton, Karl Compton, R. C. Tolman, Harry Smyth, Harold Urey, I. I. Rabi, and J. Robert Oppenheimer, with Tolman as Chairman. Feynman was asked to attend their meeting because 'I understood the theory of the process of what we were doing, and so they'd ask me questions and talk about it.'[2] In these discussions, points were made by one member after another, and sometimes clarifications were called for by someone who had already given his opinion. 'At the end, the decision [was] made as to which idea was the best—summing it all up—without having to say it three times. So that [to me] was a great shock. These were very great men indeed.'[2]

It was ultimately decided that the project in Princeton would not be the one they were going to use to separate the uranium isotopes, and that they would actually be starting the project to build the atomic bomb at Los Alamos, New Mexico, and all of them from Princeton would go there. In the early months of the project, Feynman invited his friend Elmer Heller to work on war-related problems, too; Heller worked at the Palmer Laboratories from December 1941 to May 1942.

Before Los Alamos got ready to receive people, Robert Wilson tried to make use of the available time by, among other things, sending Feynman to the so-called Metallurgical Laboratory in Chicago to find out all one could about the atomic bomb and problems related to it. Then, in the laboratories at Princeton, they could start building the equipment, counters of various kinds, etc., that would be useful when they got to Los Alamos; thereby no time would be wasted. Feynman went to Chicago and helped various groups at the Metallurgical Laboratory with his suggestions for solving problems.

Upon Feynman's return from Chicago to Los Alamos, his friend Paul Olum, the mathematician, remarked to him: 'When they make a [movie] about this, they'll have the guy coming back from Chicago to make his report to Princeton men about the bomb. He'll be wearing a suit and carrying a briefcase and so on—and here you're in dirty shirtsleeves and just telling us about it, in spite of its being such a serious and dramatic thing.'[3]

Robert Wilson went to Los Alamos to find out what was holding things up. He found that the construction company was working very hard and had finished the theater and a few other buildings, the details of which they understood. Then and there Wilson decided how the laboratories had to be set up with all the connections for water, gas, and the other things. When Wilson returned, Feynman and the others at Princeton were ready to go and getting impatient; all of them decided to go anyway.

Robert Oppenheimer, as director of the Manhattan Project, was in charge of the various people. He paid attention to everybody's problems, including worrying about Arline, Feynman's wife, who was ill with tuberculosis; he found a suitable clinic for her in Albuquerque, New Mexico, not too far from Los Alamos. Feynman recalled: 'It was the first time that I met him in such a personal way; he was a wonderful man.'[3]

The scientists going from Princeton, New Jersey, to Albuquerque, New Mexico, had been asked not to buy their train tickets in Princeton, which was a very small station; if everybody bought train tickets for Albuquerque in Princeton, it would arouse suspicion and cause gossip. Everybody else bought his train ticket somewhere else, except Feynman, because he figured— rightly—that he would be one of the few to buy their tickets in Princeton. 'So when I went to the train station and said, "I want to go to Albuquerque, New Mexico," the railway clerk said, "Oh, so all this stuff is for *you*!" We had been shipping crates full of counters for weeks and expecting that they wouldn't notice that the address was Albuquerque. So at last I explained why it was that we were shipping all those crates; *I* was going out to Albuquerque.'[4]

When the first group arrived, the houses and dormitories were not yet ready; all of them stayed at the ranch house, and were driven to the laboratory each morning. 'The first morning I drove in, it was tremendously impressive. The beauty of the scenery, for a person from the East who didn't travel much, was sensational. There are the great cliffs . . . You'd come up from below and be very surprised to see this high mesa.'[4]

The theoretical physicists started their work immediately. There were no blackboards, except one on wheels. They would roll it around, and Robert Serber would explain to everyone the things that they had thought of in Berkeley about the atomic bomb, nuclear physics, and all such things. Feynman began to meet many people whose names were familiar to him from their papers in the *Physical Review*. The experimental physicists began to help with the construction and planning of the laboratories.

Feynman worked very hard in those days, studying, reading, and calculating, having all in all a very hectic time. But he also had luck: 'All the big shots except Hans Bethe happened to be away at the time, and what Bethe needed was someone to talk to, to push his ideas against. Well, he came to this little squirt in an office and started to argue, explaining his idea. I said, "No, no, you're crazy. It'll go like this." And he said, "Just a moment", and explained to me how he's not crazy, I was crazy. And we kept on going like this. You see, when I hear about physics, I just talk about physics, and I don't know whom I'm talking to, so I say dopey things like "No, no, you are wrong", or "You're crazy!" But it turned out to be exactly what he needed. I got a notch up on account of that and I ended up as a group leader under Bethe with four guys under me [Julius Ashkin, Frederick Reines, Richard Ehrlich, and Theodore Welton].'[4]

It was at this encounter that Richard Feynman first met Hans Bethe. Feynman was deeply impressed by Bethe's analytical powers, physical intuition, stamina, erudition, his unaffected and forthright simplicity of manner, and above all his integrity. Feynman got along exceedingly well with Bethe, especially because both of them shared a robust sense of humor.

Bethe and Feynman's early interactions at Los Alamos have been vividly described by Stephane Groueff: 'Richard Feynman's voice could be heard from the far end of the corridor: "No, no, you're crazy!" His colleagues in the Los Alamos Theoretical Division looked up from their computers and exchanged knowing smiles. "There they go again!" one said. "The Battleship and the Mosquito Boat!"

'"The Battleship" was the division leader, Hans Bethe, a tall, heavy-set German who was recognized as a sort of genius in theoretical physics. At the moment he was having one of his frequent discussions with Dick Feynman, the "Mosquito Boat", who from the moment he started talking physics, became completely oblivious of where he was and with whom he was talking. The imperturbable and meticulous Bethe solved problems by facing them squarely, analyzing them quietly, and then plowing straight through them. He pushed obstacles aside like a battleship moving through the water.

'Feynman, on the other hand, would interrupt impatiently at nearly every sentence, either to shout his admiration or to express disagreements by irreverent remarks like "No, you're crazy!" or "That's nuts!" At each interruption Bethe would stop, then quietly and patiently explain why he was right. Feynman would calm down for a few minutes, only to jump up again with "That's impossible, you're mad" and again Bethe could calmly prove it was not so.'[5]

Feynman had a lot of interesting experiences with Hans Bethe. Bethe knew a lot about making numerical calculations in his head; he had a whole lot of tricks about taking squares, cubes, and various roots of numbers. 'So he knew all his arithmetic, and he was very good at it, and that was a challenge to me. I kept on practicing. We used to have a little contest. Every time we'd calculate anything, we'd race to the answer, he and I, and I would lose. After several years I began to get in there once in a while, maybe one out of four. You have to *notice* the numbers, and each of us would notice [them] in a different way. We had lots of fun.'[6]

The dormitories had not been built yet. From the ranch house, the physicists moved to the Mechanics' Lodge, which had been part of the old boys' school. From the Mechanics' Lodge, they moved to the Big House, which had a balcony all around the second floor, and where all the beds were lined up next to each other along the wall. At last the dormitory was ready, and Feynman was asked to pick his room. 'You know what I did? I looked to see where the girls' dormitory was, and then I picked a room that looked right across—though later I discovered a big tree was growing right in front of the window of that room.'[5]

Feynman was told that two people would occupy one room, but that would be temporary, and there would be double-decker bunks in each room. But Feynman did not want anyone else in his room. He had some of his wife Arline's things (at this time she was at the clinic in Albuquerque), like a nightgown and other sundry things. He opened the top of the bed and carelessly spread the nightgown on it, took out her slippers and placed them in the room, and threw some talcum powder on the floor of the bathroom, making it look as if the room was occupied by a couple. In the evening he found the beds properly made, the pajamas and nightgown properly folded and the room made up nicely. Feynman would do that every night, and the next day the beds and the room would be made up properly.

This matter was evidently reported to the authorities, and a rule was handed down which said: 'No Women in Men's Dorm.' The matter was debated, and Feynman was elected to represent the dormitory on the Town Council. After almost a year and a half he admitted his ruse to Hans Bethe, who was a member of the top Governing Council of the town.

There was a matter of censorship at the project. All the people had voluntarily agreed that they would leave the outgoing mail unsealed so that the censor could scrutinize them and seal them, while the incoming mail would be censored anyway. Feynman had many scrapes with the censor people, because he and Arline began to use codes. They would, of course, not include the key, and it was fun for them to decipher each other's messages. The censor would make a fuss each time. Feynman told the censor: 'I challenge them [my correspondents] to send me a code that I can't decipher, see? So they're making up codes at the other end, and they're sending them in, and they're not going to tell me what the key is.'[7] So the censor told him to ask his correspondents 'kindly' to send the key with the code, which they would take out before forwarding the mail to him. Feynman had a lot of fun and irritation in dealing with the censors at the Manhattan Project. But, as a result of these experiences, he knew exactly what could get through the censor and what couldn't.

One day, Feynman discovered that the workmen who lived farther out and wanted to come into the project complex were too lazy to go around through the gate and had cut for themselves a hole in the fence. So, Feynman went through the gate, went over to the hole in the fence and came in, went out and came in, and kept on doing it to attract the attention of the sergeant at the gate, who began to wonder what was happening. How come this guy is always going out, but never coming in? Of course, the sergeant's natural reaction was to call the lieutenant and try to put Feynman in jail for doing this. Then Feynman explained that there was a hole in the fence, and the security staff was responsible for the breach of rules that was taking place. Feynman was always trying to point out such things to the authorities in an indirect manner.

Feynman mastered the technique of picking locks and opening safes, by inferring the lock combination numbers in an uncanny fashion, and leaving behind notes for his victims that their security had been breached. In the case of physicists he had a hunch that for the combinations of their locks they would use the numerical values of constants like e, the base of natural logarithms, or the value of π. Feynman would try various combinations of the six digit numbers and often the combinations would work. He also read books by locksmiths, and 'found out how big a range you need to open the combination, how close you have to be. And then I invented a system by which to try all the necessary combinations.'[7] He used to practice opening safes 'like a cardsharp practices cards'.[7] To go through the papers in the locked desk of Edward Teller was a piece of cake, but he found the combination to the safe of Frederic de Hoffman by psychology: he thought that it might be some permutation of the numerical value of π ($= 3.14159$) or e ($= 2.71828$). He tried 31–41–59, 13–14–95, 95–14–13, but it didn't open. Then he tried 27–18–28, and it flung open. Moreover, all the filing cabinets in Freddie de Hoffman's office had the same combination for the locks, and Feynman had all the secrets of the atomic bomb at his disposal.

From Los Alamos, Robert Christy was to be sent to Oak Ridge to examine plant safety, but he got pneumonia and Feynman had to go instead. He was instructed by Oppenheimer to say: '*Los Alamos cannot accept the responsibility for the safety of the Oak Ridge plant unless they are fully informed as to how it works.*' So he went there and, in a meeting, this is just what he said. At Oak Ridge, they were all very attentive to what Feynman had to say about neutrons, about how cadmium absorbs neutrons, etc. They had to redesign the plants, and Feynman discussed the details of the new plant where the separated fissile material was going to be handled with construction designers and civil and chemical engineers.

The people at Oak Ridge asked Feynman to return in a few months, which he did. Then they spread out the blueprints on a very long table. Feynman was worried that, when there was an evaporator working which was trying to accumulate the material, it would explode if the valve got stuck and too much material accumulated. So they explained to him that if any valve got stuck nothing would happen; it needed at least two valves everywhere for that to happen. Ultimately, Feynman found a square with a cross through it on the blueprint; he did not know whether it was a valve or a window. Not being sure, he just put his finger on it and asked what would happen if that valve got stuck. They first tried to tell him that it was a window, but checked and found that it was indeed a valve; after that they folded up their plans to rectify them, and hailed Feynman as a genius.

At the Manhattan Project, Richard Feynman came to be in charge of the Theoretical Computations Group. Ultimately, the membership of this group, with Feynman as leader, comprised: Julius Ashkin, John Kemeny, Richard Ehrlich, Murray Peshkin, Frederick Reines, and Theodore Welton. Feynman's group made computations in parallel with other groups. One of their tasks was to calculate 'critical masses in a system with spherical symmetry and monoenergetic, isotropically scattered neutrons. The problem involved was approximately formulated by Hopf (the sun's limb darkening) and so beautifully solved by Wiener and Hopf, but the mathematics (integral equations) was thoroughly unfamiliar to all of us. There was a clear necessity to devise useful and general approximations, Wiener–Hopf being of no use except in a very idealized situation. Dick [Feynman], who was never shy about proposing physical ideas, and had long admired the variational method in quantum mechanics, piped up with the suggestion that the criticality problem might be usefully approximated as a variational problem. Hans Bethe (probably among many) considered this to be nonsense and said so. Dick rose immediately to the challenge and when next seen had performed a simple, elegant, and convincing calculation. As an important result, Hans [Bethe] (who combines a certain fair-mindedness with his talent for physics) correctly decided that [Feynman] was a man to be trusted with complex physical problems, and [he] shortly found himself to be in great demand.'[8]

The calculations were done on Marchant and Monroe calculators; they were self-powered (with electric motor) calculators, and everyone was provided with one on his desk. These machines were about a foot across and several inches high; each one of them occupied a good part of the desk. By pushing their appropriate levers, one could add, subtract, multiply, divide, etc. They were numerical gadgets, which failed often. So, against the manufacturer's advice, the members of the computations group would take off their covers, and Feynman himself became an expert at repairing them, just as someone else in the group undertook to repair the typewriters.

The entire computational section was run by a mathematician, Donald Flanders. Since he had many ladies working in his section, doing the computations, Donald was called 'Moll Flanders'.[9]

One of the problems they had to work on was to determine exactly how much energy would be released in the explosion of the atomic bomb. They divided up the total problem into all the various numerical steps that had to be done. They set up girls in a room, each with a Marchant calculator. Each one had a different function: one was an adder; the other a multiplier; this one squared; and the next one cubed, etc. Each one would do what she had to do, and then send the index card to the next one. They went through their cycles and got all the bugs out. This way of doing things was much faster than if all the steps had to be done by one person at a time. The girls would get tired after some time, but the machines didn't—especially when they were kept in a good state of repair—and the next shift would take over the calculations.

Before Feynman took charge of the Theoretical Computations Group (T4), the people who were doing the various steps did not know what all this work was for. Then Feynman obtained permission from Oppenheimer to explain to the crew the goal of the project—how important and necessary their contribution was for war work—and he gave them a lecture about what was being done and what it was for. After that the technical people worked with great excitement. There was a complete transformation: they didn't need much supervising anymore, and would even work nights and overtime.

Near the end of the war, just before the atomic bomb test was to be made, the question arose: How much energy would be released from various designs of the bomb, and then from the specific designs that were going to be used in the actual bombs, and how much fissile material was needed in each case? Robert Christy came to the computation group and told them that they had less than one month to calculate the answer; it was a big problem and the time allowed for computation was too short. So they stopped work on all other problems and concentrated on this one.

Then Arline died in Albuquerque, and Feynman had to go down there. When he returned after three days, he found that his group was extremely busy, fully occupied with the problem, juggling index cards—white, blue, and yellow cards. They had found some means of making corrections in the calculation that had been done wrongly earlier. The calculations were very elaborate and difficult, and yet they succeeded in finding the answers on time.

Enrico Fermi came down from Chicago to consult with Feynman's group. Feynman explained to him the problem on which he and his group were working, and Fermi made an on-the-spot order-of-magnitude calculation. Feynman was good at such things, but 'Fermi was ten times better. That was quite a lesson to me!'[10]

Feynman's leadership of the Technical Computations Group was universally admired. Frederick Reines recalled: 'He was a marvelous guy. He looked like a hick and talked like a New Yorker. He was very considerate and kind, a very fine boss. My wife and I visited Arline several times in the hospital at Albuquerque. Feynman loved drums. He used a "pablum" box—a box of baby cereal—to beat like a drum. The general aura that Feynman created was of being very clear and definite. Being around Feynman, Bethe, and Fermi was bound to give a young guy inferiority complex. There was a certain quality about them; but they talked like fine and considerate human beings.'[9]

Ted Welton also recalled Feynman's interactions with his colleagues: 'We all saw him diplomatically, forcefully, usually with humor (gentle or not, as needed) dissuade a respected colleague from some unwise course. We all saw him forcefully rebuke a colleague less favored by his respect, frequently with ungentle humor. Only a fool would have subjected himself twice to such an experience.'[8]

Apart from his great love and admiration for Hans Bethe, which the latter fully reciprocated, Feynman had other notable encounters and influences at Los Alamos. There was the great mathematician John von Neumann. 'We used to go for walks on Sunday. We'd walk with Hans Bethe, von Neumann, and Robert Bacher. It was a great pleasure. And von Neumann gave me an interesting idea: that you don't have to be responsible for the world you're in. So I have developed a very powerful sense of social irresponsibility as a result of von Neumann's advice. It's made me a very happy man ever since. But it was von Neumann who put in the seed that grew into my *active* irresponsibility.'[11]

At Los Alamos, Feynman also met Niels Bohr. His pseudonym at the Manhattan Project, for security reasons, was Nicholas Baker, and his son Aage Bohr was called Jim Baker. 'Even to the big guys, Bohr was a great god.'[11] At meetings, Bohr had observed that Feynman always spoke his mind, without being weighed down by the importance and authority of the people present. 'I was always *dumb* about one thing. I never knew who I was talking to. I was always worried [only] about physics. If the idea looked lousy, I said it looked lousy. If it looked good, I said it looked good. Simple proposition. I've always lived that way. It's nice, it's pleasant—if you can do it . . . I'm lucky in my life that I can do this.'[11]

So, the next time Bohr came to attend an important meeting about the bomb at Los Alamos, he decided to talk to Feynman about his ideas before calling in the other people. Aage Bohr, Niels's son, gave Feynman a call inviting him to discuss things with his father. They did so for about two hours, 'going back and forth over lots of ideas, back and forth, arguing. The great Niels kept [on] lighting his pipe; it always went out.' Finally, lighting his pipe, Bohr said, 'I guess we can call in the big shots *now*.'[11] Then they called all the other guys and had a discussion with them.

Then Aage Bohr told Feynman what had happened. 'The last time he was [at Los Alamos], he said to his son, "Remember the name of that little fellow in the back over there? He's the only guy who's not afraid of me, and will say [so] when I've got a crazy idea. So *next* time when we want to discuss ideas, we're not going to be able to discuss it with these guys who say everything is yes, yes, Dr Bohr. Get that guy and we'll talk to him first.'[11]

The next thing that happened, of course, was the test, 'after we'd made the calculations. I was actually at home [in Far Rockaway] on a short vacation at that time, after my wife died, and so I got a message [from Hans Bethe] that said, "The baby is expected on such and such a day." '[12]

Feynman flew back to New Mexico, and arrived *just* in time when buses were leaving for the test site. There he, with his group (including William Lawrence of the *New York Times*), waited at a distance of twenty miles, while others waited six miles away. They had been issued dark glasses to witness the sight of the explosion of the atomic bomb. Feynman knew that the only thing that could hurt the eyes was ultraviolet radiation, and he took a place behind the windshield of a truck; ultraviolet light would be absorbed by the glass of the windshield.

Then the explosion took place and Feynman saw it. 'A tremendous flash out there . . ., white light changing into yellow and then into orange. The clouds formed and disappeared again; the compression and the expansion formed and made the clouds disappear. Then finally a big ball of orange, the center was so bright, became a ball of orange that started to rise and billow a little bit and got a little black around the edges, and then you saw it was a big ball of smoke with flashes on the inside of the fire going out, the heat. All this took about one minute. It was a series from bright to dark, and I had *seen* it. I am about the only guy who actually looked at the damn thing—the first Trinity test. Everybody else had dark glasses, and the people at six miles couldn't see it because they were told to lie on the floor. I'm probably the only guy who saw it with [naked] human eyes.

'Finally, after about a minute and a half, there was a sudden tremendous noise—BANG, and then a remarkable thunder—and that's what convinced me. Nobody had said a word during this whole thing. We were all just watching quietly. But this sound released everybody—released me particularly because the solidity of the sound at that distance meant that it had actually worked. The man standing next to me said, "What's that?" I said, "That was the bomb!" The man was William Lawrence.'[12]

After the bomb went off and the test was successfully completed, there was tremendous excitement at Los Alamos. All of them ran around, and everybody had parties. Feynman sat on the end of a jeep and beat drums by beating metal trash cans. 'But one man, Bob Wilson, was just sitting and moping. I said to him, "What are you moping about?" He replied, "It's a terrible thing that we made." I said, "But you started it. You got us into it." '[13]

From Los Alamos, Feynman went to teach at Cornell University. His first impressions after returning to normal life were very strange. 'I can't understand it anymore, but I felt very strongly then. I sat in a restaurant in New York, for example, and I started to look out at the buildings, and I began to think about how much the radius of the Hiroshima bomb damage was and so forth . . . How far from here was 34th Street? . . . All those buildings, all smashed, and so on. And I would go along and see people building a bridge, or they would be [building] a new road, and I thought, they're *crazy*, they just don't *understand*. Why are they [building] new things? It's so useless. But, fortunately, it has been useless for [so many] years, hasn't it? So I've been wrong about it being useless to [build] bridges and I'm glad that those other people had the sense to go ahead.'[13]

Notes and References

1. R.C. Hewlett and O.E. Anderson, *The new world*, 1939/1946. *A history of the United States Atomic Energy Commission*, Pennsylvania University Press, State Park, Pennsylvania, Vol. 1, p. 59.

2. R.P. Feynman, *Engineering and Science*, January/February 1976, p. 12.

3. R.P. Feynman, Ref 2, p. 13.

4. R.P. Feynman, Ref. 2, p. 14.

5. S. Groueff, *Manhattan Project: The untold story of the making of the atomic bomb*, Little, Brown and Company, Boston, 1967.

6. R.P. Feynman, Ref. 2, p. 15.

7. R.P. Feynman, Ref. 2, p. 16.

8. T.A. Welton, Memories of R.P. Feynman. Unpublished manuscript, 1983.

9. Personal communication from Frederick Reines to Jagdish Mehra, 27 May 1990.

10. R.P. Feynman, Ref. 2, p. 27.

11. R.P. Feynman, Ref. 2, p. 28.

12. R.P. Feynman, Ref. 2, p. 29.

13. R.P. Feynman, Ref. 2, p. 30.

A 'dignified professor' at Cornell University

At Los Alamos Feynman had enjoyed very close contacts with Hans Bethe, whom he greatly loved and admired. Bethe recalled that, at Los Alamos, 'Feynman was very lively from the beginning . . . I realized very quickly that he was something phenomenal. The first thing he did since we had to integrate differential equations, and at that time had only hand computers, was to find an efficient method of integrating third-order differential equations numerically. It was very, very impressive. Then, within a month, we cooked up a formula for calculating the efficiency of a nuclear weapon. It is named the Bethe–Feynman formula, and it is still used. I thought Feynman perhaps the most ingenious man in the whole division, so we worked a great deal together.'[1] Since Bethe was from Cornell University, he proposed to Feynman that after the war he should go to Cornell with him, an idea which appealed to Feynman greatly.

Already on 30 October 1943, a few months after Feynman had been at Los Alamos, Bethe had proposed to R. C. Gibbs, chairman of the physics department at Cornell, that Feynman be hired at Cornell. He wrote from Los Alamos: 'We have here an exceedingly brilliant young theoretical physicist, Richard Feynman. He is in the opinion of all the wise men here as good as [Julian] Schwinger, but at the same time quite an extrovert and, therefore, much more useful to any department or laboratory such as this. I wonder whether it would not be possible to secure this man for our department before he gets other offers, which he undoubtedly will. I think that he himself would rather enjoy coming to Cornell and continuing the work with me and also with Weisskopf. Feynman is very young, I believe twenty-four, and at this time he has no permanent position. He used to be in Princeton . . . I should think that an offer of an acting assistant professor with about $3000, and with the promise of striking out 'acting' after one year if he is satisfactory, would be sufficient to induce him to come.

'You know me well enough to know that I would not write this letter unless I considered this an absolutely unique opportunity. I believe that men like Feynman occur only about once every five or ten years [!].

'I do not know of course whether we are in a position to get another theoretical man. I thought we could use as part of the necessary money the fund of $2000 a year which I have at my disposal for a research associate. If it is very difficult to obtain this money, I know that Weisskopf would be anxious to have Feynman part time at Rochester. I should think that some arrangement of this kind could be worked out with [Lee] DuBridge [who, at that time, was the head of the physics department at the University of Rochester, later to become president of the California Institute of Technology].'[2]

On 28 February 1944, Robert F. Bacher, who also belonged to the physics department at Cornell University and was at Los Alamos, wrote to R. C. Gibbs in support of Feynman's appointment at Cornell. He wrote: 'I would like to confirm my previous telephone conversation with you regarding Dr Richard Feynman, who is a member of the staff here. Feynman is a young man who took his degree in theoretical physics at Princeton two years or so ago, and I knew very little about him until my association with this [i.e. Manhattan] project. I believe that there is no doubt at all that he is one of the most promising young theoretical men I have seen in the last ten years. In addition to his very considerable ability in theoretical physics, he has a particular ability to correlate his theoretical work with experiments, and has a very keen insight into physics as a whole. Regarding his possible abilities as a teacher I believe he has not had any great experience, but he has a fine reputation here for explaining things to other people and giving reports. He has a particular knack for taking complicated situations and explaining them in simple terms. In short, while I know very little of his background and teaching experience, I believe that he has the necessary personality and fundamental ability which would make him an excellent teacher.'[3] Bacher referred to the letter that Bethe had previously written to Gibbs, and further added his voice in support of attracting Feynman to Cornell.

Professor Gibbs acted on the proposal of Bethe and Bacher to appoint Feynman to an assistant professorship at Cornell University. All that he needed to proceed further with the president's office at Cornell was Feynman's full name and his date and place of birth, 'partly as an indication of his citizenship,'[4] which Feynman himself supplied.[5] Feynman also sent Gibbs a one-page 'History of Richard P. Feynman'.[6]

On 8 August 1945, Feynman wrote to Gibbs: 'I appreciate the confidence you must have in me to make such a fine offer to me without our having met. I do hope that when I take up my duties at Cornell you will not be disappointed. You can be sure that this will occur as soon as the war situation will permit me to come to Ithaca. I am very anxiously looking forward to this time.'[7]

On 11 August, Bethe wrote to Gibbs and thanked him 'for your very prompt and very successful action on Feynman. He is completely satisfied and you may already have his letter containing his decision to stay at Cornell [in preference to going anywhere else]. I am, of course, very happy about this decision.'[8] In this letter, Bethe also hinted about the successful completion of work on and use of the atomic bomb, by writing: 'You certainly have heard that our work here has led to final success. Naturally, under these circumstances, it is no longer a secret who of the Cornell staff worked on this problem. If there is any interest in this, please feel completely free to mention our names in any connection in which you consider this useful.'[8]

Bethe further informed Gibbs: 'No decision has yet been made about the future of the laboratory [at Los Alamos], but I am very happy to know that any or all of us may return to Cornell either November 1st [1945] or March 1st [1946]. I hope, in the near future, to be able to tell you a more definite date.'[8] Finally, Bethe expressed the 'hope . . . that when this letter arrives, there will be Peace'.[8] With the dropping of the atomic bomb on 6 August on Hiroshima and on 9 August on Nagasaki, the war with Japan ended, and finally World War II came to an end.

Feynman's appointment at Cornell finally began on 1 November. Professor Gibbs wrote to him on 15 September that 'we would like to have you here at the start of the Fall term, that is about the first of November. Indications from correspondence and telephone calls are that we shall have a sizable increase in our graduate group at that time, some of them just starting out in graduate work and others ready for a more advanced work. Then there will be some who will be working on theses and will want or need an opportunity for consultation with someone versed in theoretical physics. I understand from Bethe that you are anxious to get started on this work and I hope that everything can be arranged as suggested. I shall now attempt to discuss the courses that you might advantageously offer but will leave it for Bethe to advise you in further detail upon his return to Los Alamos [from Cornell, where Bethe and Bacher, as well as Bruno Rossi and Lyman Parratt, planned to visit and then return to Los Alamos around 20–22 September] which I take it will not be long delayed.

'I hope we may have an opportunity to discuss your future plans and wishes in connection with work here with Bethe before he gets away on the 20th so that my discussion with him regarding them may be as realistic as possible. Then when he returns you will be able to obtain from him a clearer picture of what it will be desirable to plan for.

'We were all greatly pleased to learn of your decision to continue your connection with Cornell. I am very optimistic about future opportunities here for I believe we shall have the unique opportunity to develop a field of physics, both in teaching and research, to a higher level than ever and of a character that properly belongs in a university.'[9]

Again, on 30 October, Gibbs wrote to Feynman informing him that 'when Professors Bethe, Bacher, Rossi, and Parratt were here last week we were assured that your release from Los Alamos Laboratory could be arranged in time to enable you take up your duties at Cornell at the beginning of the Fall term which is November 1, 1945. To that end I have already recommended that your leave of absence be cancelled effective November 1, 1945, and I anticipate there will be no hesitation in making it official by Trustees' action at either one of two meetings that are to be held within the next ten days . . . I shall write to you again in regard to what courses we shall find it desirable for you to offer. They will probably include two courses of a theoretical nature for first and/or second year graduate students.'[10]

Feynman sent a telegram to Gibbs on 23 October, informing him, 'Plan to arrive Ithaca October 31,' and asked him 'What courses am I to teach?'[11] Further correspondence was really not necessary. Through Hans Bethe's influence at Cornell, Feynman had received the job offer as an assistant professor there for the fall of 1944, and had been immediately granted a leave of absence to continue his work at Los Alamos.

Richard Feynman wanted to follow Hans Bethe very much to Cornell. He did not give consideration to offers from any of the other places. 'I got offers from other places, but I just did not consider them because I wanted to be with Hans Bethe. I like him very much, and I never regretted that decision. I just decided to go to Cornell.'[12] They offered Feynman what he 'thought was a fair salary. But they hadn't realized what was going on in the world, what was happening after the war when the salaries offered were much higher all over.'[12] What happened as a result was that every once in a while Feynman would receive a notification from Cornell that he had received an increment in salary. He hadn't gone to Ithaca yet, but he got several raises from there while he was still at Los Alamos. These increments in salary came as a result of Bethe's knowledge of the various offers that were being made to Feynman, which he was refusing, irrespective of the position or salary offered, 'simply on the basis that I wanted to go to Cornell because Bethe was going to be there and he sounded like a guy to work with. All I remember was the amusing thing that I got a series of raises, three or four, without any effort on my part whatsoever. The people at Cornell were moving in line with the prevailing wages of the day [which, in Feynman's case, came to $3900 per annum at the time he finally joined Cornell].'[12]

One of the other people who very much wanted to lure Feynman was Robert Oppenheimer. Oppenheimer sought to arrange an appointment for him at the University of California at Berkeley, where he wrote to Raymond T. Birge, chairman of the physics department: 'As you know, we have quite a number of physicists here [at Los Alamos], and I have run into a few who are young and whose qualities I had not known before. Of these there is one who is in every way so outstanding and so clearly recognized as such, that I think it appropriate to call his name to your attention, with the urgent request that you consider him for a position in the department at the earliest time that is possible. You may remember the name because he once applied for a fellowship in Berkeley: it is Richard Feynman. He is by all odds the most brilliant young physicist here, and everyone knows this. He is a man of so thoroughly engaging a character and personality, extremely clear, extremely normal in all respects, and an excellent teacher with a warm feeling for physics in all its aspects. He has the best possible relations both with the theoretical people of whom he is one, and with the experimental people with whom he works in very close harmony.

'The reason for telling you about him now is that his excellence is so well known, both at Princeton where he worked before he came here, and to a number of "big shots" on this project, that he has already been offered a position [at Cornell] for the postwar period, and will most certainly be offered others. I feel that he would be a great strength for our department, tending to tie together its teaching, its research, and its experimental and theoretical aspects. I may give you two quotations from men with whom he has worked. Bethe has said that he would rather lose any two other men than Feynman from this present job, and Wigner said: "He is a second Dirac, only this time more human." '[13] (Eugene Wigner had known Feynman at Princeton and, during the war, he was at the Metallurgical Laboratory of the University of Chicago from 1942 to 1945.)

Birge replied to Oppenheimer that he could not make permanent appointments while so many tenured professors were still on leave. The Berkeley physics department had a lot of lower-division students, and he had hired people to teach them. However, he requested further information about Feynman.[14]

Oppenheimer broached the matter again with Birge six months later. 'I must say that I am not nearly so much in sympathy with the attitude expressed toward Feynman. It is not an unusual thing for universities to make commitments to young men whom they wish to have after the war. I surely do not know of all the cases where such commitments have been made, even to members of this project, but there are three which come to mind: [Robert] Christy has been offered an assistant professorship by Compton at the University of Chicago, although he had no connection with the university before the war. [Norman] Ramsey has been offered a position by Columbia University, to become effective after the termination of this project. Feynman, as you know, has been offered an assistant professorship by Cornell.

'As for Feynman himself, I perhaps presumed too much on the excellence of his reputation among those to whom he is known. I know that [Robert] Brode, [Edwin] McMillan, and [Louis] Alvarez are enthusiastic about him, and it is small wonder.[15] He is not only an extremely brilliant theorist, but a man of the greatest robustness, responsibility, and warmth, a brilliant and lucid teacher, and an untiring worker. He would come to the teaching of physics with both a rare talent and a rare enthusiasm. We have entrusted him here [at Los Alamos] with the giving of a course for the staff of the laboratory. He is one of the most responsible men I have ever met. He does not regard himself as a privileged artist but as one of a group of hard-working men for whom the development of physical science is an obligation and a pleasure. He spends much of his time in the laboratories and is always closely associated with the experimental phases of the work. He was associated with Robert Wilson in the Princeton [OSRD] project, and Wilson attributed a great part of the success of that project to his help. We regard him as invaluable here; he has been given a responsibility and his work carries a weight far beyond his years. In fact he is such a man as we have long needed in Berkeley to contribute to the unity of the department and to give it technical stength where it has been lacking in the past.'[16]

With Oppenheimer's insistence, as displayed in his letters to Birge, Feynman was finally offered an assistant professorship at Berkeley at a salary of $3900 per annum. Birge wrote to him that, 'during the period that the department was being built up by the addition of men like Lawrence, Brode, Oppenheimer, Jenkins, and White, and more recently by McMillan and Alvarez, no one to whom we made an offer ever refused it. If you come to Berkeley, I am certain you will never regret the decision.'[17] But Feynman did refuse.[18] In this connection, Oppenheimer informed Birge: 'Several months ago Dr Feynman accepted a permanent appointment with the physics department at Cornell University. I do not know details of salary and rank, but they are presumably satisfactory to him. I shall of course do my best to call to your attention any men who are available and whom we should want to recommend strongly for the department. I am afraid that at the present time this may involve some conflict since we are all eager to add personnel here and since in the nature of things I tend to go after men in whom I have the greatest overall confidence.'[19]

Oppenheimer was evidently miffed that Raymond Birge had not pursued his recommendation to offer an appointment to Feynman more vigorously. But Feynman was very content with the thought of going to Cornell and being close to Bethe. Other people from Los Alamos were going all over the country, trying to decide which place offered them the best opportunity. There was a lot of jockeying around; the universities were looking for suitable people, and a lot of people were seeking and getting jobs. There may have been competition from places like Berkeley and Chicago. So far as Feynman was concerned, he had decided to go to Cornell, and that was that. Bill Woodward and Robert Wilson were also going to Cornell, as was Philip Morrison, and Feynman was happy that these people also wanted to be close to Hans Bethe—just as he did. Some other people had been offered jobs at Cornell, but were doubtful that they wanted to go there; Feynman tried to convince them that Cornell was the place to go to, for he thought that it would be great if they were there too. 'We were a lot of friends by that time, and you wanted to know whether your pal was going to be at the same place that you were going to be later. But I don't remember ever thinking of not going to Cornell. All I remember is trying to do my best to convince anybody else that I wanted to be with to come to Cornell. Perhaps Robert Wilson was one of those about whom I was worried the most, who [ultimately] did not go.'[12] Wilson first went to Harvard for one year and then to Cornell.

Feynman left Los Alamos earlier than most people. He left in time to begin the fall term at Cornell. On the way to Ithaca, Feynman stopped at the Iowa State University to give a talk. He traveled on a train all the way from Albuquerque to Ithaca by way of Ames, Iowa. Since Feynman had been told to appear for his duties at Cornell on 1 November, he thought that classes would begin on that day. On the train Feynman began to plan and prepare the course he was going to teach; it was a graduate level course on the mathematical methods of physics. 'On the train I prepared the outline and worked out the whole course. I had never taught a course before, and I figured it all out on the train.'[12]

Richard Feynman arrived at midnight on 31 October at Ithaca. He got off the train and slung his suitcase on his shoulder as he was always used to doing. Then he said to himself, 'Wait a minute! You're a professor, and you have to act like one.' A porter asked him: 'Can I carry your suitcase?' Feynman first told him, 'No, I can carry my own', and then he realized, 'I have got to start living in a dignified way.' So he let the porter carry his suitcase to a taxi, and sat down elegantly in the back seat. The taxi driver asked him, 'Where to?' He said, 'To the biggest hotel in town, please!' The driver said, 'That would be Hotel Ithaca.' On the way he asked Feynman if he had made a reservation at the hotel, which, of course, he hadn't. The driver told him that the hotel situation in Ithaca was tough. He said, 'I'll take you there, but I'll wait for you. They probably haven't got a room.'[20]

Feynman went in and, sure enough, the hotel didn't have a room for him. He went to another hotel, and no room was available there either. He left his suitcase there and started to walk around in search of a place to stay. He found another man who was wandering around, also in search of a place to stay; they walked around together in various directions, but found nothing. They thought of stopping at someone's home to ask if they knew of a place where to stay. Just then they noticed a building, into which they could see through the windows, and saw that there were a lot of beds, including several double-decker beds. Evidently it was a dormitory for students. They went in to ask if there was an extra bed available. They went in through the door, but there was nobody there; the place was completely deserted. They walked through the place, went upstairs, saw beds, and thought that they would sleep there. But again, it occurred to Feynman that he was now a professor and he shouldn't sleep at a place without permission, for if it was found out that he had slept there without permission it wouldn't be good for his 'image as a professor'.[20] So he and his companion trooped out and roamed around the campus some more. Then, suddenly, they saw a building with couches in the lobby. Feynman went around to find the janitor, who was still working at 2:00 a.m. He asked him if it would be all right to sleep on the couches in the lobby. He said it would be fine, and that's where Feynman and his chance acquaintance spent the rest of the night. In the morning, Feynman went to the men's common washroom, where he washed and got ready, and promptly at 9:00 a.m. showed up at the physics department in Rockefeller Hall. There he wanted to find out the time at which his first class would take place, and learned that he had been asked to arrive in Cornell one week before classes so that he would have time to get settled.

Feynman was still so tense from having worked long and hard for several years at the Manhattan Project, first in Princeton and then at Los Alamos, that he did not realize that the pace of academic life in upstate New York was somewhat slower. Then he inquired at the physics office where he should sleep, where he should stay? He was advised to go to the Willard Straight Hall, where someone would help him with housing. Feynman went there. He looked very young, almost like a student. He asked at the booth about where he should stay, and the fellow there replied: 'Listen, buddy, the room situation is tough. In fact, it is so tough that, believe it or not, a professor had to sleep in the lobby last night.'[20] Feynman suddenly realized that he had slept in the lobby of the Willard Straight Hall.

Feynman was amused and bothered to find that he was being talked about right away. He had come to Cornell as quietly as he could, without making any waves, and yet rumor about him was making the rounds already. In any case, he found a room with a landlady, not a very nice and comfortable one, but one in which he could and did stay for a long time.[21] He immediately began to spend as much time as possible in preparing his lectures on the mathematical methods of physics.

The course had been very well prepared. In fact, it was so well done that neither Feynman had difficulty teaching it nor did the students encounter any difficulty in learning from it. It was a one-year course on mathematical physics. 'I did have some success in teaching; it worked out all right. They learned everything!'[12] The first seminar which Feynman had given at Princeton to 'monster minds' had been a shock,[22] but at Los Alamos he had developed a knack for speaking; he'd had many occasions to speak before audiences, and give talks on scientific, technical, or more popular subjects, and therefore he had no trouble in teaching his first course of lectures at Cornell. In fact, in future, he would think all these lectures through carefully and prepare the briefest notes for guidance; all his published scientific and popular books would be based on the notes of lectures taken by young people assigned to do so, or taken directly from tape-recordings, transcribed and mildly edited.[23] In due course, Feynman became a most accomplished and inimitable lecturer and public speaker.

Feynman's course on the mathematical methods of physics treated all the fundamental mathematical techniques and devices a physicist needs during the course of his actual study of and research on physical problems. In his lectures, Feynman discussed *mathematical topics* that would be useful to physicists. But the motivations and standards of rigor were drawn from physics; that is, the choice of subjects was dictated by their usefulness in physics, and the level of rigor was intended to reflect current practices in theoretical physics.

In his course, Feynman treated a large variety of illustrative problems, and assigned others from which the students could learn the detailed applications of each topic that he covered. He did not choose his topics to flow in a smooth logical pattern. Occasionally a new subject was introduced without the students having been carefully prepared for the blow. This was intended to reflect the way it often is in physics: theoretical physicists frequently need to plunge into the middle of an unfamiliar subject, and Feynman's course was intended to give practice and confidence in dealing with problems for which the student's preparation was incomplete. In his lectures on mathematical methods of physics, Feynman employed a considerable, deliberate non-uniformity of presentation. Certain subjects were skimmed, while very detailed applications were worked out in other areas. Feynman believed that if the course was to give practice in doing physics then the student must be given a chance to gain confidence in his ability to do detailed calculations. On the other hand what Feynman was giving was a course on the mathematical methods used in physics that could be covered in one year, rather than develop a reference work; it was therefore not possible to go into everything as deeply as one might like. Still, after having mastered this course, it would have been possible for a student of theoretical physics to move comfortably into various areas of investigation and research.

Robert Walker, one of those who attended Feynman's course of lectures at Cornell, later on developed a course on the mathematical methods of physics at the California Institute of Technology, which he patterned after Feynman's course at Cornell. At Caltech, this course (given by Robert Walker and Jon Matthews) was taken by senior undergraduate and first year graduate students, not only from physics but other departments as well.[24] Feynman looked at a number of standard texts in this field, especially the two volumes of Courant–Hilbert,[25] but they didn't quite appeal to him. He said to himself, 'Why don't I teach them mathematics the way I do it', because he had his own special way of doing everything.[21] 'Sometimes he did things in a certain way just because nobody did them that way. He would teach ways of doing integrals, ways of summing series, by using various tricks. A lot of those tricks are known to mathematicians, but they are not usually taught in any of the textbooks. For example, he taught complex variables, but did not include anything on contour integration, because during the war he had developed a sort of game with himself that he would tell people he could do any integral without contour integration that they would bring to him. He was trying to make sure that we learned all the [nonstandard] ways of performing integrals, but his may not have been a very wise decision because, of course, it is very useful to be able to do contour integration in the complex plane, and do many integrals that way. In my lectures on mathematical methods of physics I made a combination of the standard things and the things we had learned from Feynman.'[21]

When Feynman first arrived at Cornell, Bethe and Bacher were still away, but Lyman Parratt was there, as were R. C. Gibbs and Lloyd P. Smith, who became chairman of the physics department upon Gibbs's retirement. But there were not many other people whom Feynman knew. However, within a month or two of his leaving Los Alamos, all of them returned to Cornell.

Feynman's first year at Cornell was quite interesting. With his wife Arline dead, he was now a bachelor. At first he found the girls at Cornell rather interesting. He would go to freshmen parties (mixers), and since many people had come from the war to resume their education they often looked older. Feynman himself, since he looked young, could have passed for an undergraduate. 'So, while I was a professor, I could act very much like a student, even a freshman. I could be mistaken for a freshman in a very legitimate way.'[20]

Feynman recalled the first dance he went to. He wasn't sure of himself. He had danced with Arline, but he hadn't danced with a girl to try to get her to like him in so many years—so that was a bit experimental. When he went to the first mixer, the freshmen girls were there. He would dance with one, and the dancing was fine. Then the girl would start talking to him, ask him some questions, and then, after the first dance she would make some excuse like, 'I've to powder my nose,' and leave him. This went on with several girls. For example, the girl would ask him who he was; he would reply truthfully, 'I'm a professor.' 'What did you do during the war?' He'd reply, 'I worked at Los Alamos on the atomic bomb.' 'I suppose you saw the atomic explosion in New Mexico!' He would reply, 'Yes.' 'You are a damned liar', she would say and walk off. All of them assumed that Feynman was fibbing about his exploits during the war and also doubted that he was a professor. So he decided to conceal his background, and when he met a new girl to dance with he didn't tell her the truth and was successful in getting her attention. 'The girls were all too smart to believe that baloney [the truth about his background]; it was much easier to believe that I was some kind of faker!'[20]

During the first year, Feynman taught his classes with great enthusiasm. Apart from the course on the mathematical methods of physics, he taught another one on electricity and magnetism. He was very busy preparing his courses—that was hard work—but he didn't do much about his research. Other than teaching classes, he would rest. He was burned out from war work at Los Alamos. He would go to the library and sit there for hours reading the *Arabian nights*. He tried to meet girls at parties. He found that preparing his courses was a full time job, and he devoted himself fully to that. He didn't believe that it was very important work, and he thought he should be doing research. The more he taught courses—and in due course he would teach all the fundamental theoretical courses (classical mechanics, quantum mechanics, statistical mechanics, relativity theory, etc.)—and stayed away from research, the more depressed he became. He believed that he was completely burned out and wouldn't accomplish anything.[20] At first, all this—preparing and teaching courses, reading the *Arabian nights*, meeting girls, going to dances, playing drums in his room, sitting in the sun, and generally fooling around—was a vacation. All the other time he worked on preparing lectures for classes, but almost never could get down to research work. 'And I began to think this was the end.'[20]

Feynman continued to get raises in salary. He was still in demand from other places outside; they wanted to lure him away to departments in other universities. When another place offered him more money and would invite him to take a new job, he would just refuse it, but the departmental secretary knew what was going on and she would probably tell the chairman, and Feynman would continue to get raises in salary that were intended to keep him at Cornell. However, these raises in salary did not help Feynman at all, and he felt inadequate to cope with what was happening and that greatly affected his psychology.

This went on for quite a long time. Every now and then someone would bring him a problem, say on gamma rays, and he would try to become interested in it; he would talk and discuss a little bit about it, but it wouldn't go far. Even his students would ask him why he was not doing anything, but he had no answer. He did a few tiny things, but not the kind of things he had done before. Feynman tried many things to overcome his lethargy and depression, like trying to get up early and working hard, but nothing helped well enough. Feynman visited his family in Far Rockaway just before the beginning of the fall semester in 1946. At the invitation of Judah Cahn, the new rabbi at the local synagogue, he gave a talk on the atomic bomb at the Temple Israel on the day after Yom Kippur. Although Melville and Lucille Feynman were atheists, they attended the programs at the temple from time to time. Melville suffered from uncontrollable high blood pressure, for which he had even gone to consult the physicians at the Mayo Clinic at Rochester, Minnesota, in the spring of 1945. The family worried about his health all the time. Melville was now very proud of what his son Richard had achieved in science and that he would spend his life among the great scientists of the world. On 7 October 1946, Melville suffered a stroke and died the next day; Richard signed his father's death certificate, his second in less than two years—the first one had been upon the death of Arline in summer 1945. Melville was interned at the Bayside Cemetery in Queens.

A few weeks later, H. D. Smyth, the chairman of the physics department at Princeton, informed Feynman that the University and the Institute for Advanced Study (where Albert Einstein was) would like to make an 'offer of a permanent position at a substantial salary'.[26] It was intended that he would spend half the time at the university and the other half at the institute, free of teaching duties; they knew about his feeling that there was too much thinking in vacuum at the institute, and not enough contact with students and the fundamental world, so they tried to give Feynman something special—the possibility to teach and do research in his own way. It was 'even a notch better than Einstein, in the sense that I would have contact with students that I desired, and the freedom to do research at the institute.'[20] Besides, he wouldn't have much of a teaching load, and would get a salary much higher than what he was getting at Cornell. From Princeton, Eugene Wigner congratulated Feynman, and expressed the hope that he would accept.[27] Feynman decided to stay on at Cornell. However, the offer from Princeton resulted in his being promoted to an associate professorship at Cornell. He also declined an offer of an associate professorship at UCLA (the University of California, Los Angeles). He did consider seriously an invitation from Berkeley for the academic year 1947–48 and another one for the following year, but Robert Oppenheimer accepted the directorship of the Institute for Advanced Study in the spring of 1947, which convinced Feynman to stay on at Cornell.

To Feynman, given his psychological situation, all these invitations appeared to be very strange. The offer from Princeton seemed so strange, so mistaken, that he concluded: 'They must be crazy to think that I was worth all that!'[20] Feynman thought that clearly they did not know that he was all that good. Next morning, while shaving, the thought occurred to him that he was not responsible 'for such crazy dumbness like this, that I could not—and didn't have to—live up to other people's idiotic impression of my abilities. I never said that I was all that good, and I have no responsibility to try to measure up to others' impression of how good I am! Therefore I shouldn't try at all. This thought released me from a feeling of guilt.'[20] Feynman imformed Frank Aydelotte, director of the Institute for Advanced Study, of his decision to stay on at Cornell.[28]

Feynman's close associates at Cornell, such as Hans Bethe (with whom he had constant invigorating discussions) and Philip Morrison (in their shared office), did not have any idea that Feynman was suffering from depression or psychological difficulties. As Philip Morrison remarked: 'Feynman depressed is just a little more cheerful than any other person when he is exuberant.'[29] On the other hand, to Theodore Welton, who was 'entranced as always by the flow of ideas' when he met Feynman at the meetings of the American Physical Society, 'it was clear that his mind was not where it properly belonged.'[30]

Then two things happened. First, Robert R. Wilson, whom Feynman had known at Princeton and Los Alamos, and who was now head of the newly established Newman Laboratory for Nuclear Studies at Cornell, and was in some ways responsible for Feynman, called him in one day for a chat in the spring of 1947. Feynman confided his concern to Wilson that Cornell had made a 'bad bet' with him. Wilson told Feynman that when Cornell hired a professor, the risk was the university's as to what the professor would or would not grow into by his work in scientific research. Moreover, the probability that someone would really accomplish something really important in research was not high, and that many professors just try to do a good job of teaching their classes and that was just fine. Feynman should not blame himself that at that moment he was not achieving very much. Most of all, Feynman should not feel guilty, and just do whatever he was happy in doing.[20]

This conversation with Wilson led Feynman to think that in high school, at MIT, and at Princeton, he did things because he enjoyed doing them. He used to play games with things about which he felt curious or intrigued. It occurred to him that he should continue to play with ideas just as he had done when he was younger—play at finding the relationship between things, and do just whatever he felt like doing. He didn't have 'to work on a problem because it was important, or because someone expected me to do something important.'[20] He was no longer working for his Ph.D. thesis, nor was he working on war-related projects; he didn't even have to live up to the reputation he had obtained at Princeton and Los Alamos or live up to anything else. With these thoughts his anguish, strain, and guilt disappeared, and he decided to recapture the feeling of play in his work on physics.

This feeling of release was the second thing that happened, and it worked wonderfully. Just a few days later, Feynman was in the (Cornell) students' cafeteria for lunch. He used to go to the cafeteria rather than to the faculty club, because he liked to look at pretty girls.[20] While he was eating and watching, he noticed that some guy, fooling around, threw up a plate in the air; the plate went up and then started to come down. The plate had emblazoned upon it the emblem of Ezra Cornell, the founder of Cornell University. 'As the plate went up in the air I saw it wobble, and I noticed that the [blue] medallion on the plate was going around. It was pretty obvious to me that the medallion went around faster than the wobbling. I had nothing to do, so I started to figure out the motion of the rotating plate. I discovered that when the angle [of the wobble with the horizontal] is [very small], the medallion rotates twice as fast as the wobble rate—two to one. It's a cute relationship; it came out of a complicated equation.'[20, 31]

Feynman ultimately worked out the equation of motion of the rotating–wobbling plate. 'I wanted to understand this motion from Newton's laws alone. I wanted to see the forces, not just set up the Lagrangian and differentiate all the equations. I wanted to see how [Newton's] law of motion applied to the disk.'[20, 32]

After solving the problem of the spinning–wobbling plate, Feynman ran to Bethe's office and blurted out to him, 'Hey, I saw something funny about a disk'; he told him about what he had seen in the cafeteria and what he had calculated. Bethe asked him, 'But what's the importance of that?' Feynman told him that it had no importance, nor did he care if it had any importance, but it was fun. 'That's all I am going to do from now on: have fun!'[20]

This episode rekindled his love for 'playing around with physics'. Then he thought about the problem of the rotations of the spinning electron in relativity, of how to represent them by path integrals in quantum mechanics, and worked on the Dirac equation in electrodynamics. And before he knew it (it was just a short time), he was playing around with the same problem that he had loved so much, which he had stopped working on when he went to Los Alamos: his thesis type of problems, 'all those old-fashioned, wonderful things. It was effortless. It was very easy to play with these things. It was like uncorking a bottle: everything flowed out effortlessly. I almost tried to resist it! There was no importance to what I was doing, but ultimately there was. The diagrams that I got the Nobel Prize for came from that piddling around with the wobbling plate.'[33]

Something else happened in the fall of 1946 that gave Feynman the assurance that his intuitive Lagrangian formulation of quantum mechanics in his Ph.D. thesis had been correct. This was the time Feynman was called upon to introduce P. A. M. Dirac, who was giving a talk at the bicentennial celebration of Princeton University. Dirac had sent Feynman a handwritten copy of his paper and he had carefully studied it.[34] To introduce Dirac would have been important at any time, but it took place *before* Feynman's release from his psychological situation.

Afterwards, in conversation with Dirac, Feynman found that the discovery he had made in the spring of 1942 (in his thesis at Princeton), which had led him to make the functions proportional, had not been noticed at all by Dirac. Since Feynman did not know whether Dirac knew this, he verified it directly from him.

After the episode of the spinning-wobbling plate, Feynman again became interested in physics as play. Within a week or so from that time, the things which interested him were the old things like path-integrals, how to formulate the problem of the rotation of spinning electrons with path-integrals, and Feynman spent a tremendous amount of time on them. He wanted to formulate and solve the problem of obtaining a path-integral solution of spin. He studied quaternions in the mathematics library; he read all about Hamilton's work in this field. William Rowan Hamilton, like James Clerk Maxwell, was one of Feynman's heroes. With the help of quaternions and path integrals, Feynman tried to formulate the relativistic theory of an electron in one dimension. He felt confident that he could do it in four dimensions (of space and time), but he could not do it in a satisfactory way. Feynman reported his research activities at the beginning of 1947 in a letter to Ted Welton: 'I am engaged now in a general program of study—I want to understand (not just in a mathematical way) the ideas of all branches of theor[etical] physics. As you know I am now struggling with the Dirac Equ.'[35]

From the fall of 1946 up to the spring of 1948, Feynman lived at the Telluride House at Cornell. Telluride House was not an ordinary dormitory; it was a residential community founded around 1911 by a wealthy man who had been deeply impressed by the English college system in universities, and wanted to establish a house as an intellectual community on an American university campus, for which he chose Cornell. He built and endowed this house, a residential intellectual community of about thirty-five people, with a couple of faculty members as senior guides, who lived on the premises and to whom the younger students could turn for advice and counsel. In physical appearance it was very much like a fraternity house, but in actual functioning and selection criteria it was different.

Previous people who had the same guesthood at the Telluride House included Mark Kac, the mathematician. 'Cornell's most distinguished visitors would often stay at Telluride House during their visits. For example, Paul A. Fleury, the polymer chemist, stayed at the House, and many people stayed there who were not scientists. Freeman Dyson stayed there when he first came to Cornell in September 1947, until he found some other place to live.'[36]

The young people would often have dinner with Feynman at the same table. On these occasions, Feynman would regale them with the stories of his wartime exploits at Los Alamos. Feynman's story of his encounter with the Draft Board in the fall of 1946, at which he was examined by several psychiatrists and whom he fooled by giving cheeky answers and acting mentally deficient, resulting in being assigned to the 4F (total rejection) category, would always bring the house down and leave his listeners roaring with laughter.[37] Just as he used to do at Princeton, he would challenge his young friends at Telluride House to give him problems, which he would solve then and there in his head. Theodore Schultz recalled several problems, some very complicated ones, which he gave Feynman to solve, and which he solved in record time without any difficulty. These problems, at times, included such difficult challenges as the asymptotic behavior of a Bessel function, but Feynman would manage to give the correct solution each time. He would always carry a lot of sundry information, including mathematical tricks, magnitudes of physical quantities, and the like in his head, and he could make order-of-magnitude calculations with great facility.[36]

At the Telluride House Feynman loved to drum. As Schultz recalled: 'I don't think he had any drums of his own at that time; that was the time before he acquired a set of bongo drums. Telluride House had all this wood-paneling that had beautiful resonance, and he would use these wood panels as his drumming surfaces. There were also some benches that were built into the walls as you went down the grand stairway and the landings, and I can still see Feynman sitting on the bench and beating on the wood-paneled back of the bench, like a big piece of plywood. It would act like a drumhead, and he would beat upon it. Even then his drumming was very attractive, interesting, and involved. Everybody would just listen enraptured while he performed, for that's what he was doing, "performing"!'

'In Beethoven, for instance, you play three notes with one hand and two with the other all the time, and that's not easy, but you learn how to do that. Feynman would get people together and say, 'I'm going to beat five against six, or now I'm going to beat twelve against thirteen', and he would do that; that was really overwhelming.

'And he would entertain us in other ways. He claimed once that he could move one eyeball while keeping the other fixed. He challenged us to do that. I'm convinced that he could do it. I was told by an ophthalmologist that it was impossible to be able to do so, but Feynman *did* it.

'I remember I took a course, an introduction to atomic physics, one term at Cornell. It was the unfortunate scheduling of that course; it met three days a week. In the next room, a course on statistical mechanics was being given by this young Professor Feynman, and roars of laughter used to come through the wall of that classroom in the Rockefeller Hall. We would hear these gales of laughter coming in all the time. If you have been in a foreign country, where people speak a language that you don't know, you are quite content 90% of the time until someone laughs, then you know you've missed something. That's very frustrating. We had that feeling many times when we heard all that laughter coming from the next room.

'I recall going to a "work-in-progress" seminar on the ordered operator calculus by Feynman; this lecture would have been in 1949. Most of his paper on the ordered operator calculus, with all its detailed theorems, was there. After the lecture, somebody in the audience asked Feynman, 'Isn't this what Dyson did?', and Feynman replied, 'Well, where do you think he got it?' He said it in his inimitable mocking–insulting combination of tones that only he could do.'[36]

At the American Physical Society meeting in January 1947, Herbert C. Corben—who had returned, after spending several years in his native Australia, to join the faculty of the Carnegie Institute of Technology (now the Carnegie-Mellon University)—met Feynman. Feynman talked about his new ideas with Corben; these had to do with the space–time (path-integral) approach to nonrelativistic quantum mechanics and others arising from the recent episode of the spinning–wobbling plate in the Cornell cafeteria, but he found it difficult to write it all down. Herbert and Mulaika Corben invited him to come to Pittsburgh at the end of the term, stay with them at their house on the campus, and get his ideas on paper. After the Shelter Island Conference early in June 1947, Feynman decided that he had to write up his ideas and publish them before he could expect anyone to understand them, and he accepted the Corbens' offer to stay with them in Pittsburgh and write up the paper.

In Pittsburgh, 'he played with our children—aged 2, 3, and 4. We all spent a day at a local fair, and he regaled us with stories and told more of them at the parties we threw—cracking safes at Los Alamos, holding out his hands, one palm up and the other one down, to the psychiatrist who was examining him for possible induction in the army and who responded by saying, 'Turn them over!', and Feynman again turned over one palm up and the other down, and many other stories that were published later [in *Surely you're joking, Mr Feynman!*]. The *Kinsey Report* had just come out and Feynman spent most of one day sitting in the living room and reading it from beginning to end.

'At that time, Alfred Schild was on the faculty of the Carnegie Tech mathematics department, and he and his wife lived in the same house. Elliot Montroll was at the University of Pittsburgh nearby and had been thinking of a method of calculation, in the context of statistical mechanics, that to some extent overlapped with Feynman's ideas. He suggested to Feynman that he should write down these ideas before someone else did it for him. But Feynman liked to "mess around", to speculate occasionally, add an extra term to an equation to see what it would do, but was quick to spot if it led to nonsense. One time I sat at the table in the living room with him and Alfred Schild, looking at an extra term that Feynman had cooked up and added to the Dirac equation. It looked interesting and might have had some useful consequences, if not for the electron than for some other particle [such as the neutrino]. Suddenly Feynman jumped up and said, "We are idiots! It doesn't conserve parity." [It was the same equation which he would resurrect in treating the V–A interaction in the summer of 1957.]

'Finally he retired to his room and started to write. He was told by my wife [Mulaika] that he could not come out again until he had at least a rough draft. When that draft appeared, we did not think it did justice to guide him through the work and made some suggestions. He settled down huffily to write again and three weeks after he had arrived the paper was complete, to everyone's enthusiastic satisfaction. [Julius Ashkin, who had been a member of the Technical Computations Group at Los Alamos, was then at the Carnegie-Mellon University at Pittsburgh, read Feynman's paper very carefully and corrected any mistakes that had crept in.] Soon after that, Feynman left to drive West, and the paper was sent for publication. [Feynman first sent the paper to the *Physical Review*, but it was suggested to him that he should send it to the *Reviews of Modern Physics*.]'[38]

When Feynman was at Cornell, he was asked to give a series of lectures once a week at an aeronautics laboratory in Buffalo. Cornell University had made an arrangement with the laboratory, which included evening lectures in physics to be given by somebody from the university. Someone had already been doing it, but there were complaints about him, so the physics department approached Feynman to do it. Since Feynman was a young professor at that time, he could not very well afford to say no, and he agreed to take on the job.

To go to Buffalo one had to fly by a one-plane airline, called Robinson Airlines, which later became Mohawk Airlines. Mr Robinson was the owner and pilot of that airline. Although Feynman did not particularly relish the idea of going to Buffalo every Thursday night, he was being paid an extra thirty-five dollars in addition to his expenses. Since he had grown up in the Depression, he didn't want to refuse this money, which was a considerable sum in those days. Suddenly he conceived the idea that in order to make the trip to Buffalo more attractive for himself, he should spend this money on enjoying things, for this was money he would otherwise not have had. So he decided to spend the thirty-five dollars to entertain himself each time he was in Buffalo.

Not having had much experience of the world, Feynman asked his taxi driver, Marcuso, owner of cab number 169—who would always pick him up at the airport and deliver him to the place of his lecture—to guide him through the ins and outs of entertaining himself in Buffalo. Marcuso told him that an elegant bar, called the Alibi Room, was the scene of much interesting activity, where he could meet lots of people and have fun; he would drive him there after his Thursday evening lectures. Marcuso also advised him to order Black and White label whiskey with water on the side when he would come into the bar. This became his routine every Thursday night. Just when he would come in the bartender would pour his shot of Black and White label whiskey with water on the side. Feynman would down the drink in one gulp; after about twenty seconds he would have a sip of water. After practicing this kind of drinking for some time, he didn't need water anymore.

At the Alibi Room and other bars Feynman had extensive experiences of bar brawls, hookers, and con artists. These encounters would serve Feynman as the fodder for his funny stories for the rest of his life and become a permanent part of the Feynman lore.

Notes and References

1. J. Bernstein, Hans Bethe, *New Yorker*, October and November 1947; 1979.

2. H.A. Bethe, Letter to R.C. Gibbs, 30 October 1943, The Feynman file at the Department of Physics, Cornell University, Ithaca, New York.

3. R.F. Bacher, Letter to R.C. Gibbs, 28 February 1944, The Feynman file (Ref. 2).

4. R.C. Gibbs, Letter to Hans Bethe, 8 August 1944, Feynman file (Ref. 2).

5. R.P. Feynman, Letter to R.C. Gibbs, 19 September 1944. The Feynman file (Ref. 2).

6. R.P. Feynman, The History of R.P. Feynman. The Feynman file (Ref. 2).

7. R.P. Feynman, Letter to R.C. Gibbs, 8 August 1945. The Feynman file (Ref. 2).

8. H.A. Bethe, Letter to R.C. Gibbs, 11 August 1945. The Feynman file (Ref. 2).

9. R.C. Gibbs, Letter to R.P. Feynman, 15 September 1945. The Feynman file (Ref. 2).

10. R.C. Gibbs, Letter to R.P. Feynman, 30 October 1945. The Feynman file (Ref. 2).

11. R.P. Feynman, Telegram to R.C. Gibbs, 23 October 1945. The Feynman file (Ref. 2).

12. R.P. Feynman, Interviews and conversations of Jagdish Mehra, in Austin, Texas, April 1970, and Pasadena, California, January 1988.

13. J. Robert Oppenheimer, Letter to R.T. Birge, 4 November 1943. Quoted in

A.K. Smith and C. Weiner (eds.) *Robert Oppenheimer, Letters and recollections*, Harvard University Press, Cambridge, Massachusetts, 1980.

14. R.T. Birge, Letter to J. Robert Oppenheimer, 26 November 1943. Birge file, Box 20, Oppenheimer Papers, Library of Congress, Washington, D.C.

15. Brode, E. McMillan and L. Alvarez were all three on leave from Birge's department, and all held responsible posts in the ordnance department at Los Alamos.

16. J. Robert Oppenheimer, Letter to R.T. Birge, 26 May 1944. Ref. 13.

17. R.T. Birge, Letter to R.P. Feynman, 5 July 1945. Feynman Archive, Caltech.

18. R.P. Feynman, Letter to M.E. Deutsch, 27 July 1945 and 8 August 1945. Feynman Archive, Caltech.

19. J. Robert Oppenheimer, Letter to R.T. Birge, 5 October 1944. Ref. 13.

20. R.P. Feynman, Ref. 12. Also, interviews with Charles Weiner (American Institute of Physics), in Pasadena, California, 1966

21. Robert L. Walker, Telephone interview with Jagdish Mehra, 29 August 1990.

22. R.P. Feynman, *SYJMF*, p. 77.

23. Richard Feynman's volumes based on lecture notes include: *Quantum electrodynamics* (Benjamin, New York, 1961); *Theory of fundamental processes* (Benjamin, New York, 1961); *Photon–hadron interactions* (Benjamin, New York, 1972); *Statistical mechanics: A set of lectures* (Benjamin, New York, 1972).

24. Jon Matthews and Robert L. Walker, *Mathematical methods of physics*. Addison-Wesley, Reading, Massachusetts, 2nd edn., 1964.

25. R. Courant and D. Hilbert, *Methoden der mathematischen Physik*. Springer, Berlin, 1933.

26. H.D. Smyth, Letter to R.P. Feynman, 23 October 1946. Feynman Archive, Caltech.

27. E.P. Wigner, Letter to R.P. Feynman, 24 December 1946. Feynman Archive, Caltech.

28. R.P. Feynman, Letter to Frank Aydelotte, 16 February 1947. Feynman Archive, Caltech.

29. Philip Morrison to S.S. Schweber, 9 August 1980. Quoted in S.S. Schweber, *Rev. Mod. Phys.* **58**, 468 (1986).

30. T.A. Welton, Memories of R.P. Feynman. Unpublished manuscript, 1983.

31. R.P. Feynman, *SYJMF*, pp. 173–74.

32. 'A torque-free plate *wobbles* twice as fast as it *spins* when the wobble is slight.

The ratio of spin to wobble rates is $1:2$ not $2:1$.' Benjamin Fong Chao, *Physics Today*, February 1989, p. 15. Consider the case of a thin disk, or any symmetrical and fairly 'flat' object such as a china plate or a Frisbee. The perpendicular axis theorem for the principal axes is, $I_1 + I_2 = I_3$, where $I = I_1 = I_2 =$ moment of inertia about the axis normal to the symmetry axis, $I_s = I_3 =$ moment of inertia about the symmetry axis. With ω as the angular velocity vector (along the axis of rotation), Euler's equations read:

$$I\dot\omega_1 + \omega_2\omega_3(I_s - I) = 0$$
$$I\dot\omega_1 + \omega_2\omega_1(I - I_s) = 0$$
$$I_s\dot\omega_3 = 0.$$

From the last equation it follows that

$$\omega_3 = \text{constant}.$$

We define a constant Ω as

$$\Omega = \omega_3 \frac{I_s - I}{I} = \left(\frac{I_s}{I} - 1\right)\omega \cos\alpha,$$

where $\omega_3 = \omega \cos\alpha$, α being the angle between the symmetry axis (3-axis) and the axis of rotation (direction of $\boldsymbol{\omega}$), giving the rate of precession of the angular velocity vector about the axis of symmetry. This precession appears as a 'wobble', and the angular rate of this precession, $\dot\phi$, comes out to be

$$\dot\phi = \omega\left[1 + \left(\frac{I_s^2}{I^2} - 1\right)\cos^2\alpha\right]^{1/2}.$$

In this case, from the perpendicular axis theorem, $(I_s/I) = 2$. If the object is thrown into the air in such a way that the angular velocity $\boldsymbol{\omega}$ is inclined to the symmetry axis by an angle α, then we have

$$\Omega = \omega \cos\alpha,$$

for the rate of precession of the rotational axis about the symmetry axis.

For the precession of the symmetry axis about the invariable line, the 'wobble' as seen from outside, is given by

$$\dot\phi = \omega(1 + 3\cos^2\alpha)^{1/2}.$$

If α is quite small, so that $\cos\alpha$ is nearly unity, then we have approximately

$$\Omega = \omega$$

and

$$\dot\phi \simeq 2\omega.$$

Thus the wobble rate is very nearly twice the angular speed of rotation.

33. R.P. Feynman, *SYJMF*, p. 174.

34. P.A.M. Dirac, Letter to R.P. Feynman, 23 July 1946. Sealy G. Mudd Library, Princeton University Bicentennial Papers, Princeton University.

35. R.P. Feynman, Letter to T.A. Welton, 10 February 1947. Feynman Archive, Caltech.

36. Theodore Schultz, Interview with Jagdish Mehra, IBM, Yorktown Heights, New York, 28 June 1990.

37. R.P. Feynman, *SYJMF*, pp. 156–63.

38. H.C. Corben. Interview with Jagdish Mehra, Athenaeum, Caltech, 20 March 1988.

10

Feynman's path to quantum mechanics

10.1 Introduction

Feynman began his 1948 paper in the *Reviews of Modern Physics*, entitled 'space–time approach to non-relativistic quantum mechanics', by stating: 'It is a curious historical fact that modern quantum mechanics began with two quite different mathematical formulations: the differential equation of Schrödinger, and the matrix algebra of Heisenberg [as well as the q-number formulation of P. A. M. Dirac]. The two, apparently dissimilar approaches, were proved to be mathematically equivalent. These two points of view were destined to complement one another and to be ultimately synthesized in Dirac's transformation theory.

'This paper will describe what is essentially a *third formulation* of non-relativistic quantum theory. This formulation was suggested by some of Dirac's remarks concerning the relation of classical action to quantum mechanics.[1] The probability amplitude is associated with [the] entire motion of a particle at a particular time.'[2]

With these words Richard Feynman introduced one of his now most well known papers. In the spring of 1947 he decided to publish the most important parts of his Ph.D. thesis. Feynman had thought about publishing this work in a regular journal earlier, but World War II intervened, and he was not able to do so: 'The war interrupted the work.'[3]

'During the war, I didn't have time to work on these things very extensively, but wandered about on buses and so forth, with little pieces of paper (in my pockets), and struggled to work on it and discovered indeed that there was something wrong. . . .'[4] He discovered that he was not able to exclude the possibility of a complex value for the energy in his quantum action-at-a-distance theory. And if this was to be the case, one would obtain obviously wrong results for the probabilities of the events in this theory. In particular, the sum of the probabilities of all possible independent events in such a theory would not be equal to one. But this sum must be equal to one, because in every case some of these events should happen.

Feynman had started to think about these things in the fall of 1946 at Cornell, but at that time he found it quite difficult to write it all down in the form of a paper. At the January 1947 annual meeting of the American Physical Society Feynman encountered Herbert C. Corben, his friend from the early days in Princeton; Corben had discouraged Feynman at that time from getting too deeply involved in the ideas of A.S. Eddington. Corben had returned to Australia in 1942, with his California-born wife Mulaika (née Barclay), where he taught at the University of Melbourne. The Corbens had returned to the United States in the fall of 1946, after Herbert had accepted the offer of an appointment at the Carnegie Institute of Technology at Pittsburgh. Feynman told them about the problems he was working on, how his work was going, and the difficulties he was having in getting it all down on paper; 'but after three weeks the paper emerged '[5]

This was not the whole story. In April 1970, Feynman recalled: 'I wrote up this paper and sent it to the *Physical Review*, and they suggested that I publish it in the *Reviews of Modern Physics*, which I did. At first, it was returned; they said it was too long, that this stuff was old hat, and that the first part in the paper was well known, which could be left out. Hans Bethe taught me a trick. He said, "You have to emphasize that this part is known, and others that are new. It will take only a few paragraphs. In fact, I will shorten it for you." Then Bethe took out one sentence, and said, "If you make a small effort in this direction you don't have to take the whole thing out." That worked. They published it.' In the paper, Feynman thanked H. C. Corben and his wife. 'She more than cooked. She was very enthusiastic, cooperating with my writing and trying to encourage me.'[3]

In his 1948 paper (herein later referred to as the RMP (1948) article), Feynman first described that part of his Ph.D. thesis that did not produce any difficulties. 'All the ideas which appear in the RMP (1948) article were written in such a form that if any generalization is possible, they can be translated. . . . The thesis contains a somewhat more detailed analysis of the general relation of the invariance properties of the (action) functional and constants of the motion. Also the problems of elimination of the intermediate harmonic oscillators is done more completely than is done [in the RMP (1948) article]. The reason I did not publish everything in the thesis is this. I met with a difficulty. An arbitrary action functional S produces results which do not conserve probability; for example, the energy values come out complex. I do not know what this means, nor was I able to find that class of action functionals which would be guaranteed to give real eigenvalues for the energies.'[6]

10.2 The path-integral

In the RMP (1948) article Feynman presented in detail his new approach to quantum mechanics. Feynman's *third way* of formulating quantum mechanics was based on the new physical interpretation of the mathematical method which he had developed in his thesis. The 'key words' which led to the new conceptual advances were 'superposition of probability amplitudes'. The important equation (6.11) can be interpreted physically as a Huygens's principle† for matter waves, and it describes the evolution of the wave function during a small time interval. In the case of quantum mechanics, the classical trajectories play the role of rays in geometrical optics. Then, instead of Fermat's principle of least time, we can apply Hamilton's principle of least action (see equations (6.1) and (6.4) in Chapter 6) for classical or 'geometrical' mechanics. The analogy between geometrical optics and wave optics was used by Schrödinger when he derived the wave equation in quantum mechanics.[8] Feynman used this analogy in a more direct way to reach the right physical interpretation of his new method. The formula (6.11) says that 'if the amplitude ψ of the wave is known on a given "surface", in particular the "surface" consisting of all x at time t, its value at a particular nearby point $t + \varepsilon$, is a sum of contributions from all points of the "surface" at t. Each contribution is delayed in phase by an amount proportional to the *action* it would require to get from the "surface" to the point along the path of least *action* of classical mechanics.'[9]

It ought to be emphasized that Huygens's principle is actually not completely correct in optics, and has to be replaced by some modification, which was given by Kirchhoff. Since the wave equation in optics is of second order with respect to time derivatives, one should—in accordance with Kirchhoff's modification—give both the amplitude and its time derivative on the adjacent surface. It is curious that Huygens's principle actually may be

---

† Huygens's principle was established by Christiaan Huygens in 1678. The wave properties of light were discovered in quite a long chain of investigations, which were started by the work of Francesco Grimaldi (1618–63) leading to the discovery of the diffraction of light. His experiments were repeated by Robert Hooke and then by Isaac Newton. In 1675 Olaf Roemer established the finite speed of light, by measuring the periods of the eclipses due to Jupiter's shadow on its innermost moon. Starting from Roemer's discovery, Huygens was able to explain the propagation of light as a wave phenomenon. This explanation says that when the wave reaches a given point in space, this point becomes the source of spherical waves, which spread out with a finite speed. The spherical waves from all space points result in the interference of the spreading waves. Thus Huygens was able to prove the rectilinear nature of light rays as a consequence of his spherical waves.

The modern idea of interference was given by Thomas Young in 1801, and then the theory of these phenomena was developed by Augustin Fresnel in 1818. Fresnel's theory was expressed in purely geometrical terms by using the famous zone construction.[7] Finally, in 1883 Gustav Kirchhoff wrote the solution of the equation for the light waves in the correct form as an integral like equation (6.11), but involving a wave derivative in time. For the partial differential equations of more general type, Kirchhoff's approach was developed by Jacques-Salomon Hadamard in 1923.

The change from Feynman's work to Schrödinger's looks like a change from Grimaldi to Kirchhoff, but only as an evolution in the opposite direction.

applied to the quantum wave equation without any modification, as Feynman showed. 'The wave equation of quantum mechanics is of first order in the time; therefore, Huygens's principle *is* correct for matter waves, the action replacing the time.'[9]

Thus the complete and clear physical interpretation of equation (6.11) was obtained. But the more important step was to arrive at the correct physical interpretation of equation (6.13), which gives the amplitude K for a finite time as the limit of the integration performed multiple times on the coordinates. What can this procedure mean physically? After some general considerations of the relation between probabilities and quantum magnitudes, Feynman arrived at an extremely nice and simple answer to this principal question. To explain how this can be done, he assumed that he had a particle moving in one dimension, which can take up various values of a coordinate x. Then he wrote the formula (6.11) in the form

$$K = \lim_{\varepsilon \to 0} \int_R \exp\left(\frac{i}{\hbar} \sum_i S(x_{i+1}, x_i)\right) \cdots \frac{dx_{i+1}}{A} \frac{dx_i}{A} \cdots, \qquad (10.1)$$

where A is a normalization factor. Here Feynman divided the time interval from the initial instant to the final instant into a large number of small intervals, given by successive times $t_1, t_2, t_3, \ldots$, where $t_{i+1} = t_i + \varepsilon$. Then the coordinates $x_1, x_2, x_3, \ldots$, which lie in some region R, could be considered as coordinates of the positions of the particle at corresponding times $t_1, t_2, t_3, \ldots$. 'From the classical point of view, the successive values $x_1, x_2, x_3, \ldots$ of the coordinates practically define the path $x(t)$. Eventually, we expect to go to the limit $\varepsilon \to 0$.'[10] By varying the values of a coordinate x_i, we will have various paths in the range R.

The quantity $S(x_{i+1}, x_i)$ in equation (10.1) is simply the classical action on the corresponding path from point x_{i+1} to point x_i. One can obtain this action function from the the formula (6.10). Hence, the sum in the exponent in equation (10.1) in the limit $\varepsilon \to 0$ goes to the classical action on the path $x(t)$: $S = \lim_{\varepsilon \to 0} \sum_i S(x_{i+1}, x_1)$. Finally, the many-time integration in equation (10.1) obviously means a summation over all possible paths in the range R, since by varying $x-s$ we will have all possible paths in this range. But this means just the *interference of the terms* $\exp(iS/\hbar)$, which corresponds to every possible path in R. Hence, Feynman's main postulate was: 'The paths contribute equally in magnitude, but the phase of their contribution is the classical action (in units of $\hbar$), i.e. the time integral of the Lagrangian taken along the path.'[11]

Later on, Feynman explained this postulate as follows: 'The total amplitude can be written as the sum of the amplitudes of each path—for each way of arrival. For every $x(t)$ that we could have—for every possible imaginary trajectory—we have to calculate an amplitude. Then we add them all together. What do we take for the amplitude for each path? Our action integral tells us what the amplitude for a single path ought to be. The amplitude is proportional to some constant times $\exp(iS/\hbar)$, where S is the action for the path. That is, if we represent the phase of the amplitude by a complex number, the phase angle is $S/\hbar$. The action S has dimensions of energy times time, and Planck's constant $\hbar$ has the same dimensions. It is the constant $\hbar$ that determines when quantum mechanics is important.'[12] 'I could see the paths . . . each path got an amplitude. (So the) clarity came from writing up the RMP (1948) article.'[13]

As a straightforward consequence of Feynman's extremely important and completely new viewpoint concerning the relation (10.1),† one can answer a three-century-old question about the meaning of the principle of least action (Section 6.2). 'Here is how it works: Suppose that for all paths, S is very large compared to $\hbar$. One path contributes a certain amplitude. For a nearby path, the phase is quite different, because with an enormous S even nearby paths will normally cancel their different phases—because $\hbar$ is so tiny. So, nearby paths will normally cancel their effects out in taking the sum—except for one region, and that is when a path and a nearby path all give the same phase in the first approximation (more precisely, the same action within $\hbar$). Only those paths will be the important ones. So in the limiting case in which Planck's constant $\hbar$ goes to zero, the correct quantum mechanical laws can be summarized by simply saying: "Forget about all these probability amplitudes. The particle does go on a special path, namely, that one for which S does not vary in the

---

† Considering the formula (6.1) from a purely mathematical point of view, one ought to emphasize that Feynman was not the first to discover such types of relations. In pure mathematics, an analogous idea was first developed by Vito Volterra.[14] He studied an ordinary linear differential equation which is similar to Schrödinger's equation, but in infinite-dimensional spaces. Volterra proved rigorously that one can represent the solution of these equations in a form similar to equation (10.1), but instead of integration there occurred summation on certain discrete indices, and instead of terms like $\exp[iS(x_{i+1}, x_i)/\hbar]$ there were matrices. Then the corresponding type of the limit in equation (10.1) will yield a so-called 'multiplicative of Volterra', which was studied by many mathematicians. Volterra also considered the case of the infinite-dimensional linear functional space like $\psi(q)$.[15]

Feynman did not know this mathematical result. He was not looking for rigorous formal proofs of his new method, but only for clear intuitive arguments. Before Feynman, nobody had ever made the attempt to visualize the summation in equation (10.1) in the intuitively clear way he did it.

The purely mathematical considerations show why the path-integral method should be extremely useful in various scientific domains, although it was invented by Feynman for quantum mechanics. The reason for this is that from the mathematical point of view the path-integral method gives the solution of a linear differential equation in a linear space with any dimension whatsoever. The basic equations in many scientific domains are of this type, hence the generality of Feynman's method.

first approximation." That's the relation between the principle of least action and quantum mechanics.'†[12]

Thus Feynman's postulate leads to the principle of least action (6.1) and gives us the right explanation as to where this principle is coming from. As far as the principle of least action, *the* most fundamental principle of classical physics, is concerned, one which leads to the classical dynamical equations in all the fundamental classical theories, one can truly say that it was Feynman who discovered the deepest import of this principle.

10.3 The new operator algebra

In several sections of his RMP (1948) paper, Feynman developed the new formalism of quantum mechanics, and proved its equivalence to the older formulations of Heisenberg and Schrödinger. He showed how one can introduce the wave function in his path-integral approach, and derived the Schrödinger equation for this wave function. We have explained Feynman's derivation of the Schrödinger equation in Section 6.4. Then he introduced his new so useful notion of the 'transition amplitude', which can now be found in textbooks on quantum mechanics. Given two quantum states with wave functions $\psi(x, t)$ and $\chi(x, t)$, Feynman called the expression $\int \chi^*(x, t'')\psi(x, t') \, dx$ the 'transition amplitude'. Here $\chi^*(x, t'')$ is the function conjugate to $\chi(x, t)$ at the instant of time t'', and $\psi(x, t)$ is taken at another

---

† A derivation of the principle of least action from quantum mechanical reasoning was first given by Dirac.[1] This served as the point of departure for Feynman's investigations on the path-integral method. Considering equation (10.1) as an approximation to the exact quantum transition function from the initial to the final instants of time, Dirac discovered that the quantum analog of Hamilton's action principle (equation (6.1)) is absorbed in the composition law (10.1), and the classical requirement that the values of the intermediate coordinates shall make the action stationary corresponds to the condition in quantum mechanics that all values of the intermediate coordinates are important in proportion to the integral (10.1). Then Dirac considered the limiting case when h tends to zero and stated that the integrand in equation (10.1) is a rapidly oscillating function when h is small. Thus the multiple integral (10.1) 'contains the quantum analog of the action principle (as far as) the importance of our considering any set of values for the intermediate [coordinates] is determined by the importance of this set of values in the integration. If we now make make h tend to zero, this statement goes over into the classical statement that ... the importance of our considering any set of values for the intermediate [coordinates] is zero unless these values make the action stationary.'[1]

From the above remarks it is clear that Dirac was very close to the interpretation of equation (10.1) as a summation over all virtual paths, and he had found the new formulation as an extremely nice and important way to explain the principle of least action as a result of quantum laws. However, Dirac was not able to complete this line of his investigation on quantum mechanics because his point of view was that the exponent of the classical action in the form of Hamilton's principal function is only an approximate semiclassical relation. Dirac was interested only in a general question: What is the quantum analog of the classical principle of least action?

instant of time t'. Thus the transition amplitude gives us the quantum amplitude for the transition from the quantum state ψ at the time t' to the quantum state χ at the time t''. Feynman showed that, in his path-integral method, the average of the transition amplitude may be regarded as unity, that is

$$\langle \chi_{t''}|1|\psi_{t'}\rangle_S = \lim_{\varepsilon \to 0} \int \ldots \int \chi^*(x'', t'') \times exp(iS/\hbar)\psi(x', t') \frac{dx_0}{A} \ldots \frac{dx_{j-1}}{A} dx_j.$$

$$(10.2)$$

In the language of ordinary quantum mechanics, if the quantum Hamiltonian operator **H** does not depend on time, this transition amplitude is the matrix element of the quantum evolution operator $exp[-(t''-t')\mathbf{H}/\hbar]$, between the quantum states $\chi_{t''}$ and $\psi_{t'}$. This operator describes the evolution of the wave function ψ from the instant t' to the instant t'': $\psi(x, t'') = exp[-(t''-t')\mathbf{H}/\hbar]\psi(x, t')$.

As a generalization of formula (10.2), Feynman introduced the formula for the averages of any functional F of the coordinates x_i for $t' < t_i < t''$. He defined the 'transition element' of the functional F between the states ψ at t' and χ'' at t'' for the action S as

$$\langle \chi_{t''}|F|\psi_{t'}\rangle_S = \lim_{\varepsilon \to 0} \int \ldots \int \chi^*(x'', t'')F(x_0, x_1, \ldots, x_j)$$

$$\times exp\left(\frac{i}{\hbar}\sum_i S(x_{i+1}, x_i)\right)\psi(x', t') \frac{dx_0}{A} \ldots \frac{dx_{j-1}}{A} dx_j. \quad (10.3)$$

Then he used these basic formulas to obtain several fundamental results from his new formulation of quantum mechanics.

The first application was the new formulation of the so-called perturbation theory in quantum mechanics.† Suppose we consider a second problem which

---

† It turns out that, historically, this was the fundamental result of Feynman's path-integral method, which was first used in important physical problems. Feynman himself used this part of his method very soon in his papers on quantum electrodynamics.

The perturbation theory plays a very important role in many physical problems. Very often one cannot solve the exact problem because of its complexity. But it may turn out that we can solve some other problem, which differs slightly from the initial one. In this case, one can say that some small 'perturbation' leads from the unperturbed solvable problem to the perturbed one that we actually wish to solve. In such a situation, the method which permits one to reach the solution of the complicated problem, using the solution of the simpler one, is needed. This method is called 'perturbation theory'. Feynman's path-integral method leads to the now very successful formulation of the perturbation theory in quantum mechanics, based on formulas like equation (10.4). Very soon after the RMP (1948) article, Feynman proposed a proper generalization of his new perturbation theory in quantum electrodynamics. Since then Feynman's perturbation theory has been one of the most useful methods in the quantum theory of various physical fields.

differs from the first because, for example, the potential is augmented by a small amount $\lambda U(x, t)$. Then in the new problem the quantity replacing S is $S' = S + \sum_i \lambda U(x_i, t)$. Substituting it into equation (10.2) leads directly to an expression, which after performing some algebra leads to an important perturbation formula. If the effect of U is small, we find

$$\langle \chi_{t'} | 1 | \psi_{t'} \rangle_{S'} = \langle \chi_{t'} | 1 | \psi_{t'} \rangle_S + \frac{i}{\hbar} \left\langle \chi_{t'} \left| \sum_i \lambda U(x_i, t_i) \right| \psi_{t'} \right\rangle_S. \tag{10.4}$$

Formula (10.4) permits one to calculate the effects of the perturbation $\lambda U(x, t)$ to first order with respect to the small parameter λ, using the solution of the more simple problem with the action function S.

The next fundamental result of Feynman's new formulation was a completely new derivation of Newton's equations and the commutation relations. By using formula (10.3), Feynman had, in his dissertation, already derived the quantum Lagrange equation.[16] In the RMP (1948) paper, he wrote Newton's equations in the form

$$0 \underset{S}{\longleftrightarrow} -\frac{m}{\varepsilon} \left(\frac{x_{k+1} - x_k}{\varepsilon} - \frac{x_k - x_{k-1}}{\varepsilon} \right) - V(x). \tag{10.5}$$

Here ε is the small difference between the successive times $t_1, t_2, t_3, \ldots$ that is, $t_{i+1} - t_i = \varepsilon$. Hence $(x_{k+1} - x_k)/\varepsilon$ is the velocity and the term $[(x_{k+1} - x_k)/\varepsilon - (x_k - x_{k-1})/\varepsilon]/\varepsilon$ presents the acceleration a of the particle. The derivative of the potential $V(x)$, taken with the minus sign, gives the force term F. Thus, the right-hand side in the expression (10.5) represents just the classical term $-ma + F$, which according to Newton, must be equal to zero. Actually, in quantum mechanics, this expression corresponds to some quantum operator, which cannot be equal to the zero operator. But the average values of this operator (with respect to some given action S, according to equation (10.3)), are zero, and that is completely sufficient for the right physical interpretation of the meaning of this operator. Feynman employed the symbol $\underset{S}{\longleftrightarrow}$ to emphasize the fact that two different functionals may give the same result for the transition amplitude between any two states or, in other words, they are equivalent under one action S but may not be equivalent under another.

So, equation (10.5) represents Newton's equations in Feynman's formulation of quantum mechanics.

It turns out that in Feynman's formulation of quantum mechanics, one can also derive the quantum commutation relations in exactly the same manner. The commutation relations between the quantum momentum operator p and the quantum position operator x, in the usual formulation of quantum mechanics, reads: $[p, x] = px - xp = \hbar/i$. Feynman showed that in his new formulation of quantum mechanics a new relation corresponds to the old one. This new relations reads

$$m\left(\frac{x_{k+1}-x_k}{\varepsilon}\right)x_k - m\left(\frac{x_k-x_{k-1}}{\varepsilon}\right)x_k \overset{\leftrightarrow}{\underset{S}{}} \frac{\hbar}{i}. \tag{10.6}$$

Since $(x_{k+1}-x_k)/\varepsilon$ corresponds to the velocity v of the particle, here $m(x_{k+1}-x_k)/\varepsilon$ corresponds to the classical momentum $p=mv$.

Taking into account the new form of the commutator relation, equation (10.6), as far as the new form of Newton's equations (10.5) are concerned, we see that 'the operators corresponding to the functions of x_{k+1} will appear to the left of the operators corresponding to the functions of x_k, i.e. *the order of terms in a matrix operator product* (in the old formalism of quantum mechanics) *corresponds* (in Feynman's new formulation) *to an order in time of the corresponding factors in a functional*. Thus, if the functional can be, and is, written in such a way that in each term factors correspond to earlier terms, the corresponding operator can immediately be written down if the order of the operators is kept the same as in the functional. Obviously, the order of factors in a function is of no consequence. The ordering just facilitates transition to conventional operator notation.'[17] *This is the essence of the new Feynman operator algebra, where the usual operator ordering is replaced by the ordering of the classical-like terms in time.*

The Hamiltonian operator is of central importance in the usual formulation of quantum mechanics. Therefore, Feynman studied in detail the functional corresponding to this operator. He preferred to define the Hamiltonian functional in a physical way by the changes made in a state when it is displaced in time. Feynman had to perform the calculations especially carefully, because of the squared dependence of the Hamiltonian on the velocity of the particle. He derived the following expression for the functional, which corresponds to the Hamiltonian operator:

$$H_k = \frac{m}{2}\left(\frac{x_{k+1}-x_k}{t_{k+1}-t_k}\right)^2 + \frac{\hbar}{2i(t_{k+1}-t_k)} + V(x). \tag{10.7}$$

The second term in this expression is proportional to Planck's constant $\hbar$. It is a very important term, because it is due to this term that the kinetic energy turns out to be finite. The first term in equation (10.7) leads only to the infinite kinetic energy because of the relation $(x_{k+1}-x_k)^2 \overset{\leftrightarrow}{\underset{S}{}} (i\hbar/m)(t_{k+1}-t_k)$, which says that the root mean square of the 'velocity' $(x_{k+1}-x_k)/(t_{k+1}-t_k)$ is of order $(t_{k+1}-t_k)^{-1/2}$, hence it goes to infinity when $t_{k+1}-t_k$ goes to zero. From the physical point of view this leads to the important conclusion that, nevertheless, the paths which give an essential contribution to the Feynman path-integral for the transition amplitude (see equation (10.1)) are continuous paths, the velocity of the particle at each point of the paths is not well defined, and goes to infinity. One can imagine such a path as a continuous line, which breaks its direction at every point. From the mathematical point of view such a 'zigzag' path is not a differentiable path, hence the velocity of the particle is not well defined. This fact does not make difficulties in the Hamiltonian, because of the second term in equation (10.7), which cancels the infinity from the first term exactly in the limit when $t_{k+1} - t_k$ goes to zero. Feynman derived the second term in equation (10.7) from the factor A in equation (10.1). One has to remember that this factor was just needed to establish the exact relation between the quantum transition amplitude and the exponent of the classical action S times $i/\hbar$, which was the starting point of Feynman's invention of the new formulation of quantum mechanics (see Section 6.5)

In this way, Feynman demonstrated the self-consistency of his path-integral method and its equivalence to the old Schrödinger and Heisenberg formulations of quantum mechanics. At the end of the general discussion of the path-integral method, Feynman mentioned the shortcomings in his formulation of quantum mechanics. He noted: 'The formulation given here suffers from a serious drawback. The mathematical concepts needed are new. At present, it requires an unnatural and cumbersome subdivision of the time interval to make the meaning of the equations clear. Considerable improvement can be made through the use of the notation and concepts of the mathematics of functionals. However, it was thought best to avoid this in the first presentation. One needs, in addition, an appropriate measure for the space of the argument functions $x(t)$ of the functionals.

'It is also incomplete from the physical standpoint. One of the most important characteristics of quantum mechanics is its invariance under unitary transformations. These correspond to the canonical transformations of classical mechanics. Of course, the present formulation, being equivalent to ordinary formulations, can mathematically be demonstrated to be invariant under these transformations. However, it has not been formulated in such a way that it is *physically* obvious that it is invariant. This incompleteness shows itself in a definite way. No direct procedure has been outlined to describe measurements of quantities other than position. Measurements of momentum, for example, of one particle, can be defined in terms of measurements of positions of other particles. The result of the analysis of such a situation does show the connection of momentum measurements to the Fourier transform of the wave function. But this is a rather roundabout method of obtaining such an important physical result. It is to be expected that the postulates can be generalized by the replacement of the ideas of "paths in a region of space–time R", or to "paths of class R", or "paths having the property R". But which properties correspond to which physical measurements has not been formulated in a general way.'[18]

Feynman then gave an outline of the generalization of his path-integral method and how it could be used to solve certain problems. We shall discuss these matters in Section 10.5, but before doing so we will give a brief historical account of functional integration before Feynman, something which he discovered independently, without any knowledge of what had been done before.

10.4 Functional integration before Feynman

As we have noted, Feynman's principal mathematical result was the new method for the calculation of averages of quantum mechanical quantities with the help of formulas like (10.2) and, in more general cases, like (10.3). From the mathematical point of view, these formulas give us the averages of certain functionals $F [(x, t)]$ on the paths $x(t)$ in the configuration space of the classical mechanical system, where the time t runs from some initial instant t_{in} to some final instant t_{fin}. As a weight in the averaging procedure, one may use the other functional, namely, the exponent of the classical action times $i/\hbar$. We will now present an outline of some landmarks in the theory of functionals, which has developed and been applied very extensively after Feynman's work.

(a) Vito Volterra

The general theory of functionals was developed in the works of Vito Volterra, long before Feynman's investigations on the new quantum mechanical formalism. We have already mentioned the contribution of Volterra in the solution of linear equations in multi- or infinite-dimensional linear spaces by means of his multiplicative integral. Developing the general theory of the functional calculus,[19] Volterra invented the way to reduce the calculations with functionals to calculations with usual functions of many variables. This procedure was of just the type which Feynman used later: namely, one has to divide the interval from the initial time t_{in} to the final time t_{fin} into a large, but finite number N of time instants t_i, and then to approximate the functional $F[(x, t)]$ with the function $F(\ldots, x_{i+1}, x_i \ldots)$, where x_i gives the value of $x(t_i)$. Then, one has to work with this function, instead of the functional $F[(x, t)]$. This procedure is called a *finite-dimensional approximation*, or discretization, of the functional $F [(x,t)]$, which itself may be considered as a function of infinitely many variables $x(t)$, with a continuous label t. After performing operations on the function $F(\ldots, x_{i+1}, x_i, \ldots)$ in the final result one has to take the limit $N \to \infty$, keeping t_{in} and t_{fin} fixed. And this is just the procedure which Feynman employed.

(b) Norbert Wiener and others

The first considerations of the average value of a functional in pure mathematics, without any connection with quantum mechanics, were given by P.J. Daniel,[20] R. Gâteaux,[21] P. Lévy,[22] and in several papers by Norbert Wiener.[23]

The first physical application of the functional machinery was Wiener's approach to the Brownian motion of very small particles in a colloidal suspension.

Brownian motion was discovered by Robert Brown, a Scottish botanist, in

1827, when he saw through the microscope the strange chaotic movement of very small particles in colloidal suspensions. The analysis of this phenomenon, given by many physicists, shows that this movement is caused by small particles being struck by the molecules of the liquid in which they were suspended. Since these hits are random, the movement is too chaotic and leads to the diffusion of the particles in the liquid. The path of a single particle looks like a zigzag line, consisting of straight lines with random orientation and length. These zigzag straight lines describe the motion of the free particle between sequential impacts.

Let us consider, for simplicity, a particle which wanders along the X axis only. Let $\phi(x, t)$ denote the probability distribution of the particle to be at the point x at at time t. In his paper on Brownian motion, Albert Einstein[24] showed that if one supposes that the particle wanders a given distance in a given time that is independent of (1) the starting position of the particle, (2) the initial instant of time when it begins to wander, (3) the direction in which it starts to wander, then the probability distribution that after a time t the particle has wandered from the origin to a position lying between x and $x + dx$ is given by

$$\phi(x, t) = (4 \pi D t)^{-1/2} \exp(-x^2/4Dt),$$

and this probability distribution satisfies the so-called diffusion equation:

$$\frac{\partial \phi}{\partial t} = D \frac{\partial^2 \phi}{\partial x^2}.$$

Here D is called the 'diffusion coefficient', and it is related to the size and the mass of the particle and to the temperature and the viscosity of the liquid. It may be connected, too, with Boltzmann's constant k and hence with the fundamental Avogadro number $N = 6.02213 \times 10^{23}$ mol^{-1}, being the number of molecules in one gram-molecule of matter. In fact, the possibility of obtaining the value of the fundamental constant from experiments stimulated Einstein and Smoluchowski to develop the theory of this phenomenon at the beginning of the century. However, from the mathematical point of view, the value of the diffusion coefficient is not essential and by a proper choice of the units one may put it equal to $\frac{1}{4}$ for simplicity. Then

$$\phi(x, t) = (\pi t)^{-1/2} \exp(-x^2/t).$$

Wiener investigated the history of the wandering particle. He assumed that this history is represented by the equation $x = x(t)$, $x(t)$ being a continuous function; then he considered 'particle histories' or 'time paths', these being the key notions, which Wiener used in the proper sense for the first time, and said: 'There are certain assemblies of time paths to which we can immediately assign a measure, a probability. These assemblies are obtained by restricting the position of the particle at certain specified times, finite in number, to certain specified finite intervals.'[23] Using Feynman's notation (see equation (10.1)), we can write this probability as

$$P_W = \lim_{\varepsilon \to 0} \int_R \left[-\sum_i (x_{i+1} - x_i)^2 / (t_{i+1} - t_i) \right] \cdots \frac{dx_{i+1}}{A} \frac{dx^i}{A} \cdots .$$

In the limit $N \to \infty$, when the time intervals $t_{i-1} - t_i$ go to zero, this expression defines a measure on the set of all paths $x = x(t)$. Wiener showed that this measure is concentrated on the set of continuous paths, which are not differentiable. In such a limit, the term in the exponent gives just twice the integral on the time of the kinetic energy of the particle with unit mass: $\int_0^1 \dot{x}(\tau)^2 \, d\tau$. Then we can denote the so-called 'Wiener measure' as

$$d_W[x(t)] = 1/C \exp\left(-\int_0^1 \dot{x}(\tau)^2 \, d\tau \right) \prod_0^t dx(t),$$

and calculate the average value of any functional $F[x(t)]$ on the path $x(t)$ according to the formula $\langle F \rangle_W = \int_R F[x(t)] \, d_W[x, t]$. In the Wiener measure, C is a normalization constant, which normalizes the infinite-dimensional integral under the condition $\int_R d_W[x(t)] = 1$.

Thus we can see that Wiener represented the corresponding probability and the average values of the functionals for Brownian particles as functional integrals, i.e. as weighted sums on all the possible paths or, in other words, on the histories of the particle.

But there exists an essential difference between Wiener's formula given above and equation (10.3) for Feyman's averages. Wiener's averages $\langle F \rangle_W$ look almost like Feynman's averages $\langle F \rangle_S$ (see equation (10.2)) for a free particle, when the action functional reduces to the integral over the time of the kinetic energy of the particle. But in the exponent of Feynman's averages there remains an imaginary factor $i/\hbar$, which makes it impossible to interpret Feynman's averages as averages with respect to some real measure. In contrast to Wiener's path integral, in Feynman's averages there exist rapidly oscillating complex exponential functions, owing to which, as we know, there exist the least action principle and classical mechanics. These rapidly oscillating integrals are not convergent and one must understand them in a proper sense. In contrast, Wiener's integrals are very well convergent because of the properties of the Wiener measure.

Taking into account the finite-dimensional case one may ask how one should include the exponent of the kinetic energy with the minus sign in Wiener's measure. Is it impossible to define the measure in the infinite case as $\prod_0^t dx(t)$? Such an expression would be completely analogous to the expression $\prod_{i=1}^N dx_i$, which gives the measure, i.e. the volume of the ranges in N-dimensional space. If this were possible, one could include the exponential factor in the functional, and one would have to take the average both in

Feynman's and Wiener's cases. Moreover, if this were possible we shall have obtained a translational invariant additive measure, like Lebesgue's, in an infinite-dimensional case, and it would be possible to treat both cases in a similar manner. Unfortunately, one can easily prove that this is impossible and such a measure does not exist in infinite-dimensional spaces.

The reason is quite simple. Suppose we have a translational invariant additive measure in the infinite-dimensional linear space, and the volume of the bounded bodies with respect to this measure is infinite. This means that the volume of each body does not depend on its position in the infinite-dimensional space and this volume is the sum of the volumes of all parts of the body. Let us put on every axis in this space one ball with radius 1, centered at a distance 1 from the origin. The volume of every such ball is a finite number V_0, but the volume of the whole set of such balls is infinite because the space is infinite-dimensional, and one will have an infinite set of balls, one in every direction, which does not intersect with another (see Fig. 10.1). Now we may consider a new ball of radius 10 with its center at the origin. It is evident that all the infinitely many initial balls will lie within this bigger ball, which must also have a finite volume V, since we have a Lebesgue-like measure. But this is impossible, since the volume of the big ball is larger than the common volume of the entire initial set of balls, which now lie within the larger one. The common volume of the small balls is infinite.

This consideration shows that it is impossible to treat Wiener's and Feynman's averages in a similar way. The fast decreasing exponential, included in the Wiener measure, allows one to use measure theory. But in the case of Feynman's averages this is impossible and one needs some completely

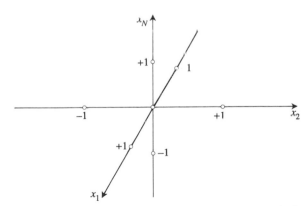

Fig. 10.1. Three-dimensional illustration of the geometrical picture we have to consider to prove the absence of the translational invariant additive measure in infinite-dimensional space. In the infinite-dimensional case there are infinitely many axes, hence, infinitely many small balls in the big ball.

different ideas to give his procedure a rigorous meaning. In spite of this problem, we should note that now there exist different approaches which can deal with Feynman's averages involving certain pseudomeasures. There exists a very suggestive short conference address given by Kirkwood,[25] in which he mentioned that one could apply to quantum physics the integration of functionals in the Wiener sense for the calculation of the statistical sum. This is the first known attempt to connect the functional integral method with quantum problems.

(c) Subrahmanyan Chandrasekhar

Wiener's treatment of the Brownian motion of the particles in liquids was approximate, because he neglected the inertia of the particle and external forces, such as the gravitational force and others, which can act on the particles. The next important step in this direction was taken by Subrahmanyan Chandrasekhar,[26] who treated Brownian motion entirely by the functional integral method, although nowhere did he mention this name.

In 1908 Paul Langevin[27] had proposed to treat Brownian motion as the motion of a classical particle of mass m under the action of a random force $f(t)$, and a frictional force $-(m/\tau)\dot{x}$, which is proportional to the velocity $\dot{x}$ of the particle. The frictional force describes the interaction of the particle with the medium, and τ is the relaxation time of the particle. In addition, there exists an external force F. Thus the so-called Langevin equation for the particles reads;

$$m\frac{d^2x}{dt^2} = f(t) - (m/\tau)\frac{dx}{dt} + F(x, t).$$

One can solve this equation with respect to the velocity $v(t) = \dot{x}$ of the particle. The result shows that the velocity of the particle is a functional of the random force $f(t)$: $v = v[f(t)]$. Then, in order to calculate the physical quantities for the Brownian particle, one has to obtain the averages of this or other functionals. To do so Chandrasekhar used Wiener's method. He assumed the probability distribution of the Wiener force to be Wiener-like; that is, the probability of finding the value of the force between $f(t)$ and $f(t) + df(t)$ in a short interval of time from t to $t + \Delta t$ to be $(4\pi a/\Delta t)^{1/2} \exp(-f^2 \Delta t)\, df$, where $a = kT\ (m/\tau)$ is a constant, k being Boltzmann's constant and T the temperature of the medium. By a proper choice of the units one may put a equal to $\frac{1}{4}$ for simplicity; then the above probability becomes equal to:

$$(\pi/\Delta t)^{-1/2} \exp(-f^2 \Delta t)\, df.$$

Chandrasekhar introduced a Wiener-like measure:

$$d_W[f(t)] = (1/C) \exp\left(\int_0^t d\tau [f(t)]^2\right) \prod_0^t df(t).$$

By calculating the functional average $\langle V \rangle_w$, Chandrasekhar showed that the average velocity of the Brownian particle does not depend on the random force $f(t)$, and the mean square displacement $\langle \Delta x^2 \rangle_w$ along any direction is proportional to the time t.

For the relaxation processes for times larger than τ, the relaxation time of the particle, we have to go back to Einstein's approximation, neglecting the inertia of the particles. This means that we have to write down the Langevin equation in a more simple form: $(m/\tau) \, dx/dt = f(t) + F(x, t)$. The solution of this equation is a functional of the random force $f(t)$: $x(t) = x[t; x_0, t_0; f(t)]$. Here x_0 is the initial position of the particle at the initial instant t_0. Chandrasekhar invented the new approach to evaluate averages of the functions $\Phi(x, t)$ of the position x of the Brownian particle at time t; this approach now has a large number of applications both in quantum mechanics and in statistical physics. The average value of the function $\Phi[x(t), t]$,

$$\langle \Phi[x(t), t] \rangle_w = \int \Phi\{x[t; x_0, t_0; f(t)]\} \, d_w[\,f(t)],$$

according to Chandrasekhar, may be represented in the form

$$\langle \Phi[x(t), t] \rangle_w = \int \Phi(x, t)\phi(x, t; x_0, t_0) \, dx,$$

where

$$\phi(x, t; x_0, t_0) = \langle \delta[x - x(t)] \rangle_w = \int \delta\{x - x[t; x_0, t_0; f(t)]\} \, d_w[f(t)],$$

is the average value of Dirac's delta-function of the corresponding argument. The point is that one can calculate this average quite simply by using certain techniques. Thus, when the external force equals zero, one obtains the result that the above function, $\phi(x, t; x_0, t_0)$, is exactly the probability distribution, first established by Einstein, and the diffusion coefficient is $D = kT(\tau/m)$.

Chandrasekhar showed that the function $\phi(x, t)$ obeys the diffusion equation for the free particle, which we have written above. This was the first derivation of this equation by the method of functional integration. Chandrasekhar used a procedure which is exactly the same as Feynman's method for the derivation of the Schrödinger equation in his dissertation (see Section 6.5). Chandrasekhar also used the same method for the derivation of the Fokker–Planck equation in the general case:

$$\partial W/\partial t = \beta \, \text{div}_v(Wv) + q \, \nabla_v^2 W.$$

Here $W(v, t)$ is the probability distribution in velocity space, $\beta = m/\tau$, and $q = kT/\tau$ is a constant.

Thus Chandrasekhar showed how one could obtain the phenomenological results of Einstein and Smoluchowski from a microscopical point of view by using functional integration. We should note that nowadays a similar approach is used in so-called statistical quantization to arrive at quantum mechanics from classical mechanics.

Chandrasekhar also solved the problem of a particle subject to both a random force and an external force, for example a harmonic oscillator under a random force. Then he used his method and results in many physical and astrophysical problems: the theory of density fluctuations, colloid statistics, thermodynamical irreversible processes, effects of gravity on Brownian motion, the phenomenon of sedimentation, the theory of coagulation in colloids, the escape of a particle over potential barriers, and various problems of stellar dynamics.

Feynman did not know anything about the achievements of functional analysis in the calculation of functional averages. He was unfamiliar with the mathematical articles in this domain, but he invented all the things he needed. 'In order to do [the path-integral method] I had to invent this new kind of mathematical structure I had thought of, which was similar to a thing called the Wiener integral . . . . I didn't know anything about that. Actually, if you look up the Wiener integral you will find, if I'm not mistaken, that what Wiener did was to suppose that the *e* (raised) to minus the kinetic energy piece was a standard weight, and you could do integrals with that weight, whereas the way I was looking at at it, that weight as well as the rest of the function was what you integrate. There's a lot of difference, maybe not as much as I thought. Anyway, never mind! I didn't know anything about Wiener or the source of the Wiener integral, except the complex plane.'[28]

'There was much in my thesis [and in the RMP 1948 article] which was of that kind, things other people had done, and I never even checked the references, but presumably other people had done them. There was, of course, a discussion of principles of least action in classical mechanics, and the problems of the definition of energy and momentum under these circumstances. [In my thesis] they were defined in a general way. I think this was quite early for this definition, but I don't know if it wasn't published earlier— certainly, it has been published since then.'[28]

10.5 Possible generalization and some applications

At the end of the RMP (1948) paper, Feynman proposed some generalization of the path-integral method, which was connected with his action-at-distance theory. For the case of the theory with a time delay he briefly sketched the generalization of the method for calculating averages of functionals of a general type.

Next, Feynman presented the main application of the path-integral method, namely, the elimination of the field oscillators. This problem had arisen from electrodynamics, which Feynman wished to modify in order to avoid the infinities at the quantum level (see Section 6.3). Feynman briefly illustrated how one could do this in the simple case of a particle with Lagrangian $L(\dot{x}, x)$, which interacts with an oscillator with Lagrangian $\frac{1}{2}(\dot{q}^2 - \omega^2 q^2)$, with the help of a term $\gamma(x, t)q(t)$. Here x is the coordinate of the particle, q is the coordinate of the oscillator, and $\gamma(x, t)$ is an arbitrary function of the coordinate $x(t)$ of the particle at time t. Then the entire classical action of this system may be written as $S = S_p + S_o + S_i$, where S_p is the action of the particle, S_o is the action of the oscillator, and S_i is the interaction term in the action of the system. Feynman showed that the solution of this complicated problem may be divided into two parts. First, one can take the path integral only on the paths connected with the oscillator degree of freedom. The result is just the elimination of the oscillator at the quantum level. Thus one obtains an intermediate problem, without the oscillator degree of freedom, which has to be solved separately. It turns out that this intermediate problem is just the action-at-a-distance theory, which Feynman first considered at the classical level in his dissertation (see Section 6.3).

The power of the new technique for the calculations of the quantum amplitudes lies in the possibility one has of separating the complex system into pieces and 'integrate out parts of it'. It is very hard to do this in the ordinary Schrödinger differential or the Heisenberg matrix form of quantum mechanics. '... Drawing on the classical analogue we shall expect that the system with the oscillator is not equivalent to the system without the oscillator for all possible motions of the oscillator, but only for those for which some property [i.e. the initial and final position] of the oscillator is fixed. These properties, in the cases discussed, are not properties of the system at just one time, so we shall not expect to find the equivalence simply by specifying the state of the oscillator at a certain time, by means of a particular wave function. *It is just for this reason that the ordinary methods of quantum mechanics do not suffice to solve this problem.*'[29]

However, there is one more extremely important result, which must be stressed. In the classical elimination of the oscillator degree of freedom there was one ambiguous choice. There we can choose different solutions of the classical oscillator equation. To make the right choice in the classical problem, Feynman had to add an additional requirement: one must derive the equations of motion of particles without the oscillator from the new principle of least action. Then it follows that one must choose just this solution of the classical oscillator equation, which contains one-half advanced and one-half retarded interaction.

Now, in the quantum problem, there is no need to require the principle of least action as an additional postulate, because it follows directly from the path-integral formulation of quantum mechanics for every system (see Section 10.2). In particular, if we have quantum mechanics for the particles without the oscillator, we shall automatically have a principle of least action for this system. Hence, Feynman's treatment leads unambiguously to the one-half advanced and one-half retarded interaction in the action-at-a-distance theory. This result is of great importance for action-at-a-distance theories.

Feynman's final result of this investigation of the particles interacting through an intermediate oscillator was that at the quantum level, as at the classical level, one can eliminate the oscillator and describe the particles as interacting at a distance, using—in both quantum and classical theories, respectively—an effective action with delay to describe such an interaction.

Feynman's method of solving complicated quantum problems, by integrating by parts the corresponding path integral, is by now a well-known powerful technique which has got a large number of applications in different kinds of theoretical investigations. In the last section of his RMP (1948) article, Feynman gave some suggestions for the applications of the path-integral method in quantum statistical mechanics and in certain relativistic problems. He considered the general problem as to how one may include the spin of the particles in the path-integral method, and suggested a formal way to do it. 'These results for spin and relativity are purely formal and add nothing to the understanding of these (problems). There are other ways of obtaining the Dirac equation which offer some promise of giving a clear physical interpretation to that important and beautiful equation.'[30]

The complete realization of this belief of Feynman's has been reached only recently in theories making use of the so-called Grassmann variables.[31]

At first, Feynman's fundamental article (RMP, 1948) did not arouse much interest among theoretical physicists, who were not familiar with Feynman's new approach to doing quantum mechanics. As Feynman recalled: 'At the Shelter Island Conference [which we shall discuss later on], a lot of exciting things were discussed and talked about. But in spite of all this, the physicists ran out of ideas. They asked me if I would explain my path-integral method for doing quantum mechanics, so I did. I must have been preparing the manuscript of my paper [RMP, 1948], so that everything was organized and I explained it. It's hard to pay attention to some new idea, and they didn't pay much attention to it.'[3] However, nowadays Feynman's RMP (1948) paper is one of the most well known and widely cited papers; it is one of the cornerstones of modern theoretical physics.

Notes and References

1. P.A.M. Dirac, The Lagrangian in quantum mechanics. *Phys. Z. Sowjetunion* 3(1) (1933).

2. R.P. Feynman, Space-time approach to non-relativistic quantum mechanics. *Rev. Mod. Phys.* 20(2), 367 (1948).

3. R.P. Feynman, Interviews and conversations with Jagdish Mehra, in Austin, Texas, April 1970, and Pasadena, California, January 1988.

4. R.P. Feynman, Interviews with Charles Weiner (American Institute of Physics), Pasadena, California 1966.

5. H.C. Corben, Interview with Jagdish Mehra, Athenaeum,, Caltech, 20 March 1988.

6. R.P. Feynman, Letter to C. Kelber, 21 February 1949. Feynman Archive, Caltech.

7. M. Born and E. Wolf, *Principles of optics*. Pergamon, New York, 1959.

8. E. Schrödinger, *Ann. Phys. (Leipzig)* 79, 734(1926).

9. R.P. Feynman, Ref. 2, p. 377.

10. R.P. Feynman, Ref. 2, p. 370.

11. R.P. Feynman, Ref. 2, p. 371.

12. R.P. Feynman and A.R. Hibbs, *Quantum mechanics and path integrals* McGraw-Hill, New York, 1965, p. 19–9.

13. R.P. Feynman, Interview with S.S. Schweber, Pasadena, California, 13 November 1980, Quoted in S.S. Schweber, *Rev. Mod. Phys.* 58 (1986).

14. V. Volterra, Sui fondamenti della teoria delle equazioni differenziali lineari. *Mem. Soc. Ital. Sci.* 6(3), 1–104 (1887); 12(3), 3–68 (1902).

15. V. Volterra and B. Hostinsky, *Opérations infinitesimales linéares,* Gauthier-Villars, Paris, 1938.

16. R.P. Feynman, The principle of least action in quantum mechanics. Ph.D. thesis, Princeton University, 1942, p. 37.

17. R.P. Feynman, Ref. 2, pp. 381–82.

18. R.P. Feynman, Ref. 2, p. 384.

19. V. Volterra, *Theory of functionals and integral and integro-differential equations.* Blackie, London, 1930.

20. P.J. Daniel, *Ann. Math.* 20, 1 (1918); 21, 281 (1919).

21. R. Gâteaux, *Bull. Soc. Math. de France* 24, 47 (1919).

22. P. Lévy, *Lecçon d'analyse fonctionelle*, 1922.

23. N. Wiener, *Proc. Natl. Acad. Sci. USA* 7, 253 (1922); *J. Math. Phys. MIT*, 2, 131 (1923); *Proc. Lond. Math. Soc.* 22, 434 (1924); *Proc. Lond. Math. Soc.* 55, 117 (1930).

24. A. Einstein, *Ann. Phys. (Leipzig)* (4) 19, 371 (1905).

25. J.G. Kirkwood, *Phys. Rev.* 44, 31(1933).

26. S. Chandrasekhar, *Rev. Mod. Phys.* 15, 1 (1943).

27. P. Langevin, *C. R. Acad. Sci. Paris* 146, 530 (1908).

28. R.P. Feynman, Ref. 3.

29. R.P. Feynman, Ref. 16, p. 66.

30. R.P. Feynman, Ref. 2, p. 387.

31. B. Gaveau, T. Jacobson, M. Kac, and L. Schulman, *Phys. Rev. Lett.* **53**, 419 (1984); B. Gaveau and L. Schulman, Dirac equation path integrals interpreting the Grassman variable. *Nuovo Cim.* D **11**, 31 (1989).

11

The development of quantum electrodynamics until mid-1947: the historical background of Feynman's work on QED

11.1 P. A. M. Dirac's theory of radiation

Although Richard Feynman decided not to pay much attention to the old quantum electrodynamics, because it had not solved the problem of the interaction of light with matter, we have to outline briefly its general development, in order to place in context the great achievements of the physicists of Feynman's generation to this field during 1947–50. For details, see Refs. 1–5.

The beginning of quantum electrodynamics as a modern theory of the interaction of light with matter, i.e. between electromagnetic light-quanta or photons and particles of matter, was made by Paul Dirac in his fundamental paper 'The quantum theory of emission and absorption of radiation,' communicated to the *Proceedings of the Royal Society* (*London*) by Niels Bohr.[6] At the very beginning of this paper, Dirac stated that 'hardly anything has been done up to the present on quantum electrodynamics'.[6] Up to that time there existed a classical theory of radiation and a sketch of certain phenomenological aspects of the quantum theory of light (Max Planck's quantum theory of blackbody radiation and Albert Einstein's revolutionary idea of the existence of light-quanta or photons) and the nonrelativistic quantum theory of particles of matter (i.e. Werner Heisenberg's matrix mechanics and Erwin Schrödinger's wave mechanics, with deep insights from Paul Dirac, Max Born, Pascual Jordan, and some others). In the papers of Born and Jordan[7] and of Born, Heisenberg, and Jordan[8] an attempt had been made (by Jordan alone) to quantize the electromagnetic field by expressing the electric and magnetic field variables as matrices and to calculate the fluctuations in the field of cavity radiation.

Dirac's idea was to apply quantum mechanics not only to the particles in atoms but also, by making use of the ideas of Paul Ehrenfest and Peter Debye, to consider the radiation field in empty space as a system of quantized oscillators which interact with atoms. Then the Hamiltonian of the whole system of atoms and radiation takes the form

$$H = H_0 + H_{int}, \tag{11.1}$$

where $H_0 = H_{atoms} + H_{field}$ is the Hamiltonian of the noninteracting atoms and field, H_{atoms} being the Hamiltonian of the atoms only, and H_{field} being the Hamiltonian of the field alone. The H_{int} term describes the electromagnetic interaction, and, for charged particles with electric charge e in a radiation field with the three-vector electromagnetic potential A, it has the form

$$H_{int} = e \int j \cdot A \, d^3x, \tag{11.2}$$

where j is the three-vector of the current density of the particles. As long as one cannot solve the whole problem exactly, Dirac proposed to treat the effects of the interaction term H_{int} as a perturbation. Then one can quantize the free Hamiltonian H_0 by parts, i.e. one may consider separately the quantum problem of the atoms with the Hamiltonian H_{atoms} (at that time only the nonrelativistic Schrödinger equation was available for this purpose), and, independently of this atomic problem, one may consider the quantization of the radiation field Hamiltonian H_{field}. When the perturbation is taken into account, the states of the atoms and the electromagnetic field are no longer stationary and transitions between different states appear to be possible. Hence, one can describe the emission or absorption of light with the help of the standard methods of quantum perturbation theory.

So, Dirac 'worked out a theory for the interaction of an atomic system with electromagnetic radiation, taking the electromagnetic radiation to be an external perturbation acting on the atomic system, and I found that this external perturbation could lead to transitions of the atomic system in which it could absorb a quantum of energy, or, alternatively, emit a quantum of energy, with a jump from one state to another. That led to a theory that reproduced the Einstein coefficient B—the coefficients that govern the absorption of radiation and stimulated emission. These are the first coefficients that were deduced on the basis of the new mechanics.'[9]

As an indirect consequence of his theory, Dirac arrived at a completely new picture for the vacuum. After Einstein had abolished the concept of the ether, the matter-free and field-free vacuum was considered as an entirely empty space. But in quantum mechanics, because of Heisenberg's uncertainty principle, the electromagnetic field oscillators cannot be strictly at rest. As a consequence, even in the ground state with the lowest possible energy, there still exist the so-called zero-point oscillations of the quantum oscillators of frequency ω, having the energy $\frac{1}{2}\hbar\omega$. Hence the oscillatory nature of the electromagnetic field of radiation leads to the zero-point oscillations of this field in the vacuum state which has the lowest possible energy. The physical vacuum is not an empty space, but is 'populated' with zero-point oscillations, which are the cause of the spontaneous emission of radiation from atoms.

Thus Dirac's theory provides the explanation for all results regarding the emission and absorption of radiation by atoms.

The numerical results, derived from the Hamiltonian (11.1), when the interaction term (11.2) is treated as a first-order perturbation, were quite satisfactory from the experimental point of view prevalent at that time. Some other radiative processes, such as the nonrelativistic Compton scattering of photons by electrons and resonance fluorescence, had been calculated with the help of Dirac's radiation theory in good agreement with the experimental data in the second order of perturbation theory, where they first appear. This theory was also able to explain the natural width of spectral lines, which had been calculated by Eugene Wigner and Viktor F. Weisskopf (1930).[10] However, there arose certain fundamental difficulties when one tried to calculate higher-order approximations in perturbation theory with the help of the Hamiltonian (11.1), which we will discuss later on. Another difficulty was the available nonrelativistic treatment of the particles of matter in this theory, which made it inconsistent with the principles of special relativity theory, and showed that one would have to regard this theory only as a first nonrelativistic approximation to the true theory.

11.2 Dirac, Heisenberg, Pauli, and Fermi's relativistic radiation theory

In 1928 Paul Dirac published two articles on a new relativistic wave equation, the famous Dirac equation for the electron. The immediate consequences of this great contribution to the foundations of physics were as follows:

(1) The new relativistic equation led unambiguously to the spin $\frac{1}{2}\hbar$ of the electron.
(2) The gyromagnetic ratio g of the electron was exactly equal to 2, and this value followed directly from Dirac's fundamental equation.
(3) Dirac's relavistic wave equation for the electron led to the correct Sommerfeld formula for the fine structure of the hydrogen spectrum.

One can obtain more profound and complicated consequences in the new theory of radiation, which is obtained by replacing the nonrelativistic Hamiltonian H_{atoms} in equation (11.1) with Dirac's new relativistic Hamiltonian for the electrons. Then the lowest orders of perturbation are able to yield: (1) the Klein–Nishina formula for the scattering of light by electrons;[11] (2) the Møller formula for the scattering of two relativistic electrons;[12] (3) the formula for the emission of photons by relativistic electrons when they are scattered by the Coulomb potential of nuclei.[13] All these results are in good agreement with experiments.

In 1929–30 Heisenberg and Pauli made another attempt to develop a consistent theory of quantum electrodynamics.[14] They tried to generalize Dirac's theory of radiation and to quantize the entire electromagnetic field, not just its radiation part. The entire electromagnetic field may be represented as a sum of two parts: the first one gives the field describing the Coulomb interaction between the charged particles, which is unambiguously determined by the position of the charged particles and represents their own fields; the second part of the electromagnetic field was called the 'free field', which describes the electromagnetic radiation. Only this radiation field oscillates with respect to the time and was included in Dirac's theory of radiation as a system of quantum oscillators.

Enrico Fermi[15] gave a simple solution of the problem of how to divide the total electromagnetic field into a Coulomb field and the radiation field. As a result of a fundamental theorem, it is possible to represent the three-vector potential A as a sum of two terms: $A = A_\parallel + A_\perp$ The so-called transverse field $A_\perp$ has a zero divergence: div $A_\perp = 0$. Its Fourier-transformed three-vector is orthogonal to the direction of propagation of the electromagnetic field, hence the name 'transverse field'. The second part $A_\parallel$ is called the 'longitudinal field' since its Fourier-transformed three-vector is in the direction of propagation of the electromagnetic field. Fermi proposed to connect the radiation field with the transverse field $A_\perp$, and the Coulomb field with the longitudinal field $A_\parallel$. This procedure leads to the simple and physically clear picture of the quantum theory of the particles and the electromagnetic field,[15] and many young physicists, including Feynman, learned quantum electrodynamics from Fermi's famous paper entitled 'The quantum theory of radiation', based upon his lectures at the University of Michigan summer school at Ann Arbor, Michigan, in 1930. Although Fermi used Dirac's relativistic equation for the electron, his approach was not completely relativistically invariant, thereby spoiling the so-called gauge invariance of electrodynamics.† Indeed, the condition div $A_\perp = 0$ satisfies a special type of gauge, called a 'Coulomb gauge', which spoils gauge invariance, besides not being relativistically invariant. This leads to difficulties when one tries to develop the relativistically invariant perturbation theory, because in Fermi's approach the transverse and the longitudinal parts of the electromagnetic field were treated differently from

---

† The so-called gauge invariance of classical electrodynamics means the following property of the theory. As one can see from equation (5.4), if one adds to the components of the four-vector of the electromagnetic potential A_μ a four-gradient $\delta_\mu \chi$ of some scalar field χ, one will obtain the same Maxwell field tensor $F_{\mu\nu}$ and the same electromagnetic forces in the problem. Hence the theories with potentials A_μ and $A'_\mu = A_\mu + \delta_\mu \chi$ will give the same physical results so long as the potential is some auxiliary quantity rather than a physical one. However, since the new potential A'_μ also has to obey the Lorentz condition (5.6), it is necessary to use only the scalar fields χ which satisfy the condition $\Box \chi = 0$. This condition allows one to preserve the form of equation (5.5), from which the potential A_μ is obtained. Gauge invariance has been shown to be a fundamental constructive principle of physical interaction in the modern gauge theories of fundamental interactions; electrodynamics was the first known theory of this type.

each other, and the separation of these parts is relativistically not invariant. It was clear, however, that, in principle, this difficulty was only a formal one; the physical results must, anyhow, be independent of the choice of gauge, but in the Dirac–Heisenberg–Pauli–Fermi theory this was not obvious.

11.3 Dirac's hole theory, spin, and statistics

In relativistic theories there existed another fundamental difficulty which had been known since 1905 when Einstein wrote the relativistic expression for the energy of the particle with rest mass m. If the momentum of this particle is p, Planck's formula for the relativistic Hamiltonian, $H = \pm c(p^2 + m^2 c^2)^{1/2}$, c being the speed of light, shows that particles with negative energies exist in addition to the ones with positive energies. The negative energy is less than the zero-point energy of the empty space. At the beginning, no one was bothered particularly by this situation, because if all classical particles start with positive energies they will have positive energies all the time, for in the classical theory a transition to a negative energy state through the barrier $2mc^2$ is impossible; hence one can simply ignore the negative energy states in classical dynamics.

In quantum mechanics, however, the situation is entirely different. Here transitions from positive energy states to negative energy states do occur, and it is impossible to exclude negative energy states from the theory. In his relativistic theory of the electron, Dirac[16] 'got the idea that because the negative energy states cannot be avoided, one must accommodate them in the theory. One can do that by setting up a new picture of the vacuum. Suppose that in the vacuum all negative energy states are filled up. The possibility of doing that arises because the exclusion principle of Pauli prevents more than one electron in any state. We then have a sea of negative energy electrons, one electron in each of these states. It is a bottomless sea, but we do not have to worry about that. The picture of the bottomless sea is not so disturbing, really. We just have to think of the situation near the surface, and there we have some electrons lying above the sea that cannot fall into it because there is no room for them.

'There is, then, the possibility that holes may appear in the sea. Such holes would be places where there is no extra energy, because one would need a negative energy to make such a hole disappear. Also, such a hole would move as though it had a positive energy. It has an absence of negative charge; so in that respect, also, it appears as a positive charge. Thus the holes appear as particles with positive energy and positive charge.'[17]

First Dirac tried the interpretatation that the holes were protons, but Hermann Weyl proved that the new particles formed by these holes must have the same mass as the electrons. The new particles were given the name 'antielectrons' or 'positrons', and were discovered in 1932 by Carl Anderson (and, shortly thereafter, by Blackett and Occhialini). The 'antiproton' was discovered twenty-five years later. Thus the resolution of the question about the negative energy states turned out to be one of the greatest discoveries of the twentieth century: the discovery of the existence of antimatter. In quantum electrodynamics, however, completely new processes are possible involving antiparticles. A negative energy electron may be lifted up into a positive energy state, if it is given enough energy, for example by the absorption of light-quanta. This process would look like the creation by a photon of an electron with positive energy and a hole with negative energy, i.e. the positron. In the inverse process of the recombination of an electron and a positron, called 'annihilation', these particles disappear and their combined energy is radiated away as photons. It was not hard to calculate the probability of annihilation of an electron and a positron into two photons;[16,18,19] moreover, the cross section for pair creation (electron and positron) by photons in the Coulomb field of atomic nuclei could also be readily calculated.[13] The theoretical results for radiative scattering and the creation of pairs were confirmed by experiments with cosmic-ray cascade showers in matter, once the incoming energy is transformed into electrons and positrons.

Dirac's interpretation of the negative energy states in the solution of the Dirac equation for the electron forced physicists to arrive at the following important conclusions. No one-particle systems exist in nature, nor even few-particle systems; these are attributed only to the nonrelativistic theory. In the true relativistic quantum electrodynamics one must take into consideration the infinite number of the electrons and positrons in the vacuum. The pair production and annihilation of electron–positron pairs, together with vacuum fluctuations and the existence of virtual pairs, leads to a theory in which the number of particles is not conserved. Hence, the particles of matter must be considered as the quanta of the corresponding field, just as the photons are the quanta of the electromagnetic field.

A new picture of forces between particles appears in quantum field theory. We can understand the interaction between two charged particles at a distance as an exchange of virtual photons, which continuously pass from one charged particle to another. These exchanged virtual particles are not directly observed as particles because of the conservation of energy, but, according to Bohr's extension of Heisenberg's uncertainty principle, $\Delta E \, \Delta t \geqslant \hbar$, such an exchange is possible for short enough time intervals. Hence, the virtual particles can be created for a very short time in the intermediate states of the physical processes, but they must be absorbed quickly enough. As a result, the charged particle is surrounded by a cloud of virtual photons. The latter can produce other virtual particles, such as electrons and positrons, by means of pair creation in vacuum, and then the electrons and positrons thus created must annihilate each other very quickly to preserve energy conservation within the limits of the uncertainty principle. Thus the cloud around the charged particle consists of photons, electrons, and positrons.

As we see, in the new relativistic quantum theory one has quite a complicated picture of the physical vacuum, of physical particles, and of physical interactions. The corresponding mathematical formalism to describe this complicated physical picture, involving infinitely many particles, was needed.

Since, in the Hamiltonian method, the treatment of the space and time coordinates is completely different, relativistic invariance is not apparent in this method. Dirac proposed the new 'many-time' formalism in which, together with the coordinates of each particle, one has to include the corresponding time variables of these particles. Thereby the theory obviously became relativistically invariant, but also quite complicated to deal with.

Pascual Jordan, Oskar Klein, and Eugene Wigner proposed another very useful method, called the method of 'second quantization'.[20] The essence of this method consisted in considering simultaneously the matter–particle field, given by the corresponding wave function, as an operator field, as well as the field of photons. Thus it became possible to deal with the corresponding creation and annihilation operators for all kinds of quanta (i.e. photons, electrons, and positrons), and then one could express all physical quantities by these operators. But there appears a very important difference between the description of photons and electrons, or speaking more generally, between particles with integer or half-integer spin. It was well known by this time that photons have spin 1 and obey the Bose–Einstein statistics, i.e. there can be an arbitrary number of such particles in the same state; they were called 'bosons'. In contrast, the particles like electrons, with half-integer spin, obey the Fermi–Dirac statistics, i.e. only one such particle occupies a given state in accordance with the Pauli exclusion principle; such particles were called 'fermions'. The nomenclature 'bosons' and 'fermions' was given by Dirac. Suppose the creation and annihilation operators of bosons are a and $a^\dagger$, respectively, and the corresponding creation and annihilation operators for fermions are b and $b^\dagger$. Then, in order to satisfy the corresponding statistics, these operators must satisfy the commutation relations. The boson operators obey the commutation relation

$$[a^\dagger, a] = a^\dagger a - a a^\dagger = 1, \tag{11.3}$$

whereas the fermion operators obey the anticommutation relation

$$\{b^\dagger, b\} = b^\dagger b + b b^\dagger = 1, \tag{11.4}$$

where 1 denotes the identity operator.

These relations were first established and used for photons and electrons only. Pauli and Weisskopf investigated the electromagnetic interactions of scalar charged particles with spin zero, described by the Klein–Gordon equation.[21] They established that the scalar field must be quantized according to commutation relations (11.3), and scalar particles do satisfy Bose–Einstein statistics. But in contrast to the photon field, now we also have the field of charged particles, and the corresponding antiparticles exist as well. Pauli, who did not like Dirac's hole theory of the positrons, was quite satisfied when he and Weisskopf proved that in the case of scalar particles one did not have to consider the sea of antiparticles. The reason was that this is simply impossible, since the scalar particles did not obey Fermi–Dirac statistics. Since, in this paper, it was shown that Dirac's hole theory was not a universal approach to negative energy states in relativistic quantum mechanics, Pauli called this paper 'our anti-Dirac paper'.[22] This work led Pauli to the discovery of the general relation between spin and statistics in connection with the commutation rules expressed by equations (11.3) and (11.4).[23] The particles with spin 0, as well as particles with values other than $\frac{1}{2}$ or 1, were not known at that time, but Pauli's important discovery of the fundamental connection between spin and statistics became part of the basic general principles of the old quantum field theory.

11.4 The infinities in quantum electrodynamics

Despite the great achievements of the theory of quantum electrodynamics before World War II, there remained serious difficulties in it, besides the fact that the theory was inconsistent. These difficulties were connected with infinities of different kinds that appeared in the theory.

Heisenberg[24] and Dirac[25] discussed the appearance of an infinite energy and infinite density of charge in a finite volume of three-dimensional space, arising from the physical properties of the vacuum in the new theory. The infinite energy was connected with zero-point oscillations of the electromagnetic field after its quantization, and the infinite charge appeared because of the Dirac sea, which was filled by the negative energy electrons with infinite density.

The resolution of these two difficulties turned out to be quite simple. Pauli first proposed the primitive solution of the infinite charge density problem by a redefinition of the charge and the current. Considering the symmetry between electrons and positrons, we can take in equal proportions the electron sea and the positron sea, with the consequence that in the resulting theory the charge of the vacuum will be zero, since the vacuum charge of the electron sea will be exactly compensated by the vacuum charge of the positron sea.

J. Robert Oppenheimer and Wendell Furry gave this idea the right mathematical form.[26] They recognized that a proper ordering of the creation and annihilation operators in the quantum electron–positron Hamiltonian will lead to the zero vacuum charge density and make Dirac's idea of a filled vacuum unnecessary. With the same ordering of the corresponding operators in the quantum Hamiltonian of photons, the zero-point vacuum energy also vanishes. This ordering of the creation and annihilation operators was called 'a normal ordering', and gives us a special kind of rule for the quantization of classical dynamical systems. It was important that this rule did not destroy the form of the quantum equations, nor the existence of vacuum fluctuations of the photon and the electron–positron field. The only effect of the normal ordering was the shift of the zero-point vacuum energy and the vacuum charge density to the correct zero values of these quantities.

In the resulting improved theory, there were now only three fundamental interactions between the electrons, the positrons, and the photons: the scattering of the fermion with the emission or absorption of the photon, and the creation or annihilation of the electron–positron pair with the emission or absorption of the photon. For treating these first-order processes the perturbation theory was perfect. But when one tried to calculate some more complicated processes in higher orders of perturbation theory, one met difficulties, because other new infinities appeared. Already in 1930, Oppenheimer had first recognized that higher-order corrections in perturbation theory would lead to infinities.[27] He calculated the effect of the interaction between an atomic electron and the quantum electromagnetic field, and discovered that this interaction leads to the infinite shift of atomic energy levels. Later on, the investigation of higher-order terms was continued by Ivar Waller[28] and others.

Among the different divergences of this type, two were the most important. In 1934, Pauli had asked the young Viktor Weisskopf, who worked as his assistant at that time, to calculate the self energy of the electron in the new relativistic quantum theory. As we have noted (Section 5.2), in classical theory this self-energy is proportional to e^2/a, where e is the charge and a is the radius of the electron. Hence, for a point electron, the classical self-energy is infinite and diverges linearly as the radius of the electron goes down to zero. In his first publication on this problem, Weisskopf made a fundamental mistake,[29] which was pointed out to him by Wendell Furry, and after correcting it Weisskopf obtained the correct expression for the self-energy of the electron in the relativistic quantum theory (in the second order of perturbation theory) in the form[29]

$$E_{self} \approx m_0 c^2 \left[1 + \frac{3}{2\pi} \frac{e^2}{\hbar c} \log \left(\frac{\lambda_C}{a} \right) \right], \qquad (11.5)$$

where m_0 is the mechanical mass of the electron at rest, and $\lambda_C (= \hbar/mc)$ is its Compton wavelength. This formula showed that the self-energy of the point electron is still infinite in quantum electrodynamics as well, but as a result of the complicated structure of the vacuum this infinity is quite a bit weaker and the self-energy diverges only logarithmically as the radius of the electron goes to zero. Another important conclusion derived from formula (11.5) is that, in quantum electrodynamics, the divergence is actually not a physical one. In fact, the logarithmic term in this formula will have the value of the order of the first term at distances of the order of 10^{-72} cm, which is extremely small compared with the Schwarzschild radius of the electron, which is only about

10^{-45} cm. At such small distances the theory will surely be wrong, because one must take into account at least the gravitational force. Nevertheless, quantum electrodynamics itself is evidently not a consistent theory because of this divergence, and may give wrong predictions at such fantastically small distances.

The second, physically important, divergence has another character. As a result of pair creation, the physical vacuum becomes a medium with dielectric properties. In the presence of a charged particle in the vacuum, virtual electron–positron pairs appear, and the induced cloud of such virtual pairs changes the value of the effective charge of the particle. The effective charge depends on the distance r from the particle and has the form $e(r) = e/\varepsilon(r)$, where $\varepsilon(r)$ is the dielectric coefficient of the vacuum. This coefficient was first calculated by Serber[30] and Uehling[31] in the second-order perturbation theory of the Coulomb field. Heisenberg and Euler[32] and Weisskopf[33] obtained an exact expression for slowly varying static fields. The result for the Coulomb field was that, at large distances r, the effective charge behaves like

$$e(r) \approx e\left[1 + \frac{3}{4\pi^{1/2}}\frac{e^2}{\hbar c}\left(\frac{\lambda_C}{r}\right)^{3/2}\exp\left(-2\frac{\lambda_C}{r}\right)\right] \quad \text{for } r \gg \lambda_C, \quad (11.6a)$$

$$e(r) \approx e\left[1 + \frac{2}{3\pi}\frac{e^2}{\hbar c}\log\left(\frac{\lambda_C}{r}\right)\right] \quad \text{for } r \ll \lambda_C. \quad (11.6b)$$

Equation (11.6a) shows that at large distances one should see the particle with the usual charge e, but from equation (11.6b) we note that at short distances the effective charge is logarithmically divergent. The reason is that the entire charge of the cloud of virtual particles around every charged particle like an electron has an infinite value. In other words, because of pair creation, the vacuum has an infinite polarization near the charged particles. The range at which this polarization has a significant value is of the order of $\lambda_C \exp(-\hbar c/e^2) \approx 10^{-72}$ cm, i.e. this effect appears at the same distance which we have discussed in connection with the self-energy of the electron, and at such short distances this theory is most likely physically inapplicable. But, in spite of this difficulty, at large distances the theory gives the usual right predictions.

Since one can reach very short distances only because of a very large energy of the particles, and the large energy of light-quanta or photons corresponds to spectral frequencies far beyond the violet range, the two divergences mentioned above were called 'ultraviolet divergences'. The real situation in quantum electrodynamics was much more complicated, because the ultra-violet divergences also appeared in higher orders of perturbation theory, and before the work of Freeman Dyson,[34] one could expect new types of divergences in each order of perturbation theory, i.e. in the following terms of the infinite Taylor series expansion in powers of the coupling constant

$\alpha = e^2/\hbar c \approx \frac{1}{137}$. The true behavior of the self-energy and the effective charge still remains an open question, which cannot be solved by formulas like (11.5), (11.6a), and (11.6b).

Finally, there also occurred certain infinities in quantum electrodynamics, which were called the 'infrared divergences'. Their physical meaning is entirely different. They are connected with the radiation of low-energy photons, hence the name 'infrared divergences'. The quantum electrodynamical result was that the charged particle emits infinitely many photons with zero frequency when it has an accelerated motion as, for instance, when an electron is scattered by a static electric field. In that case, the emitted energy does not vanish in the limit of the zero frequency of the light-quanta, in correspondence with the classical results for the electromagnetic radiation of charged particles. Felix Bloch and Arnold Nordsieck[35] and Pauli and Fierz[36] showed that the difficulty with the infinite number of zero-frequency photons is not a physical one, and may be removed by a proper contact transformation of the theory.

Thus, after 1937, the only remaining problem for the theory was how to deal with the ultraviolet divergences. One very important obstacle in the struggle with these infinities was the absence of a relativistically invariant perturbation theory. The nonrelativistic perturbation theory led to different series in different frames, and it was difficult to understand the physical meaning of the results. The only exception was several papers by Ernst C. G. Stückelberg;[37] he gave a manifestly invariant formulation of field theory, which could have been the basis for a true physical theory. But, unfortunately, these papers 'were rather obscure, and it was difficult to understand them or to make use of his methods'.[38]

11.5 The earlier attempts to overcome the infinities in quantum electrodynamics

At the end of the 1930s, it was clear to all active theoreticians in the field that quantum electrodynamics was not in a good state, and that something radically new was needed to overcome the divergences. We will briefly describe some of the proposed ideas for the solution of the problems.

In 1937 John Archibald Wheeler[39] and, independently, in 1943 Werner Heisenberg[40] proposed to give up quantum field theory entirely and to replace it with an entirely new theory, in which instead of fields one must operate only with directly measurable quantities. This approach was described as an 'S-matrix' theory.

In 1938, Heisenberg had proposed to introduce a new fundamental constant in the theory, called the 'fundamental length'.[41] His idea was that at distances less than the fundamental length, physical processes—and even geometry— are not the same as we hold them usually, and that the theory has to be changed radically at distances smaller than this fundamental length.

In 1942, Dirac proposed the notion of an 'indefinite metric', which would introduce into quantum mechanics intermediate states with negative probability. Such states were not to be observable, but they might help in obtaining convergent series rather than divergent ones.[42]

During 1940–45, Feynman and Wheeler considered the possibility of completely eliminating the electromagnetic field as the carrier of interaction between charged particles, and to replace it by an action-at-a-distance theory[43,44] (see Chapter 5). Other revolutionary approaches, such as the Born–Infeld[45] nonlinear version of classical electrodynamics and Dirac's reconstruction of the classical theory of the point electron,[46] were proposed to overcome the divergence difficulties of quantum electrodynamics, but nothing helped; the solution lay in an entirely different direction.

Léon Rosenfeld[47] had already discovered the infinite self-energy of the photon in quantum electrodynamics; it was due to the current fluctuations of the electromagnetic field in the vacuum. Here, for the first time, the notion of 'renormalization' procedure was used. The basic idea was that if the polarization of the vacuum was finite then its constant part would have been physically inessential, since no measurable physical effects would have been connected with such a constant polarization. Only the sum of the 'true' and the induced charge of the particle may be measured. It seems natural to ignore the constant part of vacuum polarization, too, in the case when it is infinite, and to take into account only the finite deviations from this constant part. Such deviations were investigated by Serber,[30] by Uehling,[31] by Weisskopf,[33] and by Serpe,[48] a student of Kramers', but the earlier attempts to measure the corresponding very small effects were unsuccessful. The first steps in the right direction were taken by Hendrik Kramers in his attempt to deal with another ultraviolet divergence connected with the self-interaction of charged particles. Kramers's idea was that, first, one has to overcome the difficulties in classical electrodynamics, and then, to build the quantum theory of it in accordance with the correspondence principle; one could expect to be free of the difficulties in the quantum case after they had been removed from the classical theory.

Kramers's program for the solution of this problem in classical theory was to use the subtractions of the infinite quantities connected with the self-interactions of the charged particles with their own fields. Following the ideas of his teacher, Hendrik Antoon Lorentz, Kramers stated that the mass m of the charged particle in equation (5.7) is not the experimental mass, but some auxilliary 'bare' mass. Then the experimental mass m_{exp} of the charged particle is the sum of the bare mass m and the electromagnetic mass $\delta m_{selfint}$ which originates from the self-interaction of the particle with its own field, $F_{\mu\nu}^{self}$, and has an infinite value for a point particle (Section 5.1):

$$m_{exp} = m + \delta m_{selfint}. \tag{11.7}$$

As far as the self-interaction of the particle with its own field, $F_{\mu\nu}^{self}$, has been taken into account by equation (5.7), we have to subtract, according to

Kramers, the field $F_{\mu\nu}^{\text{self}}$ as the entire electromagnetic field in equation (5.7), as 'mass renormalization'. Hence equation (5.7) acquires the form

$$m_{\text{exp}}c^2\ddot{a}_\nu = eF_{\nu\mu}^{\text{ext}}(a)\dot{a}^\mu, \tag{11.8}$$

where $F_{\nu\mu}^{\text{ext}} = F_{\nu\mu} - F_{\nu\mu}^{\text{self}}$ is the external field, i.e. the electromagnetic field without the field of the particle itself. Equation (11.8) has a remarkable property: it is written completely in terms of observable quantities and, despite the fact that the mass $\delta m_{\text{selfint}}$ in equation (11.7) is infinite, the mass m_{exp} is supposed to be the finite observed mass of the particle, and then there are no infinite quantities in equation (11.8) at all.

Kramers had had reservations about Dirac's theory of radiation and its later development, because he had insisted on a proper separation of bare mass and electromagnetic mass throughout the theory. Thus, according to this idea, the self-energy of the electron could be written in the form

$$E_{\text{exp}} = m_{\text{exp}}c^2 = mc^2 + W_V,$$

where W_V is the electromagnetic self-energy of the electron in some external field V. Then $W_0 = \delta m_{\text{selfint}}c^2$ is the electromagnetic self-energy of the free electron. Kramers argued that the difference of the two infinite terms, $W_V - W_0$, should lead to observable effects and may be finite.[49]

Another important example was the fluctuations of the electromagnetic field. The quantum averages, $\langle 0|E^2|0\rangle$, or $\langle 1|E^2|1\rangle$, of the square of the electric field E, both in the vacuum state $|0\rangle$ with zero photons, and in the state $|1\rangle$ with one photon, are infinite. But according to the subtraction procedure of Kramers, the difference $\langle 1|E^2|1\rangle - \langle 0|E^2|0\rangle$ is a finite and measurable quantity.[49] Kramers was able to calculate certain quantities of this type as early as 1940, but he did not actually carry through his program until 1947. He had published some of his ideas in 1938[50] and in his monograph on quantum mechanics in the chapters dealing with quantum electrodynamics.[51] However, these ideas of Kramers's were practically unknown until after the Shelter Island Conference (1947) and the Eighth Solvay Conference in Brussels.[49] Moreover, as a follower of Lorentz, Kramers had developed his ideas on the basis of the old nonrelativistic Lorentz model of the electron. Kramers emphasized the use of the correspondence principle, which, in his opinion, would have to lead to the right nonrelativistic quantum electrodynamics, and only after that Kramers intended to develop the relativistic one. Such an approach did not turn out to be useful, for in it one missed dealing with important physical phenomena, such as pair production, vacuum polarization, and the other relativistic effects. Kramers, therefore, was himself not very successful in developing his own ideas concerning the renormalization procedure, which is now widely accepted to be the right way to overcome the divergences in quantum electrodynamics. Nevertheless, it was important that as early as 1937–38 Kramers had mentioned the possibility of making corrections to the predictions of the Dirac–Heisenberg–Pauli–Fermi quantum electrodynamics for the states of the electrons in the atoms and in other physical phenomena.[49]

11.6 The earlier experimental evidence for the deviations from Dirac's theory of the electron

Already in 1937–38, experimental evidence had appeared which cast a shadow of doubt on the predictions based on Dirac's relativistic theory of the electron. William Houston and Robert C. Williams had found deviations from Dirac's theory of the hydrogen spectrum. According to Dirac's theory, the $2^2S_{1/2}$ and $2^2P_{1/2}$ levels of hydrogen must have the same energy. But the experimental evidence was against such a degeneracy in these levels.[52, 53] Simon Pasternack[54] reached the conclusion that the difference between $2^2S_{1/2}$ and $2^2P_{1/2}$ may be represented as an upward shift of the $2^2S_{1/2}$ level by approximately $0.03\ \text{cm}^{-1}$ (~ 1000 megacycles) relative to the $2^2P_{1/2}$ level. The first attempts to calculate this effect theoretically were made by Fröhlich, Heitler, and Kahn.[55] Although their calculations were in good agreement with the experimental data, they were incorrect, as was shown by Willis E. Lamb.[56]

The situation thus remained unclear, and it did not change during the years of World War II, when the attention of most physicists was directed to war-related scientific research problems.

However, as a result of war-related projects, a great improvement in experimental devices and techniques took place during the war years. These achievements had a great influence on the postwar progress, both experimental and theoretical, of quantum electrodynamics.

Certain important steps toward the new theory of quantum electrodynamics were made during wartime in Japan. In 1942, S. Sakata proposed to overcome the divergences by introducing a neutral scalar field; in 1946, the same idea was independently developed by Abraham Pais.[57] Sin-Itiro Tomonaga and Ito Koba calculated cross sections in the new theory, and discovered some mistakes in the earlier calculations of these quantities in the work of S. M. Dancoff,[58] which were quite essential for the development of the renormalization program. Tomonaga also succeeded in developing Dirac's multitime relativistic formulation of field theory. But because of the war all normal contacts and communications within the scientific community were broken, and these achievements were completely unknown in the USA and Europe until Tomonaga wrote a letter to Oppenheimer after the Shelter Island Conference in the summer of 1947.

11.7 The post-war development and the Shelter Island Conference

The main new feature of the development of quantum field theory after World War II was the emergence of quantum electrodynamics in the USA during

1947–49. In the year following the end of the war, many physicists had returned to purely scientific research problems. Many physicists, who left Europe before or during the war, also continued to do their work in America. Right after the war, physicists wished to get away from the applications of science to technology and return to work on fundamental physical problems. Another challenge was to bring the young, energetic, American-trained generation of theoretical physicists into the mainstream of the research community; they had erstwhile worked on the applications of fundamental science to engineering and technology, and now wanted to pursue research on basic physical problems. They, with their scientific elders, had been pioneers in making new devices, forging the technology of new weapons that led the Allies to victory in World War II. The government and society in the United States deeply appreciated the achievements of the scientists, especially the physicists, during the war, and when the war had been won increasing support was forthcoming for research in fundamental science. New types of national scientific organizations and institutions, such as the Manhattan Project at Los Alamos and dozens of other laboratories, had sprung up; suddenly there was great activity in the form of conferences, symposia, scientific workshops, and seminars on specialized fields under the guidance of leading experts. The era of the lone scientist, working by himself in isolation, was over, and one of the most important new ingredients of success was to 'get these guys organized', as Feynman used to say later.[59]

As a result of some conversations and exchange of letters between Karl K. Darrow, the permanent secretary of the American Physical Society, Duncan McInnes, a distinguished physical chemist at the Rockefeller Institute, Frank Jowett, then president of the National Academy of Sciences, and John Wheeler, then a young professor of theoretical physics at Princeton University, there was generated the idea of organizing several small conferences on the foundations of quantum physics. The aim was to make an evaluation of the current status of the fundamental problems, and to have serious and critical discussions among the best experts on current specific topics of interest.

The first of these conferences took place on 2–4 June 1947 at Ram's Head Inn on Shelter Island, at the tip of Long Island, and the general theme of the conference was 'Problems of quantum mechanics and the electron'. This conference turned out to be a cornerstone in the development of quantum electrodynamics. As Feynman himself recalled later on: 'There have been many conferences in the world since, but I've never felt any to be as important as this. . . . The Shelter Island Conference was my first conference with the big men. . . . I had never gone to one like this one in peacetime.'[61] The participants in this conference were: Abraham Pais, Arthur Nordsieck, Bruno Rossi, David Bohm, Duncan McInnes, Edward Teller, Hans Bethe, Hendrik Kramers, Herman Feshbach, George Uhlenbeck, Gregory Breit, Isidor Rabi, John von Neumann, John Van Vleck, John Wheeler, Julian Schwinger, Karl

Darrow, Linus Pauling, Richard Feynman, Robert Marshak, J. Robert Oppenheimer, Robert Serber, Viktor Weisskopf, and Willis E. Lamb.

In the *New York Herald Tribune* of 2 June 1947, one could read the announcement: 'Twenty-three of the country's best known theoretical physicists—the men who made the atomic bomb—gathered today in a rural inn to begin three days of discussion and study, during which they hope to straighten out a few of the difficulties that beset modern physics.'

Unlike the usual reports of participants in regular conferences, at the Shelter Island Conference there took place only extensive discussions following the comprehensive talks of the discussion leaders; the three rapporteurs were Kramers, Oppenheimer, and Weisskopf.

Weisskopf spoke first. He talked about the difficulties of the theory of elementary particles: (A) the difficulties of quantum electrodynamics—self-energies and other infinities, modifications of the classical theory and of the formalism after quantization, subtraction formalism for deriving finite results in quantum electrodynamics, high-energy limit of quantum electrodynamics; (B) nuclear forces and mesons—cosmic-ray experiments, beta decay; (C) proposed experiments, electron and proton accelerators, new machines. Weisskopf was quite pessimistic about the immediate development of the theory and finished his talk with the words: 'In view of the failure of the present theories to represent the facts and the small probability that this conference may produce a new theoretical idea, part (C) of this agenda (namely, the experiments) could become the most useful part of this conference.'[4]

Oppenheimer did not talk about the problems of quantum electrodynamics at all, but tried to adapt some field-theoretical methods to meson theory and compared the difficulties of the multiple scattering of mesons with the infrared divergences in the theory of radiation.[4]

Kramers's talk concentrated on the difficulties of quantum electrodynamics since 1927: the divergences in second-order perturbation theory, *the infinite shift of the spectral lines*, the impossibility of describing a steady state of an atom in the radiation field, and the reaction of the radiation on the atomic particles. Then he outlined his own work on the renormalization of the mass and showed 'how an electron with *experimental* mass behaves in its interaction with electromagnetic field'. Kramers stated that 'the infinite shift of spectral lines, with the Dirac Lagrangian, is immediately connected with the divergences of the electromagnetic mass for a point electron'.[62] Kramers had proposed the subtraction procedure, i.e. the mass renormalization described in Section 11.5, to obtain finite results for physical quantities. One of Kramers's very important conclusions, which he had mentioned already in 1937, was that 'as a result, we expect that the correction must be applied to the energy values of stationary states of the hydrogen atom as given in the Dirac theory of 1928'.[49]

During May 1947, the rumors of an important new experiment on the level shift in the fine structure of hydrogen, performed at the Columbia University

Radiation Laboratory were spreading. The experiment had been done by Willis Lamb, together with his graduate student Robert Retherford, and the result was the first precisely established value of the shift between $2^2S_{1/2}$ and $2^2P_{1/2}$ levels in the spectrum of atomic hydrogen (see Section 11.4). This experiment was reported at the Shelter Island Conference after Kramers's talk, and became one of the central concerns of the conference. 'The results indicate clearly that, contrary to (Dirac's) theory, but in essential agreement with Pasternack's hypothesis, the $2^2S_{1/2}$ state is higher than the $2^2P_{1/2}$ by about 1000 Mc/sec (0.033 cm^{-1}, or about 9 percent of the spin relativity doublet separation).'[63] The experiment became possible owing to 'the great wartime advances in microwave techniques in the vicinity of three centimeters wavelength.'[63]

Another important experimental result, reported at the Shelter Island Conference by Rabi, was from the work of Nafe and Nelson, and Kusch and Foley, on the hyperfine structure of hydrogen, deuterium, and more complex atoms. These experiments gave indications that another discrepancy existed between Dirac's theory of the magnetic moment of the electron and its experimental value. In the Dirac theory, the gyromagnetic ratio for the electron is $g_s = 2$. But the experimental value obtained by Foley and Kusch was $g_s = 2.000\,244 \pm 0.000\,06$.[64] It was not clear where such a small discrepancy was coming from and how one could modify Dirac's relativistic theory of the electron, one of the great triumphs of which had been the explanation of the magnetic moment of the electron. The number g_s characterizes the ratio between the strength of the electron's interaction with the external magnetic field and the strength of its own magnetic field; it is a fundamental characteristic of the electron.

At the Shelter Island Conference the other very important communication was Robert Marshak's two-meson hypothesis, about the existence of the pi-meson, which was discovered soon thereafter. But the most important discussions took place in the domain of quantum electrodynamics, which immediately after the conference reached great advances in the theoretical understanding of the physical processes involved. Robert Oppenheimer declared: 'These developments, which could have been carried out at any time during the last fifteen years, required the impetus of experiments to stimulate and verify.'[65]

Notes and References

1. J. Robert Oppenheimer, Electron theory. *Rapports du 8e conseil Solvay* 1948, Stoop, Bruxelles, 1950.
VS2. R.E. Peierls, A. Salam, P.T. Matthews, and G. Feldman, A survey of field theory. *Rep. Prog. Phys.* **18**, 424 (1955).

3. S. Weinberg, The search for unity: Notes for a history of quantum field theory, *Daedalus* **106**, 17 (1977).

4. S.S. Schweber, Some chapters for a history of quantum field theory: 1938–1952. In: *Relativity, groups and topology* II (ed. B. DeWitt and R. Sto). NATO ASI, Les Houches, XL, 1983.

5. V.F. Weisskopf, Growing up with field theory: The development of quantum Electrodynamics. In: *The birth of particles physics* (eds. L.M. Brown and L. Hoddeson). Cambridge University Press, New York, 1983.

6. P.A.M. Dirac, The quantum theory of emission and absorption of radiation, *Proc. R. Soc. Lond.* A **114**, 243 (1927).

7. M. Born and P. Jordan, *Z. Phys.* **34**, 858 (1925).

8. M. Born, W. Heisenberg, and P. Jordan, *Z. Phys.* **35**, 557 (1926).

9. P.A.M. Dirac, The origin of quantum field theory. In: *The Birth of particle physics* (ed. L.M. Brown and L. Hoddeson). Cambridge University Press, New York, 1983, p. 47.

10. V.F. Weisskopf and E.P. Wigner, *Z. Phys.* **63**, 54 (1930).

11. O. Klein and Y. Nishina, *Z. Phys.* **52**, 853 (1929).

12. C. Møller, *Ann. Phys. (Leipzig)* **14**, 531 (1932).

13. W. Heitler and F. Sauter, *Nature* **132**, 892 (1933).

14. W. Heisenberg and W. Pauli, *Z. Phys.* **56**, 1 (1929); **59**, 168 (1930).

15. E. Fermi, *Rev. Mod. Phys.* **4**, 87 (1932).

16. P.A.M. Dirac, *Proc. R. Soc. Lond.* **126**, 360 (1930); *Proc. Camb. Phil. Soc.* **26** 361 (1930).

17. P.A.M. Dirac, Ref. 9, pp. 51–52.

18. J.R. Oppenheimer and M.S. Plesset, *Phys. Rev.* **44**, 53 (1933).

19. Y. Nishina, S. Tomonaga, S. Sakata, *Sci. Papers Inst. Phys. Chem. Res.* **17** (Suppl.) 1 (1934).

20. P. Jordan and O. Klein, *Z. Phys.* **45**, 751 (1927); P. Jordan and E. Wigner, *Z. Phys.* **47**, 631 (1928).

21. W. Pauli and V.F. Weisskopf, *Helv. Phys. Acta* **7**, 709 (1934).

22. V.F. Weisskopf, Ref. 5.

23. W. Pauli, *Phys. Rev.* **58**, 716 (1940).

24. W. Heisenberg, *Z. Phys.* **90**, 209 (1934).

25. P.A.M. Dirac, *Proc. Camb. Phil. Soc.* **30**, 150 (1934).

26. W. Furry and J.R. Oppenheimer, *Phys. Rev.*, **45**, 245 (1934).

27. J.R. Oppenheimer, *Phys. Rev.* **35**, 467 (1930).

28. I. Waller, *Z. Phys.* **62**, 673 (1936).

29. V.F. Weisskopf, *Z. Phys.* **89**, 27 (1934).

30. R. Serber, *Phys. Rev.* **48**, 49 (1935).

31. E.A. Uehling, *Phys. Rev.* **48**, 35 (1935).

32. W. Heisenberg and H. Euler, *Z. Phys.* **98**, 714 (1936).

33. V.F. Weisskopf, *Kgl. Danske Videnskb. Selskab. Mat. Fiz. Medd.* **14**, 1 (1936).

34. F.J. Dyson, *Phys. Rev.* **75**, 486 (1949).

35. F. Bloch and A. Nordsieck, *Phys. Rev.* **52**, 54 (1937).

36. W. Pauli and M. Fierz, *Nuovo Cim.* **15**, 167 (1938).

37. E.C.G. Stückelberg, *Ann. Phys. (Leipzig)* **21**, 367 (1934); *Helv Phys. Acta.* **11** 225 (1938).

38. V.F. Weisskopf, Ref. 5, p. 74.

39. J.A. Wheeler, *Phys. Rev.* **52**, 1107 (1937).

40. W. Heisenberg, *Z. Phys.* **120**, 513 (1943).

41. W. Heisenberg, *Ann. Phys. (Leipzig)* **32**, 20 (1938).

42. P.A.M. Dirac, *Proc. Roy. Soc. Lond.* A **180**, 1 (1942).

43. J.A. Wheeler and R.P. Feynman, *Rev. Mod. Phys.* **17**, 157 (1945).

44. J.A. Wheeler and R.P. Feynman, *Rev. Mod. Phys.* **21**, 425 (1949)

45. M. Born and L. Infeld, *Proc. Roy. Soc. Lond.* A **144** 423 (1934); **147**, 522 (1934); **150**, 141 (1935).

46. P.A.M. Dirac, *Proc. Roy. Soc. Lond.* A **167**, 148 (1938).

47. L. Rosenfeld, *Zeits. f. Phys.* **65**, 589 (1930).

48. J. Serpe, *Physica* **VII**, 133(Feb. 1940); **VIII**, 226 (Feb. 1941).

49. H.A. Kramers, *Rapports et discussions du 8e conseil de physique Solvay* 1948, Stoop, Bruxelles, 1950, p. 241; M. Dresden, *H.A. Kramers: Between tradition and revolution*, Springer, New York, 1987, p. 375.

50. H.A. Kramers, *Hand- und Jahrbuch der Chemischen Physik I*, Abschnitt 2, Leipzig, 1938, p. 89; *Nuovo Cim.* **15**, 108 (1938).

51. H.A. Kramers, *Quantum mechanics*, Vol. 2. North-Holland, Amsterdam, 1958.

52. W.V. Houston, *Phys. Rev.* **51**, 446 (1937).

53. R.C. Williams, *Phys. Rev.* **54**, 558 (1938).

54. S. Pasternack, *Phys. Rev.* **54**, 1113 (1938).

55. H. Fröhlich, W. Heitler, and B. Kahn, *Proc. Roy. Soc. Lond.* A **166**, 154 (1939); *Phys. Rev.* **56**, 961 (1939).

56. W.E. Lamb, Jr., *Phys. Rev.* **56**, 384(1939); *Phys. Rev.* **57**, 458 (1940).

57. A. Pais, *Phys. Rev.* **63**, 227 (1946).

58. S.M. Dancoff, *Phys. Rev.* **55**, 939 (1939).

59. W.D. Hillis, *Physics Today*, February 1989, p. 70.

60. R.P. Feynman, Interviews and conversations with Jagdish Mehra, in Pasadena, California, January 1988; Interviews with Charles Weiner (American Institute of Physics), in Pasadena, California, 1966.

61. R.P. Feynman, Interviews and conversations with Jagdish Mehra, in Austin, Texas, April 1970.

62. S.S. Schweber, in *Shelter Island II*, Proceedings of the 1983 Shelter Island Conference on Quantum Field Theory and the Fundamental Problems of Physics (ed. R. Jackiw, N. Khuri, S. Weinberg, and E. Witten) MIT Press, Cambridge, Massachusetts, 1985.

63. W.E. Lamb, Jr., and R.C. Retherford, *Phys. Rev.* **72**, 241 (1947).

64. H.M. Foley and P. Kusch, *Phys. Rev.* **73**, 412 (1947).

65. J.R. Oppenheimer, Ref. 1.

12

Feynman's investigations between the Shelter Island and Pocono conferences

12.1 Hans Bethe's calculation of the Lamb shift

Right after the Shelter Island Conference, on the train from New York City to Schenectaday, New York, where he was a consultant to General Electric's Research Laboratory, Hans Bethe made his famous calculation of the Lamb shift, which he completed fully upon arrival in Schenectady. In his Nobel lecture, Feynman remarked: 'Professor Bethe, with whom I was then associated at Cornell, is a man who has this characteristic: If there's a good experimental number you've got to figure it out from theory. So, he forced the quantum electrodynamics of the day to give him an answer to the separation of these two levels ($2^2S_{1/2}$ and $2^2p_{1/2}$ levels of the hydrogen atom) . . . and thus made the most important discovery in the history of the theory of quantum electrodynamics.'[1]

At the Shelter Island Conference, 'Schwinger and Weisskopf, and Oppenheimer have suggested that a possible explanation might be the shift of energy levels by the interaction of the electron with the radiation field. This shift comes out infinite in all existing theories, and has therefore always been ignored. However, it is possible to identify the most strongly [linearly] divergent term in the level shift with an electromagnetic *mass* effect which must exist for a bound as well as for a free electron. The effect should properly be regarded as already included in the observed mass of the electron, and we must therefore subtract from the theoretical expression, the expression for a free electron of the same average kinetic energy.' This was how Bethe introduced his *published* nonrelativistic calculation of the Lamb shift.[2]†

The main idea in Bethe's calculation was to use Kramers's renormalization procedure for the self-energy of the electron in a nonrelativistic, but quantum, consideration of this problem. Bethe recalled: 'I also heard of Kramers's renormalization procedure for the first time at that time, namely, the idea that self-energy of a free electron is simply part of its mass, and you have to subtract

---

† The names of Schwinger and Weisskopf were not mentioned in the preprint note that Hans Bethe sent out to several persons. Bethe included them after hearing from Weisskopf (see Weisskopf's letter to Bethe, cited below).

that self-energy from the self-energy that you get for a bound electron. So, after Shelter Island I took that famous train ride to Schenectady and tried to write down what this difference of self-energies might be, and it turned out that you could fairly easily subtract one from the other'[3,4]

For the self-energy W of the bound electron in a quantum state m in the hydrogen atom, Bethe used the standard formula of the ordinary radiation theory:

$$W = - (2e^2/3\pi\hbar c^3) \int_0^K K \, dK \sum_n |v_{mn}|^2/(E_n - E_m + K), \qquad (12.1)$$

where $K = \hbar\omega$ is the energy of the light-quanta of the radiation field, and v_{mn} are the matrix elements of the velocity of the electron (in the nonrelativistic theory, $v = p/m = (\hbar/im)\nabla$. The sum in equation (12.1) goes over all atomic states n, and the integral is over all the quantum energies from zero up to some maximum value K, which has to be chosen later.

For the free electron this self-energy is given by the formula

$$W_0 = - (2e^2/3\pi\hbar c^3) \int_0^K K \, dK \sum_n |v_{mn}|^2/K. \qquad (12.2)$$

After integration over K and making some manipulations, and using the properties of the hydrogen wave functions, which he knew by heart, Bethe obtained the difference $W'_{ns} = W - W_0$ for the S state in the form

$$W'_{ns} = \frac{8}{3\pi} \left[\frac{e^2}{\hbar c} \right]^3 Ry \frac{z^4}{n^3} \ln \frac{K}{\langle E_n - E_m \rangle_{av}}, \qquad (12.3)$$

where Ry is the ionization energy of the ground state of hydrogen, and the average excitation energy $<E_n - E_m>_{av}$ was calculated numerically.

The nonrelativistic result in equation (12.3) is still divergent, but it diverges logarithmically (instead of linearly), when K goes to infinity, because as a result of the subtraction procedure, $W - W_0$, the linear divergent terms in the self-energy of the bound electron and of the free electron cancel each other. Bethe suggested that in the relativistic theory, where the self-energy of the electron is itself only logarithmically divergent, the difference W'_{ns}, which ought to give the Lamb shift should be finite. 'Since we expect that relativity theory will provide a natural *cut-off* for the frequency K, we shall assume that in [(12.3)]

$$K \approx mc^2 \qquad (12.4)$$

'... This would set an effective upper limit of the order of mc^2 to the frequencies K of light which effectively contribute to the shift of the level of a bound electron.'[5]

Using this value for K, Bethe obtained for the Lamb shift $W'_{ns} = 1040$ megacycles 'in excellent agreement with the observed value of 1000 megacycles. [Thus Bethe had shown that:] (1) the level shift due to interaction with radiation is a real effect and is of finite magnitude; (2) the effect of the infinite electromagnetic mass of a point electron can be eliminated by proper identification of terms in the Dirac radiation theory; (3) an accurate experimental and theoretical investigation of the level shift may establish relativistic effects (e.g. Dirac hole theory). These effects will be of the order of unity in comparison with the logarithm in equation [(12.3)].'[6]

Bethe had completed his calculation of the Lamb shift by 9 June 1947 and sent a preliminary draft of a short paper to those participants at the Shelter Island Conference who were directly interested in the problem of the theoretical calculation of the Lamb shift. In the accompanying cover letter to Oppenheimer, Bethe wrote that the calculation 'does work out. Also, the second term already gives a finite result and is not zero as we thought during the conference. In fact, its logarithmic divergence makes the order of magnitude correct. It also seems that Viki [Weisskopf] and Schwinger are correct that the hole theory is probably important in order to obtain convergence. Finally, I think it shows that Kramers cannot get the right result by his method.'[7]

Bethe's objection concerned Kramers's method to modify the conventional Dirac Hamiltonian at the classical level in terms of the experimental mass of the electron. Only then, in Kramers's approach, can one use the perturbation theory without any subtraction procedure. In 1948, Kramers finally arrived at the complete fulfilment of his nonrelativistic program, in which one has no difficulties with the self-energy of the electron, but his numerical results turned out to be quite unsatisfactory because his method did not take into account the relativistic effects and the recoil effects in the interaction of the electron with radiation.

Kramers, in turn, did not much appreciate Bethe's calculation. His comment was that 'It is difficult to make (Bethe's) argument quite rigorous, but it has certain physical plausibility.'[8] Kramers did not believe that relativity would provide a natural cut-off at mc^2, as in equation (12.4), for the upper limit of the constant K in equation (12.3), and he considered Bethe's treatment as highly arbitrary.

Bethe's achievement in calculating the Lamb shift was highly appreciated by Weisskopf. He wrote to Bethe that he was 'quite enthusiastic about the result. It is a very nice way to estimate the effect and it is most encouraging that it comes out just right. I am very pleased to see that Schwinger's and my approach seems to be right after all. Your way of calculating is just an unrelativistic estimate of our effect, as far as I can see.

'I am all the more pleased about the result since I tried myself unsuccessfully to estimate the order of magnitude of our expression. I was unable to do this, but I got more and more convinced that the method was sound.

'That the $2^2S_{1/2} - 2^2P_{1/2}$ split has something to do with radiation theory and hole theory was proposed by Schwinger and myself for quite some time.

We did not do too much about it until shortly before the conference. We then proposed to split an infinite mass term from other terms and get a finite term shift, just as I demonstrated it at the conference. Isn't it exactly what you are doing? Your great and everlasting deed is your bright idea to treat this at first unrelativistically.'[9]†

Bethe's work stimulated Bruce French and Weisskopf at MIT, Lamb and Kroll at Columbia, and Julian Schwinger—as soon as his honeymoon was over (he got married right after the Shelter Island Conference, and spent two months traveling throughout the United States)—to start hole-theoretic calculations of the Lamb shift in Dirac's radiation theory. But they used noncovariant procedures for calculation, which had been described in the second edition of Heitler's book on the quantum theory of radiation.[11] The relativistically invariant approach to calculate the quantum electrodynamical effects was hardly needed.

12.2 'I can do that for you!'

The unfolding of the story of the Shelter Island Conference, and what happened soon thereafter, is a fascinating chapter in the historical develop-

---

† In an interview with the author in May 1988, Weisskopf made the following remarks concerning Bethe's nonrelativistic calculation of the Lamb shift: 'When he [Hans Bethe] sent me this note [Bethe's draft of his calculation], I was actually really unhappy. First of all, he could have told me [that he was going to do this calculation]. I was interested in the Lamb shift problem even before the war; at that time it was called the Pasternack effect. At the Ann Arbor [University of Michigan] summer school in 1940 I had a lot of conversations with Kramers, with whom I was very close since the old Copenhagen days. He believed, as did I, that the Pasternack effect was real and he asked me to calculate it. He first brought to me the idea that true enough the self-energy is infinite, but maybe the self-energy difference between a bound and a free electron can be calculated and will be finite, and that [later on, in 1947] should be the Lamb shift. From then on I was sort of living with this problem. During the war I became occupied with other problems [at the Manhattan Project], and the Pasternack problem was put on the back burner. But, after the war, I again wanted to take it up and I definitely knew about the problem when I came to MIT [from Los Alamos after the war]. Then came the Lamb shift, Lamb's observation that Pasternack was right and one even had quantitative results.

'Schwinger and I went together on the train to New York [to attend the Shelter Island Conference], and we discussed this problem; we arrived at the conclusion that the nonreltivistic part could be calculated with matrix elements. Then I talked a lot with Hans [Bethe] about where the difficulty lies and that the nonrelativistic part is not so difficult; the difficulty lies in the relativistic region, but I did not know how to do that.

'So when he sent me that note [Bethe's preliminary calculation], because first of all he could have told me about it, and in some ways my name should have been on that paper. Personally I think that he should have asked me to publish this note together with him.

'I could actually have made the calculation myself of what then was the Pasternack effect, already in the early forties. And when Lamb measured the shift accurately, I should have won the Nobel Prize.'[10]

ment of physics in the twentieth century, and we shall try to reconstruct it here in detail.

Already at the Shelter Island Conference, Feynman had tried to make use of Kramers's suggestion about the electromagnetic origin of the Lamb shift. He tried to estimate how much his damped oscillator shifted in its frequency, but he didn't understand the real problem.[12]

Right after his calculations during the train-ride from New York to Schenectady, and their completion there, Bethe telephoned excitedly from Schenectady to Feynman, who, at that moment was visiting Bethe's house. As Feynman recalled: 'He said to me that he understood the Lamb shift, that he had calculated it, and he explained the idea about mass renormalization to me. I don't remember the details, because I didn't follow it very well. And he said that he got about 1000 megacycles for the shift; he was very excited and wanted to talk about it. Although I didn't understand it too well, but I realized it from his excitement that it was something very important.'[12]

Upon returning to Ithaca early in July, Bethe gave a lecture, in which he explained in detail his calculation of the Lamb shift. Bethe stressed the point that the self-energy of the free electron diverges linearly. However, if you take the difference of the self-energies of the bound electron and the free electron, calculated nonrelativistically, a logarithmically divergent expression is obtained. The upper limit of the integration is to be taken to be mc^2 instead of infinity, and Bethe obtained a level shift of about 1000 megacycles per second. So he knew that he was on the right track. The only problem that remained was to deal with the relativistic case precisely; exactly what do you do with the upper limit, not just cut it off arbitrarily if you get the right estimate.†

'So it was a relativistic problem. In this lecture Bethe said that you have to make so many subtractions of such large terms, really infinite terms, that it's very confusing at times, exactly what to subtract from what. And he thought that if there were any way whatever to make the theory finite, even though it didn't agree with experiment, some artificial way of cutting off electrodynamics which was relativistically invariant, then we could cut off all these things which were infinite, you could subtract them exactly, and it would be very much simpler, and then you could do the relativistic end without ambiguity. Otherwise it was very confusing.'[12,14]

After Bethe's lecture, Feynman went up to him and told him, '"I can do that for you! I'll bring it in for you tomorrow." I knew every way to modify quantum electrodynamics known to man, at that time.'[1] 'I had done electrodynamics now with path integrals. I turned it upside-down, turned it in and out. It was easy for me to handle. I could change a delta-function [see equation (5.15)] to a sharp function instead of a delta-function and take a limit

---

† Kroll and Lamb pointed out that if the effect of retardation were taken into account then the upper limit in Bethe's integration would have become $2mc^2$ instead of the arbitrary value of mc^2 which he had taken.[13]

later. There was no problem. I had complete freedom to structure it. If you were to try to change a delta-function to a Hamiltonian form, you could be in a hell of a lot of trouble because you would have to define how to come out from the differential equations for the different functions and keep the relativistic invariance and to me, by this time, nothing was difficult. I could do electrodynamics in any way I wanted. So I told Bethe that I could that.

'So I went home and, believe it or not, this shows you how stupid a man can be: because, for the first time I applied the path integrals to electrodynamics in the *conventional representations* instead of half-advanced and half-retarded scheme—just plain, ordinary, common usage of electrodynamics. I probably had written it a few times, but I had never tried to do anything with it. So, I took the normal electrodynamics, modified it, and found a way to translate what I saw into conventional description and that was effectively that you subtract the relation with the frequency k from a higher mass and integrate it over that mass. That was the idea of the convergence scheme. So I saw the convergence scheme, but now what was surprising was that I had never done any real problem—like calculating the self-energy, vacuum polarization, or the energy level shift, or anything.

'The next day I went to Bethe and told him: "Tell me how to compute the self-energy of the electron and I'll show you how to correct it, so you'll get a finite answer." I didn't know how people computed the self-energy of an electron, which was quite stupid of me; it's simply a second-order perturbation. I had gone too far on my own, but I had not looked at simple problems. So, Bethe showed me how to calculate the self-energy of the electron, and we tried to work it out. I told him the rule, and he found that the divergence went to the sixth power, instead of converging at all, which was much worse.

'So, having failed miserably, I went home and thought about it, and I couldn't figure out what was wrong, why it didn't converge. We didn't know what we did wrong, but when we went over it again, following directly the rules which I was proposing, it converged! What we had done before, I didn't know, but in the meantime I had to learn how to do it myself. So I learned how to calculate the self-energies, energy level differences, and the whole business, during that period.

'I learned how to do conventional quantum electrodynamics, still working from my path integrals. Thus I was trying to connect my path integrals with the conventional language, and saw what the perturbation theory was from the point of view of path integrals. I noticed lots of things, including the fact that several things in perturbation theory, like Coulomb correction and the transverse wave correction, were just one correction—the exchange of a photon. They could be represented by summing over the four directions of polarization. It was obvious from the path integrals that I would do that, and (other people) wouldn't understand me, but they would check and it would always be right. I thought that they must know that if they take the regular

Dirac theory, instead of using transverse waves and summing over four directions, it takes care of the Coulomb correction, but apparently they did not know. And I discovered great simplifications in the methods of calculation.

'As far as I was concerned, I was just taking path-integrals and avoiding the perturbation theory, seeing what the terms were. They were all much simpler. The reason why they were simpler is quite clear: they were all relativistically invariant. Everything I was computing was covariant. The way others had formulated everything, they had separated the Coulomb potential and the transverse waves [Section 11.2]. That depends on the coordinate system. If you say that the divergence of *A* is equal to zero, it depends on the coordinate system. So they had done everything noncovariantly and, of course, the final answer for a physical problem like the scattering of two electrons, Bhabha scattering, is simple, but it was the result of a rather complicated bunch of terms which all added together, and a whole lot of junk that was complicated was now simplified whereas when I started with my path integrals, I could see the relativistic invariance. I knew which terms went together, how they went together, and how to generalize to four dimensions from the two transverse dimensions. It was obvious; it would work; that was the fun of it. *It would always work*, I thought I was trying to learn how others did it, but I would try to do what they had done and I'd get their answers; but when I would talk to somebody, they would be so shocked that it was the right answer, and they would check and say, 'Yes, it is the right answer.' I began to realize that I already had a powerful instrument; that I was sort of flying over the ground in an airplane instead of having so many terms.'[15]

12.3 The genesis of Feynman's approach to quantum electrodynamics: between the Shelter Island and Pocono conferences

Feynman's idea concerning how to modify classical electrodynamics in the direction proposed by Bethe was very simple. He started from Fokker's action in the action-at-a-distance theory (cf. equation (5.15), which is a sum of the free particle action S_p and the action S_{int}), which describes the interaction between the charged particles:

$$S = S_p + S_{int} = \sum_a m_a \int (da_\mu \, da_\mu)^{1/2} + \tfrac{1}{2} \sum_{a,b}{}' e_a e_b \iint \delta(s_{ab}^2) \, da_\mu \, db_\mu, \quad (12.5)$$

where a_μ represents, for $\mu = 1, 2, 3$, the three space coordinates, and, for $\mu = 4$, the time coordinate of the particle *a* of mass m_a and charge e_a; $s_{ab}^2 = (a_\mu - b_\mu)(a_\mu - b_\mu)$ is the four-dimensional distance between the particles *a* and *b*, and $\delta(s^2)$ is Dirac's delta-function, which grows to infinity if $s = 0$. The prime in the second sum indicates that this summation is to be performed only over $a \neq b$, and thus one can exclude self-interaction terms, which are infinite, because of the property of delta-function, mentioned above, that $s_{aa} = 0$.[16]

Feynman proposed to replace Dirac's delta-function in equation (12.5) by some less sharp smooth function $f(s^2)$, which is different from zero and finite only in a very small range, $0 < s^2 < a$, where a is of the order of classical radius of the electron $a \approx e^2/mc^2$. As a result, we will have some deviations from Maxwell's theory at very short distances of the order of electron radius a, but the self-interaction terms will be finite, since $f(0)$ is finite, and the modified theory will be obviously relativistic so long as the new function $f(s^2)$ is relativistically invariant. Hence, we can write down a new modified action, which includes finite self-interaction terms, in the form

$$S = \sum_a m_a \int (da_\mu \, da_\mu)^{1/2} + \tfrac{1}{2} \sum_{a,b} e_a e_b \int \int f(s_{ab}^2) \, da_\mu \, db_\mu, \qquad (12.6)$$

where the summation in the second sum is to be performed over all values of a and b. The terms with $a = b$ are just the self-interaction terms, which now are finite, and that makes it possible to write down the whole interaction term in the action equation, (12.6), in the form

$$S_{\text{int}} = \int \int j_\mu(x) f(s_{xy}^2) j_\mu(y) \, d^4x \, d^4y, \qquad (12.7)$$

where $j_\mu(x)$ are the four-dimensional components of the total electromagnetic current of the charged particles.

In the limit, when a goes to zero, the function $f(s^2)$ goes to the Dirac delta-function, and the modified equations (12.6) and (12.7) reproduce the old results in the classical action-at-a-distance electrodynamics, with added (infinite) self-interaction of the charged particles. It turned out that the most convenient way to describe this limit, and to deal with the proper simple function $f(s^2)$, was to choose it in the form

$$f(s^2) = \int g(k_\mu k_\mu) \exp[-ik_\mu(x_\mu - y_\mu)] \, d^4k, \qquad (12.8)$$

where

$$g(k^2) = \int_0^\infty [\delta(k^2) - \delta(k^2 - \lambda^2)] G(\lambda) \, d\lambda, \qquad (12.9)$$

with some function $G(\lambda)$, normalized in such a way that $\int_0^\infty G(\lambda) \, d\lambda = 1$. Here Feynman's cut-off parameter λ appeared, which goes to infinity when a goes to zero. The procedure of introducing some cut-off, which makes all results in field theory finite, was called the 'regularization procedure'. As we have seen, Feynman's regularization procedure was quite simple; moreover, it was the first *relativistic* procedure. It turned out that it was convenient to describe not only the limit when the radius of the electron goes to zero in terms of Feynman's parameter λ, which corresponds to the limit when λ goes to infinity, but also the possible deviations of the properties of the real physical electron from the properties of the point electron.

The next important step was to translate this result into the conventional electrodynamics with retardation alone, rather than with the one-half advanced and one-half retarded interaction. Feynman's aim was to obtain Fermi's formulation of quantum electrodynamics (Section 11.2). For this purpose Feynman at first used his path-integral method for the elimination of the electromagnetic radiation field, which, according to the Dirac–Heisenberg–Pauli–Fermi electrodynamics, corresponds to an oscillator degree of freedom for the entire electromagnetic field. This would enable Feynman to make use of the procedure for eliminating the oscillator degree of freedom, which he had invented in his Ph.D. thesis and later published as the RMP (1948) article (Sections 6.5 and 10.2).[17] Feynman considered a system of several electrons in the quantum state χ_t and an electromagnetic field in the vacuum state ϕ_{0t} (with zero photons), and calculated the transition amplitude $\langle \chi_{t''}, \phi_{0t''} | \chi_{t'}, \phi_{0t'} \rangle$ for a transition from the state $| \chi_{t'}, \phi_{0t'} \rangle$ to the state $| \chi_{t''}, \phi_{0t''} \rangle$ of the system. After eliminating the radiation field oscillators, Feynman expressed this amplitude—analogous to equation (10.2) in Chapter 10—in the path integral form:

$$\langle \chi_{t''}, \phi_{0t''} | \chi_{t'}, \phi_{0t'} \rangle = \iint dx_{t'} \, dx_{t''} \int \mathscr{D}[x(t)] \chi_{t''}^*(x_{t''}) \exp\left(\frac{i}{\hbar} (S_p + S_{int}) \right) \chi_{t'}(x_{t'}).$$

$$(12.10)$$

Here $\int \mathscr{D}[x(t)]$ denotes the path integration over all virtual paths $x(t)$ of the particles, and the interaction term S_{int}, instead of equation (12.5), has the form

$$S_{int} = \tfrac{1}{2} i \sum_{nm} e_n e_m \iint [1 - \dot{x}_n(t)\dot{x}_m(s)] \, \delta_+\big((t-s)^2 - [x_n(t) - x_m(s)]^2\big) \, dt \, ds.$$

$$(12.11)$$

Compared to S_{int} in equation (12.5), the main difference in equation (12.11) is that the Dirac delta-function is replaced by a new function δ_+, as Feynman designated it later. This function differs from Dirac's delta-function, because in its Fourier integral representation one has to include only positive frequencies:

$$\delta_+(x) = \frac{1}{\pi} \int_0^\infty \exp(-ikx) \, dk = \delta(x) - \frac{i}{\pi x}, \qquad (12.12)$$

which reflects the absence of advanced interactions in conventional electro-dynamics. The time t was chosen as a parameter of particle paths, denoted by s

in equation (12.11). As a result, this formula looks like a three-dimensional expression, but it is actually relativistically invariant. Indeed, the expression $(t-s)^2-[x_n(t)-x_m(s)]^2=s^2{}_{nm}$ as the argument of the δ_+-function is just the four-dimensional distance $s^2{}_{nm}$ between the particles n and m, and $1-\dot{x}_n(s)=\dot{x}_{n\mu}(t)\dot{x}_{m\mu}(s)$ is just the relativistic invariant sum over $\mu=1, 2, 3, 4$.

For a single electron in the initial state $\psi_{t'}$ and final state $\psi_{t''}$, equations (12.10) and (12.11) yield the expression

$$\langle\psi_{t''}, \phi_{0t''}|\psi_{t''}, \phi_{0t'}\rangle = \iint dx_{t'}\, dx_{t''} \int \mathscr{D}[x(t)]\psi_{t''}(x_{t''})\exp\left[\frac{i}{\hbar}\left(S_p+S_{int}\right)\right]\psi_{t'}(x_{t'}),$$

(12.13)

where

$$S_{int} = \frac{ie^2}{\hbar c}\iint [1-\dot{x}(t)\dot{x}(s)]\,\delta_+\big((t-s)^2-[x(t)-x(s)]^2\big)\, dt\, ds \quad (12.14)$$

is the self-interaction term due to the interaction of the electron with the vacuum oscillations of the electromagnetic field. Here the dimensional constants $\hbar$ and c have been restored.

If there were no interaction between the electron and this vacuum electromagnetic radiation field, the term (12.14) in equation (12.13) could be neglected and the transition amplitude would have the simple form: $\langle\psi_{t''}, \phi_{0t''}|\psi\phi_{0t'}, \phi_{0t'}\rangle=\exp[-(i/\hbar)E_0\,\Delta t]$, E_0 being the energy of the electron in state ψ_t without self-interaction. In the real case, where the self-interaction should be included, one can represent the transition amplitude in the form

$$\langle\psi_{t''}, \phi_{0t''}|\psi_{t'}, \phi_{0t'}\rangle=\exp\left(-\frac{i}{\hbar}R_0\,\Delta t-\frac{i}{\hbar}E_0\,\Delta t\right),$$

(12.15)

where R_0 has been introduced to take into account this self-interaction. The term R_0 is assumed to be small enough, because the self-interaction is proportional to $\alpha=e^2/\hbar c\approx\frac{1}{137}$. Thus Feynman could use the new perturbation theory, developed in his Ph.D. thesis and published in his RMP (1948) article (see equation (10.4)), and was able to obtain, in the first order of perturbation theory, the representation of the term R_0 in the form

$$R_0 = \frac{e^2}{\hbar c}\lim_{\Delta t->0}\left\{\left(\left[\exp\left(\frac{1}{\hbar}E_0\,\Delta t\right)\right]\Big/\Delta t\right)\iint dx_{t''}\, dx_{t'}\int\mathscr{D}[x(t)]\right.$$

$$\times\psi^*(x_{t''})\exp\left(\frac{i}{\hbar}S_p\right)\iint \dot{x}_\mu(t)\dot{x}_\mu(s)]\,\delta_+\ \big((t-s)^2$$

$$\left.-[x(t)-x(s)]^2\big)\, dt\, ds\,\psi(x_{t'})\right\}.$$

(12.16)

After calculating the path integral in this expression, Feynman obtained

$$R_0 = 2\frac{ie^2}{\hbar c}\lim_{\Delta t \to 0}\left\{\left(\left[\exp\left(\frac{i}{\hbar}E_0\,\Delta t\right)\right]\Big/\Delta t\right)\iint dx_{t'}\,dx_{t'}\iint dt\,ds\right.$$

$$\times \psi^*(x_s, \Delta t - s)\dot{x}_\mu(s)K_0(x_s, s; x_t, t)\dot{x}_\mu(t)$$

$$\left.\times \delta_+\big((t-s)^2 - [x(t) - x(s)]^2\big)\psi(x_t, t)\right\}, \tag{12.17}$$

where $K_0(2,1)$ denotes the propagator of the charged particle without self-interaction, and may be represented in the form of a sum over all intermediate quantum stationary states, ψ_n, with energy E_n of this particle:

$$K_0(2, 1) = \sum_n \psi_n(x_2)\psi_n^*(x_1)\exp[-iE_n(t_2 - t_1)]. \tag{12.18}$$

Some further manipulations led Feynman to the expression

$$R_0 = 2\frac{e^2}{\hbar c}\sum_n \int \frac{\langle 0|\dot{x}_\mu e^{ikx}|n\rangle\,\langle n|\dot{x}_\mu e^{-ikx}|0\rangle}{E_0 - E_n - \hbar ck}\frac{d^3k}{2\pi k}. \tag{12.19}$$

This formula is the relativistic generalization of the expression (12.1), which Bethe used in his calculations. We should note, however, that the parameter, denoted by k in both the formulas (12.1) and (12.19), has actually two different meanings: in equation (12.1), K denotes the energy of the light-quanta, but in equation (12.19) k denotes the wave number of these quanta; hence, there is some difference in the coefficients used in these formulas. The factors $\exp(\pm ikx)$ in the matrix elements in the numerator of equation (12.19) are responsible for the retardation of the interaction in conventional electrodynamics. Hence, they take into account the finite velocity of the propagation of the interaction in the relativistic theory.

The real part of the expression (12.19) is infinite, but after Feynman's regularization, i.e. after the replacement of δ_+-function with the function given by equations (12.8) and (12.9), it becomes finite. Feynman showed that, after mass renormalization, the real part of equation (12.19) corresponds to Bethe's formula for the Lamb shift. The imaginary part of equation (12.19) gives the reciprocal of the lifetime of the state of the electron, which has been calculated in the first order of perturbation theory. The integral d^3k/k over all wave numbers k in equation (12.19), can be represented as the integral over k and all positive frequencies ω:

$$\int \frac{d^3k}{k} = 2\int \frac{d\omega}{d^3k}\,\delta(\omega^2 - k^2)$$

This representation led Feynman to his cut-off, replacing $\delta(\omega^2 - k^2)$ by $g(\omega^2 - k^2)$ in the form of equation (12.9).

However, there was one serious difficulty which still remained to be resolved. The formulas obtained by Feynman were applicable to a spinless relativistic particle, rather than the electron with spin $\frac{1}{2}$. Feynman tried unsuccessfully to derive Dirac's equation for the spin-$\frac{1}{2}$ particle through the path-integral method. In order to obtain the quantum electrodynamics for such a particle, he used a very simple intuitive procedure suggested by Bethe.[5] In Dirac's theory of the electron one has to replace $\dot{x}_\mu$ by Dirac's γ_μ matrices. Feynman simply used this rule directly in equations (12.16)–(12.19), also replacing the ψ functions with Dirac's four-component spinors, which describe the state of the Dirac electron.

In his Nobel lecture, Feynman recalled: 'Most of this was first worked out by guessing—you see, I didn't have the relativistic theory of matter. For example, it seemed to me obvious that the velocities in nonrelativistic formulas have to be replaced by Dirac's matrix α or in the more relativistic forms by operators γ_μ. I just took my guesses from the forms I had worked out using path integrals for nonrelativistc matter, but relativistic light. It was easy to develop rules of what to substitute to get the relativistic case. I was very surprised to discover that it was not known at that time that every one of the formulas that had been worked out so patiently by separating longitudinal and transverse waves could be obtained from the formula for the transverse waves alone, if instead of summing over only the two perpendicular polarization directions you would sum over all four possible directions of polarization. It was so obvious from the action [(12.7)] that I thought it was general knowledge and would do it all the time. I would get into arguments with people, because I didn't realize they didn't know that; but, it turned out that all their patient work with the longitudinal waves was always equivalent to just extending the sum on the two transverse directions of polarization over all four directions. This was one of the amusing advantages of the method.'[18]

Using the generalization of the formula (12.19) for Dirac particles, arrived at 'by guessing', and the whole set of states in the Dirac hole theory, Feynman was also able to derive Weisskopf's expression for the self-energy of the electron (see equation (11.5)) which turned out to depend logarithmically on Feynman's cut-off parameter λ.

From the letter Feynman wrote to Herbert and Mulaika Corben in the late autumn of 1947, one can see how far he had gone toward his new formulation of quantum electrodynamics. He wrote: 'I have been working very hard recently so there has been no letter. But interesting things are piling up, so I thought I had better write some of them to you.

'I sent my paper ["Space–time approach to non-relativistic quantum mechanics", RMP (1948)] to the *Physical Review* and have not heard, as yet, about it but I have continued working with electrodynamics in the range of quantum mechanics which is described in the paper. You may remember I was able to eliminate explicit reference to the field oscillation in the equations of quantum mechanics. While I was working on this, there was so much talk here about self-energy, that I thought it would be the easiest thing to calculate directly in my form. The result is exactly the same as one gets for ordinary perturbation theory (except for some nice simplification waves [*sic*; ways]). It therefore also gives infinity. I then altered the delta-function in the interaction to be a somewhat less sharp function. This corresponds to a kind of finite electron. Then the self-energy of a non-relativistic particle is finite. Actually, it comes out complex, the imaginary part represents the rate of radiation to the negative-energy states. If I cause the negative energy states to be full, then the formulation is no longer relativistically invariant and gives a finite self-energy to an electron, in fact all mass can be represented as electro-magnetic.

'It therefore seems that I have guessed right, that the difficulties of electro-dynamics and the difficulties of the hole theory of Dirac are independent and one can be solved before the other. I am now working on the hole theory, in particular, I now understand the Klein paradox, so that it is no longer a paradox and can tell you what an atom with a nuclear charge more than 137 would behave like, I still haven't solved the whole problem. The main reason I am writing to you, is to tell you about this result which I feel is of very great significance.

'It is very easy to see that the self-energy of two electrons is not the same as the self-energy of each one separately. That is because among the intermediate states which one needs in calculating the self-energy of particle number 1, say, the state of particle 2 can no longer appear in the sum because a transition of 1 into the state of 2 is excluded by the Pauli exclusion principle [see Section 11.3]. The amount by which the self-energy of two particles differs from the self-energy of each one separately is actually the energy of their electrical attraction.[19] Therefore, the electro-magnetic interaction between two particles can be looked upon as a correction to the self-energy produced by the exclusion principle. Thus Eddington is right in that it is a consequence of the exclusion principle.†

'Finally, I have learned that the classical theory with a finite electron which is deduced from a principle of least action, can show the phenomenon of pair production. The action is made a minimum sometimes by a pair which reverses itself in time, in the way we have discussed it often when I was there.'[21]‡

On 12 November 1947, on his way to attend the Tenth Washington Conference on Theoretical Physics (13–15 November 1947), Feynman gave a seminar at the Institute for Advanced Study in Princeton on 'Dirac's electron from several points of view'. Dirac himself was visiting the institute during that academic year, and he also attended Feynman's seminar. In his talk, Feynman

---

† This is a reference to A.S. Eddington's *Fundamental theory*, which Feynman had read together with his friend T.S. Welton in 1937 at MIT.[20]

‡ We have mentioned earlier that Feynman had spent part of the summer of 1947 with the Corbens in Pittsburgh, where he produced the draft of the manuscript of his RMP (1948) paper.

briefly presented the content of his RMP (1948) paper, concerning the path integral in quantum mechanics and some attempts to give a sum-over-histories formulation of quantum mechanics for the spin-$\frac{1}{2}$ particle, which obeys the Dirac equation. For this purpose, Feynman used not only paths which go forwards in time, but also paths which go *backwards* in time, in accordance with Wheeler's 1940 idea (see Section 5.3). Feynman also described his attempt to calculate the Lamb shift.[22] Harish-Chandra, who had completed his Ph.D. earlier in the spring of that year under Dirac at Cambridge, was also at the Institute for Advanced Study in Princeton, and had become acquainted with Herbert Corben and his wife, informed them: 'Dirac is very impressed by Feynman and thinks he does some interesting things . . . .'[23]

The Tenth Washington Conference on Theoretical Physics was devoted to 'Gravitation and electromagnetism'. At the conference, Julian Schwinger gave a talk on the results he had obtained since the Shelter Island Conference early in June. After the conference, Feynman reported to the Corbens: 'The meeting in Washington was very poor, don't quote me. The only interesting thing was something that Schwinger said at the end of the meeting. It was interesting because it got Oppy [J. Robert Oppenheimer] so excited but I did not have time to understand exactly what Schwinger had done. It has to do with electro-magnetic self-energy problems. One thing he did point out that was very interesting though, was that the discrepancy in the hyperfine structure of the hydrogen noted by Rabi, can be explained on the same basis as that of electro-magnetic self-energy, as can the line shift of Lamb. The rest of the meeting was concerned with gravitation and the curvature of the universe and other problems for which there are very powerful mathematical equations—lots of speculation but very little evidence.

'I met Mrs Schwinger and had hoped to come back to Princeton from Washington with them on the train. I was going to find out from Julie [*sic*: Julian] then, what he was trying to explain at the meeting. Unfortunately they did me dirt and I did not come to Princeton. I stopped off at Princeton on my way back to Ithaca to talk to Pias [*sic*: Pais] and Bohm and used up all my time with Pias—unfortunately, because I also wanted very much to talk to Bohm.'[24]

After the Washington meeting, Feynman independently calculated the radiative correction to the gyromagnetic ratio for the electron (see Section 11.7) in the first order of perturbation theory. Feynman considered the radiationless scattering of the electron in the external electromagnetic field. This field was simply incorporated in equation (12.13) and other expressions by replacing the classical action of the free particles, S_p, with the corresponding action of the particles in the external field, which was well known. The transition amplitude could then be calculated to the first order of perturbation in the radiative corrections.

At first, this problem had been treated by Dancoff within the noncovariant perturbation theory of the day, but he had missed certain matrix elements.[25] Dancoff's mistake was first established by Koba and Tomonaga[26] (see Section 11.3), and rediscovered by Lewis, who found that after mass renormalization the amplitude for radiationless scattering did not contain any ultraviolet divergences,[27] although it was infrared divergent.

Using his relativistic cut-off procedure, Feynman calculated the amplitude of the radiationless scattering and obtained the result that the radiative correction to the scattering in any potential is equivalent to the first-order correction in $e^2/\hbar c$ to the potential itself. In terms of the Dirac Hamiltonian, the finite radiative corrections to the radiationless scattering were found by Feynman to be

$$\Delta H_{\mathrm{Dirac}} = \frac{e^2}{2\pi\hbar c}\left(-\frac{\hbar e}{2mc}[\beta(\sigma\cdot B)-i\beta\alpha\cdot E]\right), \qquad (12.20)$$

where E is the electric field, B is the magnetic field, α and β are the Dirac 4×4 matrices, and σ is the Pauli matrix. Equation (12.20) showed that the interaction of the electron with radiation changes its magnetic moment by the fraction, $\alpha/2\pi = e^2/2\pi\hbar c$, which was first discovered by Schwinger in a different way (here α denotes, as usual, the dimensionless electromagnetic coupling constant).[28]

In January 1948, just prior to the New York meeting of the American Physical Society, Feynman wrote to the Corbens in Pittsburgh: 'In the last letter I wrote to you, I made a mistake.† As you know, I have been working with a theory of electricity in which the delta function interaction is replaced by a less sharp function. Then (in quantum mechanics) the self-energy of an electron including the Dirac hole theory comes out finite. The mistake in the last letter was to say that it is finite and not relativistically invariant. Actually, the self-energy comes out finite and invariant and is therefore representable as a pure mass. The magnitude of the mass change is a fraction of the order of $\frac{1}{137}$ times the logarithm of the Compton wavelength over the cut-off width of the delta function. Thus, all mass cannot be represented as electrodynamic unless the cut-off is ridiculously short. The experimental mass is of course the sum of inertia and this electromagnetic correction.

'I then turned to the problem of radiationless scattering which has always given such trouble in electrodynamics. I get the result that the cross section for scattering of a particle going past a nucleus without emitting a quantum is

---

† In 1985, Feynman recalled the story of this mistake as follows. 'As near as I can remember it, I first got the relativistic result (we were only working to order v^2/c^2). A student found an error in an early line and calculated it would not be invariant— when I wrote the first letter. But later on, several pages later, he found another error where I canceled two equal complicated terms that I should have added. The original answer I had gotten was right—it was relativistic. This miracle of two canceling errors was probably the result of a mixture of having a strong feeling for what the answer must be and algebraic carelessness.'[29]

finite. If the cut-off is made to go to zero, the answer comes out infinite. If, however, the cross section is first expressed in terms of the experimental mass and then the cut-off is made to go to zero keeping the experimental mass as a constant, when the limit is taken, the result is finite. This therefore agrees with the result of Lewis and Oppenheimer. I believe it also confirms the idea of Schwinger because I think that the terms which diverge logarithmically as the cut-off goes to zero are just the terms that Schwinger said one should subtract in a consistent electrodynamics.

'I have not computed the self-energy to the second order [in the coupling constant $e^2/\hbar c$], I only hope it is also finite. If so, I think all the problems of electrodynamics can be unambiguously solved by this process: First compute the answer which is finite (but contains the cut-off logarithm). Then express the result in terms of the experimental mass. The answer still contains the cut-off but this time not logarithmically. Take the limit which now exists, as the cut-off goes to infinity.

'I have not mentioned polarization of the vacuum for as yet I do not completely understand the problem in which it appears. However, a calculation of the phenomenon also gives a [in]finite answer for the polarizing of the vacuum. This can be removed by a renormalization of the electric charge. However, unfortunately for reasonable cut-off, the polarizability is very large as far as I can see, so that things do not look as nice as they do for self-energy.

'I am very excited by all this of course, because I think that the problem is at least solved either my way or Schwinger's. I hope to prove the equivalence or at least to compare the two ideas shortly.'[30]

Julian Schwinger reported his initial results on the Lamb shift and the calculation of the anomalous magnetic moment of the electron in an invited lecture at the meeting of the American Physical Society, which took place in New York at the end of January 1948. He reported some discrepancy between his calculations of the anomalous magnetic moment of the electron and the Coulomb field in the atom and the magnetic moment of the free electron, which he had worked out to be $\alpha/2\pi = e^2/2\pi\hbar c$. Feynman, who attended Schwinger's lecture at the APS Meeting, mentioned after the lecture that he had computed the same things as Schwinger had done. He confirmed Schwinger's results about the Lamb shift and the magnetic moment of the free electron, but he stressed the point that he had obtained the same result for the magnetic moment of the electron in the atom as for that of the free electron, contrary to Schwinger's result. The reason for this discrepancy was that Schwinger's calculation was not relativistically invariant. When the calculation procedure is relativistically invariant, there is no problem in showing that Feynman was right, and the magnetic moment of the electron in the atom also equals $\alpha/2\pi = e^2/2\pi\hbar c$.

Many years later, Feynman recalled Schwinger's talk at the APS Meeting and what he had done: 'So I got up after Schwinger's talk and said, "I have computed the same thing, and I agree with Professor Schwinger in all of his results, but that the magnetic moment of the electron in the atom is also $e^2/2\pi\hbar c$, and there is really no difficulty. If you fiddle around some more, you'll see that the magnetic moment of the electron is the same in the atom and out of the atom.

'I was not showing off, I was just trying to say that there's no problem, for I had done the same thing that he had done, and it had all come out all right. Now, Schwinger was already well known, and many people had not heard of me. Schwinger had done many things, great things, before the war, in the theory of deuteron, scattering of neutrons by helium to produce polarized neutrons, and other things. [Feynman and Schwinger had, of course, met once during the war when the latter visited Los Alamos, then at the Shelter Island Conference, and again recently at the Tenth Washington Conference on Theoretical Physics.] People knew Schwinger, but most of them did not know me. I heard later from several people who were at the APS Meeting that I sounded funny to them: "The great Julian Schwinger was talking when this little squirt got up and said, 'I have already done this, Daddy, you're in no trouble at all! Everything will be OK!'" Actually, I was quite surprised when he reported that he got another value for the electron's magnetic moment in the atom. I was actually trying to tell him that there's no difficulty at all! I had caught up with him, and I knew that everything was fine.'[12,14]

After the APS Meeting, Feynman continued his intensive work on quantum electrodynamics. On 20 March 1948, he again wrote to the Corbens: 'I have been working on my little theory of electrodynamics in which the interaction is not exact on a delta function because there was some confusion in the Schwinger–Weisskopf–Bethe camp as to what the correct answer was for the line shift. I worked that out in detail, my way. I find the shift in the magnetic moment of an electron equal to $e^2/2\pi\hbar c$. The line shift in hydrogen has two terms, one a logarithmic one proportional to the expected form of $\nabla^2 V$ and the other is a correction to the spin orbit interaction. The correction is exactly the same as the amount that you would calculate from the change of the magnetic moment, that is, everything is nicely relativistically invariant. The calculation took me four days and can be put neatly on four pages of paper. Now that I understand it, it is really a very simple problem. What I did, was to compute the change in the Dirac Hamiltonian due to the fact that an electron can emit and absorb virtual quanta when it is in a slowly varying external potential. If ϕ and A are the scalar and vector potential in a problem, the correction [Feynman did not insert a formula in the carbon copy of the letter] the answer diverges for very low energy quanta, so I have expressed it in terms of k_{min} which are the slowest momentum quanta which have been included. This avoids the infrared catastrophe and the low energy non-relativistic end can be worked out in a straightforward way, such as has already been done by Bethe. The actual shift comes around 1040 megacycles, I think.

'My theory of representing positrons as electrons going backward, is working very well but nobody believes me because I haven't got everything complete yet. I can only deal with pair production and annihilations in a complete fashion. Polarization of the vacuum still remains somewhat of a puzzle; it has not been included in the above formula for ΔH.'[31]

Many years later, Feynman still recalled: '. . . I did more problems and still more problems, and kept on working with it. There was one problem which kept on bothering me: this was the polarization of the vacuum, where a field produces a pair, and a pair annihilates again, producing a new field, which in my diagrams would have meant a closed loop. Now, because of Wheeler's original suggestion of electrons and positrons going backwards in time, I was using path integrals. I just had to translate them, operator by operator, quantity by quantity, by trial and error. Everything I did was trial and error. And I would rewrite the expression by a kind of guesswork. Then I would compare them to what I would get by the more tedious and old-fashioned methods, look them up, you see. And so I gradually developed a way of knowing what the right formulas were, relativistically. In the process, however, the problem of what to do with the pairs always bothered me. I never did understand that negative-energy stuff [meaning the Dirac sea of negative-energy electrons]. And I had some trouble.

'So I began to say, I can't do pairs this way, it's too confusing to me. And I remembered Wheeler's old idea about electrons going backwards in time. So I simply made a project—imagine what would happen if my space-time trajectories would be like the letter N in time, that they would back up for a while, and go forward again, which is famously described in one of the papers later. And I found out that I got the right formula for the positron and for the Dirac cases—you see, when you have to sum over some intermediate state, some just with electrons, some with pair productions, the mass with pair productions seemed to come right if I let this backwards path go, within a sign.

'Then I made numerical rules about the sign, by doing more and more complicated problems. You must use a minus sign for each reversal or something. So finally I found it wasn't the number of back sections. And I gradually developed empirical systems for computing everything. And I would always get the ends everybody else was putting, and I knew what I was doing. What I was doing was presumably OK.

'I did not write down these rules. I was working with them. I had them, yes. I would get to a point and say, "with the sign plus or minus", and later "the sign is equal to the number of something or the other". Then it wouldn't work. Then I would try again. So essentially I was discovering the right rules by a kind of cut and try scheme, which I have used ever since.

'At any rate, though, in this view I had about electrons going backwards in time, the idea of a pair production followed by annihilation was a closed loop. It was a ring. The electron went around, forwards and backwards in time. And I felt that it may not exist. See, in Wheeler's original idea about electrons being back sections of world-lines, the question of whether there was a world-line all by itself in a ring in space was opened. I was confused by it. One possibility was, it didn't exist. It gave me an infinity, but I didn't know how to get rid of it. So that's a certain stage I was in. I could do everything else except the polarization of the vacuum infinity. That bothered me. I hadn't got that under control when I went to the meeting at Pocono. So that tells you how I was at the meeting in Pocono. I remember the exact situation there. That was, to me, historically of some interest.'[12,14]

This development of Feynman's ideas in quantum electrodynamics in late 1947 and the first few months of 1948 was very important. Wheeler's original idea about the positrons being the back sections of the world-lines was used by Feynman in the notes he made in 1947, entitled 'Theory of positrons'.[32]

In January 1988, some three weeks before his death, Feynman recalled: 'There was a theory of holes and negative electrons. You separate the scattering into several processes, one in which the electron gets scattered directly, and another process in which it makes a pair first and then all three particles go into a negative hole, where later on the hole annihilates an electron, and so on. And that separated things unnecessarily having to do with the time. It was not covariant. The answers were always simpler. I tried to learn that, how they were doing it. I thought about this old idea about the positron being an electron going backwards in time and I simply assumed that they go backwards . . .

'. . . I was guided by path integrals and the need to keep things covariant and taking a lot of flying guesses.'[15]

As a starting point Feynman used the nonrelativistic formula for the transition amplitude $K(2, 1)$ for the transition from quantum state 1 to quantum state 2, written as a path integral (see equation (10.1) in a form

$$K(2, 1) = \int \mathscr{D}[x(t)] \exp\left(\frac{i}{\hbar} S\right). \tag{12.21}$$

This amplitude carries the wave function (1) to the wave function (2) according to the formula

$$\psi(2) = \int K(2, 1)\psi(1) \, d^3x_1, \tag{12.22}$$

which led later on to the name 'propagator' for $K(2, 1)$.

If the classical action S is represented as a sum of the free action S_0 and some perturbation, which is given by a potential $U(x)$, in a form $S = \int L \, dt = S_0 - \int U[x(t)] \, dt$, we can expand the exponent with the perturbation term in equation (12.21). This yields the perturbation theory expansion of the transition amplitude in the form

$$K(2, 1) = K_0(2, 1) - \frac{i}{\hbar} \int K_0(2, 3)U(3)K_0(3, 1) \, d^3x_3 + \cdots, \tag{12.23a}$$

where

$$K_0(2, 1) = \int \mathscr{D}[x(t)] \exp\left(\frac{i}{\hbar} S_0\right) \tag{12.23b}$$

is the free particle propagator.

In the relativistic case Feynman guessed that one could write down a formula, analogous to equation (12.22), in the form

$$\mathscr{S}(2, 1) = \mathscr{S}_F(2, 1) + \frac{i}{\hbar} \int \mathscr{S}_F(2, 3) A(3) \mathscr{S}_F(3, 1) \, d^4 x_3 + \cdots. \tag{12.24}$$

Here, the Feynman propagator $\mathscr{S}$ (2,1) for the free particle with spin-$\frac{1}{2}$ equals

$$\mathscr{S}_F(2, 1) = (i\nabla_2 + m) D_F(2, 1), \tag{12.25}$$

and obeys the Dirac equation for an electron with mass m and additional spatial conditions. Here $\nabla = \gamma_\mu \, \partial/\partial x_\mu$, and $D_F(2, 1)$ obeys the Klein–Gordon equation $(\square^2_2 - m^2) D_F(2, 1) = 0$, with the additional condition that D_F (2,1) has only positive frequency components in its Fourier integral representation if $t_2 - t_1 > 0$, and only negative frequency components if $t_2 - t_1 < 0$. As a result, the additional property has the Feynman propagator $S/_F(2,1)$ for the electron. Hence it can be written in the form

$$\mathscr{S}_F(2. 1) = \begin{cases} \displaystyle\sum_{E_n > 0} \exp\left(-\frac{i}{\hbar} E_n(t_2 - t_1)\right) \phi_n(2)\bar{\phi}_n(1) & \text{for } t_2 - t_1 > 0, \\[2em] -\displaystyle\sum_{E_n < 0} \exp\left(-\frac{i}{\hbar} E_n(t_2 - t_1)\right) \phi_n(2)\bar{\phi}_n(1) & \text{for } t_2 - t_1 < 0. \end{cases} \tag{12.26}$$

Here ϕ_n are the corresponding stationary states of the electron in the problem we are considering.

The use of the minus sign in the second line of equation (12.26) gave some difficulty to Feynman. At first, he had tried to use the equation with the plus sign in both lines. 'I'd look at it and it wouldn't work. It would be the wrong sign. I'd make a new rule: put the track in backwards and you change the sign. And I'd get the rules set up so they would work. And then I could do all these problems. It was a kind of semiempirical rule guided by the path integral. A little later I would gradually understand why it worked, why I was solving the same Dirac equation with different boundary conditions and so on.'[15]

The new rule was derived by observing that the minus sign in equation (12.26) yielded the correct expression for the self-energy of the electron, given first by the hole theory. Feynman did not like the idea of negative energy states and he replaced it with Wheeler's idea of the positrons as electrons going backwards in time. In his 1947 notes he wrote: 'We shall consider that when an electron travels along as proper time increases so does the true time. For a positron proper time increases as true time decreases. This is classically.

Quantum mechanically the situation is that the wave function has a phase (in $e^{i\phi}$ define ϕ as phase) which increases as you move in positive true time for the electron, and decreases in negative true time for a positron.'[32] This gave the interpretation of the two expressions on the right-hand side of equation (12.26), the first one being responsible for electrons and the second for positrons.

Let $\psi(x)$ denote the amplitude for the electron or the positron to arrive at a point x. For an electron to arrive at the point x, the amplitude will contain only positive energy components, insofar as this electron is coming from the past. 'If a positron were to arrive at x, it would come from a wave from the future of x & would give a $\psi(x)$ with only negative energy components.'[28]

In the first order of perturbation theory for the propagator, one must constrain the consideration to the term proportional to $\mathcal{S}(2, 3)\, A\,(3)\, \mathcal{S}(3, 1)$, which has been written explicitly in equation (12.24). Feynman had considered in a new manner the action of the potential $A(x)$: 'According to Dirac, x sends an electron, which is initially at (wave) A, into states of positive and negative energy . . . both of which spread upward in time [Fig. 12.1(a)]. We say instead that x scatters a wave B toward future representing scattered electron, and wave C toward past representing . . . ! a positron with which the electron may have annihilated by action of the potential at x . . . [Fig. 12.1(b)]'[32]

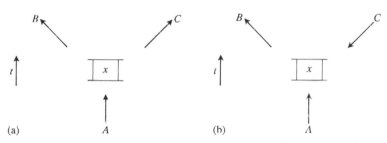

(a) A (b) A

Fig. 12.1(a). The Dirac theory.   Fig. 12.1(b). The Feynman theory.

It seems quite natural that, thinking of path-integrals and the contribution of different paths in the transition amplitude, Feynman had pictured the first-order term of the perturbation series as a diagram, which is shown in Fig. 12.2. Thus he had visualized the first-order processes in quantum electrodynamics and taken this important first step toward the invention of the famous Feynman diagrams in quantum electrodynamics, which were to be used later on in the entire field theory, in statistical physics, and in many other areas.

In the second order of perturbation theory in equation (12.24), the next term has to be taken into account. It is proportional to the product $\mathcal{S}(2, 4)A(4)\mathcal{S}(4, 3)A(3)\mathcal{S}(3, 1)$, but there exists one more term of this type:

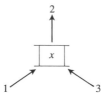

Fig. 12.2 Feynman's 'pre-diagram' for the first-order process.

$(2, 3)A(3)S(3, 4)A(4)S(4, 1)$ in which intermediate states have the opposite ordering. In the propagator in a form of equation (12.24) one must include both the terms, which corresponds to the inclusion of two different paths in the path-integral representation of the transition amplitude. These two processes were pictured by Feynman in his notes as two diagrams, as shown in Fig. 12.3.[32]

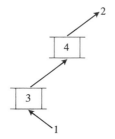

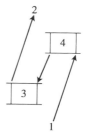

Fig. 12.3(a). Feynman's 'pre-diagram' for the second-order process.

Fig. 12.3(b). Feynman's 'pre-diagram' for the second-order process.

'The first represents scattering at x (which corresponds to the point 3 in [Fig. 12.3(a)], followed by that at y (which corresponds to point 4). The second represents a pair created at x (at point 3 [Fig. 12.3(b)]), the positron which annihil. [ates] the electron at y (at the point 4 [Fig. 12.3(b)], and the electron which is found at Z (the point 2 in [Fig. 12.3(b)]).[32]

The comparison with the hole theory showed that the contribution of the second diagram [Fig. 12.3(b)] must be taken with a minus sign. Feynman's explanation was that: 'The minus sign on the last term arises as a result of the properties of [$S(2, 1)$]. In ordinary theory it is interpreted that at (3) a hole is made in sea, electron going to (2), while hole is filled by electron (1). This represents an exchange (relative to the first process where same electron (1) gets to (2)) of electron (1) and sea electron so by exclusion principle feeds with neg. amplitude.

'According to the present theory state(s) (2) and (1) might be the same in 2nd term. Usual theory says no because then at time between t_x, t_y can't have two electrons in the same state. We say it is the same electron so Pauli principle doesn't operate. Old theory has such a term anyway for it contemplates pair created by (3) annihilated by (4) (vac. polarization type) one of which is excluded if electron is in state (1)—namely the pair created at (3) (& destroyed at (4)) whose electron is in (1). So term is subtracted relative to (infinite) vacuum if electron is in (1). This is same term as we have so both theories give same result here.'[32]

Thus the comparison with hole theory showed the equivalence of this theory and Feynman's new theory of positrons. The only problem which Feynman was not able to solve at that time was the problem of vacuum polarization. In the lowest order of Feynman's perturbation theory, vacuum polarization corresponds to the 'bubble diagram', in which a pair will be created at point 1, and then the same pair will be annihilated at point 2. The direct calculation of the contribution of this type of diagrams showed that they gave an infinite result, which had nothing to do with the infinite self-energy of the electron. Therefore Feynman's cut-off procedure was not able to make such terms in the perturbation expansion finite. But Feynman had found that correct results for the scattering amplitudes might be obtained without taking such infinite terms into account. Therefore, at first, he decided that these infinite terms, which corresponded to 'closed loops' could simply be ignored from consideration.

Thus, by the time of the Pocono Conference, Feynman had reworked almost all of quantum electrodynamics by his new methods. He had reached the most important part of his new results: namely, the relativistic formulation of quantum electrodynamics and, especially, of perturbation theory, the relativistic cut-off and the renormalization of mass, closed expressions for the transition amplitude and causal propagators, new operator calculus, rules for the calculation of the contribution to the transition amplitude in each order of perturbation theory and the idea of corresponding visualization of these rules by diagrams, Lamb shift and the anomalous magnetic moment of the electron, and cross sections of different processes. However, before the Pocono Conference, he had not published anything on quantum electrodynamics and he did not have the mathematical proofs of all his results.

12.4 Richard Feynman at the Pocono Conference

From 30 March to 2 April 1948, the second small conference on the problems of fundamental physics was held at the Pocono Manor Inn, located approximately midway between Scranton, Pennsylvania, and the Delaware Water Gap. Twenty-eight physicists participated. Kramers, MacInnes, Nordsieck, Pauling, and Van Vleck, who had attended the Shelter Island

Conference, were absent. The new participants were Niels and Aage Bohr, Eugene Wigner, Gregor Wentzel, Paul Dirac, and Walter Heitler.

At this conference, Julian Schwinger gave a marathon lecture on his version of quantum electrodynamics. As Feynman recalled at Schwinger's sixtieth birthday celebration in 1978: 'Each of us had worked out quantum electrodynamics and we were going to describe it to the tigers. He [Schwinger] described his in the morning, first, and then he gave one of these lectures which are intimidating. They are so perfect that you don't want to ask any questions because it might interrupt the train of thought. But the people in the audience like Bohr, and Dirac, Teller, and so forth, were not to be intimidated, so after a bit there were some questions. A slight disorganization, a mumbling, confusion. It was difficult. We didn't understand anything, you know. But after a while . . . he would say, 'perhaps it will become clearer if I proceed', so he continued . . .'[33]

Schwinger's lecture lasted well into the afternoon. Afterwards, Feynman gave his lecture, entitled 'Alternative Formulation of quantum electrodynamics'. Feynman recalled:

'This meeting at Pocono was very exciting, because Schwinger was going to tell how he did things and I was to explain mine. I was very nervous there and didn't sleep well at all, I don't know why. But the meeting was very exciting. Schwinger and I would talk to each other, and we would compare notes as to our respective results. He would tell me where his terms came from, and I would tell him about my result for the same; we did not know how each of us had done it, but we agreed on the answer. We would talk about the physical ideas, and see what the result of our respective calculations was. We could talk back and forth, without going into the details, but nobody there understood either of us. But Schwinger and I could talk back and forth to each other. When he tried to explain his theory, he encountered great difficulty. Now and then he would remark: 'Well, let's look at it physically.' As soon as he would try to explain the ideas physically, the wolves would descend on him; he had great difficulty. Also, people were getting more and more tired.

'Taking a cue from the response that Schwinger got, Bethe said to me: 'You should better explain things mathematically and not physically, because every time Schwinger tries to talk physically he gets into trouble.' Now, the problem for me was that all my thinking was physical. I did things by cut and try methods, which I had myself invented. I didn't have a mathematical scheme to talk about. Actually I had discovered *one* mathematical expression, from which all my diagrams, rules, and results would come out. The only way I knew that one of my formulas worked was when I got the right result from it. So, in a sense, I did have a mathematical scheme, but it was not organized in a way that I could explain it in terms that would be familiar to other people; it could not be put into any familiar mathematical language. My way of looking at things was completely new, and I could not deduce it from other known mathematical schemes, but I knew what I had done was right.

'So, following Bethe's advice, I said in my talk: "This is my mathematical formula, and I'll show you that it produces all the results of quantum electrodynamics." Immediately I was asked: "Where does the formula come from ?" I said, "It doesn't matter where it comes from; it works, it's the right formula!" "How do you know it's the right formula?" "Because it works, it gives the right results!" "How do you know it gives the right answers?" "It will become evident from what I do with it. I'll show you how the formula works, and I'll do one problem after another with its help." So, I tried to explain the meaning of the symbols I had employed, and I applied it to solve the problem of the self-energy of the electron. They got bored when I tried to go into the details. Then Bethe tried to help me by asking: "Don't worry about the details, explain to us how the formula works," and so on. Question: "What made you think that the formula was right in the first place?" Then I tried to go into the physical ideas. I got deeper and deeper into difficulties, everything became chaotic. I tried to explain the tricks I had employed. For instance, take the exclusion principle, which says that you can't have two electrons in the same state; it turns out that you don't have to pay much attention to that in the intermediate states in the perturbation theory. I had discovered from empirical rules that if you don't pay attention to it, you get the right answers anyway, and if you do pay attention to it then you have to worry about this and that. Then they asked: "But what about the exclusion principle?" "It doesn't make any difference in the intermediate states!" Then Teller asked: "How do you know?" "I know because I have worked it out!" Then Teller said: "How could that be? It is fundamentally wrong that you don't have to take the exclusion principle into account." I replied: "We'll see that later."

'Already in the beginning I had said that I'll deal with single electrons, and I was going to describe this idea about a positron being an electron going backwards in time, and Dirac asked "Is it unitary?" I said, "Let me try to explain how it works, and you can tell me whether it's unitary or not!" I didn't even know then what "unitary" meant. So I proceeded further a bit, and Dirac repeated his question: "Is it unitary?" So I finally said: "Is *what* unitary?" Dirac said: "The matrix which carries you from the present to the future position." I said, "I haven't got any matrix which carries me from the present to the future position. I go forwards and backwards in time, so I don't know what the answer to your question is."

'Everyone of these people had something in mind, and they acted as if I should know what they thought. Dirac had proved somewhere that in quantum mechanics, since you progress only forwards in time, you have to have a unitary operator. But there is no unitary way of dealing with a single electron. Dirac could not think of going forwards and backwards, and he wanted to know whether the theorem concerning unitarity applied to it. Each one of them, for different reasons, thought that there were too many gimmicks in what I was doing, and it proved to be impossible to tell them that you could actually go ahead with what I was doing.

'Bohr was also at the meeting. After I had tried many times to explain what I was doing and didn't succeed, I talked about trajectories, then I would swing back—I was being forced back all the time. I said that in quantum mechanics one could describe the amplitude of each pair in such and such a way. Bohr got up and said: "Already in 1925, 1926, we knew that the classical idea of a trajectory or a path is not legitimate in quantum mechanics; one could not talk about the trajectory of an electron in the atom, because it was something not observable." In other words, he was telling me about the uncertainty principle. It became clear to me that there was no communication between what I was trying to say and they were thinking. Bohr thought that I didn't know the uncertainty principle, and was actually not doing quantum mechanics right either. He didn't understand at all what I was saying. I got a terrible feeling of resignation. I said to myself, 'I'll just have to write it all down and publish it, so that they can read it and study it, because I know it's right! That's all there is to it.'

'Of course, there was no personal criticism in all this, no personal antagonism. Dirac was mumbling, 'Is it unitary?', Teller was excited about the exclusion principle, and Bohr was concerned about the uncertainty principle and the proper use of quantum mechanics. To tell a guy that he doesn't know quantum mechanics—well, it didn't make me angry, it just made me realize that he [Bohr] didn't know what I was talking about, and it was hopeless to try to explain it further. I gave up, I simply gave up, and decided to publish my work because I knew it was all right.

'Obviously, I had started backwards and I hadn't explained my ideas rightly in the first place; everything was all tumbled around, and all the pieces were out of joint. I was trying to explain the pieces of the puzzle rather than explaining the pattern. However, with regard to Schwinger things were different. In the lunch periods, and at other times outside the meeting and discussions, he and I would compare notes on formulas for special problems, and see that both of us had the same results. We knew where everything came from and we both knew that each of us was right, that we were both respectable. I could trust him, and he could trust me. We came at things entirely differently, but we came to the same end. So there was no problem with my believing that I was right and everything was OK. That I did not explain things properly is correct, but the rumors that I was depressed were not quite true; I just felt that there had been no communication.

'Just before the meeting broke for a brief rest after my talk, Bohr came up to me and apologized. His son Aage Bohr had told him that he didn't understand it, that I really was consonant with the principles of quantum mechanics in my presentation. I told him, "It's not necessary to apologize", and just decided to publish my work.'[12-14]

John Wheeler took the notes at the Pocono Conference, and they were distributed among the participants. They were entitled: 'Conference on

Physics, Pocono Manor, Pennsylvania, 30 March–1 April 1948'. Feynman's talk was included among them.

Notes and References

1. R.P. Feynman, The development of the space-time view of quantum electrodynamics, Nobel Lecture, 11 December 1965, Stockholm, Sweden. *Science* **153**, 699 (1966), p. 7.

2. H.A. Bethe, *Phys. Rev.* **72**, 339 (1947).

3. H.A. Bethe, in *Shelter Island II*, Proceedings of the 1983 Shelter Island Conference on quantum field theory and the fundamental problems of physics (ed. R. Jackiw, N. Khuri, S. Weinberg, and E. Witten). MIT Press, Cambridge, Massachusetts, 1985.

4. H.A. Bethe, Interview with Jagdish Mehra, in Ithaca, New York, 23 February 1988.

5. H.A. Bethe, Ref. 3, p. 340.

6. H.A. Bethe, Ref. 3, p. 341.

7. H.A. Bethe, Letter to J.R. Oppenheimer, 9 June 1947, Oppenheimer Collection, Library of Congress, Washington, D.C.

8. H.A. Kramers, *Collected works*. North-Holland, Amsterdam, p. 867. 1958.

9. V.F. Weisskopf, Letter to H.A. Bethe, 17 June 1947, Bethe Papers, Cornell University Archives, Ithaca, New York.

10. V.F. Weisskopf, Interview with Jagdish Mehra, in Cambridge, Massachusetts, 7 May 1988. Weisskopf makes the same point in his autobiography, *The joy of insight: Passions of a physicist* (Basic Books, New York, 1990), pp. 168–69.

11. W. Heitler, *The quantum theory of radiation*. Clarendon Press, Oxford, 1935, 2nd edn. 1944.

12. R.P. Feynman, Interviews and conversations with Jagdish Mehra, in Austin, Texas, April 1970, and Pasadena, California, January 1988.

13. N.M. Kroll and W.E. Lamb, Jr., *Phys. Rev.* **75**, 388 (1949).

14. R.P. Feynman, Interviews with Charles Weiner (American Institute of Physics), in Pasadena, California, 1966.

15. R.P. Feynman, Ref. 12.

16. R.P. Feynman, Notes entitled 'Brief description of the Wheeler–Feynman electrodynamics', summer 1947. Feynman Archive, Caltech.

17. R.P. Feynman, Notes entitled 'Elimination of field oscillators', summer 1947. Feynman Archive, Caltech.

18. R.P. Feynman, Ref. 1, p. 8.

19. R.P. Feynman, Notes entitled 'Self-interaction of 2 particles', summer 1947. Feynman Archive, Caltech.

20. T.A. Welton, Memories of R.P. Feynman. Unpublished manuscript, 1983.

21. R.P. Feynman, Letter to Bert and Mulaika Corben, 6 November 1947. Feynman Archive, Caltech.

22. Notes taken by Arthur Wightman, Princeton University, 1947. Feynman Archive, Caltech.

23. Mulaika Corben, to R.P. Feynman, November 1947, Feynman Archive, Caltech.

24. R.P. Feynman, Letter to Mr and Mrs Corben, 19 November 1947. Feynman Archive, Caltech.

25. S.M. Dancoff, *Phys. Rev.* **55**, 959 (1939).

26. T. Koba and S.I. Tomonaga, *Prog. Theor. Phys.* **2**, 101 (1947).

27. H.W. Lewis, *Phys. Rev.* **73**, 173 (1948).

28. J.S. Schwinger, *Phys. Rev.* **74**, 1439 (1948).

29. R.P. Feynman, Letter to S.S. Schweber, 28 January 1985. Quoted in S.S. Schweber, *Rev. Mod. Phys.* **58**, 449 (1986).

30. R.P. Feynman, Letter to Prof. and Mrs Corben, 15 January 1948. Feynman Archive, Caltech.

31. R.P. Feynman, Letter to Prof. and Mrs Corben, 20 March 1948. Feynman Archive, Caltech.

32. R.P Feynman, Notes entitled 'Theory of positrons', fall 1947. Feynman Archive, Caltech.

33. R.P. Feynman, Remarks at the banquet in honor of J. Schwinger's sixtieth birthday, February 1978. (Courtesy of R. Finkelstein, University of California, Los Angeles.)

From the Pocono Conference to the Oldstone Conference: Feynman's fundamental papers on quantum electrodynamics

13.1 The relativistic cut-off for classical electrodynamics

Right after the Pocono Conference Feynman started to publish his fundamental papers on quantum electrodynamics. In the abstract of the first of these papers, entitled 'A relativistic cut-off for classical electrodynamics' received on 8 June 1948 and published in the November issue of the *Physical Review*, he wrote: 'Ordinarily it is assumed that interaction between charges occurs along light cones, that is, only where the four-dimensional interval $s^2 = t^2 - r^2$ is exactly zero. We discuss the modifications produced if, as in the theory of F. Bopp, substantial interaction is assumed to occur over a narrow range of s^2 around zero. This has no practical effect on the interaction of charges which are distant from one another by several electron radii. The action of a charge on itself is finite and behaves as electromagnetic mass for accelerations which are excessive. There also results a classical representation of the phenomena of pair production in sufficiently strong fields.'[1]

Next, Feynman expressed his belief that a classical electrodynamics could be devised that would not contain the difficulty of self-energy, and then this theory could be quantized leading to a solution of the problem of a self-consistent quantum electrodynamics. Feynman's article concentrated on the classical theory. Its central idea may be described as follows: 'The electromagnetic potential at a point in space at a given time depends on the charge at a distance r from the point at a time previous by $t = r$ (taking the speed of light as unity). Speaking relativistically, interaction occurs between events whose four-dimensional interval s, defined by $s^2 = t^2 - r^2$, vanishes. There results, however, an infinite action of a point electron on itself. The present theory modifies this idea by assuming that substantial interaction exists as long as the interval s is time-like and less than some small length a of order of the electron radius. When t is large, since $\Delta(s^2) = 2t\,\Delta t$ this means a spread in the time of interval of a signal of amount of order $a^2/2t$. For charges separated by many electron radii, there is, therefore, essentially no effect of the modification. For the action of an electron on itself, however, there is considerable modification. The result is to reduce the infinite self-energy to a finite value. For accelerations which are not extreme, the action of an electron on itself appears simply as an electromagnetic mass. If desired in the classical theory, all the mass of an electron may be represented as electromagnetic. (In the quantum theory this cannot be done in a reasonable way as the electromagnetic mass comes out small under reasonable assumptions for a.) We have, therefore, a consistent classical theory which does not disagree with classical experience.'[2]

The mathematical formulation of Feynman's idea was based on the Wheeler–Feynman action-at-a-distance theory (see Chapter 5), although it was not strictly necessary. The starting point was the Fokker action principle for the action of a system of particles with electric charges e_a:

$$S = \sum_a m_a \int (da_\mu \, da_\mu)^{1/2} + \sum_{a,b} e_a e_b \iint \delta(s_{ab}^2) \, da_\mu \, db_\mu, \qquad (13.1)$$

where a_μ represents, for $\mu = 1$ to 4, the three space coordinates and the time coordinate of a particle a of mass m_a, s_{ab}^2 being the four-dimensional distance between particles a and b: $s_{ab}^2 = (a_\mu - b_\mu)(a_\mu - b_\mu)$. Feynman then considered the details of the action-at-a-distance theory, which we have explained in Chapter 5. He noted: 'There is no need to do so, but it is an interesting question to try to reinstate the idea of a universal field. This requires that a particle be allowed to act on itself and the term $a = b$ included in the action sum. This leads immediately to an infinite self-force. This difficulty can be eliminated if the $\delta(s_{ab}^2)$ is replaced, as Bopp has suggested, by some other function $f(s_{ab}^2)$ of the invariant s_{ab}^2, which behaves like $\delta(s_{ab}^2)$ for large dimensions but differs for small. (We shall discuss the properties of this function later, but as an example to keep in mind, consider $f(s^2) = (\frac{1}{2}a^2)\exp(-s/a)$ for $s^2 > 0$, and $f(s^2) = 0$ for $s^2 < 0$ with a of the order of the electron radius e^2/mc^2.)'[3]

Hence the action functional (13.1) will be replaced by a new one of the form

$$S = \sum_a m_a \int (da_\mu \, da_\mu)^{1/2} + \frac{1}{2} \sum \sum_{ab} e_a e_b \iint f(s_{ab}^2) \, da_\mu \, db_\mu. \qquad (13.2)$$

The term with $a = b$, which represents the self-interaction of the particle with number a, may be written in the form

$$\tfrac{1}{2} e_a^2 \iint f(s_{aa'}^2) \, da_\mu \, da_\mu', \qquad (13.3)$$

where a and a' are two points on the world-line of the particle a. The effect of the modification is therefore to change, slightly, the field of the particle on another when they are very close, and to add a self-force. Assuming that the accelerations are not very great, Feynman re-expressed the self-interaction term (13.3) in a form $m_a \int (da_\mu da_\mu)^{1/2}$, where he had set

$$m_a = \tfrac{1}{2} e_a^2 \int_{-\infty}^{\infty} f(\eta^2) \, d\eta. \tag{13.4}$$

'That is, the self-action term to this approximation represents pure electromagnetic mass. The term readily combines with $m_a \int d\tau_a$ for the mass is correctly invariant. We can go further and assume that originally m_a is zero and all mass of the electron is electromagnetic, but for protons this would then not be so.'[4]

As we can see, in this article Feynman actually abandoned the Wheeler–Feynman theory, and he turned to some modified version of the usual electrodynamics with retarded interaction only, in which he employed his new approach to overcome the self-energy problem.

Feynman then discussed the general properties of the function $f(s^2)$, which has to obey the normalization condition $\int_{-\infty}^{\infty} f(s^2) \, ds^2 = 1$. He showed that if one would represent the electromagnetic field in the modified way as a superposition of harmonic oscillators in the usual way, 'the oscillators corresponding to waves of wave number k_1, k_2, k_3 need not have a frequency k_4, equal to the magnitude of the wave number. Instead we can take the density of the oscillators to be k_4 times $g(k_\mu k_\mu) \, dk_1 \, dk_2 \, dk_3 \, dk_4$, where g is defined for positive k_4 only, and is

$$g(k_\mu k_\mu) = \frac{1}{4\pi^2} \int f(s_{xy}^2) \cos [k_\mu (x_\mu - y_\mu)] \, dx_1 \, dx_2 \, dx_3 \, dx_4.$$

'It is a function of the invariant $k_\mu k_\mu$ only. The ordinary case, $f(s^2) = \delta(s^2)$, corresponds to $g(k_\mu k_\mu) = \delta(k_\mu k_\mu)$. The condition that $f(s^2)$ be finite on the light cone implies that $g(k_\mu k_\mu)$ can be written in the form

$$g(k_\mu k_\mu) = \int_0^{\infty} [\delta(k_\mu k_\mu) - \delta(k_\mu k_\mu - \lambda^2)] G(\lambda) \, d\lambda. \tag{13.5}$$

'Here $G(\lambda)$ is normalized such that $\int_0^{\infty} G(\lambda) \, d\lambda = 1$, [in view of the normalization condition of $f(s^2)$]. The λ values for which g must exist must be large, going up to order m/e^2.'[4]

This cut-off procedure was later on called Feynman's 'regularization procedure', and the parameter λ Feynman's 'cut-off parameter'.

The electrostatic potential of the point particle in this modified theory is given by $A_4 = e \int_{-\infty}^{\infty} f(t^2 - r^2) \, dt$. For large r it is readily seen to be e/r, and it obeys Maxwell's equations. But at the origin, $r = 0$, it is finite, being $e \int_{-\infty}^{\infty} f(t^2) \, dt$ or $2m/e$. 'This has a simple interpretation if all mass is electromagnetic. The energy released in bringing a positron and electron charge together and so canceling out all external fields is just $2m$, the rest mass these particles have by virtue of their fields. Or put it otherwise, the rest mass particles have is simply the work done in separating them against their mutual attraction after they are created. No energy is needed to create the pair of particles at the same place. (These ideas do not have direct quantum counterparts since in quantum theory all mass does not appear to be electromagnetic self-energy, at least in the same simple way.)' [5]

We note that Feynman's parameter λ can be used to indicate the deviation of the modified electrodynamics from the usual Maxwellian one. Later on it was used for this purpose. H. Saleckar[6] proposed to determine the experimental radius of the electron in terms of Feynman's cut-off parameter λ. If $\lambda = \infty$, then the electron is a point-like particle with zero radius. The modern experimental data show that the electron radius is less than 10^{-17} cm. Thus Feynman's cut-off parameter λ turns out to be convenient to express experimental results.

At the end of this article, Feynman discussed the classical analog of the Klein paradox in his language. He considered a potential barrier, i.e. the potential A_4, which is zero outside a small band in x, say $|x| < \frac{1}{2}b$ (See Fig. 13.1). 'If the two points 1 and 2 are separated by a high potential barrier, there are two paths which make the action an extremum. One (solid line in [Fig. 13.1]) represents the passage of a fast electron. The other (the dotted line in [Fig. 13.1]) has a section reversed in time and is interpreted as the effective penetration of the barrier by the slow electron by means of a pair production at Q and P, section PQ representing the motion of the positron . . .

'How would such a path appear to someone whose future gradually becomes past through a moving present? He would first see a single particle at 1, then at Q two new particles would suddenly appear, one moving into the potential to the left, the other out to the right. Later at P the one moving to the

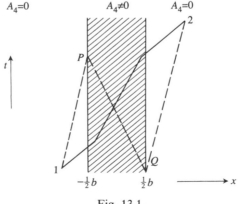

Fig. 13.1.

left combines with the original particle at 1 and they both disappear, leaving the right moving member of the original pair to arrive at 2. We therefore have a classical description of pair production and annihilation. The particle whose trajectory has its proper time in sign to the true time t (section PQ) would behave as a particle of opposite sign of db in [equation (13.2)] is equivalent to changing of sign of e_b. This idea that positrons might be electrons with the proper time reversed was suggested to me by Professor J.A. Wheeler in 1941.'[7]

We should add that in Fig. 13.1 we can see the simplest pictures from which the famous Feynman diagrams originated.

13.2 The relativistic cut-off for quantum electrodynamics

Feynman's next paper, dealing with the relativistic cut-off in quantum electrodynamics, was received by the *Physical Review* on 12 July 1948 and was published in November.[8] In it, Feynman extended his cut-off procedure to quantum electrodynamics. He introduced it by saying: 'A relativistic cut-off of high frequency quanta, similar to that suggested by Bopp, is shown to produce a finite invariant self-energy for a free electron. The electromagnetic line shift for a bound electron comes out as given by Bethe and Weisskopf's wave packet prescription. The scattering of an electron in a potential, without radiation, is discussed. The cross section remains finite. The problem of polarization of the vacuum is not solved. Otherwise, the results will in general agree essentially with those calculated by the prescription of Schwinger. An alternative cut-off procedure analogous to the one proposed by Wataghin, which eliminates high frequency intermediate states, is shown to do the same things but to offer to solve vacuum polarization problems as well.'[9]

Feynman noted that 'the main problems of quantum electrodynamics have been essentially solved by the observation of Bethe and of Weisskopf that the divergent terms in the line shift problem [the level shift of hydrogen] can be thought to be contained in a renormalization of the mass of a free electron.'[9] This principle was used at that time by H. W. Lewis[10] for the radiationless scattering of an electron in a potential and justified by Julian Schwinger,[11] who gave the general procedure for recognizing the terms which were to be identified with the rest mass, which one believed to be finite in a future correct theory. In pursuit of this belief, Feynman constructed a simple model 'for which all quantities automatically do come out finite. With this model the ideas of Bethe, Oppenheimer, and Lewis and Schwinger can be directly confirmed.'[9].

In this article, Feynman restricted himself to the consideration of those processes in which the light quanta appeared only in the intermediate states as virtual quanta. To regularize the infinite integrals, which appeared in the calculation of matrix elements for such processes, Feynman used the cut-off procedure described in the previous section, namely, he replaced the Dirac delta-function $\delta(\omega^2 - k^2)$ by some regular function $g(\omega^2 - k^2)$, given by equation (13.5), which was now written in the more convenient form as

$$g(\omega^2 - k^2) = \int_0^\infty [\delta(\omega^2 - k^2) - \delta(\omega^2 - k^2 - \lambda^2)]G(\lambda)\, d\lambda. \qquad (13.6)$$

Here ω is the frequency and k the wave number of the field oscillators of the electromagnetic field. Hence, the model depends on the normalized arbitrary function $G(\lambda)$, but it turned out that the only term that depends essentially on the form of $G(\lambda)$, and on the values of the cut-off parameter λ, is the self-energy of an electron, which can be used to renormalize the electron mass.

In order to calculate the self-energy in perturbation theory, Feynman started with the formula for the second-order corrections to the energy in Dirac's one-electron theory:

$$\Delta E = -\frac{e^2}{4\pi^2} \sum_i \int \frac{dk}{k} \left(\sum_+ \frac{(0|\alpha_i|f)(f|\alpha_i|0)}{E_f - E_0 + k} + \sum_- \frac{(0|\alpha_i|f)(f|\alpha_i|0)}{-E_f - E_0 + k} \right). \qquad (13.7)$$

Here the intermediate state arises from the initial state by the emission of a light quantum of momentum k and energy $k = |k|$, and the terms which correspond to positive and to negative energies are separated in the two sums $\sum_+$ and $\sum_-$, and the units $k = c = 1$ are used. In the usual perturbation theory of those days one assumed that the summation on the index i of the Dirac matrices α_i in this formula is only over the two directions of the transversal quanta (see Section 11.2). Hence the formula (13.7) gives only the transverse part of the self-energy.

Using the relativistic projection operators

$$\Lambda_f^\pm = (E_f \pm H_f)/2E_f = (E_f \pm \alpha P_f \pm \beta\mu)/2E_f,$$

where $H_f = \alpha P_f + \beta\mu$ is the Dirac Hamiltonian for the free electron mass μ, momentum P_f, and energy E_f in the f-state, Feynman wrote this formula in the new form

$$\Delta E = -\frac{e^2}{4\pi^2} \sum_i \int d\omega\, dk\, \delta(\omega^2 - k^2) \left(\frac{(0|\alpha_i\Lambda^+\alpha_i|0)}{E_f - E_0 + \omega} - \frac{(0|\alpha_i\Lambda^-\alpha_i|0)}{E_f + E_0 + \omega} \right). \qquad (13.8)$$

Now, instead of using the rather complicated procedure proposed by Fermi to treat the longitudinal field (see Section 11.2) and to calculate the corresponding longitudinal part of the self-energy, Feynman discovered that the entire self-energy may be obtained in the second order of perturbation theory with the help of equation (13.8) simply by performing the summation over all possible values of the index $i = 1, 2, 3, 4$. In addition, this treatment gives an obviously relativistic result and automatically insures the gauge condition for the electromagnetic potential if all the light-quanta are virtual.

Then, after evaluating the terms in equation (13.8), Feynman derived the formula for the change $\Delta\mu_0$ of the rest mass μ_0 of the free electron, based on the relativistic relation between the mass and the energy $E^2 = \mu^2 - p^2$:

$$\Delta\mu_0 = \frac{w^2}{2\pi^2\mu} \int d\omega \, dk \, \delta(\omega^2 - k^2) \left(\frac{2\mu^2 - E_0 E_f + P_0 P_f}{E_f(E_f - E_0 + \omega)} - \frac{2\mu^2 + E_0 E_f + P_0 P_f}{E_f(E_f + E_0 + \omega)} \right).$$

(13.9)

This correction for the mass of the free electron is infinite, for the integral (13.9) is logarithmically divergent. If the function $\delta(\omega^2 - k^2)$ in formula (13.9) is replaced with the function $g(\omega^2 - k^2)$, which is given by equation (13.6), the new result, denoted by $\Delta\mu$, will be finite and relativistically invariant. Feynman expressed this new result in the form

$$\Delta\mu - \mu \frac{e^2}{\mu} \left[\tfrac{3}{2} \ln(\lambda_0/\mu) + \tfrac{3}{8} \right],$$

(13.10)

where $\ln \lambda_0 = \int_0^\infty (\ln \lambda) G(\lambda) \, d\lambda$. He noted: 'Judging from the classical case we would have expected to take the cut-off parameter λ_0 of the order of 137μ, for then all mass would be electromagnetic. But $\Delta\mu$ here is too small for this to represent a real possibility. The experimental electron mass is of course $\mu + \Delta\mu$.

'The value of λ would have to be of phenomenal size ($\approx e^{137}\mu$) before $\Delta\mu$ can represent a sizable fraction of the experimental mass. However, to go to the limit of the conventional electrodynamics, λ_0 should be taken as infinite. Then the self-energy diverges logarithmically in the manner found by Weisskopf.'[12]

Feynman then studied the radiationless scattering of an electron by some potential in the first order of perturbation theory. The problem was to find the correction to the potential corresponding to the possibility of emission and absorption of the virtual quanta. He concluded: 'There will be a large change in cross section, which would be expected as the result of a change in mass of the electron plus a smaller change caused essentially by emissions to and absorption subsequent to the scattering. As in the case of the self-energy in a field and, in fact, in all such problems, we will really be interested in those effects of radiation over and above that resulting from the change in mass. It is, therefore, simpler to compute the difference between the desired quantity computed with the possibility of a virtual quantum emission and absorption with an electron of mass μ. This difference, which we shall call the *radiative correction*, can be looked upon as the result of perturbation due to the addition to the Hamiltonian of both the radiative interaction terms and the term $-\beta \Delta\mu$.'[13]

After quite complicated calculations, using certain elements from the papers of Bloch and Nordsieck[14] and Dancoff[15] seeking to solve the infrared divergence problem (see Section 11.4), Feynman derived the following correction ΔH to Dirac's Hamiltonian for the single electron in the electromagnetic field (with scalar potential ϕ and vector potential A) up to the second order of perturbation theory:

$$\Delta H = \frac{e^2}{2\pi\hbar c}\left(-\frac{\hbar e}{2\mu c}\left[\beta(\sigma B)-i\beta(\alpha E)\right]\right.$$

$$\left.+\frac{2\hbar^2 e}{3\mu^2 c^2}\,(\square^2\phi-\alpha\square^2 A)\left[\ln(\mu/\lambda_{min})-\tfrac{3}{8}\right]\right) \qquad (13.11a)$$

Here $B=\nabla\times A$ is the magnetic field and $E=-\nabla\phi$ is the electric field, and λ_{min} is the very small rest mass of the light-quanta, which one has to incorporate in order to overcome the infrared divergence according to Bloch and Nordsieck's prescription; α and β are the Dirac 4×4 matrices, and the three 4×4 matrices σ are products of the Dirac matrices, which play the role of Pauli's 2×2 matrices, describing the interaction of the magnetic moment of the electron with the magnetic field B. The first term in equation (13.11a) is the change of the magnetic moment of a Dirac electron by a fraction $e^2/2\pi\hbar c$, which was first discovered by Schwinger.

The formula (13.11a) was used by Feynman to calculate the line shift in hydrogen. For the light-quanta above the minimum wave number k_{min}, connected with λ according to the formula $\ln\lambda_{min}=\ln(2k_{min})+\tfrac{5}{8}$, Feynman derived the value of the level-shift in the form

$$\Delta H = \frac{e^2}{2\pi\hbar c}\left(-\frac{i\hbar e}{2\mu c}\,\beta(\alpha\,\nabla\phi)+\frac{2\hbar^2 e}{3\mu^2 c^2}\,(\nabla^2\phi)\left[\ln\,(\mu c^2/2\hbar k_{min})+\tfrac{5}{8}\right]\right), \quad (13.11b)$$

which gives the correct physical result, as Bethe had shown. 'Using equation (13.11b), Professor Bethe finds 1050 megacycles for the separation between $^2P_{1/2}$ and $^2S_{1/2}$ in hydrogen.'[16]

At the end of his article Feynman considered certain applications of his cut-off procedure to other processes as well as some open questions. He expressed his belief that higher-order processes will not lead to any new troubles. His basic comment was: 'The results for electrodynamics, then, after mass renormalization, depend only slightly on the form of $G(\lambda)$ and the size of λ_0. Since λ_0 may be taken to be extremely large without spoiling the smallness of $\Delta\mu$, there would appear to be good reason to drop the dependence on λ altogether. Thus $G(\lambda)$ appears only as a complicated scaffold which is removed after the calculation is done. On the other hand, electrodynamics probably does break down somewhere and it is interesting to keep the terms in λ for various phenomena to see if one might be selected which is particularly sensitive to λ. This phenomenon would then be an interesting one to study experimentally.'[17]

As examples of such promising processes Feynman pointed to the Møller scattering between two electrons and the processes with high momentum transfer in the wide angle scattering of electrons from nuclei.

The last major problem which Feynman mentioned in this article and which remained unsolved was vacuum polarization. He noted: 'In the above calculation, terms of the type discussed by Uehling[18] have been omitted. These terms represent processes involving a pair production followed by annihilation of the same pair. For example, a pair produced by the potential may annihilate again emitting a quantum. This quantum is then absorbed by the electron in state 1 transferring into state 2. These terms are infinite and are not made convergent by the present scheme. There is some point, nevertheless, to solving the problems at first without taking them into account. This is because their net effect is only to alter the effective potential in which the electron finds itself, for it may be scattered either directly or by the quantum produced by the Uehling terms. That is, if this problem of the polarization of the vacuum is solved it will mean, if there is any effect, simply that the potential A, ϕ appearing in the Dirac equation and (to a high order) in such terms as β should be replaced by new "polarized" potential A', ϕ'.'[17]

One may note how close Feynman came at that time to the idea of charge renormalization, which is the correct solution to the problem of vacuum polarization. Then he analyzed the cause of this difficulty. His conclusion was that the difficulty arises because the virtual light-quanta emitted at a given point spread out as $\delta(t^2 - r^2)$ from the origin. According to the Dirac equation, the spreading of the electron has a similar singularity. 'It is the continued coincidence of these singularities which makes the matrix element for the subsequent absorption of the quantum infinite.'[19]

Feynman's regularization procedure was based upon the smoothing of the singularity of the photon propagation. An alternative way is to smooth the electron function. If one assumes the density of electron states of energy E and momentum P to be $g(E^2 - P^2 - \mu^2)$ rather than $\delta(E^2 - P^2 - \mu^2)$, the self-energy integrals may be expressed in a form similar to equation (13.8):

$$\Delta E = -\frac{e^2}{2\pi^2} \int g(E_f^2 - P_f^2 - \mu^2)\, dE_f\, dP_f \frac{E_f}{k} \sum_i \left(\frac{(0|\alpha_i \Lambda_f^+ \alpha_i|0)}{E_f + k - E_0} - \frac{(0|\alpha_i \Lambda_f^- \alpha_i|0)}{E_f + k + E_0} \right).$$

$$(13.12)$$

A similar method was proposed by Wataghin.[20] However, the real existence of vacuum polarization at that time was not certain in Feynman's opinion. He intended to investigate this question further and to give a more complete theory in subsequent publications, but this took him rather long to do. 'It took me very long to write up the goddamn thing. I had awful trouble and difficulties in writing papers. The only two papers that I wrote relatively comfortably were the ones on "Relativistic cut-off for classical electrodynamics" and "Relativistic cut-off for quantum electrodynamics". And that was just because Rabi told me: "Just write it up the old way: get it out. You can put the improved technique later on in a more careful paper; but get it out!" I followed his advice, advice from an old fellow to a young man, and I was able to do that rather easily. In the later papers, in which I wanted to write the best way of formulating and expressing, I had great difficulty. I had worked everything out, but the act of writing it all up took an awfully long, long time. I just can't sit down and write quickly and well.'[21]

13.3 The summer and fall of 1948

For Feynman, vacuum polarization remained to be the main unsolved problem of quantum electrodynamics in the spring of 1948. Feynman recalled the situation at the time of the Pocono Conference at the end of March 1948 as follows: 'When it was my turn to talk, I began by saying, "I can do everything but I can't do closed loops, the self-energy of the photon." Schwinger immediately got up and said, "I can do everything including vacuum polarization." And he worked something out; he got a term which looked something like vacuum polarization. Actually, he had done vacuum polarization, but in his calculation he had not noticed it and left it out; in its place he had written another term which he thought was wrong, but it was vacuum polarization, and he was able to treat it. ... Actually, I had everything, too, only it took me just a little longer to recognize that I had it.'[22]

Schwinger and Feynman 'got together in the hallway (at the Pocono Conference) and although we'd come from the ends of the earth with different ideas, we had climbed the same mountain from different sides and we could check each other's equations. . . . . Our methods were entirely different. I didn't understand about those creation and annihilation operators. I didn't know how these operators that he was using worked, and I had some magic from his point of view. We compared our results because we worked out problems and we looked at the answers and kind of half described how the terms came. He would say, "Well I got a creation and then annihilation of the same photon and then the potential goes . . . ." "Oh, I think that might be that", and I'd draw a picture. He didn't understand my pictures and I didn't understand his operators, but the terms corresponded and by looking at the equations we could tell, and so I knew, in spite of being refused admission by the rest, by conversation with Schwinger, that we both had come to the same mountain and that it was a real thing and everything was all right.'[23]

The discussions between Feynman and Schwinger continued after the Pocono Conference. In fact, several weeks after the conference, they discussed these problems during Feynman's visit to MIT.[21] 'We discussed matters at Pocono and later also over the telephone and compared results. We did not understand each other's method but trusted each other to make sense—even when others did not trust us. We could compare final quantities and vaguely see in our own way where the other fellow's terms or error came from. We helped each other in several ways. For example, he showed me a trick for integrals that led to my parameter trick, and I suggested to him that only one complex propagator function ever appeared rather than his two separate real functions. Many people joked we were competitors—but I don't remember feeling that way.'[23]

Feynman was so impressed by the coincidence of his results with the ones that Schwinger had obtained in a different way that he did not foresee the possibility of any common mistakes. As he recalled: 'At the same time (as Schwinger and myself), Weisskopf [and French] also calculated the Lamb shift. That was a rather pedestrian, plodding, hard-working, old-fashioned, but careful way of doing it. Weisskopf [and French] made their calculation by following the logic of [the earlier work of] Bethe; it was accurate thinking but old-fashioned. Weisskopf did the calculation with [Bruce] French. They got a different answer than I did. He called me up on the telephone to tell me about the difference and how his formula compared with mine. His calculation was so complicated that I felt sure that he had made a mistake. And so, for a long time Weisskopf and French hesitated to publish their result; since my method of calculation was so much more efficient, they were [also] sure that they had made an error. They kept on checking and re-checking their calculation, which delayed their publication. It made me very unhappy, because they were right and had made no error.'[23]†

In 1980, Weisskopf himself recalled this incident as follows: 'J. B. French and I calculated the difference [between $^2S_{1/2}$ and $^2P_{1/2}$ energy levels in hydrogen] carefully and got a well-defined result in agreement with the experiment. We believe that we were the first to arrive at that result. Then followed a tragicomical episode. We showed our method and our result to Julian Schwinger and to Richard P. Feynman. They independently tried to repeat our calculations but found a result differing by a small additive numerical constant. Having both Feynman and Schwinger against us shook our confidence, and we tried to find a mistake in our calculation, without success. Only seven months later Feynman informed us that it was he and Schwinger who had made a mistake! We published our paper, but in the meantime, a similar calculation was made by [Norman M.] Kroll and [Willis E.] Lamb (1948), which appeared a few months earlier than ours.[24] Self-confidence is an important ingredient that makes for a successful physicist.'[25] Feynman acknowledged his error in a footnote, 'appropriately numbered' 13, in his paper on the 'Space–time approach to quantum electrodynamics'.[26]

This episode furnishes an example of the spirit that reigned in this great epoch of theoretical physics: a spirit of hard work, adventure, and friendly competition between the first-rate theoreticians of that time.

So, in the spring and early summer of 1948, neither Feynman nor Schwinger had charge renormalization in hand. 'I had two-thirds of the thing. Schwinger knew that he was missing a piece, but it's just one of those curious things.'[23] The problem was that the Wataghin-like procedure for overcoming the

---

† The correct answer had already been obtained by Kroll and Lamb before French and Weisskopf.[24]

divergence due to vacuum polarization, which Feynman had proposed at the end of his paper 'Relativistic cut-off for quantum electrodynamics',[8] spoiled the gauge invariance of electrodynamics. Feynman very carefully explained his new methods and rules to Hans Bethe at Cornell, and then he left for his summer vacation.

It was in the early summer of 1948 that Feynman travelled to Albuquerque, New Mexico, by car with Freeman J. Dyson. Dyson had been aware of Feynman's approach to quantum electrodynamics since September 1947, when he arrived at Cornell from Cambridge, England, to work with Bethe as a graduate student. After the trip, later in the summer of 1948, Dyson went from Ann Arbor to Berkeley on a vacation, as part of sightseeing required by the terms of his Commonwealth Fund Fellowship which had taken him to Cornell. He recalled that on the bus ride back from Berkeley to Chicago, where he was going to stay with friends for a week, 'it became clear in my head what the situation was with Feynman, what Feynman's theory really was. Since I was more in contact with Feynman than anybody else, I realized quite soon that it was a very great opportunity to translate Feynman into the language that other people could use. That was essentially my job . . . . Then in Chicago I really worked out the essential outline of the paper which I put together.'[27,28]

During the summer of 1948 Feynman worked on improving his computational methods in Albuquerque and Santa Fe, New Mexico. Using a suggestion of Julian Schwinger's he invented an efficient method of calculating the integrals, which appeared in his scheme, and by this more powerful method he checked again the problem of radiationless scattering. Feynman wrote to Bethe, who was spending several months in England: 'I am the possessor of a swanky new scheme to do each problem in terms of one with one less energy denominator. It is based on the great identity

$$\frac{1}{a \cdot b} = \int_0^1 dx \, \frac{1}{[ax + b(1-x)]^2} \tag{13.13}$$

so 2 energy denominators may be combined to one—reversing the parametric x integration to the indefinite future (there's the rub, of course).'[29]

Feynman believed that with this powerful new technique he would be able to calculate easily the radiative corrections to the Klein–Nishina formula and to the formula for Møller scattering (see Chapter 11). Two weeks later, he again wrote to Bethe: 'I have been working on the Compton effect & the few days I promised the answer turned into weeks. There are lots of integrals & terms to be added all together etc. & I kept looking for a new & easy way because it was so complicated. But I think it is like calculating π to 107 decimal places—there is no short cut to carry out the digits. So here I am beginning to believe that the answer is not much less simple than the steps leading to it—so I finally buckled down & did it . . . .

'I have set up & indicated how every integral can be reduced to transcendental integrals in one variable, exactly. But I have not done all the work of putting all the pieces all together & writing down the answers. I have, however, worked out a special limiting case in detail . . . .'[30]

In his lectures in England, Bethe tried to reconstruct Feynman's calculations. He found that he got everything all right, but still he obtained a wrong number and wrote about it to Feynman. 'So he wrote me a letter. "To professor from student." He said, "I tried to do your thing, blah, blah, blah, and I got into the following difficulty." So I wrote back, "Here's where you made the mistake." And he wrote back: "Well, the student flunked. Thank you very much." And then he told me, "Everyone is very excited by these methods." I knew he, Bethe, was. As a technical method, it was superior to the usual ways of calculating. "Everyone wants to learn about it." Bethe urged me to publish soon what the rules of calculation were, because the proof of the rules is a little elaborate—not today, but it was at that time. You had to explain about the path integrals, which nobody really knew. You had to explain all this crap and lead them all over the hills before you could explain where the rules came from. But the rules were simple and anybody who would accept them, without worrying (about them or disturbing me) would find them useful. So the proposal was just to explain the final conclusions and how the (quantum electrodynamics) worked, and write up the proofs sometime at leisure. That's what I did.'[23]

For the second year of his Commonwealth Fund Fellowship, Dyson went to the Institute for Advanced Study in Princeton, which Bethe had arranged for him with the help of Robert Oppenheimer. In October 1948 Dyson finished writing up his paper on 'The radiation theories of Tomonaga, Schwinger, and Feynman'[28]. Then, together with Cécile Morette, a theoretical physicist from France working at the Institute, Dyson visited Cornell to discuss the problems of quantum electrodynamics. After the visit, he wrote to his parents in England: 'Feynman himself came to meet us at the station, after our 10-hour train journey, and was in tremendous form, bubbling over with ideas and stories and entertaining us with performances on Indian drums from New Mexico until 1 a.m.

'The next day, Saturday, we spent in conclave discussing physics. Feynman gave a masterly account of his theory, which kept Cécile in fits of laughter and made my talk at Princeton a pale shadow by comparison. He said he had given a copy of my paper to a graduate student to read, then asked the student if he himself ought to read it. The student said "No" and Feynman accordingly wasted no time on it and continued chasing his own ideas. Feynman and I really understand each other; I know that he is the one person in the world who has nothing to learn from what I have written; and he doesn't mind telling me so. That afternoon, Feynman produced more brilliant ideas per square minute than I have ever seen before . . . .

'In the evening I mentioned that there were just two problems for which the finiteness of the theory remained to be established; both problems are well-known and feared by physicists, since many long and difficult papers running to 50 pages and more have been written about them trying unsuccessfully to make the older theories give sensible answers to them. Among others Kemmer and the great Heisenberg had been baffled by these problems.

'When I mentioned this fact, Feynman said "We'll see about this", and proceeded to sit down and in two hours, before our eyes, obtain finite and sensible answers to both problems. It was the most amazing piece of lightning calculation I have ever witnessed, and the results prove, apart from some unforeseen complication, the consistency of the whole theory.

'The two problems were, the scattering of light by an electric field and the scattering of light by light.

'After supper Feynman was working until 3 a.m. He has had a complete summer vacation, and has returned with unbelievable stores of suppressed energy.

'On Sunday Feynman was up at his usual hour (9 a.m.) and we went down to the Physics building, where he gave me another 2-hour lecture on miscellaneous discoveries of his . . . .'[31]

After Dyson's departure for his return to Princeton, Feynman justified the new results. He wrote to Dyson: 'I hope you did not go about bragging about how fast I could compute the scattering of light by a potential because on looking over the calculations last night I discovered the entire effect is zero. I am sure some smart fellow like Oppenheimer would have known such a thing right off.

'Any loop with an odd number of quanta in it is zero. This is because among the various possibilities which must be summed there is one corresponding to the electron going around one way and another with the electron progressing around the loop in the opposite direction. The latter is the same as the former with reversal of the sign of the charge, thus all quanta and potential interactions change sign, so if there is an odd number of them the total result is zero.'[32]

This general result about the null effect of the contribution of the loops with an odd number of electron lines which Feynman discovered in October 1948, is known as Furry's theorem, and was first established by Wendell Furry.[33]

Dyson's visit to see Feynman at Cornell had still another significance. Dyson's paper on the equivalence of the quantum electrodynamical theories of Tomonaga, Schwinger, and Feynman was ready, and Dyson had gone to inform Feynman about the awkward situation he was in. This was that his paper, to be received by the *Physical Review* on 6 October 1948, i.e. several months before the basic publications on Feynman's theory by Feynman himself, was to be the first paper published on Feynman's new method—in particular, on the now famous Feynman diagrams. Therefore, right after Dyson's paper appeared, some people began to speak about 'Dyson's graphs' and 'Dyson's method'. This did not bother Feynman. He recalled: 'Dyson is a friend of mine and I realized how the misunderstanding arose. He wasn't trying to steal anything from me; he hadn't claimed that they were his. All he was trying to do was to tell everyone that there was something good in my theory, that he had discovered the connection with the work of Tomonaga and Schwinger, and that all these different approaches were equivalent. This greatly helped people to understand the different theories. His paper had some crazy language which I couldn't understand, but others could understand it. It was like a translation of my theory, my language, for other people; of course, it's a mistake to translate something for the author. I was bothered only slightly, and I would be more concerned today if they were still called "Dyson graphs". That would not make me miserable, but I would complain a little bit about it.

'A little later, the diagrams came to be called "Dyson–Feynman graphs", with some others calling them the "Feynman graphs" through a number of people who knew about their origin a little better. Now, of course, it is as it should be. "We write down *the* diagram for this or that process." And that's the best, because it's anonymous; it's *the* diagram. It makes me feel better than the "Feynman diagram", because it is *the* rule for something, and that's just fine.'[23,34]

Many years later, Feynman remarked about Dyson's paper: 'Of course, he had my permission (to publish my work in his paper)! We were good friends. That was no problem.'[21] And Dyson recalled that when he told Feynman about the paper he had completed on the equivalence of the quantum electrodynamical theories, in which he was going to publish Feynman's work before Feynman had published it himself, 'He was absolutely delighted. He just had no qualms about giving me a free hand to publish whatever I liked. He just said: "Well, that's great! Finally I am respectable."'[27]

The general state of affairs in his approach to quantum electrodynamics in late 1948 was described by Feynman in a letter to Ted Welton, his old friend from MIT: 'In regard to "Q.E.D." as you put it, I don't have the cold dope. I can calculate anything, and everything is finite, but the polarization of the vacuum is not gauge-invariant when calculated. This is because my prescription for making the polarization integrals convergent is not gauge-invariant. If I threw away the obvious large gauge-dependent term (a procedure which I can not justify legally, but which is practically un-ambiguous) the result is a charge renormalization plus the usual Uehling term. The amount of charge renormalization depends logarithmically on the cut-off. The Uehling terms are practically independent on the cut-off and give the usual $-\frac{1}{5}$ in the Lamb shift.

'These terms come from the closed loops (in my way of talking, which I think you understand), in which two quanta are involved. Loops with a higher number of quanta always converge and in fact give definite answers practically independent of the cut-off, so that they could be computed by the conventional Q.E.D. Incidentally, it is easy to show that all loops with an odd number of quanta of field interactions give zero. You know about these things. It is widely known that the scattering of light by a potential only occurs with completed second order in the potential, i.e. probably in the fourth order in the potential. I think you told me it was so some time ago.

'To me it has become clear that all the problems of Q.E.D. appear to be involved in the simplest problems (self-energy and vacuum polarization), the more complicated ones always converge . . .

'I am very busy these days writing all my stuff on paper . . . I am working like a demon.'[35]

13.4 The APS meeting of January 1949

Feynman prepared and presented a new version of his earlier notes on the theory of positrons at the American Physical Society meeting in New York in January 1949. Although many of the technical physical ideas in his talk were the same as in his earlier notes,[36] he developed the philosophical points more fully, especially his critique of Dirac's hole theory. 'One of the disadvantages of this theory', he noted, 'is that even the simplest processes become complicated in its analysis. One must take into account besides the limited number of real particles, the infinite number of electrons in the sea. The present work results from a reinterpretation of the Dirac equation so that this complexity is not required.

'It results from a different mode of representation of phenomena of pair production. We can discuss it by a simple model. Suppose a black thread be immersed in a cube of collodion, which is then hardened. Imagine the thread, although not necessarily quite straight, runs from top to bottom. The cube is now sliced horizontally into thin square layers, which are put together to form successive frames of a motion picture. In each frame will appear a black dot, the cross section of the thread, which will move about in the movie depending on the waverings of the thread. The moving dot can be likened to a moving electron.

'How can pair production be visualized? Suppose the thread did not go directly top to bottom but doubled back for a way (somehow like the letter N with the straight parts extended to top and bottom.). Then in successive frames first there would be just one dot but suddenly two new ones would appear when the frames come from layers cutting the thread through the reversed section. They would all three move about for a while when two would come together and annihilate, leaving only a single dot in the final frames. In this way new phenomena of pair creation and annihilation can be represented. They are similar to the simple motion of an electron (and are thus governed by the same equations), but correspond to a more tortuous path in space and time than one is used to considering.

'In common experience the future appears to us to develop out of conditions of the present (and past). The laws of physics have usually been expressed in this form. (Technically, in the form of differential equations, or "Hamiltonian Form".) The formulas tell [us] what is to be expected to happen if given conditions prevail at a certain time. The author has found that the relations are often very much more simply analyzed if the entire time history be considered as all laid out in the four dimensions of time and space, and that we come upon the successive events. This is applied to simplify the description of the phenomena of a pair production in the present paper. A bombardier watching a single road through the bomb sight of a low flying plane suddenly sees three roads, the confusion only resolving itself when two of them move together and disappear and he realizes that he has only passed over a long reverse switchback of a single road. The reversed section represents the positron in analogy, which is first created along with an electron and then moves about and annihilates another electron.

'The relation of time in physics to that of gross experience has suffered many changes in the history of physics. The obvious difference of past and future does not appear in physical time for microscopic events (the connection of the laws of Newton and statistical mechanics). Einstein discovered that the present is not the same for all people. (For those in motion it corresponds to cutting the same collodion cube at slight angle from the horizontal.) It may prove useful in physics to consider events in all time at once and to imagine that we at each instant are only aware of those that lie behind us.

'The complete relation of this concept of physical time to the time of experience and causality is a physical problem which has not been worked out in detail. It may be that more problems and difficulties are produced than are solved by such a point of view. In the application to the description of positrons it should be emphasized that there still appear to be difficult unsolved problems and that the proposed point of view may eventually not prove to result in as much simplification as it appears to do at first sight.'[37]

We shall discuss the more technical details and achievements of Feynman's 'Theory of positrons', including the contents of the paper with the same title, which Feynman sent to the *Physical Review* several months after the APS meeting in January 1949, in the next section.

During this APS meeting something else also happened which had some influence on the further development of Feynman's work. One of the topics at the meeting was the scattering of electrons on neutrons. The new and quite good experimental results from the measurements of Rainwater, Rabi, and Havens[38] on the neutron–electron scattering as determined by the slow neutrons in lead and bismuth were reported. They showed the existence of the complicated structure of the neutron and some distribution of electric charge in it, described by the so-called form factors. The existence of the electric charge in the neutron does not contradict the fact that it is electrically neutral as a whole; it can be explained, in principle, by the creation of charged mesons due to the strong interaction, which form a charged cloud around the neutron in analogy with the electron–positron cloud around the electron as predicted by Dirac's hole theory. At that time only the first attempts to describe this structure had been made, and there was no good theory of it. The very description of the interaction between the neutron and the meson was unclear and different variants of the theory were tested. In particular, one had to choose between the so-called 'pseudoscalar' and 'pseudovector' couplings, comparing the theoretical predictions with the experimental data. The calculations in meson theory were performed with the help of perturbation theory, although the coupling constant here was not as small as it is in electrodynamics. Feynman had not studied this theory in detail up to the January 1949 APS meeting.

As Feynman recalled in his Nobel lecture: 'I became interested in the possible application of my methods to perturbation calculations in meson theory. But, what was meson theory? All I knew was that meson theory was something analogous to electrodynamics, except that particles corresponding to the photon had a mass. It was easy to guess that the δ-function in [the classical action] equation [(13.1)], which was a solution of the Dalembertian equals zero, was to be changed to the corresponding solution of Dalembertian equals m^2. Next there were different kinds of mesons—the ones in closest analogy to photons, coupled via $\gamma_\mu \gamma_\mu$, are called vector mesons; there were also scalar mesons. Well, maybe that corresponds to putting unity in place of γ_μ, perhaps what they called "psuedo-vector coupling" and I would guess what that probably was. I didn't have the knowledge to understand the way these were defined in the conventional papers because they were expressed at that time in terms of creation and annihilation operators, and so on, which I had not successfully learned. I remember that when someone had started to teach me about creation and annihilation operators, that this operator creates an electron, I said, 'How do you create an electron? It disagrees with the conservation of charge,' and in that way I blocked my mind from learning a very practical scheme of calculation. Therefore, I had to find as many opportunities as possible to test whether I guessed right as to what the various theories were.'[39]

At the 1949 APS meeting Murray Slotnick presented new results, which he had obtained after two years of calculation, concerning the interaction between an electron and a neutron. He had found that the answers for the pseudoscalar theory and the pseudovector theory were different. In fact, in the case of the pseudovector theory the answer was logarithmically divergent, but in the pseudoscalar theory it was convergent and gave well-defined answers. Oppenheimer, who was in the audience, asked Slotnick: 'Well, what about Case's theorem?' By this he meant the new result of Kenneth Case (who, at that time, was a postdoctoral fellow at the Institute for Advanced Study in Princeton), which was going to be reported the next day. Case had announced that he had proved that the results for both the pseudoscalar and pseudovector theories were the same. Slotnick answered: 'I never heard of Case's theorem!'

Feynman had missed Slotnick's talk, but somebody asked him about the discussion between Oppenheimer and Slotnick. He went to Slotnick and said: 'Look, I am very anxious to try out if I understand what these things mean. So just tell me what you did?' He replied, 'I scattered the electron off the neutron and I have a correction due to the mesons.'[23]

Feynman described what happened next as follows: 'This was a welcome opportunity to test my guesses as to whether I really understood what these two couplings were. So I went home, and during the evening I worked out the electron–neutron scattering for the pseudoscalar and pseudovector couplings, saw they were not equal and subtracted them, and worked out the difference in detail. The next day, at the meeting, I saw Slotnick and said, "Slotnick, I worked it out last night, I wanted to see if I got the same answers you do. I got a different answer for each coupling—but I would like to check in detail with you because I want to make sure of my methods." And he said, "What do you mean you worked it out last night? It took me six months!" And, when we compared the answers, he looked at mine and he asked, "What is that Q in there, that variable Q?" (I had expressions like $\tan^{-1} Q/Q$, etc.) I said, "That's the momentum transferred by the electron, the electron deflected by different angles." "Oh," he said, "No, I only have the limiting value as Q approaches [zero for] the forward scattering." Well, it was easy enough to just substitute Q equals zero in my answers as he did. But it took him six months to do the case of zero momentum transfer, whereas, during one evening I had done the finite and arbitrary momentum transfer. That was a thrilling moment for me, like receiving the Nobel Prize, because that convinced me, at last, I did have some kind of method and technique and understood how to do something that other people did not know how to do. That was my moment of triumph in which I realized I really had succeeded in working out something worthwhile.'[39]

Three weeks before he died, Feynman recalled that moment again. 'That day I knew I had something. Up to that time I didn't really know that my system was efficient; that it was somehow better than anybody else's. I just thought I was doing my way what other people were doing their way. But when I could do overnight what would take that guy a year and in the end it turned out he only could do a limiting case, then I knew that was a big moment!'[23]

As Feynman further recalled, next day Case reported his theorem at the APS meeting. 'And, just to be annoying, when Case finished, I said, "Yeah, but what about Slotnick's calculation?" You know, I mean Oppenheimer was imperious. If Case proved the theorem, it must be true. And I argued, "What about Slotnick's calculation? That theorem can't be true." And everybody laughed because it was perfectly logical to suppose the theorem is at fault rather than the calculation, you know. So he (Oppenheimer) said: "Well, maybe Slotnick's calculation is wrong." I said, "No, I checked it last night and it's all right. I believe it's right." That was the end of the story but I knew that I had improved the methods of calculation.

'When I wrote the paper with the rules I said what you [can] do with meson theory. Then I said that you calculate all these things, and the results don't agree with experiments, and so on. When Dyson read the paper, he suggested some corrections. Of course, he said, "You don't know what you're writing. What you're writing is that you did all the work and more, that has been backed by all these meson theories of the last five years and you're treating (all this) so cavalierly like it's nothing." And I said, "But it is." He said, "Yes, but it's too devastating. Write it just a little easier, will you?" So I modified it a little bit. But I knew that I had something. But they were doing perturbation theory and meson theory, and it was hard for them. I don't know why it was so hard. Anyway, it was fun, discovering that it really was worthwhile.'[23]

Actually the end of this story came some time after the APS meeting. Case sent Feynman the manuscript of his paper. Feynman had to learn the method of creation and annihilation operators, and he found a rather trivial algebraic mistake in Case's 'theorem'. He wrote a letter to Case and pointed out to him the mistake. The experience of learning the technique of creation and annihilation operators came in very handy when Feynman wrote his following papers on quantum electrodynamics. He expressed his feeling about the 'proofs' of physical results as follows: 'When I say I know something, that is not equivalent to "I have proved it". It doesn't have to be for me. I believe that it is possible to have knowledge with a probability that it is 99 per cent sure, and I don't believe that any proofs are sure because I have heard of the idea of mistake in the proof. In fact I myself have discovered mistakes in proofs by other people and had to send them letters (as I did pertaining to Case's proof) because they did not get the right answer according to me. I found the mistakes so I know that people do make mistakes in proofs. I don't think that proofs are that much better than checking the goddamn formula against a lot of things, than seeing its consistency and understanding that all's right. Sounds a little odd, because it's a little bit revolutionary but it's from a practical point of view absolutely true, for in physics proofs are not that good. Case's "theorem" is a good example.'[23]

13.5 The Pauli–Villars regularization

After the APS meeting in New York, there took place several important developments in Feynman's work during the early months of 1949. The most essential development was that Feynman learned about the gauge-invariant procedure to cut off the vacuum polarization processes from a communication received by Hans Bethe from Wolfgang Pauli at the end of January.[40] Pauli enclosed a copy of a letter (actually it was a short paper) which he had written to Schwinger.[41] In it Pauli proposed a new regularization method for singular integrals which appeared in quantum electrodynamics. This method was soon published in a paper by Pauli and Villars and is now known as the Pauli–Villars regularization procedure.[42]

In the simplest case, the new regularization procedure reduces to the introduction of an auxiliary mass M, and then the replacement of the badly behaved functions in the integrand, $1/(m^2 - p^2)$, which makes the corresponding integrals divergent, with the well-behaved regularized functions, according to the scheme:

$$\frac{1}{m^2 - p^2} \longrightarrow \frac{1}{m^2 - p^2} - \frac{1}{M^2 - p^2}. \tag{13.14}$$

Pauli showed that: (1) this makes the integrals convergent if the auxiliary mass M is finite; (2) this regularization procedure preserves the gauge invariance of electrodynamics (which was the most important new property of this cut-off procedure); (3) after the calculation has been performed, one must take the limit as the auxiliary mass M approaches infinity. This original idea proposed some wider possibilities of introducing several auxiliary masses M, thereby imposing some additional useful conditions upon them.

Bethe showed this regularization method to Feynman and he adopted it in place of the Wataghin-like procedure, which he had employed at the end of his article 'A relativistic cut-off for quantum electrodynamics' (see Section 13.2). Thus the main difficulty which had thus far remained in Feynman's approach up to that time was removed. As a result, by the spring of 1949 Feynman had all the essential ingredients of his new scheme for making calculations in quantum electrodynamics. Thus he had simple rules to calculate contributions of different-order processes in perturbation theory, the Feynman diagrams (the extremely useful method for visualizing these processes), efficient calculational techniques, gauge-invariant cut-off methods to make vacuum polarization and self-energy finite. Also, thanks to Dyson, he had the proof of the equivalence of his new scheme to the more conventional schemes of Tomonaga and Schwinger. At that time Feynman felt the pressure to publish his new theoretical scheme, especially from those who wanted to use it. 'They had heard that the method was good from various rumors. And Bethe had given lectures on it. I had taught it to him.'[23]

Feynman published two papers: 'The theory of positrons'[43] and 'Space–time approach to quantum electrodynamics'.[44] 'These two papers, on the theory of positrons, and on the space-time approach to quantum electrodynamics were published only in 1949. It took me an awfully long time to write them. They were prepared a long time after I knew the technical methods.'[23]

13.6 The theory of positrons

Feynman's paper on 'The theory of positrons' was received by the *Physical Review* on 8 April 1949. This was the last version of the paper on this topic on which Feynman had worked for several years. He noted: 'The problem of the behavior of positrons and electrons in given external potentials, neglecting their mutual interaction, is analyzed by replacing the theory of holes by a reinterpretation of the solutions of the Dirac equation. It is possible to write down a complete solution of the problem in terms of the boundary conditions on the wave function, and this solution contains automatically all the possibilities of virtual (and real) pair formation and annihilation together with the ordinary scattering processes, including the correct relative signs of the various terms.

'In this solution, the "negative energy states" appear in a form which may be pictured (as [done] by Stückelberg) in spacetime as waves traveling away from the external potential backwards in time. Experimentally, such a wave corresponds to a positron approaching the potential and annihilating the electron. A particle moving forward in time (electron) in a potential may be scattered forward in time (ordinary scattering) or backward (pair annihilation). When moving backward (positron) it may be scattered backward in time (positron scattering) or forward (pair production). For such a particle the amplitude for transition from an initial to a final state is analyzed to any order in the potential by considering it to undergo a sequence of such scatterings.

'The amplitude for a process involving many such particles is the product of the transition amplitudes for each particle. The exclusion principle requires that antisymmetric combinations of amplitudes be chosen for those complete processes which differ only by exchange of particles. It seems that a consistent interpretation is only possible if the exclusion principle is adopted. The exclusion principle need not be taken into account in intermediate states. Vacuum problems do not arise for charges which do not interact with one another, but these are analyzed nevertheless in anticipation of application to quantum electrodynamics.

'The results are also expressed in momentum–energy variables. Equivalence to second quantization theory of holes is proved in an appendix.'[45]

In the introduction, Feynman explained his general understanding of the theory of positrons as electrons moving backward in time. The main principle he adopted was to deal directly with the solutions of the Hamiltonian differential equations (meaning the evolution equations of any theory) rather than with these equations themselves. He stressed that in his approach, with a suitable choice and interpretation of the Dirac equation, the problems may be equally well treated in a manner which is fundamentally no more complicated than Schrödinger's method of dealing with one or more particles. In relativistic theory, although pairs may be created or annihilated, the number of particles is not conserved. Therefore, in relativistic considerations, it is better to deal with the electric charge, which is a conserved quantity; besides, it simplifies the results.

For a nonrelativistic particle, Feynman wrote the Schrödinger equation in the form

$$i\,\partial\psi/\partial t = H\psi, \tag{13.15}$$

whose solution for $t_2 > t_1$, via the Green's function $K(x_2, t_2; x_1, t_1)$ is given by

$$\psi(x_2, t_2) = \int K(x_2, t_2; x_1, t_1)\psi(x_1, t_1)\, d^3x_1. \tag{13.16}$$

He expressed the 'amplitude' $K(2, 1)$ in terms of the stationary solutions $\phi_n(x)\exp(-iE_n t)$, as follows:

$$K(2, 1) = \begin{cases} \sum_n \phi_n(x_2)\phi_n^*(x_1)\exp[-iE_n(t_2 - t_1)] & \text{for } t_2 > t_1, \\ 0 & \text{for } t_2 < t_1, \end{cases} \tag{13.17}$$

where n is the number of the stationary state with an energy E_n, and the equation which the function $K(2,1)$ obeys is given by

$$(i\,\partial/\partial t_2 - H_2)K(2, 1) = i\,\delta(2, 1), \tag{13.18}$$

where $\delta(2, 1) = \delta(x_2 - x_1)\,\delta(y_2 - y_1)\,\delta(z_2 - z_1)$ and the subscript 2 on H_2 means that this operator acts on the variable 2 of $K(2, 1)$.

For a particle in a weak potential $U(x, t)$ which differs from zero only for t between t_1 and t_2, one can express the amplitude $K(2, 1)$ in increasing powers of U:

$$K(2, 1) = K_0(2, 1) + K^{(1)}(2, 1) + K^{(2)}(2, 1) + \cdots, \tag{13.19}$$

which gives just the perturbation series expansion of K. Here $K_0(2, 1)$ is the solution of the free particle problem, i.e. when $U = 0$, and the first-order correction $K^{(1)}(2, 1)$ and the second-order correction $K^{(2)}(2, 1)$ may be evaluated according to the formulas

$$K^{(1)}(2, 1) = -i \int K_0(2, 3)U(3)K_0(3, 1)\, d\tau_3, \tag{13.20}$$

$$K^{(2)}(2, 1) = (-i)^2 \iint K_0(2, 4)U(4)K_0(4, 3)U(3)K_0(3, 1)\, d\tau_4\, d\tau_3. \tag{13.21}$$

The next important step was the visualization of the formulas (13.20) and (13.21) with the help of Fig. 13.2.

Next, Feynman dealt with the Dirac equation. 'All that would seem to be necessary in the previous equations is to consider H as the Dirac Hamiltonian, ψ as a symbol with four indices (for each particle). Then K_0 can still be defined by equation (13.17) or (13.18) and is now a 4×4 matrix which, operating on the initial wave function, gives the final wave function. In equations (13.20) and (13.21), $U(3)$ can be generalized to $A_4(3) - \alpha A(3)$, where A_4 and A are the scalar and vector potential (times e, the electron charge) and are Dirac matrices.'[45]

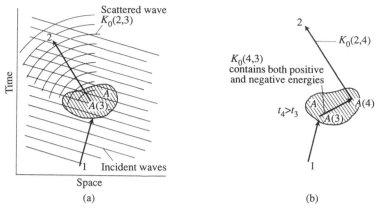

Fig. 13.2 The Schrödinger (and Dirac) equation can be visualized as describing the fact that plane waves are scattered successively by a potential. Figure (a) illustrates the situation in first order. $K_0(2, 3)$ is the amplitude for a free particle starting at a point 3 to arrive at 2. The shaded region indicates the presence of the potential A which scatter at 3 with amplitude $-iA(3)$ per cm^2 sec (equation (13.20)). In (b) is illustrated the second-order process (equation (13.21)), the waves scattered at 3 are scattered again at 4. However, in Dirac one-electron theory $K_0(4, 3)$ would represent electrons both of positive and negative energies proceeding from 3 to 4. This is remedied by choosing a different scattering kernel ($K_+(4, 3)$) (Fig. 13.3).

Feynman then introduced the new convenient relativistic notation: x_μ, where $\mu = 1, 2, 3, 4$, for the four-dimensional coordinates, with $x_4 = t$; A_μ for the scalar and vector potential; γ_μ for the Dirac matrices $\beta\alpha$ and β, which satisfy the anticommutation relation $\gamma_\mu\gamma_\nu + \gamma_\nu\gamma_\mu = 2\delta_{\mu\nu}$ (with $\delta_{11} = -1 = \delta_{22} = \delta_{33}, \delta_{44} = +1$, and the other $\delta_{\mu\nu} = 0$); the symbol $\nabla = \gamma_\mu \, \partial/\partial_\mu$; and a few others. Finally the complex conjugate ϕ_n^* in the corresponding relativistic formula of the type of equation (13.17) must be replaced by its adjoint $\bar{\phi}_n = \phi_n^* \beta$. Then, the Dirac equation for the particle of mass m in an external field $A = A_\mu\gamma_\mu$ becomes

$$(i\nabla - m)\psi = A\psi, \qquad (13.22)$$

and equation (13.18) determining the propagator of a free particle can be written as

$$(i\nabla_2 - m)K_+(2, 1) = 1 \, \delta(2, 1), \qquad (13.23)$$

where the index 2 on ∇_2 indicates the differentiation with respect to the coordinate x_2.

In the presence of the external field, the propagator $K_+^A(2, 1)$ differs from $K_+(2, 1)$ by the first-order correction

$$K_+^{(1)}(2, 1) = -i \int K_+(2, 3)A(3)K_+(3, 1) \, d\tau_3, \tag{13.24}$$

which is analogous to equation (13.20), and by the second-order correction

$$K_+^{(2)}(2, 1) = (-i)^2 \iint K_+(2, 4)A(4)K_+(4, 3)A(3)K_+(3, 1) \, d\tau_4 \, d\tau_3, \tag{13.25}$$

which is analogous to equation (13.21).

Feynman also wrote down the differential and integral equations for the propagator $K_+^A(2, 1)$ in an external field.

The essence of the article on 'The theory of positrons' was the next step: 'We would now expect to choose, for the spatial solution of equation [(13.23)], $K_+ = K_0$, where $K_0(2, 1)$ vanishes for $t_2 < t_1$ and for $t_2 > t_1$ is given by equation [(13.17)], where ϕ_n and E_n are, respectively, the eigenfunctions and energy values of a particle satisfying Dirac's equation, and ϕ_n^* is replaced by $\bar{\phi}_n$.

'The formulas arising from the choice, however, suffer from the drawback that they apply to the one-electron theory of Dirac rather than to the hole theory of the positron. For example, consider as in Fig.[(13.2a)] an electron after being scattered by a potential in a small region 3 of space–time. The one-electron theory says (as does equation (13.17) with $K_+ = K_0$) that the scattered amplitude at another point 2 will proceed toward positive times with both positive and negative energies, that is with both positive and negative rates of change of phase. No wave is scattered to times previous to the times of scattering. These are just the properties of $K_0(2, 3)$.

'On the other hand, according to the positron theory negative energy states are not available to the electron after the scattering. Therefore the choice of $K_+ = K_0$ is unsatisfactory. But there are other solutions of equation (13.23). We shall choose the solution defining $K_+(2, 1)$ so that $K_+(2, 1)$ for $t_2 > t$ is *the sum of* (13.17) *over positive energy states only*. Now this new equation must satisfy (13.23) for all times in order that the representation be complete. It must therefore differ from the old solution K_0 by a solution of a homogeneous Dirac equation. It is clear from the definition that the difference $K_0 - K_+$ is the sum of (13.17) over all negative energy states, as long as $t_2 > t_1$. But this difference must be a solution of the homogeneous Dirac equation for all times and must therefore be represented by the same sum over negative energy states for $t_2 < t_1$. Since $K_0 = 0$ in this case, it follows that our new kernel, $K_+(2, 1)$, for $t_2 < t_1$ is *the negative of the sum* (13.17) *over negative energy states*. That is,

$$K_+(2, 1) = \begin{cases} \sum_{\text{POS } E_n} \phi_n(2)\bar{\phi}_n(1) \exp[-iE_n(t_2 - t_1)] & \text{for } t_2 > t_1, \\ -\sum_{\text{NEG } E_n} \phi_n(2)\bar{\phi}_n(1) \exp[-iE_n(t_2 - t_1)] & \text{for } t_2 < t_1. \end{cases} \tag{13.26}$$

'With this choice of K_+ our equations such as [(13.24)] and [(13.25)] will now give results equivalent to those of the positron hole theory.'[46]

We should add that the propagator (13.26) is just the famous 'Feynman propagator', which plays a fundamental role in quantum field theory, and is also known as the 'causal propagator'. This propagator makes it possible to describe several different physical processes by the same formula depending on the relations of the time variables t_1 and t_2. Thus $P_v|K_+^A(2, 1)|^2$ is the probability that: (a) an electron at 1 will be scattered at 2 (and no other pairs form in vacuum); (b) electron at 1 and positron at 2 annihilate, leaving nothing; (c) a single pair at 1 and 2 is created from vacuum; (d) a positron at 2 is scattered to 1. ($K_+^A(2, 1)$ is the sum of the effects of scattering in the potential to all orders. P_v is a normalizing constant.)'[47]

Now equations (13.24) and (13.25) can be visualized as shown in Fig. 13.3.

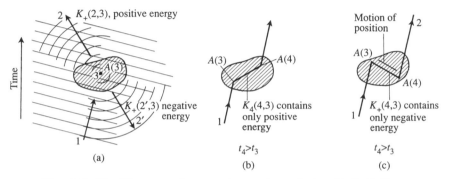

Fig. 13.3. The Dirac equation permits another solution $K_+(2, 1)$ if one considers that waves scattered by the potential can proceed backward in time as in (b). This is interpreted in the second-order processes (b), (c) by noting that there is now the possibility (c) of virtual pair production at 4, the positron going to 3 to be annihilated. This can be pictured as similar to ordinary scattering (b) except that the electron is scattered backwards in time from 3 to 4. The waves scattered from 3 to 2' in (a) represent the possibility of a positron arriving at 3 from 2' and annihilating the electron from 1. This view is proved equivalent to hole theory: electrons traveling backwards in time are recognized as positrons.

Feynman pointed out that, although he had been emphasizing scattering problems, his new method would permit one to consider also the motion of an electron and a positron in a fixed potential V, say in a hydrogen atom, and he explained the corresponding formulas.

Feynman then turned to the problem involving several charges by assuming that these charges do not interact with each other (the problem of interacting charges was treated in Feynman's next paper (Section 13.6)). In this case each particle behaves independently, and the amplitude that the particle a goes from x_1 at t_1 to x_3 at t_3 while the particle b goes from x_2 at t_2 to x_4 at t_4 is given by the product:

$$K(3, 4; 1, 2) = K_{+a}(3, 1)K_{+b}(4, 2). \tag{13.27}$$

The particles with one-half spin, such as electrons and positrons, must satisfy the exclusion principle, which requires only that one calculate $K(3, 4; 1, 2) - K(4, 3; 1, 2)$ to get the net amplitude for the arrival of charges at 3, 4. Feynman showed that no account need be taken of the exclusion principle in the intermediate states because of the definition of the propagator K_+.

Another problem arises even in the case of noninteracting charges, because the probabilities like $|K_+^A(2, 1)|^2$ are not absolute, but only relative, because the absolute probabilities result only after the multiplication of $|K_+^A(2, 1)|^2$ with some other factor P_v, which gives the true probability that if there is no particle present initially there will be no particle present finally. Hence the calculation of P_v is just a vacuum problem, and Feynman showed that $P_v = |C_v|^2$, where C_v is the amplitude for a vacuum to vacuum transition, i.e. for a transition from a vacuum state to another vacuum state through intermediate states in which an arbitrary number of particles may be present. If no potential is present during the time interval, then we consider $C_v = 1$; otherwise, Feynman showed that

$$C_v = 1 - L + \tfrac{1}{2}L^2 - \tfrac{1}{6}L^3 + \cdots = \exp(-L), \tag{13.28}$$

where L is the amplitude of a single closed loop, i.e. of the creation of an electron–positron pair in the vacuum by the potential, followed by the annihilation of the same pair. During the time interval when such a pair exists, there is the possibility to emit one or more virtual photons which will be absorbed at the end by the same particles. Feynman gave the formulas for the calculation of such processes in perturbation theory, according to which L is the sum of all single loops with a different number of virtual photons in intermediate states: $L = L^{(2)} + L^{(2)} + L^{(3)} + \cdots$, where

$$L^{(1)} = \tfrac{1}{2} \iint S_p[K_+(2, 1)A(1)K_+(1, 2)A(2)] \, d\tau_1 \, d\tau_2, \tag{13.29}$$

$$L^{(2)} = \frac{i}{3} \iiint S_p[K_+(2, 1)A(1)K_+(1, 3)A(3)K_+(3, 2)A(2)] \, d\tau_1 \, d\tau_2 \, d\tau_3, \tag{13.30}$$

etc. Then from equation (13.28) one obtains the important formula

$$P_v = |C_v|^2 = \exp(-2 \times \text{real part of } L). \tag{13.31}$$

The minus sign in the exponent in equations (13.28) and (13.31) is due to the Pauli exclusion principle for fermions. Feynman pointed-out that in the corresponding formulas for bosons one must put the sign $+$ before L. It turned out that for the electron–positron pairs the real part of L is positive and the probability P_v is not more than one, as it must be. For the bosons, for example the particles which obey the Klein–Gordon equation, the real part turned out to be negative, and the opposite sign in the formulas (13.28) and (13.31) is needed to get a meaningful value for P_v. It is important to stress another thing. In this article, and in greater detail in the next one,[44] Feynman showed that his approach to antiparticles as particles moving backward in time may be applied not only to fermions but to bosons as well. Pauli and Weisskopf[48] had shown that Dirac's hole theory does not work in the case of spin-0 particles. Hence, Feynman's approach to antiparticles, which was shown to be equivalent to Dirac's hole theory in the case of spin-$\frac{1}{2}$ particles, is actually a more general method as it works in all cases.

The last section of Feynman's paper on 'The theory of positrons', though quite technical, is very important, because it gives a useful new trick to perform the calculations. Feynman noted that the practical evaluation of the matrix elements is often simplified by working with momentum and energy, rather than space and time, variables. This is because the Fourier transform of the function $K_+(2, 1)$ is very simple, namely,

$$\frac{i}{4\pi^2} \frac{1}{p-m}.$$

On the other hand, the very function $K_+(2, 1)$, which may be represented as a Fourier integral

$$K_+(2, 1) = \frac{i}{4\pi^2} \int \frac{1}{p-m} \exp(-ip \cdot x_{21}) \, d^4p \qquad (13.32)$$

has a quite complicated form, which Feynman investigated in detail. If one expands the electromagnetic potential $A(1)$ in a Fourier integral

$$A(1) = \int a(q)\exp(-iq \cdot x_1) \, d^4q, \qquad (13.33)$$

then one can write the matrix elements in a quite simple form, using the Fourier transform $a(q)$ of the potential.

Feynman then gave some additional rules for the calculation of the matrix elements for unpolarized incident states of electrons as well as for the case when we need take into account the spin of the final state. Furthermore, in two final appendices, Feynman gave a detailed deduction of his theory from the method of second quantization. These appendices contained no new physical information, but they were useful for many people who were familiar with this method of treating quantum field-theoretic problems.

13.7 The Oldstone Conference

From 11 to 14 April 1949 there took place the third conference after the war, started by the Shelter Island Conference and followed by the Pocono

Conference, arranged by Robert Oppenheimer to discuss the fundamental problems of theoretical physics, supported by the National Academy of Sciences. The place chosen for this conference was Oldstone-on-the-Hudson in Peekskill, New York. The new participants at this conference were Freeman Dyson, George Placzek, Hideki Yukawa, and Robert Christy.

J. Robert Oppenheimer was again the chairman of the conference, who gave the following account of the previous years' theoretical developments: 'The two years since the first conference have marked some changes in the state of fundamental physics, in large part a consequence of our meetings. The problems of electrodynamics which appeared so insoluble at our first meeting, and which began to yield during the following year, have now reached a certain solution; and it is possible, though in these matters prediction is hazardous, that the subject will remain closed for some time, pending the accumulation of new physical experience from domains at present only barely accessible. The study of mesons and of nuclear structures has also made great strides; but in this domain we have learned more and more convincingly that we are still far from a description which is either logical, consistent, or in accord with experience.'[49]

While at the Pocono Conference attention was paid mainly to Julian Schwinger's achievements in quantum electrodynamics, at the Oldstone Conference Feynman's approach became the central topic of discussion. Its great power and usefulness was obvious at that time and everybody was trying to understand Feynman's rules in order to proceed with making quantum electrodynamical calculations in meson theory, which now became the central unsolved problem of fundamental physics.

Very interesting, too, was the talk given by Dyson, who reported his results on the equivalence of the theories of Tomonaga, Schwinger, and Feynman.

It became clear that quantum electrodynamics, with a proper renormalization procedure, is a good enough basis to explain the experimental data and to contribute to the development of physics in the right direction in the succeeding years. Unpublished notes of this conference were prepared by John A. Wheeler and Arthur S. Wightman, which are to be found in the Oppenheimer Collection at the Library of Congress in Washington, D.C.

Notes and References

1. R.P. Feynman, A relativistic cut-off for classical electrodynamics. *Phys. Rev.* **74**, 939 (1948).

2. R.P. Feynman, Ref. 1, p. 939.

3. R.P. Feynman, Ref. 1, p. 941.

4. R.P. Feynman, Ref. 1, p. 942.

5. R.P. Feynman, Ref. 1, p. 943.

6. H. Saleckar, *Naturforschung* **8a**, 16 (1953); **10a**, 349 (1955).

7. R.P. Feynman, Ref. 1, pp. 943–44.

8. R.P. Feynman, A relativistic cut-off for quantum electrodynamics, *Phys. Rev.* **74**, 1430 (1948).

9. R.P. Feynman, Ref. 8, p. 1430.

10. H.W. Lewis, *Phys. Rev.* **73**, 173 (1948).

11. J.S. Schwinger, *Phys. Rev.* **74**, 1439 (1948).

12. R.P. Feynman, The development of the space-time view of quantum electrodynamics, Nobel Lecture, 11 December 1965, Stockholm, Sweden, *Science* **153**, 699 (1966). p. 8.

13. R.P. Feynman, Ref. 8, pp. 1433–34.

14. F. Bloch and A. Nordsieck, *Phys. Rev.* **52**, 54 (1937).

15. S.M. Dancoff, *Phys. Rev.* **55**, 959 (1939).

16. R.P. Feynman, Ref. 8, p. 1436.

17. R.P. Feynman, Ref. 8, p. 1437.

18. E.A. Uehling, *Phys. Rev.* **48**, 55 (1935)

19. R.P. Feynman, Ref. 8, 1438.

20. G. Wataghin, *Z. Phys.* **88**, 92 (1934).

21. R.P. Feynman, Interviews and conversations with Jagdish Mehra, in Austin, Texas, April 1970, Pasadena, California, January 1988; Interviews with Charles Weiner, 1966.

22. R.P. Feynman, Ref. 21, Interviews and conversations with Jagdish Mehra, 1988.

23. R.P. Feynman, Remarks at the banquet in honor of J. Schwinger's sixtieth birthday, February 1978. (Courtesy of R. Finkelstein, University of California at Los Angeles.)

24. N.M. Kroll and W.E. Lamb, Jr., *Phys. Rev.* **75**, 388 (1949).

25. V.F. Weisskopf, Growing up with quantum field theory: The development of quantum electrodynamics. In: *The birth of particle physics* (ed. L.M. Brown and L. Hoddeson). Cambridge University Press, 1983.

26. R.P. Feynman, Space–time approach to quantum electrodynamics. *Phys. Rev.* **76**, 769(1949), p. 777.

27. F.J. Dyson, Interview with Jagdish Mehra, in Princeton, New Jersey, 25 February 1987.

28. F.J. Dyson, *Phys. Rev.* **75**, 486 (1949); *Phys. Rev.* **75**, 736 (1949).

29. R.P. Feynman, Letter to H.A. Bethe, 7 July 1948. Bethe Papers, Cornell University Archives, Ithaca, New York.

30. R.P. Feynman, Letter to H.A. Bethe, 22 July 1948, Bethe Papers, Cornell University Archives, Ithaca, New York.

31. F.J. Dyson, Letter to parents, 1 November 1948. (Courtesy F.J. Dyson.)

32. R.P. Feynman, Letter to F.J. Dyson, 29 October 1948. Feynman Archive, Caltech.

33. W.H. Furry, *Phys. Rev.* **51**, 125 (1937).

34. R.P. Feynman, Ref. 21.

35. R.P. Feynman, Letter to T.A. Welton, 30 October 1948, Feynman Archive, Caltech.

36. R.P. Feynman, Notes entitled 'Theory of positrons', fall 1947, Feynman Archive, Caltech.

37. R.P. Feynman, 'T5. The theory of positrons', unpublished manuscript of a talk given at the January 1949 American Physical Society meeting, New York. Feynman Archive, Caltech.

38. W.J. Rainwater, I.I. Rabi, and W.W. Havens, Jr., *Phys. Rev.* **75**, 1295(A) (1949).

39. R.P. Feynman, Ref 12, p. 8.

40. W. Pauli, Letter to H.A. Bethe, 25 January 1949, Bethe Papers, Cornell University Archives, Ithaca, New York.

41. W. Pauli, Letter to J.S. Schwinger, 24 January 1949. Oppenheimer Papers, Library of Congress Archives, Washington, D.C.

42. W. Pauli and F. Villars, *Rev. Mod. Phys.* **21**, 434 (1949).

43. R.P. Feynman, The theory of positrons, *Phys. Rev.* **76**, 749 (1949).

44. R.P. Feynman, Space-time approach to quantum electrodynamics, *Phys. Rev.* **76**, 769 (1949).

45. R.P. Feynman, Ref. 43, p. 749.

46. R.P. Feynman, Ref. 43, p. 752.

47. R.P. Feynman, Ref. 43, p. 753.

48. W. Pauli and V.F. Weisskopf, *Helv. Phys. Acta*, **7**, 709 (1934).

49. J.R. Oppenheimer, Letter on NAS post war conferences, 4 January 1949.

14

The space–time approach to quantum electrodynamics

14.1 Introduction

The basic principles and techniques of Feynman's new approach to quantum electrodynamics were described in his article on the 'Space–time approach to quantum electrodynamics'.[1] This article was written practically simultaneously with the preceding one on 'The theory of positrons'[2] (see Section 13.6), which was cited as I; the present article was a direct continuation of it. In this paper, Feynman considered the entire quantum electrodynamical description of the electromagnetic interaction between charged particles and the photon field, including the interaction between the charges themselves, which was neglected in I. This paper was received by the *Physical Review* on 9 May 1949, shortly after the Oldstone Conference, and published just twenty pages after 'The theory of positrons'.

Feynman introduced his new article by saying: 'In this paper two things are done: (1) It is shown that a considerable simplification can be attained in writing down the matrix elements for complex processes in electrodynamics. Further, a physical point of view is available which permits them to be written down directly for any physical problem. Being simply a restatement of conventional electrodynamics, however, the matrix elements diverge for complex processes. (2) Electrodynamics is modified by altering the interaction of electrons at short distances. All matrix elements are now finite, with the exception of those relating to problems of vacuum polarization. The latter are evaluated in a manner suggested by Pauli and Bethe, which gives finite results for these matrices also. The only effects sensitive to the modification are changes in the mass and charge of the electrons. Such changes could not be directly observed. Phenomena directly observable are insensitive to the details of the modification used (except at extreme energies). For such phenomena, a limit can be taken as the range of modification goes to zero. The results then agree with those of Schwinger. A complete, unambiguous, and presumably consistent method is therefore available for the calculation of all processes involving electrons and photons.

The simplification in writing the expressions results from an emphasis on the overall space–time view resulting from a study of the solution of equations of electrodynamics. The relation of this to the more conventional Hamiltonian point of view is discussed. It would be very difficult to make the modification which is proposed if one insisted on having the equation in Hamiltonian form.

'The methods apply as well to charges obeying the Klein–Gordon equation, and to the various meson theories of nuclear forces. Illustrative examples are given. Although a modification like that used in electrodynamics can make all matrices finite for all of the meson theories it is no longer true that all directly observable phenomena are insensitive to the details of the modification used.'[3]

In this fundamental article, Feynman explained his new perturbation theory, in which the matrix elements were worked out as expansions in powers of the dimensionless coupling constant α ($= e^2/\hbar c$). Considerable simplification in writing down these elements was achieved for complex processes mainly from the fact that the old methods unnecessarily separated into individual terms closely related processes such as the effects of longitudinal and transverse waves, etc. This separation was made on a nonrelativistic basis. In Feynman's approach, the related processes were combined in a completely relativistic manner, and the results looked quite simple.

Feynman said this about the genesis of his space–time theoretical view of quantum electrodynamics: 'The conventional electrodynamics was expressed in the Lagrangian form of quantum mechanics.[4] The motion of the field oscillators could be integrated out, the result being an expression of the delayed interaction of the particles. Next the modification of the delta-function could be made directly from the analogy to the classical case.[5] This was still not complete because the Lagrangian method had been worked out in detail only for particles obeying the nonrelativistic Schrödinger equation. It was then modified in accordance with the requirements of the Dirac equation and the phenomenon of pair creation. This was made easier by the reinterpretation of the theory of holes (I). Finally, for practical calculations the expressions were developed in a power series in $e^2/\hbar c$. It was apparent that each term in the series had a simple physical interpretation. Since the result was easier to understand than the derivation, it was thought best to publish the results first in this paper. Considerable time has been spent to make these first two papers as complete and as physically plausible without relying on the Lagrangian method [that is, Feynman's path-integral method] because it is not generally familiar. It is realized that such description cannot carry the conviction of truth which would accompany the derivation. On the other hand, in the interest of keeping simple things simple the derivation will appear in a separate paper.'[6]

Feynman's prescription of the complex processes was to deal directly with the solutions of the time evolution equations, which Feynman had called Hamiltonian equations, rather than by investigating these equations themselves. He looked at the whole space–time evolution of a given system at once, rather than tracing this evolution in detail at every instant of time. He stressed that electrodynamics can be expressed in two equivalent and complementary forms. In the more usual Hamiltonian form one has the description of the *field* by Maxwell's equations. The other form is a description of a direct action-at-a-distance (albeit delayed in time) (see Sections 5.1 and 5.2). Both the forms have some advantages and shortcomings. The action-at-a-distance form is a more impractical point of view, since it is based on the interaction of the sources with absorbers. In it many different kinds of causes may produce the same kinds of effects. In the field picture all possible processes are described as a simple emission and absorption of light. But this point of view is less practical when one considers the close collisions of charged particles, where the source and the absorber are not well distinguishable. Therefore, Feynman arrived at the conclusion that 'the field point of view is most practical for problems involving real quanta, while the interaction view is best for the discussion of the virtual quanta involved'.[7]

Here one can see an important change in the evolution of Feynman's belief about the two forms of electrodynamics. He did not insist anymore on the action-at-a-distance theory as the only right form. Instead of this he tried to use both the forms in a most practical way. In addition, his earlier experience with the action-at-a-distance theory was very useful in developing the new ideas that were needed for his theory of quantum electrodynamics.

The Hamiltonian method is not well adapted to describe the direct action between charges. In many typical quantum problems, as for example the close collisions between particles, we are not interested in the detailed description of the time evolution, and the Hamiltonian form is not really practical. Feynman noted: 'We shall be discussing the solutions of the equations rather than the differential equations from which they come. We shall discover that the solutions, because of the *overall space–time view* that they permit, are as easy to understand when interactions are delayed as when they are instantaneous.'[8]

This new philosophy was extremely useful in developing Feynman's new approach to quantum electrodynamics and in overcoming many difficulties, both technical and of principle, of the old theory. In the Hamiltonian form of the equations, one has to follow the time evolution and, therefore, to use the nonrelativistic notion of separate time and three-dimensional space coordinates. The temporal analysis of different observers will lead to different pictures in their Hamiltonian prescription of the processes, which are irrelevant because the solution is the same in space–time form. Hence Feynman's important conclusion that, 'by forsaking the Hamiltonian method, the wedding of relativity and quantum mechanics can be accomplished most naturally.'[8]

14.2 The interaction between charges

First, Feynman derived the relativistic form of the interaction between charged particles with one-half spin in quantum electrodynamics. His starting point was the amplitude $K_0(3, 4; 1, 2)$ for the case that the particle a at point x_1 at the time instant t_1 will get to the point x_3 at the time instant t_3, and the particle b at the point x_2 at the time instant t_2 will get to the point x_4 at the time instant t_4. If the particles do not interact, this amplitude is the simple product of the separate amplitudes $K_{0a}(3, 1)$ and $K_{0b}(4, 2)$, the first being the amplitude that the particle a at point x_1 at instant t_1 will get to point x_3 at time instant t_3 when the particle b does not exist, and the second being the amplitude that the particle b at point x_2 at instant t_2 will get to point x_4 at instant t_4 when the particle a does not exist; thus

$$K_0(3, 4; 1, 2) = K_{0a}(3, 1) K_{0b}(4, 2). \tag{14.1}$$

This formula was discussed in detail in paper I (Ref. 2) for noninteracting particles (see Section 13.6, equation (13.27)). For interacting charged particles the quantity $K_0(3, 4; 1, 2)$ may be defined precisely if the interaction vanishes between the instants t_1 and t_2, and also between t_3 and t_4. For practical problems this means that we have to choose such long time intervals $t_3 - t_1$ and $t_4 - t_2$ that the interaction near the end points will give relatively small effects on the final result.

Feynman guessed the form of the relativistic invariant amplitude $K(3, 4; 1, 2)$ for spin-$\frac{1}{2}$ interacting particles by using the analogy with the nonrelativistic spinless case. He first considered the interaction by a Coulomb potential e^2/r, where r is the distance between two particles. The nonrelativistic Coulomb potential does not act instantaneously. We can represent $K(3, 4; 1, 2)$ formally as an integral over all t_5 and t_6, i.e. as if the potential were on at all times. But then we must include a delta-function $\delta(t_5 - t_6)$, to ensure a contribution only when $t_5 = t_6$, in order to take into account the instantaneous character of the nonrelativistic Coulomb interaction. As a result, using the notation $r_{56} = r_5 - r_6$ and $t_{56} = t_5 - t_6$, Feynman wrote the following formula:

$$K^1(3, 4; 1, 2)$$

$$= -ie^2 \iint K_{0a}(3, 5) K_{0b}(4, 6) r_{56}^{-1} \delta(t_{56}) K_{0a}(5, 1) K_{0b}(6, 2) \, d\tau_5 \, d\tau_6. \tag{14.2}$$

But, as we know, in relativistic classical electrodynamics the Coulomb interaction is delayed by a time r_{56}, taking the speed of light as unity. To take into account this effect of the finite speed of light we must replace the expression $r_{56}^{-1} \delta(t_{56})$ in equation (14.2) by something like $r_{56}^{-1} \delta(t_{56} - r_{56})$. This turned out to be not completely right, because the Fourier transform of $\delta(t_{56} - r_{56})$ contains the frequencies of both signs. As we know, the interaction, when represented by photons, must include only quanta with positive energies, i.e. only positive frequencies in the Fourier transform of the interaction potential are admissible. This means that the delta-function $\delta(t_{56} - r_{56})$ must be replaced by the positive frequency delta-function

$\delta_+(t_{56}-r_{56})$ (see Section 12.3, equation (12.12)). This result must be averaged with the analogous term $r_{56}^{-1}\delta_+(-t_{56}-r_{56})$, which corresponds to the emission of a quantum which b receives when $t_5 < t_6$. This average value is

$$\tfrac{1}{2}[r_{56}^{-1}\delta_+(t_{56}-r_{56})+r_{56}^{-1}\delta_+(-t_{56}-r_{56})]=\delta_+(t_{56}^2-r_{56}^2)=\delta_+(s_{56}^2).$$

Hence, in the final formula, $r_{56}^{-1}\delta(t_{56})$ must be replaced by $\delta(s_{56}^2)$. But there still remains one problem. The formulas (13.20) and (13.22) are written for the scalar potential. Since, in classical electrodynamics, interaction is through the vector potential, instead of $\delta(s_{56}^2)$, we should have $(1-v_5v_6)\,\delta(s_{56}^2)$ for the classical particles (see Section 12.3, equation (12.14), and the following explanation), and

$$(1-\alpha_a\alpha_b)\,\delta(s_{56}^2)=\beta_a\beta_b\gamma_{a\mu}\gamma_{b\mu}\,\delta(s_{56}^2)$$

for spin-$\tfrac{1}{2}$ quantum relativistic particles. Hence, for the particles obeying the Dirac equation, the final form of the first-order interaction is given by

$$K^{(1)}(3,4;1,2)= -ie^2\iint K_{+a}(3,5)K_{+b}(4,6)\gamma_{a\mu}\gamma_{b\mu}\,\delta_+(s_{56}^2)$$

$$\times K_{+a}(5,1)K_{+b}(6,2)\,d\tau_5\,d\tau_6. \quad (14.3)$$

Here γ_μ and β are the corresponding Dirac matrices.

Equation (14.3) is the fundamental equation in Feynman's approach to quantum electrodynamics. After the above intuitive derivation of this equation, Feynman wrote: '... It describes the effect of exchange of one quantum (therefore first order in e^2) between electrons. It will serve as a prototype enabling us to write down the corresponding quanties involving the exchange of two or more quanta between two electrons or the interaction of an electron with itself. It is a consequence of conventional electrodynamics. Relativistic invariance is clear. Since one sums over μ it contains the effects of both longitudinal and transverse waves in a relativistically symmetrical way.

'We shall interpret equation [(14.3)] in a manner which will permit us to write down the higher-order terms. It can be understood [see Fig. 14.1] as saying that the amplitude for "a" to go from 2 to 4 is altered to first order because they can exchange a quantum. Thus "a" can go to 5 (amplitude $K_+(5,1)$), emit a quantum (longitudinal, transverse, or scalar $\gamma_{a\mu}$), and then proceed to 3 [$K_+(3,5)$]. Meantime "b" goes to 6 [$K_+(6,2)$], absorbs the quantum ($\gamma_{b\mu}$) and proceeds to 4 [$K_+(4,6)$]. The quantum meanwhile proceeds from 5 to 6, which it does with amplitude $\delta(s_{56}^2)$. We must sum over all the possible quantum polarizations and positions and times of emission 5, and of absorption 6. Actually, if $t_5 > t_6$, it would be better to say that "a" absorbs and "b" emits but no attention need be paid to these matters, as all such alternatives are contained in equation [(14.3)].'[9]

Figure 14.1 shows the simplest Feynman diagram of the first order (in $e^2/\hbar c$)

process, which describes the exchange of one photon between two electrons. According to Feynman's rules, given above, the expression (14.3) corresponds to this process, and it gives the corresponding quantum amplitude for the described process in the coordinate representation. This was indeed one of Feynman's most important inventions, namely, the visualization of fundamental processes. This achievement of Feynman's was extremely useful in understanding and developing quantum field theory in simple and natural terms, rather than only in abstract mathematical ones.

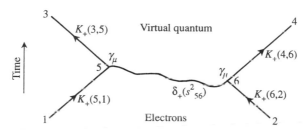

Fig. 14.1. The fundamental interaction equation (14.3). Exchange of one quantum between two electrons.

Feynman proceeded to explain the significance of equation (14.3) further: 'Although in the expression stemming from [(14.3)] the quanta are virtual, this is not actually a theoretical limitation. One way to deduce the correct rules for real quanta from [(14.3)] is to note that in a closed system all quanta can be considered as virtual (i.e. they have known sources and are eventually absorbed) so that in such a system the present description is complete and equivalent to the conventional one. In particular, the relation of Einstein's A and B coefficients can be deduced. A more practical direct deduction of the expressions for real quanta will be given in a subsequent paper. It might be noted that [(14.3)] can be rewritten as describing the action on a,

$$K^{(1)}(3, 1) = i \int K_+(3, 5)A(5)K_+(5, 1)\,d\tau_5,\qquad(14.4)$$

of the potential

$$A_\mu(5) = e^2 \int K_+(4, 6)\,\delta_+(s_{56}^2)\gamma_\mu K_+(6, 2)\,d\tau_4\qquad(14.5)$$

arising from Maxwell's equations $-\square^2 A_\mu = 4\pi j_\mu$ from a "current"

$$j_\mu(6) = e^2 K_+(4, 6)\gamma_\mu K_+(6, 2)$$

produced by particle b in going from 2 to 4. This is by virtue of the fact that $-\square\delta_+$ satisfies $-\square^2\,\delta_+(s_{21}^2) = 4\pi\,\delta(2, 1)$.'[10]

The last form of the fundamental interaction (equations (14.4) and (14.5)), given by Feynman as a footnote, is more general than the form (14.3), and allows one to describe the interaction of the Dirac particles also with external electromagnetic fields.

In this section Feynman also discussed the exclusion principle, which turned out to work exactly as in the case of noninteracting particles described in I (Ref. 2) (see Section 13.5), as well as the influence of the Bose statistics of the quanta on the results.

14.3 The self-energy problem

Feynman first used his new technique to calculate the self-energy of the electron to the first-order in perturbation theory in powers of the constant $e^2/\hbar c$. He wrote: 'Having the term representing the mutual interaction of a pair of charges, we must include similar terms to represent the interaction of a charge with itself. For under some circumstances what appears to be two distinct electrons may, according to I, be viewed also as a single electron (namely in case one electron was created in a pair with a positron destined to annihilate the other electron). Thus to the interaction between such electrons must correspond the possibility of the action of an electron on itself.'[10]

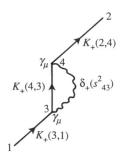

Fig. 14.2. Interaction of an electron with itself.

The corresponding first-order diagram in configuration space is shown in Fig. 14.2. To this diagram corresponds, according to the Feynman rules, the following expression for the amplitude in the first order of perturbation theory:

$$K^{(1)}(2, 1) = -ie^2 \iint K_+(2, 4)\gamma_\mu K_+(4, 3)\gamma_\mu K_+(3, 1)\, d\tau_3\, d\tau_4\, \delta_+(s_{43}^2). \quad (14.6)$$

We can connect this expression with the self-energy of the free electron if we calculate the diagonal matrix element of this amplitude between the electron states $f=g$, which are positive energy solutions of the Dirac equation for the free electron; hence, they may be represented as $u \exp(-ip \cdot x)$, where p is the energy (p_4) and momentum (p) of the electron $(p^2 = m^2)$, and u is a constant 4-index symbol (a spinor, in modern terminology). If the wave functions are normalized to unit volume, the matrix element of the amplitude (14.6) between such states gives the first-order correction, $i(\Delta E)(t_2 - t_1)$, to the factor $\exp[-i(\Delta E)(t_2 - t_1)]$ in the amplitude for arrival in state $f(2)$ at time instant t_2, starting from the state $f(1)$ at time instant t_1. Thus the whole effect is equivalent to a change of the energy ΔE, given by the expression

$$\Delta E = e^2 \int (\bar{u}\gamma_\mu K_+(4, 3)\gamma_\mu u) \exp(ip \cdot x_{43}) \, \delta_+(s_{43}^2) \, d\tau_4. \tag{14.7}$$

Similarly, one can obtain an expression for the energy shift in the hydrogen atom. For this purpose, one needs to replace the amplitude for the free electron K_+ in formula (14.7) with the corresponding amplitude K_+ of the electron in the potential $V = \beta e^2/r$ of the atom, and the free state f by a wave function (of space and time) for an atomic state. The real evaluation of expressions like (14.7) can be performed more easily by the technique which Feynman described next.

14.4 Expression in momentum and energy space: the Feynman diagrams

The calculation of matrix elements is most simple in the energy and momentum representation. The reason is quite simple. In this representation all Hamiltonian equations for free particles, like the Dirac equation, the Klein–Gordon equation, and Maxwell's equations, transform into algebraic equations which have very simple solutions. Taking into account the formula (13.32) for the Fourier transform of the K_+ function, the formula (13.33) for the Fourier transform of the electromagnetic four-potential, and the formula for the Fourier transform of the δ_+-function,

$$-\delta_+(s_{21}^2) = \pi^{-1} \int \exp(-ik \cdot x_{21}) k^{-2} \, d^4k. \tag{14.8}$$

we can rewrite all the expressions for the quantum amplitude, or its matrix elements, in the momentum and energy representation. The resulting formulas need to be justfied by some rules for giving unambiguous meaning to the corresponding expressions. For example, in equation (14.8) we have to understand the term k^{-2} as the limit $\varepsilon \to +0$ of $(k_\mu k_\mu + i\varepsilon)^{-1}$,[11] i.e. certain rules for going around the poles of the corresponding singular functions in the Fourier integrals are needed. Already in paper I,[2] Feynman had proved that such rules are equivalent to the proper choice of the solution of the quantum dynamical equations. For example, in equation (11.32), one can understand the function $(p-m)^{-1}$ as $(p-m+i\varepsilon)^{-1}$, with $\varepsilon \to +0$, to obtain just the Feynman propagator K_+.[12] All such rules can be expressed in a general rule, according to which the masses of all particles and quanta have infinitesimal negative imaginary parts.

Using these rules, Feynman represented the self-energy, equation (14.8), as a matrix between $\bar{u}$ and u of the matrix

$$(e^2/\pi i) \int \gamma_\mu (p-k-m)^{-1} \gamma_\mu k^{-2} \, d^4k, \tag{14.9}$$

which obviously has quite a simple form, and wrote: 'The equation [(14.9)] can be understood by imagining [see Fig. 14.3] that the electron of momentum p emits (γ_μ) a quantum of momentum k, and makes its way now with momentum $p-k$ to the next event [factor $(p-k-m)^{-1}$] which is to absorb the quantum [another (γ_μ)]. The amplitude of propagation of quanta is k^{-2}. (There is a factor $e^2/\pi i$ for each virtual quantum.) One integrates over all quanta. The reason an electron of momentum p propagates as $1/(p-m)$ is that this operator is reciprocal to the Dirac equation operator, and we are simply solving this equation. Likewise light goes as $1/k^2$, for this is the reciprocal Dalembertian operator of the wave equation of light. The first γ_μ represents the current which generates the vector potential, while the second is the velocity operator by which this potential is multiplied in the Dirac equation when an external field acts on an electron.'[12]

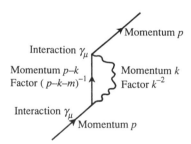

Fig. 14.3. Interaction of an electron with itself. Momentum space, equation (14.9).

These rules permit one to describe via the corresponding diagrams every process in quantum electrodynamics and to write down the matrix elements of the amplitude of this process. Today, these rules are the most well known part of Feynman's approach to quantum electrodynamics and, in general, to field theory and statistical physics. The practical usefulness of the Feynman rules and diagrams made them one of the most essential elements of the scientific training of every theoretical physicist.

As Feynman recalled many years later: '. . . The diagrams were intended to represent physical processes and the mathematical expressions used to describe them. Each diagram signified a mathematical expression. In these diagrams I was seeing things that happened in space and time. Mathematical quantities were associated with points in space and time. I would see electrons going along, being scattered at one point, then going over to another point and getting scattered there, emitting a photon and the photon goes over there. I would make little pictures of all that was going on; these were physical pictures involving the mathematical terms. These pictures evolved only gradually in my mind. There were some old pictures that were quite similar, but not as clean and as final as the diagrams I was drawing; they became a shorthand for the processes I was trying to describe physically and mathematically.

'The diagrams became very important as I began to treat more and more of these problems. They became pictorial representations of the more and more abstract things I was trying to describe. I remember that when I was at the Telluride House (at Cornell) and was working on the self-energy of the electron, there were many terms which I was trying to visualize, when it occurred to me that these pictures looked very funny. In ancient Egypt and Greece the priests and oracles used to look at the veins in sheep's livers to forecast the future, and that's the kind of pictures I was drawing to describe physical phenomena. I thought that if they really turn out to be useful it would be fun to see them in the pages of the *Physical Review*. I was conscious of the thought that it would be amusing to see these funny-looking pictures in the *Physical Review*.'[13]

The Feynman rules for the matrix elements in spinor electrodynamics in modern form are summarized in Table 14.1.[14] This is just Feynman's 'handbook on how to do quantum electrodynamics'.[15]

By making use of these rules, Feynman wrote down the matrix elements for a different kind of process in quantum electrodynamics. For example, the total matrix element for the Compton scattering of an electron in second-order perturbation theory is then

$$e_2(p_1 + q_1 - m)^{-1}e_1 + e_1(p_1 + q_2 - m)^{-1}e_2. \qquad (14.10)$$

According to Feynman's rules this expression corresponds to two possible diagrams for Compton scattering as shown in Fig. 14.4. One has to take the matrix elements of the expression (14.10) to obtain the Klein–Nishina formula.

For the radiative corrections to the scattering of the electron in the lowest order of perturbation theory, Feynman gave three diagrams, which are shown in Fig. 14.5.[16] The three diagrams differ in the ordering of the processes of scattering of the electron, and of the emission and absorption of the photon. Feynman remarked that the expressions so obtained for various processes 'are, as has been indicated, no more than the re-expression of conventional quantum electrodynamics. As a consequence, many of them are meaningless. For example, the self-energy expression [(14.7)] or [(14.9)] gives an infinite

Table 14.1. Feynman's Rules

	Element of the Feynman's diagram	Factor in the matrix element
1	Electron in the initial state with momentum p 	$(2\pi^{-3/2}u^{s,-}(p)$
2	Positron in the initial state with momentum p 	$(2\pi^{-3/2}\bar{u}^{s,-}(p)$
3	Electron in the final state with momentum p 	$(2\pi^{-3/2}\bar{u}^{s,+}(p)$
4	Positron in the final state with momentum p 	$(2\pi^{-3/2}u^{s,+}(p)$
5	Photon in the initial or final state with polarization e_v and momentum k 	$\dfrac{e_\mu^v}{(2\pi)^{3/2}\sqrt{2k_0}}\ (v\neq 0)$
6	Motion of an electron from 1 to 2 (or of a positron from 2 to 1) 	$\dfrac{1}{(2\pi)^4 i}\displaystyle\int d^4p\ \dfrac{m+p}{m^2-p^2-i\varepsilon}$
7	Motion of a photon between vertices with summation indices μ and v 	$\dfrac{q^{\mu v}}{(2\pi)^4 i}\displaystyle\int d^4k\ \dfrac{1}{k^2+i\varepsilon}$
8	Vertex with summation index v with electron line p_1 and photon line k incoming, and electron p_2 outgoing 	i.e. $\gamma^v(2\pi)^4\delta(p_2-p_1-k)$

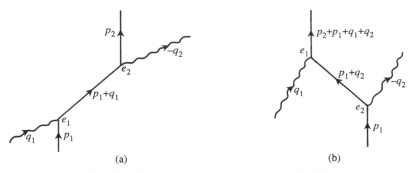

Fig. 14.4. Compton scattering, equation (14.10).

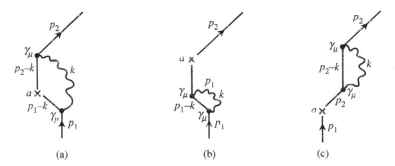

Fig. 14.5. Radiative correction to scattering, momentum space.

result when calculated. The infinity arises, apparently, from the coincidence of the δ-function singularities in $K_+(4,3)$ and $\delta(s_{43}^2)$. Only at this point is it necessary to make a real departure from conventional electrodynamics, a departure other than simply rewriting expressions in a simpler form.'[16]

In order to overcome the difficulties with the divergences connected with virtual quanta, Feynman made use of the regularization procedure which he had invented earlier[5, 17] (see Sections 13.1 and 13.2). Using this procedure with a little modification, he obtained for the expression (14.10), which gives the self-energy of the free electron, the result,

$$(e^2/2\pi)\{4m[\ln(\lambda/m)+\tfrac{1}{2}]-p[\ln(\lambda/m)+\tfrac{5}{4}]\}, \qquad (14.11)$$

up to terms in higher order of the ratio λ/m of Feynman's cut-off parameter λ and the mass m of the electron. When applied to the state of the free electron with momentum p, satisfying the Dirac equation, the equation (14.7) gives the change of the mass,

$$\Delta m = m(e^2/2\pi)[3(\ln(\lambda/m)+\tfrac{3}{4}]. \qquad (14.12)$$

For the radiation corrections to the scattering, the sum of three terms (which corresponds to the three Feynman diagrams in Fig. 14.5 leads [for small momentum transfer q ($\sqrt{q^2} = 2m \sin \theta$, θ being the scattering angle)] to the result:

$$(e^2/2\pi) \left\{ \frac{1}{2m}(qa - aq) + \frac{4q^2}{3m^2} a \left[\ln\left(\frac{m}{\lambda_{\min}}\right) - \frac{3}{8} \right] \right\}. \tag{14.13}$$

Here a is the amplitude of the four-dimensional electromagnetic potential $A = A_\mu \gamma_\mu$, which is supposed to be of the form $a \exp(-iqx)$, and $\lambda_{\min}$ is the small mass of the proton: $\lambda_{\min} < m < \lambda$, which has to be introduced to avoid infrared divergences, according to Bloch and Nordsieck (see Section 11.4). This formula shows the change of the magnetic moment of the electron in accordance with Schwinger's result, and the Lamb shift as was interpreted in greater detail by Feynman previously[17] (see Section 13.2). It is remarkable that the result (14.13) does not depend on the regularization procedure at all, assuming that the mass m is the experimental mass of the electron.

Feynman then discussed some of the difficulties of his regularization procedure, which is good enough only in the limit when λ goes to infinity, after mass renormalization. He concluded: 'I have no proof of the mathematical consistency of this procedure, but the presumption is very strong that it is satisfactory.'[18]

14.5 The problem of vacuum polarization

In his article on the 'Space–time approach to quantum electrodynamics', Feynman published for the first time his point of view on the problem of vacuum polarization. The problem arises, for instance, in the analysis of the radiative corrections to scattering, where one type of term was not considered until now. The potential, on which the electron scatters, was assumed to vary as $a_\mu \exp(ip \cdot x)$, and the direct scattering on this external potential—in the lowest order of perturbation theory—corresponds to the diagram shown in Fig. 14.6(a). This diagram is a part of the diagrams shown in Fig. 14.5. But the same potential may create an electron–positron pair (see Fig. 14.6(b)) which then reannihilates, emitting a quantum with momentum $q = p_a - p_b$. This quantum scatters the original electron from state 1 to state 2.

The matrix element connected with the diagram for the process indicated in Fig. 14.6(b) is given by the expression

$$-(e^2/\pi i)\bar{u}_2 \gamma_\mu u_1) \int S_p[(p_a + q - m)^{-1} \gamma_\nu (p_a - m)^{-1} \gamma_\mu] q^{-2} a_\nu \, d^4 p, \tag{14.14}$$

where no regularization has been made. One can imagine that the closed loop of the electron–positron pair is equivalent to the current

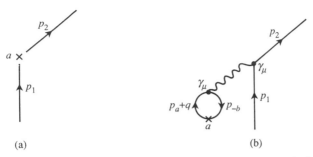

Fig. 14.6. (a) Direct scattering of the electron; (b) vacuum polarization
effect on scattering, equation (14.14).

$$4\pi j_\mu = J_{\mu\nu} a_\nu,\tag{14.15}$$

which produces the quantum acting on the electron. The quantity $J_{\mu\nu}$, characteristic of the vacuum polarization problem in the lowest order of perturbation theory, is then given by

$$J_{\mu\nu} = -(e^2/\pi l)\,(\bar{u}_2\gamma_\mu u_1)\int S_\mathrm{p}[(p_a+q-m)^{-1}\gamma_\nu(p_a-m)^{-1}\gamma_\mu]\,d^4p.\tag{14.16}$$

The integral in equation (14.16) is badly divergent. The use of the Feynman regularization was not able to lead to a convergent result here, because in equation (14.16) there is no photon propagator which could be modified by such a procedure. In his 1948 paper,[17] Feynman had proposed an analogous modification of the electron propagator. Although it does lead to the convergence of the expression (14.16), this procedure has another difficulty: it spoils the gauge invariance and, thereby, the corresponding fundamental law of conservation of the electric charge and the current j_μ. In the momentum and energy representation the conservation of the electric current leads to the condition

$$q_\mu J_{\mu\nu} = 0\tag{14.17}$$

for the symmetric quantity $J_{\mu\nu} = J_{\nu\mu}$, which turned out to be broken under the Wataghin-like renormalization of the electron propagator, when Feynman had first tried to overcome the vacuum polarization divergence (see Section 13.2).

Now, however, this problem could be treated because 'A method of making [(14.16)] convergent without spoiling the gauge invariance has been found by Bethe and by Pauli. The convergence factor for light can be looked upon as the result of superposition of the effects of quanta of various masses (some contributing negatively). . . .. (If) the quantity [(14.14)], integrated over some finite range of p, is called $J_{\mu\nu}(m^2)$ and the corresponding quantity over the same range of p, but with m replaced by $(m^2 + \lambda^2)^{1/2}$ is $J_{\mu\nu}(m^2 + \lambda^2)$ we should calculate

$$J^p_{\mu\nu} = \int_0^\infty [J_{\mu\nu}(m^2) - J_{\mu\nu}(m^2 + \lambda^2)]G(\lambda)\, d\lambda, \tag{14.18}$$

the function $G(\lambda)$ satisfying the conditions $\int_0^\infty G(\lambda)\, d\lambda = 1$ and $\int_0^+ G(\lambda)\lambda^2\, d\lambda = 0$. Then in the expression for $J^p_{\mu\nu}$ the range of the p integration can be extended to infinity as the integral now converges. The result of the integration using this method is the integral on $d\lambda$ over $G(\lambda)$ of

$$J^p_{\mu\nu} = \frac{e^2}{\pi}(q_\mu q_\nu - \delta_{\mu\nu}q^2)\left\{ \tfrac{1}{3}\ln\left(\frac{\lambda^2}{m^2}\right) - \left[\frac{4m^2 + 2q^2}{3q^2}\left(1 - \frac{\theta}{\tan\theta}\right) - \tfrac{1}{9}\right]\right\}, \tag{14.19}$$

with $q^2 = 4m^2 \sin\theta$.

'The gauge invariance is clear, since $q_\mu(q_\mu q_\nu - q^2\, \delta_{\mu\nu}) = 0$. Operating (as it always will) on a potential of zero divergence, the (quantity) $(q_\mu q_\nu - q^2\, \delta_{\mu\nu})a_\nu$ is simply $-q^2 a_\mu$, the Dalembertian of the potential. The term $-\tfrac{1}{3}[\ln(\lambda^2/m^2)]\,(q_\mu q_\nu - q^2\, \delta_{\mu\nu})$ therefore gives a current proportional to the current producing the potential. This would have the same effect as a *change in a charge*, so that we would have a difference $\Delta(e^2)$ between e^2 and the experimentally observed $e^2 + \Delta(e^2)$, analogous to the difference between m and observed mass. This charge depends logarithmically on the cut-off, $\Delta(e^2)/e^2 = -(2e^2/3\pi)\ln(\lambda/m)$. After this renormalization of charge is made, no effects will be sensitive to the cut-off.

'After this is done the final term remaining in [(14.12)] contains the usual effects[19, 20] of polarization of the vacuum. . ..

'Closed loops containing a number of quanta of potential interactions larger than two produce no trouble. Any loop with an odd number of interactions gives zero (as noted in I). Four or more potential interactions give integrals which are convergent even without a convergence factor, as is well known. The situation is analogous to that for self-energy. Once the simple problem of a single closed loop is solved there are no further divergence difficulties for more complex processes.'[21]

This was the complete resolution of the renormalization problem. In Dyson's paper[22] it was proved that, in higher-order terms no new divergences occurred, and all divergences may be connected with either the mass or the charge renormalization. Thus the full renormalization program had been realized.

While discussing the problem of higher-order terms dealt with in the paper on the 'Space–time approach to quantum electrodynamics', Feynman looked for the following remark he had made in it: 'The methods of calculation given in this paper are deceptively simple when applied to lower order processes. For processes of increasingly higher orders the complexity and difficulty increases rapidly and these methods soon become impractical in their present form.'[1]

'An honest man, you know! I'm proud of doing things in a clean and honest fashion. I think you should always point out where your thing is good and where it stops and is no good.'[13]

14.6 Some other results and concluding remarks

In the following sections of the article, Feynman gave several new results. First, he gave a discussion of the unique treatment of longitudinal and transverse waves in the general case in quantum electrodynamics. The relativistic invariance of the notion of 'unpolarized light' was derived on this basis, and new rules for calculating the cross sections for such light were given. In the next section, Feynman considered scalar charged particles obeying the Klein–Gordon equation and extended the application of the new methods to these particles. The self-energy of such particles of momentum P_μ was written in the form

$$(e^2/2\pi im) \int \lceil 2p-k)_\mu((p-k)-m)^{-1}(2p-k)_\mu-\delta_{\mu\mu}]k^{-2}C(k)\,d^4k \qquad (14.20)$$

with some regularization factor $C(k)$. The integral without this factor is quadratically divergent, and therefore $C(k)$ must satisfy stronger conditions than in the case of Dirac particles.

Feynman showed that the lowest order of contribution of a closed loop to vacuum polarization, which, for particles obeying the Bose statistics has an opposite sign, gives

$$J^p_{\mu\nu} = \frac{e^2}{\pi}(q_\mu q_\nu - \delta_{\mu\nu}q^2)\left\{\tfrac{1}{6}\ln\left(\frac{\lambda^2}{m^2}\right) - \left[\frac{4m^2-q^2}{3q^2}\left(1-\frac{\theta}{\tan\theta}\right)+\tfrac{1}{9}\right]\right\}, \qquad (14.21)$$

using the same notation as in equation (14.19).

The radiative corrections to scattering after mass renormalization are sensitive to the cut-off just as for Dirac particles.

In the last section, dealing with the meson theories, Feynman wrote: 'The theories which have been developed to describe mesons and the interaction of nucleons can be easily expressed in the language used here. Calculations, to the lowest order in the interactions can be made very easily for the various theories, but agreement with experimental results is not obtained. Most likely all of our present formulations are quantitatively unsatisfactory. We shall content ourselves therefore with a brief summary of the methods which can be used.'[23]

Feynman then described different processes with nucleons and mesons of different kind (scalar mesons, pseudoscalar and pseudovector coupling, etc.). In several appendices at the end of the article, Feynman demonstrated the details of the calculation of integrals that occurred, the calculation of the self-energy of the electron, and more complex processes of higher order in quantum electrodynamics: higher-order corrections to the Møller scattering, to the Compton scattering, and the interaction of the neutron with an electromagnetic field by virtue of the fact that the neutron may emit virtual negative mesons. Here Feynman described the results which he had obtained during the 1949 APS meeting in connection with Slotnick's calculations (see Section 13.3).

Feynman's paper on the 'Space–time approach to quantum electrodynamics' was truly fundamental in that it had a great influence on the development of quantum electrodynamics, quantum field theory, and statistical physics—in which the same methods were adopted later, and on physical thinking as a whole in the postwar period. The initial reactions of the physicists to this paper were described by Feynman himself as follows:

'And I went out into the world; [the paper] was published. At that time, Schwinger had invented a method. Now he could explain his method better because it was closer to the normal, it was very ingenious and wonderful, but it was a little closer to the conventional ways of thinking, so he had it easier. Great difficulties, but [still] he had it easier [in] explaining where it came from. So at the beginning, when people would write down problems, things on quantum electrodynamics, it would be an eight-page paper on some problem. And somewhere around the sixth or seventh page of grinding formalism, they would write something down and [then] they would say this is what you would write immediately according to the intuitive methods of Feynman. That's all they would say. And then they would go and solve the problem and there would be integral tricks, and so on. But to get to that they went through a lot of pages of algebraic shenanigans with psi's and psi-bars, and they would sort of always seem to be surprised that somehow I was already there . . . . These methods were not intuitive; they were hard work. It's just that I hadn't published. So, it was a bit unfortunate that [until then] I had not published where it came from, but still in a way fortunate because it was a long ways around. This went on for a while. And then [came my] first paper. When you wrote a paper you said, "We want to study this problem. According to Feynman's principles, the formula for this is so and so." After that, more people had the courage to start right out trusting that it would work. Dyson proved that [all three theories of Feynman, Tomonaga, and Schwinger] were equivalent.' [24]

At the end of November 1948, David M. Dennison had invited Richard Feynman to give a series of nine lectures, beginning 11 July 1949 (three lectures per week) on his space–time formulation of quantum mechanics and quantum electrodynamics at the Symposium on Modern Physics at the University of Michigan summer school.[25] Feynman gladly accepted this invitation and gave lectures on his 'work and experience in the field of quantum electrodynamics', which Dennison wanted him to do. By the summer of 1949, Feynman's work in this field had been completed and he gave a full report on it at the symposium. The other speakers at the symposium in Ann Arbor were Gregor Wentzel, Bruno Rossi, Frederick Seitz, and Louis Alvarez. In the summer of 1948 Julian Schwinger had given a series of lectures on his formulation of the theory of quantum electrodynamics.

Notes and References

1. R.P. Feynman, Space-time approach to quantum electrodynamics. *Phys. Rev.* **76**, 769 (1949).

2. R.P. Feynman, The theory of positrons. *Phys. Rev.* **76**, 749 (1949).

3. R.P. Feynman, Ref. 1, p. 769.

4. R.P. Feynman, Space-time approach to non-relativistic quantum mechanics. *Rev. Mod. Phys.* **20**(2), 376 (1948).

5. R.P. Feynman, A relativistic cut-off for classical electrodynamics, *Phys. Rev.* **74**, 935 (1948).

6. R.P. Feynman, Ref. 1, p. 770.

7. R.P. Feynman, Ref. 1, pp. 770–71.

8. R.P. Feynman, Ref. 1, p. 771.

9. R.P. Feynman, Ref. 1, pp. 772–73.

10. R.P. Feynman, Ref. 1, p. 773.

11. R.P. Feynman, Ref. 1, p. 775.

12. R.P. Feynman, Ref. 2, p. 757.

13. R.P. Feynman, Interviews and conversations with Jagdish Mehra, in Austin, Texas, April 1970, and Pasadena, California, January 1988.

14. N.N. Bogoliubov and D.V. Shirkov, *Quantum fields*. Benjamin-Cummings, London, 1983.

15. R.P. Feynman, The development of the space–time view of quantum electrodynamics, Nobel Lecture. *Science* **153**, 699 (1966), p. 8.

16. R.P. Feynman, Ref. 1, p. 776.

17. R.P. Feynman, A relativistic cut-off for quantum electrodynamics, *Phys. Rev.* **74**, 1430 (1948).

18. R.P. Feynman, Ref. 1, p. 778.

19. E.A. Uehling, *Phys. Rev.* **48**, 55 (1935).

20. R. Serber, *Phys. Rev.* **48**, 49 (1935).

21. R.P. Feynman, Ref. 1, p. 780.

22. F.J. Dyson, *Phys. Rev.* **75**, 486 (1949); *Phys. Rev.* **75**, 1736 (1949).

23. R.P. Feynman, Ref. 1, p. 783.

24. R.P. Feynman, Ref. 13.

25. D.M. Dennison, Letter to R.P. Feynman, 30 November 1948. Feynman Archive, Caltech.

15

The mathematical formulation of quantum electrodynamics

15.1 Introduction

In 1950–51 Richard Feynman wrote two papers in which he described the mathematical formulation of his method in quantum electrodynamics. The first paper was entitled 'Mathematical formulation of the quantum theory of electromagnetic interaction'; it was received on 8 June 1950 and published in the *Physical Review*.[1] The second paper, entitled 'An operator calculus having applications in quantum electrodynamics', was received on 23 May 1951 and published in the October issue of the *Physical Review*.[2] Both of these papers were aimed at giving the mathematical basis of Feynman's methods, which had been published in the previous papers without giving proper derivations. In the 1950 paper Feynman used the methods of his Ph.D. thesis (see Chapter 6) and his 1948 paper in the *Reviews of Modern Physics* (see Chapter 10) to derive the basic equations and principles of his method. In the second paper,[2] Feynman gave further development of the formalism and discussed the new idea of how to proceed with noncommuting quantities. 'No results which are new are obtained in this way, but it does permit one to relate various formulas of operator algebra in quantum mechanics in a simpler manner than is often available. In particular, it is applied to quantum electrodynamics to permit an easier way to seeing relationships among the conventional formulation, that of Schwinger[3] and Tomonaga[4] and that of the author.'[5,6]

In these articles, besides deriving the old formulas, Feynman obtained many new relations and derivations, and invented new approaches to solve different mathematical problems in quantum mechanics and quantum field theory. But, in a strict sense, these two papers were not entirely mathematical, for in them one cannot find purely mathematical proof of theorems and formulas. On the contrary, at many places Feynman's statements required more careful analysis and proofs, and sometimes they were incorrect in a rigorous mathematical sense. For instance, in these articles Feynman paid no attention to the divergence problem at all, and left the dangerous points for future investigation; still, these two papers were very constructive and quite formal mathematically. The main point was to describe all the steps that were needed to derive Feynman's rules and Feynman's approach to quantum electrodynamics from the path-integral method and to offer new ideas for obtaining a convenient general method with obvious physical applications.

15.2 Mathematical formulation of the quantum theory of electromagnetic interaction

In the paper with this title,[1] Feynman established the validity of the rules given in previous papers[5] for the solution of the problems in quantum electrodynamics. Starting with Fermi's formulation of the field as a set of harmonic oscillators, he integrated out the effect of the oscillators in the Lagrangian form of quantum mechanics. There resulted an expression for the effect of all virtual photons valid to all orders in $e^2/\hbar c$. Feynman showed that the evaluation of the expression as a power series in $e^2/\hbar c$ gives just the terms expected by the aforementioned rules.

In addition, Feynman established a relation between the amplitude for a given process in an arbitrary unquantized potential and in a quantum electrodynamical field. This relation permitted a simple general statement of the laws of quantum electrodynamics.

Feynman gave a description, in Lagrangian quantum mechanical form, of particles satisfying the Klein–Gordon equation. It involved the use of an extra parameter analogous to the proper time to describe the trajectory of the particle in four dimensions. In the special case of photons, Feynman discussed the problem of finding what real processes were implied by the formula for virtual processes.

By the Lagrangian form of quantum mechanics Feynman meant his path-integral method. He used the results of his Ph.D. thesis (see Chapter 6) and the 1948 paper in *Reviews of Modern Physics* (see Chapter 10) to give a detailed derivation of the rules, which he had proposed for calculations in quantum electrodynamics. He started from Fermi's assemblage of independent harmonic oscillators for the transverse part of the electromagnetic field, using the notations of Heitler.[7] The classical Lagrangian for the system of the electromagnetic field and the charged particles has the form

$$L = L_p + L_I + L_C + L_{tr}, \tag{15.1}$$

where L_p is the Lagrangian of the noninteracting particles (in the nonrelativistic case, $L_p = \frac{1}{2}\sum_n m_n \dot{x}_n^2$ (see Section 6.2, where Feynman first used this form to illustrate his ideas); $L_I = \sum_n e_n \dot{x}_n A_n^{tr}(x_n)$ is the interaction Lagrangian, i.e. that part of the total Lagrangian which describes the interaction between the particles and the transverse electromagnetic field with potential $L_C = -\frac{1}{2}\sum_n\sum_m e_n e_m/r_{nm}$ is the Coulomb Lagrangian, which describes the Coulomb interaction connected with the longitudinal part of the electromagnetic field; and, finally, the Lagrangian of the free transverse electromagnetic field, i.e. the radiation field, is $L_{tr} = \frac{1}{2}\sum_K\sum_r[(\dot{q}_K^{(r)})^2 - k^2(q_K^{(r)})^2]$. Hence, the classical action of this system is

$$S = \int L \, dt = S_p + S_1 + S_C + S_{tr}. \qquad (15.2)$$

According to the principles of the path-integral method (see Chapters 6 and 10), the quantum amplitude for the transitions of the system from one quantum state to the other is the sum of terms $\exp[(i/\hbar)S]$ over all virtual paths in the classical configuration space of this system. In our case the system consists of two different parts: the classical electromagnetic field and the particles of matter. Using the technique which he had invented in his Ph.D. thesis for integrating out the oscillator variables (see Section 6.5 and Chapter 10), Feynman showed that in the present case the elimination of the oscillator degrees of freedom, i.e. the elimination of the transverse electromagnetic field, leads to the effective classical action (for the charged particles only) in a form $S_p + R$, where

$$R = -\frac{1}{2}\sum_n\sum_m \int_{-\infty}^{+\infty}\int_{-\infty}^{+\infty} e_n e_m[1 - \dot{x}_n(t)\dot{x}_m(s)]\,\delta_+((t-s)^2$$
$$-[x_n(t) - x_m(s)]^2)\,dt\,ds. \qquad (15.3)$$

The real part of this term includes the δ-function instead of δ_+-function, and is just the Fokker classical action in the action-at-a-distance theory if the summation is performed only on the different values of n and m, i.e. if one includes the self-interaction of charged particles (see Chapter 5).

To obtain the transition amplitudes including the effect of the field, one must calculate the transition elements of $\exp(iR)$:

$$\langle \chi_{t''}|\exp(iR)|\psi_{t'}\rangle_{S_p}$$

(see Chapters 6 and 10). Expanding the exponent in a Taylor series, we obtain the perturbation expansion of the transition amplitude in powers of $e^2/\hbar c$ (in the calculations, $\hbar = c = 1$ is assumed) insofar as the expression (15.2) for R is proportional to this dimensionless interaction constant. Hence we have

$$\langle \psi_{t''}|\exp(iR)|\psi_{t'}\rangle_{S_p} = \langle \psi_{t''}|1|\psi_{t'}\rangle_{S_p} + i\langle \psi_{t''}|R|\psi_{t'}\rangle_{S_p} + \cdots,$$

and the calculation of the first-order term by the path integral method yields

$$\langle \psi_{t''}|R|\psi_{t'}\rangle_{S_p} = -e^2 \int dt \int ds \int \psi^*(x_{t''}, t'')K(x_{t''}, t''; x_t, t)\,\delta_+((t-s)^2$$
$$-(x_t - x_s)^2)K(x_t, t; x_s, s)K(x_s, s; x_{t'}, t')\psi(x_{t'}, t')\,d^3x_{t''}\,d^3x_t\,d^3x_s\,d^3x_{t'},$$

$$(15.4)$$

which is just the starting formula for applying Feynman's method.

However, this derivation was only for the nonrelativistic particles. The corresponding extension of the formulas for the relativistic Dirac particles was derived by Feynman in a formal manner. Feynman did not succeed in deriving the Dirac equation from first principles by the path integral method, because the relativistic classical action did not lead directly to a spin-$\frac{1}{2}$ relativistic particle. For this purpose a proper generalization of the very classical mechanics of the relativistic particles is needed; namely, one has to involve the so-called Grassmann anticommuting variables, which are important ingredients of the modern supersymmetric theories. This approach has been successfully developed recently,[8] a long time after the fundamental work of Feynman. But one can find its roots already in the Feynman paper which we are discussing. The Grassmann variables can be presented as some matrices with suitable properties.

In Section 6 of his paper, entitled 'Extension to Dirac particles', Feynman gave the formal derivation of the relativistic formulas for spin-$\frac{1}{2}$ particles, considering the transition amplitude $(x_{t'}|x_{t'})$ for a Dirac particle as a 4×4 matrix (or $4^N \times 4^N$ matrix if we deal with N electrons). For such a matrix propagator, i.e. for the transition amplitude, the usual formulas from the path-integral method are still correct, and the path-integral-like representation of this amplitude was given by Feynman in the form

$$\langle \chi_{t'}|\exp(iR)|\psi_{t'}\rangle = \lim_{\varepsilon \to 0} \int \chi^*(x_{t''}^{(1)}, x_{t''}^{(2)}, \ldots)$$

$$\times \prod_n \left(\Phi_{p,n}^{(0)} \, d^3 x_{t''}^{(n)} \, d^3 x_{t''-\varepsilon}^{(n)} \cdots d^3 x_t^{(n)} \right)$$

$$\times \exp(iR)\psi(x_{t'}^{(1)}, x_{t'}^{(2)}, \ldots), \tag{15.5}$$

where $\Phi_p = \prod_i^n (x_{i+1}|x_i)$ is a 4×4 matrix product for one-electron theory, or a $4^N \times 4^N$ matrix product if we deal with N electrons. The matrix expression $(x_i + 1|x_i)$ is the propagator of the true Dirac particle, which is analogous to the expression $(x_i + 1|x_i) = A^{-1} \exp[iS(x_{i+1}, x_i)]$ in Feynman's path-integral method (see Chapters 6 and 10); for a Dirac particle in an electromagnetic field it must be replaced by

$$(x_{i+1}|x_i)A = (x_{i+1}|x_i)^{(0)} \exp\{-i[SA_4(x_i, t_i) - (x_{i+1} - x_i)A(x_i, t_i)]\},$$

which Feynman verified directly from the Dirac equation.

A careful analysis of this procedure shows that it is equivalent to the modern one, using Grassmann's variables, and it may be considered as the first step in this direction.

Using the same procedure as in the nonrelativistic case, Feynman derived directly from equation (15.5) the formula

$$\langle \psi_{t'}|R|\psi_{t'}\rangle_{S_p} = -e^2 \int \psi^*(x_{t''})K_0(x_{t''}, t''; x_t, t)\beta\alpha_\mu$$

$$\times \delta_+((t-s)^2 - (x_t - x_s)^2)K_0(x_t, t; x_s, s)\beta\alpha_\mu$$

$$\times K_0(x_s, s; x'_{t'}, t')\beta\psi(x_{t'}) d^3x_{t''} d^3x_t d^3x_s d^3x_{t'} dt \, ds. \quad (15.6)$$

Here one has to change the notation, $\beta\alpha_\mu = \gamma_\mu$ and $\psi^*\beta = \bar\psi$, and to replace the propagator K_0 by Feynman's K^+ to take into account Feynman's theory of positrons as particles moving backwards in time, instead of the Dirac hole theory to which the propagator K_0 corresponds. As a result of this, one obtains the fundamental formula of Feynman's approach to quantum electrodynamics,[9] which is the basis for the Feynman rules and diagrams in the lowest orders of perturbation theory.

In order to get his rules in the general case of arbitrary order in perturbation theory, Feynman derived the new equation for the quantum transition amplitude $T_e^2[B]$ in the external field B. He considered the dependence of this amplitude, $T_e^2[B]$, on the square of the charge, e^2, of the particles of matter, and he derived the new equation for the amplitude as

$$\frac{dT_{e^2}[B]}{d(e^2)} = \tfrac{1}{2}i \int\int \frac{\delta^2 T_{e^2}[B]}{\delta B_\mu(1)\, \delta B_\mu(2)} \delta_+(s_{12}^2)\, d\tau_1\, d\tau_2. \quad (15.7)$$

Here $dT_{e^2}[B]/d(e^2)$ is the derivative of the amplitude $T_{e^2}[B]$ as a function of e^2, and $\delta T_{e^2}[B]/\delta B(x, t)$ is the corresponding functional derivative of the amplitude as a functional of the external field B; $s_{12}^2 = (x_{\mu,1} - x_{\mu,2})(x_{\mu,1} - x_{\mu,2})$ is the four-dimensional distance.

This formula permits one to derive in a simple manner the Taylor series of the amplitude as a function of the charge e^2, i.e. its perturbative expansion. It may also be considered as a differential-functional equation for the amplitude $T_{e^2}[B]$ with intial condition $T_0[B]$—the amplitude for the noninteracting particles with $e^2 = 0$, which was obtained by Feynman in his previous paper.[10]

Equation (15.7), and the corresponding formalism of functional derivation with respect to external fields, is very convenient for general considerations of the perturbation series in quantum field theory and is now generally used.

Using this powerful formalism, Feynman derived in Appendix C of this article the new equation for the relativistic electron; this generalization of the Dirac equation reads:

$$(i\nabla - m)\Phi_{e^2}[B, x] = B(x)\Phi_{e^2}[B, x] + ie^2\gamma_\mu \int \frac{\delta\Phi_{e^2}[B, x]}{\delta B_\mu(1)} \delta_+(s_{12}^2)\, d\tau_1. \quad (15.8)$$

Here $\nabla = \gamma_\mu \partial_\mu$, $B = \gamma_\mu B_\mu$, and $\Phi_{e^2}[B, x]$ is the Dirac four-component spinor as a function of the charge square e^2 and as a functional of the external field B. Without the last term, equation (15.8) represents the usual Dirac equation. The new (last) term, included by Feynman, takes into account the self-interaction of the electron due to the quantum electrodynamical effects (the propagation of the electron with the emission and absorption of the virtual photon). Effects of vacuum polarization are left out. Equation (15.8) actually includes all the advances in the theory of the electron that were made after Dirac's original discovery of his famous equation.

In his 1950 paper Feynman gave one more formal mathematical trick, which continues to play a definite role in theoretical investigations up to now. This trick was connected with the extension of Feynman's theory to relativistic spin-0 particles, which obey the Klein–Gordon equation. Feynman invented an elegant trick to deal with such particles in his path-integral method. The formal obstacle in using the path-integral method directly for the Klein–Gordon equation was the fact that this equation is of second order with respect to time. This was necessary to ensure the relativistic invariance, but the path-integral method may be used without proper modification only for first-order evolution equations (see Chapter 10).

Starting from the Klein–Gordon equation

$$(i\, \partial/\partial x_\mu - A_\mu)^2 \psi = m\psi \tag{15.9}$$

for the scalar relativistic field $\psi(x, t)$, Feynman proposed to describe the classical trajectory in space–time by giving the four variables $x_\mu(u)$ as functions of some fifth parameter u, rather than expressing x_1, x_2, and x_3 as functions of the time x_4. This parameter u may be considered as the proper time of the particle, which increases as we go along the trajectory, whether the trajectory is proceeding forward $(dx_4/du > 0)$ or backward $(dx_4/du < 0)$ in time. Instead of the function $\psi(x, t) = \psi(x)$ of four variables, one can introduce the new one, $\phi(x, u)$, a function of five variables, which obeys the new evolution equation of the first order with respect to u:

$$i\, \partial\phi/\partial u = \tfrac{1}{2}(i\partial/\partial x_\mu - A_\mu)^2 \phi. \tag{15.10}$$

This equation is analogous to the Schrödinger equation, and one may use the path-integral method to solve it in the usual manner. Moreover, it turned out that the corresponding relativistically invariant classical action for the classical particles, which corresponds to equation (15.10), reads:

$$S = -\int_0^\infty [\tfrac{1}{2}(dx_\mu/du)^2 + (dx_\mu/du)A_\mu(x)]\, du. \tag{15.11}$$

One can see that this action functional is quadratic with respect to the velocities dx_μ/du. Hence, it leads to the solvable Gaussian path integral.

After the solution of equation (15.10) has been found, one can obtain the solution of the Klein–Gordon equation according to the formula

$$\psi(x) = \int_{-\infty}^{\infty} \exp\left(-\tfrac{1}{2}im^2 u\right)\phi(x, u)\, du, \qquad (15.12)$$

i.e. by a simple Fourier transformation.

The analysis of this procedure according to the path-integral method, proposed by Feynman, showed that it is quite a general one, and led to the theory of path integral of constrained systems, which is a very important part of modern theoretical methods and has many applications in physics.

15.3 An operator calculus having applications in quantum electrodynamics

Feynman's 1951 article with this title[2] was extremely rich in new mathematical ideas and inventions which he proposed to use in quantum theory, especially in quantum electrodynamics. He wrote: 'It is felt, in the face of daily experimental surprises for meson theory, that it may be worth while to spend one's time expressing electrodynamics in every physical and mathematical way possible. There may be some hope that a thorough understanding of electrodynamics might give a clue as to the structure of the more complete theory to which it is an approximation. This is one reason that this paper is published, even though it is little more than a mathematical re-expression of old material. A second reason is the desire to describe a mathematical method which may be useful in other fields.

'The mathematics is not completely satisfactory. No attempt has been made to maintain mathematical rigor. The excuse is not that it is expected that rigorous demonstrations can be easily supplied. Quite the contrary, it is believed that to put the present methods on a rigorous basis may be quite a difficult task, beyond the abilities of the author.'[11]

The main new mathematical idea in this article was the introduction and development of the new operator algebra which originated from Feynman's Ph.D. thesis (see Section 6.5) and from the 1948 *Reviews of Modern Physics* article (see Section 10.3).

It is well known that the principal mathematical difference between classical and quantum mechanics is that in the former all physical quantities are described as numerical functions of proper variables—coordinates and momenta of the system under consideration (see Section 6.2), while in quantum mechanics these quantities are described with corresponding operators in Hilbert space. These operators do not commute, i.e. the result of their action depends on the order in which they act. Usually this ordering, which is essential for the results, is described by the position in which the operators are written. Thus the product AB of the operators A and B means that one must first act by the operator B and then by operator A. This product has a different action in comparison with the operator product BA, which means that one must first act by the operator A and then by the operator B. The impossibility of changing the places of the operators in quantum formulas without changing the very formulas is extremely inconvenient, and leads to great difficulties when one deals with quantum theory.

In Feynman's path-integral method there are no operators at all, but the same fundamental property of quantum theory reflects on the time ordering of the quantities in different formulas (see Section 10.3).

It seems quite natural to combine these two ways of describing the same property of the quantum variables, and to try to simplify the technique one uses in quantum theory. This is what Feynman did in his 1951 article.[2] He proposed to endow each operator A with an additional index s, writing the operator as A_s. Then the operator $A_s B_{s'}$ equals the usual operator product AB if $s > s'$, and to the usual operator product BA if $s < s'$. The order of the actual action of the operators no longer depends on their position on paper, so that the ordinary processes of analysis may be applied as though A_s and $B_{s'}$ were commuting variables. The indices s and s' are responsible for the right ordering of the action of the operators, since all mathematical manipulations are performed on the expressions we have to deal with.

For example, Feynman showed that the exponential function of the sum of two commuting operators α and β may be written in the form

$$\exp(\alpha + \beta) = \exp\left(\int_0^1 (\alpha_s + \beta_s)\, ds\right), \tag{15.13}$$

where one has to consider α and β formally as functions of the ordering parameter s.

For a commuting (classical) quantity we have the simple relation $\exp(a + b) = \exp(a) \cdot \exp(b)$, which is no longer true for the noncommuting operators α and β: $\exp(\alpha + \beta) \neq \exp(\alpha) \cdot \exp(\beta)$. But, after Feynman's invention is made use of, we have

$$\exp\left(\int_0^1 (\alpha_s + \beta_s)\, ds\right) = \exp\left(\int_0^1 \alpha_s\, ds\right) \cdot \exp\left(\int_0^1 \beta_s\, ds\right) \tag{15.14}$$

by analogy with the classical commutative case. As Feynman noted: 'Any operator function of $\alpha + \beta$ can, by replacing $\alpha + \beta$ by $\int_0^1 \alpha_s\, ds + \int_0^1 \beta_s\, ds$, be manipulated in a manifold of ways, many of which lead to useful formulas. (In a like manner, more complicated operator expressions can be rewritten using ordering indices. They may then be manipulated using all of the results of ordinary analysis.)'[12]

Feynman then added the presumption to use the subscript s as a formal argument of the corresponding operators, and to write down these operators as $A(s)$. This notation is convenient in the more general case in which the operator A actually depends explicitly on the order parameter. In this case we should have strictly to write $A_s(s)$, but Feynman proposed to omit the subscript when no ambiguity will result from the change.

Another important remark was about the general sense of the mathematical expressions, which appeared in Feynman's new formalism. The expressions like $\int_0^1 \alpha_s \, ds$ are considered not as usual integrals, which have to be calculated, but as some functional. Hence the complete expression like (15.13) is a functional of the argument functions $\alpha(s)$, $\beta(s)$, etc. 'With each such functional we are endeavoring to associate an operator. The operator depends on the functional in a complex way (the operator is a functional of a functional) so that, for example, the operator corresponding to the product of two functionals is not (in general) the simple product of the operator corresponding to the separate factors. (The corresponding statement equating the sum of the functionals and the sum of the corresponding operators is true, however.) Hence, we can consider the most complex expressions involving a number of operators M, N, as described by functionals $F[M(s), N(s), \ldots]$ of the argument functions $M(s), N(s), \ldots (M_s, N_s, \ldots)$. For each functional we are to find the corresponding operator in some simple form; that is, we wish to disentangle the functional. One fact we know is that any analytic rearrangement may be performed which leaves the value of the functional unchanged for arbitrary $M(s), N(s), \ldots$ considered as ordinary numerical functions. Besides, there are a few special operations which we may perform on $F[M(s), N(s), \ldots]$, to disentangle the expressions, which are valid only because the functional does represent an operator according to our rules. These special operations (such as extracting an exponential factor) are, of course, proper to the new calculus; and our powers of analysis in this field will increase as we develop more of them.'[13]

The first example of this new operation, disentangling of the operator functionals, which Feynman invented, was the new proof of the basic formula of the time-dependent perturbation theory:

$$\exp(\alpha + \beta) = \exp \alpha + \int_0^1 \exp[(1-s)\alpha] \cdot \beta \exp(s\alpha) \, ds + \cdots. \qquad (15.15)$$

Another very useful result was the generalization of the well-known theorem which says that, if we replace the operators $M(s), N(s), \ldots$ in the functional $F[M(s), N(s), \ldots]$ by $M'(s) = U^{-1}M(s)U$, $N'(s) = U^{-1}N(s)U, \ldots$, where U is some constant operator, then

$$F[M'(s), N'(s), \ldots] = U^{-1}F[M(s), N(s), \ldots]U. \qquad (15.16)$$

This formula is a result of a special kind of disentangling of operators. Feynman generalized it for the case when U depends explicitly on the ordering parameter $U = U(s)$, and it obeys the following operator differential equation:

$$dU(s)/ds = P(s)U(s). \qquad (15.17)$$

In this general case the corresponding formula, derived by Feynman, reads:

$$F[M'(s), N'(s), \ldots] = U^{-1}(1)F[M(s), N(s), \ldots]\exp\left(\int_0^1 P(s)\, ds\right)U(0),$$

(15.18)

where $M'(s) = U^{-1}(s)M(s)U(s)$, $N'(s) = U^{-1}(s)N(s)U(s)$, ...; $U(O)$ is the operator $U(s)$ for $s = O$, and $U(1)$ is the operator $U(s)$ for $s = 1$. The formula (15.16) is obviously the special case of equation (15.18) and follows from it when $P(s)$ equals zero, i.e. when U is a constant operator, since from equation (15.17) one obtains

$$U(s) = \exp\left(\int_0^s P(s')\, ds'\right)U(0).$$

(15.19)

Feynman called the procedure, described by the formula (15.18), a disentangling of an exponential factor.

15.4 Applications in quantum mechanics and quantum electrodynamics

In his 1951 article[2] Feynman demonstrated many physical applications of the new operator calculus, which he had invented and developed. In the applications, the ordering parameter is usually the time t, and Feynman's new formalism became the time-ordered operator calculus. Thus, one can speak of the time-ordered exponent of an operator, etc.

The first example of the applications of this new calculus was the derivation of the expressions for the quantum evolution operator $\Omega(t_1, t_2)$. This unitary operator may be written as $\Omega(t_1, t_2) = \exp[(-i(t_2 - t_1)H]$, if the quantum Hamiltonian operator does not depend on the time t. Feynman wrote this operator in the form of a time-ordered exponential: $\Omega(t_1, t_2) = \exp(-i\int_{t_1}^{t_2} H_t\, dt)$. In the case of an explicitly time-dependent Hamiltonian $H(t)$, we have to replace H_t by $H_t(t)$, but using the convention described in the previous section Feynman wrote the formula for the operator in the form

$$\Omega(t_1, t_2) = \exp\left(-i\int_{t_1}^{t_2} H(t)\, dt\right).$$

(15.20)

If the Hamiltonian is written as a sum of some zero-order Hamiltonian $H_0(t)$ and some perturbation $U(t)$, i.e. $H(t) = H_0(t) + U(t)$, we can immediately use the formula (15.15), and as a result of disentangling of the operators in the time-ordered exponential (15.20) we will get the perturbative expansion of the corresponding evolution operator $\Omega^U(t_1, t_2)$ in powers of the perturbation $U(t)$. Hence the first term in this expansion will be

$$-i \int_{t_1}^{t_2} \Omega^{(0)}(t_2, t)U(t)\Omega^{(0)}(t, t_1)\, dt, \tag{15.21}$$

where $\Omega^{(0)}(t_1, t_2)$ is the evolution operator of the unperturbed problem, with the Hamiltonian $H_0(t)$. If $K(x_2, t_2; x_1, t_1)$ is the coordinate integral kernel of the operator $\Omega(t_1, t_2)$, this formula reads:

$$-i \int_{t_1}^{t_2} K^{(0)}(x_2, t_2; x, t)U(x, t)K^{(0)}(x, t; x_1, t_1)\, dx\, dt. \tag{15.22}$$

This is exactly the result which Feynman had used in his previous papers on quantum electrodynamics; there it was derived by the path-integral method, which leads to the same formula.

The next application of the new calculus was the derivation of the method of treating the complex physical system by parts, which Feynman had invented in his Ph.D. thesis using path-integrals. Now the method had been generalized and the derivation was independent of the path-integral method. Feynman considered the system consisting of two separate parts (a) and (b) with Hamiltonians $H^{(a)}$ and $H^{(b)}$. These two parts do interact with each other, and the interaction term in the Hamiltonian is $U[x^{(a)}, x^{(b)}]$. Hence, the entire Hamiltonian of the composite system is $H^{(a)} + H^{(b)} + U[x^{(a)}, x^{(b)}]$. Disentangling the time-ordered exponent in the matrix element m of the evolution operator of the system, where

$$m = \langle \psi_2 \phi_2 | \exp\left(-i \int_t^{t_2} H^{(a)}(t)\, dt - i \int_t^{t_2} H^{(b)}(t)\, dt \right.$$
$$\left. -i \int_t^{t_2} U[x^{(a)}(t), x^{(b)}(t)]\, dt \right) |\psi_1 \phi_1\rangle \tag{15.23}$$

Feynman showed that this element may be represented in the form

$$m = \langle \phi_2 | \exp\left(-i \int_t^{t_2} H^{(b)}(t)\, dt \right) T^{(a)}[x^{(b)}(t)] | \phi_1 \rangle, \tag{15.24}$$

where

$$T^{(a)}[x^{(b)}(t)] = \langle \psi_2 | \exp\left(-i \int_t^{t_2} H^{(a)}(t)\, dt - i \int_t^{t_2} U[x^{(a)}(t), x^{(b)}(t)]\, dt \right) |\psi_1\rangle \tag{15.25}$$

is the matrix element for the system (a) alone, considering that in the interaction potential $U[x^{(a)}, x^{(b)}]$ all operators referring to (b) are arbitrary numerical functions of t.

Feynman concluded that in this way we can analyze one part of the pair of interacting systems without having yet analyzed the other. The influence of a

on b is completely contained in the operator functional $T^{(a)}[x^{(b)}(t)]$. Feynman thought that this separation may be useful in the analysis of the theory of measurement and of quantum statistical mechanics,[14] which makes that form useful in analyzing quantum properties of the electromagnetic field. Feynman expected therefore that with the present operator notation it should be equally easy to make this analysis. That this is indeed true is shown by an example later on. Since this, the main advantage of the Lagrangian form, can be so easily managed with the new notation for operators, this may take the place of the Lagrangian form in many applications. It is in some ways a more powerful and general form than the Lagrangian. It is not restricted to the nonrelativistic mechanics in any way. A possible advantage of the other form at present might be a slight increase in *anschaulichkeit* offered for the interpretation of nonrelativistic quantum mechanics.[15]

The third application of the new operator calculus was the introduction of the interaction representation for the evolution operator. This is the most convenient representation to perform real calculations in the time-dependent perturbation theory, and it gives the simplest form of this theory. Starting from the expression

$$\Omega^U(t_1, t_2) = \exp\left(-i \int_{t_1}^{t_2} H^{(0)}(t)\, dt\right) \exp\left(-i \int_{t_1}^{t_2} U(t)\, dt\right) \quad (15.26a)$$

for the evolution operator of the system with Hamiltonian $H(t) = H_0(t) + U(t)$, and using the formula (15.18), Feynman derived the interaction represent-ation of the evolution operator in the form

$$\Omega^U(t_1, t_2) = S(t_2) \exp\left(-i \int_{t_1}^{t_2} U'(t)\, dt\right) S^{-1}(t_1), \quad (15.26b)$$

where $U'(s) = S^{-1}(t)U(t)S(t)$ is the perturbation in the interaction represen-tation, and

$$S(t) = \exp\left(-i \int_0^t H^{(0)}(t)\, dt\right) \quad (15.27)$$

is the evolution operator of the nonperturbed system. Hence the time-dependent perturbation theory simply comes to evaluating

$$\Omega'(t_1, t_2) = \exp\left(-i \int_{t_1}^{t_2} U'(t)\, dt\right). \quad (15.28)$$

by expansion in power series of the exponential in this formula.

Feynman then applied the new formulas to calculate matrix elements of the evolution operator of the system coupled to a harmonic oscillator. Here he obtained the old results reached by the path-integral method in his earlier papers.[16,14,1]

The next important application of the new technique was in quantum electrodynamics, where the evolution operator was written down in the form

$$\exp\left(-i\int_0^t [H_m(t)+H_f(t)+H_i(t)]\, dt\right).$$ (15.29)

Here $H_m(t)$ is the Hamiltonian of the electron–positron field, $H_f(t)$ is that of the electromagnetic field, and $H_i(t)$ represents the interaction of these fields. Disentangling the exponential factor

$$\exp\left(-i\int_0^t [H_m(t)+H_f(t)]\, dt\right),$$

Feynman arrived at the interaction representation, and the problem was reduced to the analysis of the operator $\exp(-i\int_0^t H_i'(t)\, dt)$. Omitting the prime for the interaction representation, and considering the case for $t_1 \to -\infty$, $t_2 \to +\infty$, Feynman simplified the problem to the study of the operator

$$S-\exp\left(-i\int_{-\infty}^{+\infty} j_\mu(x, t)A_\mu(x, t)\, d^3x\, dt\right).$$ (15.30)

This operator is just the Heisenberg S-matrix in the interaction representation. Feynman also introduced the evolution operator in the interaction representation in the form

$$\Omega(\tau)=\exp\left(-i\int_{-\infty}^\tau j_\mu(x, t)A_\mu(x, t)\, d^3x\, dt\right)$$ (15.31)

and then derived the differential equation for this operator:

$$i\, d\Omega(\tau)/d\tau = \left(\int j_\mu(x, \tau)A_\mu(x, t)\, d^3x\right)\Omega(\tau).$$ (15.32)

This is the Schrödinger equation for quantum electrodynamics written in the interaction representation.

Feynman noted that 'the apparent lack of covariance implied by time to define the differential equation can be removed by analyzing S in a slightly different manner, suggested by Tomonaga and Schwinger.[17,18]

The integration over the variables x in equation (15.30) may be replaced by integration on some three-dimensional space-like surface in four-dimensional space–time. Then one has to consider the evolution operator as a functional of the surface σ: $\Omega=\Omega(\sigma)$. The evaluation of the variational derivative of this functional with respect to the surface element of the surface leads directly to the Tomonaga–Schwinger equation:

$$\frac{\delta\Omega(\sigma)}{\delta\sigma(x, t)} = -ij_\mu(x, t)A_\mu(x, t)\Omega(\tau).$$ (15.33)

Thus one can see the relation between Feynman's approach and that of Tomonaga and Schwinger.

15.5 Dyson's elaboration of the theories of Feynman, Schwinger, and Tomonaga

A detailed comparison between the different approaches to quantum electrodynamics proposed by Feynman, by Tomonaga, and by Schwinger was given by Freeman Dyson.[19] He stressed that 'the advantages of the Feynman theory are simplicity and ease of application, while those of Tomonaga–Schwinger are generality and theoretical completeness.'[20] At that time, when much of Feynman's theory was still unpublished, Dyson (who knew about Feynman's work from personal discussions with him) undertook to investigate the relations between these three approaches, which at first seemed to be completely different from each other, and to establish their equivalence. Dyson started from the Schrödinger equation in quantum field theory. One may consider the classical field as a mechanical system with some energy density in the volume d^3x around the point x in three-dimensional space, given by the Hamiltonian density $H(x)$. Then the Hamiltonian of this system will be $\int H(x)\,d^3x$. If one replaces the classical Hamiltonian by the quantum operator $H(x)$, the Schrödinger equation will be the following generalization of equation (15.32):

$$i\hbar\,\partial\Phi/\partial t = \left(\int H(x)\,d^3x\right)\Phi.$$

In this form of the field equation the relativistic invariance is not transparent. In order to reach a relativistic invariant form, Tomonaga used Dirac's many-time formalism in field theory and then developed his version of quantum electrodynamics.[21] Schwinger used in his approach,[22] as a leading idea, another invention of Dirac's, namely Dirac's formalism of canonical transformations. But both Tomonaga and Schwinger started from a Schrödinger-like equation for the quantum state $\phi(\sigma)$ in the relativistically invariant form

$$i\,\frac{\delta\Phi(\sigma)}{\delta\sigma(x)} = H(x)\Phi(\sigma).$$

It is equivalent to equation (15.33).

The Hamiltonian may be represented in the form $H(x)=H_0(x)+H_1(x)$, where $H_0(x)$ is the energy density of the free electromagnetic and electron fields, and $H_1(x)$ is that of the interaction of these fields. We can make a canonical transformation, $\phi(\sigma)=T(\sigma)\psi(\sigma)$, of the interaction representation by the operator $T(\sigma)$, defined as

$$T(\sigma)=\exp\left(-i\int t(x)H_0(x)\,d^3x\right).$$

The Schrödinger-like equation in this representation reads:

$$i\frac{\delta\Psi(\sigma)}{\delta\sigma(x)}=H_1(x)\Psi(\sigma),$$

where $H_1(x, t)=T(\sigma)^{-1}H_1(x)T(\sigma)=H_1(x)$ is the time-dependent interaction Hamiltonian in the interaction representation $[x=(x, t)]$.

The term $H_1(x)$ is a sum of the Hamiltonian $H_i(x)$ of the interaction between electron–positron and photon fields and the Hamiltonian $H_e(x)$ of the interaction with the external electromagnetic field. The elimination of the radiation field oscillators in Feynman's theory corresponds in Schwinger's theory to a canonical transformation $\Psi=\Omega(\sigma)\Theta(\sigma)$. The operator $\Omega(\sigma)$ satisfies the equation

$$i\frac{\delta\Omega(\sigma)}{\delta\sigma(x)}=H_i(x)\Omega(\sigma),$$

analogous to equation (15.33). For quantum electrodynamics, the time-dependent form of the interaction Hamiltonian is $H_i(x, t)=j_\mu(x, t)A_\mu(x, t)$. Hence we have arrived at the same equation as (15.33).

The solution of the equation for $\Psi(\sigma)$ may be written in the form

$$\Psi(\sigma)=\Omega(\sigma)\Theta,$$

where the state vector Θ is constant if the external field vanishes; otherwise it obeys the equation

$$i\frac{\delta\Theta(\sigma)}{\delta\sigma(x)}=H_T(x)\Theta(\sigma).$$

Here $H_T(x)=\Omega(\sigma)^{-1}H_i(x)\Omega(\sigma)$ represents the interaction of the charged particle with the external field, taking into account radiative corrections. This equation describes the deviation of the state vector of the single charged particle in an external field from the constant state vector of the free particle.

The operator $\Omega(\infty)$, as we know, is just the Heisenberg S-matrix operator, which describes all transitions from some initial state Θ_{in} to corresponding final state Θ_{out}. If the system with state vector Θ undergoes no transitions with the passage of time, the state vector Θ is called 'steady'. Hence, the steady vector obeys the equation $\Omega(\infty)\Theta=\Theta$.

The definition of the state vectors $\Theta(\sigma)$ via the state vectors $\Psi(\sigma)$ is unsymmetrical between past and future, and a new type of state vector, denoted by Θ', may be defined by the equation $\Theta'(\sigma)=\Omega(\infty)\Theta(\sigma)$. Since $\Omega(\infty)$ is a unitary operator, independent of σ, the state vectors Θ and Θ' are the same vector in different coordinate systems. For the steady states they are simply identical.

As we know, to avoid the divergence in quantum electrodynamics, one must perform the renormalization of the mass of the bare electron–positron field $\psi(x)$. The corresponding renormalized Hamiltonian will be denoted as $H_1(x) = H_i(x) - \delta m \bar{\psi}(x)\psi(x)$, δm being the (infinite) mass renormalization constant.

Now we are ready to explain the relation between the Feynman theory and the Schwinger–Tomonaga theory, as discovered by Dyson.[19] 'The Schwinger theory works directly with equations [for Θ and H_T], the aim being to calculate the matrix of the "effective external potential energy" H_T between states, specified by their state vectors $[\Theta]$.'[23]

The $\Omega(\sigma)$ operator is given by the formula

$$\Omega(\sigma) = 1 + (-i) \int_{-\infty}^{\sigma} H(x_1)\, dx_1$$

$$+ (-i)^2 \int_{-\infty}^{\sigma} dx_1 \int_{-\infty}^{\sigma(x)_1} H(x_1)H(x_2)\, dx_2 + \cdots,$$

and the interaction Hamiltonian with radiative corrections is

$$H_T(x_0) = \sum_{n=0}^{\infty} (i)^n \int_{-\infty}^{\sigma} dx_1 \int_{-\infty}^{\sigma(x_1)} dx_2 \ldots \int_{-\infty}^{\sigma(x_n)} dx_n$$

$$\times [H_1(x_n), [\ldots, [H_I(x_2), [H_1(x_1), H_1(x_0)]] \ldots]].$$

The repeated commutators are typical of Schwinger's theory, and their calculation is quite long and difficult. Nevertheless Schwinger was able to find all basic quantum electrodynamical effects up to second order in perturbation theory.

As Dyson noted, 'In the Feynman theory the basic principle is to preserve symmetry between past and future. Therefore, the matrix elements of the operator H_T are evaluated in a "mixed representation"; the matrix elements are calculated between an initial state specified by its state vector $[\Theta_1]$ and a final state specified by its state vector $[\Theta_2']$.'[23]

The matrix element of H_T between two such states in the Schwinger representation is

$$\Theta_2^* H_T \Theta_1 = \Theta_2' \Omega(\infty) H_T \Theta_1,$$

and, therefore, in Feynman's theory the operator H_T is replaced by the new operator $H_F(x) = \Omega(\infty)H_T(x)$. The corresponding formula for this operator is

$$H_F(x_0) = \sum_{n=0}^{\infty} \frac{(-i)^n}{n!} \int_{-\infty}^{\infty} dx_1 \ldots \int_{-\infty}^{\infty} dx_n P[H_e(x_0)H_1(x_1)\ldots H_1(x_n)].$$

Here the letter P denotes the symmetrization with respect to all indices of the variables x_i. This formula is simpler than Schwinger's formula for the operator H_T. In addition, the operator $H_F(x)$ now appears to be a function only of the variable x, instead of being a functional of the surface σ.

Replacing the operator H_e with the unit matrix, instead of the more complicated formula in Schwinger's theory, one can obtain from here the following formula for the Heisenberg S-matrix in the Feynman theory:

$$\Omega(\infty) = \sum_{n=0}^{\infty} \frac{(-i)^n}{n!} \int_{-\infty}^{\infty} dx_1 \ldots \int_{-\infty}^{\infty} dx_n \, P[H_1(x_1) \ldots H_1(x_n)].$$

Both equations (15.32) and (15.33) define the operator (15.30), which can be written down in the invariant form

$$S = \exp\left(-i \int j_\mu(1) A_\mu(1) \, d\tau_1 \right). \tag{15.34}$$

The matrix taken between states in which the field is empty of photons initially and finally was written by Feynman in the form

$$S_{00} = \exp\left(-\tfrac{1}{2} i e^2 \iint i_\mu(1) j_\mu(2) \, \delta_+(s_{12}^2) \, d\tau_1 \, d\tau_2 \right). \tag{15.35}$$

Then, disentangling the exponent of the photon operators A in the general case, Feynman arrived at the following expression for the operator S:

$$S = \exp\left(-i \int j_\mu(1) A_{\mu+\infty}^-(1) \, d\tau_1 \right)$$

$$\times \exp\left(-\tfrac{1}{2} i e^2 \iint j_\mu(1) j_\mu(2) \, \delta_+(s_{12}^2) \, d\tau_1 \, d\tau_2 \right)$$

$$\times \exp\left(-i \int j_\mu(2) A_{\mu-\infty}^+(2) \, d\tau_2 \right). \tag{15.36}$$

Here the $A_{\mu t}^+$ operator annihilates photons, and the $A_{\mu t}^-$ operator creates them at the instant t. In the expression (15.36) these operators are completely disentangled and one can very easily calculate the matrix elements.

Finally, Feynman noted: 'Taken between states empty of photons the result is S_{00} of equation (15.35), for the annihilation operator A^+ on the state of zero photons is zero, and the creation operator A^- has zero amplitude for leaving a state without photons. If there is one photon present initially and we ask that no photon remain, we shall have to annihilate it and create none, so that A^- and A^+ exponentials are expanded in power series, we must take only the term linear in A^+ and independent of A^-. This is equivalent to a first-order action of potential . . . in perturbation. The corresponding rules for higher numbers of real photons are readily derived from equation [(15.36)]. In this way we have completed an independent deduction of all the main formal results in quantum electrodynamics, by use of the operator notation.'[24]

15.6 The Dirac equation

Feynman described the applications of the new operator calculus to the Dirac equation in three sections and one appendix of his 1951 article. First, Feynman derived by his new method the basic results of his 1949 article on the theory of positrons.[25] He considered the electron in the external nonquantized electromagnetic field $B = \gamma_\mu B_\mu$, first omitting the contribution of the closed loop diagrams.[26] The solution of the Dirac equation with a source function F,

$$(i\nabla - B - m)\Psi = F, \tag{15.37}$$

was written in the form

$$\Psi = (i\nabla - B - m)^{-1}F, \tag{15.38}$$

with the help of the inverse operator $(i\nabla - B - m)^{-1}$, which may be interpreted in the definite sense implied by the limit of the operator when mass m has a vanishing negative imaginary part. From the definition of the propagator $K_+^B(2, 1)$ in the 1949 article,[25] we can write

$$K_+^B(2, 1) = (i\nabla - B - m)^{-1}i\,\delta(2, 1). \tag{15.39}$$

Then the operator identity

$$(A + B)^{-1} = A^{-1} - A^{-1}BA^{-1} + A^{-1}BA^{-1}BA^{-1} - \cdots, \tag{15.40}$$

written in the space-coordinate representation for $A = (i\nabla - m)$ and B simply leads to the perturbation expansion of the propagator $K_+^B(2, 1)$,

$$K_+^B(2, 1) = K_+(2, 1) - i\int K_+(2, 3)B(3)K_+(3, 1)\,d\tau_3$$

$$- \iint K_+(2, 4)B(4)K_+(4, 3)B(3)K_+(3, 1)\,d\tau_3\,d\tau_4 + \cdots. \tag{15.41}$$

The contribution of the closed loops is the factor $C_v = \exp(-L)$ (see Section 13.6, equation (13.28)), where L is not very easily defined directly by the operators. But the first-order change on changing the potential B to $B + \Delta B$ is

$$\Delta L = \text{trace}\{[(i\nabla - B - m)^{-1} - (i\nabla - m)^{-1}]\Delta B\}, \tag{15.42}$$

where the 'trace' means the diagonal integral in coordinates. It should be noted that this approach of Feynman's is the basis of the modern description of closed-loop effects in quantum field theory.

In the next section of his article, Feynman gave a new representation of the inverse operator $(i\nabla - B - m)^{-1}$, which makes it possible to write down the formula directly for the quantity L, instead of equation (15.42). This representation was based on the formula $\int_0^\infty \exp(iWx)\,dW = i/x$ (or rather $\lim_{\varepsilon \to 0}[i/(x+i\varepsilon)]$), which leads to the representation

$$(i\nabla - B - m)^{-1} = \int_0^\infty \exp[i(i\nabla - B - m)W]\,dW, \qquad (15.43)$$

or, involving the ordering operator w, to the new representation

$$(i\nabla - B - m)^{-1} = \int_0^\infty \exp\left(i\int_0^W [i(i\nabla(w)) - B(w)]\,dw\right)\exp(-imW)\,dW. \qquad (15.44)$$

Starting from this equation Feynman derived the following formula for L:

$$L = \int_0^\infty \mathrm{trace}\left\{\exp\left(i\int_0^W [i(i\nabla(w)) - B(w)]\,dW\right)\right\}\exp(-imW)\,\frac{dW}{W}, \qquad (15.45)$$

and gave the regularization procedure for this divergent quantity.

Another important result, derived from representation (15.44) was the formula for the expectation value R for a single charge between photon-free states:

$$R = \int_0^\infty \exp\left(-\int_0^W \nabla(w)\,dw\right)\exp\left(-\tfrac{1}{2}ie^2 \int_0^{w'}\int_0^{w''} \gamma_\mu(w')\gamma_\mu(w'')\,\delta_+(s_{w'w''}^2)\right)$$

$$\times \exp(-imW)\,dW. \qquad (15.46)$$

This expression gives a description of a Dirac electron interacting with itself. An extra factor $\exp[\ i\int_0^W B(w)\,dw]$ will describe such an electron in an external field with potential B. Feynman also gave a proper generalization of this result for a many-particle system, which gives the possibility also to calculate the effects of closed loops.

Thus the new operator calculus was shown to lead to a complete description of all quantum electrodynamical effects, and to give new powerful tools for solving the problems in quantum mechanics and quantum field theory.

In his 1951 article Feynman took one more step in the investigation of the Dirac equation. By analogy with the case of the Klein–Gordon equation (15.9), he proposed to introduce a fifth variable w for the Dirac equation, and to consider the spinor wave function $\Phi(x, w)$, which obeys the equation

$$-i\,\partial\Phi/\partial w = (i\nabla - B)\Phi, \qquad (15.47)$$

analogous to equation (15.10). The solution of the original Dirac equation may be obtained from the solution of equation (15.47) according to the formula

$$\Psi(x) = \int_{-\infty}^{\infty} \Phi(x, w) \exp(-imw)\, dw, \tag{15.48}$$

which is analogous to equation (15.2).

Another version of this idea was developed in Appendix D of this article. It was closer to the ideas of Fock[27] and Nambu.[28] Now the Dirac equation, $(i\nabla - B)\Psi = m\Psi$, was written in the form

$$[(i\, \partial/\partial x_\mu) - B_\mu]^2 \Psi - \tfrac{1}{2}\sigma_{\mu\nu}F_{\mu\nu}\Psi = m\Psi, \tag{15.49}$$

which is analogous to the form (15.10) of the Klein–Gordon equation. Here the matrices $\sigma_{\mu\nu} = \tfrac{1}{2}i(\gamma_\mu\gamma_\nu - \gamma_\nu\gamma_\mu)$ are 4×4 matrices, analogous to those of Pauli, and $F_{\mu\nu} = \partial B_\nu/\partial x_\mu - \partial B_\mu/\partial x_\nu$ is the field tensor. Adding the fifth parameter u in the spinor wave function $\Psi(x, u)$, Feynman wrote down the equation for $\Phi(x, u)$ in the form

$$i\, \partial\Phi/\partial u = \tfrac{1}{2}[(i\, \partial/\partial x_\mu) - B_\mu]^2 \Phi - \tfrac{1}{4}\sigma_{\mu\nu}F_{\mu\nu}\Phi, \tag{15.50}$$

It can then be analyzed by the Lagrangian method. The final result is the sum over all trajectories $x_\mu(u)$ of the hypercomplex amplitude

$$\exp\left(-i\int_0^{u_0} \left[\tfrac{1}{2}(dx_\mu/du)^2 + (dx_\mu/du)B_\mu(x) - \tfrac{1}{4}\sigma_{\mu\nu}(u)F_{\mu\nu}(x(u))\right] du\right). \tag{15.51}$$

We can see how close Feynman came to the current ideas of how to treat the Dirac equation via the path-integral method using hypercomplex numbers. The further development of this idea was successful, and led to the application of the Grassmann variables for this purpose, as a special kind of hypercomplex number.

Another suggestion in this direction was given in Appendix B, after the operator (15.46) for self-action was disentangled and represented, using $C_\mu(W) = \int_0^W \gamma_\mu(w)\, dw$ and $\dot{C}_\mu(w) = \gamma_\mu(w)$, in the form

$$R = \int_0^{\infty} \exp[ip_{\mu,\infty}C_\mu(w)]\exp\left(-\tfrac{1}{2}ie^2 \int_0^{w'} \int_0^{w''} \dot{C}_\mu(w')\dot{C}(w'')\right.$$

$$\left. \times \delta_+[\{\dot{C}_\mu(w') - \dot{C}_\mu(w'')\}]^2\, dw'\, dw''\right)\exp(-imW)\, dW. \tag{15.52}$$

Feynman noted: 'Not much has been done with this expression. (It is suggestive that perhaps coordinates and the space–time they represent may in

1 Riding his bicycle in Far Rockaway. (Courtesy: WGBH TV, Boston.)

2 A family portrait with parents Melville and Lucille, and sister Joan, at their Far Rockaway home. (Courtesy. WGBH TV, Boston.)

3 Feynman and Arline in their wedding announcement photograph. (Courtesy: Elmer Heller.)

4 Cracking the safe at Los Alamos. (Courtesy: California Institute of Technology, Pasadena, California.)

5 At the Shelter Island Conference, June 1947.
Standing: Willis E. Lamb, Jr and John A. Wheeler.
Seated: Abraham Pais, Feynman, Hermann Feshbach, and Julian Schwinger.
(Courtesy: National Academy of Sciences Archives.)

6 With Murray Gell-Mann, mid 1950s. (Courtesy: California Institute of
Technology, Pasadena, California.)

7 With Professor and Mrs Hideki Yukawa in Kyoto, Japan, 1956. (Courtesy: Yukawa Hall, Kyoto, Japan.)

8 Posing for the author; 10 May 1962.

9 A conversation with P. A. M. Dirac in Warsaw, 1962. (Courtesy: Polish Academy of Sciences.)

10 With children Carl and Michelle on a visit to Yorkshire, England. (Courtesy: California Institute of Technology, Pasadena, California.)

11 Playing bongo drums at Caltech. (Courtesy: California Institute of Technology, Pasadena, California.)

12 Standing in front of the blackboard in his office. (Courtesy: California Institute of Technology, Pasadena, California.)

13 The press conference at the Athenaeum, Caltech, after the Nobel Prize announcement, October 1965. (Courtesy: California Institute of Technology, Pasadena, California.)

14 With Princess Sibylla of Sweden during the Nobel banquet. (Courtesy: the Nobel Foundation.)

15 Dancing with Gweneth Feynman after the Nobel banquet. (Courtesy: the Nobel Foundation.)

16 At the Nobel prize ceremony, December 1965. (Courtesy: the Nobel Foundation.)

17 With Julian Schwinger in Stockholm, 1965. (Courtesy: the Nobel Foundation.)

18 Caltech Nobel Laureates: Carl Anderson, Murray Gell-Mann, Max Delbruck, Feynman, George Beadle. (Courtesy: California Institute of Technology.)

19 With his teachers Abram Bader and Joe Johnson on a visit to Far Rockaway High School after receiving the Nobel Prize, 1966. (Courtesy: Abram Bader.)

20 'The handsomest cowboy physicist' with a fashion editor from *Vogue*. (Courtesy: *Vogue* and Helen Tuck.)

21 Feynman standing in for Sir Isaac Newton. (Courtesy: California Institute of Technology, Pasadena, California.)

22 Three children have a close look at Feynman's book on Quantum Electrodynamics. Feynman kept this picture in his office. (Courtsey: Helen Tuck.)

23 The author with Feynman, 14 January 1970.

24 In front of his office blackboard, 1972. (Courtesy: California Institute of Technology, Pasadena, California.)

25 Receiving the Niels Bohr International Gold Medal from the Queen of Denmark, 1973. (Courtesy: the Niels Bohr Institute.)

26 Giving the commencement address at Caltech, 1974. (Courtesy: California Institute of Technology, Pasadena, California.)

27 Feynman at the drums in the 1981 Caltech production of *South Pacific*. (Courtesy: California Institute of Technology, Pasadena, California.)

28 Feynman with diagrams. (Courtesy: California Institute of Technology, Pasadena, California.)

29 At the *Challenger* disaster hearing on 11 February 1986, Feynman provides a sample O-ring with an ice water demonstration. (Courtesy: California Institute of Technology, Pasadena, California.)

30 The last photograph of Richard Feynman, 27 January 1988; he died on 15 February 1988. (Photograph by the author.)

31 Poster hung at Caltech's Millikan Library, 16 February 1988. (Courtesy: California Institute of Technology, Pasadena, California.)

some future theory be replaced completely by an analysis of ordered quantities in some hypercomplex algebra).'[29]

15.7 Functional integration and the path-integral method

In the Appendices A, B, and C of his 1951 paper, Feynman desribed a new development and generalization of the functional methods and especially of his path-integral method. He wrote: 'In this Appendix [A,B,C] an attempt will be made to discuss some properties of ordered operators and of functionals in a somewhat general way. Almost certainly many of the equations will be incorrect in their general form. This is especially true of those involving the Fourier transform in function space. However, it is expected that they are correct in special cases in which the formulas have been applied in the main part of this paper. Therefore, at least at first, when new results using these methods are derived, care should be taken to check the final result in some independent way. It is analogous to using power series expansions, or Fourier transforms, in a calculation in a situation in which the conditions for the validity of the power expansions or of the transform have not been checked, or are not known to be satisfied. The physicist is very familiar with such a situation and usually satisfied with it, especially since he is confident that he can tell if the answer is physically reasonable. But mathematicians may be completely repelled by the liberties taken here. The liberties are taken not because the mathematical problems are considered unimportant. On the contrary, this appendix is written to encourage the study of these forms from a mathematical standpoint. In the meantime, just as a poet has license from the rules of grammar and pronunciation, we should like to ask for 'physicists' license' from the rules of mathematics in order to express what we wish to say in as simple a manner as possible.'[30]

These words of Feynman indicate the spirit of his mathematical investigations, which were far from being mathematically rigorous, but very, very constructive.

As far as it is clear what the linear combination and the exponent of an arbitrary operator is, and, on the other hand, in the analysis of commuting variables, more complicated functions may be represented as a superposition of the exponents, using Fourier transformation, Feynman proposed to extend this idea to the case of the functionals for which the operators are defined. 'Thus the superposition rule permits a wide increase in the class of functionals for which we have defined the operators. In fact, with some mathematical license, we have defined the operator for any functional. We wish to imagine that any functional can be represented as a superposition of exponential ones in a manner analogous to the representation of an arbitrary function as a superposition of exponential functions. Thus, we expect to be able to write for any functional $F[M(s)]$ (the true mathematical restrictions are completely unknown to me)

$$F[M(s)] = \int \exp\left(i \int_0^1 \mu(s)M(s)\, ds\right) \mathscr{F}[\mu(s)] \mathscr{D}\mu(s), \qquad (15.53)$$

where $\mathscr{F}[\mu(s)]$ is a new (complex) functional, the functional transform of $F[M(s)]$, and $\int \ldots \mathscr{D}\mu(s)$ represents (some kind of an) integration over the space of functions $\mu(s)$. For simplicity, we take the case of just a one-argument function $M(s)$. If $F[M(s)]$ is given, $\mathscr{F}$ can be determined perhaps from

$$\mathscr{F}[\mu(s)] = \int \exp\left(-i \int_0^1 \mu(s)M(s)\, ds\right) F[M(s)] \mathscr{D}M(s), \qquad (15.54)$$

with suitable normalization. Then, if $\mathscr{F}$ is known, we define the operator $F[M(s)]$ as

$$F[M(s)] = \int \exp\left(i \int_0^1 \mu(s)M(s)\, ds\right) \mathscr{F}[\mu(s)] \mathscr{D}\mu(s), \qquad (15.55)$$

where $\mu(s)$ is a numerical function. Since we have already defined the operator $\exp(i \int_0^1 \mu(s)M(s)\, ds)$ (by some proper differential equation), we now simply require superimposition of such operators for various $\mu(s)$. The extension to functionals of several variables is evident.'[30]

This presents Feynman's idea of how to define the functional of an operator argument, using the functionals of different functions. Unfortunately, the further development of this idea showed that it is impossible in general, in a strict mathematical sense, to carry out the operations which Feynman had proposed to use only in quite restricted cases. Especially, it is hard to define proper integration in the space of functions in general (see Section 10.41).

In Appendix B Feynman used this method in the very important case of functionals of the type $F[P(s), Q(s)]$, where P and Q are quantum mechanical momentum and position operators, which obey the canonical commutation relation

$$PQ - QP = -i. \qquad (15.56)$$

Using Fourier transformations (15.53) and (15.54) of the functionals and representation (15.55) of the functional of operator arguments, combined with his disentangling procedure, Feynman showed that the matrix elements of the functional $F[P(s), Q(s)]$ between arbitrary states, with wave functions $g(Q)$ for the initial state and $f(Q)$ for the final state, may be written in a form

$$(g^*Ff) = \int\int g^*(q_1) \exp\left(i \int p(s)\dot{q}(s)\, ds\right) F[p(s)q(s)] \mathscr{D}p(s)\mathscr{D}q(s) f(q_0)\, dq_0\, dq_1.$$

$$(15.57)$$

Here $p(s)$ and $q(s)$ are the usual functions, which give the path in phase space of the classical system, being in correspondence to the quantum one. In the formula (15.57) all operators have been eliminated. It represents the matrix elements of the ordered operator $F[P(s), Q(s)]$ as a path-integral of the corresponding functional $F[P(s) Q(s)]$ on the phase space of the classical system. Here the path integral on the phase space of the classical system was first introduced by Feynman. Its rigorous definition is still an open problem.

Feynman immediately applied this result to the case of the operator functional $S = \exp(-i \int_0^T H(t)\, dt)$, where $H(t)$ is the quantum Hamiltonian of the system. This operator functional is just the evolution operator of the quantum system. For example, for the Hamiltonian $H(t) = (1/2m)P^2 + V(Q, t)$, according to the formula (15.57) we have the matrix elements

$$(g^* Ff) =$$

$$\iint g^*(q_1) \exp\left(i \int_0^T p(t)\dot{q}(t)\, dt - i \int_0^T (1/2m)p(t)^2\, dt - i \int_0^T V(q(t), t)\, dt \right)$$

$$\times f(q_0)\mathscr{D}p(t)\mathscr{D}q(t)\, dq_0\, dq_1. \quad (15.58)$$

The integral on the functions $P(t)$ can be easily done, because the functional in the exponent in (15.58) depends quadratically on $P(t)$. The corresponding technique was developed by Feynman in the following Appendix C. The result is

$$(g^* Sf) = \iint g^*(q_T) \exp\left(+i \int_0^T [\tfrac{1}{2}m\dot{q}(t)^2 - V(q(t), t)]\, dt \right) f(q_0)\mathscr{D}q(t)\, dq_0\, dq_T.$$

$$(15.59)$$

That is, the transition amplitude from point q_0 at $t=0$ to q_T at $t=T$ is the integral over all trajectories connecting these points of $\exp(\int_0^T L[\dot{q}(t), q(t)]\, dt)$, L being the Lagrangian for this problem. 'This is the fundamental theorem on which the interpretation of [Feynman's path-integral formulation of quantum mechanics] is based.'[31] Thus, starting from his operator calculus Feynman derived his old path-integral method.

In Appendix C of the 1951 article,[2] Feynman developed the technique for the calculation of the so-called Gaussian functional integrals, which is the basis of such types of calculations in field theory even up to now. Practically, this is the only working method to apply functional integration in field theory, and by now it has been highly modified and developed. In a large number of problems the operators appear in exponentials only up to the second degree. For this reason, it is handy to have available a formula for the integration of Gaussian functionals. We can define a Gaussian functional $G[y(s)]$, of one function $y(s)$, as one of the form $G[y(s)] = \exp iE[y(s)]$, with $E[y(s)]$ quadratic. Thus, we have

$$E[y(s)] = \tfrac{1}{2} \int_0^1 \int_0^1 A(t, s)y(t)y(s)\, dt\, ds + \int_0^1 B(s)y(s)\, ds, \tag{15.60}$$

where $A(t, s)$ and $B(s)$ are functionals, independent of y (that is, Gaussian if the second functional derivative of $\ln G$ is independent of y).

For this type of functional Feynman obtained the explicit results for functional integrals

$$\int \exp\{iE[y(s)]\}\mathcal{D}y(s) = I[A, B], \tag{15.61a}$$

$$\int \exp\{iE[y(s)]\}y(t)\mathcal{D}y(s) = \tilde{y}(t)I[A, B], \tag{15.61b}$$

$$\int \exp\{iE[y(s)]\}y(t)y(t')\mathcal{D}y(s) = [\tilde{y}(t)\tilde{y}(t') + iN(t, t')]I[A, B], \tag{15.61c}$$

and so on for higher powers of y. Here, in equations (15.61a–c) all terms on the right-hand sides were explicitly determined by coefficients $A(t, s)$ and $B(s)$ of the quadratic form (15.60). The function $\tilde{y}(t)$ is the solution of the integral equation

$$\int_0^1 A(t, s)\tilde{y}(s)\, ds = -B(t).$$

so $\tilde{y}(t) = \int_0^1 N(s, t)B(s)\, ds$, and it gives the extremum of the functional $E[y(s)]$; $N(s, t)$ is the kernel of the inverse integral operator, which corresponds to the integral operator defined by the kernel $A(t, s)$. Finally,

$$I[A, B] = G[\tilde{y}(s)]I[A, 0].$$

Feynman used these formulas to rederive some basic relations in quantum mechanics and quantum electrodynamics. Feynman's formulas for the Gaussian functional integrals have been proved to be strictly correct. They have been generalized and justified for different types of functional integrals, including the ones on Grassmann's noncommuting variables. These formulas have provided a convenient basis for many original investigations in quantum field theory, in statistical physics, in probability theory, and in other domains of physics and mathematics.

15.8 Some concluding remarks

Feynman's two articles of 1950 and 1951 which we have treated in this chapter were the final ones in the sequence of his fundamental articles on quantum electrodynamics. Feynman described these papers as follows. 'I had invented a new mathematical method [the operator calculus] for dealing with operators according to a parameter which, to this day, I feel is a great invention, and which nobody uses for anything; nobody pays any attention to it. Some day it will be recognized as an important invention. I still think it is something very important, just as important as I felt when I first wrote it.

'I had used it to formulate quantum electrodynamics. I invented it to do that. It was in fact the mathematical formulation that I expressed at the Pocono Conference—that was this crazy language. Dates don't mean anything. It was published in 1951, but it had all been invented by 1948. I called it the operator calculus.'

'I published it at that time because, after I had given the rules, and proved that they were the same as the other things [of Schwinger and Tomonaga], it was important [to show it formally]. Dyson had already given a proof. People don't bother to read my proof because it's too elaborate and funny, odd notations and path integrals, etc., but I had to do it in my own way for my own purposes. My paper on the 'Mathematical formulation of the quantum theory of electromagnetic interaction' was a rather unnecessary paper, because Dyson had done it in some way, and all I wanted to say was how I did it. But the other paper, on the operator calculus[2] was not completely empty; I felt it was important. In the years since I had invented it I had accumulated a whole lot of debris. For instance, I had noticed certain ways of representing spin-0 particles with path integrals, I had the operator calculus, and a whole lot of other things which I did not know where to put. Most of it was, of course, the operator calculus, but in the various appendices I included a whole variety of other things. With this paper I disgorged myself of all the things I had thought about in the context of quantum electrodynamics; this was an entire backlog of valuable things. I still think that the central item, the operator calculus, was an important invention.

'With this paper I had completed the project on quantum electrodynamics. I didn't have anything else remaining that required publishing. In these two papers,[1,2] I put everything that I had done and thought should be published on the subject. And that was the end of my published work on this field.'[32]

Feynman was never completely satisfied with his work on quantum electrodynamics, especially the renormalization procedure. As he recalled: '. . . I had answered Bethe's original request for a way of cutting it off so that all shenanigans with subtraction will be straightened out. In other words, it was obvious to me that it was renormalizable in the manner that Bethe proposed it would be, that by changing the mass and the charge, we would have expressed everything in terms of experimental mass and charge, all the results would be finite and one wouldn't need all these shenanigans.

'While I believed at the time that I wasn't finished, that I would find a satisfactory way of cutting off, I knew that the way I had cut it off destroyed unitarity, for instance, temporarily. Only the limit was presumably OK. I believed that there was a way of cutting the theory off somehow which wouldn't destroy anything, that wasn't artificial, or just a mathematical trick. It could be solved. With the finite cut-off the theory would also be sound by itself. And that the real theory was the limit of that, and that was the way it should be. So I delayed a little bit my publication. I was urged to publish it anyway, and you'll find it in that paper[25] [The theory of positrons, 1949] a kind of apology, that I apologized for publishing it before I had straightened this little thing out, this minor problem! And thank God I did, because it has never been straightened out to this day. This minor problem! I thought that perhaps Schwinger had straightened it out because he had a great reputation, but when I thought about what he did, I realized that he had in his work the same problem in another form. And I mentioned it in that paper and explained it. I knew that we both hadn't solved it. And that we hadn't really solved quantum electrodynamics in the sense of finding a sound theory that the limit of which is electrodynamics; we couldn't prove that the electrodynamics we were writing was self-consistent and possibly not unitary, possibly incorrect, and very likely is so, but it's never been resolved. It has never been proved one way or the other whether electrodynamics renormalizes a consistent theory.'[33]

As we see, up to the very end Feynman had not changed the opinion which he had expressed in his Nobel lecture: 'Therefore, I think that the renormalization theory is simply a way to sweep the difficulties of the divergences of electrodynamics under the rug. I am, of course, not sure of that.'[34]

In October 1961, Feynman would be invited to give a report at the twelfth Solvay Conference on the general theme of quantum field theory to celebrate the fiftieth anniversary of the famous 1911 Solvay Conference on radiation theory and quanta, at which Einstein, Planck, and Sommerfeld had presented their wonderful results on quantum theory. On this occasion, it was the same subject: the quantum theory of the interaction of light and matter. A large group of people, including Bethe, Weisskopf, Schwinger, and Dyson, were invited to attend this conference. Feynman was invited to give a report on the (then) current status of quantum electrodynamics.

Upon receiving the invitation to attend the Solvay Conference, Feynman felt rather honored, 'because these conferences always had a reputation. I remember when Bethe was invited sometime back [1948], he took very seriously the writing of his report for the conference. So, like father, like son: when I was invited to the Solvay Conference, I had to write a report and I took it very seriously, just as Bethe had done, imitating him in a way. In my report I discussed the subject as if I were addressing those people who had been present in 1911, telling them how far the problems which they had considered had evolved.'[32]

At the 1962 Solvay Conference, Feynman would declare: 'Considerable evidence for the general validity of QED is, of course, provided by the enormous variety of ordinary phenomena which, under rough calculation, are seen to be consistent with it. The superfluidity of helium and the superconductivity of metals having been recently explained, there are to my knowledge no phenomena occurring under known conditions where quantum electrodynamics should provide an explanation and where at least a qualitative explanation in these terms has not been found. The search for discrepancies has turned from looking for gross deviations in complex situations to looking for large discrepancies at very high energies, or by looking for tiny deviations from the theory in very simple, but very accurately measured, situations. [No discrepancies have been found.]' [35]

Would the basic ideas of quantum electrodynamics be violated by a future theory? Feynman's answer was yes. Does there exist a tendency for that? 'No. I don't see any tendencies, though I think it would be violated. I am just guessing. Would it be violated at higher energies? Probably yes. I don't see any tendencies. I can't say that a thing is right if I think it will be violated.' [32]

Feynman would enjoy his visit to Brussels, where not only all his friends in the field— including great personalities like Dirac, Heisenberg, and Wigner— were present, but he would also meet the king and queen of Belgium. His preoccupation with the problems of quantum electrodynamics had been over for quite some time, but he would continue to make use of the physical conceptions and mathematical techniques he had pioneered in this field.

Notes and References

1. R.P. Feynman, Mathematical formulation of the quantum theory of electromagnetic interaction. *Phys. Rev.* **80**, 440 (1950).

2. R.P. Feynman, An operator calculus having applications in quantum electrodynamics. *Phys. Rev.* **84**, 108 (1951).

3. J.S. Schwinger, Quantum electrodynamics. III. The electromagnetic properties of the electron—radiative correction to scattering. *Phys. Rev.* **76**, 790 (1949).

4. S. Tomonaga, On infinite field reactions in quantum field theory. *Phys. Rev.* **74**, 224 (1948).

5. R.P. Feynman, Space–time approach to non-relativistic quantum mechanics. *Rev. Mod. Phys.* **20**(2), 376 (1948); A relativistic cut-off for classical electrodynamics. *Phys. Rev.* **74**, 939 (1948); A relativistic cut-off for quantum electrodynamics. *Phys. Rev.* **74**, 1430(1948); The theory of positrons. *Phys. Rev.* **76**, 749 (1949); Space-time approach to quantum electrodynamics. *Phys. Rev.* **76r**, 769 (1949); Mathematical formulation of the quantum theory of electromagnetic interaction. *Phys. Rev.* **80**, 440 (1950).

6. R.P. Feynman, Ref. 2, p. 108.

7. W. Heitler, *The quantum theory of radiation*. Clarendon Press, Oxford, 1935, Chap. 3, §2.1.

8. See, for example, B. Gaveau and L.S. Schulman, Dirac equation path integral: Interpreting Grassmann variables. *Nuovo Cim.* **11**, 31 (1989).

9. R.P. Feynman, Ref. 1, formula 6.3.

10. R.P. Feynman, The theory of positrons, Ref. 5.

11. R.P. Feynman, Ref. 2, p. 108.

12. R.P. Feynman, Ref. 2, p. 110.

13. R.P. Feynman, Ref. 2, pp. 110–11.

14. R.P. Feynman, Space–time approach to non-relativistic quantum mechanics, Ref. 5.

15. R.P. Feynman, Ref. 2, p. 112.

16. R.P. Feynman, Ph.D. thesis, see Chapter 6.

17. J.S. Schwinger, *Phys. Rev.* **74**, 1439 (1948).

18. R.P. Feynman, Ref. 2, p. 117.

19. F.J. Dyson, The radiation theories of Tomonaga, Schwinger, and Feynman. *Phys. Rev.* **75**, 486 (1949).

20. F.J. Dyson, Ref. 19, p. 486.

21. S.I Tomonaga, *Prog. Theor. Phys.* **1**, 27 (1946); S.I Koba, S.I Tati, and S.I. Tomonaga, *Prog. Theor. Phys.* **2**, 101 (1947); S. Kanesawa and S.I. Tomonaga, *Prog. Theor. Phys.* **3**, 1 (1948); S.I. Tomonaga, *Phys. Rev.* **74**, 224 (1948).

22. J.S. Schwinger, *Phys. Rev.* **73**, 416 (1948); *Phys. Rev.* **74**, 1439 (1948), and Ref. 3.

23. F.J. Dyson, Ref. 19, p. 491.

24. R.P. Feynman, Ref. 2, p. 119.

25. R.P. Feynman, The theory of positrons, *Phys. Rev.* **76**, 749 (1949).

26. R.P. Feynman, Ref. 25, §2, eqn. (8).

27. V. Fock, *Phys. Z. Sowjetunion* **12**, 404 (1937).

28. Y. Nambu, *Prog. Theor. Phys.* **5**, 82 (1950).

29. R.P. Feynman, Ref. 2, p. 126.

30. R.P. Feynman, Ref. 2, p. 124.

31. R.P. Feynman, Ref. 2, p. 125.

32. R.P. Feynman, Interviews and conversations with Jagdish Mehra, in Austin,

Texas, April 1970, Pasadena, California, January 1988. Interviews with Charles Weiner (American Institute of Physics), Pasadena, California, 1966.

33. R.P. Feynman, Ref. 32, January 1988.

34. R.P. Feynman, The development of the space–time view of quantum electrodynamics, Nobel Lecture. *Science* **153**, 699 (1966), p. 9.

35. R.P. Feynman, The present status of quantum electrodynamics. In: Jagdish Mehra, *The Solvay Conferences on Physics: Aspects of the development of physics since* 1911. Reidel, Dordrecht, Holland, 1975, p. 275.

16

From Cornell to Caltech via Copacabana and Kyoto

What bothered Feynman the most at Cornell, in Ithaca, in upstate New York, was the weather. One day it had suddenly become very cold, rainy, and slushy, as it often did there. Feynman's car began to skid and he had to put chains on the tires. The effort of putting on chains on the tires and putting clamps on them in the bitterly cold weather was painful and unpleasant, and it dawned on him that he could avoid all that nuisance by getting out of that part of the country and going somewhere more pleasant.

As a faculty member in the sciences at Cornell Feynman was deeply bothered by the fact that not only all the humanities—such as history, philosophy, literature, psychology, sociology, etc.—were fully represented in the university, but so were animal husbandry, home economics, and hotel management. It seemed to him very strange that, as with physics, a student could study home economics or hotel management for four years and obtain a degree from Cornell; Feynman thought that these were not intellectual pursuits, and should not be represented at the university.

Feynman himself did enjoy learning about the history of the Aztecs and the Incas, but he did not meet many people at Cornell—especially in the humanities—who were really excited by what they were doing. He found some colleagues quite interesting, such as a biologist who had discovered that bats use radar in flying and was then studying seagulls and fish noises; that was fun. But such intellectual stimulation was rare; this dilution due to the availability and pursuit of so many diverse fields at Cornell bothered Feynman. 'If you did something unusual and interesting and tried to explain it to somebody, you always got dumb stares back. The resistance and dopiness of all kinds were a kind of morass, and I couldn't stand it anymore.'[1] Feynman used to eat in the university cafeteria, rather than the faculty club, where he would go with students, especially since he loved to watch beautiful young girls. In talking to students all he met with was dopiness. 'That's all right if you are talking to a secretary, but it's not all right if you are talking to students and professors. That bothered me enormously.'[1]

Robert F. Bacher, who, with Hans Bethe, had been instrumental in bringing Feynman to Cornell had, in the meantime, gone to the California Institute of Technology as head of the Division of Physical Sciences and director of the Norman Bridge Laboratory of Physics. In the fall of 1949, Bacher invited Feynman to give a series of lectures on quantum electrodynamics, meson theory, and nuclear forces. Bacher had already discussed the possibility of such a visit to give a series of lectures at Caltech with Feynman at Cornell during the summer, and had also cleared the matter with Bethe. In planning to visit Caltech, Feynman applied for leave from Cornell for the period 30 January to 1 March, which was routinely granted, and he gave a series of twelve lectures on 'Quantum electrodynamics and meson theories' in February 1950; I. I. Rabi and J. Robert Oppenheimer had been the first two invited in this series of lectures delivered at Caltech by eminent visiting scientists.

Feynman greatly enjoyed his stay at Caltech. Robert Bacher discussed with him the possibility of a permanent move to Caltech, offering him sufficient inducements to leave Cornell to come to California. Above all else, two things especially attracted Feynman by the prospect of such a move. First, of course, the pleasant climate. Second, but more important, was the character of Caltech as an institute of technology There were many science departments at Caltech, with really active people. They had the same way of thinking as Feynman. He could talk to all the people in astronomy, biology, and all the other different fields, without any trouble, from which he got a great deal of pleasure. 'The odds against meeting or talking to someone whose conversation I would find dopey—unlike Cornell—were very great. I immediately decided that Caltech was my kind of place.'[1]

In thinking of leaving Cornell the thing that worried Feynman the most was his relationship with Hans Bethe. 'That was very hard. That was a negative pressure. Actually, it was very difficult to leave. I made a joke at that time about the donkey who is exactly between two piles of hay. Which way should he go? Everytime he moves towards one pile, the other one would grow bigger. What they would do at Cornell was this: whenever I gave an indication that I wanted to move [say, to Caltech], they would fix things in [my] favor [making it very difficult for me to decide].'[2] Soon after his return from Caltech to Cornell in the spring of 1950, Bacher offered Feynman a professorship of theoretical physics. At Cornell Feynman was entitled to a sabbatical leave during the academic year 1951–52, and Caltech offered to give it to him at their expense in the beginning of his duties there.

From 24 to 30 April 1950, there took place the International Colloquium on Fundamental Particles and Nuclei, to which Feynman—together with an international cast of most of the eminent physicists in the field—was invited to attend by Alexandre Proca in Paris. Feynman first informed Proca that, having recently returned from a private visit to Brazil, he could not afford to attend the conference. On 20 February Proca informed Feynman that his trip would be paid for by the Rockefeller Foundation, and invited him to give a report on the current status of the theories of elementary particles on 24 April, the opening day of the conference. Feynman decided to travel by air, rather than join Niels Bohr, Wolfgang Pauli, and others who were traveling by boat from the United States to Europe. At the conference, Pauli gave a report on quantum electrodynamics, and Feynman's talk turned out to be his own contribution to it. Feynman had a wonderful time in Paris. 'I had met several of the girls who were dancing at the Lido in Paris, at Las Vegas. I watched rehearsals at the Lido, went backstage, and had all kinds of fun.'

The International Colloquium on Fundamental Particles and Nuclei featured almost all the great names in modern particle physics and quantum field theory. In Paris, Feynman again met Bohr, Dirac, Peierls, and Pauli. Among the others present were Walter Heitler, Christian Møller, Hendrik Kramers, Enrico Fermi, Markus Fierz, Oskar Klein, Léon Rosenfeld, Max Born, Nevill Mott, Erwin Schrödinger, Maurice Pryce, Gregor Wentzel, George Uhlenbeck, H. B. G. Casimir, Gilberto Bernardini, Abraham Pais, and Julian Schwinger. Feynman's work on his quantum electrodynamical theories was in its last stages of development, and in Paris he talked about his own work. He was not quite satisfied with his lecture at the conference. First, there was the language problem in explaining his ideas to a large multinational audience; he talked rather fast in English, and the audience could not comprehend him most of the time. Also his ideas and techniques were still new and not quite familiar to most physicists as they would become within a few years.[3]

Wolfgang Pauli, with whom Feynman had become acquainted already in his Princeton days, was deeply impressed with him and his work. He invited Feynman to visit Zurich for a few days after the conference in Paris. In Zurich, Feynman addressed the joint University–ETH (Swiss Federal Institute of Technology) colloquium and gave several other lectures on his path-integral formulation of quantum mechanics and on his work on quantum electrodynamics. This was Feynman's first visit to Europe and he enjoyed it thoroughly; he would return to Europe time and again both for business and pleasure.

Upon his return to the United States from Europe, Feynman made the necessary arrangements to leave Cornell University and join the California Institute of Technology. During the summer of 1950 Feynman worked as a consultant at the Institute for Numerical Analysis at the University of California Los Angeles. Mark Kac from Cornell also worked there during that summer; it was in fact Kac who had arranged Feynman's summer appointment there. At this Institute, they began to call each other Monte [Kac] and Carlo [Feynman], with reference to the Monte Carlo method of random sampling techniques to obtain approximate solutions to mathematical and physical problems.

Feynman had arranged with Robert Bacher that his appointment at Caltech for the academic year 1950–51 would begin on 1 July. It was also arranged that Feynman would stay at the Athenaeum, Caltech's faculty club, as a long-term guest for the entire year. Feynman had not fully committed himself to staying on at Caltech permanently; he still harbored unsettled feelings about life and the world and was not quite sure what he wanted to do with the rest of his life. He was even toying with the idea of moving permanently to South America, for which he had developed a strong liking. Thus, rather tentatively, began Feynman's association with the California Institute of Technology, where he would spend the rest of his life.

While he was still at Cornell, Feynman once picked up a hitchhiker who told him how interesting and exciting South America was, and that he ought to visit there. Feynman decided that was a good idea: he would go to South America! Foreign language classes were available at Cornell. They used a method which had been employed during the war: a group of about ten students thrown together with one native speaker of the language; they would only speak that language and nothing else. Since Feynman looked so young, he decided to take the foreign language class as a regular student. He did not yet know where in South America he intended to go. However, he decided on Spanish, because Spanish is spoken in a large majority of South American countries.[1,2]

When the time came to register, Feynman was standing in line to sign up, and a beautiful young blonde woman came up. He thought he would join the same class as her, but she was going to register for Portuguese, not Spanish. Feynman felt like taking Portuguese, too, so as to be close to her, but he thought the better of it and decided that was not good enough reason to give up Spanish—and, much to his later regret, he signed up for Spanish.

Early in January 1949, Feynman went to give a seminar at Princeton. There he met Jaime Tiomno and Walter Schützer from Brazil, who were working with John Wheeler. He told Tiomno that he was learning Spanish to go to South America. Tiomno suggested that he should go to Rio de Janeiro, where Cesar Lattes and J. Leite Lopes had established the Brazilian Center for Research in Physics (CBPF: Centro Brasileiro de Pesquisas Fisicas), and where a visiting position could be arranged for him during part of the summer. Feynman agreed to do so, but now he had to convert all the Spanish he had learned into Portuguese. He found a Portuguese graduate student at Cornell, from whom he took lessons twice a week and learned the rudiments of the Portugese language.[1]

In July 1949 Feynman went to Rio de Janeiro. He had a refuelling stop in Trinidad and he got into conversation with a Brazilian neurosurgeon who had studied in Maryland; they talked in Portuguese, which Feynman was able to understand. Feynman got off the plane in Recife; from there to Rio de Janeiro his fare was going to be paid by the Brazilian government. At Recife, Feynman was received by the wife and father-in-law of Cesar Lattes (the director of CBPF in Rio de Janeiro). There came an announcement on the intercom that the flight to Rio was canceled; so Feynman was obliged to spend the weekend in Recife, which he found to be a very nice town, and he immediately took to the relaxed way of life in Brazil.

In Rio, Feynman was received by Cesar Lattes and his arrival was filmed by the national television network, but without sound. The cameraman asked them both to keep talking while the pictures were being taken. They discussed the question of whether Feynman would give his lectures at the Center for Physical Research in the mornings or afternoons. Lattes told him that the students would prefer him to give the lectures in the afternoon, but the beach was also very nice in the afternoon, 'So, why don't you give your lectures in the mornings? Do what you find most convenient and enjoyable.'[4]

Feynman found that, unlike the United States, the attitude to life in Brazil was relaxed. They were in no hurry. So Feynman gave his lectures on nuclear theory in the mornings and enjoyed the beach in the afternoons. He found Rio de Janeiro so delightful that he wished that he had learned Portuguese in the first place rather than Spanish.

At first Feynman had thought that he would give his lectures in English, but then decided to give them in Portuguese, even though his pronunciation was not perfect and he had difficulties with the grammar. Now he had many friends in Brazil and he took the opportunity to speak as much Portuguese as possible. Cécile Morette (later Mrs Bryce DeWitt) was visiting CBPF that year from France, and Feynman felt at home among friends.

During that first time in Brazil, which lasted six weeks, Feynman was invited to give a talk at the Brazilian Academy of Sciences about his work on quantum electrodynamics. He prepared his talk in Portuguese with the help of a couple of students; he wrote the talk himself and the students corrected the grammar. The talks preceding Feynman's—one by a Brazilian chemist—were given in English. They spoke English with an awful pronunciation, which Feynman could not understand. When his turn came to speak, he wondered aloud that he had not realized that the official language of the Brazilian Academy was English, but he would nonetheless give his talk in Portuguese. 'So, for all I know, I changed the tradition of the Brazilian Academy of Sciences!'[5]

Feynman did not realize that the other speakers were speaking in English as a mark of courtesy to him. The Portuguese language was difficult for Feynman, but being persistent he kept on working at improving it by reading newspapers, giving his lectures, and talking in Portuguese. Still he found it difficult to understand the language spoken in the marketplace or by hearing people who conversed with each other rapidly.

In 1951, a new building was inaugurated to house the CBPF at the campus of the University of Rio de Janeiro. Leite Lopes invited Jaime Tiomno back to Brazil, and Guido Beck joined its faculty from Argentina. He invited Feynman for a longer stay at CBPF in 1951 and applied for support to the Point Four Program of the US State Department for his visit. Feynman decided to take his sabbatical year (to which he had been entitled from Cornell) at Caltech's expense; they paid half of his salary for a whole year. He stayed at CBPF from August 1951 to June 1952, a period of ten months. He enjoyed the beaches and the whole atmosphere of Rio; he liked the institute and helped in building it up.

At that time, after his well known success in quantum electrodynamics, Feynman was working on meson theory. He proposed to Leite Lopes that they investigate whether the pseudoscalar meson theory would give some results in the description of the deuteron which could be experimentally checked in spite of the difficulty of the $1/r^3$ singularity, at the origin, of the Yukawa potential. The results of this study were published in an article entitled 'On the pseudoscalar meson theory of the deuteron', in the proceedings of the Symposium on New Research Techniques in Physics, 15–29 June 1952.[6] Many physicists from Europe and the United States attended this symposium.

In Rio, Feynman stayed at the Miramar Palace Hotel in Copacabana. 'I had a room on the thirteenth floor, from where I could look at the ocean and watch the girls on the beach.'[7] People from the airlines—pilots and stewardesses—used to stay at Hotel Miramar on the fourth floor during their layovers in Rio. Feynman got to know them and, to be sociable, he would often go out with them at night to bars to have a few drinks. He began to enjoy this activity of going out to bars with the stewardesses. One day, at about 3:30 in the afternoon, as he was going past a bar on Copacabana beach, he felt a tremendous urge to have a drink. Suddenly he realized that it was only the afternoon, there was no social reason to have a drink as there was no company and no party, and he began to wonder why he had this great urge to have a drink. It occurred to him that he was getting used to drinking and, then and there, he forswore drinking. He had suddenly felt scared and decided not to drink again. 'That strong feeling [to have a drink] that I didn't understand frightened me . . . . I get such fun out of *thinking* that I don't want to destroy this most pleasant machine [my brain] that makes life such a big kick. It's the same reason that, later on, I was reluctant to try experiments with LSD in spite of my curiosity about hallucinations.'[8]

There was a young official at the US embassy in Rio de Janeiro who knew that Feynman liked samba music. During his first visit to Brazil, he had heard samba bands practicing in the streets, and he wanted to learn more about Brazilian music. The man from the embassy told him that a small group practiced at his apartment every week, and he could come and listen to them play. There were three or four people—one was the janitor of the apartment house—and they played rather quiet music in his apartment; they had no other place to play. One guy had a tambourine, called a *pandeiro*, and another guy had a small guitar. Feynman kept on hearing the sound of a drum somewhere, but there was no drum! Finally he figured out that the tambourine player played his instrument in a complicated way, twisting his wrist and hitting the skin with his thumb; Feynman found it very interesting and more or less learned to play the *pandeiro*.

Then, in February 1952, the Carnival time came around, and new music would be presented. That was exciting. The janitor himself was the composer for one of the small samba groups (called 'schools') called *Farcantes de Copacabana*, meaning the 'Fakers of Copacabana'. He invited Feynman to join the group. This samba school consisted of some people from the poor section of the city, called the *favelas*; they would practice their music for the Carnival in a parking lot behind the apartment house. Feynman began to play the '*frigideira*', a toy frying pan made of metal, about six inches in diameter, with a little metal stick to beat it with. At first, Feynman had difficulty, but gradually he became accomplished and a small group—the trumpet, the guitar, the *pandeiro*, the *frigideira*, and the singer—prepared samba music for a small party as a group. Afterwards, the bandleader collected money to pay for some costumes for the members of the band. Feynman had become quite a successful *frigideira* player.

Feynman took part in the pre-Carnival march. There took place a special competition between the samba schools of the three beaches—Copacabana, Ipanema, and Leblon. They marched down Avenida Atlantica. Although Feynman felt uncomfortable marching down in his costume, the costumes were Greek, he decided that he was as much Greek as the Brazilians and should not worry about wearing the costume. The march of the bands provided a great spectacle. There were huge crowds on both sides of the Avenida Atlantica, people were leaning out of the windows and standing on chairs and tables, and there were huge gatherings of people everywhere. Feynman played the *frigideira* with great gusto. He was recognized by his waiter friend as the band marched past the Miramar Palace Hotel—as well as by other acquaintances—who complimented him for 'being very good'. 'I had succeeded at something I wasn't supposed to be able to do.'[9]

During the Carnival itself, several members of Feynman's samba band didn't show up. They didn't believe that they could win against the really big samba schools of the city. Even as they were marching around in the street, some of the band wandered off. For them, the main excitement and fun had been to try to win the contest of the beaches, where most of them felt that their level was. And they did win. A photograph of Feynman disguised as Mephistopheles in a Carnival ball at the Municipal Theater of Rio de Janeiro appeared in the weekly magazine *O Cruzeiro* (15 March 1952, p. 49, Rio de Janeiro).

While it was all very enjoyable in Rio, it was not all fun and games. Apart from the collaboration with Leite Lopes on the pseudoscalar meson theory of the deuteron, Feynman became interested in calculating the energy levels of lighter nuclei, up to magnesium, on which experimental work was being done at the Kellogg Laboratory at Caltech in Pasadena. Feynman established contact with the experts at Caltech with the help of a ham radio operator and a student of his back home. These two amateur radio operators would help Feynman in establishing the exchange of information between the experimentalists at Caltech and himself. Thus, for example, he would ask information about the spacing between certain levels of boron, which he was calculating, and the experimental data helped him to adjust his constants. What Feynman was looking for was a deeper understanding of nuclei. He wrote a long letter about this work to Enrico Fermi in Chicago.[10] 'I was never quite convinced that it was very significant, so I never did anything with it.'[1]

At the University of Rio, Feynman taught two courses: one on the mathematical methods of physics and the other on electricity and magnetism. The students would learn the text all right, but they wouldn't turn in any assignments. The reason for this, it became clear to Feynman, was that they *couldn't* do the assignments. This experience led to a larger concern with the problem of teaching and learning science in Brazil and, in fact, throughout Latin America. Jaime Tiomno, Cesar Lattes, Leite Lopes, and others invited Feynman to discuss with them the structure of the educational system in Brazil. In particular, they showed him the textbooks in physics that were being used in high school and university. The Brazilians at that time were trying to introduce reform in the physics curriculum. In an invited lecture, Feynman criticized these books and other aspects of education by rote learning in Brazil.

At a meeting attended by university professors, members of CBPF, and the head of science education in the Brazilian government, Feynman expressed his views about science and science education. He started out by defining science as an understanding of the behavior of nature. He talked about the utility of science and its contribution to the improvement of the human condition. The problem of teaching physics in Latin America was only part of the wider problem of teaching physics, or anything, anywhere, for which there is no known satisfactory solution. There are many new plans in many countries for trying to teach physics, which shows that nobody is satisfied with any method. The fact is that nobody knows very well how to tell anybody else how to teach. It is at the same time a serious problem and an opportunity for new discoveries. The problem of teaching physics in Latin America reminded Feynman of the problem of doing *anything* in Latin America.

Physics is a basic science, and as such is used in engineering, chemistry, and biology, and has all kinds of applications in technology. Physics is the science, or knowledge of nature, that tells us how things work. Therefore, those who know physics will be much more useful at coping with technical problems arising in local industry. 'I think it is vitally important to improve the technical ability of the peoples of Latin America. By education, the man with the higher technical ability is able to produce more, and I believe that in the improvement of the technical ability, and thus the productivity, of the people of Latin America lies the source of real economic advancement.'[11]

It is not economically sound to import, on a continual basis, technically skilled people. If Latin American people were educated technically they would find positions in the developing industries in Latin American countries; it would soon be realized by the people who now import such workers that there is a supply of really able men right there, and this local supply has many advantages. The local people would not demand such high wages, would know the customs and ways of the country, and would be glad to take more permanent positions.

The truth is that 'Latin Americans with the same degrees in science or engineering as their foreign counterparts seem to be much less able. *This is because they have not really been taught any science.* [Let us examine the reasons why one should learn science.] One reason for teaching physics, or any experimental science, is that it incidentally teaches how to do things with your own hands. It teaches techniques of measurement and calculation, which have much wider applications than the particular field of study.

'A second reason for teaching physics is the science itself: Science as an activity of men; to many men it is a great pleasure and it should not be denied to the people of a large part of the world simply because of a fault or lack in the educational system. In other words, one of the reasons for teaching science is to [create] scientists, who will not just contribute to the development of industry but also contribute to the development of knowledge, joining in this great adventure of our times, and, of course, obtaining enormous pleasure from doing so.

'Thirdly, there is good reason to study nature, to appreciate its wonder and its beauty, even though one may not become an actively working professional scientist. This knowledge of nature also gives a feeling of stability and reality about the world and drives out many fears and superstitions.

'A fourth value of science is to teach how things are found out. The value of questioning, the value of free ideas—not only for the development of science, but the value of free ideas in every field, becomes apparent. Science is a way to teach how something gets known, what is not known, to what extent things *are* known (for nothing is known absolutely), how to handle doubt and uncertainty, what the rules of evidence are, how to think about things so that judgments can be made, how to distinguish truth from fraud, from show. These are certainly important secondary yields of teaching [and learning] science, and physics in particular.

'Finally, in learning science you learn to handle by trial and error, to develop a spirit of invention and of free inquiry which is of tremendous value far beyond science. One learns to ask oneself: "Is there a better way to do it?" We must try to think of some new gimmick or idea, to find some improvement in technique. This question is the source of a great deal of free independent thought, of invention, and of human progress of all kinds.'[12]

Some of the major characteristics of science education in Latin America that are of special concern, are, first and most serious, teaching and learning by means of pure, abject, rote memory. This in no way teaches physics as a science. Nothing is understood; it is only remembered. This in no way satisfied the reasons which Feynman had outlined for teaching science. 'Memorization of laws does not permit one to make applications of these laws to new situations; it cannot teach any techniques with hands. From memorizing, knowledge is not understood, and the beauty of nature is not appreciated. It does not tell how things were found out, or reveal the value of an inventive free mind.'[13]

Feynman gave several examples. He considered the cases of polarization and Brewster's angle, and the telescope. He had found that the students knew about the definitions by rote, but could not actually demonstrate the ideas with an actual polaroid sheet looking out at the sea, or what one did with an actual telescope; the construction and functions of the various types of the latter were memorized without requiring any understanding. Feynman declared that the main point of his talk was that no science was being taught in this way; whatever was being learned was by rote memorization, which was utterly useless. This was also the case with pages upon pages of textbooks. He opened the textbook on a page dealing with *triboluminescence*. Triboluminescence, the book said, is the light emitted when crystals are crushed. What have you learned? You have only described it using different words. But if, instead, the book had said: when you take a lump of sugar and crush it with a pair of pliers in the dark, you can see a bluish flash; some other crystals do that too, but nobody knows why, and this phenomenon is known as triboluminescence! Then, one would have learned something new about nature. 'It was incomprehensible to people in my country when I reported how material is memorized in Latin America completely without understanding.'[14]

Feynman reported that when he asked in his class what Brewster's law was, advanced students answered in a flash: 'Light impinging on a material of index n is 100% polarized with electric field perpendicular to the plane of incidence if the tangent of the angle of incidence equals the index of refraction.' To these same students Feynman said: 'Look out at the bay from which the sunlight is being reflected. If I look at the reflection through this piece of polaroid and turn it [around] what will happen?' All that Feynman received from the students was blank stares; no one knew. But when they tried looking through the polaroid and turned it around, he got cries of surprise and delight and saw the reflection getting brighter or dimmer. 'This shows something completely wrong. There is no knowledge whatsoever of nature ... Memorization is useless. These students are like books, no more. I can look in the index of a book under "Brewster's law" and find a reference equivalent to the students' reply. But in the index I cannot find "the sun reflecting on the bay".'[15]

The things that can be looked up in the book are only part of knowledge. Who wants such a student to work in a plant when a book requiring no food or maintenance stands day after day always ready to give just as adequate answers? Who wants to *be* such a student, to have worked so hard, to have missed so much interest and pleasure, and to be outdone by an inanimate printed list of 'laws'? This, Feynman thought, was one of the main failures in the education of students in Latin America.

Another problem in Latin America is that the students are all alone. They cannot converse with other students; they cannot see how stupid some fellow students are. This is mainly for some psychological reason. They do not wish to be found unsure, for they will be ridiculed. So, to save face, they all put on a show of knowledge, thereby frustrating free discussion and the exchange of ideas—one of the most pleasant and easiest way of learning things.

A third problem is the lack of freedom in the university structure. You cannot move around from one subject to another or from one laboratory to another. Those who go abroad to learn find it difficult to communicate their knowledge easily and directly to the university students when they return—for they cannot find a place in, and are not welcomed into, the university structure. For some reason or other, it becomes necessary for such people to create new and separate research institutes. The spirit of excitement which prevails in these institutions as their research progresses is not found in the universities.

Still another problem in Latin America is that there is very little outlet for the students who do not want to become complete scientists. It is not easy for them to obtain jobs in the developing industries there.

Gibbon said: 'The power of instruction is of little efficacy, except in those happy dispositions where it is nearly superfluous.' This is true of good instruction. But bad instruction can be very efficacious indeed in impressing on one how impossibly dull some subject is. In Latin America, the professors emphasize rote learning and regurgitation in the examinations of the material learned.

Feynman remarked: 'The creative scientists should have a dignity and a power to control their own destiny, and that of science and science education in their countries. It will be in safe, loving hands. It is from the fountain of research workers who understand what science is really about that the true spirit of inquiry rains onto their students, and their students' students, and ultimately, if things are organized right, permeates the entire educational system and speeds the [technological] development of the country. The problem, then, is how to get these research workers back in the universities where they belong. Then the "rain" will have a far easier and direct passage to the students, the new scientists of the country.'[16]

It is, of course, most important to do these things in a steady, continuous, and modest way. Maintenance is lacking in many of these projects. It should not be done with a big show, the big money, with much advertising, unsupported by any effective maintenance. A research group becomes world famous only after years of fruitful research.[17]

After Feynman's talk, the head of the science education department got up and said: 'Mr Feynman has told us some things which are very hard for us to hear, but it appears to be that he loves science, and is sincere in his criticism. Therefore, I think we should listen to him. I came here knowing that we have some sickness in our system of education; what I have learned is that we have *cancer!*' And he sat down. That gave other people freedom to talk and discuss, and there was much excitement.[1,2]

Since Feynman had gone to Brazil under the Point Four Program sponsored by the US government, he was asked by the State Department to write a report about his experiences in Brazil. So he wrote the essentials of the speech he had given there. He learned later through the grapevine that the reaction of somebody in the State Department was: 'That shows you how dangerous it is to send somebody to Brazil who is naive. Foolish fellow; he can only cause trouble. He did not understand the problems!' Feynman thought that it was persons like this one in the State Department who were naive and foolish; before going to Brazil, he had only read about the courses and their descriptions, which did not describe the reality of the situation.[1,2]

Feynman's dislike of artificial ceremonies and his human qualities were put in evidence during a meeting of the Physical Society at Belo Horizonte in 1952. In one of the excursions outside Belo Horizonte, Feynman had occasion to see a number of poor children in slums. He expressed his revolt openly and spontaneously when the authorities entered solemnly to begin the conference dinner. At the sound of music which announced the arrival of the special guests, Feynman could not resist his protest by openly leaving the ceremony. His friends from CBPF later joined him in a restaurant, where 'he was relaxed, beautifully playing with his hands on the table as if it were a drum.'[18]

Apart from his collaboration with Leite Lopes in Brazil on the meson theory of the deuteron, Feynman had extensive discussions with David Bohm about the latter's hidden variable interpretation of quantum mechanics, which was being developed at that time. Bohm and Feynman also interacted with each other at the meeting of the Physical Society (Brazilian Society for the Progress of Science, SBPC) in Belo Horizonte.

Towards the end of his stay in Brazil, Feynman took an airline hostess—'a very lovely girl with braids'[1]—to visit the museum. As they went through the Egyptian section, Feynman began telling her all he knew about the Egyptian lore, about the meaning of wings on the sarcophagus, the use of vases for the entrails, etc. Then he realized that he had learned all that from Mary Louise Bell (referred to as Mary Lou below), whom he had met at Cornell. She came from Michigan, and was deeply interested in art history. When Feynman went to Caltech in Pasadena, he found that she was living nearby in Westwood (near UCLA). Although they often had arguments, he liked her. So, after taking these airline hostesses out for a year and not getting anywhere in trying to develop a stable relationship, he became frustrated. Then, on that day with the airline hostess in the museum, he again thought of Mary Lou, that she was quite wonderful and that they should not be having all those arguments.

Feynman wrote to her and proposed marriage. 'When you are [far] away and you've got nothing but paper, and you're feeling lonely, you remember all the good things and you can't remember the reasons you had the arguments.'[19] Somebody wise enough would have told him that it was dangerous to propose marriage from such a long distance.[1]

After a stay of ten months in Brazil, Feynman decided to return to Caltech and accepted to stay there permanently. Soon after his return from Brazil, Feynman married Mary Lou Bell on 28 June 1952. But things did not work out between them: the arguments started right away, and the marriage lasted only a few years. She wanted him always to act, dress, and behave solemnly as a dignified professor of the California Institute of Technology, which, given his natural playfulness, humor, and sense of the ridiculous about all pomposity, he was not willing to do. They got divorced in 1956.

In the summer of 1953, Feynman toured Mexico with Mary Lou. He was invited to spend the summer term at CBPF in Rio de Janeiro, and he went with her there. 'He came to the laboratory fully dressed in necktie and jacket, which allowed us to guess when Mary Lou left before him (via Bolivia and Peru)— from that day on Feynman came to the laboratory [in shirtsleeves] without necktie and jacket.'[18]

In 1953, UNESCO sent a mission of physicists to CBPF for a year, composed of Giuseppe Occhialini, Ugo Camerini, Gert Molière, and Hans Joos. Two students from Buenos Aires, Daniele Amati and Alberto Sirlin, who had completed their undergraduate studies at home, applied for fellowships and came to Rio de Janeiro to work at CBPF. They were among those who profited the most from their activities at CBPF and from Feynman's lectures and seminars. Feynman taught a course on quantum mechanics. Feynman always maintained that 'even in teaching graduate school I can never see if I did anything; I don't have any sense of accomplishment.' Amati and Sirlin had learned physics on their own in the total vacuum of proper instruction in Argentina, 'and from me they learned quantum mechanics. The vessel was empty before they came to my class, so I believe that what they learned in quantum mechanics was put in there by me.'[1]

By the summer of 1953, Feynman had already been thinking about the problem of the superfluidity of liquid helium for a couple of years almost constantly. During his stay in Rio de Janeiro in 1951–52, several ideas came to him concerning the solution of various aspects of this problem and he discussed them with Leite Lopes. Then, in September 1953, he went to Japan to attend the International Conference of Theoretical Physics, which took place partly in Tokyo (for the ceremonial and welcoming sessions) and the rest in Kyoto (for scientific sessions) from 14 to 24 September. It was the first international gathering of physicists in Japan after World War II, and everyone who was invited went there to attend it, believing that it was good for Japan and would give a lift to the Japanese physicists—which it did indeed succeed in doing.

John Wheeler had sent to the various American participants of his acquaintance, who were going to Japan, a small army booklet of the simplest phrases in Japanese, so that when they asked a few simple questions they could express themselves politely. Feynman was very excited to go to Japan. He had heard much about Japan and something about its cultural aspects. He studied the booklet thoroughly and learned the phrases in Japanese. A Japanese lady, the friend of a friend in Rio de Janeiro, helped him with the pronunciation of the Japanese phrases and the observance of various courtesies in Japan.

Feynman learned all he could about Japan, including practicing eating with chopsticks by lifting pieces of paper with chopsticks, so that he could eat in a Japanese restaurant when he would be there. At that time Japan was very mysterious to him, and he thought it would be interesting to go to such a strange and wonderful country; he worked very hard to learn all he could about life, customs, and culture in Japan.

When the conference participants arrived in Tokyo, they were taken to a hotel designed by Frank Lloyd Wright; it was an imitation of a European hotel, with waiters and bell boys dressed as they are in European or American hotels. This was like being in America. Feynman decided that he had not gone to all the trouble of learning about Japan and Japanese phrases for nothing. He had read about the Japanese-style hotels, which were supposed to be very different from the American or Continental hotels like the one in which he had been put up. So the next morning he called up the Japanese guy looking after the arrangements of their stay and insisted that in Kyoto he wished to stay in a Japanese-style hotel. The difficulties of how to be picked up for the meetings of the conference were settled, and when the conference moved to Kyoto Feynman moved into Hotel Miyako. When Abraham Pais learned from Feynman about it, he also wanted to try it, and they agreed to share the room in the hotel.

As soon as 'I got there, I knew it was worth it. It was lovely! There was a place at the front where you take your shoes off, then a girl dressed in the traditional outfit—the obi—with sandals comes shuffling out, and takes your stuff; you follow her down a hallway that has mats on the floor, past sliding doors made of paper, and she is going cht-cht-cht-cht with little steps. It was all wonderful!'[20]

It was a really graceful room. There were all the usual, standard Japanese things there, which were all new to Feynman. 'There was a little alcove with a painting in it, a vase with pussywillows nicely arranged, a table along the floor with a cushion nearby, and at the end of the room were two sliding doors which opened on to a garden.'[20] The lady who was supposed to take care of Feynman was a middle-aged woman. She helped him undress and gave him a *yukata*, a simple white robe to wear in the hotel.

Feynman pushed opened the doors and admired the lovely garden. He sat down to do a little work. He had hardly been there for fifteen or twenty minutes when he saw, sitting at the entrance to the door, draped in the corner, a very beautiful Japanese woman, in a lovely outfit. When he looked at her, she asked him if he would like to see the garden. Feynman put on his shoes and in his *yukata* he went out with her in the garden. She took his arm and showed him around.

Sometime later, the woman who took care of Feynman's room asked him if he was ready to take his bath. Feynman was eager to take one because he had learned that the Japanese baths were a complicated ritual. He went into the lavatory section of the bathroom, where he found that someone else was occupied with taking a bath. When this person—he was the great Japanese physicist Hideki Yukawa—heard the noise of some movement outside, he peered to look out and seeing Feynman there told him: 'Professor! That's a very bad error to go into the lavatory when someone else has the bath!' Yukawa told him that the woman in charge would inform him when the bath was ready for him.[20]

Hotel Miyako was just delightful, 'especially when people came to see me there. The other guys would come into my room and we'd sit on the floor and start to talk. We wouldn't be there more than five minutes when the woman who took care of my room would come in with a tray of candies and tea. It was as if you were a host in your own home, and the hotel staff was helping you to entertain your guests.'[20]

Eating meals at the hotel was also different. 'And the food was wonderful. For instance, the soup comes in a bowl that's covered. You lift the cover and there's a beautiful picture: little pieces of onion floating in the soup just so; it's gorgeous. How the food looks on the plate is very important.'[21] Feynman did not like to eat fish at home in the United States. But in Japan he ate a lot of it. He found that fish in Japan was very, very fresh unlike at home in America.

Feynman had been working at that time on the theory of liquid helium, and had figured out how the laws of quantum dynamics explain the strange phenomena of superfluidity. He was very proud of this achievement, and gave a talk on 'The atomic theory of liquid helium' in the Symposium on Liquid Helium and Superconductivity on 24 September at the international conference in Kyoto. A day or so later, when Feynman was in his hotel room, the telephone rang; it was from the *Time* magazine. The correspondent of *Time* told him that they were very interested in his work, and would he please send them a copy of his paper. Feynman felt quite elated by this interest of the press, because he had not been written about before in a news magazine. He carefully took down the address, and then the correspondent said, 'Thank you, Mr. Pais!' Feynman realized that the message was not for him but for his roommate Abraham Pais. When Pais returned to the room, Feynman told him about *Time* magazine's interest in his work. Pais commented: 'Aw! Publicity is a whore!' Feynman was taken aback by this; he had thought at first that it would be wonderful to be mentioned in *Time* magazine.[22]

That was the first time Feynman was in Japan. He was eager to go back, and he told the Japanese physicists that he would go to any university that wanted to invite him. The Japanese arranged a whole series of visits and lectures for Feynman at various places, and he—with his wife Mary Lou—went to Japan in the summer of 1955. They were entertained wherever they went. At one place, their hosts put on a whole ceremony with dancing, usually performed for large groups of tourists, especially for them. At another place, they were met right at the boat by all the students. At still another place they were received by the mayor. 'One particular place we stayed was a little, modest place in the woods, where the Emperor would stay when he came by. It was a lovely place, surrounded by woods, just beautiful, the stream selected with care. It had a certain calmness, a quiet elegance. That the Emperor would go to such a place to stay showed a greater sensitivity to Nature, I think, than we were used to in the West.'[23]

At all these places everybody working in physics would tell Feynman what they were working on and he would discuss it with them. They would tell him the general problem they were working on, and would begin to write a bunch of equations. But Feynman wanted them to give him specific examples, special cases of the problem they wanted to solve. In this way things would come into better focus. So, in Japan, he wouldn't discuss anybody's work unless they could give him a physical example. When an example was available, it could be solved by a much simpler method of analysis. 'Since I was perpetually asking *not* for mathematical equations, but for physical circumstances of what they were trying to work out, my visit was summarized in a mimeographed paper circulated among scientists with the title, "Feynman's Bombardments, and Our Reactions".'[24]

While Feynman was in Japan, he tried to learn Japanese with a vengeance. He worked very hard at it and got to the point that he could go around in taxis and do things. He took lessons from a Japanese man for an hour everyday. He found that in Japanese there were different ways of saying the same thing, depending on what one wanted to say. For instance, if you asked someone, 'Would you like to see my garden?' the implication was: 'Would you like to take a glance at my *lousy* garden?' But if you wanted to see the other person's garden, your words would imply, 'I would be honored to see your beautiful garden.' On account of this duplicity of expression, Feynman decided that the Japanese language was not for him.

After his return to Pasadena from Japan, Feynman wrote to Leite Lopes: 'We [Feynman and Mary Lou] enjoyed Japan very much. I worked hard— lots of lectures and discussions at many cities and universities. I spent most of the time at Yukawa's place in Kyoto. Still I am trying to understand superconductivity. I worked very hard at it in Japan but couldn't solve it. Finally back here I ran out of ideas and ambition. I haven't been able to work on anything much for the last 4 or 5 months. I'm in the doldrum. I guess it's psychological—perhaps it is the shock of discovering a problem I cannot solve. I cannot work on anything else because that's admitting failure, and I can't work on it because of the unadmitted failure. I haven't accomplished anything in the last year [1955]. I haven't even written those articles for you on the interpretation of quantum mechanics that I wanted to. Ricardo Feynman.'[25]

Notes and References

1. R.P. Feynman, Interviews and conversations with Jagdish Mehra, in Austin, Texas, April 1970, Pasadena, California, January 1988.

2. R.P. Feynman, Interviews with Charles Weiner (American Institute of Physics), in Pasadena, California, 1966.

3. A. Proca, Letter of invitation to R.P. Feynman, 20 February 1960, Feynman Archive, Caltech.

4. R.P. Feynman, *SYMFJ*, p. 202.

5. R.P. Feynman, *SYMFJ*, p. 203. J. Leite Lopes took serious objection to this jocular remark of Feynman's. 'At the Brazilian Academy of Sciences when there is a visitor, people always speak in English as a courtesy. Would Feynman in Japan lead the Japanese Academy of Sciences to adopt the Japanese language because Feynman would speak in Japanese whereas the Japanese would speak in English in his presence? Well, the whole book [*"Surely you're joking, Mr Feynman!"*] is clearly a set of jokes.' Personal communication from J. Leite Lopes to Jagdish Mehra, 20 October 1988.

6. J. Leite Lopes and R.P. Feynman, On the pseudoscalar meson theory of the deuteron. *Symposium on the New Techniques in Physics*, CBPF, 15–19 June 1952, Rio de Janeiro, Brazil.

7. R.P. Feynman, *SYMFJ*, p. 204.

8. R.P. Feynman, *SYMFJ*, pp. 204–205.

9. R.P. Feynman, *SYMFJ*, p. 210.

10. R.P. Feynman, Mimeographed letter to E. Fermi. Feynman Archive, Caltech.

11. R.P. Feynman, *Engineering and Science*, November 1963, p. 21.

12. R.P. Feynman, Ref. 11, p. 24.

13. R.P. Feynman, Ref. 11, p. 25.

14. R.P. Feynman, Ref. 11, p. 26.

15. R.P. Feynman, Ref. 11, p. 26.

16. R.P. Feynman, Ref. 11, p. 30.

17. This speech was based on the transcript of a keynote speech on 'The problems of teaching physics in Latin America', given by Richard Feynman at the First Inter-American Conference on Physics Education in Rio de Janeiro in June 1963. It was

based on the speech which he gave before the assembled audience of scientists and educators in 1952 at the University of Rio de Janeiro with reference to physics education in Brazil.

18. J. Leite Lopes, Richard Feynman in Brazil: Recollections, Reprint No. ISSN 0101–9228 of CBPF.

19. R.P. Feynman, *SYMFJ*, p. 205.

20. R.P. Feynman, *SYMFJ*, p. 239.

21. R.P. Feynman, *SYMFJ*, p. 241.

22. R.P. Feynman, *SYMFJ*, pp. 242–243.

23. R.P. Feynman, *SYMFJ*, p. 244.

24. R.P. Feynman, *SYMFJ*, p. 245.

25. R.P. Feynman, Letter to J. Leite Lopes, 15 February 1956, Ref. 18.

17

The cup runneth over: Feynman and the theory of superfluidity†

17.1 Introduction

Richard Feynman wound up his work on relativistic quantum electro-dynamics at Cornell University by writing a paper on the 'Mathematical formulation of the quantum theory of electromagnetic interaction',[1] in which he sought to establish the validity of the mathematical rules he had employed in developing his theory of the positrons[2] and the space–time approach to quantum electrodynamics.[3] The full justification of these rules and methods was developed in a later paper, entitled 'An operator calculus having applications in quantum electrodynamics',[4] which he began writing at Cornell, but completed at Caltech—where he had accepted a position as professor of theoretical physics—and the Centro Brasiliero de Pesquisas Fisicas at the University of Brazil in Rio de Janeiro, where he was spending a sabbatical year before starting his regular duties at Caltech on a permanent basis. By this time he had completed his doctoral thesis at Princeton, had participated in the Manhattan Project at Los Alamos, had started work at Cornell, and had attended the Shelter Island, Pocono Manor, and Oldstone-on-the-Hudson conferences. His reputation as a virtuoso physicist and gifted lecturer had been built up and the 'Feynman legend'—Feynman as a superb and unique phenomenon in the world of physics—had started to grow, being helped generously by Feynman's own achievements and antics as a 'curious character'. By the end of 1951, Feynman had disgorged himself from his tremendous fascination and absorption in the theory of quantum electrodyn-amics, a program which he had dimly conceived as an undergraduate at MIT and which now stood complete and ready as his contribution to the very

† Raj K. Pathria of the Department of Physics, University of Waterloo, Waterloo, Ontario, Canada, has kindly collaborated with me as the coauthor of this chapter. Russell J. Donnelly, Department of Physics, University of Oregon, Eugene, Oregon, kindly provided me with a detailed communication on his 'Memories of Richard Feynman and Lars Onsager' (December 1990).

language of theoretical physics in the form of the ubiquitous Feynman diagrams and the path-integral method. In later years, Feynman, with Paul Dirac, would maintain that, in solving the problem of infinities in quantum electrodynamics, the fundamental question—that is, the physical explanation of why those infinities arise in the first place—'had been shoved under the rug'.[5-8] But Feynman was pleased and proud to have developed powerful techniques which would continue to be used widely.

Feynman had become deeply involved in the problems of quantum electrodynamics by his reading of the books of Dirac[9] and Heitler,[10] in which the basic difficulties had been recognized and the fundamental questions still to be resolved had been raised. Feynman had taken these problems as a personal challenge, and in his thinking and work from 1939 to 1951 he had devoted himself to resolving them. During this period he became familiar with a large variety of fundamental physical problems, which were being asked all around by the physicists, and Feynman thought about them also from time to time and dealt with some of them in his lectures to graduate students at Cornell and later at Caltech. From then on, he would seize upon some problem that was discussed in the physics colloquia or journals and work on it. He treated such problems as puzzles which he enjoyed solving by his own methods; he also found great satisfaction in solving problems and paradoxes, which had already been treated by other techniques, in which he would test the power of his own mathematical methods. This approach of finding new problems to work on and puzzles and paradoxes to solve would remain with Feynman throughout his life; in fact, 'if he could not resolve them right away, he liked it even better, because he would then have a challenge and he would continue to be excited by the chase until he had run them down. It gave him great thrill.'[11]

In the spring of 1952, a few months after Feynman had joined the physics faculty at the California Institute of Technology, Mark Kac, the famous mathematician with whom Feynman had developed a close and mutually enjoyable friendship at Cornell, was invited to give a series of lectures on probability theory and statistical mechanics at Pasadena. Kac was deeply in love with the 'Onsager problem'—Lars Onsager's celebrated solution of the phase transition in the two-dimensional Ising model.[12] In one of these lectures, at the physics colloquium, Kac talked about how he could get the capacitance of any shape by applying a technique he had used before in the random walk problem, and, after he was done, Feynman said: 'That's the same thing as my path-integral method; you do the same thing that way!' Kac looked at Feynman and said, 'In the famous words of Molière, do you mean I have been speaking prose all my life?'[13]† Apart from the problem of

---

† Molière, *Le bourgeois gentilhomme*. Monsieur Jourdain: 'Par ma foi! Il y a plus de quarante ans je dis de la prose sans que j'en susse rien, et je vous suis le plus obligé du monde de m'avoir appris cela.' (Act II, scene IV.)

calculating capacitance in general, Kac also mentioned the Onsager problem and the problem of the superfluidity of liquid helium.

After Kac's visit, Feynman 'began to work on the Onsager problem with some crazy business with the path integrals. Since I had developed the path integral method and the operator calculus, what I would almost always do when I would hear about a new problem of some complexity in quantum mechanics or another field, I would wheel up these two machines, so to say, and try to see if I could apply them to these problems. So I began to fiddle around with the Onsager thing, but I got stuck and confused: at first, I thought that I was making a mistake, and I found that my method was not going to work. So I said to myself, 'well, if the method does not work here, it could probably be useful in the helium problem, how the ^{4}He transition comes about.'

'I had been concerned with the helium problem before, because it was one of the well-known puzzles of physics. But I had understood the puzzle. When I was at Cornell during 1945–50, a young man called Kirschner gave a lecture on the ^{4}He problem, and he told us that there were two theories [of superfluidity]. One was that it was a consequence of quantum hydrodynamics, that it was some general quantum mechanical property of any liquid, and was due to [Lev Davidovich] Landau, and the other—due to [Fritz] London and [Laszlo] Tisza—was that it was analogous to Bose condensation of a gas, and had to do with the statistics of helium, that the wave function must be symmetrical.

'I did not know that over the years these questions had been resolved, and the views of people—including Landau's—had changed. They were all now convinced that it was due to Bose transition, whereas at the time I heard the lecture at Cornell I got the impression that certain people, including Landau, believed that it was due to general quantum hydrodynamics, and I thought that was nuts. It seemed to me perfectly obvious that if a gas has a transition, a liquid is going to have a transition as well; *it has got to do with statistics*. So I thought that Landau's hydrodynamics was not worth much, and the problem was to show that there would be a transition in the liquid analogous to a transition in the gas, and I proved it to myself and, I believe, to others that it would be so. Mine was a physical argument, of a kind that was not popular and not properly understood because it was not shown mathematically rigorously which, I thought, would take just too much work. However, I did show that the transition in liquid helium will take place just as it occurs in a gas, although the curves for the transition and the specific heat would be different, but I did understand the transition in helium. . . . I did not know that meanwhile people were convinced that it was a matter of statistics, in particular because they had examined ^{3}He and didn't find such a transition there. My work did not seem to be much to other people, but to me it was a big deal!

'Liquid helium had a number of strange properties. And now that I knew why the transition occurred, I thought that I ought to be able to understand how these properties arose. So I was engaged in the problem of helium and its superfluidity for a number of years—first alone, then with Mike Cohen.'[6,8]

As it turned out, during the years 1953–58, Feynman published some eight or nine papers (three in collaboration with his graduate student Michael Cohen, who also wrote his doctoral thesis on the problem of the superfluidity of liquid helium), in which he laid down a theory of superfluidity based on first principles—a theory which not only put the work of Landau (who had based his considerations on empirical information, phenomenological reasoning, and semitheoretical analysis) on a firm footing but also paved the way for subsequent investigations into the problem.[14–21] To capture the essence of Feynman's work in this fascinating field of physics, we must look back on the times when the phenomenon of superfluidity in liquid ^{4}He was just beginning to engage the attention of some notable theoreticians such as Tisza, London, and, of course, Landau.

17.2 Historical background

In 1908—at Leiden in Holland—Heike Kamerlingh Onnes succeeded in liquefying helium (critical temperature 5.2 K). His principal interest was in extending the range of available temperatures to lower and lower values in order to investigate the behavior of different substances at those temperatures. At first, he did not expect that helium itself had any intrinsic interest, but he soon found that liquid helium possessed unusual and unexpected properties—quite different from and unlike most other substances—which had to be investigated. That something peculiar happens to liquid helium at about 2.2 K was noticed by Kamerlingh Onnes by 1911, when he also discovered the phenomenon of superconductivity of metals at very low temperatures.[22] These investigations continued to be carried on exclusively at Leiden[23] for the next twenty years and, later on, in laboratories in other countries, such as in Cambridge, England, at the Royal Society's Mond Laboratory, by Peter Kapitza[24] (for whom the laboratory had been specially built with the support of none other than Ernest Rutherford himself) and his collaborators like Frederick Lindemann and—later on—Franz Simon, Kurt Mendelssohn, Nicholas Kurti, and others.

Kamerlingh Onnes found that when helium is cooled below 2.2 K, it starts to expand instead of continuing to contract as most other substances do. In elaborate measurements, made by Kamerlingh Onnes and Boks,[25] it was found that the density–temperature function of the liquid had a sharp maximum, with a *discontinuity of slope* (discontinuous thermal expansion coefficient), at that temperature (see Fig. 17.1). A few years later, W. H. Keesom and M. Wolfke[26] found that the dielectric constant of liquid helium underwent a sudden change as the temperature of the liquid passed through

The cup runneth over

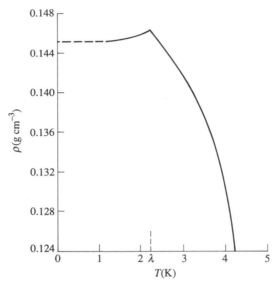

Fig. 17.1. Density of liquid helium as a function of temperature (after Kamerlingh Onnes and Boks[22]).

the same special value that had been discovered by Kamerlingh Onnes and Boks. They inferred that the liquid was undergoing some sort of a phase transition at a critical temperature (~ 2.2 K), and they named the phase at higher temperatures *liquid helium I* (or He I) and the phase at lower temperatures *liquid helium II* (or He II). Next, Keesom, in collaboration with K. Clusius and Miss A. P. Keesom, carried out detailed measurements of the specific heat of the liquid[27] and found that, as the critical temperature of 2.19 K was approached, the specific heat, from either side of the critical temperature, rose and produced a shape on the (c_V, T)-plot that very much resembled the greek letter lambda (see Fig. 17.2). Impressed by the shape of the specific heat curve, Keesom gave this transition the name lambda transition. Subsequently, Peter Kapitza at Moscow and Jack Allen at Cambridge studied the flow properties of the liquid and found dramatic results unseen before; while He I was observed to behave like any ordinary viscous liquid, He II, within certain limits, could creep along thin films and flow through narrow capillaries with annoying ease—as if it met practically no resistance in doing so. Detailed measurements showed that this property of 'superfluidity' exhibited by He II became more pronounced as the temperature of the liquid fell.

Other curious aspects turned up in flow experiments involving temperature gradients. If two containers of liquid helium II, at a common pressure P but at temperatures T and $T + \Delta T$, were connected by a superleak, the liquid would rush from the container at lower temperature towards the one at higher

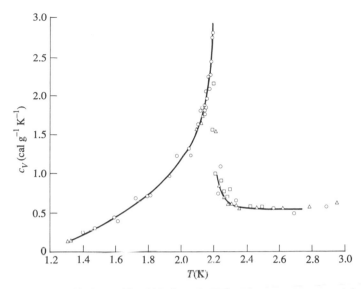

Fig. 17.2. Specific heat of liquid helium under its own vapor pressure (after Keesom and Clusius[27] and Keesom and Keesom[35]).

temperature till a pressure difference ΔP ($= \rho s\, \Delta T$) was established; here, ρ is the density and s the specific entropy of the liquid. This unusual effect is known as the 'thermomechanical effect'. If the second container is in the form of a thin tube, the resulting pressure head may cause a fountain of liquid helium to erupt—hence the name fountain effect. Conversely, if the containers were at a common temperature T but at different pressures P_1 and P_2 such that $P_1 > P_2$, then the liquid will flow from container 1 to container 2, which is not surprising. What is surprising, however, is the fact that, as a result of this flow, the temperature of the liquid in container 2 drops—the so-called 'mechanocaloric effect'. This curious interplay of thermodynamics and hydrodynamics was something entirely new in physics, and it was now time that someone explained theoretically what was going on here.

17.3 The two-fluid model of Tisza and London

To understand this unusual behavior of liquid He II, Lazlo Tisza[28] proposed a phenomenological two-fluid model according to which He II consisted of an intimate mixture of two components: a superfluid component, of density $\rho_s(T)$, that flowed without resistance, and a normal component, of density $\rho_n(T)$, that acted like an ordinary viscous fluid. As the temperature of He II decreased from the transition temperature T_λ down to $T=0$, the superfluid density $\rho_s(T)$ increased from zero to full helium density ρ, while the normal fluid density $\rho_n(T)$ decreased from the full value ρ to zero. Thus, at $T=T_\lambda$, liquid He II was all normal fluid, while at $T=0$ it was all superfluid; needless to say, the liquid continued to be normal at temperatures above T_λ. Tisza further assumed that the superfluid component was endowed with properties characteristic of the absolute zero of temperature and hence was entropyless, with the result that the entropy of the liquid arose entirely from its normal component: $s = (\rho_n/\rho)s_n$. It is not difficult to see that these special attributes of the superfluid component explain both the thermomechanical effect and the mechanocaloric effect rather straightforwardly. In the case of the former, since the fraction ρ_s/ρ is larger in the container at the lower temperature T, the superfluid component will flow through the superleak into the container at the higher temperature $T + \Delta T$ where this fraction is smaller. By the same argument, the normal component should flow in the opposite direction; being viscous, however, it cannot make its way through the superleak connecting the containers. The net result is that the flow is unidirectional, which leads to the buildup of a pressure head which finally stops the flow. In the case of the mechanocaloric effect, it is again only the superfluid component that flows through the superleak; being entropyless, it causes a decrease in the specific entropy of the liquid in the second container and hence in its temperature.

While Tisza's model does provide a practical means of understanding the curious behavior of liquid He II, it is purely phenomenological in character and gives no hint of the physical basis on which the liquid is split into two components, one of which does not even seem to have a right to exist at temperatures above absolute zero. A theoretical argument that leads naturally to a model consisting of two interpenetrating components (not unlike Tisza's) was put forward by Fritz London at about the same time as Tisza advanced his model. Struck by the similarity between the specific-heat curve of liquid ^{4}He and that of an ideal Bose gas as it passed through its critical temperature T_c—a problem first studied by Albert Einstein[29]—London proposed that the phase transition that occurs in liquid ^{4}He at $T = T_\lambda$ might well be a manifestation of the phenomenon of Bose–Einstein condensation taking place in the liquid (see Figs 17.2 and 17.3). Indeed, if one substitutes data pertaining to liquid ^{4}He in

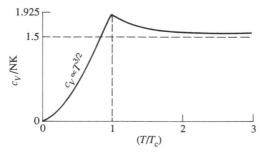

Fig. 17.3. Specific heat of an ideal Bose gas as a function of the temperature parameter (T/T_c).

the formula for the critical temperature of an ideal Bose gas, one obtains a value of about 3.13 K which is not too far from the observed transition temperature of the liquid. The important thing here is that the interpretation of the phase transition in liquid ^{4}He as a Bose–Einstein condensation provides a viable theoretical basis for the two-fluid model which, as Tisza had already shown, explained quite well the physical behavior of the liquid below the transition temperature.† According to London, the $N_0(T)$ particles, out of a total number N, that occupy a single entropyless state ($\varepsilon = 0$) could be identified with the superfluid component of the liquid and the remaining $N - N_0(T)$ particles that occupy excited states ($\varepsilon > 0$) could be identified with the normal component. As required by the model of Tisza, the 'superfluid' component in the Bose gas makes its appearance only at temperatures below the transition temperature T_c, builds up as the temperature falls until at $T = 0$ the whole of the fluid becomes superfluid. Of course, the temperature dependence of the two fractions, and of other physical properties of liquid He II, might be significantly different from what the simple-minded ideal Bose gas would suggest. London expressed the hope that the inclusion of intermolecular interactions into the calculation would improve the quantitative agreement between the two systems. Although in subsequent investigations this expectation has to some extent been vindicated, other ideas were advanced by people such as Lev Landau which provided alternative ways of looking at the helium problem.

17.4 Landau's theory of elementary excitations: phonons and rotons

Landau[37,38] developed an independent theoretical scheme which explains quite well the behavior of liquid helium II at temperatures not too close to the

---

† It should be mentioned here that, soon after Einstein discovered the phenomenon of Bose–Einstein condensation, George Uhlenbeck, in his doctoral thesis at Leiden,[30] criticized Einstein's derivation (in which *sum-over-states* appearing in the theoretical expressions for the various physical quantities pertaining to the system had been replaced by *integrals*, without examining the resulting errors) and cast doubt on the very existence of the phenomenon. London, in his *Physical Review* paper,[31] improved upon Einstein's derivation considerably, obtaining essentially the same results as Einstein had obtained earlier in 1925. At the same time, R. H. Fowler and H. Jones[32] produced a rigorous derivation, based on certain properties of Jacobi's theta functions, which left no doubt that the conclusions arrived at by Einstein and London were indeed correct. Convinced that the phenomenon was real, Uhlenbeck, in a paper written jointly with Boris Kahn,[33] withdrew his objection completely. The controversy, so long as it lasted, prompted London[34] to remark that 'if the lambda-phenomenon of liquid helium had been discovered between the years 1925 and 1927, one would perhaps have tried at once to interpret it as the condensation predicted by Einstein.' For a detailed exposition of the 'royal' manner in which the Fowler–Jones approach enables one to derive Bose–Einstein condensation in an ideal Bose gas, see Refs. 35 and 36.

transition point. According to this scheme, the liquid is treated as a weakly excited quantum mechanical system in which deviations from the ground state ($T=0$) are described in terms of a 'gas of elementary excitations' of the system against a *quiescent* background. The gas of excitations corresponds to the normal fluid while the quiescent background represents the superfluid. At $T=0$, there are no excitations present in the system ($\rho_n=0$) and the whole of the fluid constitutes the superfluid component ($\rho_s=\rho$). At higher temperatures, one could write

$$\rho_s(T)=\rho-\rho_n(T),\tag{17.1}$$

until, at $T=T_\lambda$, $\rho_n=\rho$ and $\rho_s=0$; thereafter, the liquid behaves in all respects as a normal fluid. As in the model of Tisza, the two components in the Landau picture were capable of maintaining a relative motion between themselves, so that the total current density in the liquid could be written as

$$j=\rho_n v_n+\rho_s v_s,\tag{17.2}$$

where v_n and v_s are the velocities of mass motion of the normal and the superfluid components, respectively.

Landau showed that the various properties of liquid He II could be computed directly on the basis of the energy–momentum relationship of the elementary excitations. At low enough temperatures, where their number was not expected to be very large, the excitations could be treated as mutually noninteracting. Moreover, since these excitations are supposed to obey Bose–Einstein statistics and their total number is not conserved, the mean occupation number $n(\varepsilon)$ appropriate to them would be

$$n(\varepsilon)=(e^{\beta\varepsilon}-1)^{-1}\quad(\beta=1/k_B T),\tag{17.3}$$

k_B being the Boltzmann constant. The free energy density of the liquid would then be given by

$$f=\frac{4\pi}{\beta h^3}\int_0^\infty \ln(1-e^{-\beta\varepsilon})p^2\,dp,\tag{17.4}$$

while the density of the normal fluid at *low* velocities would be given by

$$\rho_n=\frac{4\pi\beta}{3h^3}\int_0^\infty e^{\beta\varepsilon}(e^{\beta\varepsilon}-1)^{-2}p^4\,dp.\tag{17.5}$$

The evaluation of these expressions clearly requires a knowledge of the function $\varepsilon(p)$.

Guided by considerations based on quantum hydrodynamics and relying heavily on empirical information, Landau proposed an energy–momentum relationship $\varepsilon(p)$ for the elementary excitations in liquid He II along the following lines. At low momenta, this relationship would be linear,

$$\varepsilon = pc, \tag{17.6}$$

c being the speed of sound in the liquid; obviously, the excitations in this regime were *phonons*. At higher momenta, the situation turned out to be rather tricky. In his first attempt at this problem, Landau[37] argued that the nature of the higher-momentum excitations was such that the energy–momentum relationship would be essentially similar to the conventional expression $p^2/2m$, but with two important differences. First, these excitations would be separated from phonons by an energy gap Δ'; second, their effective mass would be considerably larger than the free-particle mass m. Thus, at higher momenta, we would have

$$\varepsilon = \Delta' + p^2/2m'. \tag{17.7}$$

Landau believed that these excitations were endowed with a rotational motion on an atomic scale, which was one reason why the creation of such an excitation required a minimum energy Δ'; accordingly, he called these excitations *rotons*. Preliminary estimates indicated that, at all temperatures of interest, $e^{\beta \Delta'} \gg 1$; expression (17.3) then shows that the roton occupation number may well be approximated by the Boltzmannian form

$$n_{\text{rot}}(\varepsilon) \approx e^{-\beta \varepsilon}. \tag{17.8}$$

It further follows that, at very low temperatures, the roton contribution to the thermodynamic properties of the system might become altogether negligible and the resulting situation may be determined solely by the phonons. Landau, therefore, concluded that, in the low-temperature regime ($T < 0.5$ K), one would have, on the basis of equations (17.4)–(17.6),

$$f = -\frac{4\pi^5 k_B^4}{45 h^3 c^3} T^4, \tag{17.9}$$

$$s = \frac{16\pi^5 k_B^4}{45 h^3 c^3} T^3, \tag{17.10}$$

$$c_V = \frac{16\pi^5 k_B^4}{15 h^3 c^3} T^3 \tag{17.11}$$

$$\rho_{\text{n}} = \frac{16\pi^5 k_B^4}{45 h^3 c^5} T^4. \tag{17.12}$$

At temperatures between 1 and 2 K, on the other hand, one could employ the roton spectrum alone, with the results

$$f = \bar{n}_{\text{rot}} k_B T, \quad \bar{n}_{\text{rot}} = \left(\frac{2\pi m' k_B T}{h^2} \right)^{3/2} e^{-\Delta'/k_B T}, \tag{17.13}$$

$$s = \bar{n}_{\text{rot}} k_B \left(\frac{5}{2} + \frac{\Delta'}{k_B T} \right),$$
(17.14)

$$c_V = \bar{n}_{\text{rot}} k_B \left\{ \frac{15}{4} + 3 \frac{\Delta'}{k_B T} + \left(\frac{\Delta'}{k_B T} \right)^2 \right\},$$
(17.15)

$$\rho_n = \bar{n}_{\text{rot}} \langle p^2 / 3 k_B T \rangle = \bar{n}_{\text{rot}} m'.$$
(17.16)

By comparing the theoretical results for c_V with the experimental measurements of Keesom and Keesom,[39] Landau inferred that $\Delta'/k_B \sim 8$–9 K, while $m'/m \sim 7$–8. Landau further argued that, if the foregoing results were applicable right up to the transition temperature T_λ (which is doubtful because near $T = T_\lambda$ the number of excitations present in the system would be too large to allow the assumption that they are mutually noninteracting), then T_λ could be determined simply by equating the normal fluid density ρ_n with the total density ρ of the liquid. Landau showed that, using the empirical values of Δ' and m', one obtained a transition temperature of 2.5 K. Although this seemed to be a considerable improvement over the result obtained by London, 3.1 K, on the basis of his ideal-gas picture, the presence of two adjustable parameters in Landau's theory could not make a very convincing case unless one measured the quantity $\rho_n(T)$ over a comparable range of temperatures and checked the extent to which those measurements conformed to the theoretical expressions (17.12) and (17.16).

17.5 The experiments of Andronikashvili and Peshkov

Experiments along these lines were undertaken by some of Landau's colleagues at the Institute of Physical Problems in Moscow, which led to both direct and indirect determinations of $\rho_n(T)$. The direct determination came from the experiments of Élevter Andronikashvili whose apparatus consisted of about one hundred thin aluminum disks (each about 10 microns thick), stuck on a common aluminum axis parallel to one another (to an accuracy of about 1 in 100), with spacings of about 0.2 mm in between. The whole set up was designed to possess exact axial symmetry when assembled and was suspended on a fine torsion fiber to execute small-amplitude oscillations about its axis. The normal fluid, by virtue of its viscosity, was expected to 'stick' with the disks and participate fully in their motion, contributing to the moment of inertia of the system and hence affecting the time period of the oscillations. The superfluid, on the other hand, was expected to 'slip' by the disks and not participate in their motion at all. Clearly, the time period of the oscillations would decrease as the temperature of the liquid fell, providing a direct measure of the quantity $\rho_n(T)$. The painstaking experiments of Andronikashvili,[40] did bear fruit. They showed conclusively that liquid He II indeed possessed *two* states of motion: one that went hand in hand with the asssembly of oscillating disks and the other that stayed immune to the process. Andronikashvili found that the normal fraction ρ_n/ρ fell from its maximum value unity at $T = T_\lambda$ down to about 0.5 at $T = 1.9$ K but, unfortunately, the quantitative agreement with Landau's theory was not satisfactory.

The indirect determination of $\rho_n(T)$ came from the experiments of Vasya Peshkov,[41] who carried out a detailed study of the phenomenon of second sound, which had also been predicted by Landau. This phenomenon is somewhat akin to that of ordinary sound, which is well known to be a pressure wave in which the (total) density of the fluid at any given point fluctuates while the wave advances through with speed $c - (\partial P/\partial \rho)_s^{1/2}$. The second sound, on the other hand, is a temperature wave in which, while the total density of the fluid in any given region of space remains constant, the relative densities of the normal and superfluid components fluctuate out of phase (and hence the specific entropy of the fluid undergoes variations) while the wave advances through with speed

$$c_2 = \left(\frac{\rho_s T s^2}{\rho_n \rho c_V}\right)^{1/2}. \tag{17.17}$$

Expressions (17.13)–(17.16), when substituted into (17.17), tell us how c_2 should vary with T in the roton regime, while expressions (17.10)–(17.12) provide similar information in the phonon regime; in the intermediate regime, one has to employ both sets of expressions. It turns out that c_2 is zero at $T = T_\lambda$ and grows sharply as T decreases; after attaining a maximum at about 1.6 K, it falls again reaching a minimum in the region of 1 K rising again and finally approaching a limiting value, $c/\sqrt{3}$, as $T \to 0$. Peshkov's measurements, conducted around the same time as Andronikashvili's and covering essentially the same temperature regime (1.75–2.15 K) verified most of these predictions qualitatively. The quantity ρ_n/ρ derived from these measurements, however, did not agree quantitatively with the theory of Landau. While the results of Androvikashvili and of Peshkov agreed with one another reasonably well, deviations from Landau's theory were rather significant. More disturbingly, the deviations from theory increased as T decreased, which was quite opposite to what Landau had expected—for he had argued that, the further one goes from T_λ, the more plausible the assumption of rotons being noninteracting would be, and hence the agreement between theory and experiment should be better. Landau could not fail to realize that, while the basic premises of his theory were probably right, all was not well with his rotons.

17.6 The new roton spectrum

A closer look at the theoretical expressions and the experimental data revealed that the roton effective mass m', instead of being a constant, varied with the temperature of the system; within experimental error, it varied inversely with T. Landau thereby inferred (see equation (17.16)) that the mean square momentum $\langle p^2 \rangle$ of the rotons was essentially *independent* of temperature; he called this quantity p_0^2. Clearly, one faced a dilemma here: while the mean energy $\langle \varepsilon \rangle$ of the rotons increased with T (after all, the system had a well-defined specific heat), their mean square momentum stayed constant. Landau thereupon proposed a new roton spectrum, one in which the energy $\varepsilon(p)$ varied parabolically around a characteristic momentum p_0, so that both $\langle \varepsilon \rangle$ and $\langle p^2 \rangle$ could have the desired variations with T. He wrote,[38]

$$\varepsilon(p) = \Delta + (p - p_0)^2 / 2\mu, \tag{17.18}$$

where Δ was once again the energy gap that represented the minimum energy required for the creation of a roton, p_0 gave the location of the minimum, while μ measured the curvature of the $\varepsilon(p)$ curve at the minimum (see Fig. 17.4) Expressions (17.13)–(17.16) were then replaced by

$$f = \bar{n}_{\text{rot}} k_B T, \qquad \bar{n}_{\text{rot}} = \frac{4\pi p_0^2}{h^3} (2\pi \mu k_B T)^{1/2} \, e^{-\Delta / k_B T}, \tag{17.13a}$$

$$s = \bar{n}_{\text{rot}} k_B \left(\frac{3}{2} + \frac{\Delta}{k_B T} \right), \tag{17.14a}$$

$$c_V = \bar{n}_{\text{rot}} k_B \left[\frac{3}{4} + \frac{\Delta}{k_B T} + \left(\frac{\Delta}{k_B T} \right)^2 \right], \tag{17.15a}$$

$$\rho_n = \bar{n}_{\text{rot}} (p_0^2 / 3 k_B T). \tag{17.16a}$$

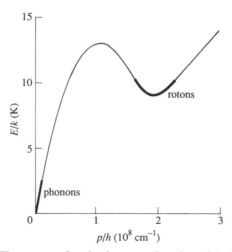

Fig. 17.4. The energy of excitations as a function of their momenta.

The determination of the parameters Δ, p_0, and μ now becomes much more complex. With hardly any guidance from theory, this determination could only be done through a detailed comparison with the experimental results of Andronikashvili on the normal fluid density ρ_n and of Peshkov on the specific heat c_V and the velocity of second sound c_2. This task was entrusted to Isaak Khalatnikov whose painstaking analysis showed that the experimental data available at that time could indeed be fitted well with the theoretical expressions derived on the basis of the new spectrum, provided that

$$\Delta/k_B = 9.6 \text{ K}, \qquad p_0/\hbar = 1.95 \text{ Å}^{-1} \qquad \mu/m = 0.77. \qquad (17.19)$$

The new spectrum thus proved to be an instant success, though its unusual features were quite baffling.

It is remarkable that Landau never attempted to derive the parameters Δ, p_0, and μ from first principles; he did, however, make some important observations on the nature of the spectrum as a whole. For instance, he emphasized that the phonons and the rotons may not be regarded as two separate disjointed branches of the $\varepsilon(p)$ relationship but rather two parts of a single continuous curve separated by a maximum which rendered rotons stable against disintegration into phonons. This unified picture of the elementary excitations does make one wonder as to why some of them should be endowed with rotational motion while others are not. The new spectrum was, nonetheless, a feat of matchless intuition which successfully tracked down a crucial element in the experimental data and converted it into a theoretical model that defied all conventional wisdom but turned out to be a correct representation of the underlying truth. At the same time it would be fair to say that a proper theoretical justification for the existence in liquid He II of elementary excitations of the type envisaged by Landau was seriously lacking.

17.7 Bogoliubov's theory of quasi-particles in an imperfect Bose gas

The first consistent step in the desired direction was taken by Nikolai Bogoliubov around the same time that Landau introduced his new spectrum. Bogoliubov[42] developed a perturbation scheme to study weakly excited states, including the ground state, of a system of N bosons confined to volume V and interacting mutually through a hard-sphere potential of diameter a. The scheme applied only to situations for which $Na^3/V \gg 1$; unfortunately, this did not strictly hold for liquid He II, for which $Na^3/V \simeq 0.2$. One did, nonetheless, hope that a study along the lines initiated by Bogoliubov would take us an important step beyond London and give us a glimpse of the influence that interparticle interactions might have on the low-temperature behavior of the Bose system. Using the method of second quantization, supplemented by a transformation (now known as Bogoliubov transformation) which takes one from the scheme of interacting particles to one of noninteracting *quasi-particles*, Bogoliubov established the following important facts.

(i) The ground state $(T=0)$ of the interacting Bose gas is *not* characterized by the condensation of *all* the particles of the system into the state with $p=0$. Particles with nonzero momentum are present as well; their number is given by

$$N(p>0) = \frac{8}{3}\left(\frac{N\alpha^3}{\pi V}\right)^{1/2} N, \tag{17.20}$$

while their mean square momentum is of order $\hbar^2 aN/V$. The condensate fraction at $T=0$ is, therefore, less than unity:

$$\frac{N_0}{N} = 1 - \frac{8}{3}\left(\frac{Na^3}{\pi V}\right)^{1/2}, \tag{17.21}$$

which contrasts sharply with the fact that the superfluid fraction ρ_s/ρ at $T=0$ is, by definition, exactly equal to 1. Apparently, the relationship between the Bose condensate on one hand and the superfluid component on the other needed to be redefined.

(ii) The ground-state energy of the system turns out to be

$$E_0 = \frac{2\pi\hbar^2 aN^2}{mV}\left[1 + \frac{128}{15}\left(\frac{Na^3}{\pi V}\right)^{1/2}\right], \tag{17.22}$$

which leads to a ground-state pressure

$$P_0 = \frac{2\pi\hbar^2 aN^2}{mV^2}\left[1 + \frac{64}{5}\left(\frac{Na^3}{\pi V}\right)^{1/2}\right]. \tag{17.23}$$

The velocity of sound then turns out to be

$$c = \left(\frac{4\pi\hbar^2 aN}{m^2 V}\right)^{1/2}\left[1 + 8\left(\frac{Na^3}{\pi V}\right)^{1/2}\right]. \tag{17.24}$$

Substituting appropriate values of the various parameters, one gets $c \sim 160 \text{ m s}^{-1}$, which may be compared with the actual value of 238 m s^{-1} found in He II. This lack of agreement between the theoretical and actual values of c need not be too disheartening for, after all, the theory of Bogoliubov pertained to a low-density gas whose molecules interacted via a hard-sphere potential rather than to a real liquid.

(iii) The excited states $(T>0)$ of the system are characterized by the appearance of excitations (in the form of quasi-particles) which obey Bose–Einstein statistics and possess an energy-momentum relationship $\varepsilon(p)$ given by

$$\varepsilon(p) = [p^2 u^2 + (p^2/2m)^2]^{1/2}, \qquad u = \left(\frac{4\pi\hbar^2 aN}{m^2 V}\right)^{1/2} \simeq c. \qquad (17.25)$$

It is remarkable that for $p \ll mu \sim \hbar(aN/V)^{1/2}$ the quasi-particles of Bogoliubov were essentially the same as Landau's phonons, with $\varepsilon \simeq pc$, while for $p \simeq mu$ they corresponded to Landau's rotons of 1941, with $\varepsilon \simeq (p^2/2m) + mu^2$, implying that $\Delta' = mu^2$ while $m' = m$. Although these findings lent much credence to Landau's picture of elementary excitations in liquid He II, their derivation by Bogoliubov made it quite clear that the excitations Landau had called rotons had nothing to do with rotational motion of any sort. At the same time, the energy spectrum (17.25), which is strictly *monotonic*, showed no resemblance at all to the new spectrum (17.18) which Landau had put forward in 1947 and which had been vindicated admirably well by the experimental data available at that time.

17.8 Enter Feynman

It was at this stage that Richard Feynman entered the scene. He set himself the task of providing a theoretical understanding of the problem of liquid helium on an atomic basis, which could only be done if one approached the problem from first principles. While he admired very much Landau's contributions to and successes in the field, Feynman[14] pointed out several weaknesses in Landau's theory. Firstly, Landau's quantum hydrodynamical approach treated liquid He II as a *continuous* medium which right from the beginning sacrificed the atomic structure of the liquid and thus forestalled the possibility of calculating the various characteristics of the system, such as the parameters Δ, p_0, and μ, on an atomic basis; one could not even argue why the system should at all make a transition from phase I to phase II. Secondly, in Landau's theory the precise role of the statistics obeyed by the helium atoms was not very clear; as Feynman asserted a few years later, Landau's approach of treating the density ρ and the velocity v of the fluid as operators and proposing a set of commutation relations for these operators was equivalent to treating the system as made up of *nonidentical* molecules (obeying neither Bose nor Fermi statistics) whose momenta and coordinates obeyed appropriate commutation relations *independently* of one another. Feynman felt that this was quite an unsatisfactory situation, for he regarded statistics as a vital element of the picture. He was indeed conscious of the fact that while ^{4}He underwent a peculiar transition from phase I to phase II, the lighter isotope ^{3}He did not do anything of the sort; it is significant, however, that Feynman did not dwell too much on the distinction between ^{3}He and ^{4}He, though he did choose to make Bose statistics the basis of his attack on the problem of ^{4}He. Thirdly, Feynman questioned Landau's reasoning for the existence of the energy gap Δ which represented the minimum energy required to create in the liquid excitations other than phonons. He argued that, unless Bose statistics intervened, excitations involving *large-scale* motions of the atoms could be created with as little energy as one wants; it was only because the situation was governed by Bose statistics that large-scale motions became redundant and one was forced to invoke motions on an atomic scale, which in turn required a finite minimum energy to get excited. Feynman, therefore, decided to attack the problem of liquid ^{4}He at the place where London's theory of the ideal Bose gas had left it.

17.9 Feynman's theory of a Bose liquid

Feynman's first two papers[15] on the subject appeared in the spring of 1953. The main thrust of the first paper was to show that, despite interparticle interactions, liquid ^{4}He did, by virtue of the symmetry of its states, undergo a phase transition very much like the one experienced by an ideal Bose gas; in other words, the suggestion made by London in 1938 that the transition observed in this liquid might be a manifestation of the phenomenon of Bose–Einstein condensation was basically correct. To demonstrate this, Feynman resorted to his space–time approach to quantum mechanics[43] and expressed the partition function of the liquid in the form of a *path-integral*, which took into account the fact that the sum-over-states was to be carried only over those states that were symmetric with respect to the exchange of particles, and went on to determine the class of trajectories that contributed most to this integral. He showed that the most important trajectories corresponded to situations in which the displacements of the individual atoms went hardly beyond their nearest neighbors; in other words, only those permutations of the coordinates were important in which the atoms were either left in their original positions or were moved to a neighboring location. The problem was thus reduced to determining the behavior of a 'sum of contributions' arising from a variety of nonintersecting polygons that can be constructed on a three-dimensional lattice. Each polygon of side r contributes a term proportional to y^r, where y is a measure of the probability of having an atomic displacement over the nearest-neighbor distance d, that is,

$$y = \exp(-2\pi^2 m k_B T d^2 / h^2), \qquad (17.26)$$

with $d = 3.6$ Å (which is the cube root of the atomic volume of liquid ^{4}He); the factor y at 2.2 K is about 0.3. Now, if the number of polygons of side r turns out plausibly to be proportional to s^r, where s is a number that depends on the structure of the lattice (one expects s to be about 3 or 4), then the sum in question takes the form

$$q \sim \sum_r (sy)^r. \qquad (17.27)$$

Clearly, the behavior of the sum q, and hence of the partition function of the system (of which this sum is a factor), would change drastically as, coming from higher temperatures, one hits a critical temperature T_c, where the quantity sy assumes the critical value 1. The partition function will become singular at $T = T_c$, signalling the occurrence of a phase transition. One cannot fail to notice that the structure of the sum (17.27) is such that the transition will be of the same nature as the one met with in the ideal Bose gas; in fact, the quantity sy corresponds precisely to the fugacity z of the ideal gas.[44]

The above conclusions rested very much on the argument that, despite interparticle interactions, the motion of one atom through the others is not opposed by a potential barrier because the others simply move out of the way. This renders the atoms essentially 'free' of one another, though it does increase their effective mass from the actual mass m to m', which Feynman expected to be not much larger than 2 or 3 times m. It is indeed this special feature of the particle motion that singles out a particular set of trajectories which makes the partition function of the system very much like that of an ideal gas. One is thereby led to a third-order phase transition (a transition accompanied by a continuous specific heat, with a discontinous slope) in contrast to the second-order phase transition actually met with in helium. Towards the end of this paper, Feynman did express the hope that if the evaluation of the path-integral (which involved the enumeration of a much larger variety of polygons) was carried out more accurately, the resulting transition may well turn out to be second-order. This hope has indeed been realized by the computational work of Ceperly and Pollock,[45] more than thirty years after Feynman first put forward his theory. It is, however, important to note that although the physical contents of the results obtained by Feynman in this paper were so close in spirit to the ones obtained earlier by London, neither phonons nor Landau rotons made an appearance here.

At this point we would like to narrate a delightful encounter that Feynman had with Lars Onsager at the International Conference on Theoretical Physics held at Tokyo, Japan, in August 1953. In Feynman's own words: 'When I went to Japan, I thought I had worked out the reason for the transition in liquid helium. I hadn't worked out all the properties of helium yet—particularly, the order of the transition—but I had worked out the transition itself. So at the dinner before the first meeting, I found myself sitting next to Onsager. I sat down first and he came in and sat down beside me and said, "I understand you think you have understood the transition in liquid helium." And I said, "Yes, I think I do." He said, "Humph". You know he never says a damn thing. And he didn't say any more through the whole dinner. So I thought he doesn't believe me. The next day I gave my talk at the meeting, where Onsager was present, and I explained that I understood the transition and how it worked and all this, except that I didn't have enough precision to determine exactly the order of the transition and I considered this really unsatisfactory, that I don't know the order of the transition and, therefore, perhaps I don't understand it. At that point Onsager got up, and you have to understand my feeling from the night before, and he said, "Professor Feynman is new to the problems of statistical mechanics and liquid helium and so on, and I think it is up to us to tell him what he doesn't seem to know." I now thought that I was really going to get it from him! He continued, "The fact that he doesn't get the order of the transition right is of no importance and significance at this point, because no one has ever gotten the order correct for any transition by a theoretical method yet. And he shouldn't criticize himself so severely because he doesn't get the order of the transition!" It was just the opposite of what I thought he was going to say, but I am sure he knew in the back of his mind that he was teasing me when he started out by saying that there's something we should tell him.'[6–8]

In his second paper of 1953 Feynman[15] investigated the situation near absolute zero and argued that, while the lowest excited states of the system were compressional waves (phonons), particle-like excitations that could in principle be present were necessarily separated from phonons by an energy gap Δ'. On the face of it this conclusion was essentially the same as the one arrived at by Landau in 1941 but the line of argument was substantially different. Feynman's approach stemmed from the feeling that the most fundamental properties of liquid helium II should be derivable, or at least understandable, on the basis of the quantum mechanical principles and the Schrödinger equation of the system. He therefore decided to undertake a close examination of the ground-state wave function Ψ_0 and thereupon construct a wave function Ψ that represented an excited state of the system characterized by particle motions other than density fluctuations. While it was obvious that, as a result of interparticle interactions, such motions would entail an effective mass m' instead of the actual mass m of the helium atom, the requirement of symmetry of the wave functions ruled out any large-scale motions of the atoms (which simply permute the atoms and do not yield anything truly different from the ground state). The only way an excited state involving particle motions could be different from the ground state was that it should allow motions on an atomic scale which in turn requires a minimum energy of excitation. Feynman emphasized that no such problem arises if one considered a Fermi liquid instead or, for that matter, disregarded statistics altogether. In either case, one could have large-scale motions with excitation energy $\varepsilon(=p^2/2m')$ as small as one likes; these excitations would be more than a match for phonons in determining the low-temperature properties of the system and hence would dominate the scene in that temperature regime. In the case of a Bose liquid, however, low-lying states such as these were not possible and one had to contend with excitations whose energy–momentum relationship was $\varepsilon = \Delta' + p^2/2m'$ instead (cf. Landau's spectrum (17.7) of 1941). Such excitations would not appear in significant numbers if $T \ll \Delta'/k_B$; accordingly, the low-temperature regime of a Bose liquid would be governed solely by phonons. In this paper Feynman did not attempt to evaluate Δ' on an atomic basis, for the precise nature of the particle motions involved in these modes of excitation was not yet clear.

17.10 Feynman's derivation of the energy spectrum of elementary excitations

The real breakthrough came with Feynman's third paper[17] which appeared early in 1954. Here Feynman looked into the question of the mathematical form that the wave function $\Psi(r_1, \ldots, r_N)$ pertaining to an excited state of the system might have and of the excitation energy that would be associated with such a wave function. He considered three most likely modes of excitation: one involving the 'rotation of a small ring of atoms', another involving the 'excitation of an atom in a local cage formed around it by its neighbors', and a third one involving the 'motion of a single atom with wave number $k \sim 2\pi/d$, where d is the atomic spacing, the other atoms moving about to get out of the way in front and to close in behind'. Feynman's arguments were again based on the requirements of symmetry of the wave function and in each of the three cases led him to conclude that the excited state wave function Ψ must be of the form

$$\Psi = \Psi_0 \sum_{i=1}^{N} f(r_i), \tag{17.28}$$

where $f(r)$ is *some* function of the position coordinates r; in the case of the third possibility, the function $f(r)$ was expected to be of the form $\exp(ik \cdot r)$, but its form in the other two cases was not very clear.

To determine an appropriate form for the function $f(r)$, Feynman made use of the variational principle which is based on the minimization of the expectation value of the Hamiltonian of the system under suitable constraints. The minimization condition turned out to be

$$\varepsilon \int p(r_1 - r_2) f(r_2) \, d^3 r_2 = -\frac{\hbar^2}{2m} \nabla^2 f(r_1), \tag{17.29}$$

where $p(r_1 - r_2)$ is the probability of finding an atom in a unit volume centered at the point r_2 when another atom is known to be at r_1; by definition, $p(r) \to \rho_0$, the mean particle density in the system, as $r \to \infty$. Equation (17.29) possesses a straightforward solution $f(r) = \exp(ik \cdot r)$, so that

$$\Psi = \Psi_0 \sum_i \exp(ik \cdot r_i) = \Psi_0 \rho_k^\dagger, \tag{17.30}$$

while

$$\varepsilon(k) = \hbar^2 k^2 / 2m S(k), \tag{17.31}$$

where

$$S(k) = \langle \Psi_0 | \rho_k^\dagger \rho_k | \Psi_0 \rangle / N \tag{17.32a}$$

$$= \int p(r) \exp(ik \cdot r) \, d^3 r. \tag{17.32b}$$

Here, $\rho_k^\dagger$ is the Fourier transform of the particle density $\rho(r)$, while $S(k)$ is the Fourier transform of the pair distribution function $p(r)$, also known as the *structure factor* of the liquid; the latter is a function only of k, the magnitude of $\mathbf{k}$. Since the function $S(k)$ could be determined experimentally (through the scattering of neutrons or X-rays), the function $\varepsilon(k)$ could be derived readily from equation (17.31).

The realization that the function $f(r)$ for three different possible modes of excitation was essentially the same was a moment of great excitement for Feynman. 'I cannot remember exactly how it happened. I was walking along the street . . . and zing! I understood it! The form (of the wave function) had to look like this.'[6] There was no doubt, then, that the excitation energy $\varepsilon(\mathbf{k})$ had to look like 17.31.

Feynman's attention now turned towards the form of the structure factor $S(k)$. He was aware of the fact that $S(k)$ rose linearly with k for small k, while it approached unity for large k. For intermediate k, he chose to follow a recipe he had learnt from Hans Bethe at Cornell: 'If you know the ends of a curve, you just take the smoothest thing in between and you are always right. So I made an artificial formula which had those two properties and was smooth in between . . . And I put that in to compute the specific heat of the liquid. But it did not work.'[6-8]

Feynman checked and rechecked his calculations but found nothing wrong with them. The problem, he concluded, lay with the structure factor alone. After a week of agonizing, he suddenly realized that, in order to produce the right results, the function $S(k)$ must first rise above the asymptotic value 1, pass through a maximum, and then come down towards the asymptote. The moment he saw that, he said to himself, 'But, of course, that is just what liquids must do. If you are measuring X-ray diffraction, then because of the spatial structure of the liquid, which is almost like a solid, there will be a maximum corresponding to the first diffraction ring of the X-ray pattern! That was a terrific moment! It was most interesting. I say this because it illustrates a moment when discovery was made. In a terrific flash of a few seconds, I saw that, since $S(k)$ appeared in the denominator, this peak in $S(k)$ would make a notch in the curve of excitation energy, so that the curve of excitation energy would be linear for low momenta, which would correspond to phonons, and at higher momenta there would be a minimum around some p_0. I suddenly realized that I now understood this thing that Landau was talking about.'[6-8][†]

Feynman was now quick to note that, since the liquid structure factor $S(k)$ would exhibit a maximum at $k \sim 2\pi/d$, where $d\,(=3.6\,\text{Å})$ is the atomic spacing, the excitation energy $\varepsilon(k)$ would exhibit a minimum in the neighborhood of

---

[†] Contrast this with the initial reaction of Feynman when someone, in the early fifties, had brought this nonmonotonic spectrum to his attention. 'When I looked at the thing, I thought it was crazy. After all, p is a vector, and subtracting p_0 from p which are *magnitudes*, rather than vectors, . . . it was so unsymmetrical and lopsided-looking that I thought Landau was nutty.'[6-8]

$k \sim 2$ Å^{-1}, which is of the same order of magnitude as the k_0 of Landau's rotons. Around the minimum, the function $\varepsilon(k)$ could indeed be written in the form (17.18) and the parameters Δ, ρ_0, and μ could, in principle, be derived from a knowledge of the function $S(k)$. Thus, to all intents and purposes, the *nonmonotonic* spectrum of Landau[38] had been derived from first principles.

It is remarkable that the experimental determination of the function $S(k)$ for liquid ⁴He had been initiated only a year earlier by Henshaw and Hurst through neutron scattering.[46] Using their preliminary results, Feynman could show that the behavior of $\varepsilon(k)$ near the minimum was qualitatively similar to the one postulated by Landau, though the values of the various parameters were not quite the same (see Fig. 17.5). In particular, the value of Δ/k_B was found to be about 18 K, which was quite large in comparison with the Landau figure of 9.6 K. In any case, since a variational treatment only gave an upper limit to the quantity $\varepsilon(k)$ in question, one could reasonably hope that a better wave function than the one employed here would yield results closer to the ones following from other sources.

Feynman also observed that, though the intent of his investigation was to examine particle-like excitations, the resulting formulation encompassed phonons as well! This happened because the wave function (17.30) also represented normal modes associated with sound waves of wave number k. He showed that the function $S(k)$ in the case of phonons was exactly equal to $\hbar k/2mc$,† and hence $\varepsilon(k)$ was exactly $\hbar kc$. Thus both phonons and rotons merged into a single, unified scheme in which they represented different parts of a common (and continuous) energy spectrum $\varepsilon(k)$, as determined by the structure of the liquid through the function $S(k)$. Clearly, no motion of a rotational character was involved, though the name roton has continued to be used.

17.11 An earlier attempt by Bijl

It seems appropriate to mention at this point that, soon after the work of London which advocated a connection between the phase transition in liquid ⁴He and the phenomenon of Bose–Einstein condensation, A. Bijl[47] investigated the mathematical structure of the wave functions appropriate to an interacting Bose gas and the excitation energy associated with those wave functions. His picture corresponded very closely to what Feynman called the 'third possibility', viz. a single atom moving through a crowd of others, and hence to the wave function (17.30). Bijl successfully derived an expression for

---

† It may be remarked here that the function $S(k)$ for the phonons may not seem to follow directly from equation (17.32b). On the basis of (17.32a), however, one can relate $S(k)$ to the 'mean energy associated with a phonon mode of wave number k', with the result that $S(k) = \langle E(k) \rangle / mc^2$. At $T = 0$, all oscillators are in the ground state, so that $\langle E(k) \rangle = \frac{1}{2}\hbar/\omega = \frac{1}{2}k$ and hence $S(k) = \hbar k/2mc$.

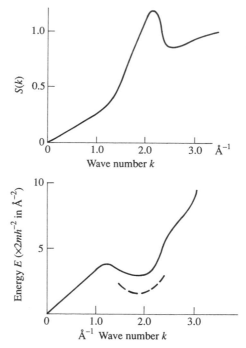

Fig. 17.5. The upper curve gives the liquid structure factor determined from neutron diffraction and extrapolated to zero k. The lower curve gives the energy spectrum of excitations as a function of wave number (momentum $\cdot h^{-1}$) which results from the formula $E = h^2 k^2 / 2mS(k)$ derived in the test. The initial linear portion represents excitation of phonons while excitations near the minimum of the curve, where it behaves as $\Delta + h^2(k - k_0)/2\mu$, correspond to Landau's rotons. However, data on the specific heat indicate that the theoretical curve should lie lower, closer to the dashed curve.

$\varepsilon(k)$ which was exactly the same as Feynman's [see equations (17.31) and (17.32b)]. Unfortunately, Bijl could only make a limited use of his result, primarily because he leaned heavily on the expansion

$$S(k) = S(0) + C_2 k^2 + C_4 k^2 + \cdots, \tag{17.33}$$

which, as we now know, represents neither phonons nor rotons. Bijl argued that $S(0)$ is identically zero (which is indeed true at $T = 0$), whereas $C_2 > 0$ and $C_4 < 0$. The energy $\varepsilon(k)$ then took the form of equation (17.7), with

$$\Delta' = \hbar^2 / 2mC_2, \qquad m' = mC_2^2 / |C_4|. \tag{17.34}$$

Bijl did, therefore, anticipate something equivalent to Landau's rotons of 1941,[37] but his theory did not have any room for the phonons. In fact, he vehemently argued that the interacting Bose gas, just like its mentor ideal Bose gas, could not support compressional waves and hence its specific heat at low temperatures would *not* follow a power law; it would instead be governed primarily by the factor $\exp(-\Delta'/k_B T)$.

It is only fair to say that Bijl's theory did contain the ingredients of a correct atomic theory of liquid He II, but he could not extract much from it, possibly because of a lack of foresight that Landau displayed when he tackled the same problem soon after or to a lack of hindsight that Feynman possessed in the wake of Landau's work. One might wonder why Bijl did not return to this problem after Landau had cleared some of the stumbling blocks: the reason was that Bijl perished in a Nazi concentration camp in 1941.

17.12 The Feynman–Cohen treatment of the 'backflow'

In his paper of 1954 Feynman discussed several other aspects of the problem of superfluidity which were closely related to the energy spectrum $\varepsilon(p)$.[17] He examined the thermodynamic properties of He II on the basis of this spectrum, essentially along the lines of Landau, but emphasized the fact that, as one got closer to the transition temperature, the number of excitations would become sufficiently large that one could not ignore their mutual interaction; clearly, this would present problems for one trying to determine T_λ from these considerations. Next, he studied the motion of the fluid as a whole—first of the superfluid alone, then of the superfluid carrying an excitation along with it, and finally of a mixture of the superfluid and the normal fluid. These studies elucidated a number of issues such as the curl-free motion of the superfluid, the possibility of quantized circulation in the superfluid, the critical velocity of superflow, the relative concentration of the two components of the two-fluid model, and so on. These issues are discussed in detail in later sections; for the present we mention an unexpected problem that Feynman identified in these studies. He noted that the roton picture emerging from his analysis failed to meet the requirement of particle conservation as one attempted to describe the excitation through a wave packet that drifts with a group velocity $v = \partial \varepsilon / \partial p$ but carries a current p/m; the roton at the minimum of the (ε, p) curve was the extreme example of this, for it drifted with a vanishing group velocity but carried a sizeable current with it. Feynman suggested that this difficulty could be resolved if one allowed for a 'backflow' of the fluid surrounding the excitation, for that would reduce the current overall and, with proper adjustments, would enable one to satisfy the requirement of conservation. He argued that this backflow would be bipolar at large distances from the excitation and that the coupling of the roton with the backflow would not only lower its energy, thus bringing the parameter Δ closer to the Landau value, but would also provide a mechanism for the roton–roton interaction.

Feynman now proceeded to investigate the influence of the backflow on the energy spectrum of the excitations in the roton regime, hoping that this would also clarify the physical nature of the roton. In collaboration with his graduate student Michael Cohen,[19] he incorporated backflow into the problem by modifying the wave function of the system from its original form (17.30) to

$$\Psi = \Psi_0 \left(\sum_i \exp(i\boldsymbol{k} \cdot \boldsymbol{r}_i) \right) \exp\left(i \sum_{j \neq k} g(\boldsymbol{r}_{jk}) \right). \tag{17.35}$$

The calculation was still very demanding, for it involved computation of both two-atom and three-atom correlation functions; for the latter, the authors employed the well-known Kirkwood approximation in which a three-body correlation function is replaced by a product of three two-body correlation functions. The net result of this painstaking calculation was that, over the whole range of interest, the excitation energy $\varepsilon(k)$ turned out to be much lower than that obtained by Feynman alone;[17] in particular, the new value of Δ/k_B turned out to be 11.5 K, way down from the previous value of 18–19 K and much closer to the Landau value of 9.6 K. The other parameters turned out to be $k_0 = 1.85$ Å^{-1} and $\mu/m \simeq 0.2$. While this result may seem to be a great improvement over the previous one of Feynman, more recent calculations of Manousakis and Pandharipande,[48] who are supposed to have done the same job more accurately, show that the energy spectrum resulting from the Feynman–Cohen wave function is not as close to the empirical spectrum as the original work would have us believe; for instance, the value of Δ/k_B obtained by the later authors is more like 14 K. It thus appears that, for a correct representation of the roton, we possibly need a better wave function than the one employed in these calculations. The fact remains that the microscopic investigation carried out by Feynman and Cohen was indeed a step in the right direction.

According to Feynman and Cohen, the roton state represented by the wave function (17.35) may be described *roughly* as that of a 'vortex ring of such small radius that only one atom could pass through its center'. Such a ring would have a very low drift velocity because, as it is already as small as possible, there will be hardly any force tending to shrink it—which force in a classical ring is balanced as a consequence of the forward drift. The energy associated with this structure is considerably smaller than $\hbar^2 k^2/2m$ because there is a correlated motion of many atoms moving together, sharing the total momentum $\hbar k$ and making the effective inertia of the excitation considerably larger than m; at $k = k_0$, where $\varepsilon(k) = \Delta$, the effective inertia is close to $2.5m$.

17.13 Direct determination of the energy spectrum

For Landau the energy–momentum relationship of the elementary excitations in liquid He II was essentially an input that enabled him to calculate the thermodynamic properties of the liquid as functions of T. These calculations were then compared with the corresponding experimental results and, if sensible agreement was found, the values of the various parameters occurring in the spectrum could be ascertained empirically. Feynman, on the other hand, had developed an atomic formulation on the basis of which the values of these parameters could be 'derived' directly from a single experimental property—the liquid structure factor. The question still remained, do these excitations really exist *as such* and, if so, could their energy and momentum be measured on an individual basis and the truth of the energy spectrum $\varepsilon(k)$ ascertained without the intervention of any macroscopic property of the system?

Feynman took a hint from the suggestion that Placzek and van Hove[49] had made concerning the observation of phonons in a solid. They had suggested that the phonon spectrum could be determined most directly by studying the energy distribution of very slow neutrons scattered inelastically and coherently from the solid; if the incident neutron beam was monochromatic and if the scattering process involved only the production or annihilation of a single phonon, then the conservation of energy and momentum implied that neutrons scattered at any given angle could have only discrete energies. The energy momentum relationship for the phonons could then be derived from the angular variation of this discrete spectrum. Feynman proposed that the same technique might be used for the determination of the energy spectrum of the elementary excitations in liquid He II. Thus, if a neutron of initial wavelength λ_i scattered at an angle ϕ and had a final wavelength λ_f, then the energy ε and momentum p of the excitation created in the liquid would be given by

$$\varepsilon = h^2(\lambda_i^{-2} - \lambda_f^{-2})/2m_n, \tag{17.36}$$

$$p^2 = h^2(\lambda_i^{-2} + \lambda_f^{-2} - 2\lambda_i^{-1}\lambda_f^{-1} \cos \phi), \tag{17.37}$$

where m_n is the mass of the neutron. With λ_i fixed, one could vary ϕ and, from the observed values of λ_f, map the entire spectrum of the excitations.

For a feasibility study of this proposal, Feynman again collaborated with Michael Cohen and together they looked into several questions that seemed to have a bearing on this problem.[50] They studied the cross section for the scattering of neutrons from liquid He II and concluded that a major part of the scattering at a fixed angle arises from the production or annihilation of a single excitation and would appear as a sharp line in the neutron spectrum. Other processes such as the production or annihilation of multiple excitations would create a continuous background; luckily, however, such processes would occur at a negligible rate if the incident neutrons were slow ($\lambda_i \gtrsim 4$ Å) and the liquid cold ($T < 2$ K). Cohen and Feynman also studied the question of linewidths in the spectrum of the scattered neutrons, for that would affect their resolution and in turn contribute to errors in the final analysis of the data; they found that, because of the long lifetime of both phonons and rotons, the spectrum lines, for all practical purposes, would be true delta-functions if the temperature of the liquid did not exceed 1 K. The stage was now set for the experimentalists to forge ahead.

The first set of experiments along these lines were conducted at Stockholm by Harry Palevsky of Brookhaven, in collaboration with K. E. Larsson and K. Otnes. They were soon followed by a group led by John Yarnell at Los Alamos and by D. G. Henshaw and A. D. B. Woods at Chalk River in Canada. The qualitative agreement between the theory and experiment was striking; the elementary excitations in liquid He II were indeed of the type envisioned by Landau[38] and established by Feynman.[17] Quantitatively too, the results were in very good agreement with the information that had accumulated so far on empirical grounds.

Yarnell and his collaborators[51] were among the first to carry out an exhaustive investigation of this problem; their results, obtained at 1.1 K, are shown in Fig. 17.6. The most significant features of these results are worth noting.

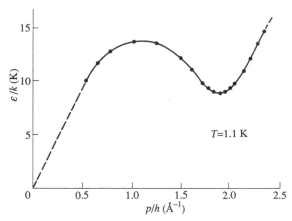

Fig. 17.6. The energy spectrum of the elementary excitations in liquid He II at 1.1 K (after Yarnell *et al.*[17]); the dashed line emanating from the origin has a slope corresponding to the velocity of sound in the liquid, viz. $239(\pm 5)$ m s^{-1}.

(1) If one fits a linear phonon-like spectrum, $\varepsilon = pc$, to points in the vicinity of $p/h = 0.55$ Å^{-1}, one obtains for c a value of 239 ± 5 m s^{-1}, which is in excellent agreement with the measured value of the velocity of sound in the liquid, viz. 238 m s^{-1}.

(2) The spectrum passes through a maximum value of $\varepsilon/k_B = 13.92 \pm 0.10$ K at $p/h = 1.11 \pm 0.02$ Å^{-1}.

(3) The spectrum then goes through a minimum around which it may be represented by the roton spectrum (17.18), with

$$\Delta/k_B = 8.65 \pm 0.04 \text{ K}, \qquad p_0/\hbar = 1.92 \pm 0.01 \text{ Å}^{-1}, \qquad \mu/m = 0.16 \pm 0.01.$$

(4) Above $p/\hbar \simeq 2.18$ Å^{-1}, the spectrum rises linearly, again with a slope equal to c.

Experiments were also done at temperatures of 1.6 and 1.8 K. The spectrum was found to be of the same general shape as at 1.1 K; only the value of Δ was slightly lower.

Subsequently Henshaw and Woods[52] extended the range of observation at both ends of the observed spectrum; their results are shown in Fig. 17.7. On the lower side, they carried out measurements down to 0.26 Å^{-1} and found that the experimental points indeed lay on a straight line, with slope ~ 237 m s^{-1}. On the higher side, they pushed their measurements up to 2.68 Å^{-1} and found that, after passing through a minimum of 1.91 Å^{-1}, the curve rose with an increasing slope until about 2.4 Å^{-1} at which point the second derivative $\partial^2 \varepsilon/\partial p^2$ changed sign; the subsequent trend suggested the possible existence of a second maximum in the spectrum.

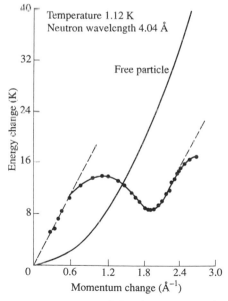

Fig. 17.7. The energy spectrum of the elementary excitations in liquid He II at 1.12 K (after Henshaw and Woods[47a]); the dashed straight lines have a common slope corresponding to the velocity of sound in the liquid, viz. 237 m s^{-1}. The parabolic curve rising from the origin represents the energy spectrum, $\varepsilon(p) = p^2/2m$, of free *helium* atoms.

The last two features of the spectrum had, in fact, been predicted theoretically. That the slope of the roton curve beyond $p = p_0$ would not exceed c had been pointed out by Feynman himself[17] on the grounds that, if the slope $(\partial \varepsilon / \partial p)$ exceeded c, the resulting roton would be unstable against the possibility of disintegration into a roton and a phonon. That the spectrum would terminate at a critical momentum p_c, with $\varepsilon_c = 2\Delta$ and $(\partial \varepsilon / \partial p)_c = 0$, was predicted by Lev Pitaevskii[53] as being a threshold that signals the decay of a roton into two rotons. The fact that the observed spectrum conformed to such specific predictions of the theory is a further testimony to the soundness of the picture developed by Landau and Feynman.†

17.14 The flow phenomena

We shall now turn our attention to the problems associated with superflow. The fact that liquid helium can flow through narrow channels with practically no resistance was discovered as early as 1911. The problem came into sharp focus only after it was realized that the liquid underwent a peculiar phase transition at 2.19 K and that below the transition temperature it displayed highly unusual behavior both thermodynamically and hydrodynamically. Measurements on viscous flow, for instance, led to two strikingly different sets of results. If one measured the coefficient of viscosity $\eta(T)$ of the liquid using a pair of coaxial cylinders rotating relative to one another, one obtained a result that varied smoothly with T, right through T_λ. If, on the other hand, one studied flow through a narrow capillary, one obtained values of η that depended critically on both T and the flow velocity v; while for $T > T_\lambda$ it was essentially of the same nature as the values of η measured by using coaxial cylinders, for $T > T_\lambda$ it was found to be practically zero for flow velocities less than a critical velocity v_c but rose sharply for velocities above v_c. One also found that the critical velocity v_c varied systematically with the diameter of the capillary, being larger for narrower capillaries; for diameters ranging from 10^{-3}–10^{-5} cm, the critical velocity fell in the range 2–20 cm s^{-1}.[55]

---

† After making valuable contributions to the theory of superfluidity, Feynman became interested in the theory of polarons, a topic to which he was attracted by the work of Herbert Fröhlich (see Chapter 19), as a part of his program to understand the phenomenon of superconductivity and develop a microscopic theory of that phenomenon from first principles. Soon thereafter he turned his attention, for a time, to quantum field theory and elementary particle physics—more precisely, the theory of weak interactions, a subject which had come to the forefront right after T.D. Lee and C.N. Yang's work on the conservation of parity in beta decay in the fall of 1956. Landau, on the other hand, went on to develop a microscopic theory of Fermi liquids,[54] which became the cornerstone of all subsequent work on the theory of liquid ^{3}He and of nuclear matter. For his overall contributions to the theory of quantum fluids, Lev Landau was awarded the Nobel Prize for physics in 1962. Three years later, in 1965, Richard Feynman, Julian Schwinger, and Sin-Itiro Tomonaga shared the Nobel Prize for their work on quantum electrodynamics.

Qualitatively, the foregoing results could be understood readily on the basis of the two-fluid model of Tisza and Landau. One could argue that in the experiments with rotating cylinders one was essentially measuring the viscosity of the normal component of the liquid, while in the experiments with narrow capillaries the normal component was practically 'stuck' to the walls of the capillary, so one was in effect measuring the viscosity of the superfluid. The existence of a critical velocity thus marked the 'breakdown' of the superfluid character of the flow, which in turn implied the onset of a dissipation of some sort. The obvious problem now was to determine the nature of the dissipative process responsible for the breakdown of superfluidity.

17.15 Landau on the critical velocity of superflow

Once again Landau[37] was the first to provide a partial answer to this question. He suggested that the nondissipative character of the superflow was based on the fact that the flow was a *potential* one, i.e.

$$\text{curl } \mathbf{v} = 0 \tag{17.38}$$

(for simplicity, we are now dropping the subscript s of the superfluid velocity). This would enable the fluid to 'slip' past the walls of the capillary, without interacting with them and hence without losing energy in the conventional manner (viz. by viscous dissipation). The only way the fluid could lose energy was by creating an elementary excitation $\varepsilon(p)$ which, as Landau showed, required a minimum flow velocity v_c. Landau's argument went as follows. Consider a mass M of the superfluid moving with velocity $\mathbf{v}$. To lose energy and at the same time maintain the irrotational character of the flow, the entire body of the fluid would have to slow down; the consequent change of energy would be given by $\delta E = M\mathbf{v} \cdot \partial \mathbf{v} = \mathbf{v} \cdot \partial \mathbf{p}$. If this change was related to the creation of an excitation of energy ε and momentum p, then, by reasons of conservation, we must have $\varepsilon = \mathbf{v} \cdot \mathbf{p} < vp$. Thus, to create such an excitation the velocity of the fluid must at least be equal to the ratio ε/p. Keeping in mind excitations of all types, one thus obtains for the critical velocity of superflow

$$v_c = (\varepsilon/p)_{\min}. \tag{17.39}$$

Using this criterion, Landau found that to create a phonon one required $v_c = c$, the velocity of sound, which was close to 240 m s^{-1}, while to create a roton (of the 1941 model)[37] one required $v_c = (2\Delta'/m')^{1/2}$, which was of the order of 60–70 m s^{-1}. To create a roton (of the 1947 model),[38] which is now standard, one required instead $[(p_0^2 + 2\mu\Delta)^{1/2} - p_0]/\mu \simeq \Delta/p_0$; this too turned out to be $\sim$60–70 m s^{-1}. Clearly, the values of the critical velocity resulting from these considerations were far larger than the observed values of v_c. Not only that, but one did not see in this argument any relationship whatsoever between the width of the capillary through which the liquid was flowing and the velocity at which dissipation set in.

17.16 Feynman's theory of quantized vorticity

Feynman attacked this problem in a comprehensive paper that appeared in *Progress in Low Temperature Physics*.[18] He argued that the only way dissipation could set in at lower velocities was 'for small parts of the fluid to stop or slow down *without* the entire fluid having to slow down at once.' In other words, the energy loss must be accompanied by flow which is *not* irrotational, that is, flow that entails local circulation. To understand this, he said, we must add to our picture of phonons, rotons, and potential flow a new element, viz. quantized vortex lines, which had been suggested several years earlier by Lars Onsager[56] but had now been derived independently by Feynman. To develop this line of thought, we go back to the wave function and see what happens to it when flow is imposed on the system.

Once again, if Ψ_0 represents the ground state of the system, then the imposition of a *uniform* velocity v on the whole body of the fluid would lead to a new wave function Ψ such that

$$\Psi = \Psi_0 \exp[i(P \cdot R_0)/\hbar] = \Psi_0 \exp\left[im\left(v \cdot \sum_i r_i\right)\bigg/\hbar\right] = \Psi_0 e^{i\phi}, \quad (17.40)$$

where $P = Nmv$ and $R_0 = N^{-1} \sum_i r_i$. If v were *nonuniform*, then the wave function Ψ might be significantly more complicated than (17.40) but the phase change $\Delta\phi$ resulting from a 'set of local displacements' would still be given by the expression

$$\Delta\phi = m \sum_i (v_i \cdot \Delta r_i)/\hbar, \quad (17.41)$$

where v is now a function of r. Equation (17.41) may now be applied to calculate the net phase change resulting from a displacement of atoms constituting a ring, from their original positions in the ring to the neighboring ones, so that on displacement we obtain a configuration that is physically indistinguishable from the initial one (see Fig. 17.8). In view of the symmetry of the wave function, the net phase change resulting from such a displacement must be an integral multiple of 2π:

$$m \sum_i (v_i \cdot \Delta r_i) = nh \quad (n = 0, \pm 1, \pm 2, \dots). \quad (15.42)$$

the summation $\sum$ going over all the atoms constituting the ring. If the ring were of a macroscopic size, one could regard the fluid as a continuum; equation (17.42) then takes the form

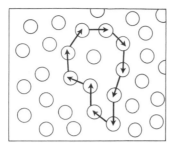

Fig. 17.8. The wave function must not change as a result of a permutation. If all the atoms are displaced around a ring, as shown, the phase change must be a multiple of 2π.

$$\oint v \cdot dr = n\frac{h}{m} \quad (n = 0, \pm 1, \pm 2, \ldots). \tag{17.43}$$

Feynman thus arrived at the remarkable result that the 'circulation of the flow associated with any circuit of integration in the fluid must be quantized in units of h/m'. One cannot fail to observe the striking resemblance this result has with the quantum condition of Bohr, viz.

$$\oint p \, dq = nh; \tag{17.44}$$

however, the region of application of equation (17.43) is macroscopic rather than microscopic!

The argument for quantized vorticity presented here was developed by Feynman in his essay of 1955.[18] The way 'quantized vortex lines' came originally to him has been described in detail in his paper of 1957.[20] In his interviews of 1966 and April 1970,[6] Feynman dwelt at length on this problem and spoke enthusiastically of the times when 'I was lying awake at nights. I tried to imagine how helium could set itself into rotation or circulation. In order for the liquid to have circulation, I visualized the following situation, which was kind of forced. I imagined that the liquid on one side of an impenetrable infinitely thin membrane, made of some material that doesn't exist, moving at a uniform velocity v, but the liquid on the other side was not moving. Now, I knew the wave function on each side of the membrane. The one on the top differed in the way that if you move an atom a distance x then the phase of the wave function would change proportionally with x, the rate at which the phase changed would depend on v. On the lower side, the phase would not change. The question now was: how could I fit the two together?

'Then I realized that the phase which is varying across the top is varying sinusoidally, and let us say that at $x = 0$ the phase at the top and the bottom is the same. So an atom could move from the top surface to the bottom surface without changing anything in the wave function. Then, if we go a certain distance, corresponding to a phase change of 2π, further on, the phase would again be like it was at $x = 0$, so that atoms could once again move up and down freely. There would be no surface tension energy between the two liquids, at little patches, every so often.' This led Feynman to think of contours of circulation that corresponded to a net phase change of 2π. By modifying the velocities step by step, he could visualize situations where the velocity field, almost everywhere, was continuous while the phase change arose principally due to a small core of atomic dimensions. 'I saw that I had invented (quantized) vortex lines. I had understood the pattern of circulation in liquid helium and, with excitement, I jumped out of the bed.'[6,7]

As mentioned earlier, equation (17.43) had been suggested several years previously by Onsager in a footnote to a paper dealing with classical vortex theory and the theory of turbulence.[56]† Onsager did not follow his announcement with detailed papers. His next important comment on the subject appeared in London's book on superfluids,[57] where London quotes, on p. 151, an unpublished remark by Onsager at the 1947 Low Temperature Physics Conference at Shelter Island. There, Onsager considered a picture of the rotating superfluid helium in terms of a 'set of (cylindrical) vortex sheets with quantized circulation'—a model on which London dwelt at considerable length; subsequently, the same model was adopted by Landau and Lifshitz[58] as well. In contrast, Feynman emphasized the importance of vortex *lines*, rather than *sheets*, for understanding the manner in which superfluid helium set itself into rotation. As will be seen in what follows, the concept advocated by Feynman was the one finally vindicated by experiment.

Using Stokes's theorem, equation (17.43) could be written in the form

$$\int_S \mathrm{curl}\ v \cdot dS = n\frac{h}{m} \quad (n = 0, \pm 1, \pm 2, \ldots), \qquad (17.45)$$

where S denotes the area enclosed by the circuit of integration. If this area was *simply-connected* and the velocity v was continuous throughout the area, then the domain of integration could be shrunk in a continuous manner without limit. The integral on the left-hand side then decreases continuously and finally tends to zero. The right-hand side, however, cannot be varied

---

† According to Russell Donnelly (private communication), the idea of quantized circulation in superfluid helium was suggested to students and colleagues at Yale University by Onsager as early as 1946. Onsager enjoyed the drama of an important scientific announcement and made public his discovery in a remark following a paper by C. Gorter on the two-fluid model at the Conference on Statistical Mechanics in Florence in 1949. He said, in part: 'Thus, the well-known invariant called the hydrodynamic circulation is quantized; the quantum of circulation is h/m. . . .. In the case of cylindrical symmetry, the angular momentum per particle is h.'

continuously. One, therefore, concludes that in such a case the quantum number n must be zero, and the condition

$$\text{curl } v = 0 \qquad (17.46)$$

must hold everywhere in the region—which is precisely the condition postulated by Landau as a basis for his understanding of the hydrodynamic behavior of superfluid helium.

Clearly, the Landau condition was only one special case of the circulation theorem of Onsager and Feynman. More generally, in a *multiply-connected* domain, which cannot be shrunk continuously to zero without encountering singularities in the velocity field, the Landau condition may not hold as a rule; one may well face an irrotational flow with quantized circulation. A simple example of such situations is provided by a *vortex flow*, which is a planar flow possessing cylindrical symmetry, such that

$$v_\rho = 0, \qquad v_\phi = K/2\pi\rho, \qquad v_z = 0, \qquad (17.47)$$

where ρ is the distance from the axis of symmetry while K is the circulation of the flow around the axis:

$$\oint v \cdot dr = \oint v_\phi(\rho \, d\phi) = K \quad (K - nh/m). \qquad (11.48)$$

Writing (11.48) in the form

$$\int_S \text{curl } v \cdot dS = \int_S \left(\frac{1}{\rho} \frac{\partial}{\partial \rho} (\rho v_\phi) \right) (\rho \, d\rho \, d\phi) K, \qquad (17.49)$$

we notice that while, at *all* $\rho \neq 0$, curl v is zero, at $\rho = 0$, where v_ϕ is singular, curl v must diverge in a manner that makes the integral in (17.49) finite. Feynman also observed that the energy associated with a unit length of such a vortex would be given by

$$\frac{\mathscr{E}}{L} = \int_a^b \frac{1}{2}(2\pi\rho \, d\rho \cdot mn_0 \left(\frac{K}{2\pi\rho} \right)^2 = \frac{mn_0 K^2}{4\pi} \ln \frac{b}{a}, \qquad (17.50)$$

where mn_0 is the (mean) mass density of the fluid, b is a length parameter related to the lateral size of the vortex while a is a linear measure of the structure of its core; for obvious reasons, a is expected to be comparable to the interatomic separation.

17.17 Feynman on the critical velocity of superflow

Having established the possibility of the existence of quantized vortex lines in superfluid helium, Feynman went on to examine the role that they might play in causing the breakdown of superfluidity at sufficiently high flow velocities.

He considered the probable patterns of flow of liquid helium emerging from the orifice of a slot-like channel of width d and worked out conditions for the formation of quantized vortices at the expense of the kinetic energy associated with the flow. He argued (see Fig. 17.9) that the number of vortex lines created

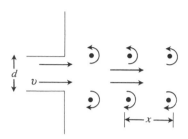

Fig. 17.9. Idealization of suposed vortex rings formed when superfluid helium issues at high speed from an orifice.

per unit length in the jet would be approximately v/K, where v is the velocity of the fluid in the channel (and hence in the mainstream of the jet), while $K(=h/m)$ is the circulation around a line; obviously, it would be cheaper to create vortices of unit circulation than ones of higher circulation. The number of lines created *per unit time* would, therefore, be $\sim v^2/K$ and the energy needed to create them (per unit length of the slot) would be $\sim (1/4)v^2 m n_0 K \ln(d/a)$. The total kinetic energy available per unit volume of the fluid was $\frac{1}{2}mn_0 v^2$ and hence per unit time (per unit length of the slot) it was $\frac{1}{2}mn_0 v^3 \, d$. If one now defines v_c to be the velocity at which the flow energy available is just large enough to create these lines, one finds that

$$v_c \sim \frac{h}{md} \ln (d/a). \tag{17.51}$$

For $d = 10^{-5}$ cm, this gave Feynman a critical velocity of about 1 m s^{-1} which, happily for him, was considerably lower than the values Landau had obtained by applying his criterion (17.39) to the possibility of creation of phonons or rotons in the flow. Compared with experimental values, however, the result obtained by Feynman was still too high. It was, nevertheless, important not only to bring the theoretical estimate of v closer to reality but to find a mechanism that made v_c dependent on the geometry of the apparatus used; at the same time, the qualitative variation of v_c with d was in the right direction. As discussed later, a more satisfactory resolution of this problem came from the possibility of the creation of quantized vortex rings rather than lines.

17.18 The 'rotation' of the superfluid

The other problem in which Feynman saw a role for his vortex lines was the problem of the 'rotation' of the superfluid. In view of the Landau condition, curl $v=0$, it seemed natural to conclude that superfluid helium was incapable of acquiring rotation in the manner normal liquids do when they are contained in a rotating vessel. Ordinarily, uniform rotation of a cylindrical vessel, with angular velocity ω about the axis of symmetry of the vessel, results in the whole mass of the fluid rotating with the same angular velocity as the vessel, the resulting velocity field v being such that $v=\omega\rho$ and

$$\text{curl } v = 2\omega \neq 0. \tag{17.52}$$

The shape of the free surface of the rotating fluid is determined jointly by the gravitational pull on the fluid and the centrifugal force resulting from rotation. In equilibrium, the surface turns out to be parabolic in shape, with curvature determined by the ratio ω^2/g:

$$z(\rho) = z(0) + (\omega^2/2g)\rho^2. \tag{17.53}$$

In the case of liquid He II, however, one would expect that, while the shape of the free surface should still be parabolic, its curvature would be less than that of a classical liquid, for, although the whole of the liquid would experience the pull of gravity, it is *only* the normal component of the liquid that would be subject to the centrifugal force; not only that, the curvature would depend on temperature as well. One may in this case write

$$z(\rho) = z(0) + [f(T)\omega^2/2g]\rho^2, \tag{17.54}$$

where $f(T)$ is the fraction of the normal component in the liquid.

The first experimental results on this question were reported by Donald Osborne of Cambridge,[59] who in 1950 studied the free surface of liquid helium II contained in a vessel rotating at an angular velocity of 10 rad s^{-1}. Surprisingly, the shape of the surface was found to be in conformity with equation (17.53) rather than (17.54), which means that the superfluid component was also participating fully in the rotation of the liquid.

It should be remarked here that the question of the rotation of superfluid helium had also been studied by Andronikashvili,[60] who, four years earlier, had followed the same approach as Osborne's and had obtained essentially the same results. However, a serious lack of approval from his colleagues, notably Landau, had prevented him from publishing his results. In addition, Andronikashvili had also probed this question somewhat differently, viz. by setting liquid He I (which is entirely normal) into rotation and then cooling it down through the lambda point so that it became 'liquid He II in rotation'; he found that, for all practical purposes, the part of the liquid that became superfluid continued to rotate as before. He even mentions the sighting of a 'thick vortex that passed through the whole column of the rotating liquid down to the bottom. A thick hollow axis formed inside the liquid. Later, as the liquid cooled, this hollow axis started to be dragged down and to shorten and, having reached the meniscus, it formed a cone on the vertex of the paraboloid of the free surface.' Andronikashvili reports to have observed this phenomenon once again but unfortunately could not capture it on film. One wonders as to what the consequences would have been had Andronikashvili conducted this experiment *prior* to the well-known stack-of-disks experiment which demonstrated so convincingly the existence of two distinct modes of flow operating side by side in the liquid; surely, the reception accorded to Landau's theory would have remained mixed for quite some time.

Feynman undertook the task of reconciling these mutually contradicting elements. On the one hand we have the observed rotation of the superfluid which is very much like that of a normal liquid; on the other we have the Landau condition, curl $v=0$, which advocates an irrotational flow. The reconciliation, according to Feynman, simply required the 'generation of quantized vortex lines in the superfluid', which would give the fluid an *overall* velocity field v similar to the one acquired by a normal fluid in rotation but, at the same time, would make curl v vanish almost everywhere in the region except at the axes of the vortices where it would diverge (so that its *average* value in the fluid would be precisely 2ω). Since curl v denotes the (average) circulation per unit area in the plane of rotation, Feynman argued that all one needed in the case of the superfluid was to provide for a 'uniform array of quantized vortex lines, parallel to the axis of rotation, with number density $2\omega m/h$ per unit area of the surface'—a recipe commonly referred to as the *Feynman rule*. The consequent mean spacing b between the lines would be $\sim (h/m\omega)^{1/2}$, which, for a typical value of ω, turns out to be a fraction of a millimeter—certainly much larger than the core of a vortex, which should be a few angstroms. Thus, practically everywhere in the fluid curl $v=0$, and it is only over infinitesimally small regions of space that curl v is infinitely large. It is not difficult to show that this arrangement of vortex lines gives the fluid a velocity field which, on a macroscopic scale ($\rho \gg b$), is practically the same as the one met with in a normal liquid.[61,44] Of course, if the vortex lines are strictly localized (which, in practice, may not be the case), then one may expect to observe a 'depression' in the surface at the location of each line caused by the large centrifuge effect felt near the axis of the line.

Feynman also calculated the energy required to generate the above-mentioned pattern of flow and showed that, expressed in terms of the energy required for a solid body-like rotation, the excess needed here was about $4\hbar m^{-1} R_\omega^{-2} \ln(b/a)$, where R is the radius of the vessel; for typical values of ω and R, the excess was no more than 1 percent. He, therefore, concluded that if rotating *solid* helium (that is, helium under excess pressure) were allowed to melt by releasing the pressure, the angular velocity distribution in the resulting liquid would differ imperceptibly from uniformity and the surface should appear parabolic just as for a normal liquid.

The theoretical framework developed by Feynman indeed required some direct experimental backing. This came, first indirectly, from the work of Wheeler, Blakewood, and Lane (WBL) at Yale, and of Hall and Vinen at

Cambridge, on the attenuation of second sound in liquid He II arising from mutual friction between the normal component of the fluid and the quantized vortices in the superfluid. While Wheeler *et al.*[62] studied the propagation of d.c. second-sound pulses in the space between two coaxial cylinders with the inner one rotating (thus enabling them to examine the alteration of the state of He II in a *shear flow*), Hall and Vinen observed second-sound attenuation in a rotating resonator with He II in *uniform rotation*. In each case the experiment was performed, or at least planned, before the publication of Feynman's work. In fact, it was during the question period after the presentation of the WBL paper at the 1955 American Physical Society meeting at New York that Feynman, who was in the audience, stood up and described the state of rotating helium in terms of vortices 'hanging down like strings in the fluid'. He attributed the (extra) attenuation of second sound to friction with these strings—an idea being formulated simultaneously, and independently, by Hall and Vinen.[63]

Direct evidence for the existence of quantized vortex lines came from the subsequent work of Vinen,[64,65] who, following a reminder by Feynman that the 'force experienced per unit length by a vortex line equals the density of the fluid times the vector cross-product of the circulation K and the velocity of the fluid v where the vortex is located', carried out an ingenious set of experiments utilizing this effect. Vinen in effect 'created' vortices around a fine wire immersed in rotating liquid He II at the location of the axis of rotation and measured the circulation K around them by means of the influence it exerts on the transverse vibrations of the wire. He found that, while vortices with circulation h/m were exceptionally stable, those with higher multiples too made appearance. Later on, repeating Vinen's experiment with thicker wires, Whitmore and Zimmermann[66] were able to observe stable vortices with circulation up to three quanta. The existence of quantized vorticity, with all its ramifications, was thus established beyond doubt.

17.19 Feynman and the quantized vortex rings

In his paper of 1955 Feynman[18] also considered the possibility of the existence of quantized vortices that were not linear. In particular, if a vortex line did not terminate on the walls of the container or on the free surface of the liquid, it may well have to close on itself, resulting in the formation of a vortex ring. The ring would obey the same quantization condition as the vortex line, viz. equation (17.48), but would have a velocity field very different from that of a line. One can readily see that the velocity field of a vortex ring, including the ring itself, and would move in a direction perpendicular to the plane of the ring with a drift velocity $v \sim h/2mr$ [see equation (17.47), with $K = h/m$ and $\rho \sim 2r$, where r is the radius of the ring]. An estimate of the energy associated with the ring may be obtained from equation (17.50), with $L = 2\pi r$, $K = h/m$, and $b \sim r$:

$$\varepsilon \sim 2\pi^2 \hbar^2 n_0 m^{-1} r \ln(r/a). \tag{17.55}$$

And, in analogy with a classical vortex ring, the associated momentum may be written as

$$p = 2\pi^2 \hbar n_0 r^2. \tag{17.56}$$

Equations (17.55) and (17.56) together provide a better estimate of the drift velocity of the ring, viz.

$$v = \frac{\hbar}{2mr} \ln(r/a). \tag{17.57}$$

Feynman's motivation in pursuing vortex rings was twofold. Firstly, he felt that, once a vortex line gets formed in the liquid, it would gradually get distorted and ultimately break up into vortex rings, thus providing a mechanism for the dissipation of energy of the flow, the breakdown of superfluidity, and the onset of turbulence. Secondly, he thought that the smallest vortex ring that could exist in the liquid—one so small that only one atom at a time could pass through it—might provide a model for the roton. It is only fair to say that, while the first suggestion seems to have worked rather well, there hasn't been much substantiation for the second, primarily because it hasn't been possible to demonstrate that the energy ε and momentum p associated with a vortex ring, however small, would ever mimic the characteristics of the roton spectrum.

There has indeed been some success in solving the riddle of the critical velocity on the basis of the formation of quantized vortex rings. Applying Landau's criterion (17.39), in conjunction with equations (17.55) and (17.56), one obtains, in the case of flow through a capillary,

$$v_c = (\varepsilon/p)_{\min} \sim \frac{\hbar}{mR} \ln(R/a), \tag{17.58}$$

where R is the radius of the capillary; the choice $r = R$ corresponds to the ring being of the largest possible size that can be formed inside the tube and hence to the smallest possible value of the ratio ε/p. Numerically, equation, (17.58) differs very little from the one obtained by Feynman on the basis of the formation of quantized vortex lines *outside* the tube, see equation (17.51), but the physical picture of the process and the derivation of the results are much clearer in terms of rings rather than lines. The situation was considerably improved when Al Fetter[67] pointed out that, as the radius r of the ring approaches the radius R of the tube, the influence of the 'image vortex' becomes quite important. The energy of the flow falls below the asymptotic value given by equation (17.55) by a factor of 10 or so. This, in turn, reduces the critical velocity by a similar factor; Fetter, in fact, obtained

$$v_c \approx \tfrac{11}{24} \hbar/mR, \tag{17.59}$$

devoid of the (inconvenient) logarithmic factor. The theoretical values of v_c were now in much better agreement with experiment.

Observational support for the existence of quantized vortex rings in liquid He II was provided by Rayfield and Reif,[68] who in 1964 performed an impressive set of experiments that enabled them to observe the velocity–energy relationship of free-moving charge-carrying vortex rings created in the liquid by suitably accelerated helium ions. Vortex rings carrying positive as well as negative charge were observed; dynamically, however, they behaved alike, as indeed was expected because the velocity and energy of a ring are determined by the properties of a large amount of fluid carried along with the ring rather than by the small charge coupled to it. Fitting experimental results with the notion of vortex rings, Rayfield and Reif concluded that their rings carried a circulation of $(1.00 \pm 0.03 \times 10^{-3} \text{ cm}^2 \text{ s}^{-1})$, which is pretty close to the quantum h/m ($= 0.997 \times 10^{-3} \text{ cm}^2 \text{ s}^{-1}$); at the same time, they seemed to have a core radius of about 1.2, which indeed is compatible with the interatomic separation in the liquid.

As for the relevance of quantized vorticity to the problem of turbulence in liquid helium II, we quote from Feynman's review of 1955:

'In ordinary fluids flowing rapidly with very low viscosity the phenomenon of turbulence sets in. A motion involving vorticity is unstable. The vortex lines twist about in an ever more complex fashion, increasing their length at the expense of the kinetic energy of the main stream. That is, if a liquid is flowing at a uniform velocity and a vortex line is started somewhere upstream, this line is twisted into a long complex tangle further downstream. To the uniform velocity is added a complex irregular velocity field. The energy for this is supplied by the pressure head.

'We may imagine that similar things happen in helium. Except for distances of a few angstroms from the core of the vortex, the laws obeyed are those of classical hydrodynamics. A single line playing out from all points in the wall upstream (both ends of the line terminate on the wall, of course) can soon fill the tube with a tangle of line. The energy needed to form the extra length of line is supplied by the pressure head. (The force that the pressure head exerts on the lines acts eventually on the walls through the interaction of the lines with the walls.) The resistance to flow somewhat above initial velocity must be the analogue in superfluid helium of turbulence, and a close analogue at that.'[18]

The subject of turbulence in superfluid helium has been discussed at length by Donnelly in his book *Experimental superfluidity*.[69]

Notes and References

1. R.P. Feynman, *Phys. Rev.* **80**, 440 (1950).

2. R.P. Feynman, *Phys. Rev.* **76**, 749 (1949).

3. R.P. Feynman, *Phys. Rev.* **76**, 769 (1949).

4. R.P. Feynman, *Phys. Rev.* **84**, 108 (1951).

5. R.P. Feynman, Interview with Jagdish Mehra, in Geneva, Switzerland, 14 December 1965.

6. R.P. Feynman, Interviews and conversations with Jagdish Mehra, in Austin, Texas, 18 April 1970.

7. R.P. Feynman, interviews with Charles Weiner (American Institute of Physics), in Pasadena, California, 1966.

8. R.P. Feynman, Interviews and conversations with Jagdish Mehra, in Pasadena, California, January 1988.

9. P.A.M. Dirac, *The principles of quantum mechanics.* Clarendon Press, Oxford, 2nd edn., 1935.

10. W. Heitler, *The quantum theory of radiation.* Clarendon Press, Oxford, 1935.

11. M. Cohen, Interview with Jagdish Mehra, in Philadelphia, Pennsylvania, 24 March 1989.

12. L. Onsager, *Phys. Rev.* **65**, 117 (1944).

13. A.R. Hibbs, Interview with Jagdish Mehra, at the Athenaeum, Caltech, Pasadena, California, 23 March 1988.

14. R.P. Feynman, Atomic theory of liquid helium. In: *Proc. Int. Conf. Theoretical Physics*, held at Tokyo and Kyoto (under IUPAP), 1953, p. 895.

15. R.P. Feynman, *Phys. Rev.* **90**, 1116 (1953); **91**, 1291 (1953).

16. R.P. Feynman, *Phys. Rev.* **91**, 1301 (1953).

17. R.P. Feynman, *Phys. Rev.* **94**, 262 (1954).

18. R.P. Feynman, In: *Progress in Low Temperature Physics*, Vol. 1 (ed. C.J. Gorter). North-Holland, Amsterdam, 1955.

19. R.P. Feynman and M. Cohen, *Prog. Theor. Phys.* **14**, 261 (1955); *Phys. Rev.* **102**, 1189 (1956).

20. R.P. Feynman, *Rev. Mod. Phys.* **29**, 205 (1957). (*Proc. Int. Conf. Theoretical Physics*, held at Seattle, Washington, USA, in September 1956 under IUPAP.)

21. R.P. Feynman, *Physica* **24**, S.18 (1958). (From *Proc. Kamerlingh Onnes Conf.*, held at Leiden.)

22. H. Kamerlingh Onnes, *Proc. R. Acad. Amsterdam* **13**, 1903 (1911).

23. W.H. Keesom, *Helium.* Elsevier, Amsterdam, 1942.

24. P.L. Kapitza, *Nature (Lond.)* **141**, 74(1938); *J. Phys. USSR* **4**, 181 (1941); **5**, 59 (1941).

25. H. Kamerlingh Onnes and J.D.A. Boks, *Rep. Int. Conf. Refrigeration*, London, 1924; *Leiden Communications* Nos. 170a,b.

26. W.H. Keesom and M. Wolfke, *Proc. R. Acad. Amsterdam* **31**, 90 (1928); *Leiden Communication* No. 190b.

27. A.P. Keesom and K. Clusius, *Proc. R. Acad. Amsterdam* **35**, 307 (1932); *Leiden Communication* No. 219c.

28. L. Tisza, *C.R. Acad. Sci. Paris* **207**, 1035, 1186 (1938).

29. A. Einstein, *Berliner Ber.* **1**, 3 (1925).

30. G.E. Uhlenbeck, Dissertation (Leiden), 1927.

31. F. London, *Nature (Lond.)* **141**, 643 (1938); *Phys. Rev.* **54**, 947 (1938).

32. R.H. Fowler and H. Jones, *Proc. Camb. Phil. Soc.* **34**, 573 (1938).

33. B. Kahn and G.E. Uhlenbeck, *Physica* **5**, 399 (1938).

34. F. London, *J. Phys. Chem.* **43**, 49 (1939).

35. S. Greenspoon and R.K. Pathria, *Proc. Camb. Phil. Soc.* **34**, 2103 (1974).

36. R.M. Ziff, G.E. Uhlenbeck and M. Kac, *Phys. Rep.* **32**, 169 (1977).

37. L.D. Landau, *J. Phys. USSR* **5**, 71 (1941); *Phys. Rev.* **60**, 354 (1941).

38. L.D. Landau, *J. Phys. USSR* **11**, 91 (1947).

39. W.H. Keesom and A.P. Keesom, *Proc. R. Acad. Amsterdam* **35**, 736 (1932); *Physica* **3**, 359 (1936).

40. E.L. Andronikashvili, *J. Phys. USSR* **10**, 201 (1946); *JETP USSR* **18**, 424, 429 (1948).

41. V.P. Peshkov, *JETP USSR* **10**, 389 (1946); *JETP USSR* **18**, 857, 951 (1948).

42. N.N. Bogoliubov, *J. Phys. USSR* **11**, 23 (1947); *JETP USSR* **18**, 622 (1948).

43. R.P. Feynman, *Rev. Mod. Phys.* **20**, 367 (1948).

44. R.K. Pathria, *Statistical mechanics.* Pergamon, Oxford, 1972.

45. D.M. Ceperley and E.L. Pollock, *Phys. Rev. Lett.* **56**, 351 (1986).

46. D.G. Henshaw and D.G. Hurst, *Phys. Rev.* **91**, 1222 (1953).

47. A. Bijl, *Physica* **7**, 869 (1940).

48. E. Manousaki and V.R. Pandharipande, *Phys. Rev.* E **30**, 5062 (1954).

49. G. Plaszek and L. van Hove, *Phys. Rev.* **93**, 1207 (1954).

50. M. Cohen and R.P. Feynman, *Phys. Rev.* **107**, 13 (1957).

51. J.L. Yarnell, *et al.*, Phys. Rev. **113**, 1379, 1386 (1959).

52. D.G. Henshaw and A.D.B. Woods, *Phys. Rev.* **121**, 1266 (1961).

53. L.P. Pitaevski, *Sov. Phys. JETP* **9**, 830 (1959).

54. L.D. Landau, *JETP USSR* 30, 105891956), English translation, *Sov. Phys. JETP* **3**, 920 (1959).

55. K.R. Atkins, *Adv. Phys.* **1**, 169 (1952).

56. L. Onsager, *Nuovo Cim.* **6** (Suppl. 2), 249, 261 (1949).

57. F. London, *Superfluids*, Vol.2. Wiley, New York, 1954.

58. L.D. Landau and E.M. Lifshitz, *Dokl. Akad. Nauk SSR* **100**, 669 (1955).

59. D.V. Osborne, *Proc. Phys. Soc.* A **64**, 114 (1951).

60. E.L. Andronikashvili, *Reflections on liquid helium*. American Institute of Physics, New York, 1989.

61. C.T. Lane, *Superfluid physics*. McGraw-Hill, New York, 1962.

62. R.G. Wheeler, C.H. Blakewood, and C.T. Lane, *Phys. Rev.* **99**, 1667 (1955).

63. H.E. Hall and W.F. Vinen, *Proc. R. Soc. Lond.* A **238**, 204, 215 (1956).

64. W.F. Vinen, *Nature (Lond.)* **181**, 1524 (1958).

65. W.F. Vinen, *Proc. R. Soc. Lond.* A **260**, 218 (1961).

66. S.C. Whitmore and W. Zimmermann, *Phys. Rev. Lett.* **15**, 389 (1965).

67. A.L. Fetter, *Phys. Rev. Lett.* **10**, 507 (1963).

68. G.W. Rayfield and F. Reif, *Phys. Rev. Lett.* **11**, 305(1963); *Phys. Rev.* A **136**, 1194 (1964).

69. R.J. Donnelly, *Experimental superfluidity*. University of Chicago Press, 1967.

18

Unwelcome recognition and establishing a routine

By this time Feynman's work had become well known and he had become a highly recognized and famous physicist. He was surprised to recall his earlier desire to be written about in *Time* magazine. He had come to believe that formal recognition did not mean anything to him. 'I feel I have received recognition when I see more and more people using my stuff; for example, when I see more and more people using the diagrams I cooked up, or when I saw that my backwards-moving electrons had appeared in one of the science fiction magazines; things like that are enough recognition for me.'[1]

In January 1954 Richard Feynman was selected winner of the Albert Einstein Award, consisting of a $15 000 cash prize, a gold medal, and a citation. The Albert Einstein Award, one of the highest honors in science, was established on 15 March 1949 on Einstein's seventieth birthday, by Lewis S. Strauss, Chairman of the Board of Trustees of the Institute for Advanced Study, Princeton, and Chairman of the United States Atomic Energy Commission, in memory of his parents, and was to be awarded every three years by the Lewis and Rosa Strauss Memorial Foundation for an outstanding contribution to knowledge in the mathematical and physical sciences. It was first awarded in 1951 jointly to Kurt Gödel of the Institute for Advanced Study and Julian Schwinger of Harvard University.

One day Feynman received a telephone call at home, and the operator said, 'Mr Lewis Stauss wants to talk to you.' Feynman turned to his wife, Mary Lou, and said: 'Hey, some guy named Lewis Strauss from Washington wants to talk to me.' She told him that Strauss was chairman of the Atomic Energy Commission (AEC). Strauss told him about the Einstein Award which he had established in memory of his parents, and that Feynman had been given that award. All the time Feynman was thinking that Strauss wanted him to do something either for the AEC or to judge candidates for the Einstein Award. On hearing that he was the awardee himself, he exclaimed, 'Won? Hot dog!' Strauss said, 'It's interesting to hear a serious scientist saying something like "hot dog!"' Feynman replied, 'Listen, you call up any serious scientist and tell him that he has won $15 000, he'll say "hot dog!"' So he had to go to Washington to collect the award in March 1954.

That was soon after the Oppenheimer hearings in which Robert Oppenheimer's clearance for secret work for the US government had been denied; Feynman's cousin Frances, who was a reporter for the Associated Press, had a copy of the hearings. Feynman was with his sister Joan before going to receive the award, and he read the entire proceedings during the night.

When the news of the Einstein Award to Feynman was announced, 'I knew what had happppened to Oppenheimer, and that Strauss had something to do with it, and I didn't like it. And I didn't like Strauss. I thought, "I'm going to fix him." It was not nice, and I was worried about it. I talked to Professor Rabi about it, who was visiting Caltech, and Rabi said, "You should never turn a man's generosity as a weapon against him. Any virtue that a man has, even if he has many vices, should not be used as a weapon against him." That's the way he put it. "You shouldn't use a man's virtue as a weakness to take advantage." I saw that's what I would be doing; if I refused him and made publicity about him by saying that I won't accept the award because he's such a stinker. That would be a terrible thing to do.

'This is the way Rabi put it. This is the way he acts, behaves, and walks around. He likes to think of himself as an elder statesman or adviser. He's like a father figure to a young scientist. I liked him very much; we were good friends. "A man's generosity should never be used as a weapon against him." Rabi was a wise man, an old philosopher. So I decided to accept the prize graciously. It was a generous move and it wasn't fair to turn on him [Strauss] because he had become generous.'[1,2]

In Lewis Strauss, Feynman saw what a prejudiced man was like. 'That was the first time I met a prejudiced man. He disregarded everything that was in Oppenheimer's favor, and stuck to what could be used against him. As for Teller and others who spoke against giving the clearance to Oppenheimer at the hearings, they were all against him. If Teller were to come here to see me, we'd just talk fine. I don't think he was stupid or venal, although he may be; I'm not sure. I just thought he misinterpreted Oppenheimer's motives. He had a paranoia, an utterly absurd paranoia, about the Russians. There was one time when he was seriously worried—this had to do with the problem of making an agreement with the Russians not to test atomic weapons in space. And his [Teller's] worry was how we could be sure that they wouldn't do it behind the moon, where we can't see them. He was serious. He was a little crazy, quite paranoid.' Strauss ranted a lot against Oppenheimer, and whenever he made a point against him Feynman rebutted him. Finally he did accept the Einstein Award from the hands of Lewis Strauss, albeit reluctantly.[1,2]

In April 1954 Feynman was elected to the US National Academy of Sciences. 'I had trouble with the National Academy of Sciences, because I had never heard of it. I received the notice of my election to membership, and I did not know what it was. I went to somebody to ask about it; he told me that [Paul S.] Epstein [who was a member] would know. Robert Bacher was out at that time. I told Epstein, "Professor Epstein, I don't want to join it, because as far as I know they don't do a damned thing." He said, "But they publish these *Proceedings* [*of the National Academy of Sciences*]. They have meetings." "Yeah, but I don't read the *Proceedings*." It was supposed to be a publication, but the articles on physics in it were not very impressive. I never had to refer to it; I never knew it was there. And I never knew anything that the academy did; all they said was that "it was an honorary society".

'When I was a kid in high school, there was a society called Arista, which was an honorary group for the students, and the only thing we did in Arista was to select other students who might become members of this society. So it was a mutual back-patting society, and I looked at what we were doing, and I thought: "That's not right. All we do, we get into this thing, and we give honor to the next guy by electing him a member. What a position to be in! Kingpin Joe, he's going to permit somebody else to have this marvelous honor that is so wonderful to have attained." So, it was my decision not to be a member of an honorary society, if it was merely an honorary society. If this damned thing did something, it would be all right.'[1,2]

Feynman made his objection known to Epstein; he just didn't like the idea of joining the National Academy of Sciences. Epstein told him that it was very important, what a great honor it was, that his many friends in the organization had worked very hard to get him elected into the National Academy, and he would probably disappoint many friends if he said no to joining; it would make a big noise, which was unnecessary. So Feynman said OK and quietly accepted membership of the academy. But he did not pay any dues and wrote to them not to send him their journal, and tried to forget the whole thing.

Feynman went to attend his first meeting of the academy. He thought he should give them a chance. It was just as he had imagined it to be. There was a lot of talk about getting new members. They were discussing: 'We have to stick together in the physics group, because we have only so and so many votes; we have to kind of agree on it among ourselves on which physicists we are going to vote for, because if we don't we're not going to have the votes to counter the number of votes of the chemists, and so on.' To Feynman, all such talk was for the birds. If the chemist is better, why should he not be voted in? He wouldn't stand for it.

Feynman listened to the talks that were presented. Their quality was variable. One member described an experiment to show the effect of stress on rats. He took a jar and put the rats in water, and he screwed the lid on so that they could not quite come up high enough when they were swimming to get a good breath, and they were drowning. And the experimenter watched how long it would take them to drown under certain circumstances.

Nothing was measured scientifically. There was no sense to the experiment. The rats got very nervous, and they swam faster. It was a most cruel, stupid, and unnecessary thing. Other than the fact that the experiment was not with human beings, it was like one of those Nazi experiments, in which they did not know what they were doing—carrying on the experiment without purpose. It was just like a kid who would do an experiment on drowning the rats. Feynman was ready to jump up and complain about it, and thought that someone else might do it and say that it was scientifically poor and had no sense to it; he thought that since he was a new member he should not complain right away. But nobody else complained. Feynman was very bothered by this scientifically bogus experiment in which nothing was estimated or measured. And *this* in a *scientific* organization; it was a useless, misinterpreted activity!

In another talk by a medical man, there was a report on some activity of the heart and nerves, and many curves were drawn from which conclusions had been arrived at. This doctor had second and third derivatives on curves as well. Feynman asked him if he could show how he drew the curves, but he refused to do so.

So, Feynman came to the conclusion that the National Academy of Sciences was not critical enough about its own conclusions on science, that it was a merely honorary society, and did not want to have anything to do with it. He wrote to Detlev W. Bronk, the president of the National Academy of Sciences, and asked him if there was some way by which he could get out of the academy quietly. He did not wish to be associated with it, but he did not wish to make a fuss publicly either. He told Bronk that if he remained he would be one reluctant, unhappy member. Bronk replied that in his view he should remain a member. When Frederick Seitz followed Detlev Bronk as president, Feynman resigned his membership of the academy.

In March 1954 Feynman went to the University of Chicago as a guest professor; there he gave some lectures about liquid helium and discussed the problems of the superfluidity of liquid helium with Enrico Fermi. Fermi listened to all of Feynman's lectures and tried to learn about this important and fundamental problem. He would ask all the appropriate and penetrating questions, and Feynman was also invited to the Fermi home several times. 'Whenever Fermi lectured about any subject whatever that he had thought out before, the clarity of the exposition and the perfection with which everything was put together to make everything look so obvious and beautifully simple gave me the impression that he did not suffer from a disease of the mind, which I suffer from, namely confusion.

'Fermi was both a theoretician and an experimentalist. But I thought of him as a theorist all the time. He was one of the very great physicists. I personally do not rank them. There's no order because their qualities are so different. Each one has a way, and Fermi's way was a clarity of physical reasoning; that was his expertise. So I don't make any order among them; for instance, I could not say who among Bethe and Fermi qualifies to be the better physicist. That, to me, is unimportant. Oppenheimer, Bethe, Pauli, and Fermi—they are all very great guys. And Fermi was someone I loved to talk to, that I thought was marvelous, a very great physicist indeed.'[1,2]

Shortly after Fermi's death the faculty at the University of Chicago were looking for someone to take his place. A couple of people from Chicago visited Feynman at his home and told him all kinds of wonderful things about the University of Chicago, how they had lots of great people there, and began hinting that if he wanted to know how much they would pay he had just to mention it. Feynman told them: 'Oh, no! I've already decided to stay at Caltech. My wife Mary Lou is in the other room, and if she hears how much the salary is, we'll get into an argument. Besides, I've decided not to decide any more; I'm staying at Caltech for good.' Feynman did not let them tell him the salary they were offering.[3]

About a month later, Feynman was at a meeting, and Leona Marshall from the University of Chicago's physics department came over and told him: 'It's funny you didn't accept our offer at Chicago. We were so disappointed, and we couldn't understand how you could turn down such a terrific offer.' Feynman told her that it was easy because he never let them tell him what the offer was. A week later he got a letter from her, and in the first sentence she told him what his salary was going to be, and asked him: 'Maybe now you want to reconsider, because they've told me that the position is still open, and we'd very much like to have you.' Feynman wrote her back a letter and said: 'After reading the salary, I've decided that I *must* refuse. The reason I have to refuse a salary like that is that I would be able to do what I've always wanted to do— get a wonderful mistress, put her up in an apartment, buy her nice things. . . . With the salary you have offered, I could actually *do* that, and I know what would happen to me. I'd worry about her, what she's doing; I'd get into arguments when I come home, and so on. All this bother would make me uncomfortable and unhappy. I wouldn't be able to do physics well, and it would be a *big mess*! What I have always wanted to do would be bad for me, so I've decided that I can't accept your offer.'[3]

After returning from Brazil, Feynman had indeed felt more and more at home at Caltech. There had been only one occasion, when he hadn't yet been at Caltech very long, that there was a serious attack of smog. He was standing at a corner, trying to cross the street, and his eyes were watering, and he said to himself: 'This is crazy! This is absolutely insane. It was all right back at Cornell. I'm getting out of here.'[4]

Feynman thought of his friends like Mark Kac, Willy Feller, Hans Bethe, Philip Morrison, Melvin Calvin, with whom he so much used to enjoy talking at Cornell, and he thought he should return. So he called up Cornell, and asked them if they thought it would be possible for him to go back. They said, 'Sure, we'll set it up and call you tomorrow.'[4] The next day Feynman's psychological circumstances changed completely. 'I was walking up to my office, and a guy came running up to me and said, "Hey, Feynman! Did you hear what happened? Baade found that there are *two* different populations of stars! All the measurements we had been making of the distances of galaxies had been based on Cepheid variables of *one* type, but there's *another* type, so the universe is twice, or three, or even four times as old as we thought!"

'I knew the problem. In those days, the earth appeared to be older than the universe. The earth was four and a half billion, and the universe was only a couple, or three billion years old. It was a great puzzle. And this discovery resolved all that. The universe was now demonstrably older than was previously thought. And I got this information right away—the guy came running up to me to tell me this.

'I didn't even make it across to the campus to get to my office, when *another* guy came up—Matt Meselson, a biologist who had minored in physics. (I had been on his committee for the Ph.D.) He had built the first of what they call a density gradient centrifuge—it could measure the density of molecules. He said, "Look at the results of the experiments I have been doing!" And he told me all about his tremendously exciting, important, and fundamental discoveries about bacteria. And I realized, as I finally got to my office, that this is where I've got to be. Where people from all different fields of science would tell me stuff, and it was all exciting. It was exactly what I wanted, really.

'So when Cornell called a little later, and said they were setting everything up, and it was nearly ready, I said, "I'm sorry. I've changed my mind again." But I decided *never* to decide again. Nothing—absolutely nothing—would ever change my mind again.

'When you're young, you have all these things to worry about—should you go there, what about your mother. And you worry, and try to decide, but then something else comes up. It's much easier to just plain *decide*. Never mind—*nothing* is ever going to change your mind. I did that once when I was a student at MIT. I got sick and tired of having to decide what kind of dessert I was going to have at a restaurant, so I decided it would *always* be chocolate ice cream, and never worried about it again—I had the solution to *that* problem. Anyway, I decided it would always be Caltech.'[5]

Soon after Feynman's settling down at Caltech after his sabbatical year in Brazil, a coterie of graduate students seeking to work for their Ph.D. began to assemble around Feynman. At Cornell there had been graduate students, but they were also Bethe's students at the same time; the separation between them was not too large. But at Caltech, Feynman was beginning to attract his own research students. Given his youthful looks and behavior, he did not look much older than a graduate student himself. One of the earliest collaborations of Feynman with a graduate student was with Michael Cohen, who came for graduate studies at Caltech in 1951 and later began to work on his thesis with Feynman. Feynman and Cohen did important work together on the theory of liquid helium and superfluidity (see Chapter 17).

During his visit to Brazil in the summer of 1953, Feynman had given a talk on 'The present situation in fundamental theoretical physics',[6] in which he listed some of the great achievements as well as outstanding problems of theoretical physics. One of these problems, Feynman noted, was the difference of $2.5m_e$ (electron masses) in the mass of the proton and the neutron. He thought that this difference should be purely electromagnetic. 'But taking the simplest equation to describe the electromagnetic behavior of the two particles, one finds a mass correction of the wrong sign. The difficulty may be a clue of the greatest importance to the elucidation of the structure of these particles. How is it possible to account for the reversed sign? The subject should be investigated more thoroughly.'[7]

Feynman's graduate student Gerald Speisman worked on the problem of the proton–neutron mass difference for his Ph.D. thesis. He computed this mass difference by using quantum electrodynamics with cut-offs on the photon propagator and the anomalous magnetic moments of the proton and the neutron. This approach worked. 'Feynman told me that he had earlier done a back-of-the-envelope calculation and obtained the wrong sign for the mass difference,' recalled Speisman.[8] Feynman had looked at this problem a long time ago, when he was first working on quantum electrodynamics, to get the sign of the mass difference and it was positive: the energy of the proton should be heavier than the energy of the neutron, and yet the energy of the neutron was heavier than that of the proton. So he had concluded that there must be something wrong with electrodynamics, or there must be some peculiarity of electrodynamics, some strange way in which the neutron or the proton interacted with electric charges at high energy. So, when one does the integrals, the sign gets reversed, because Feynman could not believe that it was anything but electrodynamics. That's why Feynman asked Speisman to do the calculation, and Speisman found that it was a negative mass difference. Feynman and Speisman were only trying to show that the fact that the proton was lighter than the neutron did *not* mean that it was impossible that the difference was electromagnetic.[9] The modern view is that the proton and the neutron are composed of quarks, and the mystery is why the up and down quarks are the only quark pair that are nearly equal in mass.

Albert Hibbs also became a doctoral student of Richard Feynman's in the early 1950s and, in due course, a personal friend. He was four years younger than Feynman and they had a very good rapport with each other. By that time, Feynman had decided that a research student who wished to work on a doctoral thesis with him had to bring along his own chosen problem. 'I don't know how to handle students. I never like to give them problems that are impossible. The only way to work on problems that occur to me is by myself. I allow myself to waste my own time; I do all kinds of crazy, impossible things, in which I don't succeed, but I don't care, but I cannot give such things to a research student or assistant to work on. So I let them find their own problems.'[1] Hibbs had developed a strong interest in physical oceanography, and proposed the problem of how the wind makes the waves grow in the ocean for his thesis. Feynman did not know anything about this topic, but he was delighted to accept Hibbs as his student, for he was also going to learn something new.

Hibbs laid out the details of the problem of the formation of waves in the ocean for Feynman; it was an unsolved problem of some importance, not only because of the nonlinear effects, but it also had some industrial applications. Lord Rayleigh and Horace Lamb had done work on such problems in the old days. Feynman suggested that he and Hibbs should check with men like Walter Munk and Carl Eckart, the big guys at the Scripps Institution of Oceanography at La Jolla, about their opinion of the importance and difficulties of the problems involved in their project. After meeting with Munk and Eckart at Scripps, Feynman concluded that those people 'don't know anything; we know more about it than they do right now.'[10] During the course of the next several years, Hibbs completed his thesis with Feynman. During all this time, however, Feynman's main concern was with the problems of the superfluidity of liquid helium and superconductivity.

Albert Hibbs also wrote down the notes of Feynman's lectures on quantum electrodynamics, which were published in due course.[11] Hibbs entered into an arrangement with Feynman to assist him in the writing of his book on path integrals and quantum mechanics for the McGraw-Hill Publishing Company. 'It was his book really. I was sort of a super stenographer in a sense, translating Feynman into the written word. It developed as follows. Several publishers were coming to him all the time and asking him to write a book on quantum mechanics. He turned them all away. I happened to go to his office to discuss something that had developed in my own graduate work, when a representative of McGraw-Hill was there. I walked in on this conversation between them, and once again Feynman was turning him down. The guy went away. So I told Richard that I thought that was a terrible thing to do, that here he had this marvelous approach to quantum mechanics, terribly insightful, one that got many students who would otherwise be left out were now brought into theoretical physics because of his approach; he had twenty people a year who were learning this and there was a world full of others who could learn it if only he would write the book. He looked at me in his characteristic way, and said, "OK, Hibbs. You help me and I'll write it." So it began. Neither of us was dedicated to getting the thing out in a hurry and McGraw-Hill was constantly beating on us to try turn in yet another chapter. The basic idea, of course, was his path-integral approach. The writing went on for several years until, ultimately, the book was published.'[10,12]

In the early 1950s Feynman was still married to Mary Lou, when Albert Hibbs obtained some impressions of their life together. 'She was impossible. Feynman came quite often to parties of graduate students including once to a friend of mine who lived quite close to me. It was a wild kind of party as graduate student parties were, several people were kind of drunk. Feynman no longer drank at that time; he had taken drinks previously in his life, but had stopped entirely. But he acted—he paced his acting—so that he was always afterwards a little drunker than the drunkenest person there. His wife, Mary Lou, sat quietly in a corner of the room and would begin to reprimand him, saying, "Richard, Richard! Stop that! You're acting like a fool, stop that!" Finally she would get up and insist that they leave. It made quite a bad scene. This was not unusual; she would repeat it all the time. She felt that he did not behave as a proper professor of a place as prestigious as Caltech; he was not professorial in his social activities. That Richard did not always act in a dignified way really upset her because she felt that was important—for her sense of herself. She wanted to be married to a dignified professor and she wasn't. She would tell other young faculty wives that all physicists were boors and they should neither go to physics meetings nor associate with physicists socially.' [10]

Murray Gell-Mann recalls that 'Mary Lou would lose our invitations. Margaret [Gell-Mann's wife] would phone her and invite them and she would forget to tell Dick. And apparently that was a habit. Once, when they were just beginning to eat dinner, she told him, "Oh, by the way, I forgot to tell you, Tommy Lauritsen called and said that we should come over tonight and have dinner over there to meet an old bore. But I didn't think you would be interested in that, so we're having dinner at home." And he said, "What did Tommy Lauritsen say? To meet an old bore? Or to meet the old Bohr?" And she, "Oh, maybe he said one or the other. What difference does it make?" And he said, "Well, the spelling is different for one thing!"' [13]

Matthew Sands remembers an informal physics department picnic, to which the faculty members, graduate students, and their families were invited, that Mary Lou came to formally dressed in high heels. She became visibly annoyed when the small playful children touched her with their grubby hands, and insisted upon leaving the picnic with her husband; she could not be persuaded that it was all part of good-natured fun. Feynman refused to go along, and she left alone in a huff without him.

Mary Lou could not stand Richard's playful moods; they rubbed each other the wrong way. His behavior was very upsetting to her, and he could not stand her constant argumentativeness. Finally they got divorced in 1956.

After taking his Ph.D. with Feynman, Hibbs had gone back to work full time at the Jet Propulsion Laboratory (JPL). The Soviet *Sputnik* went up in October 1957. US response was a little late. 'I had asked Feynman to come and help us track *Explorer II* when it went up. This was in March 1958. We had launched the first one at the end of January and this was number two. Feynman was very excited by this, and I said "Come up and join us, we'll give you a challenge; we'll give you all the tracking data as fast as we get it." So he was working with me in a room at the Jet Propulsion Laboratory and these were very exciting times for everybody. Dr Lee DuBridge was president of Caltech and he was visiting JPL. Feynman was working beside a couple of other people at a very long table as fast as he could. DuBridge came up, stood beside him for a little while, and said, "Well, what are you doing up here?" And

Feynman, without turning around, said, "Leave me alone. I'm busy." Then he recognized the voice and he turned around and said, 'Excuse me very much, Dr DuBridge.' DuBridge was laughing by this time. He said, 'That's all right. Keep working.' And he left.

'But Feynman took the tracking data as it was coming in; that data was the most reliable that we had. It was the Doppler shift of the radio signal from the satellite picked up at various tracking stations. So this meant that what we had was line of sight speed from known points on the surface of the earth. From this, it was a geometric problem to determine the orbit. Feynman solved this piece of geometry before the computer succeeded in doing so. There were two computers: one at Cape Canaveral, being used by the Range Safety Officer, and the other one was at JPL. Feynman worked with the raw data as it was coming in, and he finally said, "OK. It's in the ocean. I don't know what else I can do for you." We looked at his numbers and agreed with him. After some time, the Range Safety Officer informed us that *Explorer II* had come down in Tampa, Florida. Everybody was just delighted with Feynman's performance; he beat the computers! He came over there a few other times to look over data and join in the problem, figuring out where things were going. But eventually, of course, the computers became highly reliable and very rapid, and there was no point in doing it by hand anymore, even for Feynman.'[10]

After his divorce from Mary Lou, Feynman would often visit Las Vegas, where he could relax and enjoy himself. He had read a book, called *The big con*, which was published about that time in paperback about confidence games. He admired the tricks of the confidence men described in that book, and hoped he would meet a confidence man himself in Las Vegas. He sat around bars drinking orange juice hoping that a confidence man would approach him. None did. So, he decided, 'All right. If I can't *meet* one, I'll *be* one.' In the bars, occasionally one of the girls would walk up to him and ask him who he was and what he was doing. He would reply, 'Well, I'm sort of in the same business you are.' She would say, 'What, what?' He would reply, 'I'm a confidence man on vacation.' And immediately he was surrounded by people. He became the guide for George Hearst, one of the offspring of William Randolph Hearst, the publishing magnate, and he had a delightful time.[10]

George Hearst took him on as his aide, and asked if he would like to have the job while he was not doing anything else, as he was on vacation; Hearst would take care of all his bills if Feynman would make sure that he was well entertained. Feynman joined Hearst's little entourage, went to shows with him, and watched the girls. At one show, Hearst turned to Feynman and said, 'You know, I'd like to meet that girl.' He pointed one out and said, 'See if you can arrange that.' Feynman had never done this before in his life, but it didn't stop him for a minute from trying. He went backstage and looked for the woman in charge of keeping discipline in the chorus line; he found her without difficulty and told her: 'How do you do? My name is Richard Feynman (this was before the public knew who Richard Feynman was). And I represent Mr George Hearst, of the Hearst publishing family. He expressed a desire, if it could be arranged, to ask one of your girls, one of the beautiful young ladies in the dance group, to join him at the table for conversation.' The lady in charge of the chorus line replied: 'Well, that's very difficult to arrange. There are rules against it.' Feynman said: 'I realize how difficult it is. I don't want to upset any rules or break any discipline, I just want . . .' So they played this dance with each other for a while and, of course, within fifteen minutes or so the girl was sitting at the table with Mr Hearst, who was overjoyed but didn't quite know what to do, and after a while the girl was paying more attention to Feynman than she was to Hearst. This embarrassed him, Hearst got mad at him, and Feynman decided he had better leave this party before something really awful happened.

Shortly after Feynman had finished his calculation at the Jet Propulsion Laboratory, concluding that *Explorer II* had come down in the Atlantic ocean, he returned to Las Vegas, where Albert Hibbs joined him. Hibbs now was his companion as another confidence man. They got hooked up with some show dance group and went off to a party the girl dancers were giving for the boy dancers. At this party, the girls discovered that Feynman knew something about the planets. So he started talking about the planets and what they were and the girls lost interest. Hibbs told him, 'Wait a minute, Richard. You're saying the wrong things. They are not interested in planets as objects; they want to know their horoscopes.' So then Hibbs asked one of the women what sign she was born under, and immediately they had the attention of everybody right away. Feynman talked about the effect of planets on life on earth, which he totally made up. The girls loved it. Feynman and Hibbs had a very pleasant time in Las Vegas for a few days, after which they returned to Pasadena.[14]

Feynman had settled down into a routine of research and teaching by this time. For relaxation he would take vacations in Las Vegas and, for longer trips, he would visit the Centro Brasileiro de Pesquisas Fisicas in Rio de Janeiro, or some other interesting place on the map. After his divorce from Mary Lou, he felt a great sense of relief and again began to enjoy his bachelorhood. His old friend, Herbert Corben, had also gotten divorced from his wife Mulaika and had come to work at the TRW Corporation in Los Angeles. Corben and Feynman would double date occasionally, Corben going out with Beverly, whom he married soon thereafter, and Feynman escorting different young ladies. On one occasion Feynman and his mother, who was visiting from Far Rockaway, invited Herbert and Beverly Corben to dinner. They were served Cornish gamehen, and Feynman called the dinner 'plain Cornish gamehensmanship' making a pun on his constant games one-up-manship. Feynman and his mother also visited the Corbens after their wedding; Lucille brought an electric frying pan as a wedding present, and Richard presented Herbert a volume in Latin of Ovid's *The art of love*.[15]

Notes and References

1. R.P. Feynman, Interviews and conversations with Jagdish Mehra, in Pasadena, California, January 1988.

2. R.P. Feynman, Interviews with Charles Weiner (American Institute of Physics), in Pasadena, California, 1966.

3. R.P. Feynman, *SYJMF*, p. 236.

4. R.P. Feynman, *SYJMF*, p. 234.

5. R.P. Feynman, *SYJMF*, pp. 234–35.

6. R.P. Feynman, The present situation in fundamental theoretical physics. *An. Acad. Brasiliera Ciencias* 26, no. 31, January 1954.

7. R.P. Feynman, Ref. 6, p. 53

8. G. Speisman, Personal communication to Jagdish Mehra, 11 November 1988.

9. R.P Feynman and G. Speisman, Proton–neutron mass difference. *Phys. Rev.* 94, 500 (1954).

10. A.R. Hibbs, Interview with Jagdish Mehra, at the Athenaeum, Caltech, Pasadena, California, 23 March 1988.

11. R.P. Feynman, *Quantum electrodynamics*. Notes taken by A.R. Hibbs, corrected by E.R. Huggins and H.T. Yura. Benjamin, New York, 1965.

12. R.P. Feynman and A.R. Hibbs, *Quantum mechanics and path integrals*. McGraw-Hill, New York, 1965.

13. M. Gell-Mann, Interview with Jagdish Mehra, at Caltech, Pasadena, California, 11 July 1990.

14. A.R. Hibbs, Ref. 10.

15. H.C. Corben, Conversation with Jagdish Mehra, at the Athenaeum, Caltech, Pasadena, California, 20 March 1988. Ovid: *Ars amore*.

19

'Enjoying the scenery': Feynman and the polaron problem

19.1 Introduction

One day, towards the end of August 1954, Feynman was feeling low, with nothing to do, and felt like goofing off. At that time there was a pretty librarian working at the Caltech library, so he went to the library to look at her. There, as a cover, he just picked up a journal in order to have something to do to appear busy, and it was an issue of *Advances in Physics*: there was an article in it by Herbert Fröhlich on slow electrons moving in a polarizable crystal like sodium chloride. Fröhlich described the problem, and said that if this problem were solved it would go a long way toward understanding superconductivity, a remark which Feynman did not understand in the slightest; it was, in fact, not correct.[1]

At any rate, Feynman found the problem interesting. It was to find the energy of interaction of an electron with the phonons of the crystal; such an electron in a polarizable medium was called a 'polaron'. This was just like the field theory problem of a particle in interaction with a meson field, except that the complications of relativity were removed, and all the divergence difficulties did not exist. Feynman had developed methods of doing these kinds of things with finite coupling constants, which is what this problem was: to find the interaction energy with finite coupling constants. Fröhlich had gotten to the point of writing down an idealized Hamiltonian, in which many of the parameters of a real crystal were imitated by simple forms. It was a kind of standard problem then to solve this Fröhlich Hamiltonian, which was a typical polaron problem, that is, an electron in a polar crystal which distorts the field around it.

Feynman looked at this problem and he saw that by means of his path-integral technique he could do a great deal. One of the things he could do was to be able to integrate out some of the coordinates. 'Now, it would be an electron interacting with the oscillators (phonons) of the crystal, and if I wrote it down as a path-integral, I could integrate all the oscillators out *exactly* and just have it as a path-integral on the motion of the electron. It would work out. So I started to fiddle around and I got the formula immediately for the path integral involving an amplitude, an action in terms of the motion of the electron alone directly. All the fields would integrate out; I was already ahead, because I had done the phonon part exactly.

'At that time I had an assistant, by the name of Michael Baranger, to whom I had given nothing to do because I did not wish to waste his time with my half-assed problems. I went to him and said, "I have a problem for you." I had got to the point where I thought that maybe it was really good and could be worked out. So I said to Baranger, "I think there must be a variational principle of some kind for estimating path integrals, and I think you should try to find it." He asked me, "Well, how would you go about it? How would you make a start on it?" I tried to explain to him, and went through a number of steps and obtained the variational principle. He said, "Doesn't that just solve the problem?" I said, "Yes, I'm sorry." As I was explaining to him what to do, I solved it. So he had never anything to do, the poor guy. The point was that by that time it was so clear to me that there was a solution somewhere, that when I looked at it in detail and explained to Baranger, I found the solution. Obviously, I wasn't going to give him something that was impossible, so apparently intuitively, I knew that it was almost ready to go. But I didn't realize it was so close.

'I solved it in half an hour as I was explaining the problem. So I got excited and tried this variational method on the polaron problem. I discovered that with my variational method I could calculate the energy and also the mass of the polaron for all values of the coupling constant smoothly and continuously from one edge of the perturbation theory up to high energy, and at both ends it agreed with the best that others had done; I convinced myself that it was very accurate and it turned out in fact that it was a complete solution of a problem that people had done an awful lot of work on. As a matter of fact, up to today it's hard for anybody to get a better answer for this problem. It was really quite exciting, for I had discovered a variational principle at least for estimating path integrals, and it deepened my understanding. That turned out to be as powerful a discovery as the method of path integrals itself.'[1]

On 8 September 1954, Richard Feynman wrote to Herbert Fröhlich: 'We have very pretty librarians. Last week I went to enjoy the scenery and picked up *Advances [in] Physics* as a cover. I read your article.[2] I became more interested in it than in the librarians and resolved to accept your challenge to find a method uniformly valid over the entire range of [the coupling constant]. Enclosed is my solution. . . . What do we have to do to understand superconductivity?'

19.2 The historical background of the polaron problem

What Feynman had done was to apply his path-integral method to determine the properties of the polaron. A *polaron*† is a quasiparticle formed by the reaction back on a *slowly* moving electron of the polarization it induces in its vicinity (*via* its Coulomb field) during its motion in the conduction band of such

---

† This terminology is due to Pekar.[3]

an otherwise insulating polar crystal. This reaction results in: (i) a lowering of the energy of the electron's ground state, through the acquisition of a (finite) negative self-energy E_0; (ii) an enhancement of the Bloch effective mass m^* to a value m^{**}.

Although recognition of the possible importance of this reaction can be traced to von Hippel[4] (in connection with the mechanism of dielectric breakdown) and to Landau[5] (in an ill-fated attempt to understand the origin of F-centers in terms of an 'autolocalization' of the electron, as an extreme consequence of this reaction), the full significance of the *dynamical* nature of the electron–lattice interaction only became apparent in 1950 with the appearance of the work of Fröhlich, Pelzer, and Zienau[6] (FPZ); basic to this work was the treatment of the induced polarization in terms of the 'polarization' waves, already introduced by Fröhlich in his 1937 work[7] on dielectric breakdown in polar materials. The frequency ω of these waves is that of the longitudinal optical mode of vibration of the polar lattice in which the positive and negative ions move in antiphase, giving rise to a nonzero electric dipole moment, i.e. to a polarization. In the case of the slow conduction electron under consideration, the dominant interaction is with polarization waves of *long* wavelength (the frequency of which is, to a good approximation, independent of wavelength)—a circumstance which permits the dielectric to be treated as a *continuum*. FPZ were thus led to study the interaction of a moving, nonrelativistic particle (with Bloch effective mass m^* and electric charge equal to $-|e|$) with a field frequency ω, whose energy is quantized in units of $\hbar\omega$—the particle–field interaction being completely parametrized by a single dimensionless coupling constant α (whose role is analogous to that of Sommerfeld's 'fine structure constant' in quantum electrodynamics), defined by

$$\alpha \equiv \frac{e^2}{2\hbar\bar{\varepsilon}}\left(\frac{2m^*}{\hbar\omega}\right)^{1/2}, \qquad (19.1)$$

where $\bar{\varepsilon} \equiv (1/\varepsilon_\infty - 1/\varepsilon_s)^{-1}$, and ensures that only the 'inertial' polarization associated with the displacement of the heavy positive and negative ions is included in the electron–lattice interaction; ε_s is the static dielectric constant, and ε_∞ the dielectric constant at frequencies well above those to which the ions can respond, but below those associated with transitions of the electrons localized in the closed shells of the ions. The Hamiltonian of this system is given by

$$H = \frac{\hbar^2 k^2}{2m^*} + \hbar\omega \sum_w b_w^\dagger b_w$$

$$- i\hbar\omega \left(\frac{\hbar}{2m^*\omega}\right)^{1/4}\left(\frac{4\pi\alpha}{\Omega}\right)^{1/2} \sum_w \frac{1}{|w|}(b_w^\dagger e^{-iw \cdot X} - b_w e^{+iw \cdot X})$$

$$\equiv H_{el} + H_{lat} + H_{int}, \qquad (19.2)$$

where Ω is a cubic volume of the dielectric continuum to which periodic boundary conditions are applied, and $b_w^\dagger$ (b_w) create (annihilate) longitudinal polarization quanta with wave vector w, whose number is given by the eigenvalues of the operator $b_w^\dagger b_w$. H_{int} describes the interaction[†] of the single Bloch electron with coordinate X (whose kinetic energy is represented by H_{el}) with the optical modes of the polar lattice whose (harmonic) vibrational energy (excluding zero-point energy) is given by H_{lat}.

For $\alpha \ll 1$ (weak coupling) the *ground state* of this 'polaron' Hamiltonian can be studied (as first done by FPZ) using (second-order)[‡] perturbation theory, in the context of which the induced polarization and its reaction back on the electron is described in terms of the *virtual* emission and reabsorption by the electron of longitudinal polarization quanta—in analogy with the case of the meson–nucleon system, treated earlier by Fröhlich, Heitler, and Kemmer.[8] When there is never more than one quantum *virtually* excited, perturbation theory yields the following results for the (*zero-temperature*) electron self-energy F_0 and polaron effective mass m^{**}:

$$E_0 = -\alpha\hbar\omega, \tag{19.3}$$

$$m^{**} = m^*/(1 - \tfrac{1}{6}\alpha). \tag{19.4}$$

Unfortunately, however, most polar materials do not satisfy $\alpha \ll 1$; in NaCl, for example, $\alpha \sim 5$. Accordingly more powerful variational approaches were soon developed,[9–11] based on trial wave functions containing an *arbitrary* number of virtual quanta, but with the provisos that they all have *different* wave vectors and that correlations between successively emitted quanta (induced by the electron's recoil) can be neglected; for $\alpha < 6$, these (so-called 'intermediate' coupling) approaches yield the *same* expression for E_0 as given by equation (19.3) but replace equation (19.4) by

$$m^{**} = m^*(1 + \tfrac{1}{6}\alpha). \tag{19.5}$$

This result for m^{**} is extremely important, since it indicates that the singularity in equation (19.4) at $\alpha = 6$ is of *no physical significance*;[§] for at $\alpha = 6$, m^{**} is no longer validly given by equation (19.4), but rather by equation (19.5), which entails only a doubling in the value of m^{**}.

The validity of such 'dynamic' approaches is restricted to frequencies ω sufficiently high that too few virtual quanta ($= \tfrac{1}{2}\alpha$) are emitted for the neglected correlations to be important. At such high frequencies (or weak coupling,

---

[†] This particular form of H_{int}, derived by using a Lagrangian formalism, first appeared in Fröhlich's 1954 review article[2] in *Advances in Physics* (entitled 'Electrons in lattice fields'), which Feynman happened upon (accidentally) later that year.

[‡] In *first* order, H_{int} leads to *no* change in the electron's ground-state energy, since at $T = 0$ there is no thermal excitation of (real) polarization quanta; neither can such be emitted by the electron, since its kinetic energy is too low (recall that the electron is assumed to be a *slow* electron!)

[§] In particular, it is *not* indicative of any kind of autolocalization of the electron such as envisaged by Landau.[5]

$1 \gg \alpha \sim \omega^{1/2}$) *most* of the polarization field—in particular, that beyond a distance† of order $u^{-1} \sim (\hbar/2m^*\omega)^{1/2}$ from the electron—can follow the electron adiabatically on its peregrinations through the lattice continuum, accompanying it with the classical (Coulomb) polarization field of a point charge and endowing it with the enhanced mass m^{**}; at closer distances ($< u^{-1}$), however, the polarization is *less* than the classical value, and the response of the polarization field to the passing electron, and, in turn, the electron's *self-energy*, is here governed by the field's *dynamical* properties. Consistency with the adopted *continuum* treatment of the crystalline lattice necessarily requires, of course, that u^{-1} be much larger than the associated lattice distance; this is why such polarons are sometimes called 'large' polarons.

At low frequencies (i.e. in the strong coupling limit, $\alpha \gg 1$), on the other hand, where the number of virtual quanta is large ($\sim \alpha^2$) the correlations between successively emitted quanta predominate to such an extent that they actually result in the establishment of a *polarization potential well* (of radius of order $(\alpha u)^{-1}$) around the electron, whereby—in addition to an enhanced effective mass—the polaron acquires an *internal structure*, arising from the possibility of electronic excitation within this well.

Thus, in *both* limits, in consequence of the recoil of the electron, its *point* charge is effectively spread over a *finite* volume, the linear extent of which in the strong coupling limit is reduced by a factor α, in consequence of the predominance there of interquanta correlations. It is this spreading which essentially ensures (*without* having to introduce any kind of *cut-off*) the *finiteness* of the self-energy E_0, the order of magnitude of which increases from $e^2/\bar{\varepsilon}u^{-1}$ to $e^2/\bar{\varepsilon}(\alpha u)^{-1}$ at $\alpha \ll 1$ and $\alpha \gg 1$, respectively.

The latter (strong-coupling low-frequency) ground-state solution to the polaron Hamiltonian (equation (19.2)) was obtained by Fröhlich[2] by using a variational trial wave function $\Psi(r, \xi)$ of the form adopted by Pekar[12] in his attempt to treat the polarization field of the vibrating lattice *quantum mechanically*, rather than semiclassically as in his pioneering work of 1946[3] (in the course of which the name polaron‡ was first proposed), where it was

---

† This is essentially a measure of the quantum mechanical uncertainty in the electron's spatial coordinate as it recoils following the virtual emission or absorption of polarization quanta of energy ω.

‡ In Pekar's paper[3] the 'symbiotic' nature of the polaron was emphasized in terms of the self-consistency of the processes involved, whereby the self-induced polarization is considered to give rise to a potential well in which the electron is confined; in turn, this spatially confined electron maintains the polarization of the crystal which continues to keep the electron localized and '... *such local, self-consistent quantum states of the electron in the crystal we shall briefly call POLARONS* ...'[3]. Treating the lattice as a *classical* dielectric continuum, the potential well due only to the 'inerial' polarization connected with the ion displacements, which (unlike that associated with deformation of the electron shells of the ions) is unable to follow the electron *instantaneously*, was calculated. The behavior of the electron was then solved *quantum mechanically* via the time-independent Schrödinger equation and its ground-state energy obtained.

assumed that the electron experienced only the *average* field of the vibrating ions, which was the same as that of the ions at *rest* at their *displaced* positions, so that the electron's self-energy was necessarily *independent* of ω. After taking into account the change in elastic energy entailed in having to polarize the lattice in the first place, Pekar[3] found

$$E_0 = -0.0544 \frac{m^* e^4}{\hbar^2 \bar{\varepsilon}^2}. \tag{19.6}$$

Fröhlich's result for E_0—obtained by using the Pekar[12] *ansatz* for $\Psi(r, \xi)$, i.e.

$$\Psi(r, \xi) = \psi(r)\chi(\xi), \tag{19.7}$$

in which the electronic wave function ψ (taken to be hydrogenic) is assumed to be *independent* of the coordinates ξ of the polarization field—is

$$E_0 = -\tfrac{25}{256}\alpha^2 \hbar\omega \ (= -0.0977\alpha^2 \hbar\omega). \tag{19.8}$$

It should be appreciated, however, that despite the appearance here of ω, the product $\alpha^2\omega$ is actually *independent* of ω, so that Fröhlich's strong-coupling self-energy (equation 19.8))—like Pekar's (equation (19.6)) is independent of ω, consistent with ω being so low in this limit that here it is the *electron* which follows (adiabatically) the zero-point fluctuations of the polarization field—the converse of what obtains in the opposite weak-coupling (high-frequency) limit.

Comparison with Fröhlich's result is, however, facilitated by expressing equation (19.6) as follows, in terms of α and ω (although this is here somewhat artificial, since, as noted above, ω does *not* feature in Pekar's original (1946) analysis[2]—in contrast to Fröhlich's, where ω is an essential parameter of his Hamiltonian (equation (19.2)),

$$E_0 - 0.1088\alpha^2 \hbar\omega. \tag{19.9}$$

Fröhlich's result was even closer to that obtained in 1948 by Pekar and Deigen[13] by using a trial function based on the ground-state wave function of a harmonic oscillator (which we mention here in view of the relevance to Feynman's later work), namely

$$E_0 = -\left(\frac{1}{3\pi}\right)\alpha^2 \hbar\omega \ (= -0.106\alpha^2 \hbar\omega). \tag{19.10}$$

Following the earlier approach of Landau and Pekar,[14] Fröhlich[2] went on to derive the following expression for the polaron effective mass m^{**} by treating the (underlying) electron as a rigid charge distribution endowed with a small constant velocity of translation through the dielectric continuum:

$$m^{**} = m^*(1 + 0.0203\alpha^4).\qquad\qquad(19.11)$$

It should be noted that this strong-coupling result for m^{**}—unlike that for E_0—is (via α^4) ω-dependent ($\sim \omega^{-2}$—see equation (19.1)).

Comparison of equations (19.3) and (19.5) with (19.11) is revealing in that the same Hamiltonian (equation (19.2)) entails quite *different* expressions for the electron self-energy and polaron effective mass in the intermediate (and weak) and strong coupling limits. For $\alpha > 10$, equation (19.9) yields a more negative self-energy than does equation (19.3). At $\alpha \simeq 10$, however, although the two solutions coincide, they do *not* match *smoothly*; furthermore, the values of the polaron effective mass given by equations (19.5) and (19.11) here differ by a factor of 100!

In his 1954 article, Fröhlich[2] thus concluded that there exists a range of coupling strengths, centered on $\alpha \simeq 10$, in which neither the dynamic approaches (i.e. those of FPZ, Gurari, Lee, Low, and Pines) nor the static ones (i.e. those based on the Pekar *ansatz*, (equation (19.7)) afford a realistic description of the situation, and that '. . . *it seems to be desirable to develop a method which leads to a continuum transition between the two methods*' (emphasis added). Intuitively, the failure of the dynamical approaches can be attributed to their *complete neglect* of interquanta correlations, which at such large α values is not justified; on the other hand, at $\alpha = 10$ the coupling is too *weak* for the complete suppression of translation entailed by the strong-coupling (static) approach to be justified either.†

Feynman's 1955 paper[15] was one of two quite different responses to Fröhlich's challenge which appeared almost simultaneously in February of that year—both approaches yielding, at $T = 0$, the desired *continuous* transition between the weak- and strong-coupling limits: '. . . Fröhlich has asked for a method which works uniformly over the entire range of α . . . he considers the mismatch near $\alpha = 10$ as a serious disadvantage, which it is the purpose of this paper to avoid'[15] The more conventional approach, due to Höhler,[16] has, however, been largely eclipsed by the less conventional approach, via path integrals, adopted by Feynman,[15] basic to which was the his acceptance of Fröhlich's belief[2] that the root of the mismatch difficulties (discontinuities) near $\alpha = 10$ was the violation of translational invariance by the strong-coupling *ansatz* (equation (19.7)), which artificially binds the electron to an arbitrary *fixed* point in the continuum.

Indeed, as we shall now see, the success of Feynman's approach is essentially due to the ingenious way in which he actually *maintains* translational invariance, while at the same time retaining the essential features of the electron–field system.

---

† For the movement of the electron away from one part of the lattice permits that part to relax back to its initial undisplaced configuration, while new displacements are established in the new vicinity of the electron.

19.3 Feynman's path-integral approach to the ground-state properties of the polaron (1955)

Having read Fröhlich's 1954 paper in *Advances in Physics*,[2] in which the polaron Hamiltonian (equation 19.2)) was derived by using a *Lagrangian* formalism, Feynman (presumably) realized that Fröhlich's challenge to develop a method of finding the ground-state properties of this Hamiltonian, which would be uniformly valid over the entire range of coupling constants α could be met by a straightforward adaptation of his own *Lagrangian* (path-integral) treatment of QED. For, by replacing photons by *phonons*, and noting that in both cases the field was describable in terms of harmonic oscillators, whose interaction with the electron was *linear* in the field coordinates, the 'isomorphism' with QED was immediately apparent. Since the path integral for the forced harmonic oscillator (in terms of which this linearly coupled electron–field is described) could be obtained in *closed form*, it was again possible (just as in QED) *to eliminate completely the oscillator coordinates*†— in particular, for the ground-state properties in which there are no *real* phonons present—to obtain (via equation (19.2)) the following expression (with $m^* = \hbar = 1$) for the action S', which involves the coordinates X of the electron *alone*:

$$S' = \frac{1}{2} \int \left(\frac{d}{dt} X(t) \right)^2 dt + \frac{i\alpha}{\sqrt{8}} \int \frac{e^{-i|t-s|} dt \, ds}{|X(t) - X(s)|} \tag{19.12}$$

The effect of integrating out the field coordinates is to replace the original instantaneous electron field interaction (in equation (19.12)) by the *retarded* one represented by the second term on the right-hand side of equation (19.12), in which the electron *interacts only with itself*—in a way inversely proportional to the distance traveled from the previous times. This affords a novel reinterpretation of the concept of *self-energy*; for the electron now moves bearing, so to speak, the memory of its history, in the sense that at some space–time point (r'', t'') it is subject to the electric force due to the polarization which is the *accumulation* of the 'after-effects' of the 'sources' at all space–time points (r', t') with $t' < t''$. This 'memory' aspect (which is *unique* to Feynman's approach) can be regarded here as the counterpart of the field-theoretic interpretation of the electron self-energy in terms of the electron's virtual emission and (subsequent) reabsorption of polarization quanta at a later time. To actually *calculate* this energy, Feynman first noted that S' is closely connected with the Green's function of the time-dependent Schrödinger equation associated with the polaron Hamiltonian (equation (19.2)), which function is expressible in terms of the associated eigenfunctions ψ_n and

---

† This contrasts with the approach of Lee, Low, and Pines,[11] who eliminate the *electron's* coordinate by means of a canonical transformation.

eigenvalues E_n—the lowest of which, E_0, is just the required (self-) energy! The actual connection is given by

$$\int_{x'}^{x''} \exp(iS'/\hbar)\, DX(t) = \sum_n \psi_n^*(x'')\psi_n(x')\exp[-i/\hbar E_n(t'-t'')], \quad (19.13)$$

where $DX(t)$ represents the product of all possible electron paths between the space points x' and x''.

To extract E_0 from equation (19.13) it is only necessary to take the large *imaginary* time limit, since E_0 will then be the last surviving exponent. Thus introducing $T \equiv -(\tau''-\tau')$, where $\tau \equiv it$, E_0 is given (again with $\hbar = m^* = 1$) by

$$E_0 = -\lim_{T\to\infty}\left(\frac{\ln\int\exp(S)\,DX(\tau)}{T}\right), \quad (19.14)$$

where S is defined by

$$S = -\frac{1}{2}\int_{-\infty}^{\tau}\left[\frac{dX}{d\tau}(\tau)\right]^2 d\tau + \frac{\alpha}{\sqrt{8}}\int_{\tau'}^{\tau''}\int_{-\infty}^{\tau}\frac{\exp(-|\tau-\sigma|)}{X(\tau)-X(\sigma)}\,d\tau\,d\sigma \quad (19.15)$$

(The absence of the factor i in the argument of the exponential function in equation (19.14) should be noted.)

The interpretation of the second term in S of equation (19.15) is similar to that in S', except that the interaction of the electron with itself now dies out *exponentially* with the (imaginary) time difference, reflecting the fact that the lattice polarization initially induced by the electron in the (imaginary) past takes some time to die out, on account of the finite time needed for the ions to relax back to their undisplaced (equilibrium) positions; during this relaxation time the electron can still 'feel' the old lattice distortion, i.e. the one induced by itself at earlier (imaginary) times. The form of the interaction term in S thus indicates that at 'time' τ, the electron acts as though it were in a potential

$$\frac{\alpha}{\sqrt{2}}\int_{-\infty}^{\tau}\frac{\exp(-|\tau-\sigma|)\,d\sigma}{|X(\tau)-X(\sigma)|}, \quad (19.16)$$

resulting from the electrostatic interaction of the electron with the average charge density of its *previous* locations, each weighted by $\exp(-|\tau-\sigma|)$.

Unfortunately, however, the path integral in equation (19.4) associated with the second term on the right-hand side of equation (15.15) *cannot* be evaluated in a closed form. Feynman therefore proceeded by introducing another action S_1, which '... purports to be some sort of approximation to S',[15] but whose algebraic form is simple enough to permit the path integral to be performed exactly. In terms of S_1, the integral can be written *exactly* as follows:

$$\int \exp(S)\, DX(\tau) \equiv \langle \exp(S-S_1) \rangle \int \exp(S_1)\, DX(\tau), \qquad (19.17)$$

where

$$\langle \exp(S-S_1) \rangle \equiv \int \exp(S-S_1) \exp(S_1)\, DX(\tau) \bigg/ \int \exp(S_1)\, DX(\tau). \qquad (19.18)$$

From equation (19.14) and (19.17) Feynman now obtained the following *upper bound* on the true ground-state energy E_0 by making use of the (Jensen) inequality:† $\langle \exp(y) \rangle > \exp(\langle y \rangle)$ (which is entailed simply by the upward concavity of $\exp(y)$, where y is a real random variable); thus

$$E_0 \leqslant E_1 - \lim_{T \to \infty} \frac{1}{T} \langle S-S_1 \rangle, \qquad (19.19)$$

where E_1 is the ground-state energy associated with the integrable action S_1, and is defined by equation (19.14), with S replaced by S_1.

Thus the true ground-state energy (i.e. that associated with the *actual* action S of the system considered) is always *lower* than (or, at best, equal to) the energy value calculated from the right-hand side of equation (19.19) with the aid of the integrable action S_1; it is important to note, however, that the *actual* action S is still involved via the term $S-S_1$. If there are any *free* parameters in S_1 they can be chosen so as to *minimize* the value of the right-hand side of equation (19.19). Equation (19.19) is thus *Feynman's variational principle*.

Before addressing himself to Fröhlich's challenge to develop a method giving the electron self-energy E_0 over the entire range of α, Feynman gave the forms of S_1 which reproduce the expressions for E_0 already obtained, by using the 'dynamic' and 'static' methods referred to in the previous section; thus, for example, the choice

$$S_1^{(a)} = -\frac{1}{2} \int \left(\frac{dX(\tau)}{d\tau} \right)^2 d\tau \qquad (19.20)$$

yields (in units of $\hbar = \omega = 1$) the α-linear result (equation (19.3)) obtained by using the 'dynamic' methods of FPZ, Gurari, and Lee, Low, and Pines—namely

$$E_0^{(a)} = -\alpha. \qquad (19.21)$$

The α-quadratic results for the strong-coupling self-energy (obtained by using the 'static' Pekar-like) approach follow, on the other hand, by generalizing $S_1^{(a)}$ by the addition of the 'potential' term, thus

† Feynman thanked G. Speisman for emphasizing the importance of this general inequality.

$$S_1^{(a)} \to S_1^{(b)} = \frac{1}{2} \int \left(\frac{dX(\sigma)}{d\tau}\right)^2 d\tau + \int V(X(\tau)) \, d\tau. \qquad (19.22)$$

Choosing V to be a Coulomb potential, Z/R (where Z is treated as a variational parameter) yields, for $\alpha \to \infty$, Fröhlich's result (equation (19.8)); replacing V by a harmonic potential (proportional to R^2), on the other hand, yields equation (19.10) for $\alpha \to \infty$.

Feynman went on to remark that the form of S_1 given by equation (19.22) can *still* be used when α is *not* asymptotically large but that it then becomes difficult to evaluate—especially in the case of the Coulomb potential; he then noted, *most importantly*, that, although the use of the harmonic potential is, in this respect, much simpler, *no* choice of V can improve the α-linear result (equation (19.21)) if $\alpha < 6$, that is, for small α (<6), the addition of *any* potential V in equation (19.22) yields a *poorer* result than the one obtained when $V = 0$.

Feynman attributed this to the artificial binding to a special origin that a potential of the form introduced in equation (19.22) implies. (Recall the dicussion at the end of the previous section.) *He then immediately proposed a remedial approach, out of which evolved his now famous model of the polaron as an electron bound harmonically to a fictitious particle of finite mass which mimics the essentials of the electron's actual interaction with the lattice polarization.* To quote from Feynman's paper: '... To remedy this, I thought a good idea would be to use for S_1 the action for a particle bound by a potential $V(X-Y)$ to another particle of coordinate Y. This latter could have finite mass, so no permanent origin would be assumed. Of course, the action for such a system would contain both $X(t)$ and $Y(t)$. But the variables $Y(t)$ could be integrated out, at least in principle, leaving an effective S_1 depending only on X. At first I tried a Coulomb interaction for $V(X-Y)$ but it was rather complicated. ... But here we have already seen that an harmonic binding should be as good, if not better. Further, an extra particle bound *harmonically* has its variables $Y(t)$ appearing *quadratically* in the action. It may therefore be easily eliminated explicitly. The result we know from studies of similar problems in electrodynamics. We are, in this way, led to consider the choice

$$S_1 = -\frac{1}{2} \int \left(\frac{dX(\tau)}{d\tau}\right)^2 d\tau - \frac{C}{2} \iint [X(\tau) - X(\sigma)]^2 \exp(-w|\tau - \sigma|) \, d\tau \, d\sigma, \quad (19.23)$$

where C and w are parameters to be chosen later to minimize the right-hand side of equation (19.19).'[15]

This form for S_1 differs from that of the actual action S (equation (19.15)) in its replacement of the 'potential' given by equation (19.16) by a parabolic (harmonic) potential created on the average location of the electron in the past, the weight for different (imaginary) times being $\exp(-w|\tau - \sigma|)$; w is a parameter which is to be adjusted so as to minimize the error committed in using such a *harmonic* potential instead of the *actual* one.

The evaluation of the path integrals in equation (19.19)—when S_1 is given by equation (19.23) is not trivial and Feynman used some ingenious tricks, such as performing some of the integrals by solving the differential equations which they satisfy. The final result, which—it should be emphasized—*is valid for all α values*, is as follows:

$$E_0 \leqslant \frac{3}{4v}(v-w)^2 - \frac{\alpha v}{\sqrt{\pi}} \int_0^\infty \left(w^2\tau + \frac{v^2-w^2}{v}[1-\exp(-v\tau)]\right)^{-1/2} \exp(-\tau)\,d\tau,$$

(19.24)

where

$$v^2 \equiv \frac{4C}{w} + w^2.$$

(19.25)

Thus, w and v can now be used in place of the original parameters C and w, and varied *separately* to minimize the right-hand side of equation (19.24).

The integral on the right-hand side of equation (19.24) cannot be performed in closed form in the case of arbitrary α; in the limits of $\alpha \to 0$ and $\alpha \to \infty$, however, it is possible to proceed analytically. Thus, in the extreme weak-coupling limit ($\alpha \to 0$), the minimum value of the right-hand side of equation (19.24) occurs at $w = 3$, when E_0 is given by the following inequality:

$$E_0 \leqslant -\alpha - 0.0123\alpha^2 + O(\alpha^3),$$

(19.26)

which, Feynman pointed out, is *identical* (to this order) to that obtained by Lee and Pines,[17] by taking interquanta correlations into account.

In the extreme strong-coupling limit ($\alpha \to \infty$), on the other hand, the minimum occurs at $w = 1$, and E_0 takes the form†

$$E_0 \leqslant -\frac{\alpha^2}{3\pi} - 3\ln 2 - \tfrac{3}{4} + O(1/\alpha^2),$$

(19.27)

It should be noted that the two α-independent terms by which equation (19.27) differs from equation (19.10)—the physical significance of which was considered in detail by Allcock in a lucidly penetrating paper published in the *Philosophical Magazine* **5**, 412–51 (1956)—do *not* in fact occur if w is set equal to zero *ab initio*, and the right-hand side of equation (19.24) minimized only with respect to the parameter v. Feynman pointed out, however, that energy minima then exist only for $\alpha > 6$; *to handle weaker coupling, it is essential that w be allowed to be nonzero.* Thus, to obtain a treatment which is 'structurally continuous' between the limits of weak and strong coupling, it is necessary that w be allowed to *remain* nonzero—*even* for $\alpha \gg 1$, where, in order to realize an

† It should be noted that the terms of order $1/2$ could be *positive*, so that it cannot be guaranteed that the first three terms in equation (19.27) constitute an *upper* bound on E_0.

energy minimum, it is not actually essential to have $w \neq 0$—a circumstance which is (presumably) reflected in the much *smaller* minimizing value of w ($=1$) here obtained (cf. $w = 3$ near $\alpha = 0$); it is precisely in consequence of this nonzero w value (as $\alpha \to \infty$) that the two α-independent terms in equation (19.27) arise.

For α values other than $\alpha \to 0$ and $\alpha \to \infty$ it is necessary to resort to numerical evaluation of the integral in equation (19.24); this was done later by Schultz (see Section 19.4), Feynman being content to establish that in the above two limits his variational principle gave values for the self-energy which are '. . . at least as accurate as previously known results'.[15] Indeed, as is apparent from equations (19.26) and (19.27), his upper bounds on E_0 *were* lower (and therefore more accurate) than those given by the conventional intermediate- and strong-coupling approaches described in the previous section.

The final section of Feynman's paper dealt with the effective mass of the polaron. He commenced by noting that he had not been able to find the appropriate extension of his variational principle which minimizes the energy for *finite* polaron momentum, and which at the same time conserves this momentum; he thus limited himself to a nonrigorous consideration of the effective mass m^{**} valid for *low* translational velocities V of the bound two-body system in terms of which he modeled the polaron. For small V, the self-energy is augmented by a kinetic energy $\frac{1}{2}m^{**}V^2$, via which m is defined. To calculate m^{**} Feynman then considered all paths whose initial coordinate (at $\tau' = 0$) is zero and whose final coordinate (at $\tau'' = T$) is the point r, given by

$$r = UT, \tag{19.28}$$

where U is an *imaginary* velocity (in consequence of the interval T being itself imaginary) and sought a solution of $\int_{x'}^{x''} \exp(S)\, DX(\tau)$, which is of the following form for large T:

$$\int_{x'}^{x''} \exp(S)\, DX(\tau) \sim \exp[-(E_0 + \tfrac{1}{2}m^{**}\, U^2)T]. \tag{19.29}$$

It is essential to stress again that no variational principle can be invoked to support the argument. In place of the expression given by the right-hand side of equation (19.24) he now obtained (when the electron mass coefficient of the first term in equation (19.23) is reintroduced as the Bloch mass m^*)

$$\tfrac{1}{2}m^* U^2 + \frac{3}{4v}(v - w)^2 - A(U), \tag{19.30}$$

where $A(U)$ is a generalization of the integral term in equation (19.24). Expanding $A(U)$ to order U^2 then yields the following expression for m^{**}:

$$m^{**}/m^* = 1 + \frac{1}{3\sqrt{\pi}}\, \alpha v^3 \int_0^\infty [F(\tau)]^{-3/2} \exp(-\tau)\tau^2\, d\tau, \tag{19.31}$$

where $F(\tau)$ is defined by

$$F(\tau) \equiv w^2\tau + [(v^2 - w^2)/v][1 - \exp(-v\tau)]. \tag{19.32}$$

Inserting the values of v and w which minimize the right-hand side of equation (19.24) *when* $U = 0$ yields results which, to the lowest order in α, agree with those obtained by using more conventional methods (see equations (19.5) and (19.11)). For 'intermediate' values of α (including $\alpha \simeq 10$), the integral on the right-hand side of equation (19.31) must be evaluated numerically in order to obtain reliable values of m^{**}; the essential point, however, is that equation (19.31) yields values of m^{**}/m^* which vary *continuously* with α. Feynman admitted, however, that, not being based on a variational principle, it was difficult to adjudge the accuracy of the derived mass values, especially for large α.

In concluding his paper, Feynman mentioned that he had attempted to apply his method to meson problems,† but this had proved tractable only for the case of *scalar* nucleons coupled to *scalar* mesons—the more realistic case involving spin and isospin required further development. (For a report of this work see the publication of his collaborator K. Mano.[19])

Finally, Feynman concluded by saying that '. . . it would be desirable to find out‡ how this method may be expressed in conventional notation, for a wider class of trial functions might thereby become available'—the wider class extending beyond the present *quadratic* functionals which could be evaluated directly as path integrals.

19.4 Initial reception of Feynman's 1955 paper and Schultz's early elaborations

Fröhlich replied to Feynman's letter on 22 September 1954, enthusiastically encouraging him to publish his work and promising to write to him concerning the question raised by Feynman at the end of his letter of 8 September 1954 concerning the relevance of his generally valid solution of the polaron problem to the problem of superconductivity (this will be dealt with in Section 19.7). Feynman's paper appeared in the *Physical Review* on 1 February 1955, the final form differing little from the preprint originally sent to Fröhlich.

The first traceable published reference to Feynman's paper appeared the following April in a paper by Low and Pines[23] dealing with polaron mobility; another early citation was by Höhler[16]—in a paper published in October 1955, in which he compared his own method (see Section 19.2) of realizing a

---

† Application of polaron ideas to meson theory was actually first considered by Pekar himself in three papers published in Russian in 1954.[18]

‡ The first attempt in this direction was probably that of Yamazaki[20] (see also Yamazaki[21]), and more recently that of Devreese and Brosens.[22]

continuous transition between the strong- and weak-coupling limits with Feynman's. It was of particular interest in that his remarks concerning the interpretation of Feynman's integrable action S_1 (equation (19.23)) anticipated, to a certain extent, some aspects of the slightly later work of T. D. Schultz;[24] we shall describe the latter's work shortly in some detail, not only because of its importance in facilitating the acceptance of Feynman's ingenious contribution within the community of solid-state physicists (to whom the path-integral method was quite unfamiliar), but also because it motivated Feynman himself to address the important question of polaron mobility—the outcome of which was the monumental paper[25] with Hellwarth, Iddings, and Platzmann (see Section 19.5(c)) published seven years later in 1962, and its later extension to the non-Ohmic transport regime, in collaboration with Thornber[26] in 1970. Other citations of Feynman's 1955 paper appearing that year included the one (already referred) by K. Mano[19] (November 1955), that of E.P. Gross[27] (December 1955), as well as Haken's[28] review of Feynman's work—outlining his methodology and comparing his results with others then existing; the latter was the *first* mention of Feynman's polaron work to appear in a *book* (*Halbleiterprobleme*).

Turning now to the work of Schultz, his first task was to fulfill a request made to him by Feynman[29] (in a postscript of his letter of 27 May 1955) to perform the *numerical* calculations necessary to cover the range of coupling constant α from 4 to 8; Feynman, remember, had confined himself to the limiting cases $\alpha \to 0$ to $\alpha \to \infty$, which could be handled *analytically*. Schultz minimized equation (19.24) for five values of α ($= 3, 5, 7, 9$, and 11), using the Whirlwind Digital Computer, tabulating the best values of v and w for each value of α, and giving the corresponding self-energy and effective mass values. Comparison of these quantities as computed according to (a) the theories of Lee, Low, and Pines,[11] Lee and Pines,[17] and of Gross[27] (which are all exact in the weak-coupling limit) and (b) to the asymptotic formulae of Pekar,[12]† Bogoliubov[30] and Tiablikov[31] (valid in the strong-coupling limit) revealed, unequivocally, the superiority of Feynman's self-energy values over the entire range of α, and the smooth interpolation afforded for m^{**}.

The second problem to which Schultz addressed himself was the mobility of the polaron—in particular, how it could be calculated within the framework of Feynman's approach. It was in this connection that Schultz was led to elaborate a simplified model of the polaron based essentially on the integrable action S_1 (equation (19.23)) introduced originally by Feynman. Somewhat misleadingly, this model has now become known as the 'Feynman polaron'; in Feynman's own treatment, however, the *actual* action S (equation (19.15)) is

† An important (cultural) aspect of Schultz's work which should be stressed (which was evident in his MIT report, but only to a much lesser extent in his 1959 *Physical Review* article[24]) was his efforts and concern to make known in the West the contemporaneous work being done in Russia, which evolved out of Pekar's original ideas.[3]

still included via the difference $S-S_1$. Associated with S_1 alone, however, is the energy E_1 given by

$$E_1 = \tfrac{3}{2}(v-w)\hbar\omega, \tag{19.33}$$

which differs from that given by the right-hand side of equation (19.24), appropriate when S is included via $S-S_1$.

The essence of Schultz's approach was that—at least insofar as the calculation of the mobility of the polaron is concerned—the polaron can be modeled by S_1 alone—the difference in the value of the associated ground-state energy (E_1) from the self-energy upper bound calculated by Feynman is correctable by the inclusion of an appropriate constant in S_1. Schultz deduced the following. (a) The total mass m_1^{**} $(=m^*+M)$ of the two-particle system based on S_1 is a (zeroth) approximation to the actual polaron mass given by

$$m_1^{**} = m^* + M \rightarrow m^*(v^2/w^2). \tag{19.34}$$

By using his earlier optimal values of v and w (for various values of the coupling constant α), Schultz evaluated equation (19.34), finding values of m_1^{**} remarkably close to (but always *lower* than) those of m^{**} yielded by Feynman's original full blown approach of equation (19.31); so close in magnitude is m_1^{**} to m^* that for most practical purposes m_1^{**} suffices, so obviating the necessity to solve equations (19.31) and (19.32). (b) In terms of m_1^{**} and the reduced mass M_{red} $(\equiv(m_1^* + m^{-1})^{-1})$, the Hamiltonian H_1 can be written as follows:

$$H_1 = \frac{|P|^2}{2m_1^{**}} + \frac{|\pi|^2}{2M_{red}} + \tfrac{1}{2}M_{red}v\omega|\rho|^2 + U_0, \tag{19.35}$$

where P is the momentum operator canonically conjugate to the center of mass coordinate $R-(m^*X+MY)/(m^*+M)$, whilst the momentum π is canonically conjugate to the relative coordinate $\rho(=X-Y)$; U_0 is a constant.

In the (two-particle) polaron model described by H_1, the actual 'polaron' itself is to be identified with the center of mass of the system which moves freely (i.e. the first term on the right-hand side of equation (19.35)); the two 'ingredient' particles are themselves coupled as a three-dimensional harmonic oscillator with frequency $(K/M_{red})^{1/2}(=v\omega)$. Thus the 'harmonic' *ansatz* introduced by Feynman is essentially connected with the (internal) relative motion—the polaron (as a whole) being able *to translate freely through the lattice*, as required by the translational invariance of the system. It should be noted, however, that this translational motion is suppressed if $m^{**}\rightarrow\infty$, which it does (see equation (19.34)) when $w\rightarrow0$. Furthermore, in terms of this two-particle model, the conventional weak- and strong-coupling limits correspond, respectively, to $m^* \gg M$ and $m^* \ll M$.

Schultz went on to assess the status of the continuum treatment of the polar lattice subsumed in Fröhlich's polaron Hamiltonian (equation (19.2)), the validity of which, it turned out, could not be unequivocally guaranteed even for coupling strengths as low as $\alpha = 5$,[†] which is typical of the alkali halide NaCl, for example. When the polaron radius $R_p \gg a$ (where a is a typical interatomic distance approximately equal to the lattice constant), the continuum treatment must be abandoned and the discrete ionic structure of the lattice retained; this reformulation leads to what is known as 'small' polaron theory,[33] which is governed by a Hamiltonian quite different in form from that given in equation (19.2). It would thus appear that the validity of the continuum (or 'large') polaron theory is restricted to coupling strengths which can be handled by other, more conventional, 'intermediate' coupling approaches, thereby *appearing* to rob the Feynman approach of much of its utility. While this is indeed so with regard to its description of ground-state properties at stronger coupling (where the approximation of the lattice by a continuum is no longer justifiable) the unique possibilities which Feynman's path-integral approach offers—already in the intermediate- and weak-coupling regimes—in connection with the calculation of (finite-temperature) polaron mobility are unrivalled; it is to this subject that we now turn.

19.5 Polaron mobility and the contributions of Schultz, FHIP, and Thornber

(a) Generalities

The mobility $\mu(T)$ of a polaron is its average velocity per unit electric field, calculated for vanishingly small fields. In a perfect ionic lattice at finite temperature, μ is limited by the polaron's interaction both with the acoustic vibrational modes of the lattice (in which the positive and negative ions move 'in phase') and with the optical modes (whose *virtual* excitation at $T=0$ by the electron's own Coulomb field is, of course, the origin of polaron formation in the first place). At finite temperature, however, in contrast to the situation at $T=0$, where virtual emission must precede reabsorption, *real* vibrational quanta *already exist*, and *can* be absorbed (without the necessity for any prior emission by the polaron which is scattered accordingly. All this assumes that the entity being scattered by the real absorption of thermally excited vibrational field quanta is the *same* as that formed at absolute zero by the *virtual* emission and reabsorption of quanta of the longitudinal polarization field associated solely with the antiphase (optical) vibrational modes, i.e. a polaron! It is thus assumed that it is possible to separate the system into the free (i.e. real) quanta (which exist in consequence of finite temperature) and the

---

† Indeed, being based on the *slow* electron, the carrier itself has *insufficient* kinetic energy to emit such a quantum.

'bound' (i.e. virtual) quanta (which 'dress' the electron into the quasiparticle we call the 'polaron').

Precisely this problem was referred to by Schultz (in May 1955) in a letter to Feynman (intended as a follow-up to a short conversation they had in Washington—at the meeting of the American Physical Society—in which Feynman expressed his belief that one might apply his path-integral formulation to '. . . specific processes in which polarons are involved'). After discussing some other matters connected with the polaron, Schultz went on to say: '. . . A question of direct interest experimentally is the mobility of the polaron. This then is one important concrete problem' on which he hoped Feynman's formulation could 'throw some light'.

(b) Schultz's contribution

In his more detailed reply of 7 June 1955, Feynman took up the mobility problem, raising two questions. The first of these was answered by himself, in collaboration with Hellwarth, Iddings, and Platzmann seven years later in 1962,[25] while his suggestions as to how the second should be attacked (see below) led to the *first* application of Feynman's path-integral formulation to the mobility problem by Schultz in his 1956 MIT thesis,[24] where the case of resonance scattering was treated. Feynman's two questions were as follows: '(1) What happens when the temperature is so high that many phonons are interacting or scattering from the electron at once? (2) If the temperature is low, or for other reasons question (1) is not of importance, how would I calculate the scattering cross section for one phonon scattering from a polaron?'

After sketching a possible approach to answering the first question, in the course of which he asked Schultz to provide him with numerical magnitudes of $h\omega$, α, and the temperature '. . . so that I can keep track of what is large and small',[†] he went on to outline his approach to the second question which, he assured Schultz, '. . . does not confuse virtual and real processes[‡]. Feynman's confidence in this respect derived from the fact that he had already considered essentially the same problem in QED.[§]

In his letter to Schultz, dated 30 June 1955, Feynman wrote: 'Now let us turn to the case of low temperatures—or, more specifically, the problem (2) of the scattering of a phonon by a polaron—supposing the only free phonons are the initial and scattered one. According to the theory, like quantum

---

[†] The outcome of this survey appeared in Schultz's 1956 MIT Thesis and, later, in his paper.[24]

[‡] Feynman actually used the word 'mesons' here.

[§] In particular, in Section 9 of his 1950 paper,[29] where he extended the work of Section 4, which dealt exclusively with virtual transitions (i.e. where there are no real photons in the initial and final states, and upon which his 1955 polaron work was based), to the case in which there are real photons in the initial and final states.

electrodynamics, the process we want can be diagrammed as follows: that is, a phonon of momentum K_1 is incident a polaron of total momentum P_1. This polaron is 'surrounded' by hosts of virtual phonons being emitted and reabsorbed. It absorbs the K_1, goes on for a while and finally emits the outgoing phonon K_2 leaving the polaron (with its set of virtual phonons) with total momentum P_2, $(P_1 + K_1 = P_2 + K_2)$. The external phonons act exactly as an external potential in first order perturbation (each). The virtual phonons make up the same effect as before, namely an effective action S'. Thus let the Hamiltonian be that on page 655 of my article.[15] The effective action S' due to all the *virtual* phonons is then like equation (4) (but suitably generalized from the case ω_k = constant, C_k = const./K). Then the transition amplitude for our process is exactly:

$$\int (\exp S') \left(\int_0^T (2\omega_1)^{-1/2} C_{K_1} \exp[-iK_1 \cdot X(t_1)] \, dt_1 \right.$$

$$\left. \times \int_0^T (2\omega_2)^{-1/2} C_{K_2} \exp[+iK_2 \cdot X(t_2)] \exp(+i\omega_2 t_2) \, dt_2 \right) DX(t)$$

where the paths are such that before t_1 and t_2 they correspond to a particle of momentum P_1 and afterwards to one of momentum P_2.'

In Fig. 19.1, the wavy lines starting and finishing on the continuous straight lines denote the emission and reabsorption by the electron (denoted by the straight continuous line) of virtual phonons whereby it becomes 'dressed' as the polaron quasiparticle. The incoming K_1 (outgoing K_2) wavy lines with arrowheads denote the absorption and re-emission of *real* optical phonons. The 'Feynman diagram' drawn by Feynman is identical to that involved in *resonance* scattering. Feynman's comment that S' needs be '... suitably generalized from the case ω_k = constant, C_k = const./K', arose from the recognition that what is being scattered by the real (thermal) phonons is *not* an electron but a *polaron*—the associated virtual emission and absorption resulting in renormalization, not only of the electron into a polaron but also of the polaron system itself.

By 23 August 1955, Schultz was able to report that he had succeeded in applying Feynman's QED treatment for the case where real phonons exist in the initial and final states to the above *resonance* (Compton-like) *scattering* process for the polaron. Chapter 6 of his thesis (published the following year) contained the corresponding mobility result, calculated by using his simplified (zero-temperature) model of Feynman's polaron, already discussed in Section 19.4:

$$\mu_o = \frac{|e|}{2m^*\omega\alpha} \left(\frac{m^*}{m_1^{**}} \right)^{3/2} \frac{1}{Z_s(\alpha)} [\exp(\hbar\omega/kT) - 1], \qquad (19.36)$$

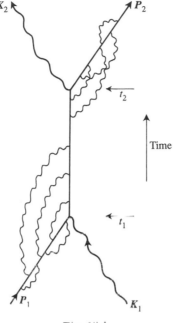

K_2 P_2

t_2

Time

t_1

P_1 K_1

Fig. 19.1.

where m_1^{**} is the zeroth-order Feynman effective mass $(=m^*(v/w)^2)$ evaluated at $T=0$, and $Z_s(\alpha)$ is a coupling constant renormalization factor defined by

$$Z_s(\alpha) \equiv \exp\left[-\frac{K^2}{2vM_{red}}\left(\frac{M}{m_1^{**}}\right)^2\right], \qquad (19.37)$$

where K and M are given, respectively, by $M/m^* = (v^2/w^2 - 1)$, and $K/m^* = (v^2 - w^2)\omega^2$. The appearance of $Z_s(\alpha)$ is connected with the necessary generalization of Hamiltonian parameters already anticipated by Feynman (in his letter of 7 June 1955 to Schultz) in respect of the fact that the real phonons scatter *polarons* and *not* electrons. For weak coupling ($\alpha \ll 1$), $Z_s(\alpha) \to 1$, while for strong coupling ($\alpha \gg 1$), $Z_s(\alpha) \to 0$ rapidly ($Z_s(\alpha=7)=0.096$, for example); the mobility is thus sensitively dependent on $Z_s(\alpha)$.

Finally, from an analysis of available experimental data, Schultz concluded that the range of T in which both the underlying Boltzmann equation treatment of the (resonance) scattering and the slow-polaron approximation are jointly valid may be relatively small, and that *other* scattering mechanisms, such as that due to acoustic phonons (which are not included in the Fröhlich Hamiltonian (equation (19.2))) or to imperfections could well be here nonnegligible.

(c) FHIP's contribution (1962)

As already mentioned, the work of Feynman, Hellwarth, Iddings, and Platzman had its origin in the *first* of two questions which Feynman formulated in his letter (of 7 June 1955) to Schultz, asking what happens when the temperature is so high that many phonons are interacting or scattering from the electron at once. As noted by Feynman, this is a 'fascinating' problem. For in consequence of the very short intervals between successive scattering events, the polaron's energy is insufficiently sharp to validate the use of the Boltzmann equation; quantum interference between successive collisions must then be anticipated, such that the cross section for scattering from one phonon becomes dependent on the presence and behavior of the others—whence the situation approaches one of *continuous* interaction!

In a technically highly intricate paper FHIP addressed themselves to this situation and developed a density matrix approach,† permitting calculation of the *impedance* of the polaron as a function of the frequency v of the applied electric field (assumed *weak*)‡ for arbitrary values of α and T. Their method consisted in calculating the linear response function from the perturbed density matrix of the total Hamiltonian, $H - X \cdot E$, where E is the weak frequency-dependent applied electric field and X is the electron's position vector. The density matrix is first transformed to a Feynman path integral in which the electron's interaction with the lattice is replaced by its interaction *with itself* at earlier locations. The path integral is expanded to second order§ in E to obtain the linear response function from the the expansion coefficient, and hence the impedance Z, to which the mobility μ is related via

$$\mu^{-1} = \lim_{v \to 0} \text{Re}[Z(v)], \tag{19.38}$$

where $Z(v)$ itself is defined *via* an appropriate generalization of Ohm's law.

FHIP eventually obtained a generally valid expression for the polaron impedance Z as a function of the frequency v of the applied field in the form

$$ivZ(v) = -[v^2 - \chi(v)], \tag{19.39}$$

---

† The origins of this approach can be identified in Feynman's letter of 7 June 1955 to Schultz. The first density matrix approach to polaron mobility, utilizing Feynman's trial function S_1 to describe the states of the polaron before and after scattering, was that of Osaka.[33] In contrast to Schultz, Osaka incorporated the properties of S_1 at *finite* temperatures (obtained by applying the Jensen inequality to the *free* energy F, rather than simply to the energy) and obtained, at low temperatures, a polaron mobility whose α dependence was quite different from Schultz's.

‡ In Feynman's later work with Thornber,[26] the case of arbitrarily *large* applied fields was dealt with (see Section 19.5(d)).

§ In this respect, FHIP[25] differs from Osaka,[35] which is based on Kubo's (linear) response theory in which the response function is expressed in terms of the change in the density matrix which is *linear* in E.

where the first term on the right-hand side of equation (19.39) is the purely inductive contribution associated with the generalization of the (integrable) action S_1, in respect of the new Hamiltonian, $H - X \cdot E$, which is now relevant, while the second (resistive) contribution—which accounts for the lifetime effects (i.e. *mobility*) due to interaction with real (thermal) phonons—originates from the corresponding generalization $S - S_1$.

Before discussing mobility, FHIP noted that at $T = 0$, their impedance expression entailed no dissipation† for applied frequencies v lower than ω of the longitudinal field; in such a field, the polaron is simply accelerated,‡ since at $T = 0$ there are *no* real phonons to scatter it! Resistance sets in only as v increases through ω, when real phonon emission becomes possible. (Of course, in a d.c. field, the polaron will eventually gain sufficient energy to emit an optical phonon and thereby dissipate its energy; this, however, is a *nonlinear* ('hot' carrier) effect which is *not* described by a theory of impedance, such as used by FHIP, but rather by that of Thornber and Feynman;[26] see Section 19.5(d).) In the limit of low, but finite v, the polaron behaves as a free particle with an effective mass m^{**}, *which turns out to be identical to that derived by Feynman in his 1955 paper*.[15]

In terms of the resistive contribution $\chi(v)$ to the impedance, the d.c. mobility $\mu(\text{FHIP})$ is given by

$$\mu(\text{FHIP}) = \lim_{v \to 0} \text{Im}[\chi(v)/v], \qquad (19.40)$$

which, at low T ($kT \ll \hbar\omega$), yields

$$\mu = \frac{|e|}{2m^*\omega\alpha} \frac{3}{2}\left(\frac{w}{v}\right)^3 \exp\left(\frac{v^2 - w^2}{w^2 v}\right) \left(\frac{kT}{\hbar\omega}\right) [\exp(\hbar\omega/kT) - 1]. \quad (19.41)$$

As a function of α, μ at first (for small α) decreases (as α^{-1}), passes through a minimum near $\alpha = 7$ (just as does Osaka's mobility[33]), and then increases at large α as $\alpha^{-7} \exp(\alpha^2)$, provided that the polaron wave function is taken to be Gaussian (as it is in Schultz's method).

In the weak coupling limit ($\alpha \ll 1$), where the 'best' variational parameters satisfy $w \simeq v$, equation (19.41) reduces to

$$\mu(\text{FHIP}) \, (\alpha \ll 1) \to \frac{3}{2}\left(\frac{kT}{\hbar\omega}\right) \frac{|e|}{2m^*\alpha\omega} \cdot \exp(\hbar\omega/kT)$$

$$= \frac{3}{2}\left(\frac{kT}{\hbar\omega}\right) \mu(\text{FPZ}). \qquad (19.42).$$

The early work of Howarth and Sondheimer[34] indicated, however, that for

---

† Z is purely imaginary, i.e. inductive.

‡ In a more realistic description this is not actually so, since resistance will arise from any excitations having energies less than hv—such as acoustic phonons.

$\alpha \ll 1$ the mobility is given correctly by the calculation of FPZ, i.e. μ(FPZ), whence in this limit μ(FHIP) is *incorrect*—as explicitly noted by FHIP: '. . . The origin of this (incorrect) temperature dependence is interesting and will be discussed at some length [later]' (Section VI of Thornber and Feynman[26]).

That some trouble should arise in μ(FHIP) in consequence of their having to take the limit $v \rightarrow 0$ (in order to get μ (equation (19.41)), is evident from the way in which Z was initially (correctly) related to linear response functions associated with the generalizations of S_1 and $S - S_1$, which is only admissible provided $v \neq 0$ (since, otherwise, no matter how small α is, the resistive part $\chi(v)$ of $Z(v)$ *exceeds* the inductive part (proportional to v_2); it should be emphasized, however, that for $v \neq 0$, there is no problem with v in the FHIP result for $Z(v)$.

The remainder of the FHIP paper essentially dealt with the frequency dependence of the polaron impedance, and opened the way for optical studies of polaron properties, such as those of Devreese *et al.*[35] in 1972.

(d) *The contribution of Thornber and Feynman*[26]

Eight years after the publication of the FHIP paper, Thornber, in collaboration with Feynman, published an extension of FHIP to cover *finite* d.c. applied electric field encountered in cold-cathode tunnel emission devices, in an attempt to ascertain whether or not optical photon scattering could account for the very large rate of loss of electron energy which, some years earlier, had been found to occur in the insulating part of these devices. For now, not only is the Boltzmann equation again inapplicable,† but also the magnitude of the electric fields used in the devices *exceeds* that for which the FHIP treatment is valid; thus Thornber and Feynman (TF)[26] essentially extended the FHIP analysis[25] (which already covered arbitrarily large couplings and temperatures) to arbitrarily large applied electric fields, thus permitting the nonlinear response of ('hot') polarons in this 'non-Ohmic' regime to be studied.

The key question TF asked themselves was this: 'For a specific velocity, what field is necessary to maintain that velocity?' or more specifically, '. . . what energy is lost per unit distance by an electron whose expectation velocity is specified?' This, it should be noted, is a subtle inversion of the usual question: What is the velocity acquired for a given field? Another crucial step was the introduction of a frame of reference based on the center of mass of the Feynman–Schultz two-particle polaron model. Having determined the required field E in terms of the expectation value of the *net* rate of emission R of the longitudinal optical phonons (i.e. the rate of emission less the rate of absorption), TF proceeded with an approximate evaluation of R by a path-

---

† Owing to quantum interference between emitted phonons which destroys the required *independence* of collisions.

integral approach similar to that used by FHIP to calculate the impedance of electrons in polar crystals (in the case of small oscillatory fields), but extended to the case of the static fields of arbitrary strength now under consideration.

Concerning the associated linear (weak field) d.c. polaron mobility μ, the following points should be noted. (1) $\mu_{TF} = \mu_{FHIP}$, and hence, as in the case of FHIP, μ_{TF} is in error at low temperatures and for weak coupling by the factor $\frac{3}{2}(kT\hbar\omega)$. (2) In the case of μ_{TF}, the 'order of limits' argument advanced by FHIP to account for this discrepancy cannot, of course, be invoked, since in TF's case the field is d.c. (i.e. static). To quote TF: '... At present we do not understand this disagreement.' To this day this problem remains unsolved.

Using Fröhlich's polaron Hamiltonian, TF went on to present numerical calculations of the velocity dependence of the field (or, equivalently, the energy loss per unit distance) for three values of α. The results obtained reveal that, with increasing velocity, firstly the strong T-dependent, low field mobility found by FHIP in the limit of a static field is valid, while the subsequent behavior depends on whether or not the initial temperature of the lattice is above or below that corresponding to the longitudinal optical phonon energy $\hbar\omega$.

Using only the experimentally measured values of $\hbar\omega$, ε_s and ε_∞, TF calculated an energy loss of 0.025 eV Å^{-1} for electrons for energies near threshold in Al_2O_3, a value close to that found experimentally (0.03 eV Å^{-1}); accordingly they concluded that optical phonon scattering can indeed produce the high rates of energy loss found experimentally in tunnel-cathode devices.

19.6 Contemporary developments à la Feynman

The most prolific single research group having the longest standing involvement with Feynman's polaron 'heritage' must be that of J. Devreese and his collaborators in Antwerp, Belgium; from their extensive output over the past thirty years, the following should be mentioned:

(1) assessment[35] of the accuracy of Feynman's path-integral approach by applying it to a modification of an *exactly soluble* polaron model[36] in which the polarization field is assumed to have only a *single* (longitudinal) wave vector: it was found that Feynman's self-energy values were within 1.42 per cent of the exact values for all values of α, the largest discrepancy occurring in the 'intermediate'-coupling regime;

(2) calculation[37] of the optical absorption of polarons (at rest and at $T = 0$) within the framework of FHIP,[25] and the attendant possibility of experimentally probing the *internal structure* of the Feynman–Schultz two-particle model of the polaron;

(3) rederivation[38] of the Thornber–Feynman result[26] *without* the use of

path-integrals, based on calculating the electron density correlation function starting from the Feynman–Schultz two-particle model;

(4) the elucidation[39] of the mysterious $\frac{3}{2}(kT/\hbar\omega)$ factor which characterizes μ(FHIP);

(5) The alternative derivation[40] of FHIP *without* the use of path-integrals, thereby permitting the various scattering processes implicit in FHIP to be identified;

(6) the realization[22] of Feynman's (1955) request[25] to re-express his formulation in 'conventional notation'.

In the USA,† Thornber continued his investigations into the Feynman polaron and its transport properties until the mid-1970s, publishing within a year of TF[26] a paper entitled 'Linear and non-linear electronic transport in electron–phonon systems: Self-consistent approach with the path-integral formulation,[4]—in which, among other things, he considered the case in which both electric and magnetic fields are applied to the system, calculating the cyclotron mass, Hall mobility, and magnetoresistivity. He followed this in 1974 by: 'Sum rules satisfied by Feynman-approximation solutions to the polaron problem'—in which he derived a free-energy theorem for polarons, as a finite temperature extension of the zero-temperature ground-state theorem of Lemmens *et al.*[42] These theorems relate the exact free energy of the polaron to the exact absorption spectrum integrated over frequency, and are in fact valid for *any* Feynman approximation to the polaron problem. In addition, Thornber made valuable contributions to the 1971, 1975, and 1977 NATO Advanced Study Institute Meetings organized by Devreese, which were published in 1972, 1976, and 1978, respectively.

19.7 Connection with superconductivity

Feynman's entry into polaron theory was (at least partially) catalyzed by the prospect (noted by Fröhlich in the introduction to his article[2] in *Advances in Physics* in 1954) of solving the more fundamental problem (to Feynman's mind) of *superconductivity*, *if* a technique could be developed which was capable of treating, realistically, the range of coupling constants where neither weak- nor strong-coupling polaron theories (which was all that existed prior to 1955) sufficed (as indicated in Section 19.2, this range is centered on $\alpha = 10$, where the mismatch problem manifests itself). That Feynman was certainly intrigued by Fröhlich's somewhat cryptic remark is clear from the penultimate sentence of his letter to Fröhlich of 8 September 1954, which asked: 'What do we have to do to understand Superconductivity?', the implication being '. . .

---

† One of longest-standing workers in the theory of the polaron, other than Devreese, must surely be E.P. Gross, who had worked originally in von Hippel's lab at MIT.

I've given you a method which yields the continuous transition between the weak- and strong-coupling regimes which you (i.e. Fröhlich) asked for, and which you claimed could be of use for superconductivity—*how now do we get superconductivity?!*'

To elucidate the connection between these two problems—as perceived by Fröhlich—it is necessary to recall that between the publication in 1950[6] of his idea that his phonon-mediated attractive interaction between conduction electrons near the Fermi surface of a metal was basic to the phenomenon of superconductivity, and the publication of his polaron review article[2] in 1954, Fröhlich had succeeded[2] in obtaining (in late 1953) an *exact* solution to a one-dimensional model which exhibited superconductivity, but no isotope effect! This model assumed a wave function for the combined electron–phonon system which was of the Pekar product from equation (19.7), which from *polaron theory* is known to be appropriate only in the limit of extremely strong coupling ($\alpha \to \infty$). The absence of an isotope effect is thus understandable, since, in this limit, the dynamic properties of the lattice are effectively *suppressed*! Accordingly, Fröhlich believed that, in order to retrieve the experimentally established isotope effect, it was surely necessary to readmit the *dynamic properties of the lattice*—but not to the extent which obtains in the weak-coupling limit of polaron theory, which *was* treatable using perturbation theory. In the case of superconductivity, however, the *impossibility* of a perturbative approach had become very evident from the nonanalyticity of his one-dimensional solution, with its essential singularity in the attractive electron–electron interaction—a feature subsequently shared by the Bardeen–Cooper–Schrieffer (BCS) solution![43] Thus he was convinced† that a realistic treatment of the intermediate regime of coupling in the case of the *polaron problem* was a necessary prerequisite for a successful solution to the *superconductivity* problem. In this connection it is thus of considerable interest to note[44] that Schrieffer was led to the now famous BCS *ansatz* via an adaptation of the 'intermediate coupling' polaron wave function of Lee, Low, and Pines.[11]

For Feynman, 'the whole polaron problem had been a side issue from the beginning, as a sort of exercise and game, which gave me some pleasure. But it was only a side issue, not a central challenge. It's just that I happened to notice in the library that this problem was within the range of my tools, and I worked on it. For me, the central challenge was the problem of superconductivity, and I spent an awful lot of time in trying to understand it and doing everything by means of which I could approach it. I did an awful lot of calculations and developed a lot of methods, which I have gradually seen other people develop after me. But I did not solve the original problem: Where does superconduc-

---

† In the case of the polaron, the fact that the electron's interaction with the ionic lattice did *not* here entail any significant enhancement of the Bloch effective mass m^* (for $\alpha \sim 6$, equation (19.5) yields a polaron effective mass m^{**} which is only twice m^*) played an important role in fostering this conviction.

tivity come from? I never published anything on it, and there is a big gap [in my publications] at that time, which was due to my attempts to solve the superconductivity problem—which I failed to do. I developed an emotional block against the problem of superconductivity, so that when I learned about the BCS paper I could not bring myself to read it for a long time. When I did read it, it was of course the right solution.'[44] At the same time as his work on the origin of superconductivity, Feynman was also trying to understand the turbulence of fluids, but he was not successful in this either.

Notes and References

1. R.P. Feynman, Interviews and Conversations with Jagdish Mehra, in Pasadena, California, January 1988.

2. H. Fröhlich, *Adv. Phys.* **3**, 325 (1954).

3. S.I. Pekar, *J.Phys. USSR* **40**, 341, 347 (1946).

4. A. von Hippel, *Z. Phys.* **68**, 309 (1931); **75**, 105 (1932).

5. L.D. Landau, *Sov. Phys.* **3**, 664 (1933).

6. H. Fröhlich, H. Pelzer and S. Zienau, *Phil.Mag.* **41**, 221 (1950).

7. H. Fröhlich, *Proc. R. Soc. Lond.* **160**, 230 (1937).

8. H. Fröhlich, W. Heitler, and N. Kemmer, *Proc. R. Soc. Lond.* **166**, 154 (1938).

9. M. Gurari, *Phil. Mag.* **44**, 329 (1953).

10. T.D. Lee and D. Pines, *Phys. Rev.* **90**, 297 (1953).

11. T.D. Lee, F. Low and D. Pines, *Phys. Rev.* **90**, 297 (1953).

12. S.I Pekar, *JETP (USSR)* **19**, 796 (1949).

13. S.I. Pekar and M.F. Deigen, *JETP (USSR)* **18**, 481 (1948).

14. L.D. Landau and S.I. Pekar, *JETP (USSR)* **18**, 419 (1948).

15. R.P. Feynman, *Phys. Rev.* **97**, 660 (1955).

16. G. Höhler, *Nuovo Cim.* II(4), 691 (1955).

17. T.D. Lee and D. Pines, *Phys. Rev.* **92**, 883 (1953).

18. S.I Pekar, *JETP (USSR)* **27**, 398, 411, 579 (1954).

19. K. Mano, *Prog. Theor. Phys.* **14**, 435 (1955).

20. K. Yamazaki, *Prog. Theor. Phys.* **15**, 508 (1956).

21. K. Yamazaki, *J. Phys.* **16**, 3675 (1983).

22. J.T. Devreese and F. Brosens, *Phys. Rev.* **45**, 6459 (1992).

23. F.E. Low and D. Pines, *Phys. Rev.* **98**, 414 (1955)

24. T.D. Schultz, *Phys. Rev* **116**, 526 (1959), based on Technical Report No. 9 of the Solid State and Molecular Theory Group of MIT (1956).

25. R.P. Feynman, R.W. Hellwarth, C.K. Iddings and P.M Platzman (FHIP), *Phys. Rev.* **127**, 1004 (1962).

26. K.K. Thornber and R.P. Feynman, *Phys. Rev.* **1**, 4099 (1970).

27. E.P. Gross, *Phys. Rev.* **100**, 1571 (1955).

28. H. Haken, Contribution to *Halbleiterprobleme*, Band II (ed. W. Schottky). Viewig, Braunschweig, 1955, pp. 1–99

29. R.P. Feynman, *Phys. Rev.* **80**, 440 (1950).

30. N.N. Bogoliubov, *J. Ukrainian Math.* **2**, 3 (1950).

31. S.V. Tiablikov, *JETP (USSR)* **21**, 277 (1951).

32. T.D. Schultz, Contribution to *Polarons and excitons* (ed. C.G. Kuper and G.D. Whitfield). Oliver and Boyd, Edinburgh, 1963, pp. 71–121.

33. Y. Osaka, *Prog. Theor. Phys.* **25**, 517 (1961).

34. D.G. Howarth and E.F. Sondheimer, *Proc. R. Soc. Lond.* **219**, 53 (1953).

35. J.T. Devreese *et al.*, *Phys. Rev.* **5**, 2367 (1972).

36. F.M. Peeters and J.T. Devreese, *Phys. Rev.* **23**, 1936 (1981).

37. F.M. Peeters and J.T. Devreese, *Phys. Rev.* **28**, 6051 (1983).

38. J.T. Devreese, *Physica Scripta* T25 309 (1989).

39. J.T. Devreese, Ref. 36.

40. J.T. Devreese, Ref. 36.

41. K.K. Thornber, *Phys. Rev.* **4**, 1929 (1971).

42. L.F. Lemmens *et al.*, *Phys. Rev.* **8**, 2777 (1973).

43. D. Pines, In: *Physics Today*, February 1989, pp. 61–66.

44. R.P. Feynman, Interviews and conversations with Jagdish Mehra, in Pasadena, California, January 1988.

20

Excursions into diverse fields

20.1 Bringing quantum mechanics to engineering

Every summer Richard Feynman used to go off in his automobile to different parts of the country or visit some other country for sightseeing and new experiences. After completing his 1955 work on the polaron he decided that, instead of going to another country, he would stay at Caltech and start making excursions into diverse scientific fields for which he harbored great interest, such as engineering and biology, and act as a catalyst for innovations into new areas of scientific and intellectual endeavor. One of the earliest opportunities presented itself in electronic engineering.

The first atomic amplifiers and oscillators (called 'maser devices') became available in 1954, and Robert Hellwarth did experiments on microwave spectroscopy for a Ph.D. degree under Brebis Bleaney at Oxford University, completing it the following year. From Oxford Hellwarth went to Caltech in the fall of 1955 as a research fellow in the physics department, where he gave a seminar on the maser, which aroused Feynman's interest. Feynman invited Hellwarth to have regular discussions with him about this new field. An engineering research student, Frank Vernon, who worked at the Aerospace Corporation, also joined Hellwarth and Feynman in these discussions. They discussed the papers of Townes and co-workers, who had written the early papers in this new field.[1]

Normally, in a maser one sends ammonia atoms through a microwave cavity, and the cavity generates very pure microwaves. Townes and co-workers were working to explore what might happen if the ammonia atoms were sent through two microwave cavities, because Norman Ramsey at Harvard had invented the double microwave region method where one could have a much higher resolution by using separated beams. In fact, Hellwarth had made use of Ramsey's method in his thesis at Oxford and made small variations in it as part of his work for the doctorate.

After the original device, which was the ammonia beam maser amplifier and oscillator, there came proposals for the variations of this device. The engineering people had to deal with questions of noise values and the sources of sensitivities in instruments. Hellwarth and Vernon talked to Feynman about how to deal with these problems with the help of quantum mechanics. Feynman would explain these things to them in his own way, in this case with geometrical analogies.

In order to analyze the original ammonia maser, as well as subsequent variations, the expected electrical dipole moment $m(t)$ of a two-level atom in an arbitrary electric field $E(t)$ had to be calculated as a function of time t, often to arbitrary orders in the field E. There existed straightforward, though tedious, methods for proceeding from the Schrödinger equation to do this. Ordinary time-dependent pertubation theory was one such method. Unfortunately, no closed-form solution exists for $m(t)$ in terms of $E(t)$ for the two-level atom. Worse yet, perturbation theory often produced pages of formulas as answers to relatively simple problems, such as that of calculating the power from the ammonia beam maser and the maser frequency.

Feynman, Hellwarth, and Vernon set out to make such calculations simple for the student and error-free for the expert. The idea was to create, in typical Feynman fashion, simple diagrams that one could draw on paper which organized the calculations into easy pieces and, in addition, made the answer easy to visualize beforehand. One such diagram is shown in Fig. 20.1. In it, the real vector called r simply precesses around the real vector Ω in a fictitious three-dimensional space. For a two-level system (in which the transitions take place between two energy levels), this almost yields all that the Schrödinger equation yields. The three components of r each have a simple physical meaning: they are the components of the expected dipole moment p_t and

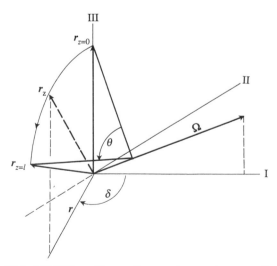

Fig. 20.1. MASER oscillator diagram in rotating coordinates.

internal energy of the two-level atom. The three components of the ω vector represent important properies of the perturbing electric field vector. The maser oscillator properties (derived previously by Townes and co-workers in many pages[1]) were rederived in the Feynman–Vernon–Hellwarth paper[2] in a few lines. The clarity of the simple derivation of FVH showed that the results worked for a much wider range of oscillator frequency than had been thought previously. For instance, the paper reduced the previously difficult analysis of 'Dicke superradiance' to a transparent one.

By the time of the advent of the initial theoretical proposal of the 'laser' (first called the 'optical maser') in 1958 by Townes and Schawlow, the maser problems were forgotten and the FVH paper was not used until Abella, Hartman, and Kurnit[3] used it in 1964 to carry over the phenomenon of 'spin echoes' from the microwave region to the now common 'photon echoes' observed at optical frequencies. Spin echoes had always been thought of with the aid of the diagram (shown in Fig. 20.1), because, in this case, the three-space reduced to real space. This development renewed the popularity of these diagrams, and today they are commonly taught in graduate courses and appear in textbooks. The FVH paper turned out to be a very useful introduction to quantum mechanics involved in the theory of lasers and masers, for it represented the way of looking at quantum mechanics easily. In due course, this paper became one of Feynman's most often cited papers.

Robert Hellwarth joined the Hughes Aircraft Company in Culver City, California, in 1956. He arranged for Feynman to give lectures for scientists, engineers, and technicians at Hughes on subjects of mutual interest. Since Feynman's range of scientific interests was large, the lectures could cover almost everything of interest to him. Feynman started giving lectures for two hours (with a break) every Wednesday. He continued to give these Wednesday lectures regularly when the Hughes Research Laboratory moved to Malibu, and did so well into the last decade of his life. He liked the contact with engineering and engineers. One such engineer was Frank Vernon, who became Feynman's research student after the joint work with Feynman and Hellwarth.

Vernon wrote a Ph.D. thesis under Feynman, entitled 'The theory of a general quantum system interacting with a linear dissipative system.'[4] Feynman and Vernon gave an exact quantum mechanical solution for the behavior of a quantum system (such as a two-level maser atom) interacting with a dissipative system (such as the lossy mode—causing attenuation or dissipation of electrical energy—of a microwave cavity). Vernon had started work on his Ph.D. thesis with Feynman in 1957, soon after the completion of the FVH paper; by that time the molecular beam quantum amplifier or oscillator, known as the maser, had existed for several years. Feynman and Vernon wished to place on a firm quantum footing the exact nature of the already postulated low-noise capability of the maser as a linear rectifier, an aim which their article achieved.

The questions arising with the new devices were of the following kind: What happens with quantum detectors? What are the interactions, especially when there is a weak signal (say from a very distant star, the stars being taken in a classical approximation), and in what sense is the signal quantum when it reaches the delicate detector?

Feynman and Vernon worked out a general theory of the interaction of a weakly coupled distant system with a quantum system. If, for example, the quantum system is coupled to a star, it is coupled to each atom with an extremely weak coupling. Their general theory was capable of answering questions about the noise background and about the signal to noise ratio in attempting to measure signals from distant sources and allowing for all the quantum effects of the detectors. In this process, Feynman and Vernon formulated a simple statement of the quantum mechanical result, which they hoped would enable any working engineer, not knowledgeable in quantum mechanics, to calculate the noise in any linear quantum 'circuit' (in which, for instance, atoms were the elements) by following a few simple rules.

Feynman and Vernon's work was done entirely from the point of view of path integrals and was very powerful. With the path integrals, one could integrate away the variables of the entire emitting system and be left just with the detector. As in the Hamiltoniam system, one did not have to have the Hamiltonian for the emitter *and* the detector. 'I feel it was a fundamental, interesting, and satisfactory analysis of the quantum system, in which the far away sources are classical. It was quite powerful. But it wasn't much used by people. They derived the same results by more conventional methods with which they felt more comfortable.'[5] Hellwarth essentially rewrote the Feynman–Vernon article in Hamiltonian form, for he hoped that in this way the work might reach more readers, and also formulated the results in more of an engineering style; his paper was, however, rejected by the *Physical Review* 'on the (correct) grounds that this was [by then] old stuff.'[6]

Feynman had used this sort of path-integral treatment of dissipation before in his calculation of the ground state energy of an electron coupled to the phonons of the crystal lattice, the 'polaron'.[7] The quantum variables of the dissipative segment, the phonons in the case of the polaron, were eliminated from the problem without approximation. And, one was *not* left with an effective Hamiltonian, perhaps with a phenomenological non-Hamiltonian damping term. Rather a Lagrangian functional of the system coordinates, involving a time integral, 'remembers' exactly the history of the dissipative interactions. A rather unusual path integral must be performed to calculate the evolution of the system by using this new Lagrangian that is not local in time. The dissipative system of phonons in the polaron problem was shown by Feynman, Hellwarth, Iddings, and Platzmann (FHIP)[8] to have such complicated effects as the formation of short-lived excited states of the polaron. All of their quantum treatments of dissipation utilized, in effect, only the same old Schrödinger equation and its standard interpretation.

In their introduction,[9] Feynman and Vernon mentioned that 'the theory of measurement' involves problems similar to the maser problems requiring a proper quantum treatment of dissipation. 'Feynman thought that there was little of practical consequence left to be done in the "theory of measurement". He certainly impressed upon his students that the so-called "collapse" of the wave function, said to occur upon measurement, follows the Schrödinger equation precisely. The subtlety in the process is the same as that in any irreversible process.'[6] The Feynman–Vernon article set down clearly how irreversible phenomena are to be calculated by using the standard Schrödinger equation, or the equivalent to the path-integral formulation. Perhaps that is why, in their introduction, Feynman and Vernon cite 'the theory of measurement' as one of the motivations for their paper and mention the 'measuring instrument' as a possible dissipative quantum subsystem. 'I am reminded of one problem in measurement theory that Feynman considered unsolved. While he, Vernon, and I were working together, for many months he had a query in his own handwriting written in the corner of the blackboard in his office: "Can a man write his own wave function?"'[6]

Many situations occur in quantum mechanics in which several systems are coupled together but one or more of them are not of primary interest. Problems in the theory of measurement and in statistical mechanics present good examples of such situations. Suppose, for instance, that the quantum behavior of a system is to be investigated when it is coupled to one or more measuring instruments. The instruments in themselves are not of primary interest. However, their effects are those of perturbing the characteristics of the system being observed. A more concrete example is the case of an atom in an excited state which interacts with the electromagnetic field in the lossy mode of a cavity resonator. Because of the coupling there will be energy exchange between the field and the atom until equilibrium is reached. If, however, the atom were not coupled to any external disturbances, it would simply remain unperturbed in its original excited state. The cavity field, although not of central interest to us, influences the behavior of the atom.

Let us suppose that there are two nonrelativistic quantum systems whose coordinates are represented in a general way by Q and X, as in Fig. 20.2, coupled together through some interaction potential $V(Q, X, t)$ which is a function of the parameters of the two systems. It is now desired to compute the expectation value of an observable which is a function of the Q variables only. The complete problem, can, of course, be analyzed by taking the Hamiltonian of the complete system, forming the wave function

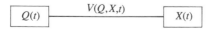

Fig. 20.2. General quantum systems Q and X coupled by a potential $V(Q, X, t)$.

$$[H(Q)+H(X)+V(Q, X, t)]\,(Q, X) = -(\hbar/i)\,(Q, X),$$

and then finding its solution. In general, this is an extremely difficult problem.

Furthermore, we realize that when this approach is used, it is not easy to see how to eliminate the coordinates of X and include its effect in an equivalent way when making computations on Q. A very satisfactory method of formulating such problems as this in a general way was made available by the introduction of the Lagrangian formulation of quantum mechanics by Feynman. Thus, in a problem where several charged particles interact through the electromagnetic field, he found that it was possible to eliminate the coordinates of the field and recast the problem in terms of the coordinates of the particles alone. The effect of the field was included as a delayed interaction between the particles.[10]

The central problem of Feynman and Vernon's investigation was to develop a general formalism for finding all the quantum effects of an environmental system (the interaction system) upon a system of interest (the test system), to investigate the properties of this formalism, and to draw conclusions about the quantum effects of specific interaction systems on the test system. They considered cases where the interaction system is composed of various combinations of linear systems and classical forces in great detail. For the cases in which the interaction system is linear, they found that parameters such as impedance, which characterize its classical behavior, are also important in determining its quantum effect on the observed system. Since this linear system may include dissipation, the results have application in a study of irreversible statistical mechanics.

It was an important paper, which gave simple rules for calculating the characteristic parameters of devices, but the Feynman path-integral method on which the formulation was based was not well known among engineers or, for that matter, among physicists, and Feynman was rather disappointed that its results were not widely used. About this work, Feynman said: 'Townes and others who knew quantum mechanics were also doing it. If I had never existed, nobody would have noticed the difference.'[5]

20.2 A 'graduate student' in biology

To Feynman, biology was a very interesting field; as a boy, his father had encouraged him to take interest in science in general and, when he was at Princeton, he had taken a course from Newton Harvey on cell physiology. Thus he was not entirely ignorant of problems in biology, which he actually found fascinating. However, all he thought he would be able to do would be to go into the laboratory, clean up, wash bottles, and hear the biologists talk among themselves about their problems, just as he had done as a youngster in the chemistry laboratory at Far Rockaway High School.

At Caltech, Feynman's interest in biology arose because he frequently used to visit Max Delbrück and other members of the biology department. On occasion he would attend biology seminars given by visitors. So, when it occurred to Feynman that he might wish to do some work in biology, he mentioned it to Delbrück, who sent him to see Robert S. Edgar, who, at that time, was a postdoctoral fellow, responsible for bacteriophage research that was still going on in Delbrück's laboratory. Delbrück, himself, was increasingly losing interest in bacteriophages as his work on the machanism on phototropism in the fungus *Phycomyces* accelerated.

Feynman proposed to Edgar that he would like to hang around his laboratory and do odd things. Edgar told him that what he had to do was act like a graduate student who would do some research. He would first have to go through the phages course, learn to handle phages, and Edgar would give him a research project and a room in the laboratory—like a graduate student, only better. That's what they did and Feynman learned how to handle the phages.

Feynman was given a special problem. It had to do with back-mutations. A mutation had been discovered in which a virus lost its ability to attack a certain kind of bacteria. Then another mutation would gain this ability back, but it was not exactly the opposite mutation, because when it got back it would do something different. For example, it would attack faster or slower; it wasn't exactly the same. And the question was to investigate what these back-mutations were.

Mutations are structural changes in the genes. Feynman's project dealt with the characterization of back-mutations, that is, mutations which appear to restore a mutant gene to its normal state. The mutant that he started with, r_{43}, is a representative of a mutation at one site within the rIIB gene that occurs at an abnormally high frequency, a mutational 'hot spot'. The notion was to explore this unusual behavior.

Using a variety of bacterial hosts, Feynman was able to distinguish various types of back-mutations (revertants); not all were identical to the normal, or wild-type, strain. He examined further some of the unusual back-mutants that were clearly not completely normal. His studies revealed that these unusual back-mutants still retained the original r_{43} mutation and had a second mutation that somehow ameliorated the effects of r_{43} mutation. These 'suppressor' mutations were, by themselves, typical mutations producing a strong mutant effect, similar to r_{43}. Nevertheless, when combined with r_{43}, these suppressor mutations produced a near normal effect on the phage.

Feynman went on to show that when these suppressors are combined with one another they do not show mutual suppression, that is, reduction in the mutant effect on the phage, nor do they do so with a wide variety of other rII mutations tested—the effect appeared to be specific for the r_{43} mutation. Feynman also showed that these suppressor mutations were located in close proximity to the r_{43} mutation.[11]

Feynman carried this study further by showing that when one started with one of these 'suppressor' mutations and looked at their back-mutations, some were found to be due to new suppressor mutations similar in characteristics to the r_{43} mutation. Thus there exist two types of mutations which we could call *plus* and *minus*. Either a *plus* or a *minus* mutation by itself produced a mutant effect on the phage. However, a *plus* mutation combined with a *minus* mutation returned the phage to almost its normal unmutated state. Feynman speculated about the possible nature of these mutations. In a conversation with Edgar, he suggested that one class caused a positively charged amino acid to be introduced in the gene product protein, while the other caused a negatively charged amino acid to be introduced; in the double mutant the original charge state of the protein could be restored.[12] (When one refers to the mutant or nonmutant 'state' of the phage, one is referring to the functional activity of the rII gene, i.e. the gene-specific protein product, when it contains no mutation, one mutation, or two mutations.)

The paper on the 'General nature of the genetic code for proteins' by F. H. C. Crick *et al.*[13] is widely regarded as one of the most important and elegant studies in the history of genetic research. In this work the authors showed that in a small region of the rII gene (the region which Feynman was studying) one can find two special classes of mutations that show mutual suppression: Feynman's *plus* and *minus* classes.

Given their notion that these mutations were additions and deletions of nucleotides, Crick and collaborators correctly speculated that this remarkable finding must be due to the fact that the gene is translated, starting from one fixed point, and that the sequence of nucleotides within the gene is read and translated by the translation machinery of the cell three nucleotides at a time. A single mutation of the addition–deletion type will have a severe effect on the translation process because the reading will be thrown 'out of phase'. Phase will be restored only in case where an addition is combined with a deletion or if three additions or three deletions are combined. Feynman had independently discovered some of the characteristics of addition–deletion, or as one now calls them 'frame-shift' mutations. However, he did not realize that they were actually addition and deletion mutations, and did not discover that '3' was a magic number. Crick and his colleagues took note of Feynman's work in their paper.

Feynman continued his biological research during his sabbatical year (1959–60), and worked with Matt Meselson on ribosomes. The ribosome work did not go very well, because Feynman was not able to reproduce his results. By the time he realized where the trouble was coming from he had to return to physics. However, he was invited to give a seminar on his work at Harvard, and during his biology sabbatical year he got to know James Watson, Francis Crick, and other well-known biologists and became friends with them.

The experience of his year in the biology department that pleased Feynman the most was the response to him as a 'graduate teaching assistant'! In biology, they put the students through a wide range of things, different kinds of techniques, and one of them was phages. So, for a week, Feynman taught them how to handle phages carefully by sucking them up the tubes containing cyanide—'you have to be damn careful!' He taught them about calculating statistics and probability. These were first year students and they did not know who Feynman really was; on their evaluation sheet they ranked him 'the best teaching assistant' they had, one 'who is excellent at explaining things'. 'I got a tremendous boost by obtaining the best score of all teaching assistants; even in biology, not my field, I could explain things clearly, and I was rather proud of it. It was great fun to be in another world and act like somebody else—a graduate student and teaching assistant!'[5]

20.3 There's plenty of room at the bottom

On 29 December 1959, at the Annual Meeting of the American Physical Society, held at Caltech, Richard Feynman gave a talk entitled 'There's plenty of room at the bottom.'[14] In this talk, Feynman sought to describe a field, 'in which little has been done, but in which an enormous amount can be done in principle.'[15] This field is not quite the same as others in that it wouldn't tell us much of fundamental physics (in the sense of 'What are the strange particles?'), but is more like solid state physics in the sense that it might tell us much of great interest about the strange phenomena that occur in complex situations. Furthermore, a point that is more important is that it would have an enormous number of technical applications. What Feynman wanted to talk about 'is the problem of manipulating and controlling things on a small scale.'[15]

Feynman recalled that, whenever he mentioned this problem to people, they would tell him about miniaturization, and how far it had progressed today. 'They tell me about electric motors that are the size of the nail on your small finger. And there's a device on the market, they tell me, by which you can write the Lord's Prayer on the head of a pin. But that's nothing; that's the most primitive, halting step in the direction I intend to discuss. It is a staggeringly small world that is below.'[15]

Feynman discussed what would be involved. The head of a pin is a sixteenth of an inch across. If we magnify it by 25 000 diameters, the area of the pinhead is then equal to all the pages of the *Encyclopaedia Britannica*. Therefore, what is necessary is to reduce in size all the writing in the *Encyclopaedia* by 25 000 times. Is that possible? The resolving power of the eye is about $\frac{1}{120}$ of an inch, which is roughly the diameter of one of the little dots on the fine half-tone reproductions in the *Encyclopaedia*. If the little dot is demagnified by 25 000 times, it is still 80 angstroms across in diameter, or thirty-two atoms across in an ordinary metal. Thus, each dot can be adjusted in size as required by photoengraving, 'and there is no question that there is enough room on the head of a pin to put all of the *Encyclopaedia Britannica* . . . There is no question that if things were reduced by 25 000 times in the form of raised letters on the pin, it would be easy for us to read it today.'[16]

The question that then arises is this: How do we write it? One way to do this might be to take light and, through an optical microscope running backwards, focus it on to a very small photoelectric screen. Then electrons come away from the screen where the light is shining. These electrons are focused down in size by the electron microscope lenses to impinge directly upon the surface of the material. Will such a beam etch away the material if it is run long enough? 'I don't know. If it doesn't work for a metal surface, it must be possible to find some surface with which to coat the original pin so that, where the electrons bombard, a change is made which could be recognized later.'[16]

That would take care of putting the entire *Encyclopaedia Britannica* on the head of a pin. Now let's consider all the books in the world. Consider three great libraries: the Library of Congress (approximately nine million volumes); the British Museum Library (about five million volumes); the Bibliothèque Nationale of Paris (another five million volumes). Discounting the duplications, let us say that there are about twenty-four million volumes of interest in the world. What would happen if we were to print all these volumes at the scale we have mentioned? That is, instead of the twenty-four volumes of the *Encyclopaedia*, we now have twenty-four million volumes. The million pinheads required for this can be put in a square of a thousand pins on a side, or an area about three square yards. That is to say, the silicon replica with the paper-thin backing of plastic, with which we have made the copies, with all this information, would occupy an area approximately the size of thirty-five pages of the *Encyclopaedia*. 'All of the information which all mankind has ever recorded in books can be carried around in a pamphlet in your hand—not written in code, but as simple reproduction of the original pictures, engravings, and everything else on a small scale without loss of resolution.'[16]

Suppose that, instead of trying to reproduce the pictures and all the information directly in its present form, we write only the information content in a code of dots and dashes to represent the various letters. Each letter represents six or seven 'bits' of information; that is, we need only about six or seven dots or dashes for each letter. Now, instead of writing everything, as we did before, on the *surface* of the head of a pin, let us use the interior of the material as well. Let us represent a dot by a small spot of one metal, the next dash by an adjacent spot of another metal, and so on. Suppose, to be conservative, that a bit of information is going to require a little cube of atoms $5 \times 5 \times 5$, that is, 125 atoms. Let's say, we need a hundred or some more atoms to make sure that the information is not lost through diffusion or some other means.

Now, estimating the number of letters in the *Encyclopaedia*'s twenty-four volumes, and assuming that each of our twenty-four million books is as big as an *Encyclopaedia* volume, then how many bits of information do we need? 10^{15}. For each bit let us allow 100 atoms. It turns out that all the information that man has accumulated in all the books in the world can be written in this form in a cube of material 1/200 of an inch wide, which is the barest particle of dust that can be made out by the human eye. 'So there is *plenty* of room at the bottom! Don't tell me about microfilm!' [17]

The fact that enormous amounts of information can be carried in an exceedingly small space is, of course, known to biologists. It resolves the mystery that existed, before it was understood clearly, of how it could be, in the tiniest cell, all of the information for organization of a complex structure such as ourselves can be stored.

The biological example of storing information on a small scale inspired Feynman to imagine what should be possible. Biology is concerned not simply with writing information; it *does something* about it. A biological system can be very small. All the information—whether we have brown eyes, or whether we think at all, or that in the embryo the jawbone should first develop with a little hole in the side so that later a nerve can grow through it—is contained in a very tiny fraction of the cell in the form of long-chain DNA molecules in which approximately fifty atoms are used for one bit of information about the cell. Many of the cells are very tiny, but they are very active; they manufacture various substances; they walk around; they wiggle; and they do all kinds of things—all on a very small scale. Also, they store information. Consider the possibility that we too can make a thing very small, which does what we want—that we can manufacture an object that maneuvers at that level!

Feynman surmized the economic possibilities of making things very small. Consider some of the problems of computing machines. It was not evident how to build computing machines—which in 1959 were very large and occupied much space—on a very small scale in a practical way. Feynman thought that we should be able to make them very small, make them of little wires and little elements—and by 'little' Feynman meant *really little*: for instance, wires should be ten or a hundred atoms in diameter, and the circuits should be a few thousand angstroms across. 'Everybody who has analyzed the logical theory of computers has come to the conclusion that the possibilities of computers are very interesting—if they could be made to be more complicated by several orders of magnitude. If they had millions of times as many elements, they could make judgments . . . If I look at your face I immediately recognize that I have seen it before. (At least I recognize that it is a *man* and not an *apple*.) Yet there is no machine which, with that speed, can take a picture of a face and say even that it is a man; and much less that it is the *same* man that you showed it before—unless it is exactly the *same* picture. If the face is changed: if I am closer to the face; if the light changes—I recognize it anyway. Now, this little computer I carry in my head is easily able to do that. The computers that we build are not able to do that. The number of elements in this bone box of mine are enormously greater than the number of elements in our 'wonderful' computers. But our mechanical computers are too big; the elements in this box are microscopic. I want to make some that are submicroscopic.' [18]

Ultimately, when our computers get faster and faster and more and more elaborate, we will have to make them smaller and smaller. But there's plenty of room (at the bottom) to make them smaller. There is nothing in the physical laws that says the computer elements cannot be made enormously smaller than they are now. In fact, there may be certain advantages.

How can we make such devices? What kind of processes would we use to make them? One possibility would be to consider (as in writing by putting atoms down in a certain arrangement) would be to evaporate the material, then evaporate the insulator next to it. Then, for the next layer, evaporate another position of a wire, another insulator, and so on. So, one simply keeps on evaporating until one has a block of material that has the elements—coils and condensers, transistors, and so on—of exceedingly fine dimensions.

We should not be afraid to consider the final question as to whether, ultimately ('in the great future'), we can arrange the atoms that we want; the very *atoms*, all the way down! 'What would happen if we could arrange the atoms one by one the way we want them (within reason, of course; you can't put them so that they are chemically unstable, for example)?' [19]

Up to now, we have been content to dig in the ground to find materials. We do all kinds of things with them on a large scale to get a pure substance with just so much impurity, and so on. But we must accept some atomic arrangement that nature gives us. 'We haven't got anything, say, with a "checkerboard" arrangement, or with impurity atoms arranged just exactly 1000 angstroms apart, or in some other peculiar pattern.' [19] What could we do with layered structures with just the right layers? What would the properties of materials be if we could really arrange atoms the way we want them? That would be very interesting to investigate theoretically. 'I can't see exactly what would happen, but I can hardly doubt that when we have some *control* of the arrangement of things on a small scale we will get an enormously greater range of possible properties that substances can have, and of different things we can do.' [19]

When we get to the very, very small world—say, circuits of seven atoms— we will have a lot of new things that would happen that represent completely new opportunities for design. Atoms on a small scale behave like *nothing* on a large scale, for they obey the laws of quantum mechanics. So, as we go down, and 'fiddle with the atoms down there', we are working with different laws than the ones that operate at the macroscopic level, and we can expect to do different things. We can manufacture in different ways. We can use, not just circuits, but some system involving quantized energy levels, or interactions of quantized spins, etc.

At the atomic level, there are new kinds of forces, and there will be new kinds of possibilities and effects. The problems of manufacture and reproduction of materials will be quite different. 'I am,' said Feynman, 'inspired by the biological phenomena in which chemical forces are used in a repetitious fashion to produce all kinds of weird effects (one of which is me [Richard Feynman]).' [20]

Feynman then announced that he would 'offer a prize of $1000 to the first guy who can take information on the page of a book and put it on an area 1/25 000 smaller on a linear scale in such a manner that it can be read by an electron microscope. And I want to offer another prize—if I can figure out how to phrase it so that I don't get into a mess of arguments about definitions—of $1000 to the first guy who makes an operating motor—a rotating electric motor which can be controlled from the outside and, not counting the lead-in wires, is only 1/64 inch cubed. I do not expect that such prizes will have to wait very long for claimants.' [20]

After this announcement, which was published in the February 1960 issue of Caltech's *Engineering and Science* magazine, Feynman was besieged by inventors of miniature motors; it was a rare day when Feynman was not interrupted in his office by someone eager to show him what usually turned out to be a very *large* small motor.

In November 1960, William McLellan, a senior engineer at Electro-Optical Systems in Pasadena, California, walked into Feynman's office in the Biology Department with *his* small motor. It looked like the same old story, because McLellan was carrying his invention in a big grocery carton. OK, said Feynman wearily, he would look at the thing—but there was no money in it for anybody; it had been his *intention* to set up the prize, but never got around to doing it.

This was all right with McLellan. It was a challenge that had set him to work on the problem anyway. Then he took a microscope out of the grocery carton and let Feynman look in to see the motor he had built. It had taken McLellan two and a half months of lunch hours to make it. The motor was 1/64 of an inch cubed, or about as big as a speck in one's eye. It weighed 250 micrograms, had thirteen parts, was built with the aid of a microscope, a watchmaker's lathe, and a toothpick, and it could be controlled from the outside. As Feynman watched, McLellan set the motor going.

Feynman and McLellan spent the better part of the afternoon operating the motor. It was after he got home that night that Feynman's conscience began to bother him. After all, the motor was *exactly* what he had asked for. 'So, I sent the guy a check for a thousand bucks.' [21]

Elated as he was over the little motor, Feynman was now worried about the *second* prize: another $1000 'to the first guy who can take the information on the page of a book and put it in an area 1/25 000 smaller in linear scale in such a manner that it can be read by an electron microscope.' Feynman expected any day to meet the man who had accomplished this particular feat. And daily, the thought would haunt him—because, in the meantime, Feynman got married (1960), bought a house, and, what with one thing and another, hadn't 'got another $1000.' *Engineering and Science* announced a public appeal 'to all inventors who are now at work trying to write small and collect the second Feynman Prize—TAKE YOUR TIME! WORK SLOWLY! RELAX!'[21]

The general reaction to Feynman's talk at the APS meeting was amusement. Most of the people who heard him thought that he was trying to be funny as usual; 'it simply took everybody by surprise'.[22] Actually, Feynman had always been interested in the limits that physics puts on the things one would like to do. When he theoretically probed the possibilities of what kind of 'room was there at the bottom', he conceived of a realm that is rapidly being realized in laboratories thirty years later: etching lines a few atoms wide with beams of electrons, building circuits on the scale of angstroms to make new kinds of computers, manipulating atoms to control the very properties of matter. This is the new science of 'nanotechnology'. Just as Feynman did, the nanotechnologists—who exploit the atomic scale for making new devices—credit their inspiration to molecular-scale processes and information systems of living things. Feynman's talk 'was so visionary that it didn't really connect with people until the technology caught up with it.'[23] Many of those who manipulate atoms using the scanning tunneling microscope (STM) did not know about Feynman's talk until after they got into the atom-moving business. As Don Eigler of the IBM Almaden Research Center in San Jose, California, who uses STM to manipulate atoms, recalled: 'I felt the ghost of Feynman behind me while I was reading, saying, "Look, I thought of these things 30 years ago." '[24]

The tiny circuits, lasers, mirrors, and mechanical devices that take shape at laboratories like the National Nanofabrication Facility at Cornell University, Ithaca, New York, are built layer by layer, often using higher-resolution versions of the techniques now commonplace in the microelectronics industry. For each layer, engineers transfer a pattern to the surface—usually silicon, gallium arsenide, or some other semiconductor—through stencil-like masks. Then they etch out the patterned region, deposit new materials on it, or modify it with beams of ions. Several iterations of the process yield completed devices: tiny technoscopes sculpted in high relief and criss-crossed with metal connections of varying conductivity.

In 1990, researchers at IBM spelled 'IBM' by lifting and depositing individual, supercooled xenon atoms on to a nickel substrate with a scanning tunneling microscope (STM). Less than a year later, Shigeyuki Hosoki, an electronics researcher at Hitachi Central Research Laboratory (HCRL) in Tokyo, carved 'PEACE '91 HCRL' into a sulfur medium using an STM—but unlike the IBM team, he did it at room temperature, without the need of a massive cooling system. Soon afterward, several other Japanese electronic equipment manufacturers moved in with further improvements on the US technique, reducing from hours to seconds the time needed to etch lines just a few atoms wide in silicon, thus boldly realizing Feynman's vision about there being 'plenty of room at the bottom'.[25]

20.4 Selecting school textbooks for science and mathematics

In 1963 Richard Feynman was still giving his lectures on physics for sophomores when one day Tom Harvey, who, as technician, assisted him in putting together the demonstrations, said to him: 'You ought to see what is happening to mathematics in schoolbooks! My daughter comes home with a lot of crazy stuff!'[26] Feynman did not pay much attention to what Harvey said, but the next day he got a call from Mr Norris, a well-known lawyer in Pasadena, who was then a member of the State Board of Education. Mr Norris asked Feynman if he would serve on the State Curriculum Commission, which had to choose new schoolbooks for the State of California. California had a law that all schoolbooks used by all the kids in all public schools of the state had to be chosen by the State Board of Education. So they had a committee, the Curriculum Commission, to examine the books and give them advice on which books to approve. As a successor to C. C. Trillingham, Los Angeles County Superintendent of Schools, Feynman became a member of the State Curriculum Commission in the fall of 1964.

Immediately he was swamped by mathematics books, several hundred pounds of which were delivered to his house. He had special shelves put in the basement of his house, in all about seventeen or eighteen feet of shelf space. As soon as Feynman agreed to become a member of the State Curriculum Commission, he immediately began to receive letters and telephone calls from book publishers. They all expressed the feeling that it was wonderful that a scientific person like him had joined the commission, and they wanted to give him any *extra* explanation that he might need about the books published by them. Feynman let them know that they did not have to explain; the books will speak for themselves.

Feynman represented the area comprising most of Los Angeles, except the city itself, which was represented by one Mrs Whiteside. Mrs Whiteside told Feynman how the members of the commission normally rated the new schoolbooks. They would get a relatively large number of copies of each book and would give them to various teachers and administrators in their school district. Then they would get reports back on what these people thought about the books. Feynman, however, felt that by reading the books himself he could make up his mind as to how the books looked to *him*, and he chose to read all the books carefully himself.

Feynman found that the choice had to be made from among the books submitted by the publishers and few really good books were submitted. His wife, Gweneth, recalled that during the period Feynman read and examined the books, loud noises of disapproval would emerge from the basement: 'it was like living over a volcano'.[27] The reason was that 'the books were so lousy. They were false. They were hurried. They would *try* to be rigorous but the definitions were not accurate. They weren't *smart* enough to understand what was meant by "rigor". They were faking it. They were teaching something they did not understand, and which was, in fact *useless*, at that time for the child.'[27]

The term 'new mathematics' was used a great deal in connection with this program. Many of the books went into considerable detail on subjects that are only of interest to pure mathematicians. Pure mathematicians have a point of view about the subject which is quite different from that of *users* of mathematics. A pure mathematician is very impractical; he is not interested in—in fact, he is purposely *uninterested*—in the meaning of symbols, letters, and ideas. He is only interested in logical interconnections between axioms, while the user of mathematics has to understand the connection of mathematics to the real world.

Although this was a new program of mathematics teaching, it was questionable and unwise to use 'new mathematics', in the sense of very modern mathematics, for the purpose of teaching. Most people—grocery clerks, for instance—use a great deal of simple arithmetic in daily life. Mathematics used in daily life, even in the sophisticated fields of engineering—such as the design of radar antenna systems, in determining the position of orbits of satellites, in statistics, economics, and inventory control, in the design of electrical machinery, in chemical research, and even in the most esoteric forms of theoretical physics—is really old mathematics, developed before 1920. A great deal of applied mathematics and mathematics used in the more advanced work in theoretical physics, for example, was not developed by mathematicians alone, but to a large extent by theoretical or mathematical physicists themselves. The great advances made by the pure mathematicians have been in basic definitions of fundamental concepts and in seeking the interconnections between one branch of mathematics and another in a logical manner.

Take, for example, the subject of 'sets'. Almost every textbook under examination discussed the subject of sets, but the material of sets and applications of set theory were never used. The only thing that was said was that 'the concept of sets is very familiar'. However, if the book makes no use of this concept anywhere, why bring it up at all. Feynman found that already in the first-grade book on arithmetic, there occurred the sentence: 'Find out if the set of lollypops is equal in number to the set of girls.' What is clearly meant is: 'Find out if there are just enough lollypops for girls.' The previous question, in the language of sets, doesn't say any more. Later on, when the special language, such as that of set theory, becomes necessary and desirable, it should be taught, but before that the goal should be clarity.

Every subject which is present in the textbook should be presented in such a way that the purpose of the presentation should be made evident. The utility of the subject and its relevance to the world must be made clear to every pupil.

Our efforts to find new books and modify the teaching of arithmetic should be directed to make it more interesting and easier for students to learn those attitudes of mind and that spirit of analysis which are required for efficient understanding and use of mathematics in engineering, science, and other fields.

The main change required is to remove the rigidity of thought found in the older arithmetic books. It is of no real advantage to introduce a new subject to be taught in the old way. What is the best method to obtain the solution to a new problem? The answer is: any way that works. There may be several ways of adding 17 and 15, but there is only one correct answer. The dissatisfaction with the old textbook is not that any of the methods to teach addition to children are unsatisfactory; they are all good. The trouble is, there are so few methods allowed that only a rigid and formal knowledge of arithmetic can result.

Problems should be put to children in many different forms. They should be allowed to guess and get at the answers in any way they wish, in terms of those particular facts which they happen to memorize. Of course, it is necessary as time goes on to memorize ordinary methods of making additions, multiplications, and divisions, in addition to being allowed a freedom about the solution of various problems that are given to them.

When we come to consider the words and definitions which children must learn, we must be careful not to teach 'just' words. It is possible to give an illusion of knowledge by teaching the technical words which someone uses in a field (and which sound unusual to ordinary ears) without at the same time teaching any ideas or facts using these words.

Many of the mathematics books that are suggested now for adoption are full of such nonsense—of carefully and precisely defined words that are used by pure mathematicians in their most subtle and difficult analyses, and are used by nobody else. The words which are used should be as close as possible to those in everyday language; or, as a minimum requirement, they should be taught the same words used, *at least* by the users of mathematics in science and engineering.

As for the emphasis on 'precise language' in the 'new math curriculum', it is more important to use *clear* language than *precise* language. Pure mathematics is an abstraction from the real world, and pure mathematics does have a special language for dealing with its own special and technical subjects. But this precise language is not precise in any sense if you deal with real objects of the world, and it is only pedantic and quite confusing to use it unless there are are some special subtleties which have to be carefully distinguished.

Consider the subject of geometry. It is necessary in geometry to learn many new words related to mathematics. For example, one must learn what a triangle is, a square, a straight line, an angle, a curved line. But one should not be satisfied solely to learn words. At least somewhere, one should learn *facts* about the objects to which the words refer, such as the area of the various figures; the relation of one figure to another; how to measure the angles; possibly the fact that the sum of the angles of a triangle is 180°; possibly the theorem of Pythagoras; or maybe the rules that make triangles congruent; or other geometrical facts.

In order to make the 'new' mathematics worthwhile, there must be freedom of thought; we do not want to teach just words; subjects should not be introduced without explaining the purpose or reason for employing certain concepts; the material should be used to discover something interesting.

In 1965, Feynman was again made a member of the State Curriculum Commission, this time to examine books on science. He thought that the science would be different, but it was the same as math. Something that looked good at first would then turn out to be horrifying. For example, there was a book that started out with four pictures: first there was a wind-up toy; then there was an automobile; then there was a boy riding a bicycle; then something else. Under each picture, it was asked: 'What makes it go?'

Feynman thought, 'I know what it is: They're going to talk about mechanics, how springs work inside the toy; about chemistry, how the engine of the automobile works; about biology, about how muscles work.' On the next page, each time they said: "Energy makes it go".'[28] It made no sense. Feynman heard later that the 'energy-makes-it-go-book' was going to be recommended by the Curriculum Commission to the State Board of Education. 'So when I saw all these horrifying books with the same kind of trouble as the math books had, I saw my volcano process starting again. Since I was exhausted from reading all the math books, and discouraged from it all being a wasted effort, I couldn't face another year of that, and had to resign.'[29]

The man who replaced Feynman on the commission said, 'That ["energy-makes-it-go"] book was recommended by sixty-five engineers at such-and-such aircraft company.' Feynman didn't doubt that some of the engineers may have been pretty good, but sixty-five engineers represent a wide range of ability, and necessarily some pretty poor guys. 'It was once again the problem of *averaging* the length of the emperor's nose. The question was, what was the length of the Emperor of China's nose? To find out you go all over the country asking people what they think the length of the Emperor of China's nose is, and you *average* it. And that would be very "accurate" because you averaged so many people. But it's no way to find out; when you have a very wide range of people who contribute without carefully looking at it, you don't improve your knowledge of the situation by averaging.'[30]

Notes and References

1. Shimoda, Wang, and Townes, *Phy. Rev.* **102**, 1308 (1956); Gordon, Zeiger, and Townes, *Phys. Rev.* **95**, 282 (1954).

2. R.P. Feynman, F.L. Vernon and R.W. Hellwarth, Geometrical representation of Schrödinger equation for solving maser problems. *J. Appl. Phys.* **28**, 49 (1957).

3. Abella, Hartman, and Kurnit, *Phys. Rev. Lett.* **13**, 567 (1964).

4. R.P. Feynman and F.L. Vernon, *Ann. Physics* **24**, 118 (1963).

5. R.P. Feynman, Interviews and conversations with Jagdish Mehra, in Pasadena, California, January 1988.

6. R.W. Hellwarth, Interview with Jagdish Mehra, University of Southern California, Los Angeles, 31 August 1990.

7. R.P. Feynman, *Phys. Rev.* **97**, 660 (1955).

8. Feynman, Hellwarth, Iddings, and Platzman (FHIP), *Phys. Rev.* **127**, 1004 (1962).

9. R.P. Feynman and F.L. Vernon, Ref. 4, p. 119.

10. R.P. Feynman, *Rev. Mod. Phys.* **20**, 367 (1948); *Phys. Rev.* **80**, 440 (1950).

11. R.S. Edgar, R.P. Feynman, *et al.*, Mapping experiments with r mutants of bacteriophage T4D. *Genetics* **47**, 179 (1962); R.P. Feynman, Reciprocal suppression of mutants within one cistron. *Caltech Annual Report*, 1960, Item 58.

12. R.S. Edgar, Personal communication to Jagdish Mehra, 4 October 1990.

13. F.H.C. Crick *et al.*, *Nature* **192**, 1227 (1961).

14. R.P. Feynman, There's plenty of room at the bottom. *Engineering and Science*, February 1960.

15. R.P. Feynman, Ref. 14, p. 22.

16. R.P. Feynman, Ref. 14, p. 23.

17. R.P. Feynman, Ref. 14, p. 24.

18. R.P. Feynman, Ref. 14, p. 25.

19. R.P. Feynman, Ref. 14, p. 34.

20. R.P. Feynman, Ref. 14, p. 36.

21. R.P. Feynman, *Engineering and Science*, December 1960.

22. Paul Shlichta of Crystal Research in San Pedro, California, then (in 1960) a materials scientist at the Jet Propulsion Laboratory in Pasadena, California. Quoted in *Science* **254**, 29 November 1991, p. 1300.

23. R. Merkle, Xerox Palo Alto Research Center, San Jose, California, *Science* **254**, 29 November 1991, p. 1300.

24. D. Eigler, *Science*, 29 November 1991, p. 1300.

25. Report in *Science*, 29 November 1991, p. 1300.

26. R.P. Feynman, Ref. 5.

27. R.P. Feynman, *SYJMF*, p. 292.

28. R.P. Feynman, *SYJMF*, p. 297.

29. R.P. Feynman, *SYJMF*, p. 297.

30. R.P. Feynman, *SYJMF*, p. 296.

21

'The only law of nature I could lay a claim to': the theory of weak interactions

'As I thought about it, as I beheld it in my mind's eye, the goddamn thing was sparkling, it was shining brightly! As I looked at it, I felt that it was the first time, and the only time, in my scientific career that I knew a law of nature that no one else knew. Now, it wasn't as beautiful a law as Dirac's [discovery of the relativistic equation for the electron] or Maxwell's [equations of the electromagnetic field], but my equation for beta decay was a bit like that. It was the first time that I discovered a new law, rather than a more efficient method of calculating from someone else's theory (as I had done with the path-integral method for Schrödinger's equation and the diagram technique in quantum electrodynamics) or a little solution to a problem (as in the case of the polaron or even the superfluidity of liquid helium). This discovery was completely new, although, of course, I learned later that others had thought of it about the same time or a little bit before, but that did not make any difference. At the time I was doing it, I felt the thrill of a new discovery! It wasn't as wondrous as Maxwell's equations, but it was good and I was satisfied to sign it. I thought, "Now I have completed myself!"' [1]

This sense of thrill, of fulfilment, in discovering a 'law of nature'[2] concerned the so-called vector–axial vector (V–A) law of weak interactions, which Richard Feynman discovered in summer 1957. With regard to Feynman's deep feeling concerning the discovery of a law of nature, Gell-Mann remarked: 'Richard [Feynman] was always saying that he hadn't found anything which was a law of nature, he had just calculated things with other people's laws, which was mostly true. Why he felt so bad about it I don't know. As I have pointed out in my article [in *Physics Today*, February 1989], his new [path-integral] point of view on quantum mechanics may turn out to be a very important law; it may turn out to be more important than the usual way of formulating quantum mechanics. But anyway he was obsessed with this notion that he had to find a law. [In the case of V–A], it seems an unreasonable conclusion that the whole thing was really so original since Felix Boehm had told him that several of us already had this idea.' [2]

As we shall see, the phenomenon of beta decay has been connected with the fundamental laws of nature throughout its history, and it has been full of puzzles, subtleties, and surprises. Moreover, during its almost hundred-year-old history—since the discovery of radioactivity by Antoine Henri Becquerel on 1 March 1896—the names of many eminent physicists have been associated with it. Even as Feynman worked to understand the law of beta decay, unbeknown to him some other physicists were engaged upon the same problem and came independently to the same result. Some of these physicists—such as Murray Gell-Mann, E. C. George Sudarshan, and Robert E. Marshak—shared with him the excitement of that discovery. In this chapter we shall discuss how the problem of the law of beta decay arose and how it was solved.

21.1 Historical introduction[3]

The work of Antoine Henri Becquerel, Pierre and Marie Curie, Ernest Rutherford, and Paul Villard, established the existence of the phenomena of radioactivity. Three kinds of radiation—alpha, beta, and gamma rays—are emitted spontaneously by a radioactive atom, such as uranium. Alpha rays were found to be the nuclei of helium atoms, beta rays were electrons, and gamma rays consisted of high energy electromagnetic radiation. The existence of the atomic nucleus was first discovered by Rutherford in 1911. In the autumn of 1912, Rutherford suggested that the origin of beta radioactivity consisted in the expulsion of an electron orbiting around the nucleus, but it was Niels Bohr who gave the correct answer by stating that 'the nucleus is the seat of the expulsion of high speed beta particles'.[4]

In the beginning the pioneers in the field of radioactivity were confronted with the fact that the explanation of beta-particle emission was a most complicated problem, and they had neither the experimental facilties to work with nor any theory of the interaction of beta and gamma radiation with matter to guide them. The first notion which they obtained about electrons emitted from radium and other radioactive bodies was that electrons were projected with a large range of velocities, from about zero up to the velocity of light. Thus, immediately, the first great crisis involved the understanding of the continuous distribution of the beta spectrum. Well-known physicists like James Chadwick, Lise Meitner, Charles D. Ellis, and William Wooster all played an important role in identifying and establishing the origin of the continuous beta spectrum.

By about 1920, the old quantum theory was quite well established and the idea of discrete energy states was quite generally accepted. In 1922 Lise Meitner raised the important point that an atomic nucleus, which is probably quantized, should not emit electrons of varying energy.[5] What then should be the cause of the continuous energy distribution of electrons? Most physicists thought that all electrons had the same energy of disintegration, equal to the upper limit of the spectrum, and that after expulsion from the nucleus they lost energy by collisions with the outer atomic electrons. Only C. D. Ellis held on to his belief in the continuous distribution of primary beta rays. This idea was eventually established by determining the average energy of disintegration of the beta emitter in a microcalorimeter in the experiments of Ellis and Wooster[6] and Meitner and Orthmann[7] Thus, by that time, the various components of the beta spectra had been correctly identified and the theoretical difficulty of explaining the continuous distribution of the disintegration electrons was fully understood.

As soon as the experimental evidence established beyond doubt that the continuous distribution of beta rays is an intrinsic characteristic of the disintegration electrons, the physicists realized that they were faced with something really puzzling. Wolfgang Pauli had closely followed the experimental arguments with the greatest interest; he was convinced that the microcalorimetric measurements of Meitner and Orthmann were conclusive and deeply significant.

By about that time quantum mechanics had also been gradually taking hold of physics, and the understanding of the spins and statistics of nuclei was becoming clear. However, protons and electrons were still regarded as the fundamental constituents of nuclei. Thus, for example, ^{14}N should consist of 21 odd particles: 14 protons and 7 electrons. According to Ehrenfest and Oppenheimer's theory,[8] the ^{14}N nucleus must obey Fermi–Dirac statistics. Surprisingly, the determination of the statistics of ^{14}N by Heitler and Herzberg[9] revealed that it obeyed Bose–Einstein statistics, contrary to expectation, and therefore provided a strong argument against the proton–electron hypothesis of nuclear structure. The considerations of the spins of nuclei also led to the same conclusion, and it became clear that electrons would have to be excluded from the nucleus.

Niels Bohr was also very perplexed by the observed continuous distribution of the beta spectrum. In his Faraday Lecture delivered before the Fellows of the Chemical Society in 1930, Bohr declared: 'At the present stage of atomic theory, however, we may say that we have no argument, either empirical or theoretical, for upholding the energy principle [the principle of conservation of energy] in the case of β-ray disintegrations, and are even led to complications and difficulties in trying to do so . . . . Still, just as the account of those aspects of atomic constitution essential for the explanation of the ordinary physical and chemical properties implies a renunciation of the classical idea of causality, the feature of atomic stability, still deeper-lying, responsible for the existence and properties of atomic nuclei, may force us to renounce the very idea of energy balance.'[10]

As early as December 1930, Wolfgang Pauli had considered the possibility of explaining beta disintegration as a three-body process. In a letter, dated 4 December 1930, addressed to Hans Geiger and Lise Meitner (who were attending a radioactivity conference in Tübingen, and whom he addressed as 'My dear radioactive ladies and gentlemen'), Pauli pointed out that in beta decay, based entirely on the consideration of spin and statistics, not only was the energy apparently not conserved, but also spin and statistics were not conserved. Consider the well-known example of the beta decay of RaE:

$$^{210}_{83}\text{RaE} \rightarrow ^{210}_{84}\text{RaF} + \beta^-.$$

The nuclear angular momentum of RaE (mass number 210) and RaF (mass number also 210) are integral multiples of $\hbar$ (it is known that they are $\hbar$ and 0 respectively). Thus the possible change of nuclear angular momentum during the transition must be an integral amount (in this case $I = \hbar$). On the other hand, the intrinsic angular momentum is clearly not conserved in beta decay if the beta particle is the only particle emitted. In order to save the situation, Pauli went on to propose 'the outlandish idea' (for those times) of the existence of a very penetrating neutral particle of vanishingly small mass, obeying Fermi–Dirac statistics, in the beta decay. Pauli called this particle the 'neutron'; it was later called 'neutrino', the 'little neutral one' by Enrico Fermi.[11]

Pauli was 'most modest' in his plea for a hearing. He wrote: 'Nothing ventured, nothing gained. And the gravity of the situation with regard to the continuous beta spectrum is illuminated by my respected predecessor in office [Peter Debye]—"Oh, it is best not to think about it at all, like the new taxes"— so dear radioactive folks, put it to the test and judge.' Pauli himself did not attend the Tübingen meeting on account of a famous annual ball at the ETH (the Swiss Federal Institute of Technology) at Hotel Baur-au-lac.[12]

Pauli made public his proposal of the neutrino at the American Physical Society meeting in Pasadena in June 1931, but this hypothesis of a new undetectable particle met with skepticism, as it was too radical for physicists to accept with ease.[13] In October of the same year, at the Rome Conference on Nuclear Physics, neither Bohr nor Pauli mentioned the new possibility publicly. However, Pauli and Fermi discussed beta decay at length at the Rome meeting, and Fermi was at once attracted to the neutrino hypothesis.

The discovery of the positron by Carl Anderson in December 1931 and of the neutron by James Chadwick in January 1932 marked the beginning of the unravelling of the crisis that had prevailed since 1929. However, the issue of the continuous beta spectrum and the problems connected with it remained unresolved throughout the year 1932. In the latter half of 1932 Heisenberg, in his theory of nuclear structure, considered the neutron to be a composite of a proton and an electron, and said this about beta decay: 'It will be assumed that under suitable circumstances (the neutron) can break up into a proton and an electron, in which case the conservation laws of energy and momentum probably do not apply. . . .'[14] He went on to say that 'The failure of the energy law in beta decay proves the inapplicability of the present quantum mechanics to the structure of the neutron.'[15]

Soon, however, the neutron–proton hypothesis of nuclear structure fitted into the whole picture beautifully. The big breakthrough came at the seventh Solvay Conference at Brussels in October 1933. Pauli was greatly encouraged by the favorable developments, and put aside any doubts he may have had about the neutrino hypothsis.[16] By then the neutrino was assumed to have an intrinsic spin of $\frac{1}{2}\hbar$, to obey Fermi–Dirac statistics, to carry no electric charge, and to possess only vanishingly small mass. With these characteristics, the neutrino became a full-fledged member of the family of elementary particles.

21.2 Fermi's theory of beta decay

Enrico Fermi was also present at the seventh Solvay Conference in Brussels, and soon after this meeting he conceived and, a few months later, published, his famous theory of beta decay.[17] Also present at the Solvay Conference discussions was Francis Perrin, who independently wrote a paper giving the correct statistical weight factor of the states soon after the conference; furthermore, he concluded even at that early stage that the neutrino rest mass must be either very small or zero.[18]

In his greatest discovery in theoretical physics, Fermi employed the language of second-quantized field theory to discuss beta decay. He wrote: 'Electrons (or neutrinos) can be created and can disappear.... The [formalism for] the system of heavy and light particles must be chosen such that in every transition from neutron to proton there is associated a creation of an electron and a neutrino. To every inverse process, the change of a proton into a neutron, the disappearance of an electron and a neutrino should be associated.'[19]

By making use of Pauli's neutrino hypothesis, Fermi formulated the theory of beta decay, much like his earlier contributions to quantum electrodynamics.[20] In Fermi's theory of beta decay, the beta particle is created at the moment of emission just as a photon is created at the moment of emission from an electron. The neutrino is also created at the moment of emission. We may express β^- decay as

$$n \rightarrow p + e^- + v \tag{21.1}$$

and β^+ decay as

$$p \rightarrow n + e^+ + v. \tag{21.2}$$

All these five particles (p, n, $e^\pm$, v) are known to have spin $\frac{1}{2}$ and to obey Fermi–Dirac statistics and therefore could be represented by a quantized Dirac field. From the Dirac relativistic theory, for every type of spin-$\frac{1}{2}$ elementary particle there exists a pair of a particle and its corresponding antiparticle with charge and magnetic moment of opposite sign, such as an electron and its antiparticle positron. Naturally, the neutrino and its counterpart, the antineutrino, would be expected to have this property.

Whether there is an intrinsic difference between the neutrino and the antineutrino was not known at the outset.

The absorption of a normal particle is equivalent to the creation of an antiparticle, because the absorbed normal particle can be taken from a state of negative energy which corresponds to the creation of an antiparticle, and vice-versa. For mathematical convenience, it is desirable to describe $\beta^{\pm}$ decay as two particles absorbed and two particles created. Thus, instead of equations (21.1), and (21.2) we have, for β^- decay,

$$n + \bar{\nu} \rightarrow p + e^-. \tag{21.3}$$

and, for β^+ decay,

$$p + e^- \rightarrow n + \nu. \tag{21.4}$$

The neutrino ν emitted in β^+ decay is designated as the 'particle' and the one accompanying β^- decay is the 'antiparticle' (the antineutrino).

The direct field coupling between $p\bar{n}$ and $e^+\nu$ is assumed to be a point interaction with $p\bar{n}$ as source and $e^+\nu$ as lepton field such as is exemplified by electromagnetic interaction where a charge can interact with a light quantum only when they are at the same place. Beta interaction is then due to a Hamiltonian interaction term

$$H = g(\bar{\psi}_p \psi_n \bar{\psi}_e \psi_\nu + \bar{\psi}_n \psi_p \bar{\psi}_\nu \psi_e), \tag{21.5}$$

where g is the coupling constant which measures the strength of beta interaction, analogous to e (electron charge) in the electromagnetic case. Here ψ_p, ψ_n, ψ_e, ψ_ν are the field operators that destroy a proton, a neutron, an electron, a neutrino, or create an antiproton, an anti neutron, a positron, and an antineutrino, respectively; similarly $\bar{\psi}_p$, $\bar{\psi}_n$, $\bar{\psi}_e$, $\bar{\psi}_\nu$ create the respective normal particles or destroy the respective antiparticles. In writing this expression the complex conjugate quantity has been added since the Lagrangian term must be Hermitian. The first term in equation (21.5) represents β^- decay and the second term corresponds to β^+ decay.

The field operator ψ is a spinor with four components. However, since the interaction term is to be a scalar, it should be independent of the Lorentz frame used. In this connection, Pauli had shown that five, and only five, relativistically covariant quantities could be constructed under proper Lorentz transformation. These five covariants behave like scalar (S), vector (V), tensor (T), axial vector (A), and pseudoscalar (P). Fermi used only the vector interaction (V) as suggested by electrodynamics, and now it seems that he had prophesied the correct one, at least for the Fermi type of interaction. The transition rate (or half-life) is given by

$$\frac{2\pi}{\hbar} \left| g \int \bar{\psi}_p \bar{\psi}_e \psi_\nu \psi_n \right|^2 \rho(E), \tag{21.6}$$

where $\rho(E)$ represents the energy density of the final state.

In the following twenty years, from 1934 to 1955 or so, the weak interactions were studied in detail; but the next really important developments occurred only after the Sixth Rochester Conference on High Energy Nuclear Physics (1956).

21.3 Question of parity and the theta–tau puzzle[21]

For a long time, classical physics had been guided by symmetry principles. The classical explanation of the conservation of linear momentum in isolated systems is the invariance of the Hamiltonian under a translation of coordinates, while the conservation of angular momentum is due to the invariance of the Hamiltonian under a rotation of the coordinate system in which the observer makes his measurements. The world, i.e. nature, should be independent of the translations and rotations of the coodinate system in which we make measurements. The experimental verification for these laws was found long before their interpretation through spatial symmetries was discovered. Although these conservation laws form a self-contained picture of nature, they had to be experimentally confirmed.

When quantum mechanics was developed, the theory of unitary transformations immediately confirmed that quantum mechanical linear and angular momenta are similarly conserved if the quantum mechanical Hamiltonian is invariant under translations and rotations, just as in classical physics and as one expects from Bohr's correspondence principle. No experiments were done to test these ideas in the quantum mechanical case; they were just taken for granted. As we have noted, Pauli even invoked these fundamental classical ideas to postulate the existence of a neutrino to explain the missing momentum and energy in beta decay; it was a radical idea at the time to propose the existence of a particle that had no mass or electric charge.

Another additional symmetry of space, the invariance of the Hamiltonian under *inversion* of coordinates, i.e. the invariance of the Hamiltonian under the transformation $r \to -r$ (where r is the position vector), has an important quantum mechanical consequence: the conservation of the quantum number called 'parity'. This can be stated by saying that the Hamiltonian is invariant under a reflection in a mirror, that is, in natural phenomena there is a symmetry between right and left. Unlike the conservation of linear and angular momentum, the parity quantum number *does not* have a classical analog; the concept of parity implies *intrinsic* parity, i.e. the behavior of the particle's intrinsic wave function under the inversion of coordinates.

In 1954–56, particle physicists were actively engaged in trying to understand the so-called theta–tau $(\theta-\tau)$ puzzle. They clearly assumed that all interactions of elementary particles satisfied the three symmetry properties of invariance under rotations, translations, and inversions of coordinates; it was assumed that space was isotropic, without having preferred points, directions, or handedness (no distinction between right and left)—one could not distinguish one point on a straight line from another, or one point on a circle from another, or a right-handed screw from a left-handed one. Thus for instance, Newton's or Maxwell's equations were clearly invariant under inversions, and classical dynamics and electromagnetism clearly conserved parity.

In April 1956 there took place the Sixth Rochester Conference on High Energy Nuclear Physics in Rochester, New York. During the previous few years particle physicists had been excited about the concept of associated production of V-particles, which was later explained, independently, by Gell-Mann and Nishijima as the conservation of the quantum number called 'strangeness'. Their scheme was simple and elegant; it suddenly explained a vast amount of experimental data. In those days, it was popular to name the particles after their decay modes. In particular, the particles θ and τ (later to be called the two decay modes of the K-meson or the kaon), had been discovered and were known to decay as follows:

$$\tau^+ \to 2\pi^+ + \pi^-, \qquad \tau^- \to 2\pi^- + \pi^+,$$

and

$$\theta^+ \to \pi^+ + \pi^0, \qquad \theta^- \to \pi^- + \pi^0,$$

as well as

$$\theta^0 \to 2\pi^0.$$

These decay modes were studied extensively and the experimental situation was as follows:

(1) The masses of both θ and τ, within small errors, were equal.

(2) In any production reaction, at all production angles and momenta, the ratio of θ to τ had the same constant value; no matter where one looked, the ratio of θ to τ was invariable.

(3) Within experimental errors, the lifetimes of both θ and τ were the same.

(4) Since the wave function for two identical bosons must be symmetric under particle exchange, and the pions have spin 0, the conservation of angular momentum required that θ^0, since it decayed into two identical pions, should have angular momentum $J=0, 2, 4$, etc.

(5) The Dalitz–Fabri plot[22] for the decay of τ into three pions yielded a distribution compatible with phase space, indicating that the matrix element corresponded to $l=0$ and $L=0$, where l is the relative angular momentum between the like-charged pions and L is the angular momentum between the center of mass of this pair with the unlike-charged pions. Since the pions have spin 0, this tells us that θ and τ can have the

same spin, $J=0$, since the spin of τ is given by $J=L+l$. Thus the simplest possibility of nature, that they both have have spin 0, is realized.

If the facts (1) to (5) were all that was known, one would conclude that θ and τ must be the same particle and their *intrinsic parities* must also be the same quantum mechanically. Hence we must argue that:

(6) Since the θ particle decays into two identical pseudoscalar pions (the parity of the pion having been determined by studying the absorption of slow negative pions in the reaction $\pi^- + d = n + n$), the intrinsic parity of the θ meson will be

$$P_\theta = (-1)^l \times (-1)^2 = (-1)^l,$$

where $l\ (=J)=0, 2, 4, \ldots$. Thus the parity of the θ meson is $+1$, and is compatible with J^P (spin parity) assigment 0^+.

On the other hand, the parity of τ, a three-body decay, is given by

$$P_\tau = (-1)^l \times (-1)^L \times (-1)^3 = -(-1)^{l+L}.$$

For both l and L to be zero, P must be equal to -1, and has the (spin parity) assignment 0^-. Thus the intrinsic parities of θ and τ are different, and they cannot be the the same particle, since they have different parity quantum numbers.

This, then, was the well-known θ–τ puzzle. Why are there such similarities between θ and τ particles, as expressed in points (1) to (5), yet nature, through point (6), contrives to make them different?

During 1955–56, Gell-Mann and Lee and Yang had tried to reconcile the above facts by the introduction of 'parity doublets'. In essence, they suggested that the puzzle could be solved by the introduction of a *strong interaction* symmetry, used *only* for strange particles, in which each strange particle had its own doublet particle, identical in all respects except that its parity was opposite to its partner's parity, i.e. there existed $\Lambda, \Lambda', \Sigma, \Sigma', K, K'$, etc. In this scheme, τ was to be K and θ to be K'. However, if this assignment were to hold, in addition to a new strong interaction symmetry that acted *only* for strange particles (but there was no evidence for the doubling of hyperons, i.e. particles that are baryons—like protons and neutrons—but which are heavier than protons and possess the property designated by the quantum number called 'strangeness'), there had to exist a second miracle: they had to have the same lifetimes. Other less radical suggestions that were made were ruled out by the more and more accurate experimental data that were coming in, and the points (1) to (6) summarized the experimental situation regarding the θ–τ puzzle in the spring of 1956, and it was debated all around at the 1956 Rochester Conference.

As Martin Block recalled: 'By pure chance . . . , I was assigned to room with Richard Feynman, whom I had personally not met before. The first evening that I met him, just before we were ready to go to bed, I suggested to Feynman that θ and τ were really the same particle, and that parity *was not* conserved in the weak interactions. Feynman was ready to tell me how dumb I was and go to bed, when he thought for a moment. It turned out that we discussed the subject until the small hours of the morning, in a most exciting and stimulating way, as only Feynman could make possible.'[21]

21.4 Richard Feynman and the problem of weak interactions

Enter Feynman. Let us hear from Feynman directly about his involvement and discovery in the theory of weak interactions, just as he elaborated it in conversations in January 1988, about three weeks before his death:[23] 'There was the famous problem of the theta–tau (θ–τ) puzzle, which was that there seemed to be two particles, one of which disintegrated into three pions and the other into two pions. Strangely enough, these two particles seemed to have the same mass and seemed to be produced in the same proportion all the time. Now these had to be two [different] particles, because according to the law of parity conservation, that laws [of nature] should be symmetrical from right to left, the same particle cannot disintegrate into three pions and also two pions.

'We were discussing this θ–τ puzzle and that night I was sharing a room with Martin Block, an experimenter, and he said to me: "Hey, you! What is this big deal about the parity thing? Maybe they are the same particle and this [conservation of parity] is not right. Since it fits everything, they are the same particle. What would be so bad if parity were not conserved?"

'So I started to think, and since I am always intimidated by everybody else, I said: "Well, I am not an expert. (There are experts like Lee and Yang, guys who work out all this stuff, with γ_5's and what not.) It would mean that you would define right and left physically—by phenomena in physics—but I don't know whether there's anything really wrong with that altogether." So I said, "I'm not so sure. I don't know why it's necessarily wrong. It's just a guess that maybe we have [a violation of parity]. I don't know, but ask the experts. Why don't you ask?"

'He [Martin Block] said, "Will you ask them tomorrow?" I said, "What the hell! It's your idea; you ask them." Because I thought it was a good idea. A real possibility. So he said, "No, they wouldn't pay any attention to me. If you were to ask they would pay some attention." I said, "All right, I'll ask."

'So the next day we were at the meeting and we were discussing the θ–τ puzzle again. Finally, Oppenheimer said something like, "Now it's time to [open] our minds and to think of new ideas." So I thought that this was the right opportunity. And I got up and said: "I'm asking this question for Martin Block. Could it be that θ and τ are different parity states of the same particle which has no definite parity, i.e. that parity is not conserved. That is, does nature have a way of defining right- or left-handedness uniquely?"[24]

'Now the reason I said that was because I thought it was a dramatic idea and I didn't want him [Martin Block] to lose any credit for thinking of it. That's why I said that. Murray [Gell-Mann] always teases me by saying: "You said that because you had such a crazy idea that you didn't have the guts to admit it to yourself. And so you said [that] you were asking it for Block." No. It was the other way. I was asking it for Block because I thought it was a possible idea, [and] I wanted to make sure that Block got credit for it. So I said it that way, and then asked the question: "What would happen if parity were wrong? What would be wrong with that in physics?"

'[Yang] answered something complicated about matrices and operators and what not, and I didn't understand it. [Actually, what Yang said was that he and Lee had looked into this matter without arriving at any definite conclusions.] "Wigner has been aware of the possible existence of two states of opposite parity, degenerate with respect to each other because of space-time transformation properties. So perhaps a particle having both parities could exist. But how could it decay, if one continues to believe that there is absolute invariance with respect to space–time transformations? Perhaps one could say that parity conservation, or else time-inversion invariance, could be violated. Perhaps the weak interactions could all come from this same source, a violation of space-time symmetries. The most attractive way out is the nonsensical idea that perhaps a particle is emitted which has no mass, charge, and energy–momentum but only carries away some strange space-time transformation properties."[25]

'Block asked, "What did he say?" I said, "I don't understand what he said. For my money it's still possible." Block told me later that he went home on a plane with [T.D.] Lee, and he worked on Lee and explained back and forth his point of view to show him that it really was a possibility and to argue about it to convince him to investigate it, but Lee didn't accept it. But I can't vouch for it [that it's true] because I wasn't there.

'Why didn't I investigate it myself? Because I had this intimidating feeling that this stuff was something for the experts to handle, because I didn't know how to handle parity inversions and CPT was always confusing me. I don't think anybody is going to believe that I was confused about such simple things all the time. Anyhow, they all think I'm smart. That's one part of the story, and that's [quite] a story by itself.'[23]

Feynman continued: 'Then Lee and Yang got into it and tried to figure out the consequences and made some predictions from it [about the violation of parity conservation in weak interactions].[26] Then the question arose: What were the laws of the [weak] interaction?

'We had another conference at Rochester [15–19 April 1957] and Lee gave me a copy of the paper that he was going to talk about at this meeting.[27] I was visiting my sister at that time; she lived [nearby] in Syracuse. I was holding [this paper and the paper of Lee and Yang[26]] and said to her: "This is all so complicated. I don't understand all this stuff." And she said to me: 'No, what you mean is not that you don't understand it. You didn't invent it. If you sat down like a graduate student and quietly went through the paper, line by line, you'd understand it." I said, "Maybe you're right."

'So I went upstairs the day before [the session] and went through the paper line by line and I got excited. I saw a combination of $(1 + \gamma_5)$'s, which I had noticed in some other connection when I had been doing something earlier, and I saw them [Lee and Yang] writing $1 + \gamma_5$ for the muon, and I realized that the right theory must be that it's $1 + \gamma_5$ for all the particles—the muon, the electron, the neutrino, whatever. I didn't realize something else, which I realized later, that they had written $f(1 + \gamma_5)$ for muon decay, and then said that f was 1. They had determined that f was 1 empirically, by the shape of the spectrum. Then I really had a prediction. I was going to say that it had to be $1 + \gamma_5$ for every wave function because that was a way of simplifying the equation [the Klein–Gordon equation] which I knew about. I proposed that it be $1 + \gamma_5$ for all wave functions. I didn't realize even that I was making a prediction about what [they were] getting empirically. But that's not the point. I went to the meeting the next day, but I wasn't scheduled to speak at the meeting.

'At Rochester, Kenneth Case had a ten to fifteen minute paper [on the 'Majorana theory of the neutrino', in Session IX on Strange Particles and Weak Interactions, pp. IX 39–42], and he said he would give me five minutes of his time, which was very nice, because I had demolished his theorem [concerning pseudoscalar and pseudovector meson coupling] earlier on [see Section 13.4]. But he was very nice. And I gave a quick outline of my ideas.[28] Now I knew that it would work with neutron decay, because I would be getting V (vector) and A (axial vector) and the neutron [decay] was known to be S (scalar) and T (tensor) by the experts. I'll never listen to the experts again!

'So I explained how it all worked with the muon–pion decay, electron, and all this stuff—and then said that the theory can't be completely right because it's all screwed up when it comes to the neutron [decay]. There were a certain number of problems about the neutron and I tried to solve them in some awkward way. Not correctly. And that was it, and it turned out that all the spins were in the directions I had guessed, [only] slightly different from what [I] had guessed.

'Then I went away to Brazil in the summer [1957] and, after a few weeks, returned home. I knew that during that period all kinds of measurements were being made of the directions of spins of electrons coming out of sodium, just to investigate the parity violation. When I left [for Brazil] there were already a lot of measurements that were inconsistent. One guy would discover that the spin of the electron coming out of the sodium was to the right, another one to the left. Mine were always going to the left. So when they said [that] they were going to the right, that would mean I was wrong. But I wanted to find out how it was going, so upon returning to New York [from Rio de Janeiro] the first thing I did was that I stopped at Madame Wu's laboratory at Columbia University. She wasn't there, but another woman was there and she described to me all the results of experiments and what they knew. I was kind of loaded up as I got back.

'Then I came here to Caltech. The guys [Felix Boehm, A. H. Wapstra, and Berthold Stech] sat me down and began telling me all the results of experiments in their lab as well as at other places and what disagreed with what and so forth. It was all chaotic. They did experiments. They got definite results. Other laboratories would disagree. I knew these guys [at Caltech] and I knew the way they thought and how they worked. So I had a little advantage. I knew which experiments were more likely to be true than others. I assumed that the Caltech experiments by these people [Boehm and co-workers] were the right ones and they were coming out for left spins. But that didn't clear up anything for me. It was still a chaos.

'They were telling me how chaotic it was and they said, "It's such a mess; Murray [Gell-Mann] even thinks that it might be V and A instead of S and T for the neutron [decay]." I realized instantaneously that if it would be V and A for the neutron [decay] and if all the decays were the same, that would make my theory right. Everything was V and A, nothing to it! So if Murray had noticed that it could be V and A, that it wasn't completely inconsistent, goddamn it, it's got to be [that]! It was an escape, it was getting rid of the prejudice that it had to be S and T. Well, they were telling me that it was a complete mess, "such a mess that Murray even thinks that it might be V and A for the neutron [decay]". I jumped out of the seat, and I said to them, "I understand everything!" And they thought I was joking, because the way it was being done, they were telling me that it was such a chaos—and I suddenly saw through it, that it was not [a mess], and I said, "I understand everything!". I meant it; it wasn't a joke.

'But I jumped out and left them immediately, went home, and started to calculate everything, assuming it was all V and A. Then I found out how the neutron [decay] fitted and everything. The [decay] rates were [either] right or they were 9 percent off.

'Somewhere during this time I called up my sister, or she called me, and I thanked her for getting me started on this stuff, that I was at last getting somewhere with this beta-decay thing and that it looked like V and A. And then I told her that it was unfortunate [that] there was still a 9 percent deviation between the rate of neutron [decay] and the rate of muon [decay].

'Well, as the night went on—there were some personal problems of some woman bothering me during the night—and I began to check more things, I got more convinced that it was right. And I gradually forgot a little bit about the 9 per cent [deviation]. The next morning I was very anxious to come in and tell the guys [at Caltech] how I had understood everything like I said the day before. So I came in and got them all around me: [Robert] Christy (in addition he was a theorist), and the other guys were [Felix] Boehm, [A. H.] Wapstra, and [Berthold] Stech. I think those were the ones who had explained everything to me the day before. So I came running into the office and said, "I understand everything. Everything fits. The neutron [decay] rate agrees with the muon [decay] rate."

'And they asked, "What beta-decay constant did you use?" I said, "the constant in [Siegbahn's] book", which gave the standard value at that time. "Well," they said, "there's a problem. It has been found out that it's 7 per cent different." "Oh!" I said, "I was too enthusiastic. I told you everything fitted, but actually there is a 9 percent difference between the muon and the neutron. And there's a 7 percent change in the beta-decay constant to that, that's going to move it 7 percent." "Well, which way?" they asked. This was terribly nerve-wracking to get the sign right under a circumstance like that, it was so exciting, and that instant the telephone rang. It was my sister. "How's it going this morning? What happened to the 9 percent?" I said, "We just discovered that there was a 7 percent change in the [beta-decay] constant." She asked, "Which way?" "I can't tell you, I'll call you back," I said. I was that excited!

'I went into another room, quieted down, to get the sign checked out. It wasn't very hard to do; we were just too excited. Christy went into a different room and he thought it out which way the sign would move. Then we both came back and agreed that the 7 percent change in that data would make the error, instead of 9 percent, just 2 percent, which was just like having a theory and an experiment which check out the next morning. So that was convincing. It was 2 percent off; much better! I called my sister back and told her that it was 2 percent and it looked good and that was it. That was it!

'I went to tell [Robert] Bacher, the head of our department about [our] success, and he asked, "Well, where did they get the idea that it is S and T? Why don't you look up that paper?" . . . And I looked up the paper, and this was really sad. In those days I read the *Physical Review* like the *Scientific American* every month. You could do it, it was thin enough. I used to read it all the time, even those [papers] in which I was not interested. I remembered that I had seen that article; I remembered the [graph in that article] and I remembered saying to myself when I saw it, "That doesn't prove it." The experiment which was supposed to show [that it was S and T], I had read it at a time when I was completely uninterested in beta decay. I had read that article and decided that the experiment didn't prove it, because the points which proved it were the last points on the scale, always a dangerous thing. The last point is never good, because if it were good, they'd take another point. They were coming to the edge and, in fact, it turned out that the solid angle was getting harder and harder to calculate and the more uncertain. And that was where the error was. I could tell that it was wrong when I read it. But I didn't know that that was the experiment that all the experts were supporting, this enormous S and T business, and that I had really doubted it when I first read it. That was kind of amusing. Then Murray [Gell-Mann] came back.'[23]

Gell-Mann had been vacationing with his wife in northern California and had been inaccessible for several weeks. 'So Murray came back. He said he was going to write a paper [on the V,A idea], too. And I said [as did Robert Bacher] that would not be a good idea, two different papers [on an identical theme] from the same institution. I said, "We are supposed to be colleagues; let's write it together." He had done some thinking about the strangeness changing transitions, which I had not thought through as well. So we added a little bit on that and put it together, and that was the paper that we wrote. But I had done most of the thing already. At the time, when I was doing it, I felt that I knew something that no one else knew about [that] law of nature. This was nothing like the work of Maxwell or Dirac, but it was the only law of nature I could lay a claim to. That's the story.'[23]

21.5 Another important contribution to the law of beta decay

E. C. George Sudarshan 'was a top graduate student' under Robert E. Marshak in the physics department at the University of Rochester when the breakthrough on parity violation occurred, and 'I judged that he could do the best job on the problem I had assigned to him, namely to find out whether a universal Lorentz structure was possible for all known weak interactions (including strange particle decays), including the new parity-violating results that were beginning to pour out. Sudarshan and I discussed the weak interaction problem whenever the need arose, either when he had some question or I thought of a new point. Sudarshan was an independent worker and the need for consultation was less (than with some other graduate students who needed more help and direction; moreover, I was rather familiar with the rapidly growing weak interaction phenomenology and was very interested in the problem, which led to frequent discussions between Sudarshan and myself.'[29] Sudarshan's problem for his Ph.D. thesis required an analysis of all extant experimental results ('including the ones in the rumor mill') bearing on the problem.

By the time of the Seventh Rochester Conference in April 1957, unbeknown to Richard Feynman, Sudarshan had completed the analysis of the available experimental data and concluded: 'While it is clear that a mixture of vector [V] and axial vector [A] is the only universal four-fermion interaction which is possible and possesses many elegant features, it appears that one published and several unpublished experiments cannot be reconciled with this hypothesis. These experiments are:

(A) the electron–neutron angular correlation in He^6 (Rustad and Ruby);

(B) the sign of the electron polarization from muon decay (Lederman *et al.*);

(C) the frequency of the electron mode in pion decay (Anderson and Lattes);

(D) the asymmetry from polarized neutron decay (Telegdi *et al.*).

'All of these experiments should be redone, particularly some of them that contradict the results of other recent experiments on weak interactions. If any of the above four experiments stands, it will be necessary to abandon the hypothesis of V–A four-fermion interaction or either or both of the assumptions of a two-component neutrino and/or conservation of leptons.'[30]

The principal results of the work of Sudarshan and Marshak had been obtained by the time of the 1957 Rochester Conference in April. Sudarshan and Marshak had identified the problems of reconciling all the known weak interaction experiments—both parity-conserving and parity-violating—with a unique Lorentz structure and recognized that some experiments must be wrong if a universal V–A theory, which they obtained by invoking the principle of chirality invariance, were to hold.

The results of the work of Sudarshan and Marshak on the V–A theory were not presented at the Rochester Conference, neither in the session in which Feynman presented his conjectures on the V,A form of the beta-decay interaction, which he had arrived at on the previous day, nor were they brought up in the 'free for all' discussions at the end of the conference following the talks of T. D. Lee or C. S. Wu. Marshak was to have done so, but he did not do so 'because of the specter of a V,T interaction in beta decay (requiring opposite helicities for the neutrino), in favor of which Wu had argued in her talk.'[29] Marshak was reluctant to argue for V–A as the universal Fermi interaction (UFI) option as long as a consistent picture did not emerge from parity-violating experiments in weak interactions. Sudarshan, as a graduate student, was forbidden by the conference rules to give a talk or make remarks at the Rochester Conference, and since Marshak was himself giving a major talk on nuclear forces (the Signell–Marshak potential), he had hoped to mention the salient features of the Sudarshan–Marshak V–A theory in the 'free for all' discussions. Sudarshan had requested P. T. Matthews, then a visiting professor at the University of Rochester, to report on the theory, but 'for some reason Matthews failed to do so'.[31]

While Marshak and Gell-Mann were both consultants to the Rand Corporation in Santa Monica in the summer of 1957, Sudarshan visited California on a vacation and, at the request of Robert Marshak a luncheon meeting was set up by Gell-Mann early in July to discuss the status of the theory of weak interactions. At this meeting, other than Gell-Mann, Marshak, and Sudarshan, there were present Felix Boehm and Berthold Stech. Marshak and Sudarshan mentioned their conclusion concerning V–A as the law of beta decay that they had drawn, and requested from Felix Boehm, the experimentalist, an update on whether the V,T combination 'was a mirage insofar as the parity-violating beta-decay experiments were concerned.'[29]

During the spring and summer of 1957 Gell-Mann was writing a review article on weak interactions with Arthur Rosenfeld: 'I [Gell-Mann] came to the conclusion that the Universal Fermi Interaction could still be right, and have the form V–A, provided that we could ignore various experimental results. We included the idea in the review article, where we called it the 'last stand' of the Universal Fermi Interaction.'[32]

'Meanwhile, George Sudarshan, working with Bob Marshak, was making a similar suggestion, but in a more confident manner. I recall a summit meeting with them on the weak interaction at the Rand Corporation . . . there was an exchange of views, and we mentioned the section on the 'last stand', while they told us of their plans to write an article.

'I then went on vacation, after mentioning the 'last stand' to Felix Boehm, who described it to Feynman when he returned from Brazil in my absence. Feynman got tremendously excited, expanded the idea somewhat, and wrote a long paper on it. When I returned we decided to modify it and sign it together.'[33]

The Sudarshan–Marshak paper, entitled 'The nature of the four-fermion interaction', was completed in the first half of July 1957 (while both Sudarshan and Marshak were still in southern California), and an abstract was sent immediately to N. Dallaporta, Chairman of the Padua–Venice International Conference (23–28 September 1957), where Marshak presented the paper in question. Preprints of that paper were sent out from Rochester on 16 September 1957; by coincidence the Feynman–Gell-Mann paper was received on the same day by the *Physical Review*.

Still another formulation of the V–A interaction was given by J. J. Sakurai. This came about as follows. Sakurai learned about the work of Sudarshan and Marshak from their preprint, a copy of which had been sent to Hans Bethe at Cornell, where Sakurai then was. In the beginning of October Sakurai went to discuss the V–A theory with Marshak at Rochester, from whom he received copies of the preprints of the Sudarshan–Marshak as well as Feynman–Gell-Mann papers (for which he thanked Marshak in a letter dated 10 October 1957). Sakurai took over the Tiomno-Stech–Jensen language of 'mass-reversal invariance'—which is completely equivalent to Sudarshan and Marshak's chirality invariance—and then made use of the Feynman–Gell-Mann treatment of the two-component Klein–Gordon equation as the basis of his formulation of V–A.

In conformity with C. S. Wu[35] we shall give an outline of the three formulations, respectively of Sudarshan–Marshak, Feynman–Gell-Mann, and Sakurai, in their historical order.

21.6 The universal Fermi interaction[35]

The V–A form of the universal Fermi interaction was reached independently by three different theoretical approaches. All of them were based on the principal idea representing the four-component spinor ψ in terms of two two-component spinors ϕ_+ and ϕ_-. To allow only one of the two two-component spinors to appear in the interaction, different hypothetical principles were proposed to justify its restriction. These three theoretical approaches were:

(1) the chirality invariance conjectured by Sudarshan and Marshak;[30]

(2) the two-component formulation of Dirac spinors by Feynman and Gell-Mann;[36]

(3) The mass-reversal invariance proposed by Sakurai.[34]

(a) Chirality invariance

'The word 'chirality' is derived from the Greek word *kheir* (hand), and it refers to the expression of 'handedness'. The chirality transformation is defined as $\psi \to \gamma_5 \psi$. For a particle of given momentum, the Dirac equation has four solutions, each of them a four-component spinor. Now, for a mass-zero particle, e.g. a neutrino, of these four solutions, two have positive chirality, $\gamma_5 \psi = \psi$, and two have negative chirality, $\gamma_5 \psi = -\psi$.

In the case of $m \neq 0$, the general Dirac spinor is not an eigenstate of the operator γ_5. However, it can be expanded in terms of such eigenstates. We can write

$$\psi = \psi_+ + \psi_-, \tag{21.7}$$

where

$$\psi_\pm = \tfrac{1}{2}(1 \pm \gamma_5).$$

In terms of the two-component spinors I, ϕ, ξ, we have

$$\gamma_5 = \begin{bmatrix} 0 & -I \\ -I & 0 \end{bmatrix}$$

and

$$\psi = \begin{bmatrix} \phi \\ \xi \end{bmatrix} = \tfrac{1}{2}\begin{bmatrix} \phi - \xi \\ -(\phi - \xi) \end{bmatrix} + \tfrac{1}{2}\begin{bmatrix} \phi + \xi \\ \phi + \xi \end{bmatrix} \tag{21.8}$$

Thus

$$\psi_+ = \begin{bmatrix} \phi_- \\ \phi_- \end{bmatrix} \quad \text{and} \quad \psi_- = \begin{bmatrix} \phi_+ \\ \phi_- \end{bmatrix},$$

where $\phi_\pm = \tfrac{1}{2}(\phi \pm \xi)$. To express this in words: if one projects with the positive chirality operator, one obtains the two-component spnor ϕ_-; using the negative chirality operator yields the the two-component spinor ϕ_+. At this point, Sudarshan and Marshak[30] made a bold conjecture that *the total four-fermion interaction should be invariant under a* γ_5 *transformation on any of* the ψ's, $\psi_i \to \gamma_5 \psi_i$.

'Consider the four-fermion interaction

$$g(\bar{\psi}_2 O \psi_1)(\bar{\psi}_4 O \psi_3).$$

Make the transformations

$$\psi_i \to \gamma_5 \psi_i \quad \text{and} \quad \bar{\psi}_j \to -\bar{\psi}_j \gamma_5. \tag{21.9}$$

Then chirality invariance implies

$$\bar{\psi}_j O \psi_i \equiv -\bar{\psi}_j \gamma_5 O \gamma_5 \psi_i$$

where O is any operator. We have

$$O\gamma_5 = O \quad \text{and} \quad -\gamma_5 O = O$$

or

$$[O, \gamma_5]_+ = 0.$$

That means O and γ_5 anticommute.

'Of the five operators (S, V, T, A, P) only V and A anticommute with γ_5; S, T, and P commute with γ_5. Therefore the operator O must be a linear combination of V and A,

$$O = a\gamma_\mu + b\gamma_\mu \gamma_5.$$

From the condition, $O\gamma_5 = O$,

$$O = a\gamma_\mu \gamma_5 + b\gamma_\mu = a\gamma_\mu + b\gamma_\mu \gamma_5.$$

This gives $a = b$ or $O = a\,\gamma_\mu(1 + \gamma_5)$. The interaction is thus

$$g[\bar{\psi}_2 \gamma_\mu (1 + \gamma_5) \psi_1][\bar{\psi}_4 \gamma_\mu (1 + \gamma_5)\psi_3]. \tag{21.10}$$

Of course, we could have retained $(1 - \gamma_5)\psi$ instead of $(1 + \gamma_5)\psi$; then $\psi \to -\gamma_5 \psi_i$ and we get $a = -b$, which again leads to the V, A, interaction. Theoretically these two possibilities are equally good.'[35]

(b) *The two-component spinor formulation of the Dirac spinors*

'As we have noted, for $m \neq 0$, ψ_+ and ψ_- cannot be decoupled in the Dirac equation, and it is rather mystical to write down the interaction involving only ψ_+ and ψ_- for every particle. The great contribution of Feynman and Gell-Mann in this respect was to explain the situation by showing that the Dirac equation can also be expressed in terms of the two-component wave function. However, the two-component wave function must satisfy a second-order Klein–Gordon equation. Once one accepts this viewpoint, then the hypothetical principles which were proposed to restrict the interaction term to (V, A) seem to be more reasonable.

'The first-order Dirac equation for the four-component field ψ can be written in terms of the Dirac matrices as

$$H\psi = \alpha \cdot p\psi + \beta m\psi. \tag{21.11}$$

The four-component wave function ψ can be expressed in terms of the two-component spinors ϕ and ξ. Then

$$H\phi = \sigma \cdot p\xi + m\phi, \qquad H\xi = \sigma \cdot p\phi - m\xi. \tag{21.12}$$

Adding and subtracting these equations, we obtain

$$H\phi_+ = \sigma \cdot p\phi_+ + m\phi_-, \qquad H\phi_- = -\sigma \cdot p\phi_- + m\phi_+, \tag{21.13}$$

where ϕ_+ and ϕ_- have been defined earlier.

'If $m = 0$, these equations are decoupled, so the functions ψ_+ and ψ_-, which are eigenstates of the chirality operator γ_5, are also eigenfunctions of the Dirac equation. For $m \neq 0$, the two equations are coupled. However, ϕ_+ and ϕ_- satisfy the Klein–Gordon equation since

$$\phi_+ = (1/m)(H + \sigma \cdot p)\phi_-, \tag{21.14}$$

we have

$$m^2\phi_- = m(H) - \sigma \cdot p)\phi_+ = (H - \sigma \cdot p)(H + \sigma \cdot p)\phi_-$$

$$= [H^2 - (\sigma \cdot p)^2]\phi_- = (H^2 - p^2)\phi_-, \tag{21.15}$$

or

$$[(\partial^2/\partial t^2) - \nabla_2 + m^2]\phi_- = 0. \tag{21.16}$$

This is the well-known Klein–Gordon equation, which had been a plaything of Feynman's for a long time. Although ϕ_+ does not appear in the theory explicitly, nevertheless it appears via equation (21.14), expressed in terms of ϕ_- and its derivatives. This implies that the whole theory can be expressed in terms of a two-component wave function, either ϕ_+ or ϕ_-, which, however, must satisfy the Klein–Gordon equation.

'On experimental grounds, we know that the four-fermion interaction formulated in terms of ψ's is *linear in the fields and does not contain derivatives*. Now, an arbitrary interaction form, even if it is linear in ψ, in general, involves both ψ_+ and ψ_-, or in terms of two-component wave functions, both ϕ_- and ϕ_+. If expressed in terms of ϕ_- alone, the interaction must contain terms proportional to ϕ_- and also to $\phi_- \sim \partial\phi/\partial x$. If, however, we *insist* that no such derivative terms should appear, then the interaction, formulated in terms of ψ, must contain only ψ_+ and not ψ_-, i.e. only ϕ_- not ϕ_+ (or vice versa). This requirement is identical with that resulting from chirality invariance.

(c) Mass-reversal invariance

'Consider the behavior of the Dirac equation

$$\gamma_\mu p_\mu \psi = im\psi \tag{21.17}$$

under the transformation $\psi \to \gamma_5 \psi$. Since γ_5 anticommutes with each γ_μ, we have

$$\gamma_\mu p_\mu (\gamma_5 \psi) = -im(\gamma_5 \psi) \tag{21.18}$$

Thus, $\gamma_5 \psi$ is not an eigenfunction of the Dirac equation, unless we also make the transformation $m \to -m$. The Dirac equation is then invariant under the combined 'mass-reversal' transformation

$$\psi \to \gamma_5 \psi, \qquad m \to -m. \tag{21.19}$$

When one applies this transformation to each of the four fermions simultaneously and demands that the interaction be invariant, then it is equivalent to γ_5 invariance.'[35]

(d) Connection with the V–A interaction

The three hypotheses discussed above are equivalent to the assumption that the beta-decay interaction occurs only in states of positive chirality, i.e. negative helicity. The requirement of negative helicity, i.e. left-handed polarization for both neutrinos and electrons (in positive energy states) implies the existence of a (V,A) combination in beta decay, even though the coefficients are arbitrary. If we also require that the nucleons involved are left-handedly polarized (if their rest mass could be neglected), then the interaction is uniquely defined as V–A.

By using the relations $\gamma_5(1+\gamma_5) = (1+\gamma_5)\gamma_5$, the interaction can be written as follows:

$$g[\bar{\psi}_2 \gamma_\mu (1+\gamma_5)\psi_1][\bar{\psi}_4 \gamma_\mu (1+\gamma_5)\psi_3] = g\{(\bar{\psi}_2 \gamma_\mu \gamma_5 \psi_1)[\bar{\psi}_4 \gamma_\mu \gamma_5 (1+\gamma_5)\psi_3]\}. \tag{21.20}$$

Since γ_μ and $i\gamma_\mu\gamma_5$ are usually the vector and axial-vector operators, respectively, we then have the (V–A) combination. This universal (V–A) four-fermion interaction gives the unique combination (V–A), yields two-component neutrinos of negative helicity, leads to the conservation of leptons, and is invariant under the combined inversion of 'CP'.

The universal (V–A) interaction differs from the vector interaction originally proposed by Fermi,

$$(\bar{\psi}_2 \gamma_\mu \psi_1 \bar{\psi}_4 \gamma_\mu \psi_3), \tag{21.21}$$

only by the extra factor $1+\gamma_5$. It is remarkable how close Fermi came to the correct beta-decay interaction long before the understanding of beta decay was as far advanced as it became after the mid-1950s.

21.7 The conserved vector current hypothesis

'Because of the strong coupling between the nucleons and pions, the coupling constants in the old [Fermi] theory of beta decay need renormalization. Nucleons can emit and absorb virtual pions such as $n \rightarrow n + \pi^0 \rightarrow p + \pi^- \rightarrow n + \pi^+ + \pi^- \rightarrow \ldots$ Therefore, a neutron exists for only a fraction of its lifetime as a bare neutron; the rest of its life it exists as a proton surrounded by a negatively charged pion cloud or as a neutron surrounded by a neutral pion cloud, etc. The neutron in the latter state is called a dressed or physical neutron to differentiate it from a bare neutron. In the old beta-decay theory, only the bare nucleon is assumed to undergo beta decay, not the dressed nucleon.

'A muon does not have strong interactions. Its Fermi interaction strength needs no renormalization, except in higher-order process. Therefore the effective coupling constant in muon decay should equal the intrinsic one. What mystified people was that the effective interaction strength of the vector couplings in both beta decay and muon decay were found to be equal to within about 2 percent. Therefore the question arose: Why is no renormalization required between the effective and the bare interaction strength in beta decay? To explain the unexpectedly good agreement, Feynman and Gell-Mann's approach to explain the equality of vector beta interaction strength in nuclear beta and muon decay was to assume that the pions carry with them the beta-interaction strength when they are virtually emitted from the nucleons and that the vector part of the nuclear beta interaction is so arranged as to have no renormalization effects.

(a) Analogy with electromagnetism

'The fact that the vector interaction in beta decay appears to be unaffected by pionic corrections has its analogy in electromagnetism. The electron is believed to be a simple Dirac particle with no charge distribution, i.e. essentially a point charge (except for small radiative corrections of order $\alpha/2\pi \sim 10^{-3}$, while the proton is a very complicated object containing a meson cloud surrounding a bare nucleon core. Yet the total charge of the proton, which one measures in electron–proton scattering at very low energies, is the same as the proton charge one would measure if there were no pion interaction. As a matter of fact, all interactions are arranged in such a way that the equality between the physical electric charge and the bare charge is not disturbed, so that the electric charge of the proton is the same as the electric charge of the positron (of course in the presence of pion interactions, the charge of the nucleon core *alone* is not the same).

'How is this equality achieved in electrodynamics? First, electric charge conservation holds in the process

$$p \rightleftharpoons n + \pi^+,$$

that is, the π^+ has the same charge as the proton. Secondly, even while the proton is in the 'dissociated' state, the interaction of the π^+ with the electromagnetic field is the same as that of the proton. Mathematically, the vector potential A couples to the *conserved charge current* which consists of the p and π^+ currents.

'Of course, if the pion interaction with the electromagnetic field were different from the proton interaction, such as happens for the magnetic moment, this conservation law would not hold. Thus the magnetic moment of the physical proton differs from that of the bare proton.

(b) The conserved electromagnetic current

'The charge current for a proton is a polar vector whose four components are given by

$$i_\mu = \begin{cases} \psi_p^+ \alpha_\mu \psi_p = \rho(v_\mu/c) & \text{for } \mu = 1, 2, 3, \\ i\psi_p^+ \psi_p = i\rho & \text{for } \mu = 4, \end{cases} \tag{21.22}$$

in units of the electron charge e. In covariant notation we have, apart from a factor i,

$$i_\mu = \bar{\psi}_p \gamma_\mu \psi_p. \tag{21.23}$$

Of course, for neutrons there is no charge current.

'We can combine the results for the proton and neutron in terms of isotopic spin operators. For the proton and neutron, we have, respectively, $\tau_z = +1$ and -1. Thus

$$i_\mu = \bar{\psi}_N \gamma_\mu \tfrac{1}{2}(1 + \tau_z)\psi_N, \tag{21.24}$$

where ψ_N represents a general nucleon wave function. The nucleon current can be decomposed into an isotopic spin scalar and isotopic spin vector,

$$i_\mu = \underbrace{\tfrac{1}{2}\bar{\psi}_N \gamma_\mu \psi_N}_{\text{isoscalar}} + \underbrace{\tfrac{1}{2}\bar{\psi}_N \gamma_\mu \tau_z \psi_N}_{\text{isovector}} = i_\mu^S + i_\mu^V. \tag{21.25}$$

The isoscalar term satisfies the continuity equation:

$$\partial i_\mu^S / \partial x_\mu = \nabla \cdot i_\mu^S + \partial \rho / \partial t = 0. \tag{21.26}$$

The conservation of isoscalar current implies the conservation of the number of nucleons. However, the second term, which is the z component of an isotopic spin vector, is not conserved by itself, but only if it is supplemented by the pion term, i.e.

$$J_\mu^z = \tfrac{1}{2}\bar{\psi}_N \gamma_\mu \tau_z \psi_N + [\pi \times (\partial \pi / \partial x_\mu)]_z + \cdots' \tag{21.27}$$

(c) The formulation of the conserved vector current: (CVC) theory

'The novel feature of the Feynman–Gell-Mann paper was a good discussion of the CVC theory. For a conventional vector beta interaction, the nucleon current is given by

$$J_\mu^+ = (1/\sqrt{2})\bar{\psi}_N \gamma_\mu \tau_+ \psi_N \quad \text{for } \beta^- \text{ decay}, \tag{21.28}$$

where

$$\tau_+ \psi_n = [(\tau_z + i\tau_y)/\sqrt{2}]\psi_n = \sqrt{2}\,\psi_p, \qquad \tau_+ \psi_p = 0, \tag{21.29}$$

and similarly

$$J_\mu^- = (1/\sqrt{2})\bar{\psi}_N \gamma_\mu \tau \psi_N \quad \text{for } \beta^+ \text{ decay}. \tag{21.30}$$

These currents are very similar to the electromagnetic isovector current J_μ^z. The J_μ^-, J_μ^z, J_μ^- are the three components of one and the same isotopic spin current.

'Feynman and Gell-Mann[36] suggested that, just as for electromagnetism, we must supplement the nucleonic current by a pionic term, i.e. that not only J_μ^z but also J_μ^+ and J_μ^- contain a pionic vector current,

$$J_\mu^+ = (1/\sqrt{2})\bar{\psi}_N \gamma_\mu \tau_- \psi_N + [\pi \times (\partial \pi / \partial x_\mu)] + \cdots . \tag{21.31}$$

Physically, this is equivalent to attributing the same beta-interaction strength to the direct pion–lepton as to the baryon–lepton interactions. Since the strong interactions are charge independent, we have conservation of isotopic spin T, a generalization of conservation of charge, i.e. of T_z. Thus the Feynman–Gell-Mann hypothesis amounts to the assumption that the total isotopic spin current, including both nucleonic and pionic terms, is conserved.

'It is of interest to recall here the comments which Gershtein and Zeldovich made at a time when the Fermi part of the beta interaction was believed to be scalar rather than vector. They wrote: "It is of no practical significance but only of theoretical interest if the interaction is of vector type; then g_V (bare) $= g_V$ (effective). No renormalization can be foreseen by analogy with Ward's identity for the interaction of the charged particle with the electromagnetic field; in this case, virtual processes involving particles do not lead to charge renormalization of the particle." [37]

The CVC hypothesis for weak interactions has been confirmed experimentally and has served as a guiding principle for the modern gauge theory of strong and weak interactions, where it is predicted as a necessary consequence of the vector gauge theory.'[35]

21.8 Some personal consequences of the work on UFI

The Sudarshan–Marshak paper on the theory and prediction of the (V–A) universal Fermi interaction (UFI), although submitted at the same time as Feynman and Gell-Mann submitted theirs to the *Physical Review*, was published with considerable delay in the *Proceedings of the Padua–Venice International Conference* (1958),[30] and did not have the same impact as the Feynman–Gell-Mann paper, which it rightfully would have had if it had been published in a regular journal like the *Physical Review*. Although Sudarshan and Marshak published a follow-up paper in the *Physical Review*,[38], their principal work was overshadowed by the publication of the Feynman–Gell-Mann paper. Largely, only the active researchers in the field of weak interactions took note of the publication in the Padua–Venice conference proceedings. This circumstance, and the fact that no mention of the work of Sudarshan and Marshak had been made at the April 1957 Rochester Conference, by which time— several months before the Feynman–Gell-Mann paper was ready—Sudarshan and Marshak had arrived at their principal conclusions regarding the (V A) character of the law of beta decay and UFI, led to questions of priority and bitterness, especially on the part of Sudarshan, who was a young researcher at that time and this work represented the major accomplishment of his life. He never recovered from his thoughts and feelings that full recognition had been denied to him for his achievement, and he continued to give expression to his unhappiness in speeches and articles whenever he had the opportunity.[39]

Richard Feynman, when he became aware of this complex situation, tried to make amends to Sudarshan and Marshak by making the following remarks at the conclusion of a conference on weak interactions: 'So I would like to say where we stand in our theories of weak interactions. We have a conventional theory of weak interactions invented by Marshak and Sudarshan, published by Feynman and Gell-Mann, and completed by Cabibbo—I call it the conventional theory of weak interactions—the one which is described as the V–A theory.'[40]

In 1985, Richard Feynman and Robert Marshak met in Kyoto, Japan, at a conference entitled 'MESON 50', celebrating the fiftieth anniversary of the proposal of meson (as the exchange particle in strong interactions) by Hideki Yukawa, and discussed the murky situation concerning the origins of the (V–A) theory of the universal Fermi interaction. Marshak mentioned to Feynman Sudarshan's continuing unhappiness about the lack of proper recognition of his early major contribution by the scientific community. Right after Marshak's departure from Japan, Feynman wrote to him from Kyoto: 'It was great seeing you and talking. I hope someday we can get this straightened out and give Sudarshan the credit for priority that he justly deserves.

'Truly the paper Murray [Gell-Mann] and I wrote[36] was a fully *joint paper* resulting from many interchanges of ideas between us and it is hopeless to try to disentangle who did what. Nobody should try to determine sources of credit among the authors of a joint paper.

'. . . These matters all vex me—and I wish I had not caused you and Sudarshan such discomfort. At any opportunity I shall try to set the record straight—but nobody believes me when I am serious. . . . Best regards, good friend, Dick Feynman.'[41]

Even though Feynman, when he initially encountered the (V–A) law of beta decay, had felt that it was the only law of nature he could lay a claim to, he was now perfectly happy to share the credit for the discovery with Gell-Mann, Sudarshan, and Marshak.

Notes and References

1. R.P. Feynman, Interviews and conversations with Jagdish Mehra, in Pasadena, California, January 1988.

2. Murray Gell-Mann, Conversation with Jagdish Mehra, at Caltech, Pasadena, California, 11 July 1990.

3. C.S. Wu has written extensively on the historical origin and resolution of the problems of beta decay and establishment of the laws of weak interactions in books and articles, from which I have benefited greatly. Some of these works are: C.S. Wu, Experiments on the shape of beta-spectra: The interaction in beta decay, In: *Beta- and gamma-ray spectroscopy* (Ed. K. Siegbahn). Interscience, New York, 1955; C.S. Wu and S.A. Moszkowski, *Beta decay*, Chapters 1 (Historical introduction) and 7 (Recent developments). Interscience, New York, 1956; C.S. Wu, The neutrino. In: *Theoretical physics in the twentieth century* (ed. M. Fierz and V.F. Weisskopf). Interscience, New York, 1959; C.S. Wu, History of beta decay. In: *Trends in atomic physics* (ed. O.R. Frisch, F.A. Paneth, F. Laves, and P. Rosbaud). Interscience, New York, 1959; C.S. Wu, The universal Fermi interaction and conserved vector current in beta decay. *Rev. Mod. Phys.*, April 1964. I have learned from all these works, but made particular use of the last three.

4. N. Bohr, *Phil. Mag.* **26**, 476 (1913).

5. L. Meitner, *Z. Phys.* **9**, 131 (1922).

6. C.D. Ellis and W. Wooster, *Proc. Roy. Soc. Lond.* **117**, 109 (1927).

7. L. Meitner and W. Orthmann, *Z. Phys.* **60**, 143 (1930).

8. P. Ehrenfest and J.R. Oppenheimer, *Phys. Rev.* **87**, 333 (1931).

9. W. Heitler and G. Herzberg, *Naturwiss enshaften* **17**, 673 (1929); F. Rasetti, *Z. Phys.* **61**, 598 (1930).

10. N. Bohr, *J. Chem. Soc.*, **349** (1932).

11. W. Pauli, Letter to 'Radioactivity Ladies and Gentlemen', *Collected Papers*, Vol. I, Interscience, New York, 1964.

12. C.S. Wu, Subtleties and surprise. *Ann. N.Y. Acad. Sci.*, 1978, p. 39.

13. W. Pauli, *Phys. Rev.* **38**, 579 (1931).

14. W. Heisenberg, *Z. Phys.* **77**, 1 (1932).

15. W. Heisenberg, *Z. Phys.* **78**, 156 (1932).

16. W. Pauli, In; *Structures et propriétés des noyaux*, Proceedings of the seventh Solvay Conference. Gauthier-Villars, Paris, 1934, pp. 324–25.

17. E. Fermi, *Z. Phys.* **161**, (1934).

18. F. Perrin, *C.R. Acad. Sci. Paris* **197**, (1933).

19. E. Fermi, 1934, Ref. 17; *Collected Papers*, Vol. 1. University of Chicago Press, 1965, pp. 538, 559, 575.

20. F. Fermi, Quantum electrodynamics. *Rev. Mod. Phys.*, 1932.

21. This section has greatly benefited from 'Why be even-handed?', a talk presented by Martin M. Block on the occasion of his sixtieth birthday, at Northwestern University, Evanston, Illinois. I have followed these remarks of Block's in particular because he figures in the story of how Richard Feynman got started with the problem of the law of weak interactions.

22. R.H. Dalitz, *Phil. Mag.* **44**, 1068 (1953); *Phys. Rev.* **94**, 1046 (1954). E. Fabri, *Nuovo Cim.* **11**, 479 (1954).

23. R.P. Feynman, Ref. 1.

24. R.P. Feynman, *Proceedings of the Sixth Annual Rochester Conference on High Energy Nuclear Physics*, 3–7 April, 1956. Interscience, New York, 1956, p. VIII-7.

25. C.N. Yang, Ref. 24, pp. VIII-27, 28.

26. T.D. Lee and C.N. Yang, Question of parity conservation in weak interactions. *Phys. Rev.* **104**, 254 (1956).

27. T.D. Lee, *Proceedings of the Seventh Rochester Conference on High Energy Nuclear Physics*, 15–19 April 1957, Interscience, New York, Session VII, Introductory survey, pp. 1–12.

28. R.P. Feynman, Ref. 27, pp. IX-42–44.

29. R.E. Marshak, Personal communication from R.E. Marshak, 20 November 1990.

30. E.C.G. Sudarshan and R.E. Marshak, *Padua–Venice International Conference*, 1957.

31. At the Dirac Memorial Meeting in Cambridge, England, on 19 April 1985, I verified from P.T. Matthews that he decided not to mention the conclusions of Sudarshan and Marshak in view of Madame Wu's indication of a V, T interaction in beta decay.

32. M. Gell-Mann and A.H. Rosenfeld, Hyperons and heavy mesons. *Ann. Rev. Nucl. Sci.* 1957, p. 433.

33. M. Gell-Mann, Particle theory from S-matrix to quarks. Talk at the First International Conference on the History of Scientific Ideas at Sant Filiu de Guixols, Catalunya, Spain, 1983. M. Doncel, A. Hermann, L. Michel, and A. Pais (eds.), *Symmetries in physics*, 1600–1980. Barcelona, Publicaciones de la Universidad Autonoma de Barcelona, 1989.

34. J.J. Sakurai, *Nuovo Cim.* **7**, 649 (1957).

35. C.S. Wu, *Rev. Mod. Phys.*, April 1964. Sections 21.6 and 21.7 are due to C.S. Wu's treatment (1964).

36. R.P. Feynman and M. Gell-Mann, *Phys. Rev.* **109**, 193 (1958).

37. S.S. Gershtein and J.B. Zel'dovich, *Soviet Phys. JETP* **2**, 576 (1955).

38. E.C.G. Sudarshan and R.E. Marshak, *Phys. Rev.* **109**, 1860 (1958).

39. Just to give two examples: E.C.G. Sudarshan (with R.E. Marshak), Origin of the V–A theory. In: *50 years of weak interactions*, Wingspread Conference (1984) (ed. D. Cline and G. Riedasch), University of Wisconsin, Wisconsin, Madison, Wisconsin; Midcentury adventures of particle physics. In: *Pions to quarks* (ed. L.M. Brown, M. Dresden, and L. Hoddeson). Cambridge University Press, 1989, p. 492.

40. R.E. Marshak, Ref. 29; Conference in Philadelphia, 1974.

41. R.P. Feynman, Letter to R.E. Marshak, 17 August 1985. (Courtesy R.E. Marshak.)

22

Virtuoso performances as teacher and lecturer

It was very long ago when Richard Feynman had felt nervousness at having to give a seminar on the action-at-a-distance theory in the departmental colloquium at Princeton in the fall of 1940 or a ten-minute talk at the American Physical Society Meeting in New York in February 1941: they were only distant memories. Since then he had developed into an an accomplished and inspiring teacher and lecturer, who gave virtuoso performances full of showmanship, humor, with his own inimitable brilliance, style, and manner, and he would be invited to give talks and lectures everywhere he could or would. Anyone who had heard him lecture once wanted to do so again with anticipation at every opportunity that presented itself later on. His lectures had a light and airy feeling, to the extent that there were those who compared them to a Chinese meal, which one greatly enjoyed while one ate it with gusto, felt full with the feast of taste and flavor, but shortly after eating it felt hungry again.[1]

Matthew Sands joined the physics department at Caltech in 1950, at the same time as did Richard Feynman. They had known each other at Los Alamos and at Cornell, but at Caltech their acquaintance matured. After Feynman's visit to Japan in 1953, their collaboration became much closer. Matt Sands taught graduate courses in optics and electronics, while Feynman ranged over the entire spectrum of graduate level courses in theoretical physics. Sands noticed that the graduate curriculum was very traditional. The first year or so consisted of classical mechanics, electromagnetism, and thermodynamics; the students did not get any modern physics, quantum mechanics, or electron theory until much later in the second year. Sands solicited Feynman's help in trying to revise the graduate curriculum, after which they began to teach quantum mechanics and electromagnetism (in the style of Abraham and Becker) in the first year of graduate school. Feynman taught quantum mechanics and all the other advanced theoretical courses; he also introduced in the graduate curriculum the teaching of quantum electrodynamics and elementary particle theory.

At Los Alamos and afterwards at MIT, Matthew Sands had known Jerrold Zacharias. In the 1950s Zacharias was devoting his attention to the teaching of undergraduate physics in universities, and he invited Sands to become a member of the Commission on College Physics, which had been established as a national commission to work on the improvement of physics teaching. Sands served on the commission for six years, the last two as chairman. Until that time he had been teaching graduate courses and, with Feynman's help, had restructured the graduate curriculum at Caltech. Stimulated by his work on the Commission on College Physics, he took a close look at the undergraduate physics curriculum at Caltech and didn't like what he saw; they were still teaching introductory physics according to the curriculum designed by Robert Millikan, Duane Roller, and Fletcher Watson twenty years previously. Sands noticed that in the first two years, when students took chemistry, physics, and engineering, no mention was made in the physics course of atomic physics, quantum theory, and relativity—all they learned about was pith balls and inclined planes. Moreover, there were no lectures in the introductory course; it was all done with a book in recitation sections.

Sands felt unhappy with this situation and started to make noises. He felt very strongly that they should revise the undergraduate introductory courses in physics. At first, he got only a negative response from Robert Bacher, who was then head of the division of physics, mathematics, and astronomy. Bacher thought that they were doing an excellent job of teaching physics at Caltech, and did not wish to accept the fact that the curriculum could be improved. With the help of some younger colleagues, Sands began to stir things up and ultimately convinced Bacher that it would be good to modernize the program. Bacher approached the Ford Foundation and received a substantial grant for revamping the introductory physics curriculum at Caltech. He thought that Matt Sands himself was too radical, so he asked Robert Leighton, a quiet conservative, and Victor Neher—an old collaborator of Millikan's and an excellent designer of pedagogical experiments—all three to work on revising the introductory physics curriculum.

Leighton and Sands worked for several months trying to put together an outline of a course, with Neher working to devise new laboratory equipment. While Sands was working on this program, he would often consult with Feynman about the simple ways of bringing modern physics into it. 'About half way through the year [1960] I became very frustrated because Leighton kept coming back with a very traditional outline, and we could not seem to converge on a solution which would meet my requirements and his. One day I had the brilliant inspiration of saying, "Look, why don't we get Feynman to give the lectures and let him make the final decision on the contents?"' [2]

So, Sands went to see Feynman at his house and said: 'Look, Richard, you have spent forty years trying to understand physics. Now here is your chance to distill it down to the essence at the level of a freshman.' [2] Feynman thought a little about it and said, 'Hmm! That might be interesting! But, you know, I have never taught freshman physics before.'[3] Sands had seen Feynman lecture in graduate courses and seminars and was convinced that his style and thought would be very good for what he had in mind. From their discussion, Feynman obtained a good feeling for what might be possible. 'So he said he would think about it for a day or two and I saw him later on and he asked: "Do you know if there has ever been a great physicist who lectured on freshman physics?" I said, "I don't know, but I don't think so!" And he said, "I'll do it!"'[2]

Sands went to Leighton and told him that Feynman had agreed to give the introductory lectures on physics. Leighton said, 'Oh no, that would never do. He has no experience of teaching freshman and undergraduates. His head is too high in the sky. That would not be any good.'[2] At their meeting, Victor Neher said, 'Oh, that would be marvelous!'[2] Neher and Sands convinced Leighton that this was an interesting possibility. Together, all three of them went to Bacher and proposed that Feynman should give the lectures to freshmen. Bacher exclaimed: 'Oh, no! He is much too valuable for advanced courses, graduate courses, and he has never taught freshman physics. So that's not a good idea. I don't think we should do that.'[2]

Sands did some campaigning among the faculty members—like the Lauritsens (Charles and Thomas)—they were all very much on Sands's side. Since Feynman was interested in giving the introductory lectures, and several other faculty members—especially the younger ones—thought that it was a good idea, Bacher was ultimately convinced. Leighton and Sands took their two outlines and handed them to Feynman. Feynman threw away their syllabus and said that he would develop his own.

In the fall of 1961, Feynman began to give two lectures per week, with demonstrations and the whole show. He gave 100 percent of his time to the lectures. He worked from eight to sixteen hours per day on these lectures, thinking through his own outline and planning how each lecture fitted with the other parts. 'I was worried about how things would fit together; I had all this in my head and I would map and plan out the individual lectures. I would come to the lecture with a small piece of paper with a few little notes on it. I wasn't only worried about the content of each lecture, but also each lecture had to be self-contained, complete in itself. It had to be a dramatic production—which had a dramatic line, with an introduction, a development of the theme, and a denoument.'[3]

From the beginning, the lectures were recorded. It was planned that from the recordings transcripts would be made and notes would be prepared for the students. It was thought in the beginning that graduate students, who were working as teaching assistants, would work on preparing these notes. But what they produced was poor; they couldn't properly translate Feynman's spoken words into the written form. Sands and Leighton took it upon themselves to prepare the written notes of Feynman's lectures. Sands was also responsible for organizing the discussion sections of fifteen or twenty students, each with the teaching assistants. He took some of the discussion sections himself to get some feeling of how the students were doing. After every lecture, he and Leighton would meet with Feynman, usually at lunch, to discuss the lecture and what would follow.

The lectures were of course attended by the students, about two hundred in all, for whom they were intended. As time went on, there was some decrease in numbers; for some students the lectures were either too difficult or not interesting, and they stopped coming, but more than 75 percent continued to attend. The lectures were also attended by graduate students and faculty from the physics department and from other disciplines as well. 'Most of the audience members felt during Feynman's lectures that they were participating in something special. It was a beautiful performance in the sense that he had thought through not only the dramatic line but also where each thing he wrote on the blackboard would be. He would start in one corner of the blackboard and develop a little something there, which he would refer to later; so the blackboard would gradually become covered and at the end was also a dramatic piece. The entire evolution was remarkable. Of course, Feynman's physical performance as a showman was quite famous and he lived up to it. He would use gestures to illustrate a point. He spent a lot of time developing original demonstrations with the technician, Tom Harvey, and each demonstration would be gone over in advance. He did not want any "black boxes" or hidden apparatus; he wanted everything to be open and visible.' [2]

Feynman was able to organize the material in such a way that sometimes an elementary early lecture might present a problem and an idea that would be useful in a later lecture. 'I enjoyed it because I love to try to figure out how to explain things. Being a kind of showman I invented a number of interesting demonstrations with Tom Harvey, and it was kind of fun. My speech is not easily translated into [written] words. I back up often, and sometimes break in the middle of a sentence, and other funny things like that. So it was not just a matter of transcribing the lectures, but to translate my speech into something readable, while preserving my style and spirit. Sands and Leighton were both first-class physicists and they did an excellent job of writing up my lectures. In the early lectures I dealt mostly with Leighton, but in the later ones Sands was involved—it was a well-organized system.

'They had hired a special secretary. One day into this class came this *absolutely stunning* girl in a green dress with red hair. I had never seen her before and she was sitting part way up in the audience. Being weak, I gave my entire lecture to her, so to speak, and I made things as clear as I could. Then I discovered that she was the secretary who was going to help in organizing who got which lectures to work on and to make sure that the production was kept on schedule, and they had just brought her into the class to show her what the lecture was like so she could understand better what she was dealing with. But she was not a student; she was a sort of production assistant. She became my inspiration for that special lecture.

'My experience of giving lectures at that time was that I knew what I was doing. I was working very hard and did the best I could to explain all this physics. There was always a certain pleasure in discovering for myself actually that I could understand many more things than I thought I could from the elementary point of view. I would use these explanations. I had a special difficulty as I realized that all the students were not the same, and that if we had too much relativity, atoms, quantum theory, and the fireworks, that the other students would get confused. I tried to invent some kind of system to tell them what was essential and what was for the entertainment of those who could understand it. For, if you add something to keep the subject from being dull, it makes it only duller to many students because they have to learn that then too, which is pitiful. That's the way the system works; I was trying to break that. I would write a summary of the essentials on the blackboard.'[3]

The hope was that the students would just pay attention to the essentials. It didn't really work that way, because the teaching assistants, who were graduate students, were so excited at the discovery that they could understand what they thought was advanced things in terms of Feynman's elementary points of view that they could not resist telling even more to the students about these advanced things which they could now understand in an elementary way; it made things only harder for the duller student. 'So it didn't quite work, because the discussion sections with teaching assistants were supposed to make sure that the ground level got put in. The problem of making it interesting for the intelligent student, and basic enough that the duller student can understand it, is a hard one and I didn't quite solve it. I am also disappointed that in the books the summaries are not there to guide the reader as to what's the essential basic course, and what's the fireworks and interesting—but there you are!'[3]

About his teaching experience and whether he had achieved any success, Feynman remarked: 'Now, if you ask me if I think I succeeded in teaching physics well, I haven't the slightest idea. Actually I am very pessimistic. I don't think you can teach physics very well anyway to people in that manner, by giving lectures on a big scale. I think it's hopeless. I have taught all these years and I don't know whether I have been successful or not. People say I'm a good teacher. Well, *they* say! You work very hard to teach them, you give them an exam or you give them some questions and problems, and some of them are so goddamn dumb that it makes you discouraged. Then there are others; you give them a problem and they give you a rather brilliant solution, and you always get the feeling that they learned that from some other class. Otherwise, they are *no* good and you feel you are not getting anywhere. This is my psychological reaction to it. It must be wrong, because if they can get something from some other class that you can appreciate, they must also be able to get something from you for some other class. But I can never tell what it is.

'At the end of two years [1961–63] I felt that I had wasted two years, that I had done no research during this entire period and I was muttering to this effect. I remember Robert Walker saying to me: "Someday you will realize that what you did for physics in those two years is far more important than any research you could have done during the same period." I said, "You're crazy!" I don't think he's crazy now. I think he was right. The books [*The Feynman lectures on physics*] are popular, they are read by a lot of people, and when I read them over [I find] *they're good, they're all right*. I am satisfied; rather, I am not dissatisfied with them. I am just dissatisfied with the system whether it would transmit, but when you have a book and somebody from far away writes that he is learning from it, then I feel that I may have done something to a large number of other people, to people everywhere.

'They have the books on the shelves. They are used all the time. They are twenty-five years old, and they are still on the shelves. Undergraduate and graduate students use them. They look them up for fundamental ideas behind advanced subjects. There is all kinds of stuff there, more basic physical points of view, and so apparently they are useful. I must admit now that I cannot deny that they are really a contribution to the physics world.'[3]

But on an individual basis, 'I was able to do some good only in exceptional cases. A few people, including two Argentinians, did all right. When I was in Brazil, I gave a course in quantum mechanics at the Center for Physical Research there [1953], and there were two Argentinians there—[Daniele] Amati and [Alberto] Sirlin—who worked together. These guys worked very hard and did the problems, but there had been a vacuum before, they had never heard of quantum mechanics. So I know that everything they did in these problems and whenever they showed any intelligence [in their work], it was coming from what I had taught them a week or two before. Since then both Amati and Sirlin have become respectable professors of physics and have done good work in quantum theory and quantum field theory. I know that I taught them because I started with a vacuum, and when they got out of the class they were doing very well. Another case was of a man called Sam Berman.

'Sam Berman came from an unusual background. He had played saxophone in a band and he encountered difficulties in his path. He decided that he ought to do something else and he picked up physics. He was older by this time, and he applied for admission to graduate school here at Caltech. This school is very interesting; once in a while they accept someone without normal preparation, just on the odd chance to see what happens. Berman did not have the usual preparation, but he was enthusiastic. He became my student and we did some work together on beta decay. I explained everything to him and he had very little background, so I know that he got it from me, and he's another person who did reasonably well in physics.

'In these cases at least I know that the vessel was empty when I started and, of course, given a great deal of their own intelligence, I felt that I did succeed in making enough contact that they were able to do well, which was nice. I always get the feeling that if they turn out smart, they got it from somewhere else, and if they don't turn out smart, well you don't get any fun out of that!'[3]

As for the lectures on physics, 'I have put a lot of thought into these things over the years. I've always been trying to improve the method of understanding everything. I had already tried to explain the results of relativity theory in my own way to my girlfriend, Arline, and then I used the same explanations in my lectures. These things are very personal, my own way of looking at things and I recognize them. I did everything—*all of it*—in my own way. I wasn't quite as successful with electrodynamics. I tried very hard to present Maxwell's equations in my own way, but I never did discover a way that was scientifically better or clearer or somehow different from the conventional way. Now, I think I know how to do it better. But still, when I look at *The Feynman lectures on physics*, I feel a very personal sense of closeness to them.'[3]

Feynman's lecture program went on for two years from 1961 to 1963. At first it was thought that quantum mechanics could be appended to the volume on electromagnetism (Volume II), but Feynman decided to make a volume of it by itself (Volume III) by giving supplementary lectures.

Matthew Sands was responsible for getting the printed versions out as quickly as possible for the students; usually within two or three weeks after the lecture a copy of the printed version would be made available to the students. Towards the middle of the second year they decided that the notes were sufficiently useful that they should be published in book form for the future students. Several publishing companies, who had heard of these lectures and knew about Feynman, were trying to convince the organizing team to publish them. 'In the end, we picked a publisher [Addison-Wesley] who said that they could have the copies of the book in the hands of the students six months later. It was the month of March and they said they could have copies of the books available in September.'[2]

Sands had the responsibility of seeing the books through publication. He had one very interesting and instructive experience. The first chapters that came back typeset were disasters, because the editor had decided that the informal style—Feynman's use of informal language, the spoken word rather than the written style—was not appropriate, so he had gone through the text and revised the style. Sands told the publisher that this was unacceptable, that the style they had used was intentional, and if there were incomplete sentences that's the way it had to be. The understanding was reached that the publisher would follow the manuscripts that were provided—because it was not a *textbook* but a book of *lectures*. A second book was intended to go with the lectures, called the workbook; it would have worked out examples, emphases, etc., and it would be a textbook.

Sands intended to prepare that workbook the following year, but he accepted a position at the Stanford Linear Accelerator Center (SLAC) at Stanford University at the invitation of Wolfgang Panofsky. He was still working on Volumes II and III, and he completed both of them in close collaboration with Feynman. 'The key point which is related both to

Feynman's personality and intellect is that he felt that if a physicist really understands some concept, he should be able to explain it in simple language and that's what he always tried to do. Sydney Drell said that's why he was a true genius.' [2]

The way Feynman had originally planned the lectures was that after completing the course up to electromagnetism, he would have liked to teach all the difficult branches of physics by using the same equation, like the diffusion equation which applies to lots of different things or the wave equation for sound, light, and so on. So the second half of the course would have been on the mathematical methods of physics. 'The course would be organized in the usual way. It would be in terms of subjects—the point being that the equations are just the same in many fields, so the moment you deal with an equation you ought to know all fields it comes from, instead of just talking about the equation alone. That's what I had planned to do.

'But then I had another possibility. Maybe I could teach quantum mechanics to sophomores. I had a crazy upside-down way of presenting quantum mechanics, absolutely inside out, in which everything advanced came first and everything that was elementary, in the conventional sense, would come last. And I told this to the guys in the department. They kept on working on me. They said I had to teach quantum mechanics in my own way; that the mathematical things could be done by somebody else another time. They thought that doing quantum mechanics from my point of view would be unique. They knew that I would not go on for another year, unless I did something unique, even if it killed the students. So I settled upon teaching quantum mechanics.' [3]

22.1 The Feynman lectures on physics

The Feynman lectures on physics were based on lectures given by Feynman during 1961–63 to freshmen and sophomores at the California Institute of Technology. These lectures crackled with life and possessed a great artistic and philosophical depth, and anyone who had the opportunity of hearing Feynman lecture, before groups large or small, will recognize in these three volumes his humor, dramatic flair, personal philosophy, and insistence upon utter clarity. In reviewing Volume I of *The Feynman lectures on physics*, a graduate student wrote: 'I prefer to discuss the [Feynman] lectures from the point of view of a man who has had at least a liberal education in physics—mathematics through calculus and an elementary physics course—who wants to understand the natural world around him, and who is prepared to give as much effort to Feynman's lectures as he gives to James Joyce's *Ulysses*. The parallel between the two works is suggestive because both may be read for a greater understanding of the world, yet both abound in wit and humor and demand considerable concentration.' [4]

The wide range of topics and the casual tone of lectures might, at first glance, be thought to imply a shallow treatment characteristic of a survey course, but they are meant to provide a thorough grounding in physics. To an unusual degree these volumes offer the careful reader Feynman's specific brand of careful scientific spirit and philosophy. At the outset, Feynman declares that 'there isn't any solution to [the] problem of education other than to realize that the best teaching can be done only when there is a direct individual relationship between a student and a good teacher—a situation in which the student discusses the ideas, thinks about things, and talks about things', and quotes Edward Gibbon to say that 'the power of education is seldom of much efficacy except in the happy dispositions where it is almost superfluous'.[5]

Feynman asks why we cannot teach physics by just giving the basic laws on page one and then showing how they work in all possible circumstances, as we do in Euclidean geometry, where we state the axioms and then make all sorts of deductions, and answers that 'we cannot do it for two reasons. First, we do not yet *know* all the basic laws: there is an expanding frontier of ignorance. Second, the correct statement of the laws of physics involves some very unfamiliar ideas which require advanced mathematics for their description. Therefore, one needs a considerable amount of preparatory training even to learn what the *words* mean. No, it is not possible to do it that way. We can do it only piece by piece.'[6]

The generality of Feynman's approach to the learning of physics becomes immediately apparent: 'If, in some cataclysm, all of scientific knowledge were to be destroyed, and only one sentence passed on to the next generation of creatures, what statement would contain the most information in the fewest words? I believe it is the *atomic hypothesis* (or the atomic *fact*) that *all things are made of atoms—little particles that move around in perpetual motion, attracting each other when they are a little distance apart, but repelling upon being squeezed into one another.*'

'*Everything is made of atoms*. That is the key hypothesis. The most important hypothesis in all biology, for example, is that *everything that animals do atoms can do*. In other words, *there is nothing that living things do that cannot be understood from the point of view that they are made of atoms acting according to the laws of physics*.

'The most remarkable discovery in all of astronomy is *that stars are made of the same kind of atoms as those on earth* . . . Poets say science takes away from the beauty of the stars—mere globes of gas atoms. Nothing is "mere". I too can see the stars on a desert night, and feel them. But do I see less or more? The vastness of the heavens stretches my imagination—stuck on this carousel my little eye can catch one-million-year-old light. A vast pattern—of which I am a part—perhaps my stuff was belched from some forgotten star, as one is belching there. Or see them with the greater eye of Palomar, rushing all apart from some common starting point when they were perhaps all together. What is the pattern, or the meaning, or the *why*? It does not do harm to the mystery to know a little about it. For far more marvelous is the truth than any artists of the past imagined! Why do the poets of the present not speak of it? What men are poets who can speak of Jupiter if he were like a man, but if he is an immense spinning sphere of methane and ammonia must be silent?' [7]

'One of the most impressive discoveries was the origin of the energy of the stars, that makes them continue to burn. One of the men who discovered this was out with his girl friend the night after he realized that *nuclear reactions* must be going on in the stars in order to make them shine. She said, "Look at how pretty the stars shine!" He said, "Yes, and right now I am the only man in the whole world who knows *why* they shine." She merely laughed at him. She was not impressed with being out with the only man who, at that moment, knew why stars shine. Well, it is sad to be alone, but that is the way it is in the world.' [8]

'There is no historical question being studied in physics at the present time. We do not have the question, "Here are the laws of physics, how did it get that way?" We do not imagine, at the moment, that the laws of physics are somehow changing with time, that they were different in the past than they are at present. Of course, they *may* be, and the moment we find they *are*, the historical question of physics will be wrapped up with the rest of the history of the universe, and then the physicist will be talking about the same problems as astronomers, geologists, and biologists.' [9]

'A poet once said, "The whole universe is in a glass of wine." We will probably never know in what sense he meant that, for poets do not write to be understood. But it is true that if we look at a glass of wine closely enough we see the entire universe. There are the things of physics: the twisting liquid which evaporates depending on the wind and weather, the reflections in the glass, and our imagination adds the atoms. The glass is a distillation of the earth's rocks, and in its composition we see the secrets of the universe's age, and the evolution of stars. What a strange array of chemicals are in the wine? How did they come to be? There are the ferments, the enzymes, the substrates, and the products. There in wine is found the great generalization: all life is fermentation. Nobody can discover the chemistry of wine without discovering, as did Louis Pasteur, the cause of much disease. How vivid is claret, pressing its existence into the consciousness that watches it! If our small minds, for some convenience, divide this glass of wine, this universe, into parts—physics, biology, geology, astronomy, psychology, and so on— remember that nature does not know it! So let us put it all back together, not forgetting ultimately what it is for. Let it give us one more final pleasure: drink it and forget it all.' [10]

Volume I of *The Feynman lectures on physics* was devoted mainly to mechanics (motion, Newton's laws of dynamics, conservation of energy and momentum, characteristics of force, work and potential energy, the theory of gravitation, special theory of relativity, relativistic energy and momentum, space–time, rotation, moment of inertia, harmonic oscillator, resonance);

radiation (the principle of least time, geometrical optics, electromagnetic radiation, interference, diffraction, origin of refractive index, radiation damping and light scattering, polarization, relativistic effects in radiation, color vision, mechanisms of seeing, quantum behavior of radiation, and the relation of wave and particle viewpoints); and heat (kinetic theory of gases, the principles of statistical mechanics, Brownian motion, applications of kinetic theory, diffusion, and the laws of thermodynamics); sound (the wave equation, beats, modes, harmonics, different kinds of waves); and, finally, the symmetry of physical laws.

Among the major unsolved problems of classical physics, Feynman considered the analysis of *circulating or turbulent fluids*. 'Nobody in physics has really been able to analyze it mathematically satisfactorily in spite of its importance to the sister sciences. . . . If we watch the evolution of a star, there comes a point where we can deduce what should happen. A few million years later the star explodes, but we cannot figure out the reason. We cannot analyze weather [exactly]. We do not know the patterns of motion that there should be inside the earth. The simplest form of the problem is to take a pipe that is very long and push water through it at high speed. We ask: to push a given amount of water through that pipe, how much pressure is needed? No one can analyze it from first principles and the properties of water. If the water flows very slowly, or if we use a thick goo like honey, then we can do it nicely. What we really cannot do is to deal with actual, wet running water through a pipe. That is the central problem which we ought to solve some day, and we have not.' [11]

Feynman asks the question: 'Why is nature so nearly symmetrical?' And answers: 'No one has any idea why. The only thing we might suggest is something like this: There is a gate in Japan, a gate in Neiko; it was built in a time when there was great influence from Chinese art. The gate is very elaborate, with lots of gables and beautiful carving and lots of columns and dragon heads and princes carved into the pillars, and so on. But when one looks closely he sees in the elaborate and complex design along one of the pillars, one of the small design elements carved upside down; otherwise the thing is completely symmetrical. If one asks why this is, the story is that it was carved upside down so that the gods will not be jealous of the perfection of man. So they purposely put an error in there, so that the gods will not be jealous and get angry with human beings.

'We might like to turn the idea around and think that the true explanation of the near symmetry of nature is this: that God made the laws only nearly symmetrical so that we should not be jealous of His perfection!' [12]

In Volume II, devoted mainly to electromagnetism and properties of matter, Feynman discussed the following topics: electrostatics, electromagnetism, differential and vector fields, Gauss's law, the electric field in various circumstances, atmospheric electricity, dielectrics, magnetostatics, the magnetic field in various situations, the vector potential, induced currents, waveguides, electrodynamics in relativistic notation, Lorentz transformation of fields, field energy and field momentum, electromagnetic mass, the motion of charges in electric and magnetic fields, the internal geometry of crystals, refractive index of dense materials, reflection from surfaces, the magnetism of matter, paramagnetism and magnetic resonance, ferromagnetism, magnetic materials, elasticity and elastic materials, laminar and viscous flow, properties of curved spaces and the theory of gravitation.

'There is a force', said Feynman, 'the electrical force. And all matter is a mixture of positive protons and negative electrons which are attracting and repelling with this great force. So perfect is the balance, however, that when you stand near someone else you don't feel any force at all. If there were even a little imbalance you would know it. If you were standing at arms length from someone and each of you had *one percent* more electrons than protons, the repelling force would be incredible. How great? Enough to lift the Empire State Building? No! To lift Mount Everest? No! The repulsion would be enough to lift a "weight" equal to that of the entire earth!'[13]

Maxwell's equations: 'From a long view of history of mankind—seen from, say, ten thousand years from now—there can be little doubt that the most significant event of the 19th century will be judged as Maxwell's discovery of the laws of electrodynamics. The American Civil War will pale into provincial insignificance in comparison with this important scientific event of the same decade.'[14]

After treating the subject of lightning and atmospheric electricity, Feynman remarked: 'It has apparently been known for a long time that high objects are struck by lightning. There is a quotation of Artabanis, the advisor to Xerxes, giving his master advice on a contemplated attack on the Greeks—during Xerxes' campaign to bring the entire known world under the control of the Persians. Artabanis said, "See how God with his lightning ways smites bigger animals and will not suffer them to wax insolent, while those of lesser bulk chafe him not. How likewise his bolts fall ever on the highest houses and tallest trees." And then he explains the reason: "So plainly, doth he love to bring down everything that exalts itself."

'Do you think—now that you know a true account of lightning striking tall trees—that you have greater wisdom in advising kings on military matters than did Artabanis 2300 years ago? You could only do it less poetically!'[15]

Scientific imagination: 'I have asked you to imagine these electric and magnetic fields. What do you do? Do you know how? How do *I* imagine the electric and magnetic field? What do *I* actually see? What are the demands of scientific imagination? Is it any different from trying to imagine that the room is full of invisible angels? No, it is not like imagining invisible angels. It requires a much higher degree of imagination to understand the electromagnetic field than to understand invisible angels. Why? Because to make invisible angels understandable, all I have to do is to alter their properties *a little bit*—I make them slightly visible, and then I can see the shapes of their wings, and bodies, and halos. Once I succeed in imagining a visible angel, the abstraction required—which is to take almost invisible angels and imagine them completely invisible—is relatively easy. So you say, "Professor, please give me an approximate description of the electromagnetic waves, even though it might be slightly inaccurate, so that I too can see them as well as I can see almost invisible angels. Then I will modify the picture to the necessary abstraction."

'I'm sorry I can't do that for you. I don't know how. I have no picture of this electromagnetic field that is in any sense accurate. I have known about the electromagnetic field a long time—I was in the same position 25 years ago [in 1937, at the age of 19] that you are now, and I have had 25 years more of experience thinking about these wiggling waves. When I start describing the magnetic field moving through space, I speak of the E and B fields and wave my arms and you may imagine that I can see them. I'll tell you what I see. I see some kind of vague shadowy, wiggling lines—here and there is an E and B written on them somehow, and perhaps some of the lines have arrows on them—an arrow here or there which disappears when I look too closely at it. When I talk about the fields swishing through space, I have a terrible confusion between the symbols I use to describe the objects and the objects themselves. I cannot really make a picture that is even nearly like the true waves. So if you have some difficulty in making such a picture, you should not be worried that your difficulty is unusual.

'Our science makes terrific demands on the imagination. . . . The whole question of imagination in science is often misunderstood by people in other disciplines. They try to test our imagination in the following way. They say, "Here is a picture of some people in a situation. What do you imagine will happen next?" When I say, "I can't imagine," they may think we have a weak imagination. They overlook the fact that whatever we are *allowed* to imagine in science must be *consistent with everything we know*: that the electric fields and waves we talk about are not just some happy thoughts which we are free to make as we wish, but ideas which must be consistent with all the laws of physics we know. We can't allow ourselves to seriously imagine things which are obviously in contradiction to the known laws of nature. And so our kind of imagination is quite a difficult game. One has to have imagination to think of something that has never been seen before, never been heard of before. At the same time the thoughts are restricted in a strait jacket, so to speak, limited by the conditions that come from our knowledge of the way nature really is. The problem of creating something new, but which is consistent with everything which has been seen before, is one of extreme difficulty.' [16]

What can we do with our equations? 'We have written the equations of water flow. From experiment, we find a set of concepts and approximations to use to discuss the solution—vortex sheets, turbulent wakes, boundary layers. When we have similar equations in a less familiar situation, and one for which we cannot yet experiment, we try to determine what new qualitative features may come out, or what new qualitative forms are a consequence of the equations. Our equations for the sun, for example, as a ball of hydrogen gas, describe a sun complete without sunspots, without the rice-grain structure of the surface, without prominences, without coronas. Yet, all of these are really in the equations, we just haven't found the way to get them out.

'There are those who are going to be disappointed when no life is found on other planets. Not I—I want to be reminded and delighted and surprised once again, through interplanetary exploration, with the infinite variety and novelty of phenomena that can be generated from such simple principles. The test of science is its ability to predict. Had you never visited the earth, could you predict the thunderstorms, the volcanos, the ocean waves, the auroras, and the colorful sunset? A salutary lesson it will be when we learn of all that goes on each of those dead planets—those eight or ten balls, each agglomerated from the same dust cloud and each obeying exactly the same laws of physics.

'The next great era of awakening of human intellect may well produce a method of understanding the *qualitative* content of equations. Today we cannot. Today we cannot see that the water flow equations contain such things as the barber pole structure of turbulence that one sees between rotating cylinders. Today we cannot see whether Schrödinger's equation contains frogs, musical composers, or morality—or whether it does not. We cannot say whether something beyond it like God is needed, or not. And so we can all hold strong opinions either way.'[17]

Volume III of *The Feynman lectures on physics* was devoted to quantum mechanics (quantum behavior, the relation of wave and particle viewpoints, probability amplitudes, identical particles, spin-1, spin-$\frac{1}{2}$, the dependence of amplitudes on time, the Hamiltonian matrix, the ammonia maser and other two-state systems, hyperfine splitting of hydrogen, propagation in a crystal lattice, semiconductors, the independent particle approximation, the dependence of amplitudes on position, symmetry and conservation laws, angular momentum, the hydrogen atom and the periodic table, operators, the Schrödinger equation, and a seminar on superconductivity).

The uncertainty principle: 'The uncertainty principle "protects" quantum mechanics. Heisenberg recognized that if it were possible to measure the momentum and position simultaneously with a greater accuracy, then quantum mechanics would collapse. So he proposed this it must be impossible. Then people sat down and tried to figure out a way to measure the position and momentum of anything—a screen, an electron, a billiard ball, anything—with any greater accuracy. Quantum mechanics maintains its perilous but still correct existence.'[18]

More on indeterminacy: 'We have already made a few remarks about the indeterminacy of quantum mechanics, that is, that we are unable to predict what will happen in physics in a given physical circumstance which is arranged as carefully as possible. If we have an atom that is in an excited state and is going to emit a photon, we cannot say *when* it will emit the photon. It has a certain amplitude to emit the photon at any time, and we can predict only a probability for emission; we cannot predict the future exactly. This has given rise to all kinds of nonsense and questions on the meaning of free will, and of the idea that the world is uncertain.

'Of course we must emphasize that classical physics is also indeterminate in a sense. It is usually thought that this indeterminacy, that we cannot predict the future, is an important quantum mechanical thing, and this is said to explain the behavior of the mind, feelings of free will, etc. But if the world *were* classical—if the laws of mechanics were classical—it is not quite obvious that the mind would not feel more or less the same. It is true classically that if we knew the position and velocity of every particle in the world, or in a box of gas, we could predict exactly what would happen. And therefore the classical world is deterministic. Suppose, however, that we have a finite accuracy and do not know *exactly* where just one atom is, say to one part in a billion. Then as it goes along it hits another atom, and because we did not know the position to better than one part in a billion, we find an even larger error in the position after the collision. And that is amplified, of course, in the next collision, so that if we start with only a tiny error it rapidly magnifies to a very great uncertainty. To give an example: if water falls over a dam, it splashes. If we stand nearby, every now and then a drop will land on our nose. This appears to be completely at random, yet such a behavior would be predicted by purely classical laws. The exact position of all the drops depends upon the precise wigglings of the water before it goes over the dam. How? The tiniest irregularities are magnified in falling, so that we have complete randomness. Obviously, we cannot predict the position of the drops unless we know the motion of the water *absolutely exactly* . . .. It is therefore not fair to say that from the apparent freedom and indeterminacy of the human mind, we should have realized that classical "deterministic" physics could never hope to understand it, and welcome quantum mechanics as a release from a "completely mechanistic" universe. For already in classical mechanics there was indeterminability from a practical point of view.'[19]

In concluding his course of lectures, Feynman remarked: 'Finally, may I add that the main purpose of my teaching has not been to prepare you for some examination—it was not even to prepare you to serve industry or the military. I wanted most to give you some appreciation of the wonderful world and the physicist's way of looking at it, which, I believe, is a major part of the true culture of modern times. (There are probably professors of other subjects who would object, but I believe that they are completely wrong.)

'Perhaps you will not only have some appreciation of this culture; it is even possible that you may want to join in the greatest adventure that the human mind has ever begun.'[20]

The Feynman lectures on physics, taken together, turned out to be a work of art, capable of standing by itself and contributing in a fundamental way to a complex world view. Feynman presented the complex data of the physical world in wide-ranging yet penetrating detail, and his lectures were throughout replete with good humor and wit. He portrayed the natural world and points beyond it, the observed as well as the unimaginable. At the close of *The origin of species*, Charles Darwin wrote: 'There is a grandeur in this view of life, with its several powers, having been originally breathed by the Creator into a few forms or into one; and that, while this planet has gone circling on according to the fixed law of gravity, from so simple a beginning endless forms most beautiful and wondrous have been, and are being evolved.' Like Darwin, Feynman treated the complex themes of the physical world with clarity, honesty, graciousness, and unfailing charm.

22.2 The character of physical law

The Messenger lectures have taken place annually at Cornell University since 1924, when Hiram J. Messenger, a graduate of and professor of mathematics at Cornell, gave a sum of money to encourage eminent personalities anywhere in the world to visit Cornell to talk to the academic community. In establishing the fund for the lectures, Messenger specified that it was 'to provide a course or courses of lectures on the evolution of civilization for the special purpose of raising the moral standard of our political, business and social life.' In November 1964, Richard Feynman presented seven lectures, extempore style, on 'The character of physical law'. The lectures were recorded for television by the British Broadcasting Corporation, and a transcription was prepared and printed 'to serve as a guide or memory aid for the television viewers who may see the lectures and wish to have a permanent reminder to refer to'[21] The transcription was an extremely lucid, self-contained account of Feynman's lectures, and was later reprinted by the MIT Press in paperback form (1987).

In the lectures Feynman concentrated on the general characteristics common to most of the laws of physics, of which the pre-eminent example is the law of gravitation; on the role of mathematics in physics; on the symmetries of physical law; on the distinction between past and future; on probability and uncertainty in physical law; and on the techniques by which physicists seek new laws. Feynman made his discourse vivid and clear by frequent examples, taken largely, from the theory of gravitation and from quantum theory.

First of all, Feynman defined the nature of the physical law: 'As we look at the sunsets, the ocean waves, and the march of stars across the heavens, we get aesthetic pleasure from them directly on observation. There is also a rhythm and a pattern between the phenomena of nature which is not apparent to the eye, but only to the eye of analysis; and it is these rhythms and patterns which we call physical laws. What I want to discuss in this series of lectures is the general characteristic of these physical laws; that is another level, if you will, of higher generality over the laws themselves. Mainly I wish to speak about only the most overall general qualities of nature.' In choosing to treat the law of gravitation as his special example, Feynman pointed out that all of modern science is exactly in the same tradition as the discoveries connected with this law, for this law 'has been called the greatest generalization achieved by the human mind; it is a marvel that nature can obey such [elegant and simple laws].'[22]

These lectures were directed primarily at the layman, and for this reason considerable attention was paid to a detailed development of the gravitational and quantum mechanical examples. Yet, by skipping lightly over the examples and concentrating on the fundamental ideas, physical scientists and engineers could also gain new insight into the character of physical law. Of particular interest was Feynman's discussion of the relation of mathematics and physics (Chapter 2) and his description of methods for seeking new scientific laws when old ones fail (Chapter 7).

Feynman pointed out that mathematics is a way of going from one set of statements to another. It is evidently useful in physics, because we have these different ways in which we can speak of things, and mathematics permits us to develop consequences, to analyze situations, and to change the laws in different ways to connect the various statements. Now an interesting question comes up. Is there a place to begin to deduce the whole works? Is there some particular pattern or order in nature by which we can understand that one set of statements is more consequential? There are two kinds of ways of looking at mathematics, which Feynman called the Babylonian tradition and the Greek tradition. In Babylonian schools in mathematics the student would learn something by doing a large number of examples until he caught on to the general rule. Also he would know a large amount of geometry, a lot of the properties of circles, the theorem of Pythagoras, formulas for the areas of the cubes and triangles; in addition, some degree of argument was available to go from one thing to another. Tables of numerical quantities were available so that they could solve elaborate equations. Everything was prepared for calculating things out. In the Greek or Euclidean tradition, on the other hand, one had to work out everything from axioms or first principles. 'If you have a structure [of physical laws] that is only partly accurate, and something is going to fail, then if you write it with just the right axioms maybe only one axiom fails and the rest remain, you need only change one little thing. But if you write it with another set of axioms they will all collapse, because they all lean on that one thing that fails. We cannot tell ahead of time, without some intuition, which is the best way to write it so that we can find out the new situation. We must always keep all alternative ways of looking at a thing in our head; so the physicists [generally] do Babylonian mathematics, and pay but little attention to the precise reasoning from fixed axioms.'[23]

In the pursuit of seeking new laws of nature Feynman considered himself a

Babylonian unlike others, like Julian Schwinger, who, Feynman thought, pursued the Greek or the Euclidean method.

22.3 QED: The strange theory of light and matter

In the fall of 1983, Feynman gave the Alix G. Mautner Memorial Lectures at the University of California Los Angeles on quantum electrodynamics. Entitled 'QED: The strange theory of light and matter', it was delivered to large audiences comprising scientists, scholars from the humanities, laymen, and the students. Alix Mautner, the wife of Leonard Mautner, Feynman's boyhood friend, had taught English literature at the California State University in Los Angeles, but she was very interested in several aspects of modern science. She used to ask Richard Feynman questions about quantum mechanics and quantum electrodynamics, which he had promised her once to answer in detail. Upon her death, Leonard Mautner established the Alix G. Mautner Memorial Lectureship at UCLA, and Feynman was the first person chosen to give these lectures. 'So here are the lectures I really prepared for Alix, but unfortunately I can't tell them to her directly, now.'[24]

Feynman began by saying that people were always asking him about the latest developments 'in the unification of this theory with that theory, and they don't give us a chance to tell them anything about one of the theories that we know pretty well. They always want to know things that we don't know. So, rather than confound you with a lot of half-cooked, partially analyzed theories, I would like to tell you about a subject that has been very thoroughly analyzed. I love this area of physics and I think it is wonderful: it is called quantum electrodynamics, or QED for short.'[25]

What Feynman presented to his audiences was a beautiful description of quantum electrodynamics, the 'strange' theory of the interaction of light with matter, in simple, nontechnical language, yet remarkably accurate and complete. That the twin goals of completeness and accuracy could be achieved in a popular exposition is an example of creative presentation by a master craftsman. As Feynman said himself in the introduction, many 'popular' expositions of science using clever language try to present a simple *understandable* picture, but only at the expense of distortion. Feynman gave an accurate picture of *how* nature works, admitting repeatedly that nobody understands *why* nature works in that 'strange' way. He proposed a new intuition to deal with light and matter, 'the 99 per cent of all of physics'. Although addressed to laymen, a book of lectures of this quality and integrity should be also a revealing experience to all physicists, even those who work in the field of quantum electrodynamics itself, at least to remind them of the deep problems and questions that remain to be solved.

QED is our best example of a good theory. So far nothing has been found to be wrong with it, and whenever it *can* be checked it is very accurate. It is also practical ('There's nothing so practical as a good theory', said Feynman), and the bulk of his small book of four lectures was devoted to explaining everyday phenomena: the simple reflection of light from a window (an early mystery to Newton), the derivation of the laws of mirrors, diffraction gratings, mirages, reflection from crystals, double-slit experiments, and the scattering of light and electrons from matter.

Feynman's new intuition was based on little turning arrows, like the hand of a stopwatch, representing the magnitude and phase of the amplitude for each possible path of the photon or the electron. The perturbative quantum electrodynamics is based on three actions: the photon goes from one place to another, the electron goes from one place to another, and an electron emits or absorbs a photon. The rules of working with these little arrows are simple. We cannot say anything about what an individual photon will do in going, for example, from a source S, being reflected from a glass surface G, and then going to a detector A, but we can calculate the probabilities as follows. Consider all paths from S via G to A: (i) If something can happen in alternate ways, add the arrows or vectors; (ii) if the event occurs as a succession of steps (or consists of independent pieces), then multiply the arrows. The square of the final arrow gives the probability of the event. The simplicity of the three basic actions is the superiority and attractiveness of QED. Feynman takes the Feynman graphs (diagrams) seriously and is justly proud of his techniques. But he does not conceal their practical limitations, when the number of graphs or paths becomes dramatically large at higher and higher order (e.g. 'there are some 10 000 graphs with 500 terms each' in the calculation of the anomalous magnetic moments with six vertices) and in bound state problems.

The last lecture was entitled 'Loose ends', showing both the power of Feynman's techniques and the humility of his attitude. Although hardly any physicist nowadays is struggling with the infinities of renormalization, with the mathematical consistency of QED, the fine structure constant $\alpha^{-1} = 137.03597(2)$ ('one of the *greatest* damn mysteries of physics: a *magic number* that comes to us with no understanding by man. You might say that the 'hand of God' wrote that number, and "we do not know how He pushed His pencil".'), the values of the masses ('one especially unsatisfactory feature is that no theory adequately explains the observed masses of the particles—what they are, where they come from—a serious problem'), it is necessary that the present and future generation should be constantly made aware of these problems, as Dirac did, and as Feynman attempted to do eloquently in his lectures on QED.

Perhaps these questions are too difficult. On the other hand, if we carry over the methods of QED to other field theories, we do not have a completely clear conscience that all is well, because we have left QED unfinished. Feynman called renormalization a 'dippy' process, and suggested, as Dirac used to do, that 'it is not mathematically legitimate', but he was hopeful that 'someday a legitimate mathematical connection between bare coupling constant and the electric charge will be found.' It will be difficult but not impossible.[26]

Towards the end, Feynman talked about the remaining 1 percent of the physics, the nuclear phenomena, radioactivity, and the proliferation of new particles, some four hundred of them ('we cannot accept four hundred particles'), and he discussed how almost exactly the same ideas as perturbative QED have been used for quarks and gluons in the QCD (quantum chromodynamics) theory of strong interactions and how the exchange of heavy vector mesons has been used in the theory of weak interactions: 'It is very clear that the photons and three W's are interconnected somehow, but at present level of understanding the connection is difficult to see clearly—you can still see the "seams" in the theories' (presumably a reference to the problem of symmetry-breaking and Higgs particles).[27]

As for QCD, 'it is a definite theory, but yet you cannot calculate anything with it', since the coupling constant is large. Why are all three theories of the same type (spin-$\frac{1}{2}$ particles, vector meson exchange)? Feynman thought of three possible answers: the limited imagination of physicists, maybe nature repeats itself, or maybe they are different aspects of the same theory. He mentioned other complications of the theory: the utterly unknown quark mixing angles, number of flavors, and masses. Particle physics now looks like a 'terrible mix-up, . . . a hopeless mess,' but Feynman, the eternal optimist, reflected: 'It has always looked like this!'

Notes and References

1. A.R. Hibbs, Interview with Jagdish Mehra, 23 March 1988, at the Athenaeum, Caltech, Pasadena, California.

2. M. Sands, Telephone interview with Jagdish Mehra, 31 August 1990.

3. R.P. Feynman, Interviews and conversations with Jagdish Mehra, in Pasadena, California, January 1988.

4. R.R. Blandford, *Engineering and Science*, February 1964, p. 19.

5. R.P. Feynman, *The Feynman lectures on physics*. Addison-Wesley, Reading, Massachusetts, 1963, Vol. I, p. 1-5.

6. R.P. Feynman, Ref. 5, 1-1.

7. R.P. Feynman, Ref. 5, 1-2, 1-8, 3-6.

8. R.P. Feynman, Ref. 5, 3-7.

9. R.P. Feynman, Ref. 5, 3-9.

10. R.P. Feynman, Ref. 5, 3-10.

11. R.P. Feynman, Ref. 5, 3-9, 10.

12. R.P. Feynman, Ref. 5, p. 52-12.

13. R.P. Feynman, *The Feynman lectures on physics.* Addison-Wesley, Reading, Massachusetts, 1963, Vol. II, p. 1-1.

14. R.P. Feynman, Ref. 13, p. 1-13.

15. R.P. Feynman, Ref. 13, p. 9-11.

16. R.P. Feynman, Ref. 13, pp. 20-9, 10, 11.

17. R.P. Feynman, Ref. 13, p. 41-12.

18. R.P. Feynman, *The Feynman lectures on physics.* Addison-Wesley, Reading, Massachusetts, 1963, Vol. III, p. 1-11.

19. R.P. Feynman, Ref. 18, pp. 2-9, 10.

20. R.P. Feynman, Ref. 18, p. 21-19.

21. R.P. Feynman, *The character of physical law.* BBC, London 1965; MIT Press, Cambridge, Massachusetts, 1987.

22. R.P. Feynman, Ref. 21, pp. 13-14.

23. R.P. Feynman, Ref. 21, p. 54.

24. R.P. Feynman, *QED: The strange theory of light and matter*, Princeton University Press, Princeton, New Jersey, 1986. (Feynman first tried out this set of four lectures at the University of Auckland, New Zealand, in the fall of 1982, before finally giving them in the spring of 1983 as the Alix G Mautner Memorial Lectures of UCLA.)

25. R.P. Feynman, Ref. 24, pp. 3–4.

26. R.P. Feynman, Ref. 24, pp. 128–29.

27. R.P. Feynman, Ref. 24, p. 142.

23

Gravitons, partons, and quark jets

23.1 The quantum theory of gravitation

In January 1957 Richard Feynman attended one of the first conferences organized to discuss the role of gravitation in physics.[1] 'I knew that gravity must be part of nature and nature can't be half classical and half quantum mechanical.'[2] It needed to be verified that the general relativity theory must be subject to the same rules as every other 'classical' theory. It had to be shown that otherwise there would be inconsistencies in the laws of nature. This is not altogether obvious because gravitational phenomena as we know them all take place at macroscopic distance and mass scales. Indeed, Feynman in several of his lectures on gravitation gave lengthy motivations as to why he thought there must be quantum corrections to the gravitational force.[3]

Many people argue that gravitational force becomes strong at ultrashort distances (about 10^{-33} cm), and therefore that distance scale will be *dominated* by quantum gravity. So it is definitely relevant to ask the question how to reconcile general relativity with quantum mechanics. It seems that Feynman did not like this argument. The distance 10^{-33} cm, which corresponds to 10^{19} GeV (the Planck scale), is experimentally totally inaccessible, and maybe physics there does not even vaguely resemble anything we know. Nowadays we are not so pessimistic. Most physicists believe (though nobody knows) that present day field theory in its general form will be valid until close to that scale. At the Planck scale itself fundamental revisions must become necessary.

Feynman preferred to say: We don't have to go to such ridiculous energies to see the effects of quantum gravity; we could imagine instead that we do experiments with extreme accuracy (one part in 10^{120} or more). Surely there should be laws of physics telling us how in principle corrections due to quantum effects should be calculated, even if they are small.[2]

One can see why Feynman was more satisfied with this argument than the high-energy argument, but it is not necessarily superior. The real point, which is accepted by nearly everyone in the field, is that ultimately we do want a complete understanding of all laws of nature. Somehow the 'logic' of general relativity should be brought into harmony with the 'logic' of the quantum world.

In the fall of 1960 Viktor Weisskopf asked Feynman a question concerning the radiation of gravitational waves. Early in 1961 Feynman gave Weisskopf a detailed answer.[4] In his letter, Feynman discussed gravitational radiation and the lowest order of quantum description. Feynman patiently explained to Weisskopf how to calculate gravitational waves, that he thought they must be quantized just like electromagnetic waves have to be, and that 'gravitons' (quanta of the gravitational field), particles with spin 2, must be real physical particles carrying real, physical energy like all the others.

In the beginning physicists had very confused ideas about these gravitons: their existence was very much in doubt, and it was neither understood nor considered 'proven' that they really moved with the speed of light.

Feynman mentioned to Weisskopf at the outset that it is careless to write the gravitational interaction term as $\frac{1}{2}g_{\mu\nu}T^{\mu\nu}$. It depends on what you want to do with it. If you are only interested in the equation for $g_{\mu\nu}$ then it is allowed, but if you want to describe the motion of matter you must use the Lagrangians he wrote down. In those days many people preferred to work with Hamiltonians rather than Lagrangians and mistakes were made. Feynman's strict use of the Lagrangian formalism made his letter to Weisskopf look quite modern; Feynman's contemporaries, however, felt uneasy because from the Lagrangian one cannot see that the theory is unitary, has nonnegative energies, and so on. But for Feynman the Lagrangian was a natural thing to work with, because he was always thinking of path integrals.

However, Feynman did not mention one important thing. Imagine that the gravitational force had the opposite sign, so that all masses would repel each other instead of attracting each other. His arguments would have failed to work then: gravitons would carry negative energy and the gravitational field would become unstable.

Finally, Feynman expressed a sudden doubt. Should the gravitational field be quantized at all? He seemed to feel uncertain. Later on he would elaborate on this question, but he would conclude: Yes, it is inevitable, you *must* quantize the gravitational field. He was right in being vigilant. The present belief is that, yes, the gravitational field should obey the rules of quantum mechanics just like anything else, but maybe, just maybe, these rules will look different for it. At the *submicroscopic* level, i.e. at the Planck scale, it could be that our world will seem to be more classical, more *deterministic* than most physicists would presently accept.

From 25 to 31 July 1962 Feynman attended the international conference on relativity and gravitation in Warsaw, Poland. There he gave lectures on the quantum theory of gravitation.[5] Feynman began with many of the same things he had explained to Weisskopf over a year before the conference. He still felt the need to justify his interest in the subject along lines that would not be popular today: for instance, he claimed that it must be possible in principle to compute such a thing as the Lamb shift correction to the energy levels of an atom held together exclusively by the gravitational force. Apparently this argument satisfied him more than the idea that at very high energies the gravitational force would eventually dominate over all other forces.

Feynman emphasized that one should ask *physically relevant questions*: How does one formulate the rules for computing the dynamical properties of atoms held together by gravity? Can one in principle detect the quantized energy packets of the gravitational field? How do these particles, called 'gravitons', behave?, and so on. And he sharpened his arguments by computing such things as the gravitational Compton effect. Feynman was not interested in formalities that could never be checked by some experiment, such as 'quantized universes' and 'similar absurdities'. He argued, and this is very important, that one should do *perturbative expansions*. There is a systematic perturbative expansion just like the one for quantum electrodynamics. It was true then, as it is nowadays, that most general relativists had some sort of contempt for perturbation expansions. They wanted the real thing, not some approximation. In Feynman's view, if one doesn't understand what the real theory of 'quantum gravity' is, then one should better look at the perturbative expansion. The crucial importance of understanding the peculiarities of this expansion is often underestimated.

The fundamental 'field variable' in gravity is the metric tensor field $g_{\mu\nu}(x, t)$. In perturbation expansion one writes:

$$g_{\mu\nu} = \delta_{\mu\nu} + \kappa h_{\mu\nu}, \tag{23.1}$$

where $\delta_{\mu\nu}$ is the metric of flat space (a space-time without any gravitational field), κ is the gravitational constant (a very small parameter), and $h_{\mu\nu}$ describes the tiny deviations from flatness: the field of the graviton. This field is then quantized in a standard (i.e. particle physics) way and gives rise to a picture of massless spin-2 gravitons which mediate the gravitational force.

This approach was (and still is) anathema to most general relativists since it neglects much of the structure of conventional general relativity. The two specific problems in quantum gravity that are associated with Feynman's name are: (1) showing that the particle physicist's study of interacting spin-2 gravitons reproduces the field equations of general relativity; and (2) computing the correct Feynman rules to describe closed loops of gravitons.

Feynman tackled these problems by using the tools of quantum field theory, many of which he had himself developed. His approach to the first problem was just a question of applying basic ideas of elementary particle physics, although he did it with his usual outstanding physical insight. The second problem was considerably more complicated. Feynman started by computing tree diagrams (i.e. Feynman diagrams without closed loops) of the theory (which are equivalent to classical theory) and showed that they were gauge-invariant. However, he then looked at some of the loop diagrams, and it was his discovery that they were not gauge-invariant that started the long saga of the 'Faddeev–Popov' ghosts.[6] This approach was taken up and developed by Bryce DeWitt and then, in the late 1960s and early 1970s, by a whole generation of young elementary particle physicists.

Feynman's contribution to showing that the particle physicist's approach recovers traditional general relativity is part of a long chain of work that is still continuing. The first reference in this direction is usually that to S. N. Gupta,[7] then to Feynman.[5] The theme was developed further by Weinberg,[8] and then in a series of papers by Boulware and Deser, culminating in their 1975 article in *Annals of Physics*.[9] However, the results are not completely watertight, and one needs to specify the input assumptions rather carefully; for example, Wald[10] has found examples of massless spin-2 theories that are generally covariant. This line of work is still important today in, for example, assessing claims that superstring theory produces general relativity as a low-energy limit.

Feynman's second piece of work is probably the more important of the two. Feynman showed that naive perturbation rules of quantum field theory lead to diagrams that are nonunitary. He also indicated how this might be corrected by adding loops of fictitious spin-1 particles but with the 'wrong' spin-statistics relation. This idea was developed at length by Bryce DeWitt[11] and has continued to be of great use up to the present day (although mainly in the context of Yang–Mills theory, where the corresponding particles have spin 0). These days, most people associate these 'ghost' particles with the names of Faddeev and Popov, who derived the extra terms which must be added to the Lagrangian by considering a full path-integral quantization, but all this goes back to Richard Feynman.

The Yang–Mills theory continues to be of major importance, and the ideas originated by Feynman are still in daily use. However, the situation in quantum gravity is quite different. Since the early days, it was expected that quantum gravity could be nonrenormalizable (Feynman mentioned this possibility in his lectures at Warsaw) and a number of loop processes have confirmed this result. A variety of techniques have been tried to overcome this deficiency including, for example, supergravity theory (where it was hoped that the unwanted divergences could be canceled by the graviton's fermionic partners). But these days, research in quantum gravity is mainly directed along two quite different directions.

The first position maintains that general relativity cannot be quantized by using perturbative techniques of the type inaugurated by Feynman and DeWitt. What is needed is a *non*perturbative method (i.e. one that does not involve expanding the metric tensor about a flat background). However, most effort in this direction involves the canonical approach to gravity which is completely disconnected from Feynman's ideas. This approach takes far more seriously the geometrical aspects of classical general relativity and employs techniques that owe much to Dirac and nothing to Feynman! The most active branch is the study of the Ashtekar variables. A lot of work has also been done on quantum cosmology in a 'mini-superspace' approach, and related conceptual problems such as the nature of 'time' in quantum gravity.

The second position agrees that general relativity cannot be quantized perturbatively, but also maintains that there is no nonperturbative quantization only. In schemes of this type, general relativity is regarded as a 'phenomenological' theory which is only valid at low energies. The 'real' theory that must be quantized is something quite different. The most promising current example of such a system is superstring theory, although not many papers deal directly with the gravitational sector of the theory.

In this connection, Feynman stated: 'I feel I have solved the [problem of the] quantum theory of gravity in the sense that I figured out how to get the quantum principles into gravity. The result is a nonrenormalizable theory, showing it is an incomplete theory in the sense that you cannot compute anything. But I am not dissatisfied with my attempt to put gravity and quantum mechanics together. I accept whatever consequences that this putting together produces, mainly that it can't be renormalized. I was slightly disappointed that I did it only to lowest order. I could not figure out what to do with an arbitrary number of loops, which was later solved by others, but I was not dissatisfied with that. The fact that the theory has infinities never bothered me quite so much as it bothers others, because I always thought that it just meant that we've gone too far: that when we go to very short distances the world is very different; geometry, or whatever it is, is different, and it's all very subtle.

'People understand it better now than I understood it. We can say that we haven't got a consistent quantum theory of gravitation, except perhaps for the string theory, maybe! Who knows? It has got eleven dimensions. The world doesn't have eleven dimensions, so it rolls up seven. Why not six, why not four? It's a hell of a theory, isn't it? One can't even check the number of dimensions. I don't think we know anything very much. There's a lot to learn.

'People like to say that we end up with one "unified" theory. We don't know that; there could be other ways. Often someone would ask me if I am working on a unified theory, one theory of everything. I don't look at it that way. I work always to understand more about nature. If nature turns out to have seven theories then that's the way it will come out. And I'm not going to presume to tell her how it's going to have to look up there. I can't say that I am seeking the Holy Grail; there may not be a Holy Grail. What I'm trying to do is to find out more and understand more about nature, and what I find is what I'll find—I have no preconception about what nature is like or ought to be!'[2]

23.2 Partons

After his work on the V–A theory of weak interactions, Feynman surveyed the situation in the physics of strong interactions (structure of nucleons) and found it to be too complex; not enough experimental data were available. At the conference on the role of gravitation in physics at Chapel Hill, North Carolina, in January 1957, Feynman became interested in quantum gravity and, upon a suggestion of Murray Gell-Mann's, pursued it by making use of the Yang–Mills theory. The quantum theory of gravitation and the *Feynman lectures on physics* fully occupied him in the early 1960s, and it was only after receiving the Nobel Prize for physics in 1965 that he was able to turn his attention to high-energy physics. At that time, the theoretical situation in physics abounded with various approaches to the problem of strong interactions: dispersion relations, Regge asymptotics, current algebra, the *S*-matrix approach, nuclear democracy, bootstrap theory, and, of course, symmetries. Feynman thought that 'there was an awful lot of theory in those days'.[2]

In the spring of 1968, Feynman began by examining the collisions of two hadrons—say two protons or a pion and a proton—at high energies. He believed that at high collision energy the dynamical details of the strong force between them might become quite simple and amenable to calculation. Because of their high relative velocity, each proton will see the other as relativistically contracted along the direction of motion to a flat disk or pancake. Also, since the strong interactions are of short range, the two flat disks would only have a very short time to interact with each other.

During that summer Feynman was working in Santa Barbara, where he added a new element to the picture. As recorded in his notebook on 19 June, Feynman began to think of each hadron as a collection of smaller parts, of unspecified quantum numbers, which he christened 'partons'. He thought of partons as arbitrary, 'bare', ideal particles—the 'quanta of some underlying field, their exact number in any hadron being indeterminate'.

Feynman envisaged high-energy collisions of two hadrons as taking place between individual partons of each flattened disk, and, since the available interaction time would be small, he regarded the interaction of partons with a given disk as negligible: during a high-energy collision the partons of each proton would act as independent, quasifree, entities. Most of the partons in one disk would pass through the other freely, but two of them—one from each disk—would occasionally collide. This image was the basis of Feynman's 'parton model'. In this picture the probability of the two hadrons (two protons) colliding was just the sum of the probabilities of any two partons colliding.

During the next several weeks, Feynman worked out the consequences of his parton model, and looked for evidence of its validity in the scanty data then available on high-energy proton–proton and pion–proton collisions. By mid-July he felt he was on the right track. During the second week of August 1968, Feynman went to SLAC (the Stanford Linear Accelerator Center). He often used to visit his sister, Joan, who lived nearby and during these visits he would also drop by the SLAC laboratory. When he stopped by in August, the

MIT–SLAC collaboration was just beginning a second deep inelastic collision experiment.

Experiments performed in 1968 on deep inelastic lepton–nucleon scattering were designed to probe the structure of hadrons. More specifically, the study of the nucleon by the scattering of high-energy electrons showed that the nucleon is not a point-like object (particle) but has a finite size. The results of the collision would be interpreted as the scattering of the lepton by a constituent.

Historically, it was the class of elastic scattering data on e^+e^- colliders at both SLAC and DESY (Deutsche Elektron Synchrotron Anstalt), studying the e^+e^- annihilation into hadronic final states that provided the initial information about the structure of the nucleon. The class of experiments on inelastic scattering concentrated mainly on the measurement of the production of nucleon resonances. With the higher energies and intensities available, it was possible to investigate a new region of inelastic scattering. The advantage of this regime corresponds to the excitation of the continuum beyond the nucleon excitation (resonance) region.

In order to gain a better insight into the scattering of electrons by nucleons of a finite size, it is instructive to consider a simpler case of the scattering of a particle without the spin quantum number with a distribution of electronic charge spread over a finite region and characterized by a total charge Ze. This also introduces the concept of the form factor.[12] A pictorial representation of the process is shown in Fig. 23.1.

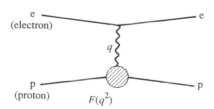

Fig. 23.1. Diagram illustrating the ep scattering process. The shaded circle at the lower end of the diagram represents the form factor of the nucleon.

By using first-order perturbation theory in quantum mechanics, it is possible to derive the expression for the cross section of the scattering process. It is given by

$$\frac{d\sigma}{d\Omega} = \left(\frac{d\sigma}{d\Omega}\right)_{\text{point}} |F(q)|^2, \tag{23.2}$$

where $(d\sigma/d\Omega)_{\text{point}}$ is the differential cross section for the scattering by a point-like charge. This is known as the Rutherford scattering. $F(q^2)$ is the form factor, which depends on the four-momentum transfer in the process, and mathematically it is expressed as the Fourier transform of the charge distribution.

In the high-energy limit of first-order perturbation theory, the expression for the point-like differential cross section is

$$\left(\frac{d\sigma}{d\Omega}\right)_{\text{point}} = \left(\frac{Ze^2}{2E}\right)^2 \frac{1}{\sin^4 \frac{1}{2}\theta},\tag{23.3}$$

where θ is the angle between the incident and outgoing electron and E is its energy.

The above formulas, describing the scattering process, are for particles without spin. An analogous consideration for the scattering of high-energy electrons by a point-like charge, but this time including the treatment of the spin of the electron, yields

$$\left(\frac{d\sigma}{d\Omega}\right) = \left(\frac{e^2}{2E}\right)^2 \frac{\cos^2 \frac{1}{2}\theta}{\sin^4 \frac{1}{2}\theta},\tag{23.4}$$

which is also known as Mott scattering.

The preceding discussion serves to illustrate the mathematics of the scattering process and defines the concept of a form factor. It is clear, however, that the theory of the scattering of the electrons by nucleons is more detailed than the simplified example discussed above. This is due to the fact that the spin and magnetic moment of the nucleon have to be taken into account appropriately.

Considering first the case of the proton, one has to think of two form factors: one is due to the space distribution of the charge, and the other is to describe the effects of the space distribution of the magnetic moment.

The process of the scattering of an electron by a proton can again be visualized as in Fig. 23.1. It can be considered as the exchange of a virtual photon between the electron and the proton. The expression for the differential cross section for the process is given by the expression

$$\frac{d\sigma}{d\Omega} = \left(\frac{d\sigma}{d\Omega}\right)_{\text{Mott}} \left(\frac{G_E^2(q^2) + (q^2/4M^2)G_M(q^2)}{1 + q^2/4M^2} + \frac{q^2}{4M^2} 2G_M^2(q^2)\tan^2 \frac{1}{2}\theta\right).\tag{23.5}$$

This is referred to as the Rosenbluth formula. In equation (23.5), M is the mass of the proton; $G_E^2(q^2)$ is the form factor attributed to the charge, while $G_M^2(q^2)$ is the form factor attributed to the magnetic moment.

The experimental results for the above are consistent with the following parametrization of the two form factors:

$$G_E^2(q^2) = G_M(q^2)/\mu_p = G_D(q^2),\tag{23.6}$$

where μ_p is the magnitude of the magnetic moment of the proton, expressed in units of the nuclear magnetons; $G_D(q^2)$ is equivalent to $1/(1 + q^2/D^2)$, with D

having a constant value of 0.71 (GeV/c^2). In the literature, this is often referred to as the scaling law with a 'dipole fit'.

In the case of the scattering of an electron by the neutron, the direct experimental determination is not possible. Instead, the cross section for the scattering of electrons by neutrons is derived from experiments on the scattering of electrons by deuterons. For this reason the accuracy of the values of neutron form factors is less precise than that of the proton form factors. The relation given by equation (23.6) is valid for the experimental range investigated: typically $q^2 \sim 0$ to 2 (GeV/c^2). At higher momentum transfers (q^2), only the experimental data on electron–proton scattering exist. Furthermore, these are sensitive to the magnetic form factor; the contributions due to the electric form factor are small and difficult to measure. In summary, the form factors obtained from the elastic scattering process provide information on the charge distribution and magnetic moment of the nucleon.

As the incident electron energy increases, it becomes possible to produce additional particles in the final state. This is known as the inelastic scattering of electrons by protons. An important feature of the experimental observations is the weak dependence of the inelastic scattering cross section on the momentum transfer (q^2) for the region beyond resonance production. This phenomenon is in marked contrast to the behavior of the elastic scattering cross section which falls off rapidly as a function of q^2

In analogy to Fig. 23.1, the process depicting the inelastic scattering of an electron by a nucleon is illustrated in Fig. 23.2. This process is characterized as follows: (1) the incident electron with energy E scatters off a nucleon at an angle θ; (2) the final state (n) consists of hadrons; (3) the process occurs via the exchange of a virtual photon of four-momentum transfer q.

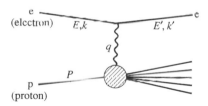

Fig. 23.2. Diagram illustrating the process of inelastic electron–nucleon scattering. The kinematical variables used are also given.

In general, the experiments observe the scattered electron, and the details of the final hadron state are not observed. One can then derive an expression for the differential cross section of the process in the reference frame of the observer (laboratory) as

$$\frac{d^2\sigma}{d\Omega\ dE'} = \frac{e^4}{4E^2 \sin^4 \tfrac{1}{2}\theta} \cos^2 \tfrac{1}{2}\theta\ [2W_1 \tan^2 \tfrac{1}{2}\theta + W_2], \tag{23.7}$$

where W_1 and W_2 are the structure functions and depend on hadron physics, and are functions of the invariant variables

$$Q^2 = q^2 \quad \text{and} \quad v = -\frac{1}{M}(q \cdot P)$$

that describe the inelastic scattering process.

It is common in the literature to introduce functions and variables derived from the above quantities, and rewrite equation (23.7) as

$$\frac{d^2\sigma}{dq^2\,dx} = \frac{4\pi\alpha^2}{q^4}\left((1-y)\,\frac{F_2(x,q^2)}{x} + \tfrac{1}{2}y^2\,\frac{2xF_1(x,q^2)}{x}\right), \qquad (23.8)$$

where

$$\left.\begin{array}{r} F_1(q^2,v) = W_1(q^2,v), \\ F_2(q^2,v) = W_2(q^2,v)/M, \\ y = v/E, \\ E'/E = 1 - y, \\ q^2 = 2MExy, \\ x = q^2/2Mv. \end{array}\right\} \qquad (23.9)$$

From the above, James D. Bjorken in 1967 produced the following argument: as q^2 and v tend to infinity, the value of the functions $F(q^2, v)$ remains finite. That is, it depends on the variable x which is the ratio of these two quantities. This is known as the Bjorken scaling hypothesis.[13]

An interpretation of scale invariance was given by Feynman in 1968 during his visit to SLAC, in discussions with J. D. Bjorken and Emmanuel Paschos, in the context of his parton model. In order to understand this, the process is schematically shown in Fig. 23.3, where the target proton has a very large momentum, so that its mass may be neglected. It is considered as consisting of constituent partons, each carrying a fraction x of the energy–momentum four-vector P. In the limit where P is large, we can again neglect the mass(es) and transverse momentum (momenta) of the parton(s). In Fig. 23.3, a parton of

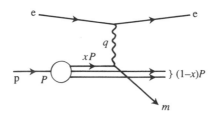

Fig. 23.3. A schematic illustration of the variables used to desdribe the parton model of deep inelastic scattering.

mass m is scattered by an elastic collision from the four-momentum (q) of the scattered electron. Applying the kinematic limits described above, it can be shown that

$$x = q^2/Mv \qquad (23.10)$$

in the laboratory system. Therefore x affords the interpretation of the fraction of the parton momentum in the above kinematic limit. One can interpret this as a parton with rest mass m in the laboratory frame, with the relation $q^2 = 2m$, and where q^2 is very much larger than M^2 we have

$$x = q^2/2Mv = m/M. \qquad (23.11)$$

Thus the 'Feynman parameter' x also represents the fraction of the nucleon mass carried by the parton. Since the cross section depends on x via the functions $F(x)$, they provide a measure of the mass distribution of the constituent partons. Thus scaling emerged as an exact prediction of the parton model.

When Feynman read Bjorken's papers later on in the fall of 1968, he saw that Bjorken had almost all these ideas, but he had expressed them in the abstract language of current algebra. In the simpler picture, in which the protons are built up of partons, these ideas could be expressed more readily. What Feynman added to Bjorken's work, besides his simpler picture, was his realization that the graph of F (Fig. 23.4) was actually a momentum distribution. When one plotted this function against his own parameter $x = q^2/2Mv$ (essentially the inverse of Bjorken's v/q^2), things got clearer still. The height of this curve at any particular value of x gave the probability of finding a parton carrying that fraction of the parton's momentum.

Feynman returned to SLAC in October to give another talk about his ideas. After that, partons swept through SLAC 'like a brushfire' in the memories of the physicists there.[14] Bjorken and Paschos soon worked out a detailed model based on quarks,[15] while another group of theoreticians took partons to be 'bare' pions and protons, without their virtual clouds. Feynman had again supplied the language, and a strikingly simple mental image, to describe what might be going on in a remote and tiny realm. 'I was always delighted', he reminisced, 'when something esoteric could be made to look so simple.'[14]

After Feynman's seminar in October 1968, the physicists at SLAC were in the grip of great enthusiasm for partons. He had provided a remarkably simple, workable framework for thinking about proton structure, one that could be used in many different ways and required urgent elaboration. The advocates of partons soon divided into two camps: those who took the partons to be bare pointlike versions of the observable mesons and baryons, and those who imagined them to be the long-sought quarks. Partons quickly became identified with quarks by most particle physicists; Gell-Mann would ridicule them as 'Feynman's *putons*'.[16] The quark-parton explanation of scaling required that the quark struck in the electron–proton interaction

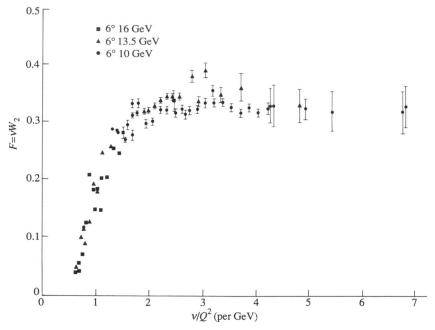

Fig. 23.4. The graph of the proton structure function that Kendall plotted
at Bjorken's suggestion.

behaves as a free particle. If this quark continued to behave as a free particle
one could expect that it would shoot out of the proton and appear among the
debris of the collision. However, quarks were not observed in the final states of
electron scattering or in any other class of interactions. The debris of the
electron scattering was just a shower of normal hadrons, and some
assumption had to be added to the parton model to explain this.[17] This
assumption was simply that, although the quark behaved as a free particle in
the initial hard interaction, it must subsequently undergo a series of soft low-
momentum-transfer strong interactions with its fellow partons. These
interactions were supposed somehow to ensure that hadrons, and not quarks,
would appear in the final state and, being soft, would not invalidate the
explanation of scaling itself. Such assumptions were unavoidable and
theoretically unjustifiable but, as the quark–parton model became central to
the approach of an increasing number of particle physicists, 'the high energy
physics community learned to live with this unsatisfactory state of affairs.'[18]

23.3 Quark jets

(a) Introduction

In the mid-1970s Richard Feynman became interested in a phenomenon
known as 'quark jets'. As he recalled: 'I made a contribution to the theory of

the structure of matter by talking about protons as being made of parts. I worked out consequences from it, consequences for a large number of possible phenomena such as if you hit two protons together very hard, and the parts come off at an angle, parts we call quarks and gluons. These particles, when they come out, would be just as similar to the pair of particles that would come out of e^+e^- [scattering], and that makes jets of hadrons finally. It was not seen at the beginning that they were jets.

'People were measuring the single pions at a perpendicular angle, at large angle and transverse angular momentum. Rick Field came into my office; he was working on calculating ahead of time trying to understand how many pions you should get at large angles. This is the way it all started. He showed me the theories of the day and I thought they were absolutely nutty. They were going to take a pion that was already in a proton and turn it around to a new angle and that would mean—since I knew that a pion is made up of at least two quarks—two quarks would have to be turned around. Very hard to do. Easy to turn one around.

'Field was trying to interpret it phenomenologically and we slowly developed our theory of this. As we went along, it turned out that the more aspects of quantum chromodynamics (QCD) that we put in, the less arbitrary guesses, the better the fit. It was a nice development. This gave rise to a series of papers[19] for the prediction of results at very high energy collisions, particularly at high transverse momenta.'[2]

Feynman continued: 'The prediction was made that there were jets of particles and jets were discovered and it turned out that there were in fact two hundred particles with each pion. So it was a series of ever-increasing consonant models which at the beginning had numbers of black boxes, where you would make up functions, say, for collision cross section between two particles or something to make it fit the data; then, later on, you would say, "No, let's say the collision cross sections be determined by the theory of quantum chromodynamics." And then you would discover, in fact, that it fit better than when you had an arbitrary black box. So, the more we were guided by the principles of QCD, the better the things fitted, and the better were the predictions—evidence for the correctness of the theory of QCD.'[2]

The experimental evidence for the phenomenon of quark jets was one of the more important developments in particle physics in the mid-1970s. The terminology of jets refers to specific features of the hadronic final states in different types of (high-energy) interactions. Experimentally, jets are observed in processes initiated by leptons, e.g. e^+e^-, ep, and νp interactions, as well as hadron–hadron interactions.

The phenomena of jets, in theoretical models, are assumed to be due to quarks that 'fragment' into hadrons (mesons and baryons). The kinematics of the reaction process is such that these hadrons move in the same direction as the original quark, when the entire interaction is analyzed theoretically in terms of the fundamental constituents.

The phenomenology of the properties of jets was developed in the context of the quark–parton model and the theory of QCD. Certain assumptions are necessary in these models, based upon experimental observations, in order to construct a framework to perform calculations. Some of the more important assumptions are the following. The quarks and gluons behave as if they are approximately free in interactions characterized by large momentum transfers at short distances. This property is referred to in the literature as asymptotic freedom, and it is due to the hypothesis that the interaction of quarks may be calculated in the theory of perturbative QCD at the relevant energy scale of interaction. At distances of the order of one fermi they are confined, and are not observed to propagate freely.

In the theoretical construction of the model, the forces that confine the quarks are called 'soft'. (Collisions at large distances—i.e. peripheral interactions—characterized by small momentum transfer, and thus low transverse momentum p_T, are 'soft' interactions; while the collisions at short distances—i.e. central interactions—characterized by large momentum transfer, and thus large p_T, are 'hard' interactions.) These processes, responsible for the confinement and production of quark–antiquark pairs out of vacuum, are characterized by small momentum transfer. Therefore, the quarks produced and the observed hadrons have a small transverse momentum with respect to the intial parton direction. This is often referred to in the literature as the 'jet direction' and is the subject of experiments.

Figure 23.5 shows the processes by which jets may be produced in the different types of collisions, as well as the vocabulary used to discuss the jet phenomenology: (a) from e^+e^- collisions; (b) from lepton–hadron collisions; and (c) from hadron–hadron collisions. The jets observed in all these processes are thought to arise from the quarks that 'fragment' into a set of hadrons, with the appropriate kinematical features.

(b) Experimental observation of jets

The observation of jet-like events in e^+e^- collisions were reported in the second half of 1970s. The lowest-order process, as illustrated in Fig. 23.5(a), for producing the final state hadrons is

$$e^+e^- \rightarrow q\bar{q}$$

where the quarks fragment into hadrons. The important assumption of the quark–parton model, which leads to the expectation of jets in these collisions, is that the transverse momenta of the fragmentation products of quarks originate from soft processes and remain small, while the longitudinal momenta of the fragmentation products can increase with the quark energy. Such a behavior was observed, and indeed found to be the dominant feature of the production of hadrons, in the data recorded by the experiments both at

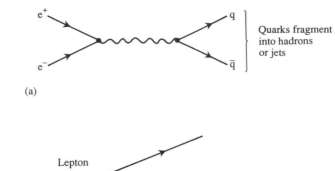

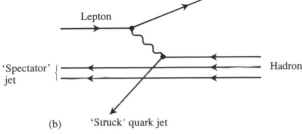

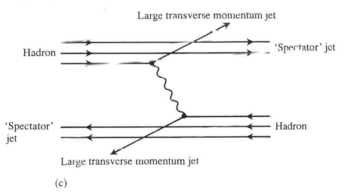

Fig. 23.5. (a), (b), and (c). Production of jets.

PEP (SLAC) and PETRA (DESY). The range of center-of-mass energies at these storage ring accelerators was between 30 and 40 GeV.

In order to characterize the hadrons in a jet, certain mathematical quantities (variables), such as sphericity, aplanarity, and thrust, have been constructed from the measured momentum and transverse momentum of the hadrons.

In analogy with the above process, at the first order in the strong coupling constant (α_s) in QCD, it is possible to have a process

$$e^+e^- \to q\bar{q}g$$

that can give rise to an event with three jets present in the final state (the third one arising from the radiated gluon g). Indeed, events compatible with three jets in the final state were observed experimentally towards the end of 1970s. The observation of such events actually was the first direct evidence for the existence of gluons, postulated within the framework of QCD.

The three jets, reconstructed from the kinematics, should be coplanar, because the sum of the momenta should add up to zero from the law of conservation of momentum. In practice, however, while analyzing the data, it is observed that there is a certain amount of ambiguity in distinguishing events with three jets from those with two jets. Again, the characteristics of these jets are studied by using the variables mentioned above.

If it is experimentally possible to isolate in the data set a 'clean' or well-characterized sample of three-jet events, it is then possible to make a comparison with the theoretical predictions. It is worthwhile to note that these comparisons are often made by using Monte Carlo simulations with fragmentation models. Thus, this procedure may be as much a test of the particular fragmentation model as a test of QCD. Sometimes, however, it may be desirable to perform the comparisons with calculations at the quark–gluon (i.e. parton) level, in which case there is only little 'sensitivity' to the fragmentation scheme.

In the category of lepton–hadron collisions (or, more generally, lepton–nucleon collisions), as shown in Fig. 23.5(b), the basic process is the lepton–quark scattering. When the center-of-mass energy is large enough, we expect to see hadrons in jets, as in the case of e^+e^- collisions. An interesting aspect in the present case, which is absent in the case of e^+e^- collisions, is the possibility of studying diquark jets, due to the mechanism of production. In addition, the kinematics of the process is such that the analysis of the jet axis can be determined independently of the sphericity or thrust analysis.

One has to be careful, however, of the fact that the appearance of a collimated set of hadrons in the q direction (Fig. 23.5(b)) does not necessarily imply a quark jet in this class of interactions. From high-energy hadron interaction theory, this could be due to the soft component of (forward) diffractive scattering. Thus, it is necessary to impose certain kinematical cuts in order to suppress the diffractive component. The possible 'higher-order' processes from QCD have the observed effects of 'broadening' the jet distribution and create events with three jets in the final state.

In hadron–hadron collisions (see Fig. 23.5(c)), the bulk of the cross section is due to numerous soft processes that cannot be 'fully' calculated from a theory starting from first principles. It is, however, possible that by applying certain kinematical cuts, one can study the observed phenomena, employing the predictions of perturbative QCD. The processes shown in Fig. 23.5(c) can give four jets in the final state. These are from each of the scattered partons as well as two jets from the so-called 'spectator' partons that continue to move along directions of the incident beams. In analogy with the process $e^+e^- \rightarrow q\bar{q}$, we expect that jets will be produced in these types of collisions when the center-of-mass energy is appropriate. For example, at the CERN proton–antiproton collider, operating at a center-of-mass energy between 540 and 630 GeV, the phenomenon of jet production is the most striking feature, characterized by events having a sum of the 'transverse energy' that is relatively large.

The experimental signature for the jets in the CERN proton–antiproton collider experiments is the large quantity of energy deposited in a cluster of the 'cells' of the calorimeter apparatus, instrumented for the purpose of measuring energy. It is experimentally observed that when both jets are contained within the fiducial volume of the calorimeter, they are separated by 180° in the azimuthal direction. It therefore provides a rather easy identification of these events.

In the hadronic interactions discussed here, there are higher-order QCD processes that can give 'higher-order' contributions to the simple configuration of partons. An example of the higher-order process is the emission (or radiation) of gluons from the incident as well as outgoing (final state) partons. It is therefore rather critical in the experiments to understand and implement appropriate jet algorithms to reconstruct the jets. In the above example, if the algorithm for the reconstruction of jets is such that the 'volume' (or cone) over which the sum of the energy in the calorimeter cells is wide enough, then the dominant configuration will lead to two jets in the final state.

Within the framework of QCD, it is expected that jets initiated by gluons are softer than quark jets. It is also necessary in the theory to parametrize 'correctly' the fragmentation function of the gluons, in analogy with the quarks.

(c) *Hadronization/fragmentation*

The quarks and gluons produced in the final states are not observed as 'free' particles. In QCD theory, the color quantum numbers are 'organized' in such a way that the final products (i.e. observables) are hadrons that do not carry the color quantum numbers.

The process of 'organization' of the quarks and gluons into hadrons is referred to as the process of hadronization or fragmentation. In the theoretical interpretation of the process, this is assumed to occur via the creation of quark–antiquark pairs. This is illustrated in Fig. 23.6. Essentially, the quark–antiquark pairs combine to produce mesons (that are hadrons), and this results in a multihadron final state.

It is worthwhile to reiterate the underlying difficulty explained in Section 23.2(a), that the process of fragmentation is governed by the 'soft' processes, for which there does not exist any theory to allow one to do the calculations from first principles. Thus, in order to 'explain' the observed phenomenon of hadrons in jets, one has to proceed in an empirical manner.

There are numerous fragmentation models, which have been incorporated

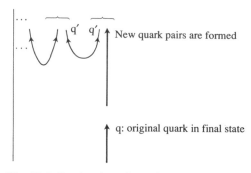

Fig. 23.6. Production of quark-antiquark pairs.

into Monte Carlo programs for the purpose of calculation. For example, the independent fragmentation model considers the hadronization process to be independent of the production process of the parton. Also, in this model, it is assumed that each parton fragments independently of the other partons. Thus, the important concepts such as quantum number conservation have to be implemented on a somewhat *a posteriori* basis. The concept of the fragmentation process can be different between quarks and gluons. Another example is the so-called *string model*, where it is assumed that the fragmentation process results from a break in a color flux tube that extends between the partons. Therefore, the fragmentation process with three partons can, in principle, be different from a process with two partons, and, in particular, the partons do not fragment independently.

In summary, the different Monte Carlo programs from different authors (or groups) have to implement a decision on how many partons are produced in the final state, using QCD theory. These partons have then to be materialized into hadrons by using different available fragmentation algorithms. Initially, the hadrons produced in the final state can be unstable (short lifetime), and themselves decay into other 'secondary' hadrons.

Before describing in somewhat greater detail the work of Feynman, Field, and Fox on the particular fragmentation scheme, it is worthwhile to give a summary of the overall fragmentation process in order to introduce some of the concepts and vocabulary. The observed hadrons do not carry the color quantum number, so in the final state the quark (which is scattered) and the so-called 'recoiling' system (which could be the antiquark or a diquark system) have a net color quantum number which is balanced. The process is envisaged in such a way that the quark and the recoiling system are connected together by a color flux tube. These flux lines 'stretch' and 'break' and create quark–antiquark pairs that group together to form hadrons (actually mesons), which do not carry color quantum number. The hypothesis that the combination takes place locally means that the properties of the quark jets are a function of the quarks' properties themselves, such as the color quantum number, other quantum numbers, and the momentum. Thus, in this picture, as a first approximation, each quark is considered to fragment independently.

Mathematically, let a parton (p), with an energy E_p, produce a hadron (h), with energy E_h. The fraction z of the energy that the hadron retains is $z = E_h/E_p$, and this can be distributed over the allowed values from 0 to 1. The probability of finding h in the energy range from z to Δz (where Δz is a small increment compared with z) is defined by the expression $D_p^h(z)\, \Delta(z)$, where D_p^h is referred to as the fragmentation function. In the rather special case (or limiting case) where the parton energy is very large with respect to the masses of the other final states as well as their transverse momenta, it can be contemplated that the z variable describes the dynamics of the process. In this limit, when the fragmentation depends on the z variable alone, one says that the fragmentation obeys the rule of 'Feynman scaling'. Different types of experiments are required in order to measure the fragmentation of different quark species (u, d, s, c, b).

The integral of the fragmentation function, i.e. $\int_z D_p^h(z)\, dz$, over the allowed physical range of z provides a knowledge of the average number of hadrons in the jet that have originated from the parton p. Thus, in one independent fragmentation picture, the hadron multiplicity in the final state, at high energies, is governed by the behavior of $D(z)$ for small values of z. Empirically, the function $D(z)$ can be parametrized by

$$D(z) = c(1-z)^n/z, \tag{23.12}$$

where c is a constant and the term $(1-z)^n$ gives the behavior at large values of z, whereas the term $1/z$ is introduced in order to be compatible with a logarithmic increase in the multiplicity of the final state hadrons at high energies, as is experimentally observed.

It is interesting to point out the parallel, conceptually, between the fragmentation functions and the parton distribution functions. The fragmentation function is the probability density for finding a hadron in the fragmentation products of a parton, whereas the parton distribution function is the probability density for finding a parton within a hadron.

(d) The independent fragmentation scheme

The first model of such schemes was due to Feynman and Field.[20] The model can be visualized as in Fig. 23.6. Basically, it is supposed that the initial quark q creates a quark pair q'q̄, and a meson (q'q̄) is formed. This meson has a fraction z of the original momentum of q. Moreover, q' can then combine in analogy to the preceding case, and so on. Thus one has a series production of the mesons. In a simplified model, it is assumed that the full process can be characterized by a function $f(z)$. The normalization of the function $f(z)$ is such that

$$\int f(z)\,dz = 1, \tag{23.13}$$

which represents the fact that the probability of an occurrence at each step, for a given value of z, is unity. Stated in another way, if the original quark's four-momentum variable (i.e. energy and the three components of the momentum) is P_μ, then each dissociation results in a hadron (meson) with four-momentum zP_μ and the remaining quark with a fraction of the momentum $(1-z)P_\mu$.

In fact, the original Feynman–Field parametrization[20] used the following definition for the z variable:

$$z = (E^h + P_1^h)/(E^q + P_1^q), \tag{23.14}$$

where E is the energy, and P_1 is the longitudinal component of the three-momentum (h refers to to the hadron and q to the quark). The expression that Feynman and Field used was

$$f(z) = 1 - a + 3a(1-z)^2, \tag{23.15}$$

where the constant $a \simeq 0.8$, as determined by the data.

A successive application of the above procedure leads to the final jet configuration. Recalling that $D(z)$ is the probability density for producing any hadron (meson) with a momentum fraction z, then the above successive application of $f(z)$ results in

$$D(z) = f(z) + \int_z f(1-z')D(z/z')\frac{dz'}{z'}, \tag{23.16}$$

which implies that the meson is either in the first chain with probability $f(z)$, or else it is a part of the subsequent chain with a probability $f(1-z')$, where z' is the new fraction of the momentum of the hadron. It is important to reiterate that the hadron spectrum $D(z)$ is an important constraint on the form of $f(z)$.

Specific aspects of the observed process are introduced or incorporated into the model 'by hand'. For example, the hadrons have a small transverse momentum distribution. This is included by a Gaussian probability distribution:

$$dN/dp_T^2 \simeq \exp(-p_T^2/2\sigma), \tag{23.17}$$

where p_T is the transverse momentum and σ is the width of the distribution. The composition of the final-state hadrons (mesons) is also 'adjusted' to agree with the experimental observations.

Similarly, it is also clear that the type of hadron produced in the final state will depend upon the initial and final quark type. The meson production then results from a series of $(q\bar{q})$ pair production. Thus the final state quark–antiquark pairs are chosen with appropriate weights.

A few other points from the work of Feynman and Field are worth noting here. (1) The independent fragmentation model, which is based on the recursive model, provides an 'easy' method to calculate the properties of quark jets in terms of only a few parameters. There are certain limitations, such the model does not include the production of baryons in the final state hadrons and, as such, is not the 'true' theory of how jets are produced. (2) The properties of jets, originating from the light quarks u and d, can be described in terms of the hadrons containing the original quark. It is not possible to distinguish these on an event by event basis. However, it is possible to distinguish them by studying their average properties. (3) The particular scheme should not be considered as a theory that confronts the experiment, but rather as a guide to what the general properties may be expected experimentally. The importance of comparing high p_T jets initiated by hadrons compared to those generated by lepton collisions is also emphasized.[19]

Feynman's work with Field on quark jets gave him much pleasure, for it represented another chase in the pursuit of an aspect of nature. He was happy that QCD worked so well, and declared, 'I am now a confirmed quarkanian!'[2]

Notes and References

1. See the *Proceedings of the Conference on the Role of Gravitation in Physics*, held at the University of North Carolina, Chapel Hill, January 18–23, edited by C.M. DeWitt, Wright Air Force Center, March 1957.

2. R.P. Feynman, Interviews and conversations with Jagdish Mehra, in Pasadena, California January 1988.

3. R.P. Feynman, Lectures on gravitation, 1962–63. A series of 16 lectures on gravitation. Lecture notes by F.B. Maringo and W.G. Wagner, Caltech, 1971. Unpublished

4. R P. Fcynman, Letter to V.F. Weisskopf, 4 January–11 February 1961.

5. R.P. Feynman, *Proceedings of the International Conference on the Theory of Gravitation*. Gauthier-Villars, Paris, 1964, pp. 697–718.

6. L.D. Faddeev and V.N. Popov, *Phys. Lett* B **25**, 29 (1967).

7. S.N. Gupta, *Phys. Rev.* **96**, 1683 (1954).

8. S. Weinberg, *Phys, Rev.* B **135**, 1049 (1964); *Phys. Rev.* **138**, 988 (1965).

9. R. Boulware and S. Deser, *Ann. Phys.* **89**, 193 (1975).

10. R. Wald, *Phys. Rev.* D **33**, 3613 (1986).

11. B.S. DeWitt, *Phys. Rev.* **160**, 1113 (1967).

12. Perhaps the first attempt to consider the form factor of the nucleon was made by W.E. Lamb, Jr., and L.I. Schiff, *Phys. Rev.* **53**, 651 (1938).

13. J.D. Bjorken, *Phys. Rev.* **163**, 1767 (1967); *Phys. Rev.* **179**, 1547 (1969).

14. M. Riordan, *The hunting of the quark.* Simon & Schuster, 1987, p. 152.

15. J.D. Bjorken and E.A. Paschos, *Phys. Rev.* **185**, 1975 (1969).

16. M. Gell-Mann, Interview with Jagdish Mehra, at Caltech, Pasadena, California, 23 March 1988.

17. R.P. Feynman, Very high collisions of hadrons. *Phys. Rev. Lett.* **23**, 1415 (1969); The behavior of hadron collisions at extreme energies. In: *High energy collisions* (ed. C.N. Yang). Gordon & Breach, New York, 1969; *Photon–hadron interactions.* Benjamin, New York, 1972; Structure of the proton. *Science* **183**, 601 (1974).

18. A. Pickering, *Constructing quarks.* University of Chicago Press, 1984, p. 140.

19. R.P. Feynman, Correlations in hadron collisions at high transverse momentum. Invited talk at *Orbis Scientiae*, Coral Gables, Florida, January 1977; Quark jets, Invited talk at the VIII International Symposium on Multiparticle Dynamics, Kaysersberg, France, June 1977; Correlations among particles and jets produced with large transverse momentum (with R.D. Field and G. Fox). *Nucl. Phys.* B **128**, 1 (1977); Quark elastic scattering as a source of high transverse momentum (with R.D. Field). *Phys. Rev.* D **15**, 2590 (1977); A quantum chromodynamic approach for large transverse momentum production of particles and jets (with R.D. Field and G. Fox). *Phys. Rev.* D **18**, 3320 (1978).

20. R.P. Feynman and R.D. Field, A parametrization of the properties of quark jets, *Nucl. Phys.* B **136**, 1 (1978).

24

The fundamental limits of computation

24.1 Introduction: Feynman's interest in computers

Richard Feynman had been interested in the problem of computing and the nature of computers since his earliest days in high school. He used to read about mathematical machines, tide predictors, area measuring devices, and 'all kinds of wonderful things' about computing in the *Encyclopaedia Britannica*. He had always had an interest in computation and also in machines intended not just for computation. 'I believe that analyzing and thinking about computing machines and what they can do uplifts one's mind philosophically to a large number of natural questions, like what is intelligence and other wonderful things. Moreoever, computation devices have a great many applications.'[1]

At Princeton, Feynman had the opportunity of learning about what John von Neumann was doing to devise computers, but at that time Feynman himself became involved in developing a mechanical director for shooting down airplanes at the Frankfort Arsenal in the summer of 1941, and did not take any direct interest in what von Neumann was doing. At Los Alamos, as leader of the Technical Computations Group in the Theoretical Division under Hans Bethe, Feynman used Marchant and Monroe calculators and learned how to repair them. Later on, when the computers started to come out, he did not do a great deal with them but played around.

At Caltech, a computer scientist, Meyer Weinstein, once invited Feynman over to his office and explained some problems he was having in designing a computer for a robot that was supposed to wander around a maze and do this or that. How would you make a computer do all that? Weinstein asked Feynman if he knew any physics students who would be interested in thinking about such things. 'And I said I did know one, myself. So he and I talked a great deal. I learned a lot about the nature of computer problems and I found the stuff so much fun that I kept on going.'[1] Feynman taught a course at Caltech for three or four years on the potentialities and limitations of computing machines. This was a course on computers, both hardware and software, and the practical problems involved in building them.

As an undergraduate, Carl, Feynman's son, worked with Daniel Hillis, who had invented a central processing machine that would take numbers—one number and then another number—add them up and put them back in the memory, and so on. The central processing was worked very hard; the memory was sitting there waiting for calls. Hillis tried to speed things up by having two, three, four, or maybe six central processors and found that it was very hard to program it to give organized results. Hillis felt that parallel processing was an obviously efficient way to do things and that he would get a better idea about what the real problems were, not by calling up six, but by making a machine with—as he liked to say—a million central processors. He actually made one with 64 000 central processors. Feynman began to do consulting work with the Thinking Machines Company, Hillis's outfit in Cambridge, Massachusetts.

John Hopfield and some others at Caltech wanted to develop a computer course that was wider than the one Feynman had taught before. They mostly specialized in hardware, in very large integration circuits. 'We had a limited view of computation and computer problems, compared to MIT, which had a much wider, more open view. I realized that the [computer] field was marvelous and very wide open and had all kinds of ramifications. At MIT they were teaching all these wonderful things, but at Caltech we were limited in our thinking on these matters.' [1]

Hopfield wanted to develop a course to widen the students' interests. Feynman agreed with him, and together they started to give the course. In the beginning, neither of them knew too much about the computer world, so the course was run by inviting experts to come and give lectures. For instance, they would get the head designer at IBM to come and tell them about the problems of computer design. People came from all over, and were very generous; they would come over as soon as they were invited. In the course run by Feynman and Hopfield, they would tell them about all the things they had experience of, and next time Feynman and Hopfield knew more about what to do in their course. The second time around, the experts were invited once a week, and then Feynman would discuss what they had talked about with the class the preceding term. Finally, Feynman and Hopfield realized that now they had discussed all the stuff in detail, and they themselves knew how to handle the course without outside speakers, except occasionally. Feynman himself became a computer expert. He interacted with a young man called Stephen Wolfram, but he did not develop any program with him. Wolfram himself went on to develop a good symbolic algebraic program, called MATHEMATICA.

During the course of these activities, a question arose that had something to do with the limitations due to the physical limitations of computers. This question first came to Feynman's attention in a lecture by Carver Mead, head of the computer department at Caltech, in which he invited physicists to look into this question. Mead asked what was the minimum energy required to operate a computer, the heat generation for a certain amount of computation. Mead himself had some ideas about it. Feynman began to work on this problem and gradually came to the conclusion that there was no limitation on energy. If you went slower, you would do it more smoothly and have less heat loss, and it was a kind of Carnot cycle; there is effectively no real limit on how much energy you actually need to make a computation. This was rather a surprise. Feynman had to argue this point with Mead, who never believed him. Feynman came into contact with Ed Fredkin, Marvin Minsky, Carver Mead, Charles Bennett, Rolf Landauer, and all the other top notch guys in the computer field.

Feynman went to a meeting on computation at MIT. There he met Charles Bennett 'who claimed that there was no lower limit on the amount of heat needed, just as I had deduced. He had done it a few years earlier, but I did not know it. He expressed so nicely and so clearly how it worked. I admired it very much and I understood him perfectly because I had deduced the same thing myself. I liked him very much and appreciated his results. The question [then] came up about limits due to quantum mechanics. The computation [device] gets smaller and smaller and faster and faster. What are the limits due to that? Ordinarily we work these things out assuming the current goes through or it does not go through; either it switches on or it does not. These things are approximations to the real world and the question was how small you could really make a computer, what are the limits due to quantum mechanics?

'I worked out a way. Bennett, in fact, came here to Caltech and gave a lecture on what other people had suggested. Their quantum mechanical computers were elaborately complicated, but I saw how I could solve some of the problems in a different way. I answered their challenge to write the Hamiltonian of a quantum mechanical system which could be used as a computer. The net result is that there's effectively no limitation due to quantum mechanics, other than things like the size. You can't write a number smaller than an atom, with spin up or down (it had to be one or zero), but there's no real limitation due to the quantum laws in particular. I designed a machine which, working entirely on quantum mechanical laws in principle, would compute.' [1]

Feynman wanted to find out what the computers could achieve, or what kind of problems they could handle. After working on these problems, 'I got a much more profound view of all this stuff. I don't have a philosophical view; everything is a practical problem. The development of increasing computer capacity, i.e. the ability to solve problems of wider and wider ranges of complexity and apparent difficulty, in recent years is very interesting. One of the things that is amusing about computers is to discover that they can do what the scientists consider themselves better at than the rest of the populace, such as thinking, doing mathematics, learning equations, and doing logic—all this can be done by computers. But you cannot make a computer today which can look at the street and when there's a dog in the street it will bark, as an actual dog would do. That's interesting. These are the things that we never pay much attention to philosophically.

'I found it amusing that the things I consider myself smart at—for instance, when I was young I was good at calculus, playing chess, and other logical things—could be done by computers. They cannot play as good chess as the *best* chess player. People want to protect themselves against machines. No machine can play better than the *best* human, but they can play better than most humans. But they always want the machine to play Beethoven and to write music like Mozart. But they can't do that. They assume the abilities of all humans because they are inhuman. It isn't so easy to build a computer that has such refined abilities in all directions. But you can go a long way for a lot of things. Mathematical and logical thinking, which we were always so proud of, that they can do. It's illogical thinking that we don't know how to do [with computers] that we do immediately, easily, as the eye jumps from one part of the scene to another and integrates the whole picture into a room with chairs and furniture and everything that we see, that's difficult. It's very interesting. Altogether, computers are fascinating and the problems that they can do are fascinating.'[1]

24.2 Information as a physical quantity

Information—this word is now so often used, yet the notion itself is not easily defined in precise terms. Information is the element of computers, whose sole task is to process it. Numerical calculations, image processing, database searches, communication—all these are different aspects of processing information. Thus before attempting any formulation of physical laws and principles influencing the operation of computers it is necessary to define the element: information. Is it a physical quantity? If yes, how can we define it and what laws govern its behavior?

Let us look at a problem which brought about the realization of the importance of information in the physical world: the Maxwell demon paradox. Before describing the problem let us recall some fundamental facts about entropy and the second law of thermodynamics. There exist various formulations of the second law of thermodynamics, and we will choose one that stresses its implications resulting in the irreversibility of certain processes.

One knows from everyday experience that most events cannot be undone. A once burned log cannot be recreated from cinders, even if we tried to include all the heat generated in the process of burning it. A rubber ball, which bounces lower and lower on a floor and finally comes to rest cannot reabsorb all its spent energy and jump back to its original height. An ice cube put on a warm plate will melt: heat flows from the warm plate to the ice cube, never vice versa. All these events are governed by the second law of thermodynamics, which, in its most general formulation, can be stated as follows: *Every physical process in nature takes place in such a way as to increase the sum of entropies of all the bodies taking part in any process. In the limit (for reversible processes) the sum of the entropies remains unchanged.*

This general formulation introduces into our discussion a new quantity: entropy. Without going into detail, let us understand entropy informally as a measure of the disorder of a system. Thus, what the second law of thermodynamics says is that disorder of a system as a whole can only grow, or at best remain constant. Whenever we order some part of a system, we do so at the expense of energy, which has to be taken from some other part of the system, and obtaining it raises entropy somewhere else. Following Léon Brillouin, one can also say that entropy measures the lack of information about the actual structure of a system. We will explore the connection between entropy and information soon. First, let us return to an interesting idea due to James Clerk Maxwell, who in 1871 in his *Theory of heat* suggested that there could in principle exist a creature which, being sufficiently small to be able to see molecules, could create a difference of temperature between two connected vessels, initially in equilibrium.

The idea was as follows. Maxwell's demon, as the creature was soon called, would sit by a hole separating the two vessels (let us call them A and B). It could open and close the hole at will. Initially both vessels will have the same temperature. The demon would open the hole in such a manner that only faster (i e. more energetic) molecules would pass from A to B and only slower from B to A. This would lead to an increase of temperature in B and a decrease in A, hence a violation of the second law of thermodynamics.

Attempts to resolve the conflict between Maxwell's demon and the second law of thermodynamics mark the history of thermodynamics. In 1912, Marian von Smoluchowski[2] showed that a simple form of the demon, consisting of a trapdoor will transfer energy to it, thus causing, at some point, its random motion due to thermal energy. This movement will, of course, prevent the trapdoor from acting as an effective demon.

Smoluchowski's reasoning does not refute an intelligent demon. The next step was taken by Leo Szilard in 1929; he argued that the observation, which is a measurement, leads to entropy increase, which in total compensates for the entropy decrease brought about by the operation of the demon. Later, in 1962, Léon Brillouin developed that argument further, by analyzing an act of observation, which, as he stated, has to be done with an expenditure of at least one photon, so the energy dissipation (and corresponding entropy increase) is equivalent to the energy of that photon.

Charles Bennett[3] closed the discussion by demonstrating that the measurement can be done with arbitrarily little energy dissipation, thus refuting Brillouin's argument. He also indicated the real source of paradox. Using the result of Landauer[4] that not the transformation of information, but rather its discarding, is thermodynamically costly, he arrived at the following conclusion: Maxwell's demon indeed increases its entropy, but not by the process of measurement itself, but rather by the preparation for the next measurement, where it has to free its memory in order to accommodate the result of the next observation, and therein lies the paradox. Even if the demon were equipped with large memory, so that it could keep the results of observations instead of deleting them, there still would be no conflict with the second law of thermodynamics. The demon would simply decrease entropy of the vessels at the expense of increasing the entropy of its own memory.

This example has demonstrated that the information about any system contributes to its entropy and that information is a well-defined physical quantity, which enters into conservation laws.

24.3 Energy dissipation as a result of information processing

In the last section, we established that discarding information raises the entropy of a system. Let us look into this problem in more detail. Before we start, let us, however, describe some basic notions underlying information processing: bits, logical operations and gates, and the like.

A unit for measuring information is one bit. A bit is the amount of information which permits selecting between two possibilities or states. We can also look at one bit of information as having true–false (or 0–1) values, thus entering the well-known realm of binary logic. We can always break down all, even very complex, operations on data into elementary logical operations such as conjunction alternative, or negation. Thus, it turns out, that the basic building blocks for computers are logic gates—systems performing logical operations *and* (conjunction), *or* (alternative) and *not* (negation). It can be shown, however, that only the so-called NAND gate, which realizes the negation of a conjunction, is sufficient to build any logical operation. Once we agree upon some way of representing objects (as, for instance, numbers) by strings of bits, we can perform equivalents of operations on them by subjecting bits in strings representing them to certain logical operations. It should be noted that we have two levels of abstraction here: first we map objects and procedures into bits and logical operations, and then we realize the latter by some physical processes typically happening in electronic devices.

The problem of heat generated during calculations had already appeared in early computers built from relays and vacuum tubes. The major source of heat was the inefficiency of electrical circuits, rather than transformations of information, whose contribution, at that time, was infinitesimally small with respect to other sources. Thus the problem of changes of entropy during computations appeared to be very academic. Nevertheless, Landauer investigated the subject and came up with the answer which was certainly contrary to the conventional wisdom of that time. Already in the 1940s, John von Neumann understood that logic signals are associated with a comparable energy. In his 1949 lecture[5] he stated that '... per elementary act of information, that is, per elementary decision of a two-way alternative and per elementary transmittal of one unit of information one pays costs of energy dissipation of the order of kT, where T is temperature and k is the so-called Boltzmann constant.' Landauer (1961)[4] carefully analyzed the relationship between speed and energy dissipation and the effects of errors induced by thermal fluctuations. He showed that entropy growth is associated only with logical operations which involve loss of information. Loss of information is equivalent to performing logical functions which do not have a single-valued inverse (are irreversible).

So we see that, contrary to early beliefs, there are no fundamental limits preventing construction of a dissipationless computer. Still, the question of whether such machines can be built remains open.

24.4 Models of classical reversible computers

In the previous section we distinguished between abstract logic and its implementation by physical processes. We should remember that there are no *a priori* assumptions on the logical level as to how the logic will be realized. The next step is to use such logic gates to construct a computer which will perform all its calculations without discarding information. Here we shall list various proposals for reversible computers, which are general enough to perform any type of calculation.

Thus far we have mentioned abstract and realistic logic gates, but now we will move one level of abstraction higher and present what can be called an abstract computer. It is a Turing machine, which serves as a general model of a computer and is often used as a device for discussing the finiteness of algorithms. It has been proved that this machine can perform any type of computation, and all existing computers are equivalent to a Turing machine. Thus, proving that a particular idea of a computer is equivalent to a Turing machine suffices to validate it as a general-purpose computer, at least from a logical point of view.

The Turing machine consists of an infinite tape divided into cells, each keeping one bit (zero or one) of information, and a head which can travel along the tape and modify the content of the cells. The head can be in various states, defined by its memory. These states can be changed during the process of computation. The head starts from one position along the tape and, according to the program or the algorithm in question, moves in steps to the right or to the left, possibly changing the content of the tape cells in the process. The whole computation ends when certain conditions defined as a part of the algorithm are met.

The Turing machine is a testbed for finite algorithms, i.e. 'execution' of an algorithm on it can check whether it ends after a finite number of steps or not. More about Turing machines can be found, for instance, in Benioff,[6] Bennett (1982),[3] and Penrose.[7] In 1973, Bennett[3] had shown that a three-tape reversible Turing machine can be constructed. It would operate in three phases: compute and record history, copy result, and then return to initial state by reversibly 'undoing' all computational steps. This result was important in establishing that the reversible computer can in principle exist, but in order to be more concrete we have to step down again to the level of basic computer building blocks: logical gates.

It was already observed by Landauer that ordinary logical operations (and thus also respective gates) are irreversible. It is easy to understand why: in order for any logical gate to be reversible the number of output lines must be equal to the number of input lines, otherwise it is impossible to recreate the input to the gate based only on the output.

Fredkin and Toffoli[8] investigated the idea of such reversible gates. In fact, the first such gate was conceived by Fredkin when he was a Sherman Fairchild Distinguished Scholar at Caltech in 1974. He was invited there by Feynman. The story of their acquaintance began in 1962 in a rather strange fashion. Ed Fredkin, together with Marvin Minsky, was in Pasadena sometime in 1962. Having nothing to do one evening, they decided to call Richard Feynman and, as Fredkin recalls, 'We sort of invited ourselves and he had us come [to his house] and we stayed until two or three in the morning. We had a long, long talk about many things, and I kept in touch [with him] from that time on.'[9] The discussion that night was mostly about doing algebra on a machine. Feynman was interested in whether a computer could perform algebraic manipulations. The seed sown that night resulted in the birth of MACSYMA, an important program for doing mathematics on a computer. Fredkin and Minsky, upon their return to Cambridge, Massachusttes, started to work on the project, and 'we got involved in trying to make that happen—Marvin [Minsky] more than me—and basically the result was this system called MACSYMA.'[9]

Fredkin's 'keeping in touch' with Feynman resulted in his being invited to Caltech as a Fairchild Scholar. Since the early 1970s Fredkin had been director of MIT's Laboratory for Computer Science. After some time he got more interested in physics and Feynman arranged for him to be invited to Caltech for a year. He was supposed to teach Feynman more about computers, and learn more from him about physics. The result, according to Fredkin, was that he learned more about physics than Feynman learned about computer science. In any case, it was during that stay that Fredkin invented his gate. After realizing that one needs at least three lines to embed ordinary logical functions, he proposed a three-input three-output gate. One of the three lines is a control line. Its output emerges unchanged. The status of the other two output lines depends on the state of the control line. It can be either a simple copy of the two input lines, or an exchange of them. An iterative use of Fredkin gates can produce all logical functions.

Later investigations by Fredkin[8] showed that not only NAND but an arbitrary Boolean function can be embedded in a conservative bijective function.

The Fredkin gate is a theoretical concept, but physical realizations of it also exist. The question of whether a gate such as proposed by Fredkin can have a physical realization at all had been raised. Fredkin, refuting critics, came up with a model of conservative-logic computer, called a billiard ball model. It consists of a plane, equipped with fixed reflectors, and balls, which collide elastically with themselves and the reflectors. The balls are prepared in a certain initial condition, with given positions and velocities. They enter the container, collide one or more times, and then emerge from it. The container with reflectors represents a computer-machine capable of performing certain manipulations on the data (as represented by the position of the balls). In order to specify the data, we can imagine a grid, overlaying the apparatus in such a way that each cell of the grid can hold exactly one ball. Then the input state can be read by looking at the grid and checking which fields are occupied by a ball (representing a logical 1) and which are empty (representing a logical 0).

In particular, one can construct such a billiard ball model of the Fredkin gate. This indeed was the case: Fredkin came up with it, and almost immediately informed Feynman about it. 'Feynman got quite excited about it. Then about a week later he sent me [Fredkin] a long letter. He'd been playing with this idea and doing various things. He discovered that it was nice to write this gate down in a sort of particular way. And it turned out that one of my students had done the same thing. And we all agreed that we'd call it the Feynman gate, because we wanted Feynman to be interested in this. And he was; he was very nice because he got very enthusiastic about it.'[9]

Fredkin's computer is 'ballistic', that is, the balls enter at a finite speed, and thus all calculations are done in a fully reversible manner in finite time. Unfortunately, such a model is not very practical. Any attempt at operating such a machine in a real world is bound to fail. Zurek[10] analyzed instabilities in its evolution and came to the conclusion that all initial errors (and in a real world we cannot set balls in their initial positions with infinite accuracy) will grow exponentially in the process of calculations. Thus, after only a few hundred steps, the accumulated errors will render the result completely meaningless. One could, of course, get rid of the errors by 'normalizing' the positions of the balls with respect to the reference grid every few steps, but that could be done only by discarding some information (reducing unwanted noise), and that is something they were trying to avoid all the time.

Other models of reversible computers were also proposed. Most of them were so-called 'Brownian' computers, where, as in many thermodynamical processes, reversibility is obtained only in the zero-speed limit, that is, the processes happening are not entirely reversible, but they become more and more so when the velocities of all moving parts approach zero. Bennett already in 1973[3] gave an example of an enzymatic apparatus of DNA replication, transcription, and translation of nature's closest approach to reversibility— the dissipation involved (from $20kT$ to $100kT$) is well below that of the computers available nowadays.

Another idea of Bennett was a clockwork Turing machine.[3] This was a rather rigid looking, frictionless clockwork device, composed of various manipulators, rotating disks and knobs, like a nineteenth-century contraption. The machine would wander back and forth through its 'computational space', but it would record an overall progress thanks to a small driving force imposed upon it by a spring.[3]

Bennett[11] also noticed that an early coupled potential-wells model of Keyes and Landauer,[12] which was invented before the advent of reversible computing, and in another context, could in fact function as a Brownian reversible computer when programmed suitably.

Landauer also proposed a 'balls and pipes model',[13] where the pipes are the mechanical information propagation channels, and balls, as in the billiard ball model, represent information by their presence (logical state 0). Unlike Fredkin's model, Landauer's pipes have friction proportional to velocity, and function reversibly only in the zero-speed limit.

Another interesting idea was that of Likharev,[14] who proposed a computing device based on the so-called Josephson junction—but in describing that we would get even further away from the main topic of this chapter, which we are trying to approach all the time, and which we shall discuss in the following two sections.

So far we have seen that it is possible to make a computer which would work without energy dissipation, and even at finite speed. Unfortunately, all these machines are macroscopic, and rather unpractical. Attempts to consider smaller ones necessarily lead us into a level at which we have to take into account the quantum mechanical description of the world. And such models are the subject of the next section.

24.5 Models of quantum mechanical reversible computers

First steps on the road to quantum mechanical computing were taken by Benioff.[15] His interest in quantum computations started from a belief that physics and mathematics are deeply intertwined and that one checks the validity of a physical theory such as quantum mechanics by making mathematical calculations of theoretical expectation values and comparing them by means of repeated experiments. Now the calculation of expectation values can be made with a computer which is a physical system. The computer plus computation process should be describable as a quantum mechanical system evolving under the quantum mechanical laws of evolution; both processes are described within the theory whose validity is being checked. In his papers, Benioff proposed a series of Hamiltonians describing the evolution of a system composed of spin-$\frac{1}{2}$ particles sitting at fixed lattice sites. The initial state of the system, $\Psi(0)$, at time 0 corresponds to the initial state of a computation. Spin-$\frac{1}{2}$ particles have only two possible states—spin-up and spin-down—which correspond to logical states 0 and 1. The initial state is equivalent to the computer input. This input evolves under the action of the Hamiltonian (which in a certain way contains information about the program of the computations), until it reaches the final state. Benioff's Hamiltonian was constructed in such a way that, at times $0, \Delta, 2\Delta, \ldots, n\Delta$, the quantum states $\Psi(0), \Psi(\Delta), \Psi(2\Delta), \ldots, \Psi(n\Delta)$ describe the completion of $0, 1, 2, \ldots, n$ steps of the calculation.

This particular construction can use either the time-independent or time-dependent Hamiltonian. The time-independent Hamiltonian model conserves energy, but it has some problems—the construction of the Hamiltonian probably requires knowledge not only of the computer program but also of computational orbits. Another undesirable feature is that the Hamiltonian contains many-particle interactions which are not localized to small lattice distances. The former problem can be cured by employing a time-dependent Hamiltonian, but the latter problem remains. Difficulties notwithstanding, Benioff's achievement was appreciated by specialists in the field: Landauer said: 'The pros and cons of the value of such description are complex, but best left to the detailed literature. As someone, who had tried to do something like this, and failed, I was impressed.'[16]

So, in the beginning of 1981 the idea of reversible computing was by no means new, but known only among a few specialists involved in this field. Fredkin's gate, conservative logic, and Benioff's quantum model were fresh additions, but again only a few read the relevant papers and thought that there really was something there. Then an important event took place which changed the situation. Fredkin, Toffoli, and Landauer organized a conference on the physics of computation, held from 6 to 8 May 1981, at MIT's conference center at Endicott House, Dedham, Massachusetts. All the people working in this and related fields were there, and Fredkin managed to convince Feynman not only to participate in the conference but to be the keynote speaker. It was not clear from the beginning that he would come. As Fredkin recalled: 'He asked what was the name of the meeting. We had a name that . . . implied that perhaps there were informational models of physics. . . . When Feynman heard that, he said, "Well, if you have that as a name, and it implies that there are computational models of physics, then I am not coming." So, we said OK, we'll change the name to something innocuous like "Physics and computation." He said, "OK, I'm coming." Then I thought it was a funny story and I relayed it to Michael Dertouzous . . . he was director of the Laboratory . . . He opened the meeting and Feynman was to be the keynote speaker and he was introducing Feynman. [Dertouzous] told the funny story which was how I wanted to call that meeting something like "Computational models of physics", but when Feynman heard that, he said that if that is the topic of the meeting he would not come. So they had to change that. When Feynman got up to speak, he said, "Yes, that's true, but, since he told me that I have changed my mind, and the talk I am going to give *is* on computational models of physics." So it was sort of first time in public that he ever admitted that he was interested in this viewpoint.'[9]

There were many other talks at the conference, and among the people who gave them were: Benioff, Bennett, Fredkin, Keyes, Landauer, Minsky, Toffoli, Wheeler, and Zuse.

Feynman's talk, 'Simulating physics with computers', almost did not touch the subject of quantum computers. He only indicated the possibility of imagining a quantum computer as a computer operating on two-state objects, by means of some kind of creation and annihilation operators. But the key element—how to write a 'program' for such a computer, how to force it to evolve in a well-defined predictable way—was missing at that time. The answer came a few years later; in the talk, instead, he concentrated on the problem of simulating the real world, which is quantum mechanical, with classical computers—computers operating on principles of classical mechanics. The interest in that stemmed to a large extent from discussions with Fredkin: Feynman had analyzed Fredkin's ideas and pinpointed their inherent flaws. The talk itself was a careful analysis of the hypothesis that we can build a general simulator which in some way will simulate physical phenomena. Now, the word *simulation* should be understood properly. By *simulation* Feynman did not mean finding some approximate solution to the equations of motion: what he wanted was an exact reproduction of physics. The example he analyzed was a two-photon correlation experiment, a phenomenon very quantum mechanical in its nature, and the proof was presented that no classical computer could imitate it.

Feynman's conclusion was: 'And I'm not happy with all the analyses that go with just the classical theory, because nature isn't classical, dammit, and if you want to make a simulation of nature, you'd better make it quantum mechanical, and by golly it's a wonderful problem, because it doesn't look so easy.'[17]

At the MIT meeting, the ideas concerning reversible computing and quantum mechanical computers were intensely discussed and, according to the testimony of other participants, Feynman took an active part in them.

In this section we have tried to review briefly some of the ideas leading to quantum computers. Although Benioff constructed the first such model, Feynman's proposal was much more elegant and actually established a method for constructing quantum mechanical Hamiltonian models of computers. We shall now give a more detailed description of Feynman's model.

24.6 Feynman's model of a quantum computer

Feynman's only paper on quantum computers is based on his talk delivered at the CLEO/IQEC Meeting in Anaheim, California, in 1984.[18] It was first published in the February 1985 issue of *Optics News*[19] and later reprinted in the *Foundations of Physics* (1986). The abstract of this paper is rather short: 'The physical limitations, due to quantum mechanics, on the functioning of computers are analyzed.' In the paper itself, Feynman acknowledged the previous work of Bennett, Fredkin, and Toffoli, but he made no reference to the work of Benioff.

In the introduction of his paper Feynman began by discussing logic gates and the definition of three reversible primitives, which are sufficient to build a reversible machine. Selection of such elements is rather arbitrary, and Feynman's choice was rather nonstandard: taking NOT (negation), CONTROLLED NOT, and CONTROLLED CONTROLLED NOT. CONTROLLED NOT is a two-inputs and two-outputs gate. One of the input lines is a data line, the other is a control line. The gate acts as a NOT gate when the control line is activated, and transmits the data line unchanged in the opposite case. Such a gate can be used for building a FAN OUT (copying one input on two outputs) and EXCHANGE (exchange of input values between two lines) gate.

Having only two lines is not sufficient to construct an arbitrary reversible logical function, thus the need for CONTROLLED CONTROLLED NOT—a gate with two control lines, which changes (produces negation of) the input data line only when both are activated. As an example of usage of this set, Feynman constructs an adder, which performs addition of two input lines. It takes into account carryover from the previous addition, and the whole process of adding is done in a reversible manner, presenting as the final result the desired output and a copy of the input data.

The next step is to build such a computer using the laws of quantum mechanics. The aim is to write a Hamiltonian which, when applied to a system composed of interacting parts, will effectively perform computations, as if it were a computer. The fundamental assumption is that the smallest 'building block' of our computer (called atom by Feynman) can have only two states, which will be represented by $|0\rangle$ and $|1\rangle$. Thus each atom will represent a single bit. Then we can introduce operators which would perform logical operations on the bits, equivalent to the action of gates described above. Such operators can be represented as two-dimensional matrices. In order to build such matrices (or operators) we can first construct two elementary operators: an annihilation operator a, which converts $|1\rangle$ to $|0\rangle$ (and leaves $|0\rangle$ unaffected), and a creation operator a^*, which moves from $|0\rangle$ to $|1\rangle$. Then $a + a^*$ would act like NOT; CONTROLLED NOT (which acts on two lines, $|a, b\rangle$) can be represented by $a^* a(b + b^*) + aa^*$, and the CONTROLLED CONTROLLED NOT is $1 + a^* ab^*b(c + c^* - 1)$.

Now we have to consider the problem of joining our elementary logical units (gates) into something performing some computation, like adder, etc. This would involve k operations $A_1, A_2, \ldots, A_k$ acting on n input lines. How shall we write our Hamiltonian so that it transforms the input state into the desired output state? Feynman's idea was to add to the existing n atoms an auxiliary set of $k + 1$ atoms, which he called 'program counter sites'. If we denote by a_i the annihilation operators for the program site i (i goes from 0 to k), then we can write our Hamiltonian as follows:

$$H = \sum_{i=0}^{k-1} a_{i+1}^* a^i A_{i+1} + \text{c.c.}$$

$$= a_1^* a_0 A_1 + a_2^* a_1 A_2 + \cdots + a_0^* a^1 A_1^* + a_1^* a_2 A_2^* + \cdots.$$

Then we also need one more assumption: we always assume that only one of the sites $0, \ldots, k$ is in the 'occupied' state. This occupied site we will call the cursor. Then the operation of this Hamiltonian would simply cause the cursor to propagate along the program counter sites, causing at the same time respective operators A_i to operate on the register n. After the cursor arrives at the site k we are sure that the entire combination $A_1, A_2, \ldots, A_k$ has operated on n as desired. In order to make this computation ballistic, we have to add some sites before and after the actual 'computational' sites $0, \ldots, k$, and start computations by putting the cursor with different amplitudes on different sites representing an initial incoming spin wave, a wide packet of nearly definite momentum.

This was the initial proposal of a Hamiltonian which could perform ballistic computation on a quantum mechanical system. Important aspects of that Hamiltonian are its time independence and locality of interaction among logical variables. All this constituted a significant improvement over Benioff's first attempt, and was a foundation for many to build upon.

24.7 Further developments of Feynman's ideas

Feynman himself did not develop his ideas further, but he had shown the way for many who followed him. His initial proposal was not perfect: there were problems with possible spreading of the wave packet, definition of input–output procedures had to be completed, some areas still remained unexplored, but the beginning was made. In fact, much more than that: Feynman's presence at the MIT conference and his interest in the field caused many people to look into the strange concepts of making computers run backward or of writing a Hamiltonian instead of a program. A lot of research has been done along directions originally indicated by Feynman by N. Margolus, A. Peres, P. A. Benioff, W. H. Zurek, and J. A. Wheeler.

It is very difficult to predict the development of computers at any timescale longer than just a couple of years. The field is developing very rapidly, old barriers are overcome, and new much better designs appear on the market almost continually. According to the estimates made by Keyes, by around 2010 (assuming that the pace of the progress in manufacturing computers will not slacken) designers will confront problems arising from the second law of thermodynamics. The gates will be so miniaturized and otherwise perfected that the amount of heat generated by performing irreversible logical operations will constitute the major source of heat in the system. So, maybe the time of reversible computers is fast approaching?

24.8 The underlying discrete structure of the universe

Another problem connected with computers has always been in the back of the minds of physicists. How does the universe know what to do? There are the laws of physics, one could say. But how are the laws of physics implemented? Exactly how it is done has always been a fundamental question of physics. How does the universe calculate the trajectories of galaxies, planets, stones, air molecules, quarks? Which computer does it use? Well, maybe it is itself a computer.

Fredkin's ideas in this matter are decidedly unorthodox, and he discussed them many times with Feynman, but neither managed to convince the other. Basically, Fredkin's view is that the whole universe is a giant computer, whose underlying structure resembles something like a cellular automaton. This cellular automaton is a discrete object, composed of cells, whose behavior is governed by simple rules. The idea of the underlying discontinuity is nothing new, but this time it seems to have been taken to its extreme. Between Fredkin's concepts and the conservative approach there lies a whole range of various questions and suggestions, and sometimes just a new angle of looking at things.

Minsky,[20] in his talk at the MIT conference, analyzed what he called a 'cellular vacuum'—space built from discrete units which contain only a finite amount of information. Then the space is 'taught' some rules of evolution, based only on the knowledge of the state of the nearest neighbors of each cell. The demand made of the space is that it obey some well-known constraints, such as, for example, the conservation of momentum. The result is that some very strange phenomena occur under such conditions. Conservation laws are different, but some sort of Newtonian law of inertia is obeyed.

John Wheeler pointed to the nature of time as a secondary, derived category in the description of nature and the transitory nature of the laws of physics. He suggested the existence of a deeper layer of elements, which he called 'elementary quantum phenomena', lying beneath particles, force fields, and space–time. From these he drew analogies between constructing physics from such elementary entities, and constructing a computer out of binary elements.

Zuse again looked into the mechanics of particles which in fact are 'moving state structures', objects existing only as collections of cells of a cellular automaton. The problem of the reversibility of time direction can be stated in this context, too, and rules paralleling those of physical particles can be derived.

Feynman, often Fredkin's adversary in their discussions about the 'digital universe', expressed his ideas in this matter in his keynote speech given during the MIT conference on physics and computation. Its conclusion was already mentioned earlier, but there was also another twist to the whole business. In Feynman's words: 'A very interesting question is the origin of probabilities in quantum mechanics. Another way of putting things is: We have an illusion that we can do any experiment we want. We all, however, come from the same universe, have evolved with it, and have come from a certain past. It is somehow that we are correlated to the experiments that we do, so that the apparent probabilities don't look like they ought to look if you assume that they are random. There are all kinds of questions like this, and what I'm trying to do is to get you people who think about computer simulation possibilities to pay a great deal of attention to this, to digest as well as possible the real answers of quantum mechanics, and see if you can't invent a different point of view than the physicists have had to invent to describe this.' [17]

For Feynman, finding out connections between quantum mechanics and the rules of computation had only been an amusement, but his passing through the stage of reversible computing put the subject in the spotlight, and drew the attention of many to this field. As Landauer remarked about the 1981 MIT conference: 'Feynman's mere participation, together with his willingness to accept an occasional lecture invitation in this area, have helped to emphasize that this is an interesting subject.' [16]

Notes and References

1. R.P. Feynman, Interviews and conversations with Jagdish Mehra, in Pasadena, California, January 1988.

2. M. von Smoluchowski, *Phys. Z.* **13**, 1069 (1912).

3. C.H. Bennett, Logical reversibility of computation. *IBM J. Res. Dev.* **17**, 525 (1973); The thermodynamics of computation—a review. *Int. J. Theor. Phys.* **21**, 905 (1982); Demons, engines and the second law. *Sci. Am.* **255** (11), 108 (1987).

4. R. Landauer, Irreversibility and heat generation in the computing process, *IBM*

J. Res. Dev. **5**, 183 (1961); C.H. Bennett and R. Landauer, The fundamental limits of computation. *Sci. Am*, **253** (1), 489 (1985).

5. J. von Neumann, *Collected works* (ed. A.H. Taub). Pergamon Press, 1963.

6. P.A. Benioff, Quantum mechanical models of computers. *Ann. N.Y. Acad. Sci.* **480**, part X, 475 (1986).

7. R. Penrose, *The emperor's new mind.* Oxford University Press, 1989.

8. E. Fredkin and T. Toffoli, Conservative logic. *Int. J. Theor. Phys.* **21**, 219 (1982).

9. E. Fredkin, Telephone interview with Jagdish Mehra, 20 June 1990.

10. W.H. Zurek, Reversibility and stability of information-processing systems. *Phys. Rev. Lett.* **53**, 391 (1984).

11. C.H. Bennett, Notes on the history of reversible computation. *IBM J. Res. Dev.* **32**, 16 (1988).

12. R.W. Keyes and R. Landauer, Minimal energy dissipation in logic. *IBM J. Res. Dev.* **14**, 152 (1970).

13. R. Landauer, Fundamental limitations in the computatational process. *Ber. Bunsenges. Phys. Chem.* **80** (11), 1041 (1976); Uncertainty principle and minimal energy dissipation in the computer. *Int. J. Theor. Phys.* **21**, 283 (1982).

14. K.K. Likharev, Classical and quantum limitations on energy consumption in computation. *Int. J. Theor. Phys.* **21**, 311 (1982).

15. P.A. Benioff, The computer as a physical system: a microscopic Hamiltonian model of computers as represented by Turing machines. *J. Stat. Phys.* **22**, 563 (1980); Quantum mechanical Hamiltonian models of discrete processes, *J. Math. Phys.* **22**, 495 (1981); Quantum mechanical Hamiltonian models of discrete processes that erase their own histories: Applications of Turing machines. *J. Stat. Phys.* **29**, 515 (1982); Quantum mechanical models of Turing machines that dissipate no energy. *Phys. Rev. Lett.* **48**, 1581 (1982).

16. R. Landauer, Fundamental physical limitations of the computational process: An informal commentary. Submitted as Visiting Fellow to the Sackler Institute of Advanced Studies, Tel Aviv University, 1988.

17. R.P. Feynman, Similuating physics with computers. *Int. J. Theor. Phys.* **21**, 467 (1982).

18. R.P. Feynman, Quantum mechanical computers. Plenary talk presented to IQEC/CLEO Meeting, Anaheim, California, 19 June 1984.

19. R.P. Feynman, Quantum mechanical computers. *Opt. News* **11**, 11 (1985); *Found. Phys.* (1986).

20. R. Minsky, *Int. J. Theor. Phys.* **21**, 537 (1982).

25

Reflections on science, religion, culture, and modern society

Beginning in the mid-1950s Richard Feynman began to give invited talks on his more philosophical reflections on science, its relation to religion, its role in the world today, and the value of scientific culture in modern society. In these talks Feynman celebrated the joys and wonders of thinking about nature, championed a boldly logical and rational point of view against mystical and irrational beliefs and practices, and expressed some highly original viewpoints. He turned the full force of his derision on superstition, magic, witch doctors, UFOs, extrasensory perception (ESP), and psychology and psychiatry. About psychiatry, he would mockingly say that 'anyone who wants to visit a psychiatrist should have his head examined'.[1] Feynman's views on the importance of a scientific, rational, and objective outlook on life and human endeavor were formed early in life; he lived by them and unfailingly expressed them, to the extent that in his pursuit of total objectivity he could sound unfeeling and rather belligerent. In this chapter, I shall give an account of Feynman's philosophical reflections on science and the vision of a rational future for mankind which he cherished.

25.1 The value of science[2]

Scientific knowledge enables us to do and make all kinds of things. If we do and make good things, then it is not only to the credit of science but it is also to the credit of the moral choice which led to the good work. Scientific knowledge is the enabling power to do either good or bad—but it does not carry instructions on how to use it. Such power has evident value, even though the power may be negated by what one does.

Feynman learned a way of expressing this common human problem on a trip to Honolulu, Hawaii. In the Buddhist temple there, he met a priest who was explaining the Buddhist religion to the tourists, and told them a Buddhist proverb: 'To every man is given the key to the gates of heaven; the same key opens the gates to hell.' It is true that if we lack clear instructions that determine which is the gate to heaven and which the gate to hell, the key may be a dangerous object to use, but it obviously has great value: we cannnot enter heaven without it. In spite of the fact that science could produce enormous horror in the world, it is of value because it can produce *something*.

Another value of science is the intellectual enjoyment which some people get from reading, learning, and thinking about it, and which others get from working on it, and this enjoyment is as important as anything else. Moreover, the world view which results from scientific effort is also important. Through science, we have been led to imagine all sorts of things, which are perhaps more marvelous than the imaginings of poets and dreamers of the past, which shows that nature's imagination is greater than the imagination of man. 'For instance, how much more remarkable it is for all of us to be stuck—half of us upside down—by a mysterious attraction [called gravitation]—to a spinning ball that has been swinging in space for billions of years, than (as man imagined in the past) to be carried on the back of an elephant supported on a tortoise swimming in a bottomless sea.' [3]

Feynman gave poetic expression to the great joy of thinking and imagining about nature as follows:[4]

> For instance, I stand at the sea-shore,
>   alone, and start to think.
> There are the rushing waves . . .
>   mountains of molecules,
> Each stupidly minding its own business
>   Trillions apart . . . , yet forming white surf in unison.
> Ages on ages . . . before any eyes could see
> Year after year . . . Thunderously pounding
>   the shore as now.
> For whom, for what? . . . on a dead planet,
> With no life to entertain.
> Never at rest . . . tortured by energy . . .
> Wasted prodigiously by the sun . . . poured into space.
> A mite makes the ocean roar.
> Deep in the sea, all molecules repeat the patterns
> Of one another till complex new ones are formed.
> They make others like themselves . . . and
>   a new dance starts.
> Growing in size and complexity . . .
> Living things, masses of atoms, DNA, protein . . .
> Dancing a pattern ever more intricate.
> Out of the cradle onto the dry land
> Here it is standing . . . atoms with consciousness
> Matter with curiosity.

Stands at the sea ... Wonders at wondering ...
I ... a universe of atoms ... an atom in the universe.

The same thrill, the same awe and mystery, come again and again when we look at any problem deeply enough. With more knowledge comes deeper, more wonderful mystery, luring one on to penetrate deeper still. With pleasure and confidence we turn over each new stone to find unimagined strangeness leading on to more wonderful questions and mysteries—certainly a grand adventure. 'Few unscientific people have this particular type of religious experience. Our poets do not write about it, our artists do not portray this remarkable thing, and the value of science remains unsung by singers. This is not yet a scientific age.' [4]

The thing which we call our individuality is only a pattern of dance of atoms. The atoms come into our brain, dance a dance, then go out, always new atoms but always doing the same dance, remembering what the dance was yesterday.

Education is a strong force, but it can be used for either good or evil. 'Communications between nations must promote understanding: that was another dream. But the machines of communication can be channeled or choked; communication can be a force [for] either good or bad. Medicines control diseases, and the record here is generally good; yet there are men patiently working to create plagues and poisons, which are to be used in warfare tomorrow. The sciences do not directly teach good or bad.' [5]

Throughout all ages men have tried to fathom the meaning of life. From the history of enormous monstrosities created by false beliefs, philosophers have realized the infinite and wondrous capacities of human beings. The dream is to find the open channel. 'It is our responsibility as scientists to proclaim the value and freedom to teach how to doubt; to doubt should not be feared but welcomed and discussed; and to demand this freedom is our duty to all coming generations.' [5]

25.2 The relation of science to religion[6]

The relation of science and religion is an old problem, and it is still with us. Feynman was invited to talk upon this subject at the Caltech YMCA on 2 May 1956. He pointed out that, in our times, where specialization prevails in all aspects of human activity, people who work in one field are often incompetent to discuss another. Yet, the problem of the relation between science and religion was one in which Feynman was always interested.

It often happens that a young man, brought up in a religious family, studies one of the sciences, and as a result he comes to doubt and disbelieve in his father's God. In fact, there are many scientists who do not believe in God in a conventional sense. Now, belief in God is a central feature of religion. Why does the young man come to disbelieve in God? It is possible that many of his teachers, from whom he learns, are atheists, and beliefs are passed on from one to the other. It is also possible that the young man, after learning more, will grow out of this 'sophomoric sophistication' and come to realize that the world is more complicated, and he will again begin to understand that there must be a God after all. Belief in science and in God—the God of religion—is a consistent possibility. In fact many scientists believe in both. However, this consistency is difficult to attain. Feynman then sought to understand two things: why this consistency is not easy to attain, and whether it is worth attempting to attain it.

When one talks about one's 'belief in God', there always arises the puzzle: 'What is God?' In Western religions, one usually has in mind a personal God to whom one prays and who had something to do with the creation of the universe and guiding morals.

There are two sources of difficulty in welding science and religion together. The first source is this: in science, it is imperative to doubt; it is necessary for the progress of science to have uncertainty as a fundamental part of your inner nature. To make progress in scientific understanding we must remain modest and allow that we do not know. Nothing is proved beyond all doubt. The statements of science are not of the nature of what is true and what is not true, but of what is known to different degrees of certainty. 'Every one of the concepts of science is graduated on a scale somewhere between, but neither end of, absolute falsity and absolute truth.' [7]

It is of great value to acknowledge ignorance not only in science but in other things as well. When we make decisions in our life we do not necessarily know that we are making them correctly; we only think that we are doing the best we can. It is of great value to realize that we do not know the answers to different questions. This attitude of uncertainty is vital to any scientist; this attitude of mind is the first one to acquire and make a habit of thought—for, once acquired, it cannot be relinquished any more.

We cannot have absolute truth. So the question, 'Is there a God?' changes to 'How sure it is that there is a God?'. Although there are scientists who believe in God, Feynman doubted if they think of God in the same way as religious people do. Science denies the absolute certainty of the existence of God, which religion affirms.

Then there are special tenets, such as the existence of an afterlife, the details of religious doctrine, and the life and divinity of Christ. The scientific attitude to these tenets is based on their scrutiny, while in religion they are a matter of certainty.

Why is it that belief in God—at least, the God of religion—should be considered unreasonable in science? The size of the universe is very impressive: we are whirling on a tiny particle (the earth) around the sun, one among hundreds of millions of suns in the galaxy, itself among billions of galaxies. Then, there is the close relation of the biological man to animals, and of one life to another. Man is a latecomer in a vast evolving drama; can the rest be but a scaffolding for his creation?

Again, there are atoms, all of which appear to follow immutable laws. All the stars are made of the same stuff as all the animals are. Like man himself, everything is made of great complexity. It is a great adventure to contemplate the universe beyond man, to think what it means without the presence of man. 'When this objective view is finally achieved, and the mystery and majesty of matter appreciated, to then turn the objective eye back on man viewed as matter, to see life as part of the universal mystery of great depth, is to sense an experience which is rarely described. It usually ends in laughter, delight in the futility of trying to understand. These scientific views end in awe and mystery, lost at the edge of uncertainty, but they appear to be so deep and so impressive that the theory that it is all arranged as a stage for God to watch man's struggle for good and evil seems to be inadequate.' [8]

Even if one obtains the conviction that prayers are not answered and God does not exist, it does not fundamentally alter the moral view one holds. It is possible to doubt the divinity of Christ, and yet believe firmly that it is a good thing to do unto your neighbor as you would have him do unto you. It is possible to have both views at the same time; in fact, many atheistic people carry themselves quite morally. Although science makes some impact on many religious ideas, it does not affect the moral content.

Religion has several aspects: it answers all kinds of questions. There are three main aspects of religion. First, the metaphysical aspect of religion answers questions about what things are, where they come from, what man is, what God is; this is the basic theological and metaphysical concern of religion. Second, the ethical aspect of religion gives a moral and ethical code. This ethical code tells us how to behave in life in general in a moral way. Even with moral values granted, human beings are weak; they must be reminded of the moral values in order that they are able to follow their consciences. It is not simply a matter of having the right conscience; it is also a question of maintaining strength to do what you know is right. Religion gives strength, comfort, and inspiration to follow moral values. The third aspect is the inspiration religion gives for the arts and all kinds of thoughts and actions as well.

These three aspects of religion are very well interconnected, and it is often thought that to attack one feature of the system is to attack the whole structure. The three aspects work as follows. The metaphysical aspect of religion gives the belief in God; the moral aspect, the moral code, enjoins us to follow righteous conduct; and the inspiration comes from working with God. The inspirational aspect brings one's actions in contact with the universe at large.

Science occasionally conflicts with the metaphysical aspect of religion. For instance, whether the earth moves around the sun or the sun moves around the earth was once a great metaphysical question. The result in such situations is a retreat of the religious metaphysical view, but it does not lead to the collapse of religion. Science is developing and new things will be found out which will be in disagreement with the present-day metaphysical theories of certain religions, but morals are not affected. The spirit of uncertainty in science is an attitude toward the metaphysical questions that is quite different from the certainty and faith that is demanded in religion. When both science and religion seek to answer questions in the same metaphysical realm difficulties arise. However, a real conflict does not arise in the ethical aspect, because moral questions are outside the scientific realm. Even when science and religion conflicted about metaphysical views, moral values did not collapse. There are good men who practice Christian ethics and who do not believe in the divinity of Christ; they find themselves in no inconsistency here.

Science can be defined as a method for, and a body of information obtained by, trying to answer only questions which can be put in the form 'If I do this, what will happen?' The technique here is fundamentally this: try it and see. All scientists will agree that a question—any question, philosphical or other—which cannot be put in this form is not a scientific question; it is outside the realm of science. Yet, there is a complete consistency between the moral view, or the ethical aspect of religion, and scientific information.

Now the inspirational aspect of religion. The inspiration comes from working with God, from obeying His will, feeling one with God. Emotional ties to the moral code—based in the manner—begin to be severely weakened when doubt, even a small amount of doubt, is expressed as to the existence of God; so when belief in God becomes uncertain, this particular method of inspiration fails. However, an absolute faith in the metaphysical aspect of religion is fundamental to maintaining the real value of religion as a source of strength and courage to most men.

Western civilization stands on two great heritages. 'One is the scientific spirit of adventure into the unknown, an unknown that must be explored; the demand that the unanswerable mysteries of the universe remain unanswered; the attitude that all is uncertain; in short, the humility of the intellect. The other great heritage is Christian ethics—the basis of action on love, the brotherhood of all men, the value of the individual—the humility of spirit. These two heritages are logically, thoroughly consistent. But logic is not all; one needs one's heart to follow an idea. How can we draw inspiration to support these two pillars of Western civilization so that they may stand together in full vigor, mutually unafraid? This is the central problem of our time.' [9]

25.3 The role of science in the world today[10]

The Institute of World Affairs organized a meeting in 1957 on 'Science reshaping world politics', but, given the tenor of the various talks, the theme of this meeting—in Feynman's view—should have been more appropriately entitled 'Political problems arising from some recent technological advances'.

From the invention of the telephone to the industrialization of the world, the *technological* advances have produced political problems. Feynman proposed to use the word 'science' as a scientist, rather than to signify 'technological engineering developments' or 'applied science'—which most people use the word 'science' to connote. By 'science' one should understand 'pure science'. To understand what is involved in these different usages, let us consider the example of the atomic bomb.

How is science involved in the development of the atomic bomb? Historically, the first thing was the study of the nuclear structure of matter by scientists. They wanted to find out the constituents of which matter was made. In 1911, Rutherford found that the outside of atoms of which matter was made was soft and squishy, made of electrons, while the inside is a very small hard core called the nucleus. The problem then arose: What constitutes the nucleus? It was finally discovered that it was made up of protons and neutrons. The neutron was discovered in 1932. The neutron was used to hit many elements as targets to see what happened. Finally, when the element uranium was hit by neutrons, something peculiar happened: the nucleus of uranium broke up into two almost equal parts. This experiment, dealing with the so-called 'fission' of uranium, was done all over the world after the first results of Hahn and Strassmann in 1938. By 1939 it was clear that when the uranium nucleus splits into two, more neutrons as well as energy are liberated· each time two neutrons are liberated, they hit another nucleus of uranium. This phenomenon clearly gave rise to the possibility of nuclear energy, and the attitude to the problem suddenly became different.

After that, a large number of technical problems arose in making an atomic bomb. These problems were many and complex, but they were all primarily applied, technical, and engineering problems. The problem of 'pure science' occurred only in the beginning: the discovery of the neutron, the structure of the nucleus, and the discovery of nuclear fission.

The motives of the scientist in making discoveries are: curiosity; the feeling of intense excitement and pleasure in making a discovery, which leads one to try to find out more things, the study of science alone is full of fun and intellectual enjoyment that exists in finding out how nature works in contemplating at least that small fraction of the great whole which has been partially revealed. When contemplating that small fraction, one cannot help wanting to know what is around the corner that has not been revealed yet— and so one soon finds oneself working on new things in science.

Scientific work of this kind is international. It has been international for the last 250 years, and there is complete cooperation among all nations about it. Scientists receive reprints from their colleagues all over the world. Thus science is a human development, a truly world affair.

How is science communicated? In America, for instance, we have a journal called the *Physical Review*, and every time we get results that are interesting we publish them. Science is no good without publishing. We want to tell our colleagues all over the world how things work. The *Physical Review* publishes the paper after a delay of about six months, and it goes all over the world. In the same way, there is in Russia the *Journal of Experimental and Theoretical Physics*, and it does the same thing. Then there are English, German, French, etc., journals and everybody exchanges information all the time.

The character of science is international. 'Professor Gell-Mann and I recently made a mild discovery, or rather an improvement on someone else's theory. When we made it, we sent it to the *Physical Review*, but we also made in mimeographed form a large number of copies, about 100, which we sent to scientists that we knew all over. So I am afraid the secret is out, for what it is worth. The modification that we made was made on a theory which was made before by [T. D.] Lee and [C. N.] Yang, who are Chinese living in the United States; they are Americans in that sense, but they are Chinese men. At the same time, exactly the same theory was being proposed by [L. D.] Landau in Russia (a Russian by the way), and exactly the same theory was proposed in England by [Abdus] Salam, who is Pakistani. So you see that it is a universal business all the way around. And the information which I needed in order to work on this theory I got from three men who were visiting California: one was a Swiss [Felix Boehm], one was a German [Berthold Stech], and one was hurriedly on his way to Israel [A. H. Wapstra]. So it is all interconnected, and there is nothing you can do about it, and I hope [no one stops] us from [doing] this.' [11] This is 'basic' or 'pure' research.

Consider the technical problems in building the atomic bomb. What is involved in these problems is not so much that we would like to find something about nature, but that we would like to make something in particular. This may also be called 'basic' research, and it is done in a completely scientific manner. This kind of work includes engineers, metallurgists, and so on. During World War II this research was done by people who would otherwise have been 'pure' scientists. This kind of research is actually 'applied research'.

For geopolitical reasons, and reasons of Cold War between the West and the Soviet Union, the engineering and technology of building atomic bombs and nuclear weapons was kept secret by the nations possessing them, as was the know-how of building rockets and putting satellites into orbit.

If nations can cooperate in pure science, why can't they also cooperate in technology? Actually, it used to be that technology was cooperatively exchanged. For instance, when the telephone was invented in the United States, it appeared within four years in countries all over the world. The same thing happened with radio, developed by an Italian [Guglielmo Marconi]. It also happened in chemistry, with the development of dyes, etc.; the patents became public knowledge. Technology used to be international—not perfectly, but then the system of patents was devised. A great many inventions are made in the laboratory by scientists trying to make measurements on something that can hardly be measured. That is, they have to invent new kinds of scientific devices and apparatus, and they publish information on these right away.

It is not that science has been shaping world affairs, but world affairs have been shaping technology, as in the case of nuclear reactors and rockets and missiles. For the sake of military and industrial measures, all the things being done in advanced technology are kept secret. Do we gain or lose by keeping technological things secret? We don't keep pure science secret, and it would be better to free technology of secrets also. The tremendous progress in pure science results from the fact that everybody communicates everything to everybody else.

What are some of the most exciting technological problems of today? One of them surely is interplanetary travel, with all its problems and excitement. Another very exciting problem is controlled thermonuclear energy; it is a technological problem of the highest caliber. The consequences of having controlled fusion energy will be great because it will make essential power supply practically free—certainly the fuel for the power (i.e. water) will be free. This will surely occur one day, unless we blow each other up before that.

Then there are applications of biological knowledge. There are fundamental genetic problems and problems of birth control. Also artificial food is another obvious problem.

An important direction in which science influences world affairs is the philosophy of science. 'After all, science is one of the few eminently successful endeavors at solving problems, and it may pay to look at some of the viewpoints or attitudes which are useful in science, and which may be of advantage in the problems of world affairs.'[12] One of these ways of looking at things is the scientist's attitude in trying to see what is actually involved rather than to see how something appears or what is said about it. This is different from propaganda and counterpropaganda.

The most important thing in the scientific attitude is that one doesn't know the answer to most questions. There is no shame in not knowing the answer. 'A man who simply says he knows the answer is not usually smarter than the one who says, "I don't know!"'[13] The best way to get the right answer, in general, is to start by admitting that you don't know. Unfortunately, the attitude all around today is quite different from this. A politician who said he didn't know the answer would be out politically. However, it would be refreshing if we could develop such attitudes a little more through studying science in schools. 'The reason we study science is not only to make an engineer, but we study science to look at the evidence, the way to realize how much baloney is there in the world, and to see what is right and wrong.'[13]

The scientist has a lot of experience with ignorance, doubt, and uncertainty, and this experience is of very great importance. 'When a scientist doesn't know the answer to a problem, he is ignorant, and when he has a hunch as to what the answer is, he is uncertain. When a scientist is pretty sure what the result would be, he is still in some doubt. This is not like everybody else.'[13] In order to make progress we must recognize the paramount importance of admitting ignorance and leaving room for doubt. 'Scientific knowledge is a body of statements of various degrees of certainty. Some of them are most unsure. Some of them are more nearly sure, but none of them is *absolutely* certain. In science, we take it for granted that it is perfectly possible to live and *not* know. It is not evident that most people realize that it's true.'[13] The scientist's freedom to doubt was born of a struggle against authority in the early days of science. It was a very deep and very strong struggle. 'Permit us to question—to doubt, that's all—not to be sure! It is important that we do not forget the importance of this struggle and thus perhaps lose sight of what we have gained.'[14]

We are all saddened when we think of the wondrous potentialities which human beings seem to have and we contrast them with their actual accomplishments. Again and again people have thought that we could do much better. 'Those of the past saw in the nightmare of their times, a dream for the future. And we, in their future, see that their dreams, in certain ways, remain dreams. The hopes for the future today are, in good measure, those of yesterday.'[15]

Once, some thought that the possibilities people had were not developed because most people were ignorant. 'With universal education, could all men not become Voltaires? But, as we saw in Nazi Germany, bad can be taught at least as efficiently as good. Education is an extremely strong force, but for either good or evil.'[15]

Applied sciences should free man of material wants at least. Medicine controls diseases. And here it looks as if the situation is all to the good. However, we know that there are today men working in laboratories trying to create new chemical and biological weapons.

Almost everybody dislikes war. Our dream today is peace. In peace, man can develop best the enormous possibilities he seems to have. But maybe future generations will find that peace, too, can be good or bad. Clearly, peace is a great force, as are material power, communication, education, honesty, and the ideals of many dreamers. We have more of these forces to control than did the ancients. And maybe we are doing a little bit better than most of them could do. But what we ought to be able to do seems gigantic compared with our confused accomplishments.

'Why is this? Why can't we conquer ourselves?' asked Feynman. 'Because,' he said, 'we find that even great forces and abilities do not seem to carry with them clear instructions on how to use them. As an example, the great accumulation of understanding as to how the physical world behaves only convinces one that this behavior seems to have a kind of meaninglessness. The sciences do not teach good and bad.'[16]

Through all ages men have tried to fathom the meaning of life. They have realized that if some direction or meaning could be given to our actions great human forces would be unleashed. Very many answers have been given to the meaning of it all. 'It is from the history of enormous monstrosities created by false belief that philosophers have realized the apparently infinite and wondrous capacities of human beings. The dream is to find the open channel, not the blind alley.' [17]

What then is the meaning of it all? What can we say to dispel the mystery of existence? Is it to find a definite goal toward which to guide our activities? 'If we take everything into account, not only what the ancients knew, but all of what we know today that they didn't know, then we must admit that *we do not know*. But, in admitting this, we have probably found the open channel.' [17]

It has always been clear to socially minded people that openness is an opportunity, that doubt and discussion are essential to progress into the unknown. If we want to solve a problem that we have never solved before, we must leave ajar the door to the unknown. 'We are at the very beginning of time for the human race. It is not unreasonable that we grapple with problems. There are tens of thousands of years in the future. Our responsibility is to do what we can, learn what we can, improve the solutions and pass them on. It is our responsibility to leave the men of the future a free hand. In the impetuous growth of humanity, we can make gross errors that can stunt our growth for a long time. This we will do if we say that we have the answers now, so young and ignorant; if we suppress all discussion, all criticism, saying, "This is it, man is saved!", and thus doom mankind for a long time to chains of authority, confined to the limits of our present imagination. It has been done many times before, and it is being tried again today.' [18]

In a prophetic statement, Feynman remarked: 'The Communist system is anti-scientific. An extension of this system throughout the world would be as fatal to science and to the future of man as was the period of the Dark Ages. The lack of freedom of discussion of ideas under the Communist system imprisons mankind in a way that the true potentialities of that future cannot evolve. Nothing can be learned, discussed, or modified, for only those in power in this system are supposed to have "true knowledge".' [19]

There always has been, and there always will be, progress when the political climate enables man to pursue ways not contemplated by the governing authority. Our hesitant and uncertain development in democracy is analogous to the uncertain development of science with its changing theories and unsure results. 'We do not know where we are going or whether what we are doing is right, but as long as we are willing to change our views as we gather new experiences, we shall progress. To think that one can give an answer now for all times is stupidity. Not to want to hear discussion or criticism nor to learn from other peoples opinions is blind stupidity, the antithesis of science.' [19] In a democracy we can change gears, and we can solve problems by admitting our mistakes and take actions to correct them.

Our responsibility 'as scientists, as citizens of a democracy, is to know the great value of a satisfactory philosophy of ignorance, the great progress that is the fruit of freedom of thought, to proclaim the value of this freedom, to teach how to doubt is not to be feared but to be welcomed and discussed, and to demand this freedom is our duty to all coming generations.' [20]

25.4 The role of scientific culture in modern society[21]

From 17 to 21 September 1964 a conference, organized by the Italian Physical Society, was held in Pisa, Italy, to celebrate the 400th anniversary of the birth of Galileo Galilei, and the theme assigned to Feynman for discussion was: 'What is and what should be the role of scientific culture in modern society?' The purpose of this conference was, on the one hand, a critical and philosophical analysis of various trends in modern physics, while, on the other hand, dealing with certain aspects of natural philosophy which are more or less common thinking among scientists from all fields. The topics of the principal lectures were chosen with a view to underlining the links between Galileo's thinking and life with the natural philosophy of today.

Galileo was the greatest exponent and founding father of the natural philosophy that grew up in his time from the abstractions drawn from his thoughts and experiments. It was this philosophy that ushered in the scientific revolution, of which our present day scientists are direct descendants, and our world view of nature is the greatest beneficiary of the evolution of ideas that have developed since Galileo's time.

After a number of technical talks dealing with the frontiers of modern theoretical physics, two lectures, dealing with general scientific and philosophical themes, were delivered, respectively, by Viktor F. Weisskopf on 'The connection between physics and other branches of science', and by Richard P. Feynman on 'What is and what should be the role of scientific culture in modern society?'

Feynman began by stating his belief that 'the proper place of scientific culture in modern society is not to solve the problems of modern society.'[22] He felt that 'it is a dream to think that to simply decide that one aspect, as to how ideally science and society should be matched, is somehow to solve all problems,'[22] and although he proposed to suggest certain modifications of the relationship between science and society, he did not expect these modifications to be the solution of society's problems.

Modern society, in Feynman's view. was subject to numerous threats. One of the greatest dangers which threatened it was 'the resurgence and expressions of ideas of thought control; such as ideas Hitler had, or Stalin in his time, or the Catholic religion in the Middle Ages, or the Chinese today ... One of the greatest dangers is that this shall increase until it encompasses all the world.'[22]

In dealing with the relation of science or scientific culture to society, the first thing that comes to mind is the applications of science. Science and its applications are parts of culture, and usually the discussion on the subject of the relation of science to society revolves around the applications of science. Moreover, the moral questions that scientists have about the kind of work they do also usually involve the applications.

Science creates a power through its knowledge; it confers a power to do things when one knows something scientifically. However, with this power, science does not provide instructions as to how to do good or fight against evil. The problem then is essentially to organize scientific applications in a way that does not do too much harm and does as much good as possible. But scientists often maintain that the manner in which scientific applications are used is not their responsibility.

Most people think of the serious problems of society in terms of physics: problems like atomic energy or the threat of nuclear armaments and holocaust. The other science which finds itself in moral difficulties due to its applications is biology, and 'although the problems of physics relative to society seem difficult, the problems of the development of biological knowledge will be fantastic.'[23] Aldous Huxley, in his *Brave new world*, had hinted on these possibilities. If energy in the distant future can be supplied freely and easily by physics, 'then it is a matter merely of chemistry to put together the atoms in such a way as to produce food from energy. The number of atoms is conserved, so that you can produce as much food as there are waste products from human beings; and there is therefore a conservation of material and no food problem.'[23]

However, in the case of biological applications, 'there will be serious social problems when we find out how to control heredity, as to what kind of control, good or bad, to use. Suppose that we were to discover the physiological basis of happiness or other feelings, such as the feeling of ambition, and suppose that we could control whether somebody feels ambitious [or not]—this will [produce moral problems of choice, one way or the other].'[23]

Finally, of course, there is the question of death. 'It is one of the most remarkable things that in all biological science there is no clue as to the necessity of death. If we want to make perpetual motion, the laws of physics tell us that either it is impossible or the laws are wrong. But there is nothing in biology yet found that indicates the inevitability of death.' Feynman expressed the view that death is 'not at all inevitable, and that it is only a matter of some time before the biologists discover what it is that is causing us trouble and that terrible universal disease [i.e. death]; then the temporariness of the human body will be cured . . . [Thus] there will [arise] social problems of a fantastic magnitude from biology.'[24]

Besides scientific applications, we should consider two other aspects of science: one is scientific ideas, a world view which science produces; and the other is the techniques (or means) of scientific investigation. To Feynman, the ideas and the world view which science produces are 'in some ways the most beautiful part of the whole thing', while some other people hold that the methods and techniques of science are really the most important. 'But the means were [intended] to produce some wonderful ends . . . [All of us] know something about the wonders of science: for instance, the fact that we are all made of atoms, the enormous ranges of time and space that there are, [our] position historically in the remarkable evolutionary sequence. Further, the most remarkable aspect of our scientific world view is its universality. One of the most promising hypotheses in all of biology is that everything the living creatures do can be understood in terms of what atoms can do, that is, in terms of physical laws ultimately. The fact that our knowledge is universal is something that is not completely appreciated: this is that the world is so wonderful in the sense that the stars are made of the same atoms as the cows and ourselves, and as stones.' [24]

From time to time we try to communicate this world view to our unscientific friends, and we get into difficulty most often because we get confused in trying to explain to them the latest developments in science, whereas they are unaware of some of the most preliminary things. For over four hundred years since Galileo, we have been gathering information about the world which they do not know. And the things that appear in the newspapers and that seem to excite the imagination are always those things which the scientifically uninformed people cannot understand, because they have not learned anything of all the much more interesting well-known things that people have found before.

The average person, the great majority of the people, are woefully and absolutely ignorant of the science of the world they live in, 'and they can stay that way. [But] we should teach [people] the wonders [of science]; the purpose of knowledge is to appreciate wonders even more . . . The knowledge is just to put into correct framework the wonder that nature is.' However, Feynman wished to answer 'the question as to why people can remain so woefully ignorant and not get into difficulties in modern society, is because *science* is *irrelevant*.' [24] It is not that it has to be, but we *let* it be irrelevant to society.

The other important aspects of science are the ideas and techniques of scientific investigation. These methods and techniques had their beginning in the time of Galileo. The most important thing is the matter of judging evidence: that is, before you begin your inquiry you must not know the answer. It is necessary to begin with doubt and uncertainty, for if you already know the answer there is no need to gather any evidence about it. 'Being uncertain, the next thing is to look for evidence, first by trials . . . A very important way is to try to enforce a logical consistency among the various things you know. It is a very valuable thing to try to connect [what] you know with [what you don't know], and try to find out if they are consistent. And the more the activity is in a direction of trying to put together the different directions, the better it is. After we look for the evidence we have to judge the evidence. There are usual rules about judging the evidence: [the most important thing] is not to pick only what you like, but to take all the evidence [and] try to maintain some objectivity about the thing . . . and not to ultimately depend on authority. *Authority may be a hint as to what the truth is, but is not the source of information. As long as it is possible we should disregard authority whenever the observations disagree with it.* The results should be reported in a disinterested way. [It does not mean] that the [scientist] does not give a darn about the results; disinterest here means that [the results] are reported in such a way as to try not to influence anyone into an idea that is different than the evidence indicates.'[25]

All these ideas and techniques are in the spirit of Galileo. 'Suppose Galileo were here and we were to show him the world today and try to make him happy, or see what he finds out. We would tell him about the questions of evidence, those methods of judging things which he developed. We would point out that we are in exactly the same tradition; we follow it exactly, even to the detail of making numerical measurements. [We will point out to him] that the sciences have developed in a very good way directly and continuously from [the] original spirit [which] he developed. And, as a result, there are no more witches and ghosts.'[25]

That, in fact, is a definition of science today. The same techniques work in physics, biology, geology, anthropology, and archaeology. We know a great deal about the past history of man, animals, and the earth by the use of similar techniques. Notwithstanding obvious difficulties, the same techniques have been applied to a limited extent to history and economics, but the results of such applications to the field of education are not very encouraging. Although 'I would like to show Galileo our world, I must show him something with great shame. If we look away from the sciences and look at the world around us, we find out something rather pitiful: that the environment we live in is so actively unscientific. Galileo could say: "I noticed that Jupiter was a ball with moons and not a god in the sky. Tell me what happened to the astrologers?" Why do we still have astrologers? Why can people write [such] books as *Worlds in collision* and similar ones with an infinite amount of crazy stuff. [The popularity of such books] shows that there is an environment actively, intensely unscientific. There are talks about telepathy. There is faith-healing galore, all over. There is a whole religion of faith-healing. There is miracle at Lourdes where healing goes on . . . If [all this] is true, it should be investigated scientifically.'[26]

If one could establish the truth, not just of the whole idea of astrology but just any one little item, it could have a profound modification on our understanding of the world. The reason we laugh a little bit is that we are so confident of our scientific world view and we are sure that one is not going to get anything by investigating miracles and astrology. Then why do we not get rid of all this? 'Because,' said Feynman, 'science [to most people] is irrelevant.'[26]

Feynman expressed the belief that there is a kind of morality which the scientists feel toward each other, or feel a kind of respect that represents this morality. What is the right way and wrong way to report results? Objectively and disinterestedly—so that the other man is free to understand precisely what you are saying, and not covering with your desires, as nearly as possible. This is a useful thing which helps each of us to understand each other so that we can pursue our science in a way relevant for the general development of ideas. 'So there is a kind of scientific morality. I believe, hopelessly, that this morality should be extended much more widely.'[27] In this kind of morality, such a thing as propaganda is a dirty word. Advertising is an example of a scientifically immoral description of products. This kind of immorality is so extensive that one gets so used to it in ordinary life, that one no longer realizes that it is a bad thing. 'One of the important reasons to increase the contact of the scientists with the rest of society is to explain the danger that comes from not having information, or having information always in a [biased] form.'[27]

The person who believes in astrology should be required to learn some astronomy. The person who believes in faith-healing might have to learn some medicine and biology. Then alone will science become relevant. All of us have read somewhere that science is all right if it does not attack religion; so long as it does not attack religion, it need not be paid attention to and nobody has anything to learn from it. So it can be cut off from modern society except for its applications, and thus be isolated. 'There was in the past an era of conversation on these matters. It was felt by the Church that Galileo's views attacked the Church. It is not felt by the Church today that scientific views attack the Church. Nobody attacks; nobody writes trying to explain the inconsistencies between the theological views and the scientific views held by people today—or even inconsistencies sometimes held by the same scientist in his religious and scientific beliefs.'[28]

A subject which Feynman considered to be most serious and important had to do with the question of uncertainty and doubt. When a statement is made the question is not whether it is true or false, but rather how likely it is true or false. 'Does God exist?' When this question is put in the form, 'How likely is it that God exists?', it makes a terrifying transformation of the religious point of view; that's why the religious point of view is unscientific. We must discuss each question with the uncertainties that are allowed. We absolutely must leave room for doubt, or there is no progress and no learning. There is no learning without having to pose a question. 'People search for certainty. *But there is no certainty.* People are terrified—*how can you live and not know*? It is not odd at all. As a matter of fact, you only think you know, most of our actions are based on incomplete knowledge and we really do not know what it is all about, or what [the] purpose of the world is, or know a great deal of other things. Then it is possible to live and not know.'[29]

The freedom to doubt is absolutely essential for the development of the sciences. It was born of a struggle with the constituted authorites of the time, namely the Church, who had a solution to every problem. Galileo was and is a symbol of that struggle. And although Galileo himself apparently was forced to recant, nobody takes the confession seriously. 'We do not feel that we should follow Galileo in this way that we should all recant. In fact, we consider the recantation as a foolishness [which] we see again and again; and we feel sympathetic to the musicians and artists of the Soviet Union who had to recant, [only] a few years ago. But the recantation is a meaningless thing, no matter how cleverly it is organized . . . Galileo was an old man and the Church was very powerful. The fact that Galileo was right is not essential to this discussion. The fact that they tried to suppress [his views] is of course [important].'[30]

In his summation of the question of the role of scientific culture in society, Feynman really waxed eloquent. He remarked: 'Men, philosophers of all ages, have tried to find the secret of existence, the meaning of it all. Because if they could find the real meaning of life, then all this human effort, all this wonderful potentiality of human beings, could then be moved in the correct direction and we would march forward with great success. [We have, therefore,] tried these different ideas. But the question of the meaning of the world, of life, and human beings, and so on, has been answered very many times by very many people. Unfortunately, all the answers are different; and the people with one answer look with horror at the actions and behavior of the people with another answer. Horror, because they see the terrible things that are done; the way man is being pushed into a blind alley by this rigid view as to what the meaning of the world is. In fact, it is really by the fantastic size of the horror that it becomes clear how great are the potentialities of human beings, and it is possibly this which makes us hope that if we could move things in the right direction, [they] would be much better.

'What then is the meaning of the whole world. We do not know what the meaning of existence is. When we look at the result of studying all the views that we have had before we find that we do not know the meaning of existence; but in saying that we do not know the meaning of existence, we have probably found the open channel. If we will allow only that, as we progress, we remain unsure, we will leave opportunities for alternatives. We will not become enthusiastic for the fact, the knowledge, the absolute truth, of the day, but remain always uncertain. The English have developed their government in this direction, it is called "muddling through", and although a rather silly, stupid sounding thing, it is the most scientific way of progressing. To decide upon the [final] answer is not scientific. In order to make progress, one must leave the door to the unknown ajar.

'We are only at the beginning of the development of the human race; of the development of the human mind, of intelligent life; we have years and years in the future. It is our responsibility not to give an answer today as to what it is all about, to drive everybody down in that direction and say: "This is the solution to it all." Because we will be chained to the limits of our present imagination, we will only be able to do those things that we think today are the things to do. Whereas, if we leave some room for discussion, and proceed in a way analogous to the sciences, then this difficulty will not arise. I believe, therefore, that, although it is not the case today, there may some day come a time, or I should hope, that the power of government should be limited. That governments ought not to be empowered to decide the validity of scientific theories. That is a ridiculous thing for them to try to do. That they are not to decide the various descriptions of history or of economic theory or of philosophy. Only in this way can the real possibilities of the future human race be ultimately developed.' [31]

Many scientists participated in the discussion following Feynman's talk: V. F. Weisskopf, G. Bernardini, S. Sambursky, I. I. Rabi, M. Fierz, G. Toraldo di Francia, C. H. Townes, S. Devons, S. Brenner, J. Monod, and others; all of them emphasized one point or the other, some in agreement, others in disagreement with Feynman. N. Dallaporta, for instance, pointed out to Feynman that from his words it might not be clear that 'there are physicists all over the world who are at the same time religious men, Buddhists, Hindus, Moslems, and Christian Catholics, for whom there is absolutely no opposition or contradiction—but perfect equilibrium—between their world views as [scientists] and their religious faith, including doctrines on theology, saints, and miracles; in the sense that the religious frame, when properly and deeply understood, is wide enough to include practically everything, and therefore also the the whole domain of [science]; while, I am afraid, the physical world may not be in a position to explain what is outside its boundaries.' [32]

Sambursky expressed the view that, in some respects, Feynman was too naive an optimist and had sought to make things sound too easy. Sambursky felt that 'there is a certain need for inconsistency, for irrationality in human nature, which will never be overcome. I further believe,' he said, 'that science will never become relevant for the majority of the people . . . Today, a business manager, for instance, in Germany, or in England or France, is as far from the Dirac equation as the Italian peasant was from Galileo's discoveries. That will never change . . . Scientists should be aware that with wrong methods you can sometimes get right results. For example, Paracelsus believed in astrology. He discovered that syphilis can be cured by the use of mercury. He arrived at this discovery because of the fact that the planets Mercury and Venus were in opposition at that time, [and it] gave him the idea that the element mercury might be used against venereal disease. Thus an important discovery was made by way of astrology . . . Scientists sometimes tend to form a closed club against fringe phenomena, as for instance extrasensory perception today, and unorthodox methods, e.g. astrology in former times. They try to push these things away and not deal with them. Furthermore, there is a certain type of superstition prevailing in science itself: people tend to believe sometimes that science can solve every question and make it into a new religion. That is as dangerous as rejecting science altogether. With regard to this trend,' Sambursky said, 'I take a much more pessimistic view than Feynman.' [33]

Markus Fierz pointed out that 'scientists [who teach], in fact, have no idea at all as to how the human mind is framed. Each scientist, if he is a little careful, knows that he dreams; and in his dreams he functions just like other people function . . . If you want to be a successful scientist you really need a broader humanistic education, that you know what men are because this is also expressed in the humanistic tradition. You can learn it by looking at different people, like Galileo, like Newton. What are the speculations they had besides what is considered today as scientific.?' [34]

In his lecture, Feynman had spoken about the unscientific and stupid attitudes of governments, churches, and authorities in general, 'dealing out lashes to the right and to the left, with commendable impartiality. The Russian delegation became restive, calmed down when criticism focused on the situation in the West, but got nervous again when it returned to the situation in the USSR. Then, after Feynman's comment about artists and musicians having to recant their views under pressure from the authorities in the USSR, the Russian delegation got up and marched out in single file, a woman at the head. Nothing was said at the moment, neither by the Russians nor by the rest of the audience, and Feynman just went on with the lecture.

'The lecture was followed by a coffee-break, during which V. F. Weisskopf and Vladimir Veksler discussed the situation. When the meeting was resumed the Russians returned. [Weisskopf had sought to calm the ruffled temperaments.]' [35]

After the coffee-break, Veksler declared that 'the problem of [promoting] understanding between scholars from various countries [is serious] . . . We must try to remove every object which is an obstacle in such collaboration.' [36] At the end of the discussion, Feynman made a final remark: 'I am sorry if I made people unhappy, but I think that as we have had all this discussion it is probably OK, because we have talked back and forth and each of us has changed his views a little, and that is what it is all for.' [37] Finally, Feynman remarked: 'I am not aware of having broken any code, written or unwritten, of the community of physicists, but if I have then I apologize.' [35]

25.5 Cargo Cult Science [38]

During the Middle Ages all kinds of strange ideas abounded, such as that a piece of rhinoceros horn would increase male potency. Then a method was discovered for sifting the ideas: this was to try one and see if it worked, and if it didn't work, to eliminate it. This method became organized as science. It developed very well, so that now we live in a scientific age. In fact, it is such a scientific age now that we have difficulty in understanding how witch doctors could have *ever* existed, when nothing that they proposed ever really worked, or very little of it did.

However, even today people talk about UFOs, astrology, various forms of mysticism, expanded consciousness, extrasensory perception (ESP), and so forth. All this led Feynman to conclude that ours is not a scientific world after all.

Feynman began to explore some of these 'wonderful' things. [39] First he started investigating various ideas of mysticism and mystic experiences. For this he went into Dr John Lilly's isolation tanks ('they are dark and quiet, and you float in Epsom salts') and got many hours of hallucinations. He also visited Esalen, 'which is a hotbed of this kind of thought', but he had no 'mystical' experience.[39]

One of the crazes in this regard was Uri Geller, 'a man who is supposed to be able to bend keys by rubbing them with his finger'. At Geller's invitation, Feynman went to his hotel room to see the demonstration of key bending by finger touch and mind reading. Uri Geller could not read Feynman's mind ('nobody can read my mind'[39]), nor did he succeed in bending the keys. Feynman found himself 'unable to investigate [rather, verify]' Geller's claims. He thought about the witch doctors of old, and wondered 'how easy it would have been to check on them by noticing that [none of their claims ever] worked.'[39]

Feynman thought that in our schools many such witch doctors' methods, cures and remedies, are applied to improve reading or mathematical skills, but they don't work and the test scores of students keep going down. Another example is how to treat criminals. No progress has been made in this regard— 'lots of theory but no progress'[39]—in decreasing the amount of crime, by the methods used in handling criminals. Yet, all these things are said to be scientific. However, 'ordinary people with commonsense ideas are intimidated by this pseudoscience.'[39] We ought, therefore, look carefully into theories that don't work, and science that isn't science.

Feynman discovered other topics, which were examples of pseudoscience, 'the efficacy of various forms of psychotherapy' being an important case.[40] He called all such examples 'Cargo Cult Science'. 'In the South Seas there is a Cargo Cult of people. During the war they saw airplanes land with lots of [material goods], and they want the same things to happen now. So they have arranged to make things like runways, to put fires along the sides of runways, to make a wooden hut for a man to sit in, with two wooden pieces on his head like headphones and bars of bamboo sticking out like antennas—he's the controller—and they wait for the airplanes to land. They're doing everything right. The form is perfect. It looks exactly like the way it looked before. But it doesn't work. No airplanes land. So I call these things Cargo Cult Science, because they follow all the right precepts and forms of scientific investigation, but they are missing something essential, because the planes don't land.'[40]

There is *one* feature generally missing in Cargo Cult Science. That is this: We learn from all examples of proper scientific investigations, that there is 'a kind of scientific integrity, a principle of scientific thought that corresponds to a kind of utter honesty—a kind of leaning backwards. For example, if you're doing an experiment, you should report everything that you think might make it invalid—not only what you think is right about it: other causes that could possibly explain your results; and things you thought of that you've eliminated by some other experiment, and how they worked—to make sure that the other fellow can tell [that] they have been eliminated.

'Details that could throw doubt on your interpretation must be given, if you know them. You must do the best you can—if you know anything at all wrong, or possibly wrong—to explain it. If you make a theory, for example, and advertize it, or put it out, then you must also put down all the facts that disagree with it. There is also a more subtle problem. When you have put a lot of ideas together to make an elaborate theory, you want to make sure, when explaining what fits, that those things it fits are not just the things that gave you the idea for the theory; but that the finished theory makes something else come out right, in addition.

'In summary, the idea is to try to give *all* the information to help others to judge the value of your contribution; not just the information that leads to judgment in one particular direction or other.'[40]

We have learned from experience that the truth will out. 'Other experimenters will repeat your experiment and find out whether you were wrong or right. Nature's phenomena will agree or they'll disagree with your theory. And although you may gain some temporary fame and excitement, you will not gain a good reputation as a scientist if you haven't tried to be very careful in this kind of work. And it's this type of integrity, this kind of care not to fool yourself, that is missing to a large extent in much research in Cargo Cult Science.'[41]

A great deal of the difficulty of the problems of Cargo Cult Science is the inapplicability of the scientific method to them. But this is not the only difficulty. "That's *why* the planes don't land—but they don't land.'[42]

However, 'this long history of learning how not to fool ourselves—of having utter scientific integrity—is, I'm sorry to say, something that we haven't specifically included in any particular course that I know of. We just hope that you've caught on by osmosis.'[42]

The first principle is 'that you must not fool yourself—and you are the easiest person to fool. So you have to be very careful about that. After you have *not* fooled *yourself*, it's easy not to fool other scientists. You just have to be honest in a conventional way after that.

'. . . You should not fool a layman when you are talking as a scientist. I am not trying to tell you what to do about cheating on your wife, or fooling your girlfriend, or something like that, when you're not trying to be a scientist, but just trying to be an ordinary human being. We'll leave those problems up to you and your rabbi. *I'm talking about a specific extra type of integrity that is not lying, but bending over backwards to show how maybe you're wrong, that you ought to do when acting as a scientist. And this is our responsibility as scientists, certainly to other scientists, and I think to laymen.*'[42]

One example of the principle is this: 'If you've made up your mind to test a theory, or you just want to explain some idea, you should always decide to publish it whichever way it comes out. If we only publish results of a certain kind, we can [always] make the argument look good. We must publish both kinds of results.'[42]

All kinds of claims are made in advertising, in doing experiments with rats in psychology, and even planning experiments in the national accelerator laboratories. Claims are made that are not based on consistent studies or those that give coherent results. So, Feynman wished [the graduating class of Caltech students] 'the good luck to be somewhere where you are free to maintain the kind of integrity I have described, and where you don't feel forced by a need to maintain your position in the organization, or financial support, or so on, to lose your integrity. May you have that freedom.' [42]

Notes and References

1. R.P. Feynman, Interviews and conversations with Jagdish Mehra, in Pasadena, California, January 1988. The observation about psychiatrists has been made by many others, of course.

2. R.P. Feynman, The value of science. *Engineering and Science*, December 1955.

3. R.P. Feynman, Ref. 2, pp. 13–14.

4. R.P. Feynman, Ref. 2, p. 14.

5. R.P. Feynman, Ref. 2, p. 15.

6. R.P. Feynman, The relation of science to religion. *Engineering and Science*, June 1956.

7. R.P. Feynman, Ref. 6, p. 21.

8. R.P. Feynman, Ref. 6, p.22.

9. R.P. Feynman, Ref. 6, p. 23.

10. R.P. Feynman, The role of science in the world today. *Proceedings of the Institute of World Affairs*, Vol. 23, 1957.

11. R.P. Feynman, Ref. 10, p. 20.

12. R.P. Feynman, Ref. 10, p. 25.

13. R.P. Feynman, Ref. 10, p. 26.

14. R.P. Feynman, Ref. 10, pp. 26–27.

15. R.P. Feynman, Ref. 10, p. 27.

16. R.P. Feynman, Ref. 10, pp. 27–28.

17. R.P. Feynman, Ref. 10, p. 28.

18. R.P. Feynman, Ref. 10, pp. 28–29.

19. R.P. Feynman, Ref. 10, p. 29.

20. R.P. Feynman, Ref. 10, pp. 30–31.

21. R.P. Feynman, The role of scientific culture in modern society, *Suppl. Nuovo Cim.* **4**(2), 492–526 (1956).

22. R.P. Feynman, Ref. 21, p. 492.

23. R.P. Feynman, Ref. 21, p. 493.

24. R.P. Feynman, Ref. 21, p. 494.

25. R.P. Feynman, Ref. 21, 496.

26. R.P. Feynman, Ref. 21, pp 497–98.

27. R.P. Feynman, Ref. 21, pp. 498–99.

28. R.P. Feynman, Ref. 21, p. 500.

29. R.P. Feynman, Ref. 21, pp. 500–501.

30. R.P. Feynman, Ref. 21, p. 501.

31. R.P. Feynman, Ref. 21, pp.502–503.

32. R.P. Feynman, Ref 21, p. 508.

33. R.P. Feynman, Ref. 21, p. 505.

34. R.P. Feynman, Ref. 21, pp. 507–508.

35. H.B.G. Casimir, Personal communication to Jagdish Mehra, 20 June 1991.

36. R.P. Feynman, Ref. 21, pp. 503–504.

37. R.P. Feynman, Ref. 21, p. 524.

38. R.P. Feynman, Cargo Cult Science. *Engineering and Science*, June 1974. Commencement Address at Caltech, 1974.

39. R.P. Feynman, Ref. 38, p. 10.

40. R.P. Feynman, Ref. 38, p. 11.

41. R.P. Feynman, Ref. 38, pp. 11–12.

42. R.P. Feynman, Ref. 38, p. 12.

26

The beat of a different drum

26.1 Settling down to married life

Richard Feynman and Mary Lou got divorced in 1956. After that Feynman
led a bachelor's life, going out on dates with various girlfriends and having fun,
but he was on the look out for a suitable partner with whom to settle down in
marriage. In late summer 1958 Feynman was in Geneva, Switzerland, to
attend the Second International Conference on the Peaceful Uses of Atomic
Energy, which took place there from 1 to 13 September, and at which he
presented a joint paper on his own behalf and that of Murray Gell-Mann on
'Theoretical ideas used in analyzing strange particles',[1] a survey of the then
current status of elementary particle physics.

Gweneth Howarth, an attractive young Englishwoman, who hailed from a
small village near the town of Millbank, high in the Yorkshire Pennines, had
lived a very uneventful, strait-laced life back home, where nothing really ever
happened. She went to school and started to become a school librarian. In her
summer vacations she would visit the Continent. Then she became dissatisfied
with her life and began to wonder if that was all she was going to be and do. She
couldn't take that; so, in the spring of 1958, she purchased a one-way ticket to
Geneva, Switzerland. She did not take enough money to buy a return ticket
back home on purpose, so that she *had* to find a job in Switzerland to survive.

Gweneth had not arranged for a job in Geneva when she left England. She
had addresses of two agencies which she had obtained from the Swiss Embassy
in London before leaving, thus she had two contacts there. She got a job as an
au pair girl with an English family in Geneva at $25.00 per month plus room
and board, working 15 hours a day, $6\frac{1}{2}$ days a week. She did not have a full day
off; she had three hours off on Thursday afternoon and three hours off on
Sunday afternoon. Of course, she couldn't live on the money she earned; she
had to buy winter clothes and occasionally a candy bar and an English
newspaper. So she had to keep writing back home to England to send her

money. At that time it was illegal to send money out of Great Britain; her family would put banknotes in personal letters; once the authorities had one of the letters opened and returned a very stiff warning note saying that no currency should be sent along with personal mail out of the country, but they kept on doing it.

One day Gweneth was relaxing and sunning herself on the beach on Lake Geneva. Richard Feynman was close by on the beach, too. He eyed this attractive young woman in her polka-dot bikini and decided that he better get acquainted with her. First he did not know what to say, and said something about the water being too cold. She thought that he was one of those pushy Americans, and wondered what she was going to do with him. But she answered him, 'Yes, it seems to be cold.' With the encouragement of this reply, he moved his towel over next to her and struck up a conversation. He told her all about California and how nice it was. Feynman eventually learned that she was in Geneva as a kind of a governess with an English family. So he asked her how much they paid her; she told him. He said to her, 'I'll pay you more than that just to take care of my house for me; I have no one to take care of it.'

Gweneth's intention at that time was to travel and go around the world. Nobody from her home had gone out to see the world. It was an awfully big jump for her to go from Switzerland to California, but she thought about it and Feynman persuaded her to come. 'I didn't particularly care about coming to the US, I was thinking of going to Australia and staying there a couple of years,' [2] then seeing more of the world and returning home to England.

Gweneth did not realize, nor did Richard at that time, that you had to get a sponsor to come to the United States, and it was not easy to find one. In order to obtain the immigration visa you had to have someone who would sign a contract that you would never become a public charge, who would have enough money and be of good moral character. You could get a visitor's visa, but without a sponsor and permanent visa you couldn't work. Feynman went to see his lawyer, who advised him that since Gweneth would be living with him in his house, he should not become a sponsor himself; for if a sexual relationship developed it might be misunderstood and might have legal repercussions. So Feynman asked his friend and colleague Matthew Sands and requested him to become Gweneth's sponsor, the implication being—for the sake of the visa—that if she did not have any other employment Sands would employ her; Feynman guaranteed that he would never suffer financially on this account. With Sands's sponsorship Gweneth got the visa and came to live in Feynman's house in Altadena in June 1959. She had her own room in the duplex, and he lived in the front part of the house. 'People in my hometown did not have the gumption to do something like going to Geneva or to Pasadena. It worked fine. When I first felt in England that I was going to take off and go to Switzerland, I had a lot of friends who said, "You're mad," and others who said, "I'd like to do it too." But nobody did.' [2]

At first nobody, except Matthew Sands and his wife, knew that Feynman had a housekeeper living at home. Then his friends and colleagues noticed that everyday he would slip out at lunchtime to go home, and somehow the news became public that 'Feynman was living with this woman!' and there was quite a scandal at the Athenaeum, Caltech's faculty club.[3] As far as Gweneth was concerned, she had boyfriends and was going out on dates, and Richard had a few girlfriends of his own in those days.

Then, all of a sudden, they discovered each other, in spite of the fact that they had been living together in the same house. She had taken care of his house and he thought she was kind of nice. 'I had no intention of marrying him. I had boyfriends here; I had a marvelous time. I would date Richard from time to time. Until suddenly, out of the blue, he proposed. I was never more surprised in my life, and I had to think about it. He wanted to get married the next week, but I said, "No, I absolutely cannot do that. It's bad enough that I have to write home and say I'm going to marry someone that nobody's ever heard of. And so we must have a Methodist marriage, because a civil marriage doesn't mean anything to my family in England. It's terribly important—it just wouldn't count."

'This was hard, of course, because Richard is very much an atheist and I'm an atheist, but I wanted to do something for my family. It was going to be very difficult for them, because nobody had ever left home before.'[2]

Feynman had gotten to know Wesley Robb, an Episcopalian minister, who was dean of the divinity school at the University of Southern California, and a very liberal person. Richard and Gweneth had a little talk with him beforehand to get around the theological problem. At Gweneth's request, Richard asked Matthew Sands if he would give her away in marriage, which, of course, he agreed to do. Dr Robb performed the marriage ceremony at the Huntington Hotel on 24 September 1960, at which Jirayr Zorthian, Feynman's artist friend, was his best man. 'It was a very nice wedding', as Gweneth recalled.[2] Gweneth's family were not able to attend the wedding, but she and Richard visited England the following year.

Already after his return from Geneva the previous year, Feynman had told Manny Delbrück, the biologist Max Delbrück's wife, that he had met this English girl in a polka-dot bikini at the beach in Geneva, and he thought he was going to marry this girl. 'Murray [Gell-Mann] has had such good luck with *his* English girl [Margaret]!' he had said. And Margaret Gell-Mann recalled: 'It wasn't only the English girl, it was also a small brown dog we had. When he acquired Gweneth he also acquired a small brown dog [named Venus]—which turned out to be a much better bargain than Murray made, in the matter of dogs, at least!'[2]

After the wedding, the story being bandied about at Caltech was: 'Feynman lived with his housekeeper, trying her out before he married her!'[3]

From the beginning Gweneth sought to make for Richard Feynman a peaceful and happy home. Richard wouldn't really discuss his work with her but he was wonderful at explaining complicated things simply, and he would explain his research work to Gweneth from time to time, and she would feel that she really understood it. She always got the feeling that he loved teaching. 'He's quite aware of how basic he's got to be when he talks to dumb people.'[2]

Their son Carl was born in 1962 and was named after the Caltech physicist, Feynman's friend, and discoverer of the positron, Carl Anderson. Feynman developed a very close relationship with his son, and sought to help him develop in the same way as his own father, Melville, had helped him, and Carl caught the spirit, too. Gweneth thought that 'Carl's mind is very much like Richard's.'[2] Six years later, in 1968, Richard and Gweneth adopted a two-month-old infant daughter and named her Michelle. Richard didn't have 'as close a relationship with her as he had with Carl, because she wouldn't let him.'[2] But he adored her; however, in childhood at least, she would keep him at his distance.[2]

Together, Richard and Gweneth loved traveling; they often went backpacking, or camping, or just visiting places. 'And when we go out to a place we like to go places on the back streets. We don't like staying in big hotels; we like unusual places. And we both love to travel in the van—it's so comfortable, with the table and all. It's a Dodge Maxivan, the biggest one there is. The four of us can sleep in it, if we have to. We prefer to sleep in bags outside.'[2] Feynman had his QED diagrams painted on the outside of the van.

The Feynman family loved visiting Yorkshire in England. 'Richard loves it; he can never get enough of it. The countryside is just [wonderful]—you can set out in any direction and walk just wherever you want, and with you go your dogs. Richard runs every morning.

'He's got half way to Mt Wilson now [1977]—four miles straight up. And he runs when we are in England. He wears his little orange shorts and runs seven or eight miles, and the word filters back from the country people around: "That man is back again. I saw him three miles over here." "Oh, did you? When I was driving my car at five o'clock yesterday morning, he was over *there!*"'[2]

Gweneth did not have the feeling that she had to be somebody important. 'I'm typically happy with what I do, and I don't feel I have to compete. I don't feel [I'm a] shadow; I'm perfectly happy—not being a servant to him—we get along very well. I know he's happy because he says it. When he comes home at night he says, "Oh, it's nice to come home." Like on a rainy winter day when we have a big fire in the fireplace and the curtains drawn and good smells coming out of the kitchen. I don't do it just for him—I do it for the family, and I like it—I like to feel comfortable. This is where my satisfaction lies and I don't have to feel important. I do things that [Richard] doesn't do, and I do them well.'[2]

Gweneth enjoyed doing volunteer work in schools. 'I spend a lot of time and get a lot of satisfaction out of that, knowing that I'm doing something that's worthwhile. It's in the public schools; setting up a library. We set one up in Edison school; they had none. And we started one in my daughter's primary school; this was the last primary school in the whole district that didn't have a library. The books were there, stuffed in a closet for a whole year, and nobody knew about it.'[2]

And then, of course, Gweneth sang with Margaret [Gell-Mann]. 'We have a group called "The Arroyo Singers"—between 16 and 20 of us. We sing all kinds of things. We're doing some *haiku* set to music by Persichetti; and we commissioned some work to be written for us. We do Bach and Brahms and all kinds of things. Sometimes we perform at the [Pasadena] Music Center.'[2]

Richard and Gweneth would go to the costume parties at the house of Albert Hibbs. Once, on April Fool's Day, Hibbs asked people to come dressed as a king, queen, a knave or a fool, the major cards. Richard came dressed as Queen Elizabeth II in a perfectly plain dress, with a dumpy white hat, a great big purse, make up, and short high heels. 'He was the perfect Queen Elizabeth, completely out of style, wrong dress, wrong hat, wrong purse. He did a strip tease which delighted everybody.'[3] At such parties, Gweneth would sit quietly in a chair, but unlike Mary Lou, who also sat quietly, she never complained. 'I'm not sure that she enjoyed these parties as much as he did', Ai Hibbs thought.

Hibbs gave another costume party one year on the occasion of the summer solstice. He asked his friends to come either as something astronomical, astrological, or as a heavenly body. Feynman came dressed in a dog-suit with a sign saying 'I'm Sirius', spelt like a star. And he had hanging on his dog-suit with a large safety pin and ribbon a little stuffed dog. 'Then when people would look at him, and this was not untypical, he wouldn't wait for them to figure it out; he had to explain it to them right away. "You know what it is, don't you?" And before they could remember that there was something called a companion of Sirius, he said, "That's the companion of Sirius!" He was very impatient; he wouldn't wait for us to figure it out. So that was the heavenly body, Sirius, the dog-star, and the little dog was the companion of Sirius. He made a pun. His wife, Gweneth, and his sister, Joan, came dressed as the Gemini twins.'[3]

On another occasion, the theme was myths and legends, and Feynman came as God. People accused him as being Moses in his white robe and long beard. He said, 'No, no, I'm God!' Hibbs had invited a newspaper reporter friend of his to this party; he went over to Hibbs and said, 'I just met Feynman. I had not met him before and he says he's God.' Hibbs told him, 'Yes, we all know about that!'[3]

On yet another occasion, Feynman announced that he was going to a costume party at which he had to go in a traditional costume from an area between latitudes 40° North and 10° South, and between longitudes 30° and 150° East. He decided to go as a Tibetan Lama. Gweneth was an accomplished seamstress, used to making elaborate costumes for Carl and Michelle each Halloween; so she looked for an article on Tibet in the *National Geographic* and soon found one on Ladakh, a remote region in the Himalayas, where the Lamaist traditions also abounded. She set out to make a distinctive Ladakhi costume for Richard, 'with pointed ear flaps sticking out prominently on each side of the hat.'[4] Richard fashioned a Lama's prayer wheel from a small circular bearing, which he bought at the local army surplus store; 'he slipped the bearing around a wooden sofa leg that he bought at a hardware store, jammed a tin can around the bearing, and attached a small chain to the can. (The weight on the chain made it possible for the Lama to turn his prayer wheel—actually a cylinder—by wobbling his wrist.) One revolution of the prayer wheel equalled one utterance of the prayer inside—a highly efficient way of fulfilling one's spiritual duties while herding yaks.'[4] The whole outfit turned Feynman looking like a perfect Lama from Ladakh.

Feynman had always been fond of children. Earlier in his life he had played with and kept amused the children of his friends and colleagues such as John Wheeler, Hans Bethe, and Viktor Weisskopf. He was greatly delighted with his own son Carl when he came along. He would be terribly patient with everything Carl did and as soon as he could he would introduce him to anything new like letters, numbers, or ideas, very patiently—never pushing— and was always proud when Carl would learn to read something. The first thing he reported Carl reading was a big manhole cover in the sidewalk where it said 'Water and Power', where you get into the underground pipes and lines, and Carl was able to read the word 'Water'; Richard reported this to his friends with great pride.

In some experiment at school Carl was given an IQ test and the teacher, very disturbed, reported to Gweneth and said, 'Was Carl sick last week? He did so badly on his IQ test. Only 126.' Gweneth said, 'Well, a chip of the old block!' When Richard had been tested for IQ in high school it was found to be 125.

Feynman would tell his friends about the steps Carl was going through as he was learning, reading, doing arithmetic, and solving problems. Once, during a ride in car, Carl asked him, 'Daddy, what's a fake estate?' 'I don't know what a fake estate is,' replied Richard. 'Well, then, what's a real estate?' asked Carl. But Carl knew exactly what he was doing when he made the joke; he was leading Feynman into the joke.[3]

Both Richard and Gweneth liked dogs. He loved Kiwi, their delightful brown mongrel dog. He had heard from somebody that dogs are unable to be taught the difference between right and left. So he taught his dog, Kiwi, to shake hands. He would say to Kiwi, 'Right foot,' and Kiwi would put out his right paw, then, 'Left paw,' and Kiwi put out his left paw. Richard showed this to a guy who claimed you couldn't teach dogs left from right. The guy said, 'Yeah, but you're saying right foot and left paw instead of just right and left.' And Feynman looked at him and couldn't understand that kind of thinking. He told this story to his friends with great hilarity.[3]

Gweneth was an excellent housekeeper and a wonderful wife; she took a load off his shoulders—things he didn't care about, such as household expenses. Feynman was very proud of his son, and very happy with his wife and family, including the dogs. At graduate student beer parties, Feynman

would be heard drumming—which he always did, although he didn't drink—
and sometimes he would sing the ditty:

> What's Murray got, that I haven't got?
> An English wife and a Basenji dog! [5,6]

26.2 The Nobel Prize

Richard Feynman had seen Elena Karina, a girlfriend of his from New York,
dance in a ballet production of *The Bloomer Girl* at the Schubert Theater in
New York City in 1949. Elena then went to Malmö, a port city in southern
Sweden, across the sound from Copenhagen, where in 1951 she danced in the
productions of *Swan Lake* and *Kiss Me Kate* at the Stadtstheater. She invited
Richard to visit Malmö to see her dance. His brief reply was: 'I shall visit
Sweden only when I come to pick up the Nobel Prize.' [7] By 1960, it had
become evident, even in Feynman's mind, that he might win the Nobel Prize
for one of the several original things he had done: the theory of quantum
electrodynamics, the theory of the superfluidity of liquid helium, or the theory
of weak interactions. For Feynman, the pleasure which he had received from
his work had been enough, and he derived much satisfaction from the fact that
other people found his work useful and employed it in their calculations; he
did not any longer look for any recognition of his work beyond what the
scientific community had already conferred upon him. Yet he did win the
Nobel Prize in physics for 1965, jointly with Julian Schwinger of Harvard and
Sin-Itiro Tomonaga of Japan, for their respective contributions to the theory
of quantum electrodynamics and the calculation of the Lamb shift, and—just
as he had promised to Elena Karina—Feynman made his first visit to Sweden
to pick up the Nobel Prize.

For many years Feynman would look, when the time was coming around to
announce the Nobel awards, at who might get them. But after a while he
wasn't even aware of when it was the right 'season' for the awards. So he had no
idea why someone would be calling him one morning at 3:30 or 4:00 a.m.
Richard and Gweneth had been to a party the previous night and had gone to
bed only at about 2:30 a.m.; they had been asleep for less than an hour when
the phone rang. 'Hello, Dr Feynman? This is the American Broadcasting
Company calling. May I congratulate you on your Nobel Prize?' 'Hey! Why
are you bothering me at this time of the morning?' asked Feynman. 'I thought
you would like to know that you've won the Nobel Prize!' 'Yeah, but I am
sleeping! It would have been better if you had called me [later] in the
morning.' And he put the phone down. Gweneth asked him, 'What was that?'
He said, 'I won the Nobel Prize.' And she said, 'Oh, go to sleep!'

Gweneth: 'Richard has a very dead-pan way of making jokes and nine times
out of ten I know that what he says is not so. But this one time it was true. Then

the phone rang again, and he said, "It's four o'clock in the morning, call me back later." And I wondered who it was who would call him back again. So he put the phone down, and I said, "Is it true?" and he said, "Yes." Then the reporters started to call from New York, and Richard took the phone off the hook. So we were lying awake after an hour's sleep with the phone off the hook, and Richard said, "I have to get up." When he's thinking he has always to pace the floor. He went down to his study and banged around for a while, then he said, "I think I'd better put up the phone"—and RING!!

'So then we decided we just had to get up, because the *Los Angeles Times* called and the *Star-News* called and the reporters were on their way. So we got up. These reporters were there at five.'[2] Gweneth made coffee. The reporter from *Time* magazine called, and Feynman told him, 'Listen, I've got a problem, so I want this thing off the record. I don't know how to get out of this thing. Is there some way not to accept the prize?' The reporter said, 'I'm afraid, sir, that there isn't any way you can do it without making more of a fuss than if you leave it alone.' Feynman told the guy from *Time* magazine: 'Some reporters want me to tell them in one sentence what it is for which I've been awarded the Nobel Prize. I can't answer that.' The reporter said, 'Tell them that if it could be said in one sentence it wouldn't be worth the Nobel Prize, would it? Feynman liked this reply and wished he had used it.[8] 'Then at ten o'clock there was a news conference at the Athenaeum, the Caltech faculty club, for radio, television, newspaper, and magazine reporters. The phone was ringing all day long and people were coming over and we didn't get to bed until midnight. That was a long day.'[2] The students at Caltech draped the top of the Throope Hall, the administration building at Caltech, with a large banner proclaiming: 'WIN BIG, RPF'.

The Swedish consul from Los Angeles called Feynman and said they were going to have a reception and party in his honor, but he thought, 'They don't have to do that; I don't really want that.' In any case, the consul said, 'You make up a list of guests whom you will invite and we'll make up a list whom we will invite and we will check them over and see who are the common ones and work it out. We'll get together tomorrow.' Feynman made up a list of about eight or ten people, all close friends and colleagues. The Swedish consul came to see him with a list of about two hundred people: the Governor, the Lt. Governor, state and city officials, the Mayor of Los Angeles, Paul Getty, big actors, and all kinds of people, 'a kind of a frightening thing'. Feynman told him, 'I don't know if I want to meet all these people!' 'Oh,' the consul said, 'Don't worry, many of them wouldn't come!' 'And I had never invited people to a party that I expected not to come; that's not my way of life. I got a feeling of revulsion against this crazy idea that he had to invite these people for some reason of protocol; that's just something he had to do and they could refuse him. The whole idea began to bother me. I just got more and more upset with what was happening. So, finally, I called the Swedish consul on the phone and asked him to cancel the whole thing, that I couldn't do it. I think he was really delighted that he didn't have to do it; anyway, he had no objection to my saying no, cancel it. Everything was OK; we don't have to go through with that.'[8]

Richard and Gweneth went to Stockholm to attend the Nobel ceremonies by themselves; no members of either families were present. Before leaving, Richard had to have a tuxedo made; he had not worn one since his days at MIT, and now needed one for formal receptions; and Gweneth purchased a few gowns.

Gweneth recalled that during the stay in Stockholm, 'You don't really have time to think very much. They take care of everything. You have your personal attendant, a junior diplomat, who is always married, so his wife took care of me. He's like a sheepdog—he makes sure you get there, where you are supposed to be. You have to go to fittings for your tails—come let's go to the tailor kind of thing. And he always reminds you of the next thing to do . . . As for the program and activities in Stockholm, [Richard] had a diary with everything written down. We were probably there eight or nine days.

'Richard did not want to accept the prize. He really didn't. He just didn't think he could face the ceremony and all the starched speechmaking. So he was in a terrible state—before we went and when we got there. I had to tread on eggs all the time. He was a nervous wreck. He had to give a ten-minute acceptance speech and a scientific lecture. The scientific lecture did not bother him.[9] He knows what he is talking about. But the acceptance speech—he agonized after that day after day.'[2]

'While I had a lot of fun,' recalled Feynman, 'I *did* still have this psychological difficulty all the way through. My greatest problem was the Thank-You speech that you have to give at the King's Dinner. When they give you the Prize they give you some nicely bound books about the years before, and they have all the Thank-You speeches written out as if they're some big deal. So you begin to think it's of some importance what you say in this Thank-You speech, because it's going to be published . . . The truth was, I really didn't want this Prize, so how do I say thank you when I don't want it? . . . Finally I figured out a way to make a perfectly satisfactory-sounding speech that was nevertheless completely honest. I'm sure those who heard the speech had no idea what this guy had gone through in preparing it.'[10]

Feynman started out by saying that he had already received his prize in the pleasure he got in discovering what he did, from the fact that others used his work, and so on. He tried to explain that he had already received everything he expected to get and the rest was nothing compared to it; he had already received his prize. But then, he said, he received, all at once, a big pile of letters, reminding him of these people whom he knew: letters from childhood friends who jumped up with joy when they read the morning newspaper and cried out, 'I know him! He's that kid I used to play with!' and so on, letters like that, which were very supportive and expressed what Feynman interpreted as a kind of love. For *that* he thanked them for the Nobel award.[11]

At the dinner at the City Hall, Gweneth sat between the King and Prince Bertil. 'The King was marvelous, he really was. Conversation was no problem at all. He's so practiced he could talk to anybody . . . Richard enjoyed sitting next to [Princess] Christina, the present King's sister. But he did have a little trouble with the old King's daughter-in-law, Sibylla, who was the epitome of a queen or a princess. White hair—not a smile—extremely dignified—ramrod straight. She wasn't really his kind of girl!' [2]

'It's not true,' recalled Gweneth, 'that Richard didn't enjoy *any* of it. He loved the thing when they blow the trumpets—these long, long golden trumpets [when you receive the award from the King]. That was kind of fun. And then the students entertain you. They have a ball, and that he enjoyed very much, because it was loose and we were dancing all over the place.' [2]

Feynman enjoyed the dancing. 'I loved it. The photographers would take pictures if I was dancing with my wife or with the wife of another dignitary, but if I was dancing with a student they wouldn't take photographs. They were very controlled and you could do whatever you wanted but they would decide when to take pictures. They protected you from yourself, so to speak. It was relatively delightful. They know how to entertain people, to take care of people, and the parties were fun and everything was OK. Especially, they had a few things involving students and student fraternities, Order of the Frog; they make a noise like a frog and I would hop and make a noise '*Brunga-in, Brunga-in*', which is just like a frog, and that was great. The way I learned that was when I picked up a book of my father's, *The frogs* by Aristophanes, a play in Greek in English translation. In the book they had the frogs making a noise *brekebek, brekebek*. I thought that was not the way a frog sounds, that was crazy. Then I started imitating it and practicing, and that's where I learned to make frog noises. I was just curious about this play, so I used it later to make a frog noise in Stockholm.' [8]

Richard and Gweneth enjoyed the trip to Uppsala. 'That was beautiful. It was the first time we saw the sun in seven days. There was a constant cloud cover; it felt it was like ten feet above your head. It was piercingly cold, with snow on the ground, and it was dark, dark, dark, all the time. Depressing. But as soon as the sun comes through the clouds, it just changes the whole world around you.' [2]

After the Nobel award ceremonies in Stockholm, Feynman went to Geneva, where Viktor Weisskopf, then the director-general of CERN (Centre Européen pour la Recherche Nucléaire), had invited him to give a lecture. At the lecture, Feynman began by saying that at Stockholm the Nobel Prize winners in physics and biology were discussing among themselves if there would be any change in their personalities as a result of the Nobel Prize, and he had to admit one. 'That is, I feel that I kind of like being in a suit [the nice suit which Feynman had had tailored to measure before going to Sweden; normally he gave lectures in open-neck shirts, without a jacket or tie]. The whole audience roared, "No, No, No", and Weisskopf got up and tore his jacket off and said "No, No, No!" It woke me up, and I realized what a stupid thing I was saying. So I took off the jacket and tie and gave the lecture in shirt sleeves [the way I usually do]. They cleaned out in two minutes all the work they had done [at Stockholm] to make a dignified man of me. But it's true, it had affected me to the point that I thought it was nice to wear a suit. What a ridiculous idea! They all roared, and I was saved by that CERN audience. They reminded me that I wasn't just some Nobel Prize winner from Sweden, that I was Richard Feynman with my own individual personality.'[8]

Feynman's lecture at CERN was attended by Ernst C. G. Stückelberg (who always went around with his dog everywhere). Stückelberg had done important work in quantum electrodynamics, some of which preceded and overlapped with Feynman's. After the lecture, Stückelberg was making his way out alone (with his dog) from the CERN amphitheatre, when Feynman—surrounded by admirers—made the remark: 'He did the work and walks alone toward the sunset; and, here I am, covered in all the glory, which rightfully should be his!'[12] For a lifetime of achievements in theoretical physics, Stückelberg was honored with the Max Planck Medal of the German Physical Society.

During his visit to CERN in Geneva, Switzerland, a wager was made between Feynman and Weisskopf at lunch, the terms of which were agreed upon as follows: 'Mr Feynman will pay the sum of Ten Dollars to Mr Weisskopf if any time during the next ten years (i.e. before 31 December 1975) the said Mr Feynman has held a "responsible position". Conversely, if on 31 December 1975, the said Mr. Feynman shall have held or be holding no such position, Mr Weisskopf will be deemed to have forfeited his wager and will be in duty bound to pay the sum of Ten Dollars to Mr. Feynman. For the purpose of the aforementioned wager, the term "responsible position" shall be taken to signify a position which, by reason of its nature, compels the holder to issue instructions to other persons to carry out certain acts, notwithstanding the fact that the holder has no understanding whatsoever of that which he is instructing the aforesaid persons to accomplish. Signed: Richard P. Feynman, Viktor F. Weisskopf, 15 December 1965.' Needless to say that Weisskopf lost the bet by a long shot; Feynman *never* held the kind of 'responsible position' mentioned in their contract in all his life.

26.3 Offer of an honorary doctorate and other honors

On 4 January 1967, two years after Feynman was awarded the Nobel Prize in physics, George Beadle, president of the University of Chicago, wrote to Feynman that the Board of Trustees, upon the recommendation of the faculties, proposed to confer upon him the honorary degree of Doctor of Science at a Special Convocation to be held on Friday, 5 May 1967. This special convocation had been arranged to mark the seventy-fifth anniversary of the founding of the University of Chicago. Beadle wrote: 'It is my hope, both personally and on behalf of the University, that you will permit us to have the privilege of recognizing your achievements on this occasion. Since honorary degrees are not conferred *in absentia*, will you please let me know, at your convenience, if the proposal to confer the degree is acceptable to you and whether it is possible for you to attend the Convocation at 3 o'clock in the afternoon of May 5? Preceding the Convocation there will be a luncheon for special guests which we hope you will be able to attend.'

Feynman replied to Beadle on 16 January: 'Yours is the first honorary degree that I have been offered, and I thank you for considering me for such an honor.

'However, I remember the work I did to get a real degree at Princeton and the guys on the same platform receiving honorary degrees without work—and felt that an "honorary degree" was a debasement of the idea of a "degree which confirms [that] certain work has been accomplished". It is like giving an "honorary electrician's license". I swore then that if by chance I was ever offered one I would not accept it. Now at last (twenty-five years later) you have given me the chance to carry out my vow. So thank you, but I do not wish to accept the honorary degree you offered.'

Naturally, after that, Feynman declined every such offer of an honorary degree. Actually, Feynman would rather not have obtained the real Ph.D. degree either. He was always a bit envious of Freeman Dyson who had only a BA from Cambridge, England. Dyson had gone to Cornell in 1947 to do graduate work with Hans Bethe, but there the circumstances turned out in such a way that Dyson did not even enroll himself as a Ph.D. student. On the basis of the merit of his work establishing the equivalence of the radiation theories of Feynman, Schwinger, and Tomonaga, Dyson was appointed professor of physics first at Cornell University, and then at the Institute for Advanced Study at Princeton. Feynman wished he was like Dyson and didn't have a Ph.D. degree, so that he could tell people (when they were doing something really stupid) how stupid they were . . . and say, 'Even I know that much, and I don't have a Ph.D.!'[8]

In the fall of 1959 Richard Feynman had been named Richard Chace Tolman Professor of Theoretical Physics, an endowed Chair named after the famous theoretical physicist Richard Tolman, at Caltech. In 1962 he was awarded the Ernest Orlando Lawrence Memorial award by the Atomic Energy Commission 'for significant contributions to nuclear science.' Early in 1965, before he was awarded the Nobel Prize, Feynman was elected a Foreign Member (a Fellow) of the Royal Society of London in honor of his contributions to quantum field theory and the theory of liquid helium. In 1971 Feynman received the Oersted Medal of the American Association of Physics Teachers for excellence in physics teaching, and in 1973 Queen Margarethe of

Denmark bestowed upon him the Niels Bohr International Gold Medal in Copenhagen.

Feynman regularly received invitations to give various lectures at prestigious universities and research institutions at home in America and abroad, which he habitually refused, pleading lack of time or the pressure of teaching obligations or some other excuse. He treated offers of visiting appointments—such as a visiting professor at University College London (from Sir Harrie Massey), the Max Planck Institut für Physik in Munich (from Werner Heisenberg), or CERN in Geneva (from Bernard Gregory)—in the same way, pleading that his teaching obligations at Caltech would not permit him to be away from Pasadena or that he liked it well enough and was happy enough in California not to wish to be away. Feynman received such invitations regularly from about 1950 up to the last year of his life, but they were all summarily refused, the few exceptions being places which he really wished to visit such as Brazil or Japan. The only invitations which he accepted readily were to address students of science in elementary or high schools or universities in southern California, and that too on condition that any of the teachers or school authorities would not be present at his lectures or be allowed to make a 'big official fuss' about his visit. He got a great kick out of talking to young people. Similarly, the door to his office was always open to students, but faculty colleagues, administrators, or other people on business had to make appointments through his secretary, who guarded his privacy.

26.4 A variety of glimpses into Feynman's life and personality

(a) Art and drawing

There used to be parties and relaxing social gatherings at the artist Zorthian's ranch. 'Jirayr' was his Armenian name, but everyone called him Jerry. 'He was educated at Yale, an artist, did a certain amount of work, never made a very big name for himself, quite a good representational artist, very fine draftsman, perfect—almost photographic—with his drawing. After a few children and divorce from a rather well-to-do woman in California, he bought a place up in north of Pasadena, privately owned piece of property, actually inside the National Forest boundaries. There he raises horses, goats, pigs, and chickens. He and his wife Daphne—she is a beautiful, tall, statuesque woman, who started out as his model many years ago; he is short and squat—live in an adobe house crowded with all kinds of stuff.'[3]

Feynman had known other artists before. He and Zorthian met at a party—shortly after the launch of the Sputnik in 1957—at the house of Wendy Miller, who was married to a publicity official at Caltech. At this party Feynman was playing drums lustily, and Zorthian was particularly excited and inspired by the drumming. Zorthian 'is a very outgoing, loud, laughing, happy social animal.'[3] He went into the bathroom, took off his shirt, put on a black wig, smeared toothpaste in funny designs all over his chest, and came out dancing wildly an African dance, with cherries hanging down from his ears. That evening, both Feynman and Zorthian were interested in pursuing a lovely Italian girl; she left with Zorthian. Zorthian met Feynman again at a program of lectures organized by the Los Angeles World Affairs Council, and soon they became good friends. Zorthian owned a vacation beach house in Playa de la Misiòn in Baja California; from his share of the Nobel Prize money, Feynman also eventually bought a small place near Zorthian's house. There they would go to the beach, play with children, and enjoy themselves. They would celebrate Thanksgiving together; one year the Thanksgiving dinner would be at Zorthian's house, the next year at Feynman's. If they were in Pasadena, they would sometimes meet at Feynman's friend Richard Davies's house for dinner. They would sing together and have a good time.

Feynman and Zorthian had arguments all the time. Feynman would say: 'Artists are lost: they don't have any subject! They used to have religious subjects, but they lost their religion and now they haven't got anything. They don't know anything about the beauty of the *real* world—so they don't have anything in their hearts to paint.' Zorthian would reply: 'Artists don't need to have a physical subject; there are so many emotions that can be expressed through art. Besides, art can be abstract. Furthermore, scientists destroy the beauty of nature when they pick it apart and turn it into mathematical equations.'[13] So, Feynman would say: 'That's not true. We can see beauty much better because we understand it at different levels and so on.'[13] Once they were having this argument late at night, and Feynman proposed to Zorthian: 'Listen, Jerry! The reason we have these arguments that never get anywhere is that you don't know anything about science, and I don't know anything about art. So on alternate Sundays, I'll give you a lesson in science, and you give me a lesson in art.' 'OK,' said Zorthian, 'I'll teach you how to draw. Of course, you'll have to work.'[13]

In high school, the only thing that Feynman was able to draw was pyramids and deserts, consisting mainly of straight lines. 'I had absolutely no talent.'[8] Feynman promised to work, but still bet Zorthian could not teach him to draw. He wanted very much to learn to draw for the reason that he felt a very private emotion about the beauty of the world. 'It's difficult to describe because it's an emotion. It's analogous to the feeling one has in religion that has to do with a god that controls everything in the whole universe: there is an aspect of generality that you feel when you think about how things that appear so different and behave so differently are all run 'behind the scenes' by the same organization, the same physical laws. It's an appreciation of the mathematical beauty of nature, of how she works inside; a realization that the phenomena we see result from the complexity of the inner workings between atoms; a feeling of how dramatic and wonderful it is. It's a feeling of awe—of scientific awe—which I felt could be communicated through a drawing to someone who had also this emotion. It could remind him, for a moment, of this feeling about the glories of the universe.'[14]

Jerry Zorthian turned out to be a very good teacher. Feynman learned to draw—a shoe, a flowerpot, flowers, and leaves. Feynman kept on trying, Zorthian kept on encouraging him, and gradually he got better. Though he was never satisfied, he practiced drawing all the time. He would draw other people. He kept a little pad of paper with him and practiced drawing wherever he went.

Feynman did not have the same success in teaching science to Zorthian. So they had a new argument: whether Zorthian was a better teacher than Feynman, or Feynman a better student than Zorthian.

Somebody who saw him drawing recommended to Feynman that he should go down to the Pasadena Art Museum where they had live models. Finally he attempted that, and—after a long while— he was able to draw the full figure of a nude in half an hour. Zorthian kept on telling him that drawings that are too full aren't any good. Feynman learned that, unlike the physics teacher, the art teacher has the problem of communicating by osmosis and not by instruction, while the physics teacher has the problem of always teaching the techniques, rather than the spirit, of how to go about solving physics problems—or so he thought, at first. Ultimately, Feynman found that he could draw the model without looking at what he was drawing. He found that his drawing had a certain kind of strength—a funny, semi-Picasso-like strength, which appealed to him. Zorthian was always telling him 'to loosen up'. He thought that 'loosen up' meant 'make sloppy drawings', but it really meant to relax and not to worry about how the drawing is going to come out.

The summer after the drawing class in 1964, Feynman was in Italy to attend a conference celebrating the 400th anniversary of Galileo's birth, and he went to see the Sistine Chapel in the Vatican. He got there very early in the morning, bought his ticket before anybody else, and *ran* up the stairs as soon as the place opened. 'I therefore had the unusual pleasure of looking at the whole chapel for a moment, in silent awe, before anybody else came in.'[8,15] Feynman walked around, looking at the ceiling for a while. Then his eye came down a little bit and he saw some big, framed pictures, and he thought, 'Gee! I never knew about these!' He thought to himself, 'I know why these panels aren't famous; they aren't any good.' Then he looked at another one, and thought, 'Wow! That's a *good one*.' And he looked at others. 'That's good too, so is that one, but that one is lousy.' He had never heard of these panels, but he decided that they were all good except two. He saw the same thing in the Raphael Room.[16]

When Feynman returned to his hotel, he looked into the guide book, which he had forgotten to take along to the Vatican. There he learned that below the panels of Michelangelo there were fourteen panels by Botticelli, Perugino, and so on, all great artists, and 'two by so and so, which are of no significance.'[16] The fact that he could distinguish between the beautiful and the other that wasn't gave him great excitement; he was not able to define it, but he could notice and feel it, just as Zorthian could do. In the Raphael Room, the secret was that only some of the paintings were made by the great master himself and the others by students; Feynman liked the ones done by Raphael, and he was able to seek them out. This gave him a great boost of self-confidence.

At a small art exhibition at Caltech, Feynman displayed two of his drawings. One of them, entitled 'The magnetic field of the sun', was bought by someone who wanted to know more about the picture. She had bought it to present it to her husband on his birthday.

Feynman finally understood what art is for really, in certain aspects. 'It gives somebody, individually, pleasure. You can make something that somebody likes *so much* that they are depressed, or they're happy, on account of that damn thing they made! In science, it's sort of general and large: you don't know individuals who have appreciated it directly . . . I understood that to sell a drawing is not to make money, but to be sure that it's in the home of someone who really wants it; someone who would feel bad if they didn't have it.'[17]

So Feynman decided to sell his paintings. However, he did not want people to buy them because he, Richard Feynman, was a physics professor who could draw. He made up a pseudonym. His friend Dudley Wright suggested 'Au Fait', French for 'thoroughly conversant'; he took it, but changed the spelling to 'Ofey'.

One of his models wanted him to make a drawing of her, but she didn't have money. She offered to pose three times free if Feynman would give her a drawing. In turn, Feynman offered to give her three drawings if she would pose once for nothing. She put up the drawings Feynman had given her on the wall in her small room, and soon her boyfriend noticed it. He liked it so much that he wanted to commission Feynman to do a portrait of her for sixty dollars. This model got the idea of becoming his agent; she thought she could earn extra money by going around selling his drawings—'this new artist from Altadena . . .' She arranged to have some of his drawings framed and put on display in the art department at Bullock's, the most elegant department store in Pasadena, although nobody bought them. 'I've done a lot of drawing by now, and I've gotten to like to draw the nudes best. For all I know it's not art exactly; it's a mixture. Who knows the percentages?'[18]

Jerry Zorthian never learned any physics. That didn't bother Feynman, because Zorthian was totally honest about it; he never claimed to know physics. Feynman did not mind that; he minded if you didn't know something and claimed you did. That's what got him; people who were fakes or phonies deeply disturbed him; with them he was not gracious, he would leave them, just walk away.

(b) *Gianonni's topless bar*

There was a period when there were restaurants and bars in Pasadena that would feature topless dancing: one could go there for lunch or dinner, and the girls would dance without a top, and after a while without anything. One of these places was only about a mile or so away from Feynman's house and he would go there often. He would sit in one of the booths and work a little on physics on the paper placemats; sometimes he would draw one of the dancing girls or one of the customers just for practice. 'My wife Gweneth, who is English, had a good attitude about my going to this place. She said, "The Englishmen have clubs they go to." So it was something like my club.' [8,19]

The owner of this restaurant-bar was Gianonni. In this place, there were pictures hanging around on the walls, which Feynman did not like. So he gave Gianonni a rather nice drawing he had made of his model, called Kathy, to put up on the wall, and he was delighted. Giving him the drawing produced some useful results. Gianonni became very friendly to him and, since Feynman did not drink any alcoholic beverages, would give him free drinks of 7-Up

Every time Feynman would go to Gianonni's restaurant-bar, a waitress would come around with his glass of 7-Up. Feynman would watch the girls dance, do a little physics, prepare a lecture, or draw a little bit. If he got tired, he'd watch the entertainment for a while, and then do a little more work. Gianonni knew that he did not wish to be disturbed, so if a drunk would come over and start to talk to him, right away a waitress would appear and get the guy out of there. On the other hand, if a girl came over to see Feynman, Gianonni would do nothing; they had a pretty good understanding.

Once Feynman was commissioned to draw a picture for a massage parlor. He drew the picture of a slave girl in imaginary Rome massaging some important Roman senator. Since she was a slave girl, she had a certain look on her face; she knows what's going to happen next, and she's sort of resigned to it. Feynman worked hard on that picture. He used Kathy as his model for the slave girl, and a muscular man for the Roman senator. He did lots of studies. Soon the cost of hiring the models alone was eighty dollars, but all Feynman cared about was the challenge of completing the commission. Finally he ended up with a drawing just as he had imagined it: a picture of a muscular man lying on a table with the girl massaging him; she's wearing a kind of a toga that covers one breast- -the other one was nude—and he got the expression of resignation just right.

One day there was a police raid on Gianonni's place, and some of the dancers were arrested. Someone wanted to stop Gianonni from putting on topless shows, but Gianonni did not wish to stop. So there was a big court case about it; it was in all the local newspapers. 'Gianonni went around all the customers and asked them if they would testify in support of him. Everybody had an excuse [not to do it]. But I [said] to myself, "I'm the only free man here. I haven't any excuse! I *like* this place, and I'd like to see it continue. I don't see anything wrong with topless dancing." So I said to Gianonni, "Yes, I'll testify."' [20]

In the court Feynman was asked if he went to other bars, and how often he visited Gianonni's bar: 'Five or six times a week!' That got in the newspapers: 'The Caltech professor of physics goes to see topless dancing six times a week.' [20] There were lots of questions in the court about whether topless dancing was acceptable to the community or not. Gianonni temporarily lost the case and his case, or another one very similar to it, ultimately went to the Supreme Court. In the meantime, Gianonni's place remained open, and Feynman continued to get his free 7-Ups.

According to Albert Hibbs, 'Gweneth did not mind [such escapades] of Richard's. She knew what kind of guy he was and she loved him. She not only knew that he adored beautiful women but she did not mind. He loved sketching nude women, and had his studio in the basement. Not only didn't she care, she sort of enjoyed the fact that he so clearly enjoyed life. She enjoyed him enjoying life. She shared that with him. She knew that Richard loved her, and she loved him with understanding, so that there was nothing to worry about.' [3]

As another artist friend of Feynman's, Tom Van Sant, recalled: 'Though Richard adored women, he was always true to Gweneth and would never do anything that would embarrass her or reflect badly on her and his family. He would say, "Gweneth and I have been together all these years and we never argue." He never came to dinner to my place scratching his head or saying that he had had an argument with Gweneth. He just appreciated her tremendously and loved her dearly. Still, he just loved women. He once made a joke saying, "When I walk down the street, I see all women but the men are just fuzzy blurs."' [21]

(c) Ceremony for blessing the animals

Every Saturday before Easter there is a ceremony, primarily for the old Mexican community of Los Angeles. It takes place at the old center, the original city of Los Angeles, called the Plaza de Los Angeles. It's a big square, actually a circle in the old Spanish or Mexican style, situated at the end of the famous tourist attraction called Olvera Street. There are Mexican restaurants, curio shops, and other tourist attractions. On this particular Saturday, people bring all their pets to be blessed. They form a huge parade around this large circular area at the center of the Plaza. On a brick wall above the walkway stands the Bishop of Los Angeles, who sprinkles holy water on all the animals.

Feynman's artist friend, Jerry Zorthian, puts a lot of animals in various trailers and hauls them down there and parks them. He is a fixture and everyone leads the animals around in a parade past the Bishop, who blesses all the animals. This is a major social activity every Saturday before Easter, and

Feynman's duty was always to pull a cart. The cart had in it a couple of chickens and usually a pig. Feynman would say, 'Jerry says this year I have to pull a cart.' Albert Hibbs would usually lead a goat or a pig, and other people would carry chickens or ride horses or whatever else.

This was a regular thing. If Feynman was in town, he would be there for the ceremony for the blessing of the animals. In the spring of 1987 Feynman was very sick, and he did not attend it; Easter 1986 was the last time he did it. As he was pulling his cart carrying Jerry's animals, someone shouted, 'Mr Feynman, you're not Catholic, are you?' He shouted back, 'No, but the animals are!' [22]

(d) *Theater and drama*

Feynman would regularly take part in the annual productions of the Caltech Drama Department, which were produced by Shirley Marneus, the director. Thus he took part in the musicals *Guys and Dolls*, *Kismet*, *Fiorello*, and numerous others. In *The Mad Woman of Chaillot*, Feynman played the role of the king of sewers, the sewers of Paris, which was a very significant part. He had many good lines and was just delightful. 'He was the perfect king of sewers!' [3] Most of the other parts he played were short, walk-on parts.

They put on the musical *South Pacific* in 1982, and one of the scenes in it was staged on the island of Bali Hai where all the natives have gone. The *South Pacific* story is about the U.S. Navy in the south Pacific and their life stuck away on the remote island, far from the war, very bored. The natives have taken all the young girls off to the other island, so the sailors can't get at them. One of the scenes in this is when one of the officers gets over to the other island to hook up with a girl (a native) he has fallen in love with. They had a lot of Caltech students dressed up like natives, and then Feynman appeared with this gigantic feather plume, all covered with feathers and a big coat, naked from the waist up and a scar from his 1981 operation very clear across his belly, upper chest covered down with a belt, and played on a hollowed out log with sticks; that started out the whole scene with a very wild piece of drumming. Ralph Leighton, who used to do a lot of drumming with Feynman, was also present in the scene, both of them drumming at the same time. 'Feynman was of course the leader of it; it was wonderful!' [3]

The last one, in 1987, they put on the musical comedy called *How to Succeed in Business Without Really Trying*. All of the action takes place in the business offices of some fictitious company in New York. Feynman played the part of a janitor; it was a walk-on part. He was supposed to walk on the stage and clear things up with a broom, but that was not enough for him. He had on a janitor's costume. He would pick up a wastebasket and then clean up the broom. Before he left, he would pick up the other wastebasket and dump it into the first one and leave. It brought the house down. 'But it was typical; he would do it whenever he got the chance, to turn a walk-on part into stealing scenes.' [3]

(e) Mayan hieroglyphics

The reason why Feynman knew anything about Mayan mathematics and astronomy was because he visited Mexico with his second wife, Mary Lou, on their honeymoon. Mary Lou was greatly interested in art history, particularly that of Mexico. On their trip to Mexico, Richard and Mary Lou climbed up and down pyramids, and she had him following her all over the place. She showed him many interesting things, such as the relationships in designs of various figures, but after a few days (and nights) of going up and down in hot and steamy jungles Feynman was exhausted.

In some little town in Guatemala, they went into a museum that had a case displaying a manuscript full of strange symbols, pictures, bars, and dots. It was a copy—made by a man called Villacorta—of the Dresden Codex, an original book prepared by the Mayans and found in a museum in Dresden in Germany. Feynman recognized the bars and dots as numbers; he remembered how the Mayans had invented zero—his father had told him that—and had done many interesting things. The museum had copies of the codex for sale and Feynman bought one. On each page at the left was the codex copy, and on the right a description and partial translation of it in Spanish. Feynman loved puzzles and codes, so when he saw the bars and dots he thought he was going to have some fun. He covered the Spanish with a sheet of yellow paper and began to play the game of deciphering the Mayan bars and dots, sitting in the hotel room, while Mary Lou climbed up and down the pyramids all day.

Feynman quickly figured out that a bar was equal to five dots, what the symbol for zero was, and so on. It took him a little longer to figure out that the bars and dots carried at twenty the first time, but they carried at eighteen the second time (thus making cycles of 360). He also figured out all kinds of things about various faces: they represented certain days and weeks.

Upon his return to California, Feynman continued to work on the codex. He found it a lot of fun to decipher something like that, because when he started he knew nothing about it, he had no clue to go by, but then he noticed certain numbers which appeared often, and added up to other numbers, and so on. There was one place in the codex where the number 584 was very prominent. This 584 was divided into periods of 236, 90, 250, and 8. Another prominent number was 2920, which represented 584×5 or 365×8. There was a table of multiples of 2920 up to 13×2920; as far as Feynman could tell, they were intended to calculate errors; only many years later did he figure out what they actually were.

Since figures denoting days were associated with the number 584, which was divided up so peculiarly, Feynman figured that it wasn't a mythical number of some sort; it might be an astronomical number. Finally he went down to the astronomy library at Caltech, looked up the relevant books, and found that 583.92 days is the period of Venus as it appears from the earth. Then 236, 90, 250, 8 became apparent: these must represent the phases that Venus goes through. At first, it is a morning star, then it can't be seen (it's on the other side of the sun), and finally it disappears again (it's between the earth and the sun). The 90 and 8 are different because Venus moves more slowly through the sky when it is on the far side of the sun compared to when it passes between the earth and sun. The difference between 236 and 250 might indicate a difference between the eastern and western horizons in Maya Land.

Feynman discovered another table nearby that had periods of 11 959 days. This turned out to be a table for predicting lunar eclipses. Still another table had multiples of 91 in descending order. Feynman did not figure that one out, 'nor has anyone else'.[23]

When Feynman had worked out as much as he could from the codex, he decided to look at the Spanish commentary of Villacorta to see how much he had been able to figure out. He found the commentary to be 'complete nonsense',[23] so he didn't have to study the commentary anymore. After that, Feynman began to read a lot about the Mayans, especially in the books of the great Mayan expert Eric Thompson. He did all the calculations over again, and figured out that those 'funny numbers', which he had at first thought were errors, were in fact integral multiples of the period 583.923; the Mayans had realized that 584 was not exactly right.

At the invitation of Nina Byers, Feynman gave a lecture on 'Deciphering the Mayan hieroglyphics' in the physics department at UCLA, and repeated it at Caltech. A few days before Feynman's lecture at Caltech, there was a big splurge in the *New York Times*, which reported that a new codex had been discovered. There were supposed to exist only three codices at that time—hundreds of thousands had been burned by the Spanish as the work of the Devil. Feynman obtained a glossy print of what the *New York Times* had published with the help of his cousin Frances, who worked for the Associated Press, and proved that it was a fake. It was in the style of the existing codices, but had nothing original in it. 'If you find something that is really new, it's got to have something different. A real hoax would be to take something like the period of Mars, invent a mythology to go with it, and then draw pictures associated with this mythology with numbers appropriate to Mars—not in an obvious position; rather, have tables of multiples of the period with some mysterious "errors" and so on. The numbers would have to be worked out a little bit.'[24]

(f) 'That wouldn't be rational!'

As usual, at a party, Feynman was drumming to the accompaniment of the piano. The piano player said, 'How about 6/8 time?' Fine. 'Waltz?' Fine. '4/4 time!' Fine. Someone shouted, 'How about pi beats to the measure?' And Feynman, without blinking an eye or stopping, replied: 'That wouldn't even be rational.'[3]

Feynman greatly enjoyed other people playing, but he neither went to concerts nor enjoyed classical music. He was delighted with his daughter Michelle's cello playing. That was something he encouraged very much and loved to hear. But he himself did not play anything apart from percussion; that satisfied some primeval sense of rhythm within him. He enjoyed Michelle's cello just because *she* played it.

(g) *Relations with students and colleagues*

Feynman used to complain that he never had any good students. He would say, 'I've put a lot of energy into students, but I think I wreck them somehow. I have never had a student that I felt I did something for, and I have never had a student who hasn't disappointed me in some way. I don't think I did very well. For instance, take Oppenheimer as a teacher; he had a group of students, he had some thirty graduate students, and had some way of running them. There have been many famous physicists who have been known as Oppenheimer students, because they were. They learned their damned stuff from him in the graduate school, directly or indirectly. He worked in some indirect way; I don't know how the hell he did it. There have been many famous people who were Sommerfeld's students. All famous guys, and they knew that they learned that crap from Sommerfeld, somehow. I don't feel that way about anybody that I had as a student. I can list my students, and everyone of them mediocre guys, somehow failures one way or the other.

'Most of my students were some kind of failures. The guys from Cornell, they were Bethe's students too. And they were no good either. Bethe was a good teacher, but he had the same trouble I had. I'll bet if we sat down together and looked at our students, we wouldn't be happy. I think Bethe probably doesn't realize it; if he sat down and thought about it, I bet he would realize it; for the hell of it I'd like to know.[8,25]

One of Feynman's former students, Phil Platzmann of the Bell Laboratories, attempted to throw some light on Feynman's relationship to his students. 'The reason why Feynman did not have many [good] students was because he was very difficult with them, because he didn't really worry about students. He somehow did not want to make sure that the student was successful; he didn't want to have anything to do with that. He had a few students, but not many. He suggested many problems in the course of lectures, seminars and discussions, but if you would go to him to ask for a problem to work on he wouldn't give it to you; you had to find one yourself.

'Working with Feynman was very difficult for students because he was very competitive with them, too, and the effect was that the students would not feel very smart. Feynman would always talk with students only about physics. If you came in and said, "I have a problem in physics, I don't understand it," he would help you. But if you came came in and said, "Help me out," rather than discuss physics, he would say, "No!" He wouldn't help you. You wouldn't go to him and say, "Give me a problem."

'Or, if you just came in and asked for help, he would say he wasn't interested. Even when you were working with him, he didn't take an interest in you or your problems, like whether you were going to get your degree, who would sign your research papers, or where you were going to get a job, etc. He wasn't interested; he was only interested in physics, not in you as a human being. He had a one-track mind. And he loved to give lectures to a group of people because he was a showman; he liked to put on a show. He would call you "stupid" or "dim wit", jocularly though; or, if you came in and just asked for his help, he would tell you to get out of his office. You would say, "Let's make an appointment", and he would say, "Well, I'm too busy to talk to you this week", and things like that. He wouldn't take students under his wing.'[26]

In his brusqueness and abrasiveness Feynman was very much like the Russian physicist Lev Davidovich Landau in many respects, including his curtness toward students. It is illustrated by Niels Bohr's visit to the USSR in 1961. Bohr was asked how he had succeeded in creating a famous and first-rate school of theoretical physics. Bohr answered: 'Probably because I have never been ashamed of admitting to my students that I'm a fool.' Bohr's remarks were translated into Russian by E. M. Lifshitz, who translated them as: 'Probably because I have never been ashamed to tell my students that they are fools.' As there was laughter after this remark, Lifshitz became aware of his mistake, corrected himself and apologized. Peter Kapitza, who was present, remarked that this translation had not been accidental at all, and continued: 'Precisely herein lies the difference between Bohr's and Landau's schools.'[27] Feynman's attitude corresponded more to Lifshitz's mistranslation of Bohr's words. But, in fairness to Feynman, we might add that he was just as willing to call himself 'dopey' or a 'fool'. Feynman (and Landau) realized, above all, that—faced with the mysteries of nature—we are all fools. But Feynman's distant and sometimes critical attitude towards his students had a disastrous effect on their self-confidence.

Feynman did not especially choose to be curt to his students. He treated one and all in the same way, and at times he could be quite charming. As William Fowler, Feynman's colleague during all his years at Caltech, recalled: 'Most of us were afraid of him. At faculty meetings if you said something with which he disagreed he would put you in your place with a sharp tongue. He didn't suffer fools at all. My impression is that no one on the faculty got close to him.'[28]

Feynman thought that people should do what they really wanted to do. Fowler would go to Feynman to discuss some difficult theoretical paper. 'You had just to tell him a few lines, and he would jump up with ideas and diagrams. He was very helpful and encouraging. Feynman was interested in everything. He seemed to know about everything you could bring up. He was just tremendous, but nobody ever got close to him.

'When Feynman first came to Caltech, we realized that there was a genius in our midst. His Nobel Prize was a wonderful thing for Caltech. Eveyone was impressed by Feynman. They realized that he was the smartest and wisest guy in the physics division.

'Feynman changed after his marriage to Gweneth. He became a much nicer guy. She was just such a sweet person; it was just the opposite with Mary Lou, who was "very strange". Mary Lou antagonized everybody; everybody was relieved when Feynman divorced her. When Feynman married Gweneth we all wondered how it would be; it turned out to be wonderful.'[28]

Feynman never attended physics division board meetings, except once or twice in the early days. He never applied for research grants nor did he write proposals, which almost all other faculty members—certainly in the sciences—had to do, but the group in high-energy physics kept his needs satisfied. Feynman thought that if Caltech wanted him to have research students, it was their responsibility to provide for them. Lee DuBridge (Caltech's president) understood Feynman perfectly; when Feynman needed anything, his needs were met by those responsible for the funding of high-energy research or by Caltech directly.

'At seminars and colloquia, Feynman would ask terrible questions of the speaker, always showing that he knew it better than the speaker.'[28] 'He used to torment the speakers who came to give the theory seminars if he thought they weren't good. The theory seminar used to take place in this small room at the Norman Bridge Laboratory at Caltech. Feynman would sit in the front row, which was maybe three feet away from the blackboard. When the speaker got there, Feynman would fall asleep in the front row, slide down in his chair, stick out his legs so that the person could not get to the blackboard without walking over his legs—just to annoy the speaker if he thought he was stupid or not to the point.'[26] If there was no speaker available for the theory seminar, Feynman would offer to give the seminar himself; he would ask the students to ask him any problem discussed in the *Physical Review* and he would treat it in his own way extemporaneously then and there, which would lead to some very interesting discussions.

'Feynman never wore a jacket and tie, only long-sleeve white shirts and gray trousers. Even in the worst weather he came without a raincoat. Gweneth used to pick him up in the evening.

'Everyone realized that his [last] illness [in 1987] would be fatal. Finally he slowed down. Feynman's passing was a terrible moment. We all thought that the whole world was ending. But it was probably the best thing when the release came from his pain and misery.

'Feynman was a very wise man, who sat very high standards for everyone. He motivated you to achieve them. Just the fact that he was around, all of us at Caltech thought that we had to live up to his standards. In this indirect way he influenced us all.'[28]

(h) *Fashions in physics*

Feynman was aware that there were different schools and fashions in physics, but personally he did not much care who was doing what. 'There are people who do certain kinds of problems; there are a lot of different ideas, there always have been. Actually, there probably are little schools, and there is a tendency for younger people to follow a leader. Once Geoffrey Chew believed that everything was going to come out of the S-matrix; then he gathered a coterie around him, who believed that they would find the answer by following that route. There has been around the school of John Wheeler concerning gravitation and geometry, the quantum theory of gravitation, and so on. Wheeler has nurtured a school of students around him; they sort of believe these wild ideas of his and have been absorbed in them. Then there was the idea of Regge poles—it was a good one—there was a whole comet tail of guys working on it. In recent years there has been the string theory. Somebody notices a good idea and starts working on it, and all the other guys rush in believing that this is *the* thing. They expect to be at the forefront of the thing; they follow the leaders who say that by working on this thing they'll be on the cutting edge. So there is a large number of people who rush, it seems to me, from one theoretical view to another theoretical view, sort of mediocre characters following their leaders. It seems odd to me that so much work is done on a few ideas at any given time. There is always a favorite "in fashion" idea; there are more fashions actually than there are schools.

'I think we have too many guys in fundamental theoretical physics, who have got nothing else to do. They just sit around all over the place, not doing anything by independent thought. They are not critical, they are not careful, the papers are sloppy, the work isn't very good. And the real work in a field is always done by a limited number of people. Of course, it is important that these people exist; but it seems to me that there are just too many people running around, following the leader, all over the field of theoretical physics.'[8]

(i) *Attitude toward nature and physics*

Richard Feynman maintained that physics was his only hobby, his primary joy and entertainment. That it was also his work was beside the point. He constantly thought about it and played with it. There was nothing in his life compared to thinking about physics and nature, everything centered upon it.

Feynman often said that he would write a book with the title 'Physics is fun'; but he did not know whether to spell fun 'PHUN' or physics 'FYSICS'. He wanted to spell them both the same way but could not decide which.[3]

Feynman believed that there were two ways of doing physics: the Babylonian way and the Greek way. The Greeks were very logical and worked on things from first principles, from axioms, where one thing depended on the other. The Babylonians just related one thing to the other. Feynman always said that he was a Babylonian, and that, in his view, men like Julian Schwinger and Sin-Itiro Tomonaga were the Greeks in that they tended to do things in a much more logical fashion. This was his approach not only to quantum electrodynamics but to physics as a whole. When he saw a problem, he always tried to relate it to what he knew about nature, about his experience; he just tried to relate one thing to another. Feynman always said, 'I'm like a little Jewish boy in the marketplace trying not to get cheated by nature.' [8]

Feynman treated the attempt to discover the laws of nature by giving the following analogy.[29] Imagine that the gods are playing some great game of chess and we don't know the rules of the game, but we are allowed to look at the board, in a little corner perhaps, from time to time. From these observations we try to figure out what the rules of the game are, what rules are obeyed by the moving pieces. After a while we might discover, for example, that when there is only one bishop around on the board that it maintains its color. Later on we might discover that the bishop moves along the diagonal, which would explain the law that we understood before that it maintains its color; this would give us a deeper understanding of the motion of the bishop on the chessboard. Then other things can happen. Everything is going well, we've got all the laws, and then all of a sudden some strange phenomenon occurs in the corner; so we investigate that: it's castling, something we didn't expect.

'In fundamental physics, we are always trying to investigate those things in which we don't understand the conclusions. We're not trying to check our conclusions all the time; after we have checked them enough we are OK. The thing that doesn't fit is the thing that's the most interesting, the part that doesn't go according to what you expected.' [29] There could also be revolutions in our understanding of the game of chess, which are comparable to revolutions in physics. For instance, after we have noticed that the bishops maintain their color and they move along the diagonal for such a long time that everybody knows that that's true; then we suddenly discover one day in a chess game that the bishop doesn't maintain its color, it changes its color. Only later do we discover a new possibility: that a bishop is captured and that a pawn went down all the way to the queen's end to produce a new bishop. That can happen, but we didn't know it. So it's very analogous to way the laws of nature are. They keep on working and, all of a sudden, some little gimmick shows that they are wrong. 'And then we have to investigate the conditions under which this bishop's change of color happened and so forth, and gradually learn the new rule that explains things more deeply.' [29]

In the chess game, the rules become more complicated as we go along. 'In physics, unlike chess, when we discover new things, it looks more simple. It appears on the whole to be more complicated because we have to learn about a greater experience.' That is, we have to learn about more particles and new things. And so the laws look more complicated again. 'But what's wonderful is that if we expand our experience into wilder and wilder regions every once in a while we have these integrations, which make everything look simpler than it looked before.'[29]

At the present time, the only way to understand the ultimate character of the physical world is through a mathematical type of reasoning. 'One cannot understand the great depth of the character of the universality of laws of nature, the relationship of things, without an understanding of mathematics. There is no other way to do it. We don't know any other way to describe accurately and well or to see the interrelationships without it.

'There are many, many aspects of the world that mathematics is unnecessary for, such as love, and which are very delightful and wonderful to appreciate and to feel awed and mysterious about.'[29]

Feynman did not mean to say that physics is the only thing in the world, but to *him* the contemplation of nature through physics was the most important thing in his life, transcending everything else.

Feynman had such an insight into physical problems; he found a wonderful joy in trying to understand nature and find how things really worked; he could almost feel it with his hands. He liked to play drums, so when he was doing physics he was doing something really with his hands. He liked to wave his arms and make sweeping gestures. He liked to do things that were sort of artistic. He shied away from too much mathematics even though he was wonderful at it.

The discussions between Feynman and Gell-Mann at the theory seminars were exciting to witness, because the two of them were on top of everything. In the words of Gell-Mann, in the course of their discussions together they 'twisted the tail of the cosmos'.[30]

Once Richard Feynman visited the Bell Laboratories. At that time the scanning tunneling microscope had just been invented and there were a number of people doing scanning tunneling microscopy. There were wonderful images of gold atoms on silicon atoms. Phil Platzmann was sitting there, looking at them, asking questions. Feynman turned around to him, and said, 'Platzmann, shut up! Those are atoms! This is religion. You shouldn't be asking questions, you just should look at the pictures. You don't have to say anything. Just look at it: Wow! That's God you know! Atoms right there!'[26] To look at the pictures of atoms in the scanning tunneling microscope was for Feynman akin to a religious experience.

Feynman's life was his love for physics. Everything else depended on it. This was the thing that enriched him always, that kept him excited and alive, and he communicated his excitement about physics and nature to others. As the *Los Angeles Times* science editor wrote: 'A lecture by Dr Feynman is a rare treat indeed. For humor and drama, suspense and interest it often rivals Broadway stage plays, and above all it crackles with clarity. If physics is the underlying "melody" of science, then Dr Feynman is its most lucid troubador.'[31]

To Feynman nature was both beautiful and simple, and he emphasized that all the time. Discussing the relation of the gravitational force to the electrical force, he would say, raising his hands ecstatically, 'Isn't nature wonderful to make something with 42 zeros? It's not much of a miracle to predict something if you know the laws about it. In other words, it's enough of a miracle that there are laws at all, but what's [really] a miracle is to be able to find them!' [8]

26.5 The space shuttle *Challenger*

In the spring of 1983 a reusable space shuttle made its maiden voyage. From the beginning there used to be problems of leaks in one valve or the other, and a variety of other difficulties inherent to the flight of space vehicles, but they were usually overcome. Richard Feynman used to read in the newspapers about shuttles going up and down all the time, apparently on so-called 'scientific' missions, and it bothered him a little bit that he never saw in any of the scientific journals the results of any experiments that were supposed to be so important and that had been performed aboard the shuttles. So Feynman never took much notice of what they did in these shuttle experiments. The space shuttle *Challenger* had an accident on 28 January 1986. Like many other people, Feynman watched the explosion of the shuttle on television, but apart from the tragedy of losing seven astronauts, he did not think much about it.

A few days after the accident, Feynman received a telephone call from William Graham, head of NASA (the National Aeronautic and Space Administration), who asked him to be a member of the commission to investigate what went wrong with the shuttle. Graham had been a student of Feynman's at Caltech and had later worked at the Hughes Aircraft Company, where he used to attend Feynman's Wednesday afternoon lectures.

Feynman learned that the investigation would take place in Washington, and his immediate reaction was not to take part in it; he did not want to go anywhere near Washington or the government. He called his friends Albert Hibbs and Richard Davies to seek their advice about what to do. He told Hibbs, 'Look, this is what I have been asked to do, should I do it?' Hibbs asked him: 'Do you think you could find anything about what happened?' Feynman said, 'Yeah, probably.' Hibbs asked, 'Do you think it would be important that that problem be solved?' He replied, 'Yeah, it would be important.' So, after a long pause, Hibbs asked him, 'Well, why are you asking me?' Feynman said, 'Thanks a lot, Hibbs!' and hung up.[3] Then he asked his wife, Gweneth; he told her: 'Look, anybody can do it. They can get somebody else.' Gweneth said, 'No. If you don't do it, there will be twelve people, all going in a group, going around from place to place together. But if you join the commission, there will be eleven people—all in a group, going around from place to place—while the twelfth one, you, runs around all over the place, checking all kinds of unusual things. There probably won't be anything, but if there is, you will find it. There isn't anyone else who can do that like you can.' [32]

The commission had to answer several questions. Figure out what went wrong with the shuttle; the next thing would be to find out what was the matter with the organization of NASA. Then there were questions like: 'Should we continue with the shuttle system, or is it better to use expendable rockets?' Then there would be even bigger questions like: 'Where do we go from here? What should our future goals be in space?'

Feynman thought that a commission which started out by trying to find out what happened to the space shuttle *Challenger* could end up as a commission trying to decide national policy, and go on forever. He felt nervous at this thought. However, he decided that he would accept to be a member, but get out at the end of six months, no matter what. He also resolved that, during the time he participated in investigating the accident, he should do nothing else. He told Graham: 'I won't be able to do any work with the physics problem I have been having fun with; I'm going to do nothing else but work on the shuttle—for six months.'[33] The next day he was informed that it was now a presidential commission, headed by William Rogers, the former secretary of state, and that he (Feynman) had been accepted as a member of the commission.

Already in his initial notes, Feynman wrote: 'O rings show scorching in clevis—check.' That meant that hot gas had burnt through the O-rings on several occasions. He also learned that the zinc chromate putty had bubbles or holes. It turned out that, indeed, the gas came through these holes to erode the O-rings.

Feynman learned a lot about the shuttle engines, and how extraordinary and complicated they were, at the Jet Propulsion Laboratory (JPL). There had been many difficulties with the engines, and Feynman learned that the moment the people who had worked on the engines saw the shuttle explode they all felt that it was the engines that had been at fault. But, of course, the television replay showed a flame coming out of the solid rocket boosters (SRB).

Feynman pursued his single-minded investigation, just like the old days at Los Alamos; he got fully briefed and 'sucked up all the information like a sponge.'[34] In Washington, by way of a visit to William Graham's office, Feynman arrived at the offices of William Rogers, the commission's chairman, a few blocks away. The first meeting was a get-together, but Chairman Rogers did discuss the importance of being careful with leaks to the press. Then the regular meetings began to take place.

In the first regular meeting of the commission, a public meeting, the NASA people—in response to questions—mentioned only a fraction of the things which Feynman had already learned at the JPL. The next day there was an executive session and it was more effective. General Donald J. Kutyna, another member of the commission, told the members in great detail what an accident investigation was like and how it was done, using the Titan missile accident as an example. Feynman was impressed with Kutyna's presentation. He also found that most of the questions he had planned to ask were indeed the kind one should ask, except that the investigation had to be conducted in a much more methodical manner than he had imagined. Feynman and General Kutyna got acquainted and, right away, Kutyna decided to take Feynman under his wing and guide him through the rigmaroles of bureaucratic meetings and hearings. Feynman was determined not to just sit and listen in committee, but to find out what was happening at first hand, and General Kutyna's guidance would prove to be invaluable.

Feynman told his colleagues on the commission that the public briefings did not work well with him; he had to talk to the technical people directly, and did not wish to lose any time doing so. There was going to be a break of five days before any further activity, such as a visit to the Kennedy Space Center in Florida, would take place. Feynman asked William Graham to arrange for him to visit the Johnson Space Center in Houston, where they take the telemetry of space flights. Chairman Rogers vetoed Feynman's idea of talking to the technical people alone by himself. But Feynman explained to him that he wanted to do something immediately rather than waste time waiting around; so he was allowed to get a private briefing at NASA on the engines and seals. It was a continuation of his JPL briefing, only more detailed, including a detailed history of all the problems that had been encountered: how the problems had been discovered early, how there had been 'burn-throughs', 'blowbys', and such things on flight after flight. After this report on the problem of seals, there came a page of recommendations that NASA had made.

Feynman looked at the recommendations and was struck by the contradiction between two major ones. The first one said: 'The lack of a good secondary seal in the joint is most critical. Ways to reduce effects should be incorporated as soon as possible to reduce criticality.' Further down, another recommendation was: 'Analysis of existing data indicates that it is safe to continue flying with existing design. . . .' There were some other conditions such as using 200 lb of pressure in the leak test. It was discovered later on that the leak itself was causing the holes in the putty and was part of the failure of the seals.[35] Feynman asked about the kind of analysis that had been made, and learned that there was only a computer model that determined the degree to which a piece of rubber will burn in a complex situation like that; Feynman found that absurd.

Feynman also noticed that there was no discussion of problems and matters causing trouble until the 'flight readiness review', where the decision was made to fly the shuttle or not. Otherwise, between flights, there was no discussion of the problem. 'So, what was really happening was that NASA had developed an attitude: If the seals leaked just a little and the flight was successful, it meant that the seal situation was not serious. Therefore the seals could leak and it would be all right—it was no worse than the time before.'[35] It was like playing Russian roulette.

Within a couple of days, Feynman received a telephone call from General

Kutyna, who said to him: 'I was working on my carburetor, and I was thinking. You're a professor,' he asked, 'what, sir, is the effect of cold on the rubber seals?' [36] The thought struck Feynman immediately that what General Kutyna was thinking of was this. The temperature was 29°F when the shuttle flew, and the coldest previous launch had taken place at 53°F. Feynman answered: 'You know as well as I do. It [the rubber] gets stiff and loses resiliency.' That gave Feynman the idea he was looking for. NASA provided him the data on the resiliency of the O-ring rubber at low temperatures, but the information they sent was for deformation and creep over *hours*. Feynman wanted to know what happens over *fractions of a second* during launch 'when the gap in the field joint is suddenly changing'.[36] So the information he received was of no use.

Next day there was going to be a public meeting, in which what had been discussed in the closed meeting would be said again for public information. In the evening Feynman was having dinner. He looked at his table and there was a glass of ice-cold water. He said to himself: '*I* can find out about the rubber *without* sending notes to NASA and getting back stacks of papers; all I have got to do is get a sample of the rubber [from the O-ring], stick in ice water and see how it responds when I squeeze it! That way I can learn something *new* in a public meeting.' [36]

Feynman asked NASA for a piece of rubber used in the O-ring, but they could not provide him one. But William Graham remembered that there were two pieces of rubber in the field joint model which NASA was going to use in the public meeting. Immediately, Feynman went to a hardware store in a taxi, where he bought screwdrivers, pliers, clamps, and so on, not knowing what exactly he would need. With the help of pliers alone, he was able to open the field joint model and get the rubber without any problem.

It was 11 February 1986, the day of the public meeting. Feynman knew he had to perform a dramatic experiment in the meeting. He knew that it would be more dramatic to do a fresh and honest experiment right at the meeting, but it would be quite a flop if it didn't work. So he tried the experiment privately first and made sure it worked. At the public meeting, when General Kutyna gave him the signal, 'Now!', he did the experiment. He demonstrated that the rubber had no resilience when it was squeezed at the temperature of ice water, and that it was the partial cause of the accident. With that experiment, performed on television in front of millions of viewers, Feynman became a hero and a celebrity.

Feynman was not beholden to anyone. He was not part of any organization that would object to his expressing his scientific opinions freely. He was truly independent and unafraid. The *New York Times* published an article after Feynman did the ice water experiment, and they explained every detail perfectly, for which Feynman himself had had no time in the public meeting. They all agreed afterwards that it was true.

The commission visited the Kennedy Space Center as scheduled, but

Feynman stayed on there for a few more days. He ran around and found out more details about the launch. Then, after getting loaded with a variety of facts, he returned to Washington, where there took place more public meetings with the engineers and management of Morton Thiokol Company about the launching of the shuttle. Then he went to Pasadena. At the JPL he discussed with the experts the enhancement of the pictures of the flame that had appeared on the side of the solid rocket booster (SRB) just before the main tank exploded. 'I had just been in Washington, having NASA engineers talk through a fog. What a difference—just like the photograph guys and the ice crew at Kennedy, everything was so direct and simple at Caltech and JPL.'[37]

Finally, there came the time to write the report for the president. Feynman wrote up what he had found out about various things, and hoped that the other members of the commission would see it and have discussion about it. He sent it to the executive officer, whom Chairman Rogers had selected to coordinate everything on the commission. The report was being written at the Marshall Space Flight Center in Huntsville, Alabama, but Rogers wanted them to return to Washington and complete the report there. Feynman found that in all the discussions, only questions of style and 'word-smithing' were brought up, but not ideas and matters of substance.

Feynman also discovered that other members of the commission did not even know that he had written a special report about his experiences in investigating engines and avionics, while the executive officer had assured him that everyone had been given a copy of his report. Feynman saw to it that they did get a copy of his report, and it was supposed to go into the commission's report as an appendix.

Finally, the commission held its last meeting. It was about the recommendations that would be made to the president. They made nine recommendations. The next day, as Feynman was standing in Chairman Rogers's office, the latter said: 'I thought we would add a tenth recommendation: "The commission strongly recommends that NASA continue to receive the support of the administration and the nation . . ."' This issue had not been discussed during the four months that the commission had been at work on its investigation, nor was it a part of the directive from the president. The commission was only supposed to investigate the accident, find out what caused it, and recommend how to avoid such accidents in the future.

Feynman did not consider the tenth recommendation as being appropriate and said so. It was only William Rogers's idea. In a letter, dictated to Chairman Rogers's secretary, which she typed and delivered to him, Feynman placed on record the reasons why he didn't like the tenth recommendation. William Rogers told him later that he had polled the various members of the commission and they were in favor of the tenth recommendation, and he (Feynman) was outvoted. Feynman decided to verify the situation and called up several members of the commission on the telephone. Some denied any knowledge of the last recommendation, while others thought that Rogers had mentioned it in the meeting. Feynman was incensed. He sent a telegram to Mr. Rogers requesting him to take off his signature from the report unless the tenth recommendation were dropped and his own report would go as an appendix without modification. As a result of this telegram, William Rogers sought a compromise. He asked General Kutyna to be the intemediary with Feynman to convince him to change his mind. Feynman ultimately agreed that, instead of making a new recommendation, the report would conclude by saying that the commission 'urges'—rather than 'strongly recommends'—the administration to continue to support NASA.

From all these experiences, Feynman concluded that when NASA's mission had been to land a man on the moon and safely bring him back to earth, everybody—engineers, scientists, and managers—cooperated to achieve the goal, just as they had done in building the atomic bomb at Los Alamos; but since that time NASA and its goals had deteriorated, and the difficulties and problems in shuttle missions were neither fully recognized nor aired. Feynman's theory was that the loss of common interest between the scientists and engineers on the one hand, and management on the other, was the cause of deterioration in cooperation that caused the *Challenger* disaster. Feynman reached the profound but obvious conclusion that 'for a successful technology, reality must take precedence over public relations, for Nature cannot be fooled.'[38]

26.6 Tannu Tuva: 'The last journey of a genius'

Ralph Leighton (the son of Richard Feynman's physicist colleague Robert Leighton at Caltech), who edited Feynman's anecdotal autobiographical sketches *Surely you're joking, Mr. Feynman!*, used to teach arithmetic and algebra in a high school in Pasadena, California. Once, during the fall of 1977, he was given an assignment to teach geography and he was talking about it to Feynman. Since Leighton listened to short-wave radio and took an interest in world affairs, Feynman wanted to tease him about it, and told him, 'So you know all about geography, huh?' Leighton replied, 'Yeah!' Feynman asked him, 'Okay, what happened to the country of Tannu Tuva?' As a boy, he knew there was a country of that name in Central Asia; it used to print interesting triangular and diamond-shaped postage stamps, which Feynman had in his stamp collection. His father had shown him on the map where this country was, and Feynman had always wondered what happened to it. Ralph Leighton had never heard about it, and he thought Feynman was kidding and making up a country that didn't exist. Feynman got the encyclopedia out and looked for it on the map. Sure enough, there was Tannu Tuva, just outside Outer Mongolia in the middle of Central Asia, far away from everything, but it was no longer an independent country: it was a part of the Soviet Union, with its capital at Kyzyl. Richard, Gweneth, and Ralph looked at the map together, grinned at each other, and decided that any country with a capital named Kyzyl had just got to be interesting.

Feynman and Leighton tried to get information about Tannu Tuva, but at first they failed. They were together in San Francisco playing drums for a ballet; in their spare time they went to the public library and sought information about this unknown country. They hit upon the *Great Soviet Encyclopaedia*, published in 1931; from it they were led to a book *Travels in Central Asia* and found other travel books of that region. In these books they didn't find about anyone who went through Tuva; people would go down below it or they went around above it, but whenever they went through Central Siberia they missed it, because it was a kind of bowl and if one went down one would have to climb out back. So, in spite of scouting through all these travel books, Feynman and Leighton found no information about Tannu Tuva.

Then one day they came across a book, entitled *Reise ins asiatische Tuwa* by the German historian and explorer Otto Mänchen-Helfen. Mänchen-Helfen was the first non-Russian to set foot in the Republic of Tuva. It took a lot of trouble for him to obtain permission to go. He went there as an ethnologist; an ethnologist was considered totally harmless by the Soviet authorities. He gave a description of the town of Kyzyl, where the electric plant worked only when the movie theater was running. Mänchen-Helfen saw the beautiful Pudovkin film *Mother* there; the subtitles were in Russian and the audience did not follow anything, but they had a great time watching the film—Tuvinians had come from far and wide to look at the wonder of cinema. Leighton also studied a guidebook about Tuva written in Russian, which he obtained on loan from the Library of Congress. This small book contained a crude map of the country, with little silhouettes of various animals: in the north-east there were foxes and reindeer; in the south, camels; in the west there were yaks.

Early in the summer of 1978, Feynman went to the doctor complaining of abdominal pains. He was diagnosed to have liposarcoma, a malignant fatty tumor, in the abdomen, and soon underwent surgery. The surgeon removed a very large mass of cancer, the size of a football, that had crushed his kidney and spleen. He needed the remainder of the summer to recover.

One day, in the fall of 1978, Feynman came across a short article in the *Los Angeles Times* that reported that a Scythian gold sculpture depicting a hunter, his dog, and a wild boar had been found in the Tuva ASSR. On 17 January 1979, after dinner at 9.15 p.m., there was a program on the short-wave radio from Radio Moscow; it dealt with Tuva and gave essentially the information which Feynman and Leighton had already obtained from the *Great Soviet Encyclopaedia*. Their adventure had begun in earnest. As Feynman recalled, 'We had discovered the Shangri-La, a place in the world where nobody visited for a long time. So we right then and there said we've to get there of course.' [39]

Leighton began an exchange of correspondence directly with Intourist, the official Russian travel agency, about the possibility of a visit to Tannu Tuva, but they informed him that they could offer very little hope of getting to Tuva. While there was no harm in going ahead and applying for a visa, the obstacles in actually going there were insurmountable.

It occurred to Feynman that actually the matter could be quite simple. He knew that he was a famous physicist. He would offer to give some lectures in the Soviet Union. 'They would be delighted, I think. I go there, and I say that the condition is that I travel to Tuva. And they say, indeed, that's fine. And then I say, but I shall give the lectures in Moscow *after* I visit Tuva, and they'll have to say that I could go. I never understood before why I didn't want to do it that way, and now I suddenly do.'[39] But the reason why Feynman didn't want to do that earlier was: 'The whole idea is to have adventure. The way to have adventure is to do things at a lower level, not to ride on the freeway and to stop at the Holiday Inn.'[39]

Feynman and Leighton received a Mongolian–Tuvan–Russian phrase book which turned out to be wonderful. Now that they had a phrase book they could write in Tuvan with its help; they thought that they would arouse somebody's interest, so they struggled. 'This is the kind of thing I love. We tried to put something together, so [we took] all the phrases and [tried] to make minimum changes in any of the phrases in the phrase book, so that they would have as few errors as possible.'[39] They were able to put together the phrases in order to say: 'Greetings to your country from ours. We've had great interest in Tuva and we hope some day to come to visit and we would look forward to see you—Greetings and good wishes, and if there's any way that you can send us tapes of your language we would appreciate it, etc. etc.'[39] They mailed this letter to an address that was given in the phrase book: Tuvan Scientific Research Institute of Languages, Literature and History, 4 Kochetova, 667000 Kyzyl, Tuva ASSR.

At first nothing happened. Then, at the end of January 1980, Leighton received a reply, dated 7 January, from the Tuvan Research Institute; he took it to Feynman that evening, and together they opened it. This letter was from Ondar Daryma; they deciphered it with the help of the phrase book and the Tuvan–Russian dictionary, and finally from Russian into English. O. Daryma and K.X. Orgu had edited a folklore volume in Tuvan, entitled *Tyva tooldar* (Tuvan tales).

Leighton introduced Feynman in his letter to Ondar Daryma. They mailed their letter in mid-February 1980. Through interlibrary loan at Caltech, they obtained *Tyva tooldar* from Columbia University. They made a xerox copy of it and began to look for a suitable story to translate from it. There were eighteen stories; they chose 'Tarbagan bile koshkar'—'The Marmot and the ram'—but they could not proceed very far with it in their first attempt. They also obtained Sevyan Vainshtein's *Istoricheskaya ethnografiya tuvintsev* (Historical ethnography of the Tuvans); this book had an extensive introduction by the British anthropologist Dr Caroline Humphrey.

Leighton obtained special license plates, marked TOUVA, for his automobile. For the fun of it they had his car parked outside Feynman's house, and they got some friends of theirs to take pictures trying to push this vehicle as if it was out of gas or something up the hill. They sent the pictures to Ondar Daryma and told him; 'See how hard we're working to get to Tuva. It's Tuva or bust.'[40] Daryma was delighted with the picture and took it to the local newspaper in Kyzyl, which printed it with the caption which Leighton and Feynman had written.

Somewhere along the line Feynman noticed an announcement in *Soviet Life* magazine that three American biologists had reached Kyzyl. They were rather disappointed that these guys had reached it ahead of them and also that they had not fully appreciated the wonderful place Feynman and Leighton imagined Tuva to be, where they still planned to go. But from the botanists they got the idea that it was easier for them to go because they had something to do in Tuva. Feynman and Leighton had to find something that would provide a good official reason to get there.

Then Leighton found out that there was going to be a great throat singing contest and conference for a week somewhere way out on the western edge of Mongolia right next door to Tuva; it was a part of Mongolia which people normally did not visit, but it was close by to Tuva. Feynman and Leighton decided to attend this conference, but it fell through because the minister of culture decided not to have a throat singing conference in western Mongolia.

In September, drumming and storytelling sessions continued at home in Altadena. One day Feynman called up Leighton, because he had something to show him. It was a twelve-inch phonograph record, called *Melodii Tuvy*. It had been delivered to him by Kip Thorne, a Caltech physicist, who had just returned from Moscow. It had come with the compliments of S. Vainshtein, with the message that a separate letter from Vainshtein to Feynman had been sent by mail and that with the help of the director of the Institute of Ethnography he was trying to arrange permission for Feynman to visit Tuva.

At the end of October 1981 Feynman had some medical tests done at UCLA. The results were 'interesting' from Feynman's point of view: the cancer in his abdomen that supposedly had been removed three years before had now spread in a complicated pattern around his intestines. Dr. Donald Morton of UCLA's John Wayne Cancer Clinic was called in to operate. He believed in cutting away an inch of good tissue around every place where he found cancer. 'I usually don't stop until I can see the operating table underneath,' he said.[41] Feynman asked, 'What are the odds in an operation like that?' Dr. Morton replied, 'Well, I've had a dozen patients, and I haven't lost one yet—but I still don't know what my limitations are.'[41]

Feynman took radiation therapy to soften up the cancerous tissue, and then underwent what turned out to be a ten-hour operation. As he was being sewn up, an artery close to his heart burst. He required eighty pints of blood before it was over. Coincidentally, there had been two other patients at UCLA with similar needs that day. An alert was sent out to Caltech and its affiliate, the Jet

Propulsion Laboratory. Within a couple of hours there was a line of a hundred volunteers from Pasadena donating blood into the 'bank account' of Richard Feynman. The surgery ultimately took fourteen hours in all. Feynman's recovery was slow, but he didn't complain—'he was already living on borrowed time'.[42]

The yearly Caltech musical in 1982 was *South Pacific*. Feynman and Leighton set the tone for the mythical island of Bali Hai in a special scene created by Shirley Marneus, the director of Caltech's drama production department. They would be 'drumming for a quartet of grass skirts slung low on shapely hips'.[42]

On the opening night Feynman did not have enough endurance; he had to sleep during most of the performance, getting up only for the Bali Hai scene. But still he commanded the drummers and dancers in Tahitian to join him on the stage in a strong and confident voice. Feynman drummed only for a few minutes, but 'with such gusto that he looked as if he had recovered one hundred percent. It was his first public appearance since that harrowing fourteen-hour operation in October [1981], so it was an emotional moment for the audience—especially for the army of volunteers, who were obviously satisfied that their blood [matching Feynman's O-type] had been put to good use.'[43]

In the fall of 1983 news came from Sevyan Vainshtein. He wrote that he had visited Tuva in June, and was surprised to find an article in *Tuvinskaya Pravda* with greetings from Richard Feynman, Ralph Leighton and Glen Cowan [a friend of Leighton's from Berkeley] from California accompanied by a photograph.

In February 1984, before heading for Esalen to conduct his first seminar on 'quantum mechanical view of reality', Feynman went with Leighton to hear the Dalai Lama of Tibet at the Pasadena Civic Auditorium. The Dalai Lama spoke with sincerity and excitement about the wonders of nature as revealed by science. Feynman greatly enjoyed the occasion, especially the way the 'simple Buddhist monk'—as the Dalai Lama referred to himself—used humor (often at his own expense) to make a point. The Dalai Lama's approach to life reminded Feynman of what Lucille, his mother, used to say: 'The highest forms of understanding we can achieve are laughter and human compassion.'[44]

At Esalen, Feynman and Leighton relaxed in the serenity of baths overlooking the ocean, and participated in drumming. At such moments of joy, Feynman would often cry out, 'Thank you, Dr Morton!'; he never forgot that he was living on borrowed time and 'often thanked that man most responsible for it in the same way that others would thank God for giving them another fine day'.[45]

Towards the end of the week at Esalen, most of which had been spent at the seminar, Feynman remarked to Leighton: 'I'm going nuts! I met a girl from Canada who's so beautiful, she looks like Arline.'[45] As he reflected on his mortality, Feynman's thoughts were turning more and more to Arline and their youth. He rarely used to talk about her before, but was now beginning to be haunted by her memory.

As the summer of 1984 drew to a close, John Boslough, a writer for *National Geographic*, who was preparing an article about time, visited Feynman. Feynman joked: 'Has the *National Geographic* run out of places in the world to write about?' 'Well, not exactly,' replied Boslough. Feynman told him that there was still a place in the world that the *National Geographic* had not written about, and told him about Tannu Tuva. Boslough recommended that Feynman should write a detailed letter to *National Geographic* about publishing an article on Tuva, and he would take it from there.[46]

At the end of April 1985 Ralph Leighton and Glen Cowan, his friend from Berkeley, flew from Los Angeles to Helsinki, Finland, and from there to Moscow, where they met Sevyan Vainshtein. In Moscow, they learned that there was a museum exhibit associated with the ancient Silk Road, which had several hundred archaeological objects—many unearthed by Vainshtein in Tuva—and this exhibit was just then touring Sweden, where it had opened in Göteborg in February. Leighton informed Feynman about the exhibit, and they thought of having the exhibit transferred to the United States, where they would act as representatives to make contact to look at sites where the things came from, to take pictures that would become part of the exhibit, and to do various other things associated with it; they would be the museum representatives who would go to Tuva. Feynman wrote to A. P. Alexandrov, president of the USSR Academy of Sciences and the corresponding member A. P. Kapitsa, the official in charge of exhibitions, about bringing the exhibit to the United States.

For several years the University of Tokyo had been inviting Richard Feynman to visit Japan. But every time he accepted their invitation, he would happen to get sick. In the summer of 1985 there was going to be an international conference in Kyoto to celebrate the fiftieth anniversary of the proposal for the existence of the meson by Hideki Yukawa, and Feynman was invited to be the chairman of one session at the MESON 1985 conference. This time he was lucky and didn't get sick; so he and Gweneth went to Japan and had many new and exciting adventures. They visited the Ise Peninsula, where they stayed in a Japanese-style inn near the small town of Iseokitsu, which they enjoyed very much. From there they returned to Tokyo and went to the University of Kanazawa. Some professors arranged to drive them along the coast of nearby Noto Peninsula. They passed through several delightful fishing villages, and went to visit a pagoda in the middle of the countryside.

Richard and Gweneth stayed in a place called Togi for several days in a Japanese-style hotel, and attended the dedication of a new shrine. 'The ceremony was wonderful. There was a ceremonial cup with branches and leaves in it; there was a group of girls in special uniforms; there were dancers, and so on. It was quite elaborate.'[47] The head priest of the shrine gestured to them to follow him; they went around the shrine and entered it from the side, where the priest introduced them to the mayor and other dignitaries. Feynman was asked to make a little speech and he said, 'I am particularly impressed by your tremendous technological change, while at the same time your traditions still mean so much, as you are showing with this shrine dedication.'[47] He tried to express the mixture he had seen in Japan: change, but without losing respect for traditions. After a wonderful vacation in Japan, Richard and Gweneth returned home at the end of August.

In October 1986, on the day after Ralph Leighton's wedding, Dr Morton again performed surgery on Feynman—'another daring operation, another lease on life'.[48] After his recovery, he and Leighton continued to make plans and contacts for a possible visit to Tuva. Feynman's zest for life was so great that after each illness and surgery he mentally cooperated with his recovery and well-being to a great extent, and would feel better soon each time. Liposarcoma is a rapidly growing cancer, and it was a miracle that Feynman was able to survive so long after its detection and first removal in 1978. After the operation in October 1986, the cancer grew even faster and massive surgery was performed in October 1987. In each operation he had organs and muscle tissue removed, so that, after the last surgery, there was nothing left in one side of him; he was bent over, and had to straighten himself with effort. After this final operation Feynman did not bounce back with the same optimism and vigor he had shown previously; now he often felt weak, tired, depressed, and in pain, but when he talked about science or something else that deeply interested him he would feel excited and color would return to his cheeks. He continued to teach a graduate course on quantum chromodynamics at Caltech. When the cancer returned in winter, Dr Morton said it was inoperable.

In the last week of January 1988, Feynman gave an interview and drumming performance (with Leighton), which was recorded by Christopher Sykes for the BBC. In this interview he talked a little about what the whole preoccupation with Tannu Tuva had been about: 'Well, getting a little philosophical and serious, let's go back and see what we're doing. One day we look at the map [of Tannu Tuva] and its capital is K-y-z-y-l; we've decided it would be fun to go there because it's so obscure and peculiar. It's a game, and it's not serious, it does not involve some deep philosophical point of view about authorities or anything, it's just the fun of having an adventure to try to go to a land that we'd never heard of, that we knew was an independent country once. It's no longer an independent country; we find out what it's like and discovered as we went along that nobody went there for a long time—and the fact that it was isolated made it more interesting. Many explorers like to go to places that are unusual and it's only for the fun of it—and I don't go for the philosophical interpretation of our deeper understanding of what we're doing. We don't have any deep understanding of what we're doing; if we tried to understand what we are doing we'd go nuts.'[39]

On 3 February Feynman was taken ill and entered the UCLA Medical Center at 7.43 p.m. He did not want any extraordinary measures—including kidney dialysis—to be taken to keep him alive. During the night of 15 February 1988 Richard Feynman died, three months' short of his seventieth birthday. The last journey of a genius was over.

A few days after his death, an invitation came from E. P. Velikhov, vice-president of the USSR Academy of Sciences: 'Dear Professor Feynman: I have great pleasure to invite you, your wife, and four of your colleagues to visit the Soviet Union. I was informed by Professor Kapitsa that you would like to visit Tuva and get acquainted [with] its sightseeing. We consider the most favorable time for such a trip to be the period of May and June 1988. Your trip will take about three to four weeks. Kindly note that the Academy of Sciences will cover your expenses. Yours sincerely: E. P. Velikhov.'

The exhibit on the 'Nomads of Central Asia' opened at Smithsonian's Museum of Natural History in Washington, D.C., in November 1989. An invitation was received for Gweneth Feynman, Ralph Leighton, and others to visit Tuva in the summer of 1990. Gweneth died on 31 December 1989 of cancer.

26.7 Final stay in the hospital

As mentioned already, Richard Feynman entered the UCLA Medical Center in Los Angeles on 3 February 1988. He knew that his ten-year battle with cancer would soon be over. His friends, Albert Hibbs, Jerry Zorthian, and Tom Van Sant would visit him in the hospital and try to cheer him up; instead they found that he would try to be jovial with them and attempt to lift up *their* spirits in the face of his own grave condition. Al Hibbs recalled: 'The last time I saw him, the Saturday before he died, I was at his hospital room. He was complaining. He said, "What am I going to do if I get back there again [to his house]? I want to keep on drawing but I don't have a studio. My daughter has taken over the studio; she is using it for all her photography stuff. I don't have any place anymore. Can I borrow a room in your house?" I said, "Sure." He said, "I was only joking!" I said, "So was I!". He said, "You're always topping me, aren't you?" Then he talked about some of the memories of his life, such as his experiences in Brazil.' [3]

A couple of days before Feynman died, Jerry and Daphne Zorthian visited him in the hospital. He told Zorthian: 'They could probably keep me alive with all kinds of devices, but the quality of life will be ridiculous, and I'm not interested in that.' At one point Feynman broke down and cried: he was remembering Arline and he said that he had finished the book '*What do you care what other people think?*', something which Arline used to say all the time. The memories of Arline and their youth together came crowding in and Feynman sobbed for a long while. The Zorthians saw that he was getting tired, and Daphne kissed him gently on the forehead. As they were walking out, Feynman's last words to Zorthian were: 'Don't worry about anything, Jerry; just go out and have a good time.'[13]

Tom Van Sant, Feynman's other artist friend, also visited him in the hospital to cheer him up. When Van Sant visited him one morning, only a few days before his death, the test results just came in, which indicated that the kidney (the only one he had now) was failing. 'I was alone waiting for him when they brought him back to the room, and he told me about the test results, and I said, "We have talked about this day coming." We had talked about it before each of the two previous operations, because his chances of survival were not all that good in either one of them, and in each one of them I had shared as much of it with him as I could until the night before the surgery. So, here we were, at that moment we had talked about, and I apparently had a distressed look on my face, because after a moment he sort of squeezed my hand a little bit and smiled and said: "Well, I think I was about seven years old when I knew that I would ultimately die. I don't see why I should start complaining about it now. It's OK, Tom. Don't worry. I don't want to have to comfort *you!*" I said, "OK, Dick." We went on talking for about an hour and a half about different things. Then he got tired and needed to sleep, so I left. I didn't see him again. He was in a coma the last few days, and he died on 15 February. The next day Gweneth called me to let me know what had happened and asked me to remember Dick the way he was.'[21]

On the afternoon of 28 March 1988, a memorial service was held for Feynman in the large Beckman auditorium at Caltech; it had to be held twice so that all those who wished to attend it could do so. It was a very moving ceremony, in which many events of Feynman's life were portrayed through a rapid-moving slide show, a good deal of fast drumming, and brief remarks by a number of friends and faculty colleagues who had been close to Feynman. The thoughts were expressed that Feynman was a marvelous teacher, who brought clarity, joy, and enthusiasm to his teaching, but he never said himself that he was a good teacher. He loved the truth and would always go to the foundation to get it, but he never claimed to know the truth. He was a most courageous man who faced the end with full knowledge of what was happening to him, but he never claimed to have any special courage. He had the kind of courage that one usually associates with someone who has very strong religious convictions and expects rewards in an afterlife, yet he had no religious conviction or expectation. He was absolutely sure that the evolutionary process terminated existence in the same way as a leaf falling from a tree and that life rolls over through genetics. The concept of consciousness in the universe manifesting itself locally through a deity or an afterlife seemed too parochial to him. He could conceive of these things, but could not fit them into his conception of an expanding universe and an evolutionary design.

Feynman had lived his life in the search for truth about nature through physics, and he was a physicist's physicist. He had concluded his Nobel lecture

in Stockholm in December 1965 with the words: 'I think the problem is not to
find the *best* or most efficient method to proceed to a discovery, but to find any
method at all. Physical reasoning does help some people generate suggestions
as to how the unknown may be related to the known. Theories of the known,
which are described by different physical ideas may be equivalent in all their
predictions and hence scientifically indistinguishable. However, they are not
psychologically identical when trying to move from that base into the
unknown. For different views suggest different kinds of modifications which
might be made . . . I, therefore, think that a good theoretical physicist today
might find it useful to have a wide range of physical viewpoints and
mathematical expressions of the same theory . . . available to him. This may be
asking too much of one man. The new students should as a class have this. If
every individual student follows the same current fashion in expressing and
thinking about [the generally understood areas], then the variety of
hypotheses being generated to understand [the still open problems] is limited.
Perhaps rightly so, for possibly the chance is high that truth lies in the
fashionable direction. But [if] it is another direction . . . who will find it?'[49]

'So spoke an honest man; the outstanding intuitionist of our age and a prime
example of what may lie in store for anyone who dares to follow the beat of a
different drum.'[50]

Notes and References

1. R.P. Feynman and M. Gell-Mann, In: *Proceedings of the Second U.N.
International Conference on the Peaceful Uses of Atomic Energy*, Geneva, 1–13
September 1958. United Nations, Geneva, pp. 38–49.

2. Gweneth Feynman, The life of a Nobel wife. *Engineering and Science*,
March–April 1977, pp. 14–24.

3. A.R. Hibbs, Interview with Jagdish Mehra, 23 March 1988, at the Athenaeum,
Caltech, Pasadena, California.

4. Ralph Leighton, *Tuva or bust!*. Norton, New York, 1991, p. 45.

5. The news of Feynman's singing this ditty had reached far and wide; I heard it on
a visit to the University of Chicago in April 1988. Gell-Mann explained to me what
a 'Basenji' dog is. 'Basenji, or Washenzi in Swahili, means wild creatures. It is an
African breed of dog. Richard's dog was not a Basenji; it was a cross-breed cocker
spaniel, whom he called Venus. My dog was in fact a Basenji. I called mine
"Ruwenzori", the name of an African mountain range lying between Uganda and
the Belgian Congo.'[6]

6. M. Gell-Mann, Interview with Jagdish Mehra, at Caltech, Pasadena, California, 11 July 1990.

7. Elena Petra, Telephone conversation with Jagdish Mehra, 9 March 1988.

8. R.P. Feynman, Interviews and conversations with Jagdish Mehra, in Pasadena, California, January 1988.

9. Feynman spoke on 'The development of the space-time view of quantum electrodynamics'. *Les Prix Nobel en* 1965. Imprimérie Royale P.A. Norstedt & Söner, Stockholm, Sweden, 1966, pp. 152, 161.

10. R.P. Feynman, *SYJMF*, pp. 307–308.

11. R.P. Feynman, Acceptance speech. *Les Prix Nobel en* 1965. Impriméric Royale P.A. Norstedt & Söner, Stockholm, Sweden, pp. 84–85.

12. I was in the group of admirers surrounding Feynman at CERN when he made this remark.

13. Jirayr Zorthian, Telephone conversations with Jagdish Mehra, 28 and 30 August 1990; R.P. Feynman, *SYJMF*, p. 260.

14. R.P. Feynman, *SYJMF*, p. 261.

15. R.P. Feynman, *SYJMF*, p. 265.

16. R.P. Feynman, *SYJMF*, pp. 265–66.

17. R.P. Feynman, *SYJMF*, pp. 267–68.

18. R.P. Feynman, *SYJMF*, p. 269.

19. R.P. Feynman, *SYJMF*, p. 270.

20. R.P. Feynman, *SYJMF*, p. 274.

21. Tom Van Sant, Interview with Jagdish Mehra at the Athenaeum, Caltech, Pasadena, California, 30 August 1990.

22. Jirayr Zorthian, Telephone conversation with Jagdish Mehra, 30 August 1990.

23. R.P. Feynman, *SYJMF*, p. 315.

24. R.P. Feynman, *SYJMF*, p. 317.

25. R.P. Feynman, Interviews with Charles Weiner (American Institute of Physics), in Pasadena, California, 1966.

26. P.M. Platzman, Interview with Jagdish Mehra at New Brunswick, New Jersey, 25 June 1990.

27. Jagdish Mehra, Lev Davidovich Landau: Some aspects of his life and personality. In: *Frontiers of physics, Proceedings of the Landau Memorial Conference*, Tel Aviv, Israel, 6–10 June 1988 (ed. E. Gotsman, Y. Ne'eman, and A. Voronel). Pergamon, Oxford, 1991, pp. 89–90.

28. William Fowler, Interview with Jagdish Mehra, 12 June 1990, at the Athenaeum, Caltech, California.

29. R.P. Feynman, The pleasure of finding things out. Public Broadcasting Company broadcast, WGBH, Boston, 25 January 1983.

30. M. Gell-Mann, *Physics Today*, The Feynman Memorial Issue, February 1989, p. 51.

31. I.S. Bengelsdorf, *Los Angeles Times*, 14 March 1967.

32. R.P. Feynman, *WDYCWOPT*, p. 117.

33. R.P. Feynman, An outsider's inside view of the *Challenger* inquiry. *Physics Today*, February 1988, p. 26.

34. R.P. Feynman, Ref. 33, p. 27.

35. R.P. Feynman, Ref. 33, p. 29.

36. R.P. Feynman, Ref. 33, p. 30.

37. R.P. Feynman, Ref. 33, p. 33.

38. R.P. Feynman, *WDYCWOPT*, p. 237.

39. R.P. Feynman, The last journey of a genius. Public Broadcasting Company broadcast, WGBH, Boston, 24 January 1989.

40. *Tuva or bust!* became the title of Ralph Leighton's book about his and Feynman's Tuvan adventure (Norton, New York, 1991).

41. Ralph Leighton, Ref. 40, p. 63.

42. Ralph Leighton, Ref. 40, p. 64.

43. Ralph Leighton, Ref. 40, pp. 71, 73.

44. Ralph Leighton, Ref. 40, p. 93.

45. Ralph Leighton, Ref. 40, p. 97.

46. Ralph Leighton, Ref. 40, p. 96.

47. R.P. Feynman, *WDYCWOPT*, p. 80.

48. Ralph Leighton, Ref. 40, p. 176.

49. R.P. Feynman, Ref. 9, pp. 190–91.

50 J.S. Schwinger, *Physics Today*, February 1989, p. 48.

INDEX OF NAMES

Note: An asterisk (*) after a name indicates that it receives fuller treatment in the Index of Subjects.

INDEX OF SUBJECTS